TRIP GENERATION

An ITE Informational Report

8th Edition • Volume 2 of 3

Trip Generation Rates, Plots and Equations

- Port and Terminal (Land Uses 000 - 099)
- Industrial (Land Uses 100 - 199)
- Residential (Land Uses 200 - 299)
- Lodging (Land Uses 300 - 399)
- Recreational (Land Uses 400 - 499)

Institute of Transportation Engineers

Trip Generation, 8th Edition

An Informational Report of the
Institute of Transportation Engineers

Volume 2 of 3

The Institute of Transportation Engineers (ITE) is an international educational and scientific association of transportation professionals who are responsible for meeting mobility and safety needs. ITE facilitates the application of technology and scientific principles to research, planning, functional design, implementation, operation, policy development and management for any mode of transportation. Through its products and services, ITE promotes professional development of its members, supports and encourages education, stimulates research, develops public awareness programs and serves as a conduit for the exchange of professional information.

Founded in 1930, ITE serves as a gateway to knowledge and advancement through meetings, seminars and publications and through its network of nearly 17,000 members working in more than 92 countries.

Institute of Transportation Engineers
1099 14th St. NW, Suite 300 West
Washington, DC 20005-3438 USA
Telephone: +1 202-289-0222
Fax: +1 202-289-7722
ITE on the Web: www.ite.org

Publication No. IR-016F
1,000/AGS/1008

ISBN-13: 978-1-933452-43-2
ISBN-10: 1-933452-43-9
Printed in the United States of America

Table of Contents (8th Edition)
Volume 2
Trip Generation Rates, Plots and Equations

Lodging (Land Uses 300-399)

Recreational (Land Uses 400-499)

Preface

Trip Generation is an informational report of the Institute of Transportation Engineers (ITE). The information in this document is based on trip generation studies submitted voluntarily to ITE by public agencies, developers, consulting firms and associations. This publication is an educational tool for planners, transportation professionals, zoning boards and others who are interested in estimating the number of vehicle trips generated by a proposed development. It is prepared for informational purposes only and does not include ITE recommendations on the best course of action or the preferred application of the data.

Volume 1 of the publication, the *User's Guide*, contains definitions of the independent variables and terms used in this report. The *User's Guide* also provides general instructional material on statistical data and helps users understand the data plots contained in the second and third volumes.

In June 2004, ITE produced a supplemental publication to offer recommendations on the preferred application of the data in this report. This publication, the *Trip Generation Handbook,* Second Edition (Publication Number RP-028B), has two primary purposes: to provide instruction and guidance in the proper use of data presented in *Trip Generation* and to provide information on supplemental issues of importance in estimating trip generation for development sites. Some additional topics covered in the *Trip Generation Handbook,* Second Edition include primary/pass-by/diverted link trips, multi-use developments, truck trip generation and transportation demand management programs.

Users are encouraged to review and become familiar with the *User's Guide* and *Trip Generation Handbook,* Second Edition prior to using the data contained in this volume.

Land Use: 010
Waterport/Marine Terminal

Description

Waterports, or marine terminals, are areas used for the transfer of materials between land and sea and possibly for the storage of these materials.

These ports generally contain ship berths for transferring cargo in bulk or containerized form; enclosed and outdoor storage areas; and office space.

Additional Data

Truck trips accounted for approximately 38 percent of the total weekday traffic at container terminals and 60 percent at break-bulk terminals.

Research conducted by the source that provided these data indicated that revenue-ton was the best indicator of traffic generation for port facilities. Trip generation rates were as follows:
— 0.45 average weekday vehicle trip ends per average weekday revenue-ton for container terminals; and
— 0.30 average weekday vehicle trip ends per average weekday revenue-ton for break-bulk terminals.

Source Number

113

Waterport/Marine Terminal
(010)

Average Vehicle Trip Ends vs: Berths
On a: Weekday

Number of Studies: 7
Average Number of Berths: 3
Directional Distribution: 50% entering, 50% exiting

Trip Generation per Berth

Average Rate	Range of Rates	Standard Deviation
171.52	38.60 - 338.57	130.72

Data Plot and Equation

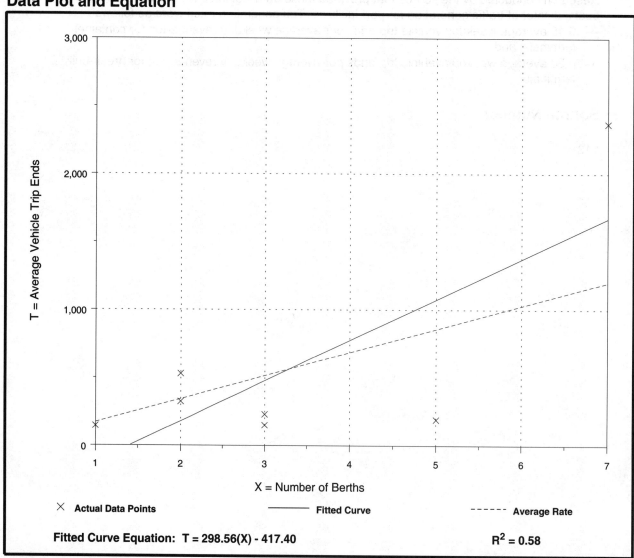

X = Number of Berths

✕ **Actual Data Points**	—— **Fitted Curve**	- - - - **Average Rate**

Fitted Curve Equation: T = 298.56(X) - 417.40 $R^2 = 0.58$

Waterport/Marine Terminal
(010)

Average Vehicle Trip Ends vs: **Acres**
On a: **Weekday**

Number of Studies: 7
Average Number of Acres: 47
Directional Distribution: 50% entering, 50% exiting

Trip Generation per Acre

Average Rate	Range of Rates	Standard Deviation
11.93	4.95 - 19.47	6.07

Data Plot and Equation

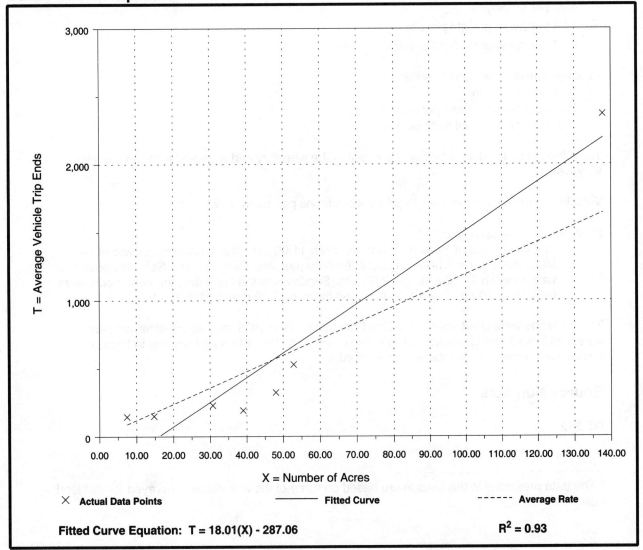

X = Number of Acres

$\times$ **Actual Data Points** ——— **Fitted Curve** - - - - - **Average Rate**

Fitted Curve Equation: $T = 18.01(X) - 287.06$ $R^2 = 0.93$

Land Use: 021
Commercial Airport

Description

Commercial airports accommodate commercial passenger service and are characterized by long runways for serving large jets and extensive terminal facilities. However, some commercial airports have shorter runways and serve exclusively intrastate and commuter airlines. The commercial airports surveyed also accommodate general aviation activities. General aviation airport (Land Use 022) is a related use.

Additional Data[1]

For the purpose of this land use, the independent variable "average flights per day" is defined as the total number of arriving and departing flights.

Average weekday transit trip ends:
— 4.97 per employee
— 48.8 per average flight per day
— 41.3 per commercial flight per day

Average weekday person trip ends:
— 18.1 per employee
— 150.3 per average flight per day
— 150.2 per commercial flight per day

Truck trips accounted for less than 1 percent of the weekday and weekend traffic at the sites surveyed.

Vehicle occupancy ranged from 1.79 to 2.42 persons per automobile.

Peak hours of the generator —
    The weekday a.m. peak hour was between 11:00 a.m. and 12:00 p.m. for two of the sites; the p.m. peak hour was between 5:00 p.m. and 7:00 p.m. The Saturday peak hour was between 11:00 a.m. and 2:00 p.m. Sunday was the peak day; the peak hours were between 12:00 p.m. and 1:00 p.m. and between 7:00 p.m. and 8:00 p.m.

Three studies were conducted in the San Francisco, CA in 1975; an additional airport was surveyed in southern California in 1983. These were moderate to major airports in terms of commercial passenger service when surveyed.

Source Numbers

90, 212

---

[1] The data presented in this section are based on three of the four studies surveyed for this land use.

Commercial Airport
(021)

Average Vehicle Trip Ends vs: Employees
On a: Weekday

Number of Studies: 3
Avg. Number of Employees: 2,649
Directional Distribution: 50% entering, 50% exiting

Trip Generation per Employee

Average Rate	Range of Rates	Standard Deviation
13.40	10.28 - 22.94	5.06

Data Plot and Equation

Caution - Use Carefully - Small Sample Size

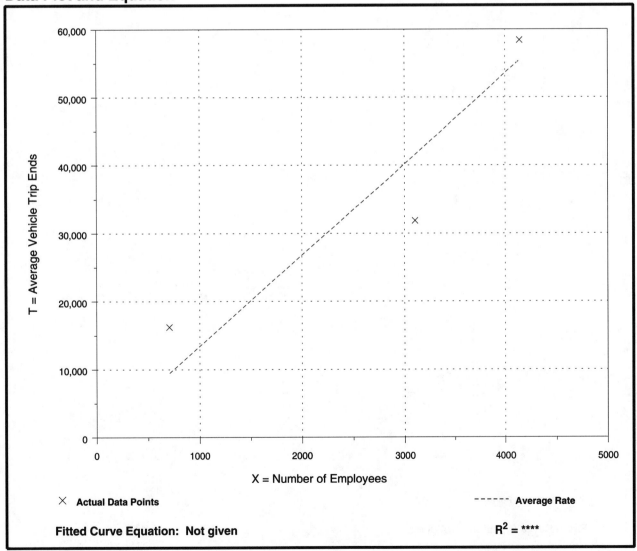

× **Actual Data Points**   ----- **Average Rate**

Fitted Curve Equation: Not given $R^2 = ****$

Commercial Airport
(021)

Average Vehicle Trip Ends vs: Employees
On a: Weekday,
Peak Hour of Adjacent Street Traffic,
One Hour Between 7 and 9 a.m.

Number of Studies: 2
Avg. Number of Employees: 2,424
Directional Distribution: 55% entering, 45% exiting

Trip Generation per Employee

Average Rate	Range of Rates	Standard Deviation
0.82	0.73 - 1.32	*

Data Plot and Equation

Caution - Use Carefully - Small Sample Size

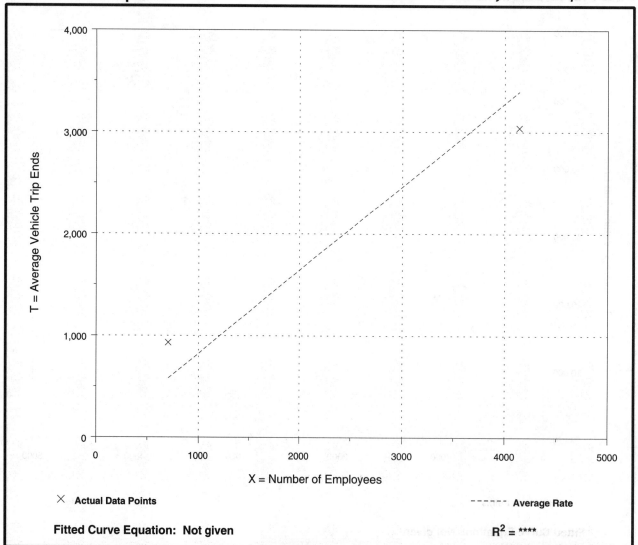

X **Actual Data Points**

- - - - - **Average Rate**

Fitted Curve Equation: Not given $R^2 = ****$

Commercial Airport
(021)

Average Vehicle Trip Ends vs: **Employees**
On a: **Weekday,**
Peak Hour of Adjacent Street Traffic,
One Hour Between 4 and 6 p.m.

Number of Studies: 2
Avg. Number of Employees: 2,424
Directional Distribution: 54% entering, 46% exiting

Trip Generation per Employee

Average Rate	Range of Rates	Standard Deviation
0.80	0.69 - 1.43	*

Data Plot and Equation

Caution - Use Carefully - Small Sample Size

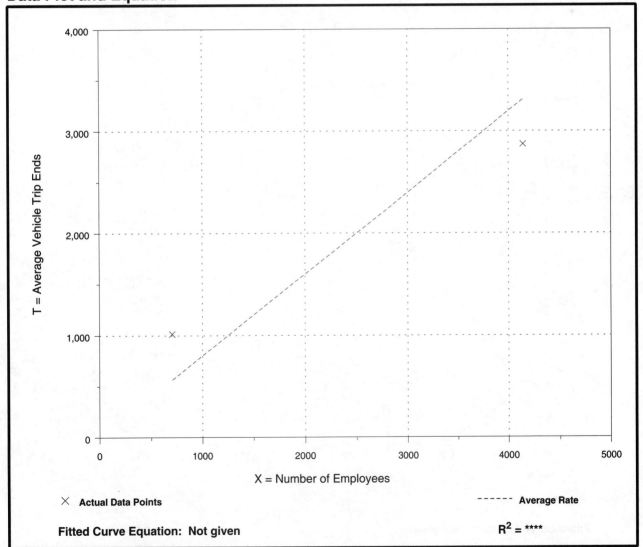

X **Actual Data Points**

- - - - - **Average Rate**

Fitted Curve Equation: Not given $R^2 = ****$

Commercial Airport
(021)

Average Vehicle Trip Ends vs: Employees
On a: Weekday,
A.M. Peak Hour of Generator

Number of Studies: 2
Avg. Number of Employees: 2,424
Directional Distribution: 45% entering, 55% exiting

Trip Generation per Employee

Average Rate	Range of Rates	Standard Deviation
1.21	1.17 - 1.48	*

Data Plot and Equation

Caution - Use Carefully - Small Sample Size

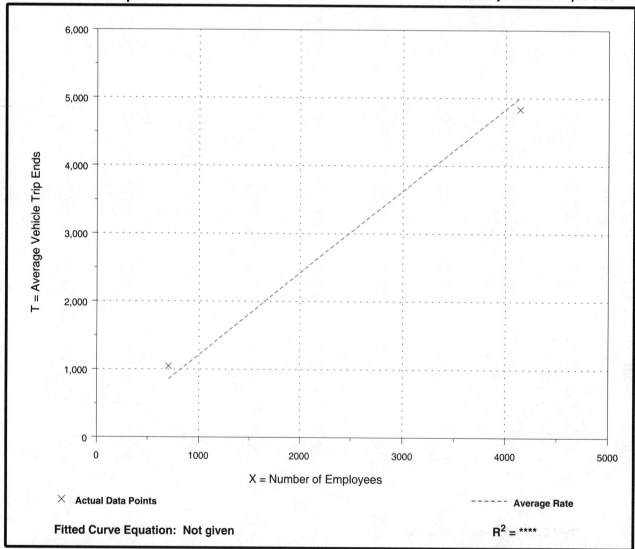

X **Actual Data Points**   - - - - - **Average Rate**

Fitted Curve Equation: Not given $R^2 = ****$

Commercial Airport
(021)

Average Vehicle Trip Ends vs: **Employees**
On a: **Weekday,**
P.M. Peak Hour of Generator

Number of Studies: 2
Avg. Number of Employees: 2,424
Directional Distribution: 47% entering, 53% exiting

Trip Generation per Employee

Average Rate	Range of Rates	Standard Deviation
1.00	0.90 - 1.60	*

Data Plot and Equation

Caution - Use Carefully - Small Sample Size

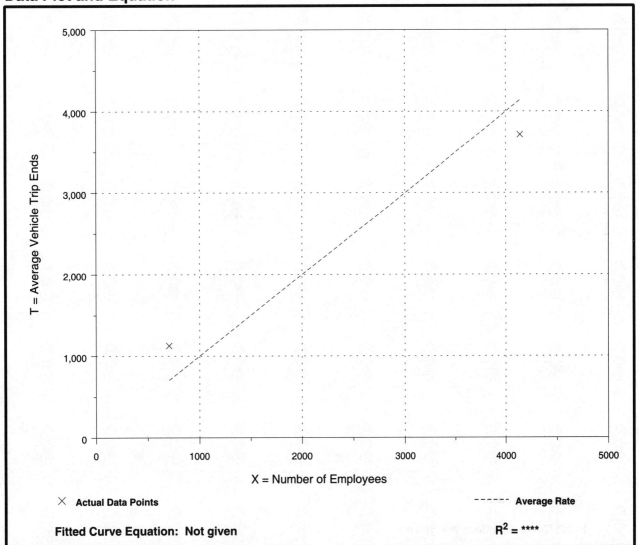

X **Actual Data Points** - - - - - **Average Rate**

Fitted Curve Equation: Not given $R^2 = $ ****

Commercial Airport
(021)

Average Vehicle Trip Ends vs: Employees
On a: Saturday

Number of Studies: 3
Avg. Number of Employees: 2,649
Directional Distribution: 50% entering, 50% exiting

Trip Generation per Employee

Average Rate	Range of Rates	Standard Deviation
12.20	8.48 - 19.65	4.87

Data Plot and Equation

Caution - Use Carefully - Small Sample Size

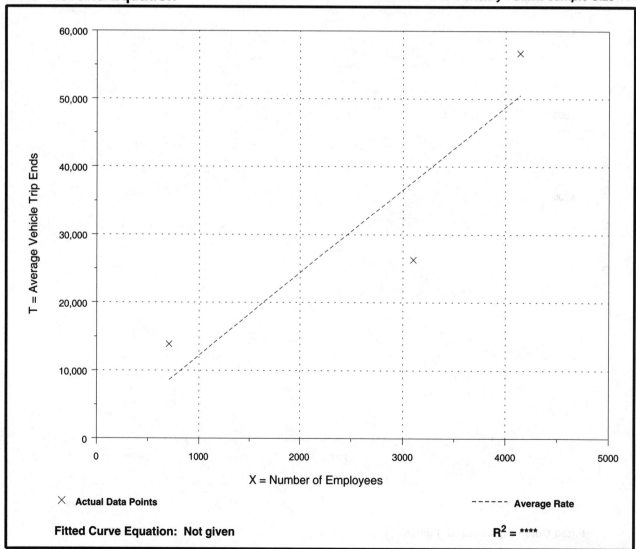

X **Actual Data Points**

- - - - - **Average Rate**

Fitted Curve Equation: Not given $R^2 = ****$

Commercial Airport
(021)

Average Vehicle Trip Ends vs: **Employees**
On a: **Saturday,**
  Peak Hour of Generator

Number of Studies: 2
Avg. Number of Employees: 2,424
Directional Distribution: 51% entering, 49% exiting

Trip Generation per Employee

Average Rate	Range of Rates	Standard Deviation
1.14	1.03 - 1.76	*

Data Plot and Equation

Caution - Use Carefully - Small Sample Size

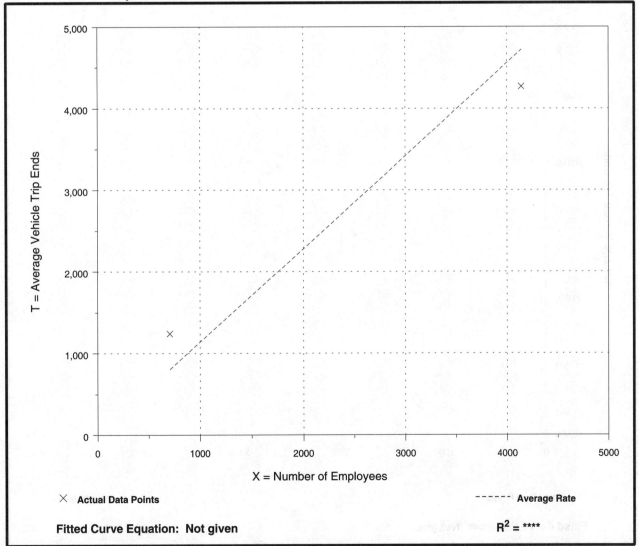

X **Actual Data Points**

- - - - - **Average Rate**

Fitted Curve Equation: Not given $R^2 = ****$

Commercial Airport
(021)

Average Vehicle Trip Ends vs: **Employees**
On a: **Sunday**

Number of Studies: 3
Avg. Number of Employees: 2,649
Directional Distribution: 50% entering, 50% exiting

Trip Generation per Employee

Average Rate	Range of Rates	Standard Deviation
14.70	10.23 - 24.27	5.67

Data Plot and Equation

Caution - Use Carefully - Small Sample Size

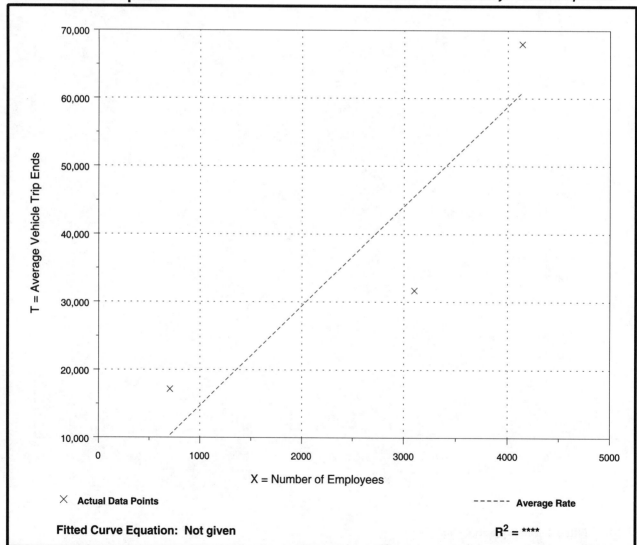

X **Actual Data Points**

- - - - - **Average Rate**

Fitted Curve Equation: Not given $R^2 = $ ****

Commercial Airport
(021)

Average Vehicle Trip Ends vs: Employees
On a: Sunday,
Peak Hour of Generator

Number of Studies: 2
Avg. Number of Employees: 2,424
Directional Distribution: 47% entering, 53% exiting

Trip Generation per Employee

Average Rate	Range of Rates	Standard Deviation
1.28	1.19 - 1.77	*

Data Plot and Equation

Caution - Use Carefully - Small Sample Size

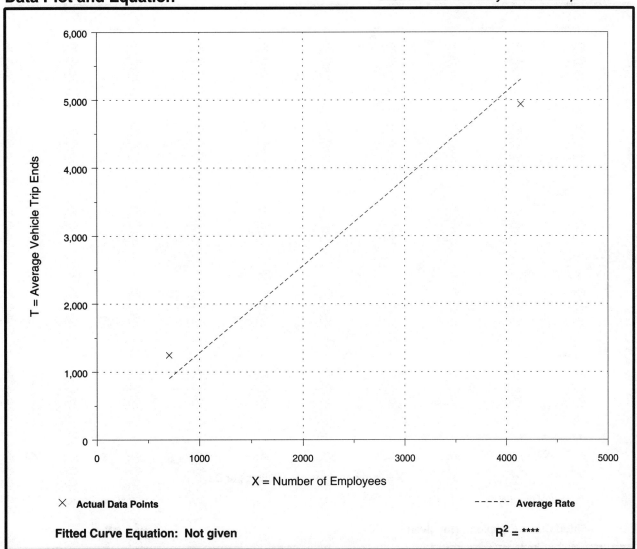

X **Actual Data Points**   - - - - - **Average Rate**

Fitted Curve Equation: Not given $R^2 = ****$

Commercial Airport
(021)

Average Vehicle Trip Ends vs: Average Flights per Day
On a: Weekday

Number of Studies: 2
Average Number of Flights per Day: 349
Directional Distribution: 50% entering, 50% exiting

Trip Generation per Flight

Average Rate	Range of Rates	Standard Deviation
104.73	65.69 - 122.97	*

Data Plot and Equation

Caution - Use Carefully - Small Sample Size

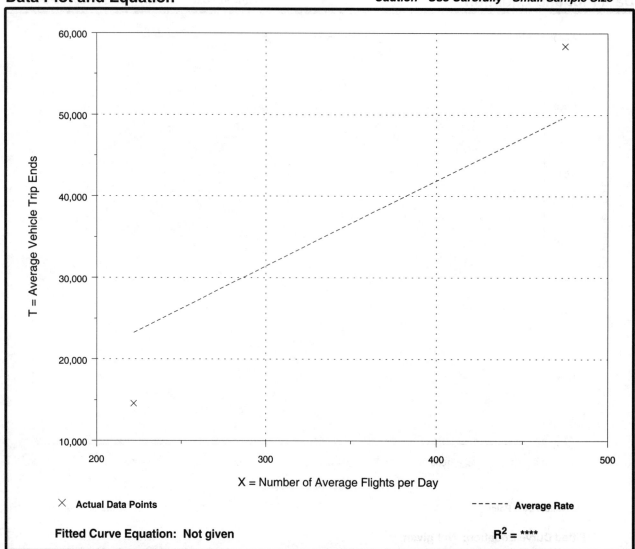

X   **Actual Data Points**

- - - - - **Average Rate**

Fitted Curve Equation: Not given $R^2 =$ ****

Commercial Airport
(021)

Average Vehicle Trip Ends vs: **Average Flights per Day**
On a: **Weekday,**
Peak Hour of Adjacent Street Traffic,
One Hour Between 7 and 9 a.m.

Number of Studies: 2
Average Number of Flights per Day: 349
Directional Distribution: 54% entering, 46% exiting

Trip Generation per Flight

Average Rate	Range of Rates	Standard Deviation
5.40	3.27 - 6.40	*

Data Plot and Equation

Caution - Use Carefully - Small Sample Size

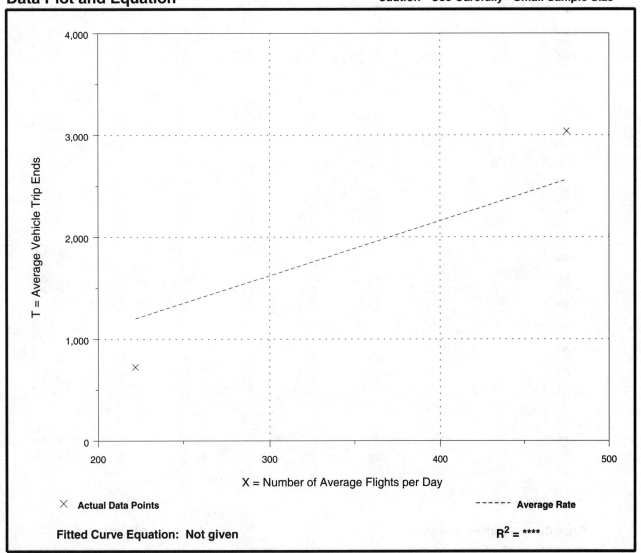

X **Actual Data Points**

- - - - - - **Average Rate**

Fitted Curve Equation: Not given

$R^2 = ****$

Commercial Airport
(021)

Trip Generation per Flight

Average Rate	Range of Rates	Standard Deviation
5.75	5.12 - 6.05	*

Data Plot and Equation

Caution - Use Carefully - Small Sample Size

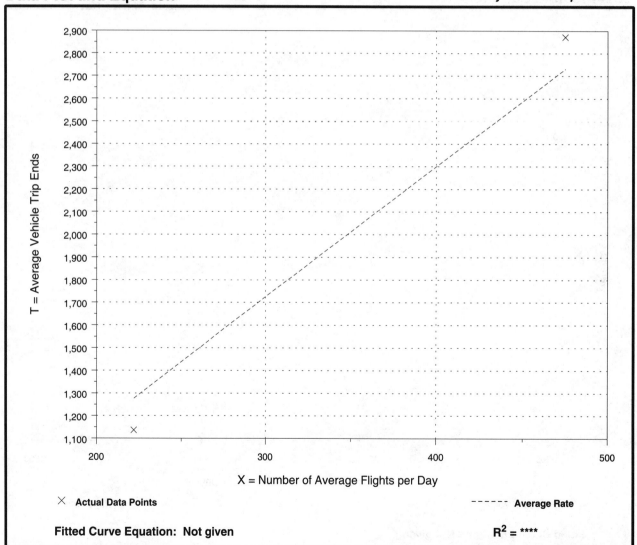

X **Actual Data Points**   - - - - - **Average Rate**

Fitted Curve Equation: Not given $R^2 =$ ****

Commercial Airport
(021)

Average Vehicle Trip Ends vs: Average Flights per Day
On a: Weekday,
A.M. Peak Hour of Generator

Number of Studies: 2
Average Number of Flights per Day: 349
Directional Distribution: 45% entering, 55% exiting

Trip Generation per Flight

Average Rate	Range of Rates	Standard Deviation
8.17	3.90 - 10.17	*

Data Plot and Equation

Caution - Use Carefully - Small Sample Size

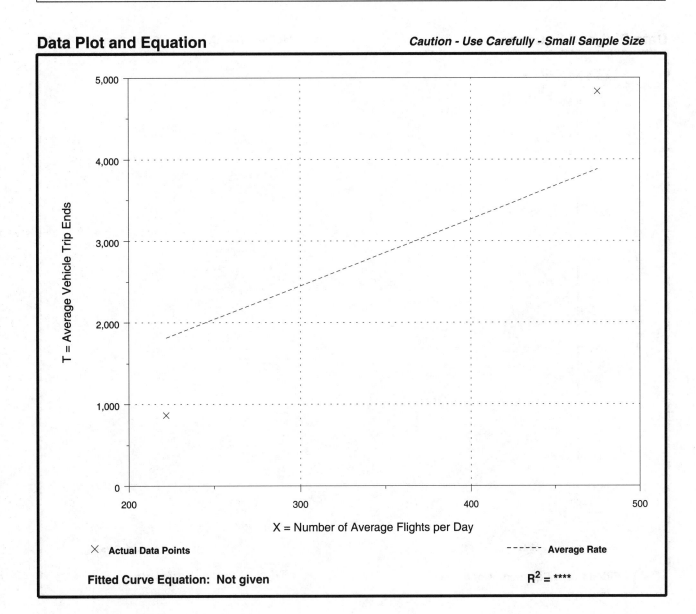

X   **Actual Data Points**   - - - - - **Average Rate**

Fitted Curve Equation: Not given $R^2 = ****$

Commercial Airport
(021)

Average Vehicle Trip Ends vs: Average Flights per Day
On a: Weekday,
P.M. Peak Hour of Generator

Number of Studies: 2
Average Number of Flights per Day: 349
Directional Distribution: 49% entering, 51% exiting

Trip Generation per Flight

Average Rate	Range of Rates	Standard Deviation
6.96	5.12 - 7.82	*

Data Plot and Equation

Caution - Use Carefully - Small Sample Size

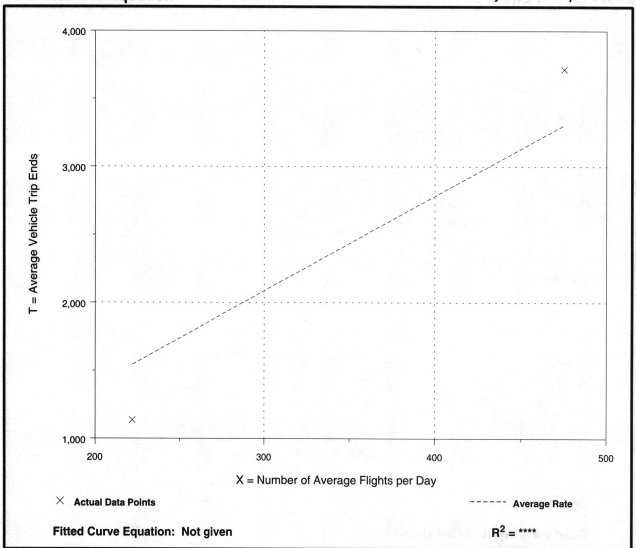

X = Number of Average Flights per Day

× **Actual Data Points**   - - - - - **Average Rate**

Fitted Curve Equation: Not given $R^2 = ****$

Commercial Airport
(021)

Average Vehicle Trip Ends vs: Average Flights per Day
On a: Saturday

Number of Studies: 2
Average Number of Flights per Day: 349
Directional Distribution: 50% entering, 50% exiting

Trip Generation per Flight

Average Rate	Range of Rates	Standard Deviation
98.46	53.56 - 119.45	*

Data Plot and Equation

Caution - Use Carefully - Small Sample Size

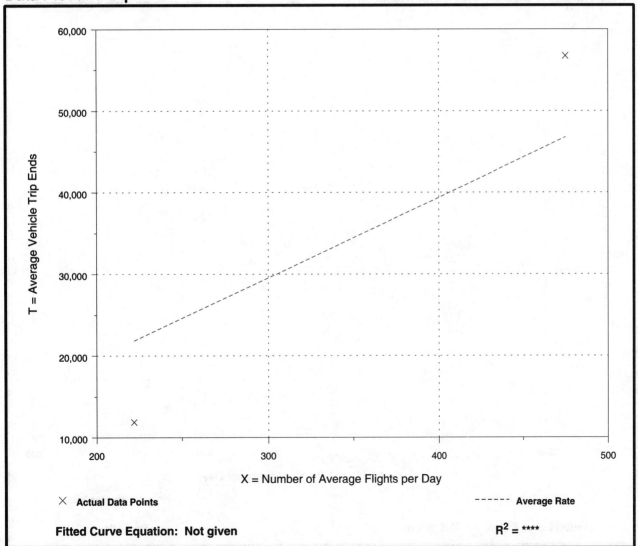

X **Actual Data Points**

- - - - - **Average Rate**

Fitted Curve Equation: Not given

$R^2 = ****$

Commercial Airport
(021)

Average Vehicle Trip Ends vs: **Average Flights per Day**
On a: **Saturday,**
Peak Hour of Generator

Number of Studies: 2
Average Number of Flights per Day: 349
Directional Distribution: 52% entering, 48% exiting

Trip Generation per Flight

Average Rate	Range of Rates	Standard Deviation
7.47	4.25 - 8.98	*

Data Plot and Equation

Caution - Use Carefully - Small Sample Size

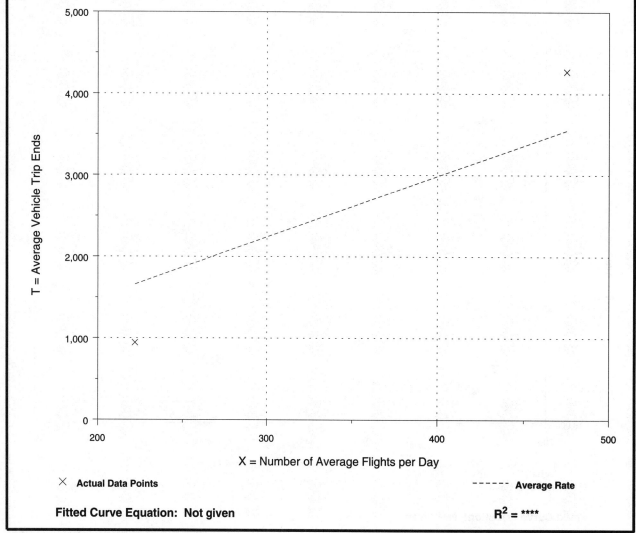

X **Actual Data Points**   - - - - - **Average Rate**

Fitted Curve Equation: Not given $R^2 = $ ****

Commercial Airport
(021)

Average Vehicle Trip Ends vs: **Average Flights per Day**
On a: **Sunday**

Number of Studies: 2
Average Number of Flights per Day: 349
Directional Distribution: 50% entering, 50% exiting

Trip Generation per Flight

Average Rate	Range of Rates	Standard Deviation
119.61	69.31 - 143.12	*

Data Plot and Equation

Caution - Use Carefully - Small Sample Size

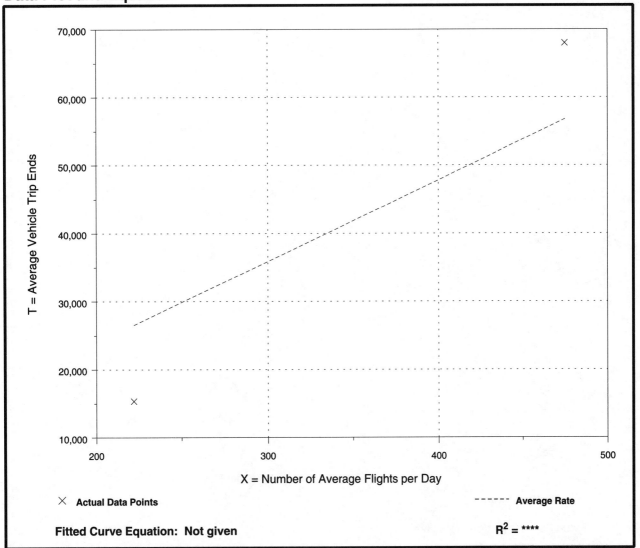

X **Actual Data Points**   - - - - - **Average Rate**

Fitted Curve Equation: Not given $R^2 = ****$

Commercial Airport
(021)

Average Vehicle Trip Ends vs: **Average Flights per Day**
On a: **Sunday,**
Peak Hour of Generator

Number of Studies: 2
Average Number of Flights per Day: 349
Directional Distribution: 47% entering, 53% exiting

Trip Generation per Flight

Average Rate	Range of Rates	Standard Deviation
8.85	5.53 - 10.40	*

Data Plot and Equation

Caution - Use Carefully - Small Sample Size

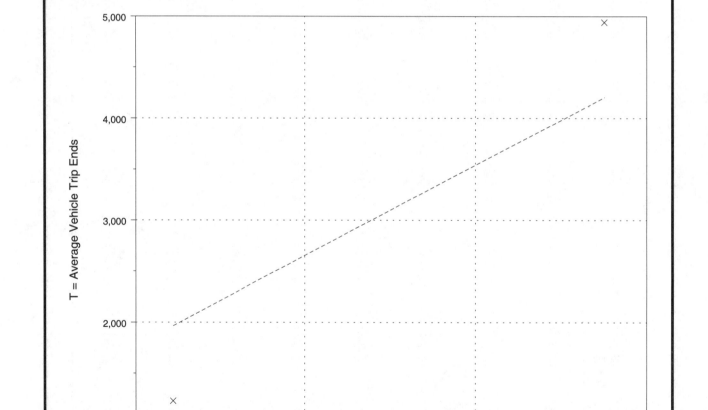

X = Number of Average Flights per Day

✕ **Actual Data Points**   ----- **Average Rate**

Fitted Curve Equation: Not given $R^2 = ****$

Commercial Airport
(021)

Average Vehicle Trip Ends vs: Commercial Flights per Day
On a: Weekday

Number of Studies: 3
Avg. Num. of Comm. Flights per Day: 243
Directional Distribution: 50% entering, 50% exiting

Trip Generation per Commercial Flight

Average Rate	Range of Rates	Standard Deviation
122.21	99.50 - 138.74	22.25

Data Plot and Equation

Caution - Use Carefully - Small Sample Size

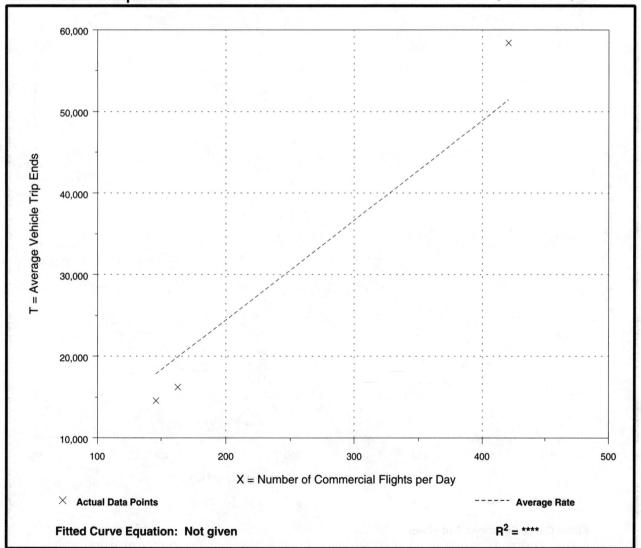

✕ **Actual Data Points**   ------ **Average Rate**

Fitted Curve Equation: Not given $R^2 = ****$

Commercial Airport
(021)

Average Vehicle Trip Ends vs: Commercial Flights per Day
On a: Weekday,
Peak Hour of Adjacent Street Traffic,
One Hour Between 7 and 9 a.m.

Number of Studies: 3
Avg. Num. of Comm. Flights per Day: 243
Directional Distribution: 55% entering, 45% exiting

Trip Generation per Commercial Flight

Average Rate	Range of Rates	Standard Deviation
6.43	4.97 - 7.22	2.71

Data Plot and Equation

Caution - Use Carefully - Small Sample Size

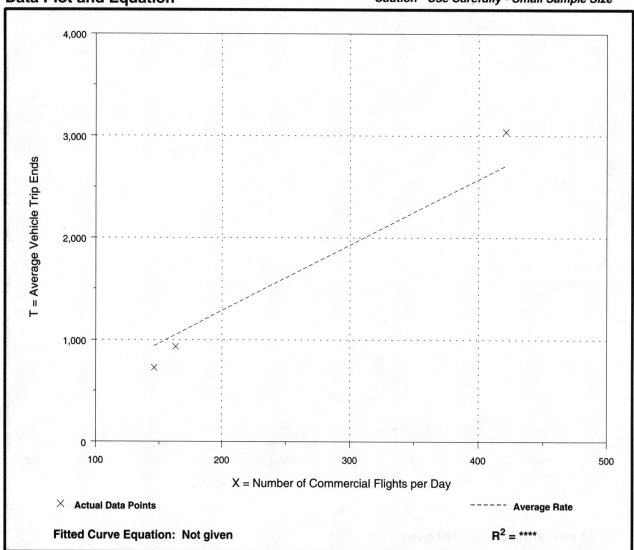

X **Actual Data Points**

‐ ‐ ‐ ‐ ‐ **Average Rate**

Fitted Curve Equation: Not given

$R^2 = ****$

Commercial Airport
(021)

Average Vehicle Trip Ends vs: **Commercial Flights per Day**
On a: **Weekday,**
Peak Hour of Adjacent Street Traffic,
One Hour Between 4 and 6 p.m.

Number of Studies: 3
Avg. Num. of Comm. Flights per Day: 243
Directional Distribution: 54% entering, 46% exiting

Trip Generation per Commercial Flight

Average Rate	Range of Rates	Standard Deviation
6.88	6.22 - 7.79	2.67

Data Plot and Equation

Caution - Use Carefully - Small Sample Size

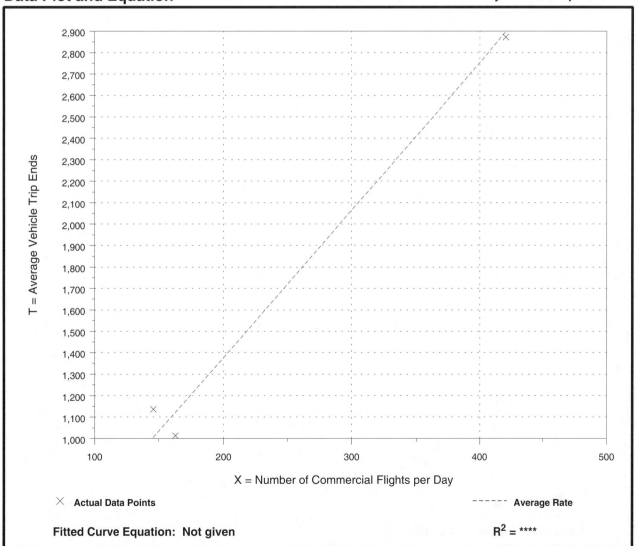

X = Number of Commercial Flights per Day

✕ **Actual Data Points**   - - - - - **Average Rate**

Fitted Curve Equation: Not given $R^2 = ****$

Commercial Airport
(021)

Average Vehicle Trip Ends vs: **Commercial Flights per Day**
On a: **Weekday,**
A.M. Peak Hour of Generator

Number of Studies: 3
Avg. Num. of Comm. Flights per Day: 243
Directional Distribution: 46% entering, 54% exiting

Trip Generation per Commercial Flight

Average Rate	Range of Rates	Standard Deviation
9.24	5.92 - 11.48	4.01

Data Plot and Equation

Caution - Use Carefully - Small Sample Size

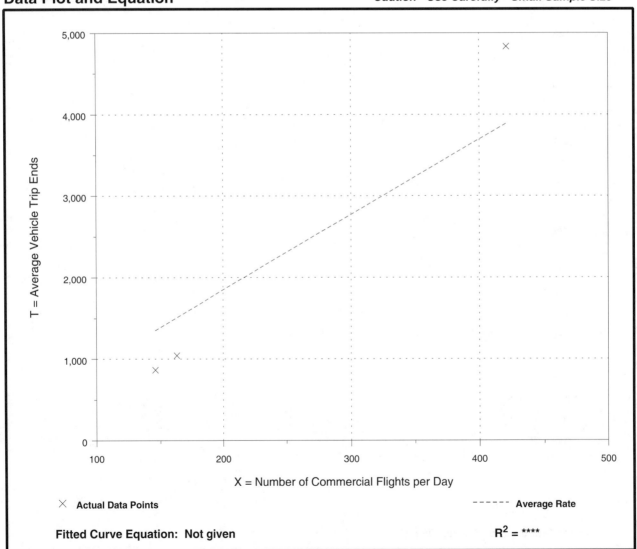

X = Number of Commercial Flights per Day

× **Actual Data Points**   - - - - - **Average Rate**

Fitted Curve Equation: Not given $R^2 = $ ****

Commercial Airport
(021)

Average Vehicle Trip Ends vs: **Commercial Flights per Day**
On a: **Weekday,**
  P.M. Peak Hour of Generator

Number of Studies: 3
Avg. Num. of Comm. Flights per Day: 243
Directional Distribution: 48% entering, 52% exiting

Trip Generation per Commercial Flight

Average Rate	Range of Rates	Standard Deviation
8.20	6.93 - 8.83	2.97

Data Plot and Equation

Caution - Use Carefully - Small Sample Size

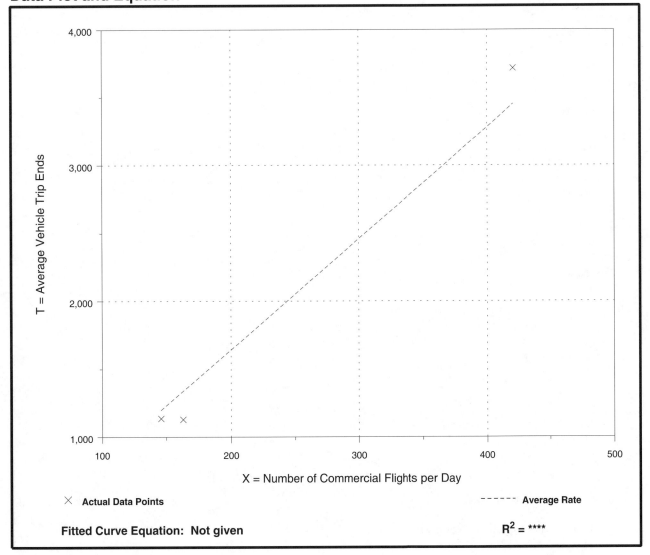

X = Number of Commercial Flights per Day

✕ **Actual Data Points**   - - - - - **Average Rate**

Fitted Curve Equation: Not given $R^2 = $ ****

Commercial Airport
(021)

Average Vehicle Trip Ends vs: Commercial Flights per Day
On a: Saturday

Number of Studies: 3
Avg. Num. of Comm. Flights per Day: 243
Directional Distribution: 50% entering, 50% exiting

Trip Generation per Commercial Flight

Average Rate	Range of Rates	Standard Deviation
113.04	81.45 - 134.77	27.54

Data Plot and Equation

Caution - Use Carefully - Small Sample Size

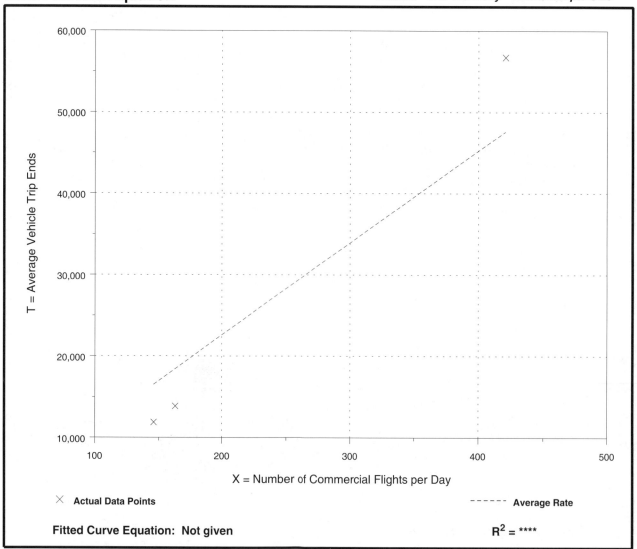

X **Actual Data Points**

----- **Average Rate**

Fitted Curve Equation: Not given

$R^2 = $ ****

Commercial Airport
(021)

Average Vehicle Trip Ends vs: Commercial Flights per Day
On a: Saturday,
Peak Hour of Generator

Number of Studies: 3
Avg. Num. of Comm. Flights per Day: 243
Directional Distribution: 51% entering, 49% exiting

Trip Generation per Commercial Flight

Average Rate	Range of Rates	Standard Deviation
8.84	6.47 - 10.13	3.35

Data Plot and Equation

Caution - Use Carefully - Small Sample Size

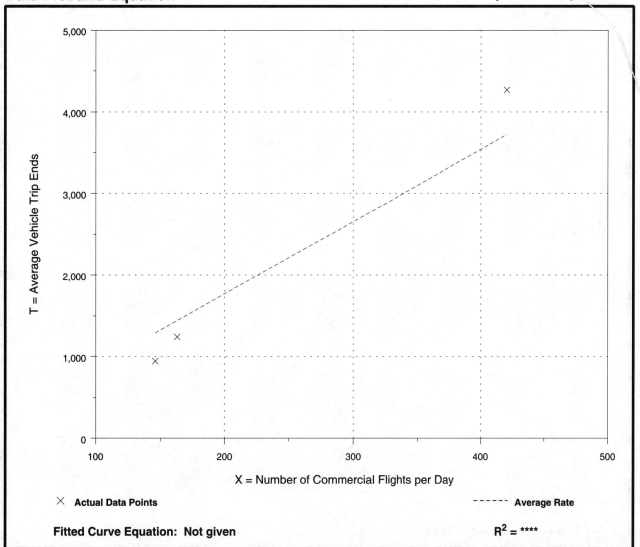

X   **Actual Data Points**

- - - - - **Average Rate**

Fitted Curve Equation: Not given $R^2 = ****$

Commercial Airport
(021)

Average Vehicle Trip Ends vs: Commercial Flights per Day
On a: Sunday

Number of Studies: 3
Avg. Num. of Comm. Flights per Day: 243
Directional Distribution: 50% entering, 50% exiting

Trip Generation per Commercial Flight

Average Rate	Range of Rates	Standard Deviation
137.71	105.29 - 161.47	30.13

Data Plot and Equation

Caution - Use Carefully - Small Sample Size

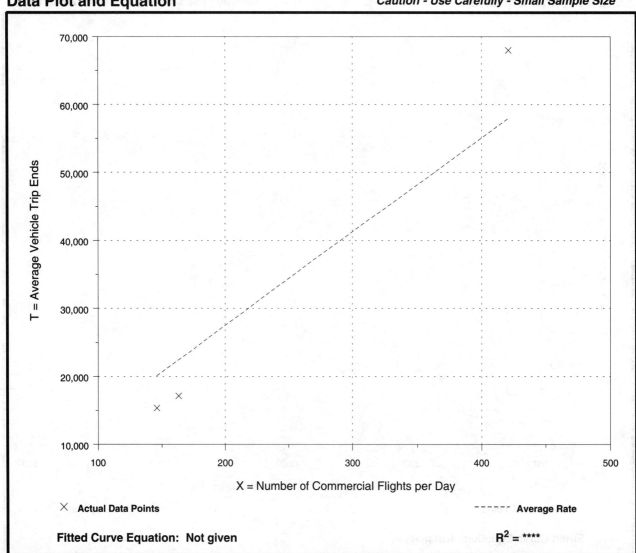

✕ **Actual Data Points**   - - - - - - **Average Rate**

Fitted Curve Equation: Not given $R^2 = ****$

Commercial Airport
(021)

Average Vehicle Trip Ends vs: Commercial Flights per Day
On a: Sunday,
Peak Hour of Generator

Number of Studies: 3
Avg. Num. of Comm. Flights per Day: 243
Directional Distribution: 47% entering, 53% exiting

Trip Generation per Commercial Flight

Average Rate	Range of Rates	Standard Deviation
10.16	7.66 - 11.73	3.68

Data Plot and Equation

Caution - Use Carefully - Small Sample Size

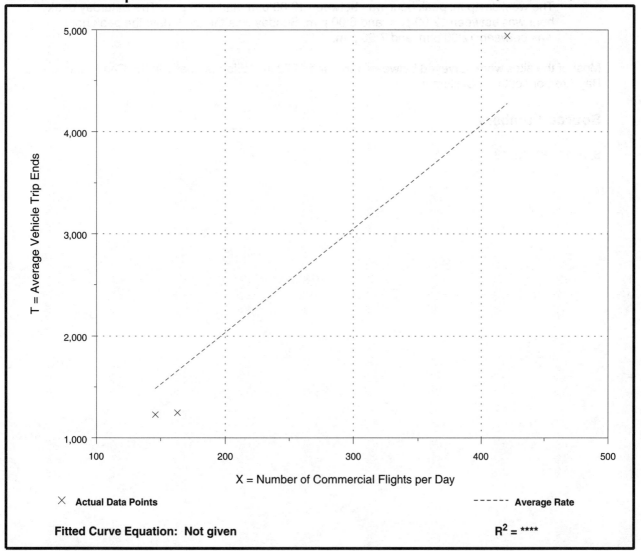

X **Actual Data Points**

- - - - - **Average Rate**

Fitted Curve Equation: Not given

$R^2 = ****$

Land Use: 022
General Aviation Airport

Description

General aviation airports are designed primarily for use by small private and corporate aircraft, not for commercial passenger service. They are usually characterized by short runways, few or no terminal facilities and many small aircraft. Commercial airport (Land Use 021) is a related use.

Additional Data

Truck trips accounted for 3 to 5 percent of the weekday traffic at the airports surveyed.

Vehicle occupancy ranged from 1.2 to 1.7 persons per automobile on an average weekday.

Peak hours of the generator —
> The weekday p.m. peak hour was between 12:00 p.m. and 6:00 p.m. The Saturday peak hour was between 12:00 p.m. and 6:00 p.m. Sunday was the peak day; the peak hour was between 12:00 p.m. and 7:00 p.m.

Most of the sites were surveyed between 1967 and 1972 in California, many in the San Francisco Bay Area or southern California.

Source Numbers

8, 9, 11, 12, 13, 18

Land Use: 022
General Aviation Airport
Independent Variables with One Observation

The following trip generation data are for independent variables with only one observation. This information is shown in this table only; there are no related plots for these data.

Users are cautioned to use data with care because of the small sample size.

Independent Variable	Trip Generation Rate	Size of Independent Variable	Number of Studies	Directional Distribution
Employees				
Weekday a.m. Peak Hour of Adjacent Street Traffic	0.69	140	1	83% entering, 17% exiting
Weekday p.m. Peak Hour of Adjacent Street Traffic	1.03	140	1	45% entering, 55% exiting
Based Aircraft				
Weekday a.m. Peak Hour of Adjacent Street Traffic	0.24	394	1	83% entering, 17% exiting
Weekday p.m. Peak Hour of Adjacent Street Traffic	0.37	394	1	45% entering, 55% exiting

General Aviation Airport
(022)

Average Vehicle Trip Ends vs: Employees
On a: Weekday

Number of Studies: 6
Avg. Number of Employees: 108
Directional Distribution: 50% entering, 50% exiting

Trip Generation per Employee

Average Rate	Range of Rates	Standard Deviation
14.24	9.79 - 122.00	10.46

Data Plot and Equation

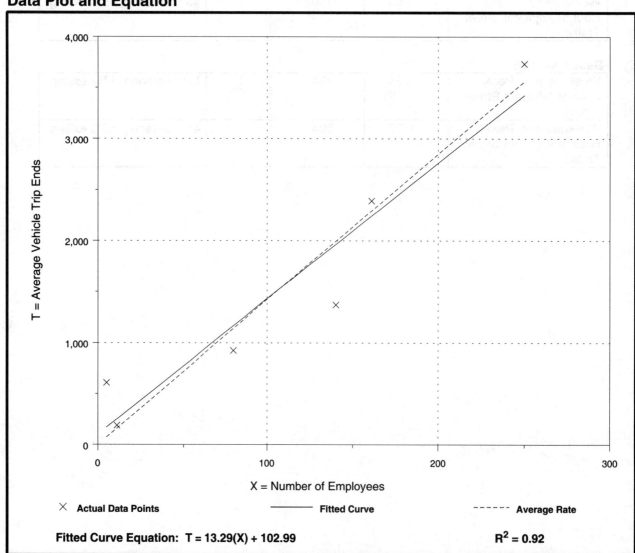

Fitted Curve Equation: T = 13.29(X) + 102.99 $R^2 = 0.92$

General Aviation Airport
(022)

Average Vehicle Trip Ends vs: **Employees**
On a: **Weekday,**
A.M. Peak Hour of Generator

Number of Studies: 5
Avg. Number of Employees: 128
Directional Distribution: 50% entering, 50% exiting

Trip Generation per Employee

Average Rate	Range of Rates	Standard Deviation
1.29	0.78 - 1.58	1.17

Data Plot and Equation

Caution - Use Carefully - Small Sample Size

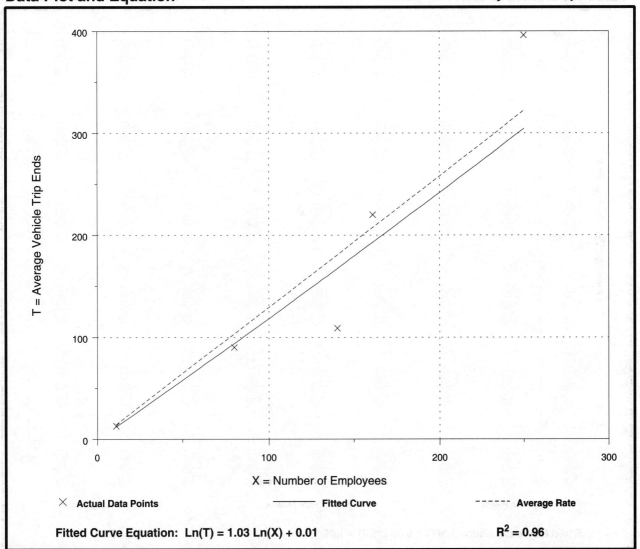

X = Number of Employees

✕ **Actual Data Points** ──────── **Fitted Curve** ─ ─ ─ ─ **Average Rate**

Fitted Curve Equation: Ln(T) = 1.03 Ln(X) + 0.01 $R^2 = 0.96$

General Aviation Airport
(022)

Average Vehicle Trip Ends vs: **Employees**
On a: **Weekday,**
  P.M. Peak Hour of Generator

Number of Studies: 5
Avg. Number of Employees: 128
Directional Distribution: 55% entering, 45% exiting

Trip Generation per Employee

Average Rate	Range of Rates	Standard Deviation
1.46	0.99 - 2.27	1.24

Data Plot and Equation

Caution - Use Carefully - Small Sample Size

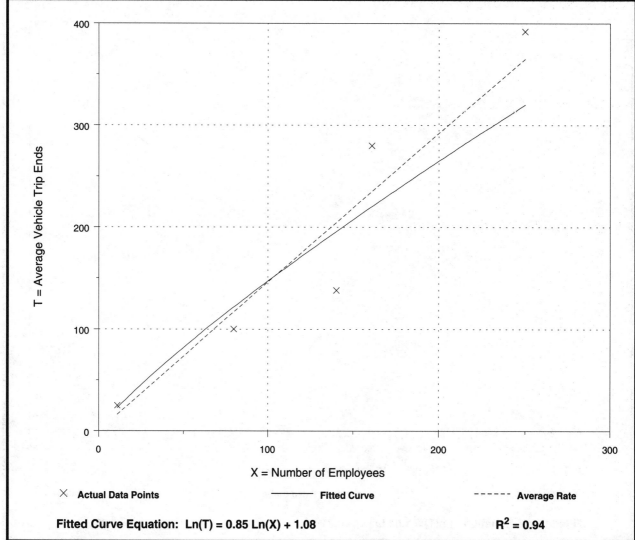

X = Number of Employees

✕ **Actual Data Points**   —— **Fitted Curve**   - - - - - **Average Rate**

Fitted Curve Equation: Ln(T) = 0.85 Ln(X) + 1.08 $R^2 = 0.94$

General Aviation Airport
(022)

Average Vehicle Trip Ends vs: **Employees**
On a: **Saturday**

Number of Studies: 5
Avg. Number of Employees: 128
Directional Distribution: 50% entering, 50% exiting

Trip Generation per Employee

Average Rate	Range of Rates	Standard Deviation
10.96	8.36 - 23.09	4.06

Data Plot and Equation

Caution - Use Carefully - Small Sample Size

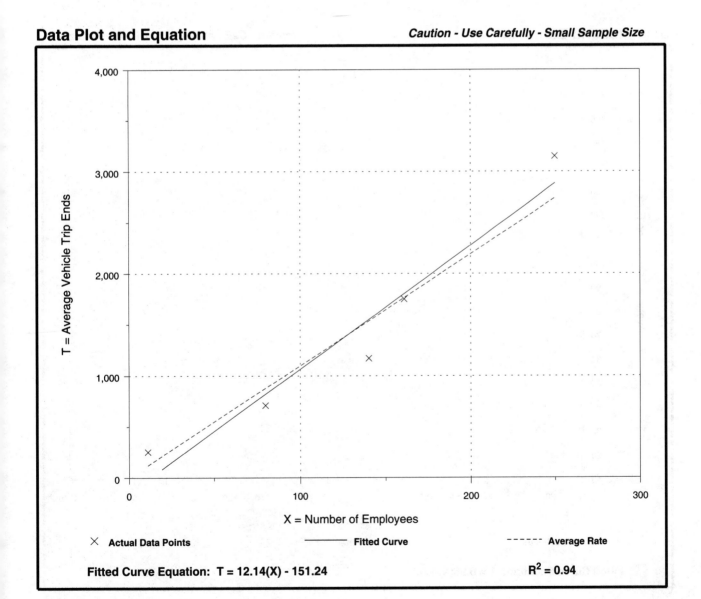

X **Actual Data Points** ——— **Fitted Curve** - - - - - **Average Rate**

Fitted Curve Equation: T = 12.14(X) - 151.24 $R^2 = 0.94$

General Aviation Airport
(022)

Average Vehicle Trip Ends vs: **Employees**
On a: **Saturday,**
Peak Hour of Generator

Number of Studies: 4
Avg. Number of Employees: 98
Directional Distribution: 61% entering, 39% exiting

Trip Generation per Employee

Average Rate	Range of Rates	Standard Deviation
1.05	0.88 - 2.64	1.06

Data Plot and Equation

Caution - Use Carefully - Small Sample Size

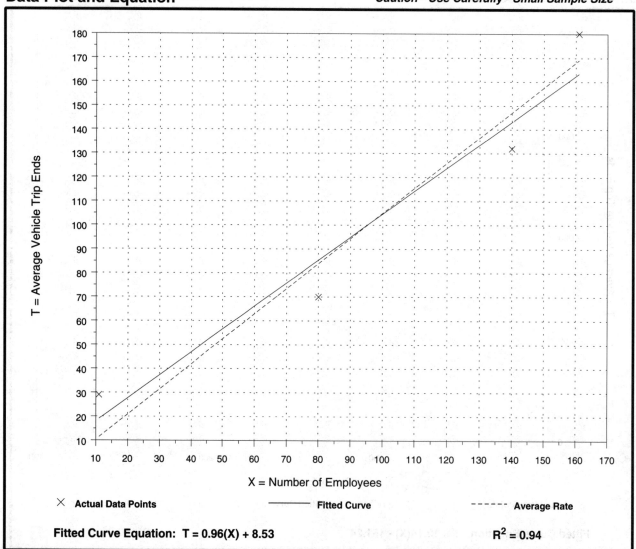

X = Number of Employees

× Actual Data Points	—— Fitted Curve	- - - - Average Rate

Fitted Curve Equation: T = 0.96(X) + 8.53 $R^2 = 0.94$

General Aviation Airport
(022)

Average Vehicle Trip Ends vs: Employees
On a: Sunday

Number of Studies: 5
Avg. Number of Employees: 79
Directional Distribution: 50% entering, 50% exiting

Trip Generation per Employee

Average Rate	Range of Rates	Standard Deviation
13.28	11.00 - 128.80	13.77

Data Plot and Equation

Caution - Use Carefully - Small Sample Size

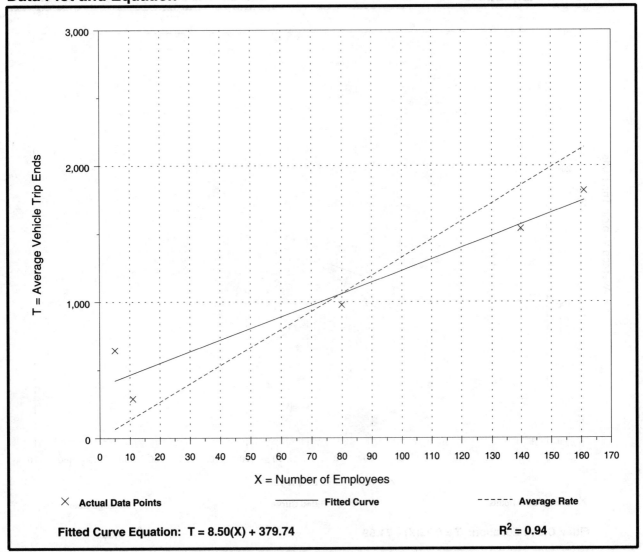

X **Actual Data Points** ———— **Fitted Curve** - - - - - **Average Rate**

Fitted Curve Equation: T = 8.50(X) + 379.74 $R^2 = 0.94$

General Aviation Airport
(022)

Average Vehicle Trip Ends vs: **Employees**
On a: **Sunday,**
  Peak Hour of Generator

Number of Studies: 5
Avg. Number of Employees: 79
Directional Distribution: 55% entering, 45% exiting

Trip Generation per Employee

Average Rate	Range of Rates	Standard Deviation
1.70	1.18 - 26.00	3.05

Data Plot and Equation

Caution - Use Carefully - Small Sample Size

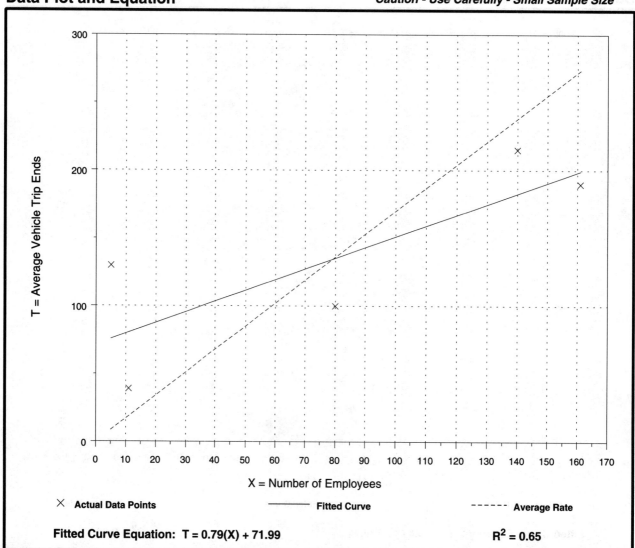

X   **Actual Data Points**   —— **Fitted Curve**   - - - - - **Average Rate**

Fitted Curve Equation: T = 0.79(X) + 71.99 $R^2 = 0.65$

General Aviation Airport
(022)

Average Vehicle Trip Ends vs: **Average Flights per Day**
On a: **Weekday**

Number of Studies: 8
Average Number of Flights per Day: 674
Directional Distribution: 50% entering, 50% exiting

Trip Generation per Flight

Average Rate	Range of Rates	Standard Deviation
1.97	0.96 - 2.81	1.58

Data Plot and Equation

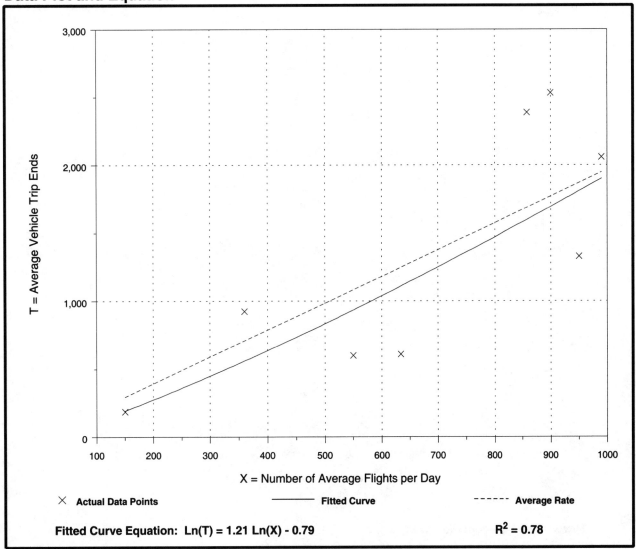

X **Actual Data Points**   ———— **Fitted Curve**   - - - - - **Average Rate**

Fitted Curve Equation: Ln(T) = 1.21 Ln(X) - 0.79 $R^2 = 0.78$

General Aviation Airport
(022)

Average Vehicle Trip Ends vs: Average Flights per Day
On a: Weekday,
A.M. Peak Hour of Generator

Number of Studies: 3
Average Number of Flights per Day: 456
Directional Distribution: Not available

Trip Generation per Flight

Average Rate	Range of Rates	Standard Deviation
0.24	0.09 - 0.26	0.49

Data Plot and Equation

Caution - Use Carefully - Small Sample Size

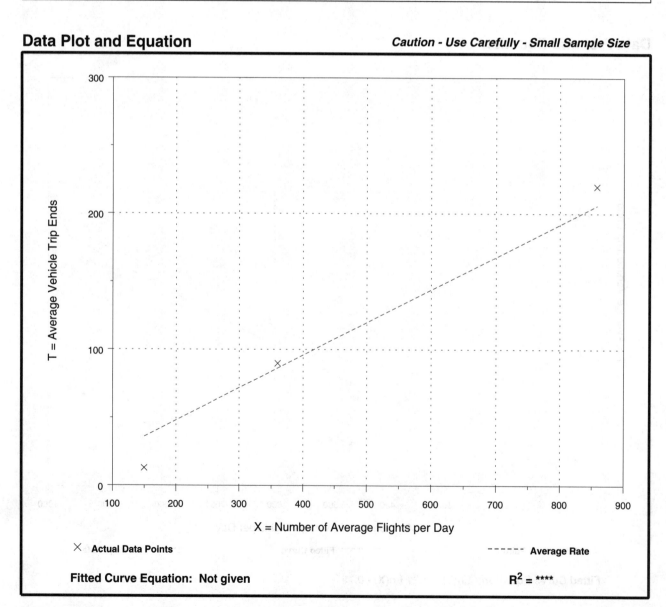

X = Number of Average Flights per Day

✕ **Actual Data Points**   - - - - - **Average Rate**

Fitted Curve Equation: Not given $R^2 = ****$

General Aviation Airport
(022)

Average Vehicle Trip Ends vs:	**Average Flights per Day**
On a:	**Weekday,**
	P.M. Peak Hour of Generator

Number of Studies: 3
Average Number of Flights per Day: 456
Directional Distribution: Not available

Trip Generation per Flight

Average Rate	Range of Rates	Standard Deviation
0.30	0.17 - 0.33	0.55

Data Plot and Equation

Caution - Use Carefully - Small Sample Size

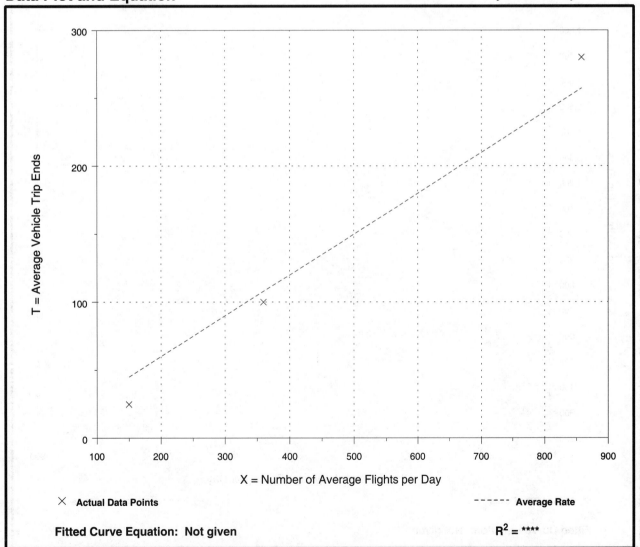

X **Actual Data Points**   - - - - - **Average Rate**

Fitted Curve Equation: Not given $R^2 = ****$

General Aviation Airport
(022)

Average Vehicle Trip Ends vs: Average Flights per Day
On a: Saturday

Number of Studies: 3
Average Number of Flights per Day: 456
Directional Distribution: 50% entering, 50% exiting

Trip Generation per Flight

Average Rate	Range of Rates	Standard Deviation
1.98	1.69 - 2.04	1.41

Data Plot and Equation

Caution - Use Carefully - Small Sample Size

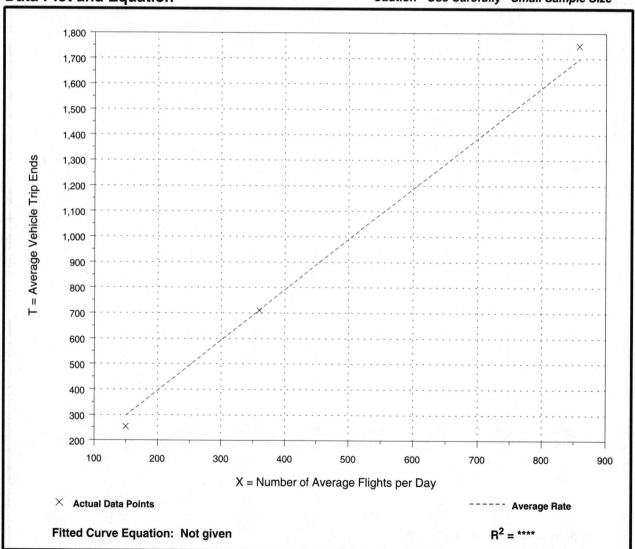

$\times$ **Actual Data Points**

----- **Average Rate**

Fitted Curve Equation: Not given $R^2 = ****$

General Aviation Airport
(022)

Average Vehicle Trip Ends vs: **Average Flights per Day**
On a: **Saturday,**
Peak Hour of Generator

Number of Studies: 3
Average Number of Flights per Day: 456
Directional Distribution: Not available

Trip Generation per Flight

Average Rate	Range of Rates	Standard Deviation
0.20	0.19 - 0.21	0.45

Data Plot and Equation

Caution - Use Carefully - Small Sample Size

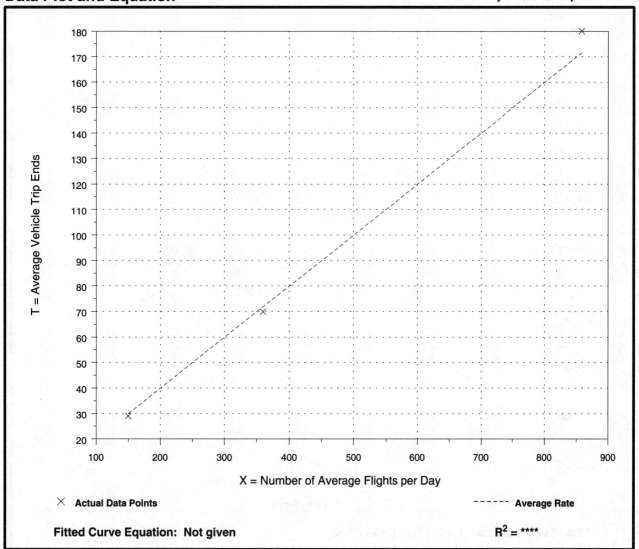

X ✕ **Actual Data Points**   - - - - - **Average Rate**

Fitted Curve Equation: Not given $R^2 = ****$

General Aviation Airport
(022)

Average Vehicle Trip Ends vs: Average Flights per Day
On a: Sunday

Number of Studies: 4
Average Number of Flights per Day: 501
Directional Distribution: 50% entering, 50% exiting

Trip Generation per Flight

Average Rate	Range of Rates	Standard Deviation
1.87	1.02 - 2.72	1.50

Data Plot and Equation

Caution - Use Carefully - Small Sample Size

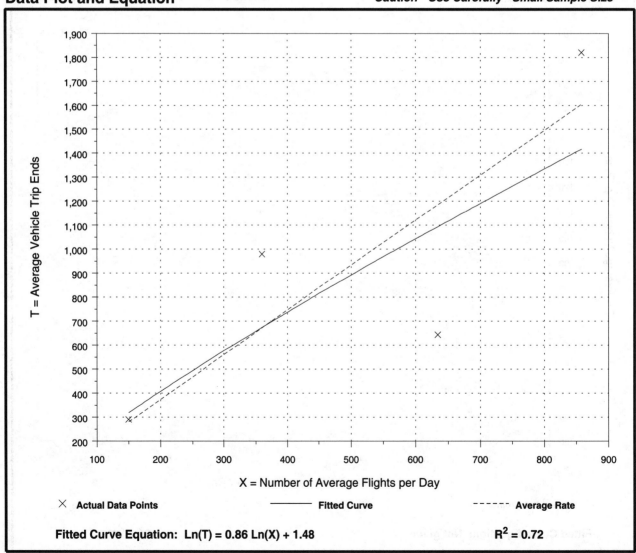

X **Actual Data Points** ——— **Fitted Curve** - - - - - **Average Rate**

Fitted Curve Equation: $Ln(T) = 0.86\ Ln(X) + 1.48$ $R^2 = 0.72$

General Aviation Airport
(022)

Average Vehicle Trip Ends vs: **Average Flights per Day**
On a: **Sunday,**
Peak Hour of Generator

Number of Studies: 4
Average Number of Flights per Day: 501
Directional Distribution: 54% entering, 46% exiting

Trip Generation per Flight

Average Rate	Range of Rates	Standard Deviation
0.23	0.21 - 0.28	0.48

Data Plot and Equation

Caution - Use Carefully - Small Sample Size

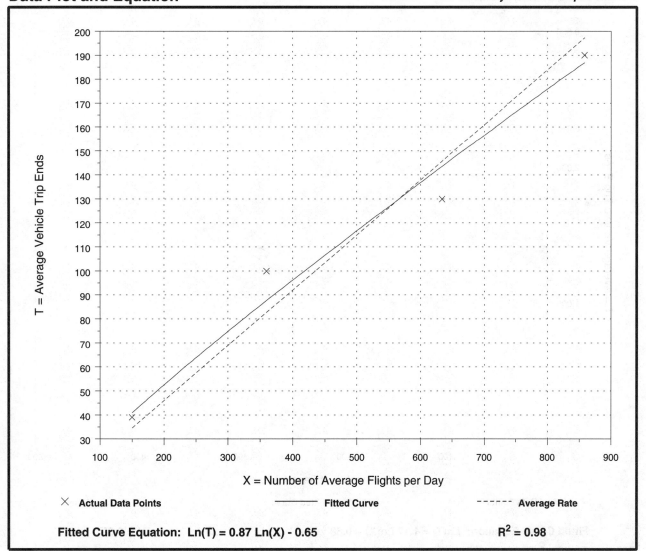

X = Number of Average Flights per Day

✕ **Actual Data Points**	———— **Fitted Curve**	- - - - - **Average Rate**

Fitted Curve Equation: Ln(T) = 0.87 Ln(X) - 0.65 $R^2 = 0.98$

General Aviation Airport
(022)

Average Vehicle Trip Ends vs: Based Aircraft
On a: Weekday

Number of Studies: 9
Average Number of Based Aircraft: 267
Directional Distribution: 50% entering, 50% exiting

Trip Generation per Based Aircraft

Average Rate	Range of Rates	Standard Deviation
5.00	2.26 - 8.30	2.94

Data Plot and Equation

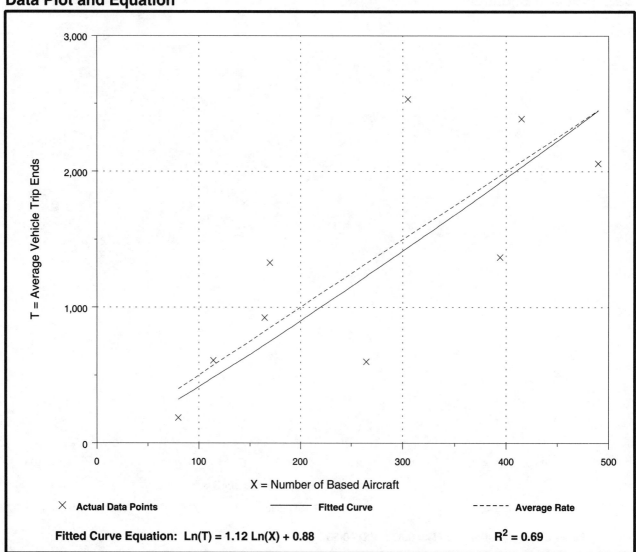

X **Actual Data Points**   ——————— **Fitted Curve**   - - - - - **Average Rate**

Fitted Curve Equation: Ln(T) = 1.12 Ln(X) + 0.88 $R^2 = 0.69$

General Aviation Airport
(022)

Average Vehicle Trip Ends vs: **Based Aircraft**
On a: **Weekday,**
A.M. Peak Hour of Generator

Number of Studies: 4
Average Number of Based Aircraft: 264
Directional Distribution: 50% entering, 50% exiting

Trip Generation per Based Aircraft

Average Rate	Range of Rates	Standard Deviation
0.41	0.16 - 0.55	0.65

Data Plot and Equation

Caution - Use Carefully - Small Sample Size

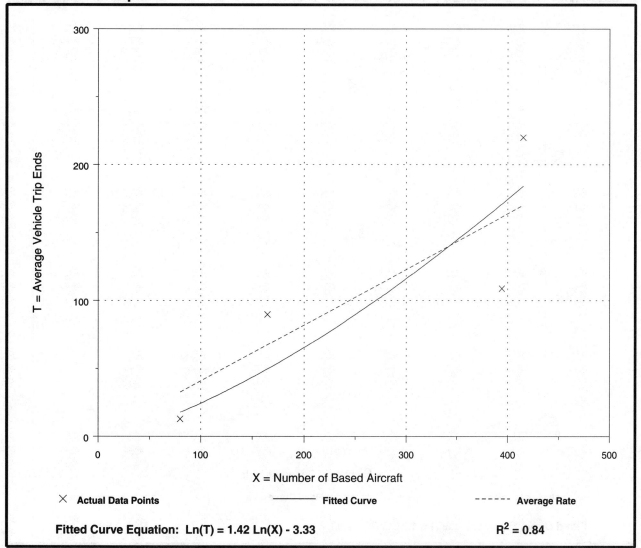

X **Actual Data Points** ———— **Fitted Curve** - - - - - **Average Rate**

Fitted Curve Equation: $Ln(T) = 1.42 \, Ln(X) - 3.33$ $R^2 = 0.84$

General Aviation Airport
(022)

Average Vehicle Trip Ends vs: Based Aircraft
On a: Weekday,
P.M. Peak Hour of Generator

Number of Studies: 4
Average Number of Based Aircraft: 264
Directional Distribution: 55% entering, 45% exiting

Trip Generation per Based Aircraft

Average Rate	Range of Rates	Standard Deviation
0.52	0.31 - 0.67	0.73

Data Plot and Equation

Caution - Use Carefully - Small Sample Size

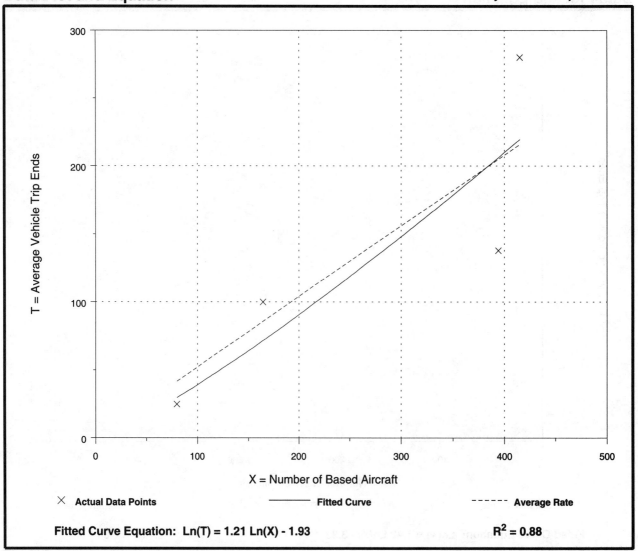

X **Actual Data Points**   —— **Fitted Curve**   - - - - - **Average Rate**

Fitted Curve Equation: Ln(T) = 1.21 Ln(X) - 1.93 $R^2 = 0.88$

General Aviation Airport
(022)

Average Vehicle Trip Ends vs: Based Aircraft
On a: Saturday

Number of Studies: 4
Average Number of Based Aircraft: 264
Directional Distribution: 50% entering, 50% exiting

Trip Generation per Based Aircraft

Average Rate	Range of Rates	Standard Deviation
3.69	2.97 - 4.30	2.01

Data Plot and Equation

Caution - Use Carefully - Small Sample Size

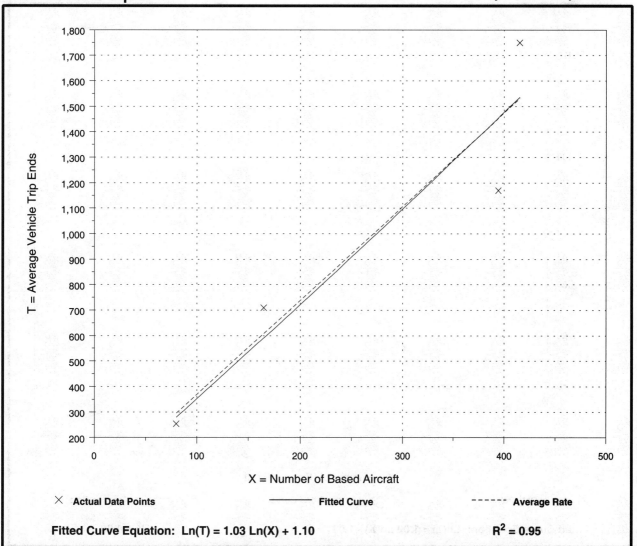

X **Actual Data Points**   ————— **Fitted Curve**   - - - - - **Average Rate**

Fitted Curve Equation: Ln(T) = 1.03 Ln(X) + 1.10 $R^2 = 0.95$

General Aviation Airport
(022)

Average Vehicle Trip Ends vs: **Based Aircraft**
On a: **Saturday,**
Peak Hour of Generator

Number of Studies: 4
Average Number of Based Aircraft: 264
Directional Distribution: 61% entering, 39% exiting

Trip Generation per Based Aircraft

Average Rate	Range of Rates	Standard Deviation
0.39	0.34 - 0.43	0.63

Data Plot and Equation

Caution - Use Carefully - Small Sample Size

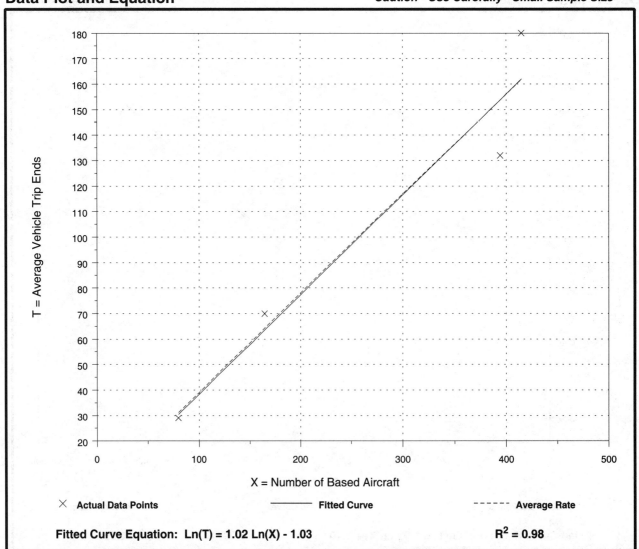

X = Number of Based Aircraft

$\times$ **Actual Data Points** ——— **Fitted Curve** ----- **Average Rate**

Fitted Curve Equation: Ln(T) = 1.02 Ln(X) - 1.03 $R^2 = 0.98$

General Aviation Airport
(022)

Average Vehicle Trip Ends vs: Based Aircraft
On a: Sunday

Number of Studies: 5
Average Number of Based Aircraft: 234
Directional Distribution: 50% entering, 50% exiting

Trip Generation per Based Aircraft

Average Rate	Range of Rates	Standard Deviation
4.51	3.63 - 5.94	2.25

Data Plot and Equation

Caution - Use Carefully - Small Sample Size

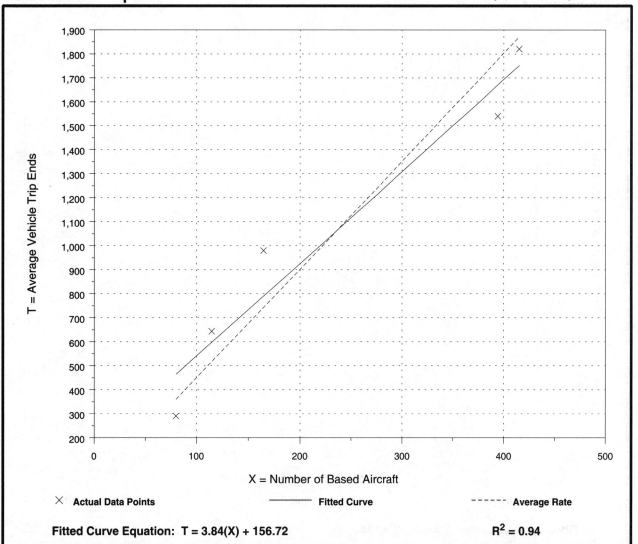

X = Number of Based Aircraft

✕ **Actual Data Points**   ———— **Fitted Curve**   - - - - - **Average Rate**

Fitted Curve Equation: T = 3.84(X) + 156.72 $R^2 = 0.94$

General Aviation Airport
(022)

Average Vehicle Trip Ends vs: Based Aircraft
On a: Sunday,
Peak Hour of Generator

Number of Studies: 5
Average Number of Based Aircraft: 234
Directional Distribution: 55% entering, 45% exiting

Trip Generation per Based Aircraft

Average Rate	Range of Rates	Standard Deviation
0.58	0.46 - 1.13	0.78

Data Plot and Equation

Caution - Use Carefully - Small Sample Size

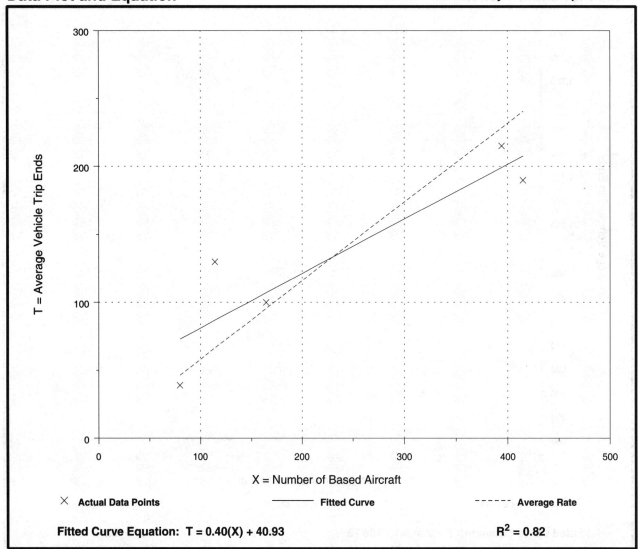

X **Actual Data Points**   ———— **Fitted Curve**   - - - - - **Average Rate**

Fitted Curve Equation: T = 0.40(X) + 40.93   **$R^2 = 0.82$**

Land Use: 030
Truck Terminal

Description

Truck terminals are facilities where goods are transferred between trucks, between trucks and railroads, or between trucks and ports.

Additional Data

Truck trips —

> At one site, an intermodal truck terminal, 70 percent of the site-generated driveway volume was truck traffic. At an additional truck terminal located on the waterfront, 34 percent of the driveway volume was truck traffic.

Vehicle occupancy was 1.16 persons per vehicle for two of the three sites surveyed.

Peak hours of the generator —

> The weekday p.m. peak hour was between 12:00 p.m. and 6:00 p.m. The Saturday peak hour was between 12:00 p.m. and 6:00 p.m.

The sites were surveyed in the 1970s and 1990s in California and Oregon.

Source Numbers

88, 443

Land Use: 030
Truck Terminal
Independent Variables with One Observation

The following trip generation data are for independent variables with only one observation. This information is shown in this table only; there are no related plots for these data.

Users are cautioned to use data with care because of the small sample size.

Independent Variable	Trip Generation Rate	Size of Independent Variable	Number of Studies	Directional Distribution
1,000 Square Feet Gross Floor Area				
Weekday	9.85	131	1	50% entering, 50% exiting
Weekday a.m. Peak Hour of Adjacent Street Traffic	0.90	131	1	40% entering, 60% exiting
Weekday p.m. Peak Hour of Adjacent Street Traffic	0.82	131	1	47% entering, 53% exiting
Weekday a.m. Peak Hour of Generator	0.90	131	1	40% entering, 60% exiting
Weekday p.m. Peak Hour of Generator	0.82	131	1	47% entering, 53% exiting
Saturday	1.89	131	1	50% entering, 50% exiting
Saturday Peak Hour of Generator	0.29	131	1	49% entering, 51% exiting
Sunday	1.02	131	1	50% entering, 50% exiting
Sunday Peak Hour of Generator	0.11	131	1	36% entering, 64% exiting
Truck Berths				
Weekday	6.79	190	1	50% entering, 50% exiting
Weekday a.m. Peak Hour of Adjacent Street Traffic	0.62	190	1	40% entering, 60% exiting
Weekday p.m. Peak Hour of Adjacent Street Traffic	0.57	190	1	47% entering, 53% exiting
Weekday a.m. Peak Hour of Generator	0.62	190	1	40% entering, 60% exiting
Weekday p.m. Peak Hour of Generator	0.57	190	1	47% entering, 53% exiting
Saturday	1.31	190	1	50% entering, 50% exiting
Saturday Peak Hour of Generator	0.20	190	1	49% entering, 51% exiting
Sunday	0.71	190	1	50% entering, 50% exiting
Sunday Peak Hour of Generator	0.08	190	1	36% entering, 64% exiting

Truck Terminal
(030)

Average Vehicle Trip Ends vs: **Employees**
On a: **Weekday**

Number of Studies: 2
Avg. Number of Employees: 164
Directional Distribution: 50% entering, 50% exiting

Trip Generation per Employee

Average Rate	Range of Rates	Standard Deviation
6.99	4.22 - 47.33	*

Data Plot and Equation

Caution - Use Carefully - Small Sample Size

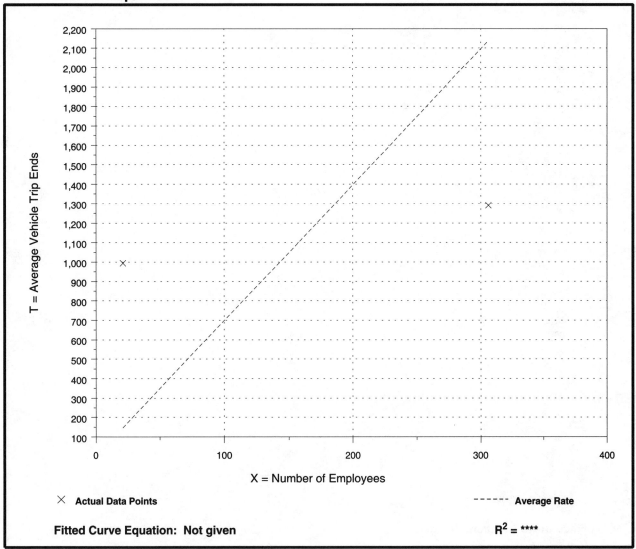

X **Actual Data Points**   - - - - - **Average Rate**

Fitted Curve Equation: Not given $R^2 = ****$

Truck Terminal
(030)

Average Vehicle Trip Ends vs: **Employees**
On a: **Weekday,**
Peak Hour of Adjacent Street Traffic,
One Hour Between 7 and 9 a.m.

Number of Studies: 2
Avg. Number of Employees: 164
Directional Distribution: 40% entering, 60% exiting

Trip Generation per Employee

Average Rate	Range of Rates	Standard Deviation
0.66	0.39 - 4.67	*

Data Plot and Equation

Caution - Use Carefully - Small Sample Size

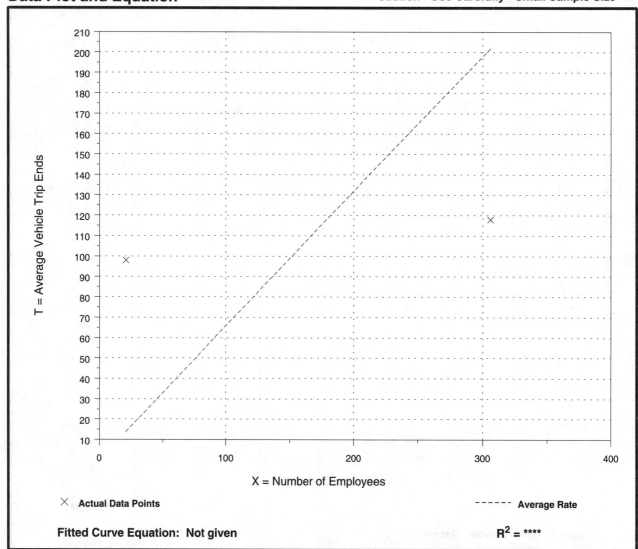

X = Number of Employees

✕ **Actual Data Points**   - - - - - **Average Rate**

Fitted Curve Equation: Not given R^2 = ****

Truck Terminal
(030)

Average Vehicle Trip Ends vs: **Employees**
On a: **Weekday,**
Peak Hour of Adjacent Street Traffic,
One Hour Between 4 and 6 p.m.

Number of Studies: 2
Avg. Number of Employees: 164
Directional Distribution: 47% entering, 53% exiting

Trip Generation per Employee

Average Rate	Range of Rates	Standard Deviation
0.55	0.35 - 3.43	*

Data Plot and Equation

Caution - Use Carefully - Small Sample Size

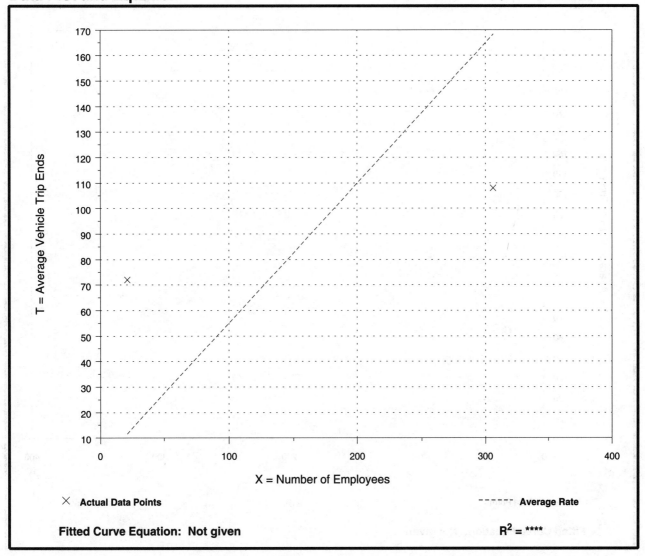

X **Actual Data Points**   - - - - - **Average Rate**

Fitted Curve Equation: Not given $R^2 = ****$

Truck Terminal
(030)

Average Vehicle Trip Ends vs: **Employees**
On a: **Weekday,**
A.M. Peak Hour of Generator

Number of Studies: 2
Avg. Number of Employees: 164
Directional Distribution: 40% entering, 60% exiting

Trip Generation per Employee

Average Rate	Range of Rates	Standard Deviation
0.66	0.39 - 4.67	*

Data Plot and Equation

Caution - Use Carefully - Small Sample Size

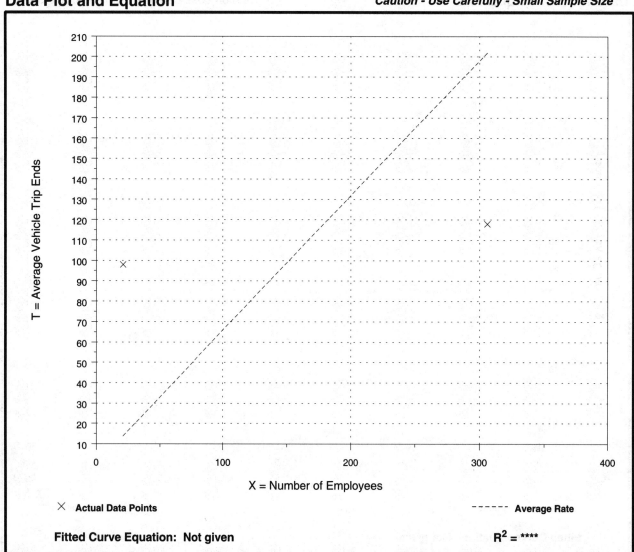

X = Number of Employees

✕ **Actual Data Points**   - - - - - **Average Rate**

Fitted Curve Equation: Not given $R^2 = ****$

Truck Terminal
(030)

Average Vehicle Trip Ends vs: **Employees**
On a: **Weekday,**
P.M. Peak Hour of Generator

Number of Studies: 2
Avg. Number of Employees: 164
Directional Distribution: 47% entering, 53% exiting

Trip Generation per Employee

Average Rate	Range of Rates	Standard Deviation
0.62	0.35 - 4.48	*

Data Plot and Equation

Caution - Use Carefully - Small Sample Size

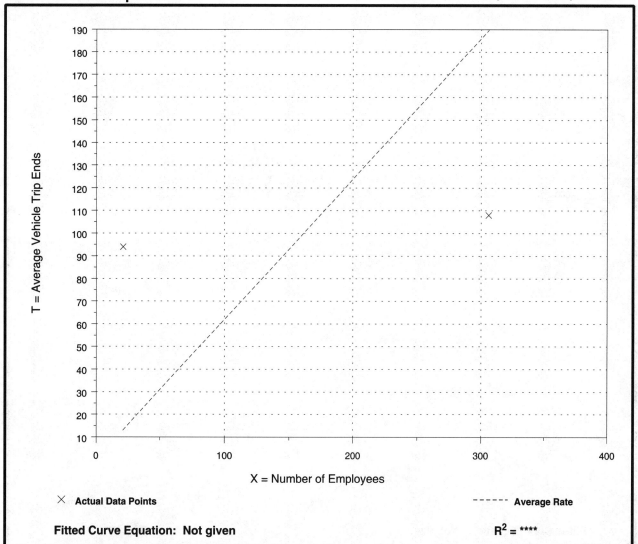

X **Actual Data Points**   - - - - - **Average Rate**

Fitted Curve Equation: Not given $R^2 = ****$

Truck Terminal
(030)

Average Vehicle Trip Ends vs: Employees
On a: Saturday

Number of Studies: 2
Avg. Number of Employees: 164
Directional Distribution: 50% entering, 50% exiting

Trip Generation per Employee

Average Rate	Range of Rates	Standard Deviation
1.47	0.81 - 11.14	*

Data Plot and Equation

Caution - Use Carefully - Small Sample Size

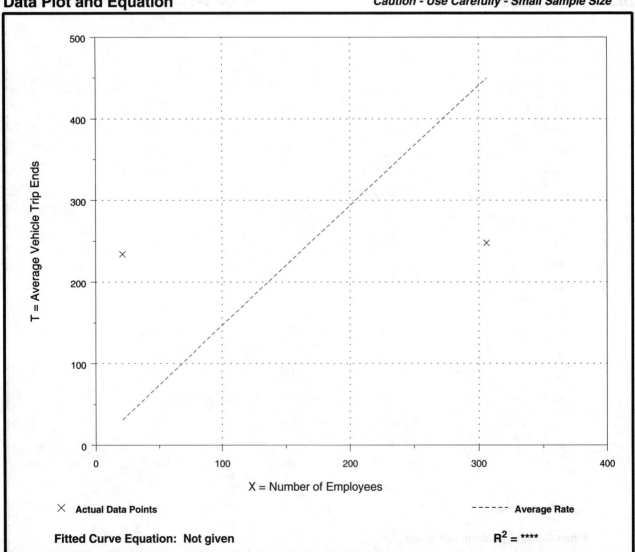

X **Actual Data Points**

– – – – – **Average Rate**

Fitted Curve Equation: Not given $R^2 = ****$

Truck Terminal
(030)

Average Vehicle Trip Ends vs: Employees
On a: Saturday,
Peak Hour of Generator

Number of Studies: 2
Avg. Number of Employees: 164
Directional Distribution: 49% entering, 51% exiting

Trip Generation per Employee

Average Rate	Range of Rates	Standard Deviation
0.20	0.12 - 1.29	*

Data Plot and Equation

Caution - Use Carefully - Small Sample Size

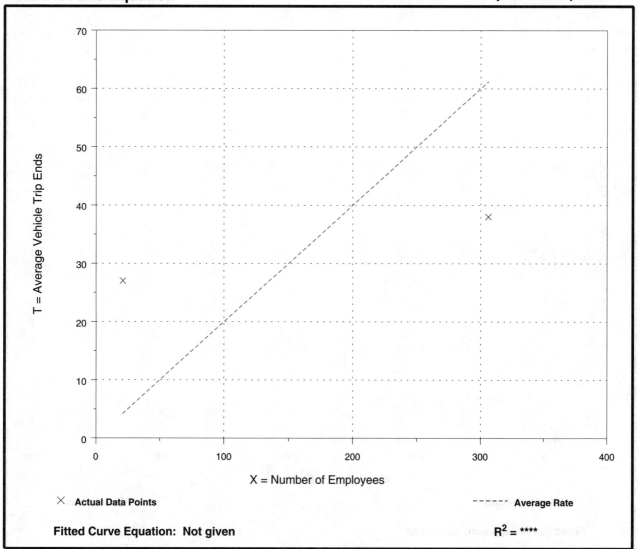

X **Actual Data Points**   - - - - - **Average Rate**

Fitted Curve Equation: Not given $R^2 = ****$

Truck Terminal
(030)

Average Vehicle Trip Ends vs: Employees
On a: Sunday

Number of Studies: 2
Avg. Number of Employees: 164
Directional Distribution: 50% entering, 50% exiting

Trip Generation per Employee

Average Rate	Range of Rates	Standard Deviation
0.92	0.44 - 7.95	*

Data Plot and Equation

Caution - Use Carefully - Small Sample Size

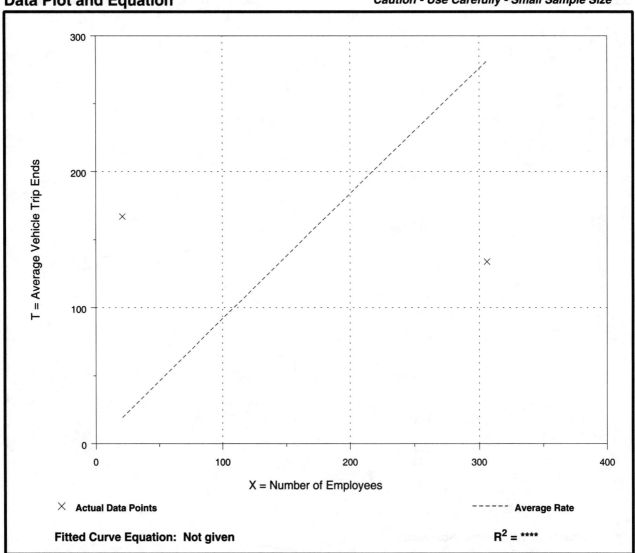

X = Number of Employees

✕ **Actual Data Points**

‑ ‑ ‑ ‑ ‑ **Average Rate**

Fitted Curve Equation: Not given $R^2 = ****$

Truck Terminal
(030)

Average Vehicle Trip Ends vs: **Employees**
On a: **Sunday,**
Peak Hour of Generator

Number of Studies: 2
Avg. Number of Employees: 164
Directional Distribution: 36% entering, 64% exiting

Trip Generation per Employee

Average Rate	Range of Rates	Standard Deviation
0.11	0.05 - 1.00	*

Data Plot and Equation

Caution - Use Carefully - Small Sample Size

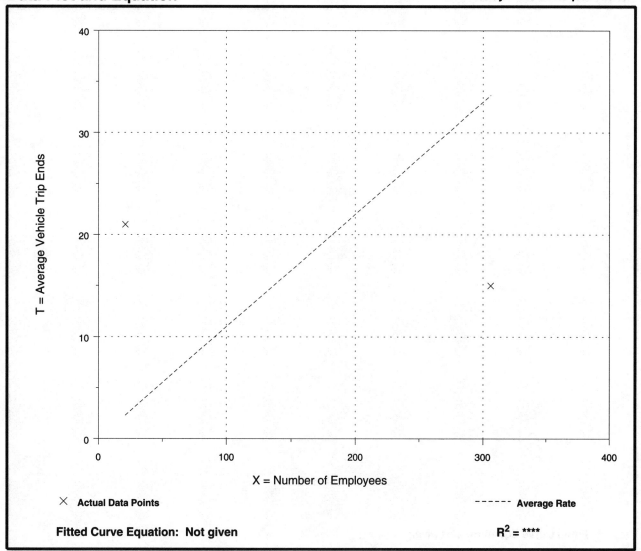

X   **Actual Data Points**   - - - - - **Average Rate**

Fitted Curve Equation: Not given $R^2 = $ ****

Truck Terminal
(030)

Average Vehicle Trip Ends vs: Acres
On a: Weekday

Number of Studies: 2
Average Number of Acres: 14
Directional Distribution: 50% entering, 50% exiting

Trip Generation per Acre

Average Rate	Range of Rates	Standard Deviation
81.90	66.27 - 100.08	*

Data Plot and Equation

Caution - Use Carefully - Small Sample Size

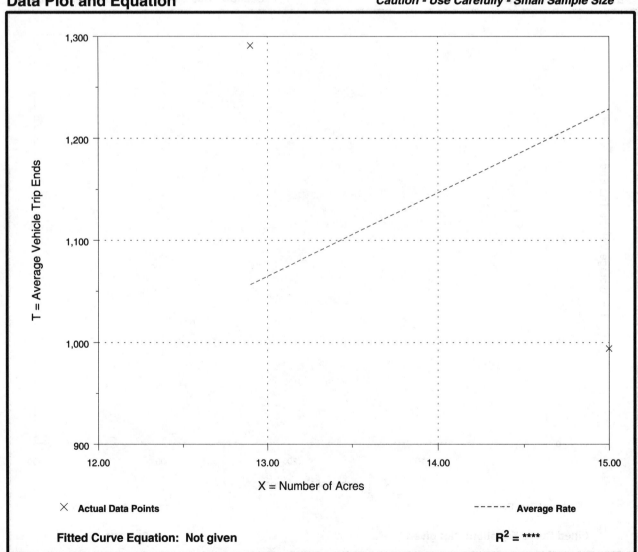

X **Actual Data Points**   - - - - - **Average Rate**

Fitted Curve Equation: Not given R^2 = ****

Truck Terminal
(030)

Average Vehicle Trip Ends vs: **Acres**
On a: **Weekday,**
Peak Hour of Adjacent Street Traffic,
One Hour Between 7 and 9 a.m.

Number of Studies: 3
Average Number of Acres: 12
Directional Distribution: 41% entering, 59% exiting

Trip Generation per Acre

Average Rate	Range of Rates	Standard Deviation
7.28	5.30 - 9.15	3.04

Data Plot and Equation

Caution - Use Carefully - Small Sample Size

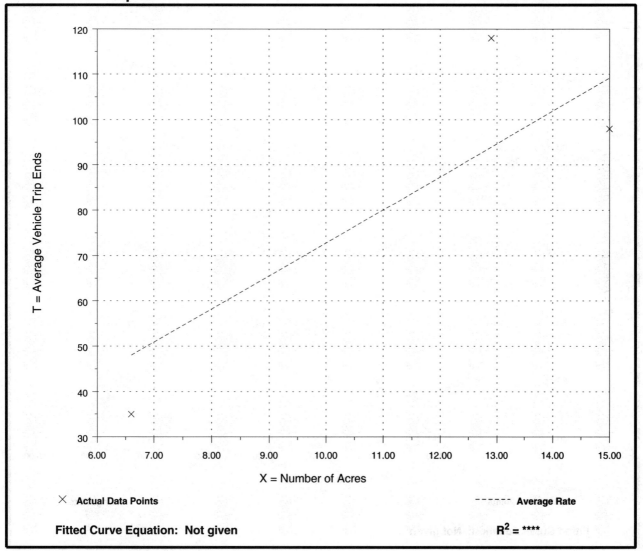

X **Actual Data Points**   ------ **Average Rate**

Fitted Curve Equation: Not given $R^2 = ****$

Truck Terminal
(030)

Average Vehicle Trip Ends vs: **Acres**

On a: **Weekday,**
Peak Hour of Adjacent Street Traffic,
One Hour Between 4 and 6 p.m.

Number of Studies: 3
Average Number of Acres: 12
Directional Distribution: 43% entering, 57% exiting

Trip Generation per Acre

Average Rate	Range of Rates	Standard Deviation
6.55	4.80 - 8.37	2.97

Data Plot and Equation

Caution - Use Carefully - Small Sample Size

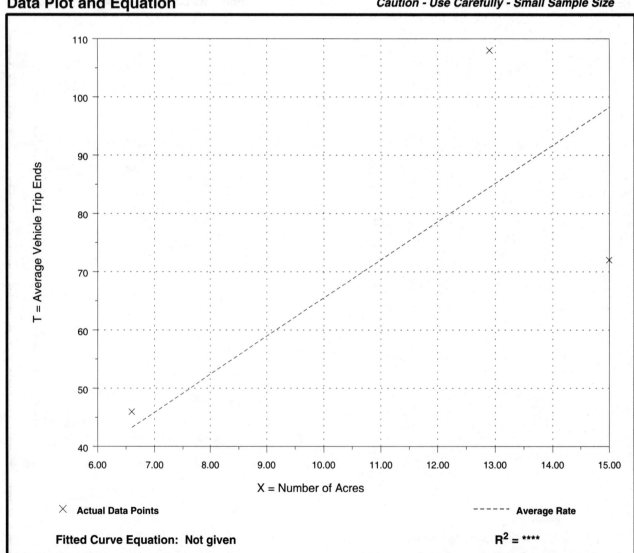

X **Actual Data Points**

------ **Average Rate**

Fitted Curve Equation: Not given $R^2 = ****$

Truck Terminal
(030)

Average Vehicle Trip Ends vs: **Acres**
On a: **Weekday,**
A.M. Peak Hour of Generator

Number of Studies: 2
Average Number of Acres: 14
Directional Distribution: 40% entering, 60% exiting

Trip Generation per Acre

Average Rate	Range of Rates	Standard Deviation
7.74	6.53 - 9.15	*

Data Plot and Equation

Caution - Use Carefully - Small Sample Size

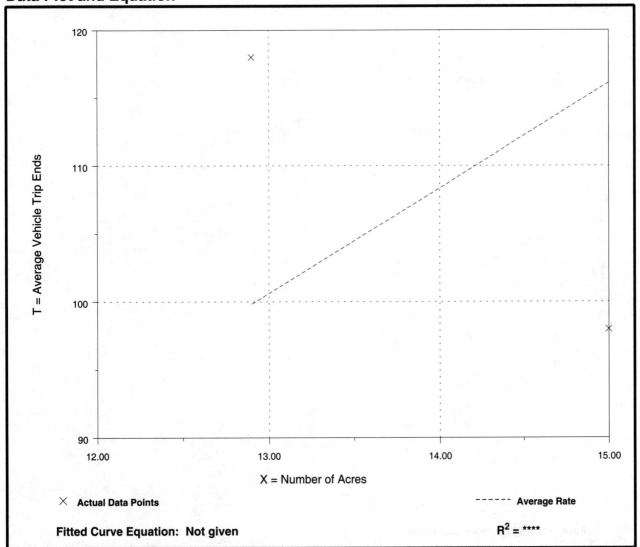

X **Actual Data Points**   - - - - - **Average Rate**

Fitted Curve Equation: Not given $R^2 = ****$

Truck Terminal
(030)

Average Vehicle Trip Ends vs: **Acres**
On a: **Weekday,**
P.M. Peak Hour of Generator

Number of Studies: 2
Average Number of Acres: 14
Directional Distribution: 47% entering, 53% exiting

Trip Generation per Acre

Average Rate	Range of Rates	Standard Deviation
7.24	6.27 - 8.37	*

Data Plot and Equation

Caution - Use Carefully - Small Sample Size

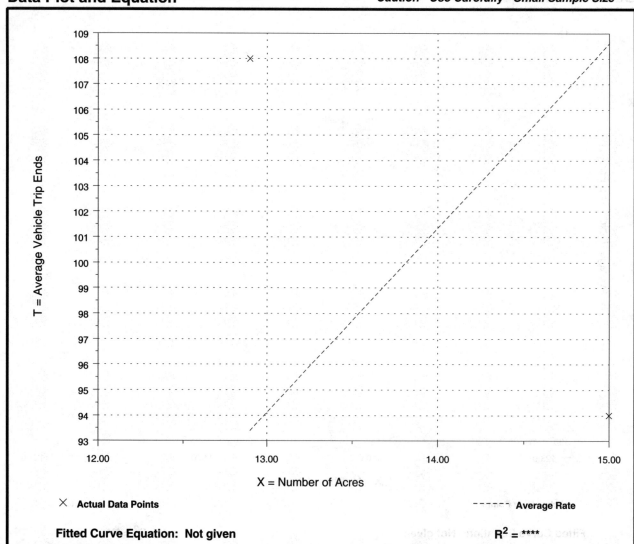

X **Actual Data Points**   ------ **Average Rate**

Fitted Curve Equation: Not given $R^2 = ****$

Truck Terminal
(030)

Average Vehicle Trip Ends vs: Acres
On a: Saturday

Number of Studies: 2
Average Number of Acres: 14
Directional Distribution: 50% entering, 50% exiting

Trip Generation per Acre

Average Rate	Range of Rates	Standard Deviation
17.28	15.60 - 19.22	*

Data Plot and Equation

Caution - Use Carefully - Small Sample Size

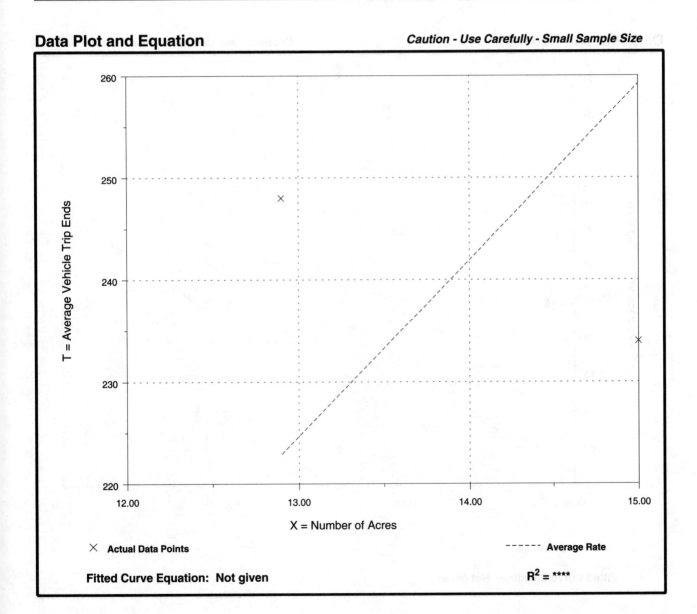

X = Number of Acres

✕ **Actual Data Points**   - - - - - **Average Rate**

Fitted Curve Equation: Not given $R^2 = ****$

Truck Terminal
(030)

Average Vehicle Trip Ends vs: Acres
On a: Saturday,
Peak Hour of Generator

Number of Studies: 2
Average Number of Acres: 14
Directional Distribution: 49% entering, 51% exiting

Trip Generation per Acre

Average Rate	Range of Rates	Standard Deviation
2.33	1.80 - 2.95	*

Data Plot and Equation

Caution - Use Carefully - Small Sample Size

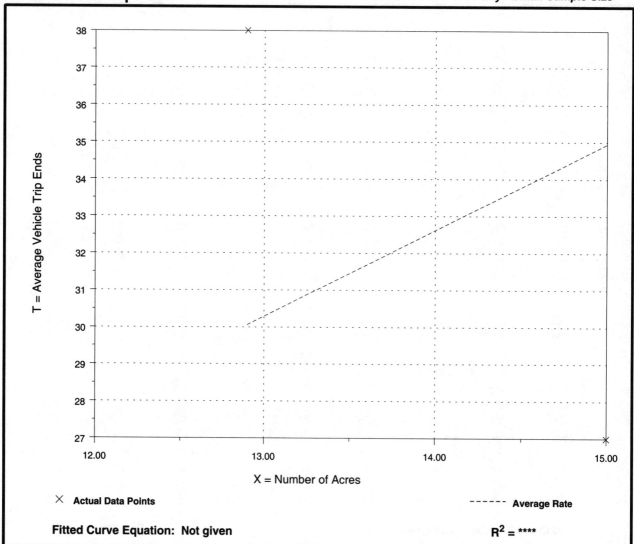

X **Actual Data Points**

- - - - - **Average Rate**

Fitted Curve Equation: Not given $R^2 = ****$

Truck Terminal
(030)

Average Vehicle Trip Ends vs: **Acres**
On a: **Sunday**

Number of Studies: 2
Average Number of Acres: 14
Directional Distribution: 50% entering, 50% exiting

Trip Generation per Acre

Average Rate	Range of Rates	Standard Deviation
10.79	10.39 - 11.13	*

Data Plot and Equation

Caution - Use Carefully - Small Sample Size

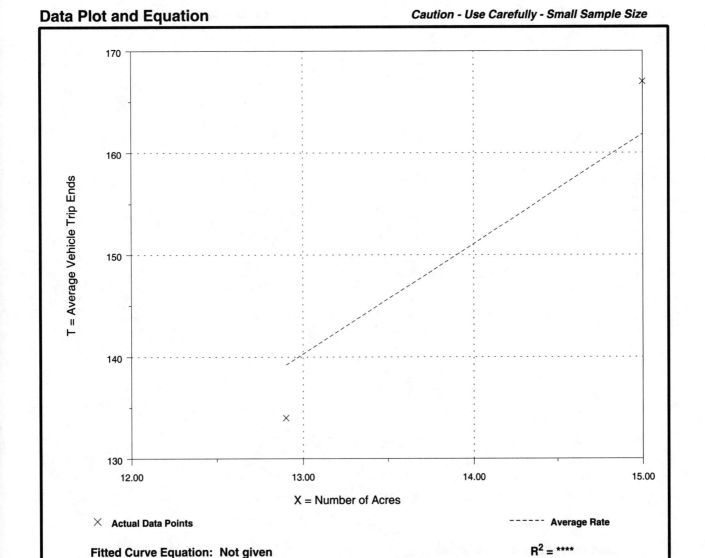

X Actual Data Points

- - - - - **Average Rate**

Fitted Curve Equation: Not given $R^2 = ****$

Truck Terminal
(030)

Average Vehicle Trip Ends vs: Acres
On a: Sunday,
Peak Hour of Generator

Number of Studies: 2
Average Number of Acres: 14
Directional Distribution: 36% entering, 64% exiting

Trip Generation per Acre

Average Rate	Range of Rates	Standard Deviation
1.29	1.16 - 1.40	*

Data Plot and Equation

Caution - Use Carefully - Small Sample Size

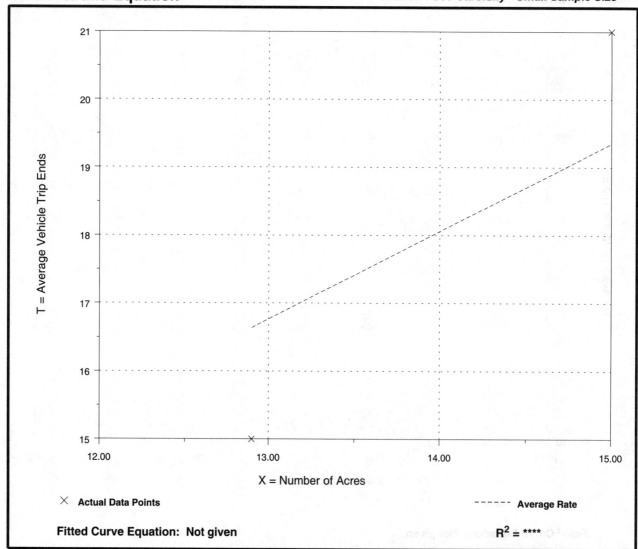

X = Number of Acres

× **Actual Data Points**

----- **Average Rate**

Fitted Curve Equation: Not given $R^2 = ****$

Land Use: 090
Park-and-Ride Lot with Bus Service

Description

Park-and-ride lots with bus service are areas used for the transfer of people between private vehicles and buses. They usually contain a bus passenger shelter, a parking lot and circulation facilities for buses, as well as for private motor vehicles. In addition to park-and-ride, a significant number of passengers are dropped off. Light rail transit station with parking (Land Use 093) is a related use.

Additional Data

The trip generation for the a.m. and p.m. peak hours of the generator typically coincided with the peak hours of the adjacent street traffic; therefore, only one a.m. peak hour and one p.m. peak hour, which represent both the peak hour of the generator and the peak hour of the adjacent street traffic, are shown for park-and-ride lots with bus services. The weekday a.m. peak hour was between 6:00 a.m. and 9:00 a.m. The weekday p.m. peak hour was between 4:00 p.m. and 6:30 p.m.

The sites were surveyed between the 1980s and the 2000s in Oregon, California, Washington and New Jersey.

Source Numbers

155, 422, 425, 435, 443, 579, 598, 611

Park-and-Ride Lot with Bus Service
(090)

Average Vehicle Trip Ends vs: Parking Spaces
On a: Weekday

Number of Studies: 4
Average Number of Parking Spaces: 256
Directional Distribution: 50% entering, 50% exiting

Trip Generation per Parking Space

Average Rate	Range of Rates	Standard Deviation
4.50	3.90 - 7.06	2.26

Data Plot and Equation

Caution - Use Carefully - Small Sample Size

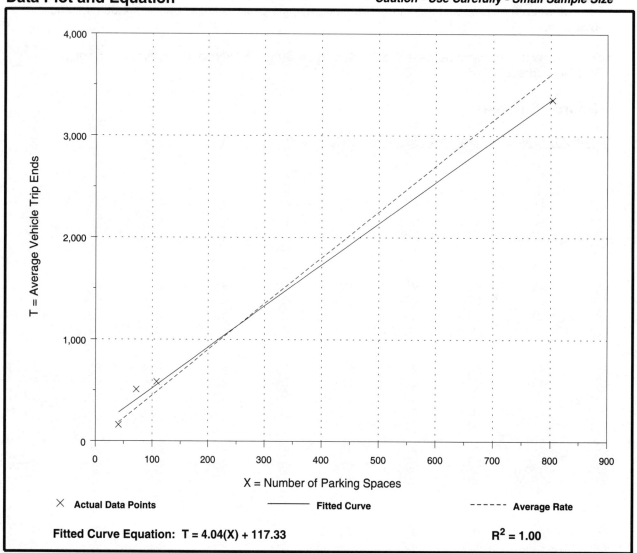

X = Number of Parking Spaces

$\times$ **Actual Data Points**   ——— **Fitted Curve**   - - - - - **Average Rate**

Fitted Curve Equation: T = 4.04(X) + 117.33 $R^2 = 1.00$

Park-and-Ride Lot with Bus Service
(090)

Average Vehicle Trip Ends vs: Parking Spaces
On a: Weekday,
Peak Hour of Adjacent Street Traffic,
One Hour Between 7 and 9 a.m.

Number of Studies: 10
Average Number of Parking Spaces: 394
Directional Distribution: 81% entering, 19% exiting

Trip Generation per Parking Space

Average Rate	Range of Rates	Standard Deviation
0.72	0.29 - 0.87	0.86

Data Plot and Equation

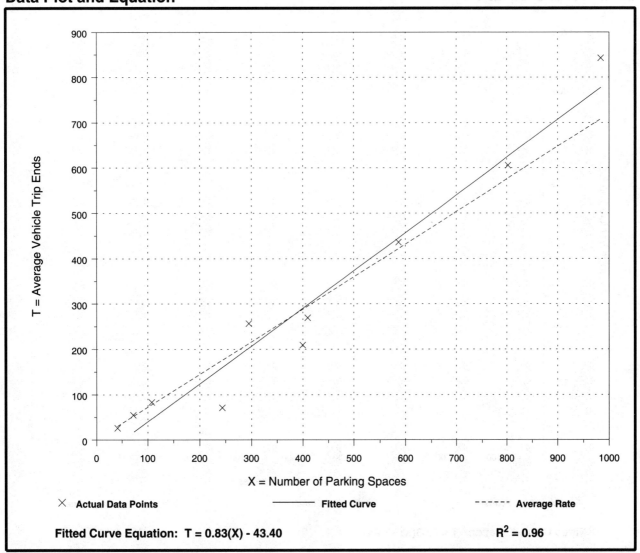

T = Average Vehicle Trip Ends

X = Number of Parking Spaces

✕ **Actual Data Points**　　　———— **Fitted Curve**　　　----- **Average Rate**

Fitted Curve Equation: T = 0.83(X) - 43.40　　　$R^2 = 0.96$

Park-and-Ride Lot with Bus Service
(090)

Average Vehicle Trip Ends vs: **Parking Spaces**
On a: **Weekday,**
Peak Hour of Adjacent Street Traffic,
One Hour Between 4 and 6 p.m.

Number of Studies: 13
Average Number of Parking Spaces: 420
Directional Distribution: 23% entering, 77% exiting

Trip Generation per Parking Space

Average Rate	Range of Rates	Standard Deviation
0.62	0.23 - 0.93	0.80

Data Plot and Equation

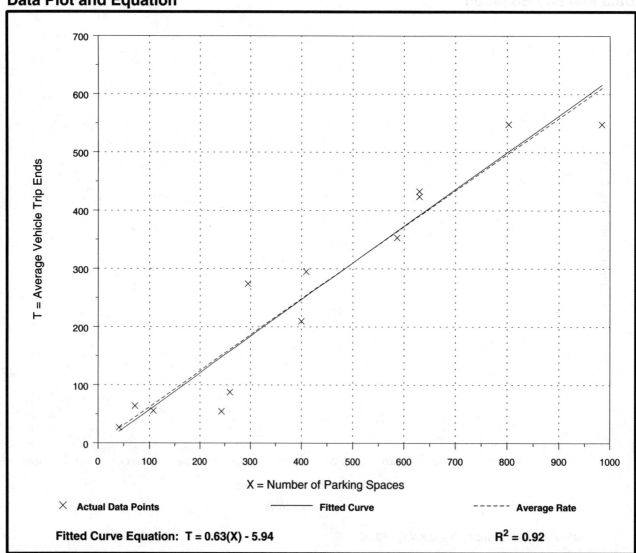

X   **Actual Data Points**   —————— **Fitted Curve**   − − − − − **Average Rate**

Fitted Curve Equation: T = 0.63(X) - 5.94 $R^2 = 0.92$

Park-and-Ride Lot with Bus Service
(090)

Average Vehicle Trip Ends vs: **Occupied Spaces**
On a: **Weekday**

Number of Studies: 3
Average Number of Occupied Spaces: 43
Directional Distribution: 50% entering, 50% exiting

Trip Generation per Occupied Space

Average Rate	Range of Rates	Standard Deviation
9.62	4.71 - 12.15	4.31

Data Plot and Equation

Caution - Use Carefully - Small Sample Size

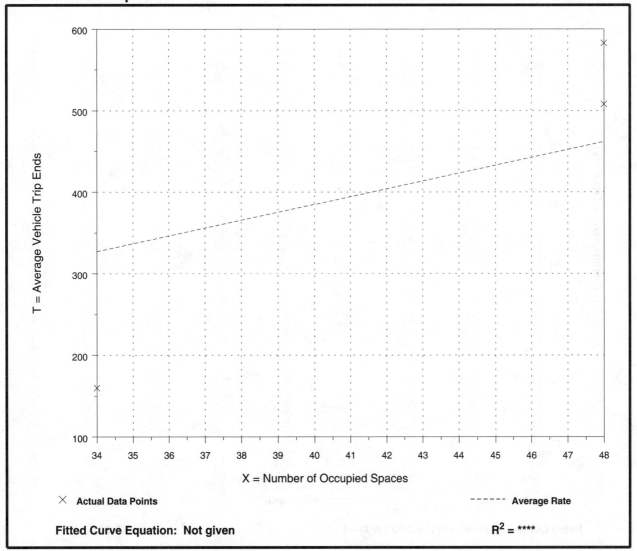

X = Number of Occupied Spaces

×   **Actual Data Points**   - - - - -   **Average Rate**

Fitted Curve Equation: Not given $R^2 = ****$

Park-and-Ride Lot with Bus Service
(090)

Average Vehicle Trip Ends vs: **Occupied Spaces**
On a: **Weekday,**
Peak Hour of Adjacent Street Traffic,
One Hour Between 7 and 9 a.m.

Number of Studies: 4
Average Number of Occupied Spaces: 47
Directional Distribution: 69% entering, 31% exiting

Trip Generation per Occupied Space

Average Rate	Range of Rates	Standard Deviation
1.26	0.76 - 1.73	1.16

Data Plot and Equation

Caution - Use Carefully - Small Sample Size

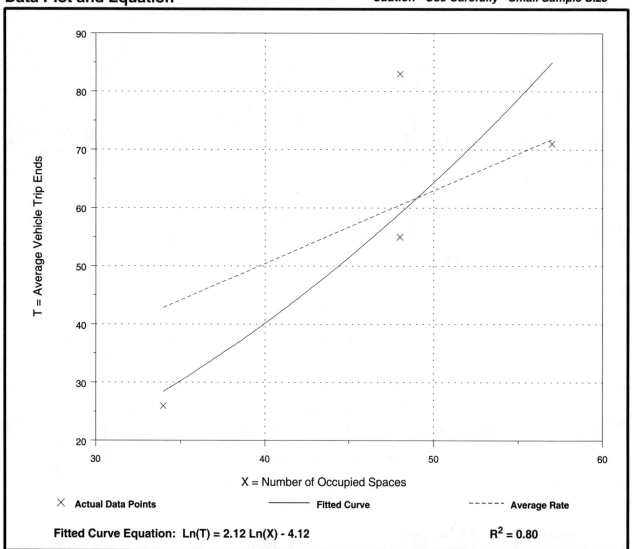

X   **Actual Data Points**   ———— **Fitted Curve**   - - - - - **Average Rate**

Fitted Curve Equation: Ln(T) = 2.12 Ln(X) - 4.12 $R^2 = 0.80$

Park-and-Ride Lot with Bus Service
(090)

Average Vehicle Trip Ends vs: **Occupied Spaces**
On a: **Weekday,**
Peak Hour of Adjacent Street Traffic,
One Hour Between 4 and 6 p.m.

Number of Studies: 6
Average Number of Occupied Spaces: 148
Directional Distribution: 28% entering, 72% exiting

Trip Generation per Occupied Space

Average Rate	Range of Rates	Standard Deviation
0.81	0.71 - 1.33	0.91

Data Plot and Equation

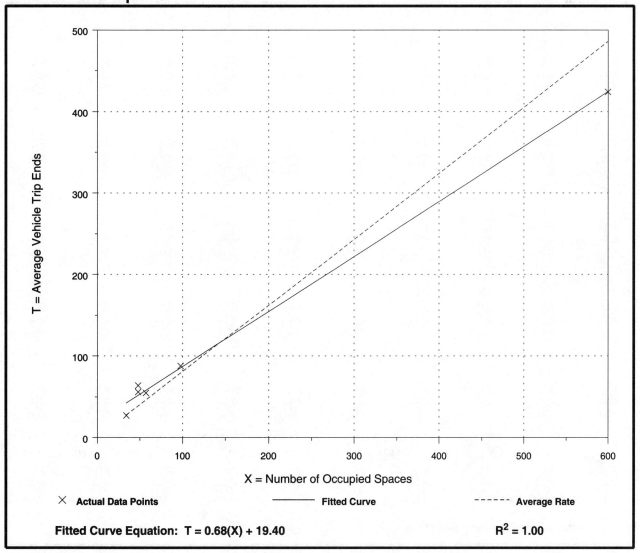

X = Number of Occupied Spaces

✕ **Actual Data Points** ───── **Fitted Curve** ----- **Average Rate**

Fitted Curve Equation: T = 0.68(X) + 19.40 $R^2 = 1.00$

Park-and-Ride Lot with Bus Service
(090)

Average Vehicle Trip Ends vs: **Acres**
On a: **Weekday**

Number of Studies: 3
Average Number of Acres: 1
Directional Distribution: 50% entering, 50% exiting

Trip Generation per Acre

Average Rate	Range of Rates	Standard Deviation
372.32	216.22 - 508.00	124.97

Data Plot and Equation

Caution - Use Carefully - Small Sample Size

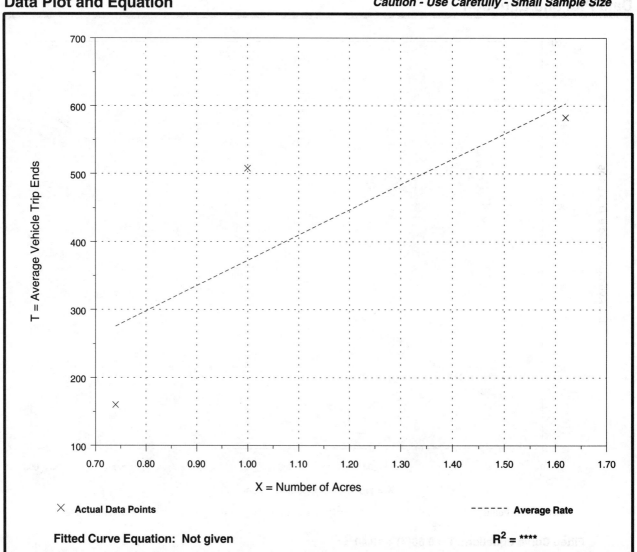

×	Actual Data Points	- - - - - Average Rate

Fitted Curve Equation: Not given $R^2 = ****$

Park-and-Ride Lot with Bus Service
(090)

Average Vehicle Trip Ends vs: **Acres**
On a: **Weekday,**
Peak Hour of Adjacent Street Traffic,
One Hour Between 7 and 9 a.m.

Number of Studies: 3
Average Number of Acres: 1
Directional Distribution: Not available

Trip Generation per Acre

Average Rate	Range of Rates	Standard Deviation
48.81	35.14 - 55.00	9.41

Data Plot and Equation

Caution - Use Carefully - Small Sample Size

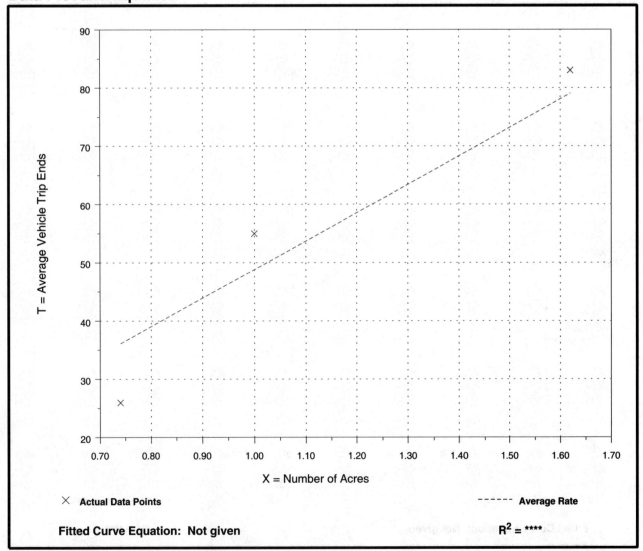

X Actual Data Points

----- Average Rate

Fitted Curve Equation: Not given

$R^2 = ****$

Park-and-Ride Lot with Bus Service
(090)

Average Vehicle Trip Ends vs: **Acres**
On a: **Weekday,**
Peak Hour of Adjacent Street Traffic,
One Hour Between 4 and 6 p.m.

Number of Studies: 3
Average Number of Acres: 1
Directional Distribution: Not available

Trip Generation per Acre

Average Rate	Range of Rates	Standard Deviation
43.75	34.57 - 64.00	15.91

Data Plot and Equation

Caution - Use Carefully - Small Sample Size

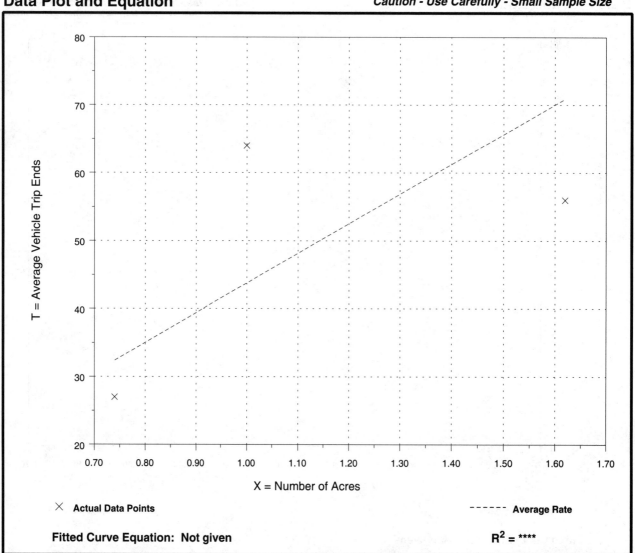

X Actual Data Points

- - - - - **Average Rate**

Fitted Curve Equation: Not given $R^2 =$ ****

Land Use: 093
Light Rail Transit Station with Parking

Description

Light rail transit (LRT) stations are defined as transportation stations that provide park-and-ride activity. These stations are for the transfer of people between private vehicles and light rail transportation. They usually contain automobile parking areas; a transfer station; a passenger shelter; ticketing facilities; and ancillary amenities, such as restrooms, vending machines and coffee/newspaper stands. Drop-off/pick-up and carpool areas may also be provided. Park-and-ride lot with bus service (Land Use 090) is a related use.

Additional Data

Peak hours of the generator —
> The weekday a.m. peak hour was between 6:00 a.m. and 9:00 p.m. The weekday p.m. peak hour was between 4:00 p.m. and 6:00 p.m.

The sites were surveyed in 1994 and 1995 in Oregon.

Source Number

443

Land Use: 093
Light Rail Transit Station with Parking
Independent Variables with One Observation

The following trip generation data are for independent variables with only one observation. This information is shown in this table only; there are no related plots for these data.

Users are cautioned to use data with care because of the small sample size.

Independent Variable	Trip Generation Rate	Size of Independent Variable	Number of Studies	Directional Distribution
Parking Spaces				
Weekday a.m. Peak Hour of Adjacent Street Traffic	1.07	391	1	80% entering, 20% exiting
Weekday p.m. Peak Hour of Adjacent Street Traffic	1.24	391	1	58% entering, 42% exiting
Occupied Parking Spaces				
Weekday a.m. Peak Hour of Adjacent Street Traffic	1.14	365	1	80% entering, 20% exiting
Weekday p.m. Peak Hour of Adjacent Street Traffic	1.33	365	1	58% entering, 42% exiting

Light Rail Transit Station with Parking
(093)

Average Vehicle Trip Ends vs: **Parking Spaces**
On a: **Weekday**

Number of Studies: 2
Average Number of Parking Spaces: 380
Directional Distribution: 50% entering, 50% exiting

Trip Generation per Parking Space

Average Rate	Range of Rates	Standard Deviation
2.51	1.78 - 3.54	*

Data Plot and Equation

Caution - Use Carefully - Small Sample Size

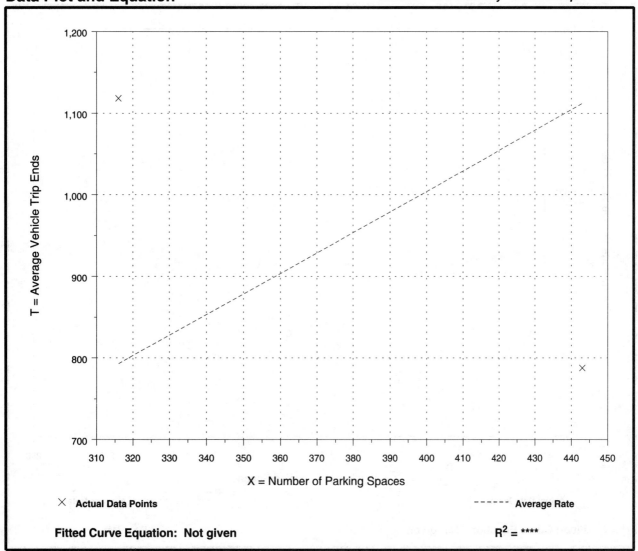

X **Actual Data Points**

- - - - - **Average Rate**

Fitted Curve Equation: Not given

$R^2 = ****$

Light Rail Transit Station with Parking
(093)

Average Vehicle Trip Ends vs: **Occupied Spaces**
On a: **Weekday**

Number of Studies: 2
Average Number of Occupied Spaces: 244
Directional Distribution: 50% entering, 50% exiting

Trip Generation per Occupied Space

Average Rate	Range of Rates	Standard Deviation
3.91	3.75 - 4.04	*

Data Plot and Equation

Caution - Use Carefully - Small Sample Size

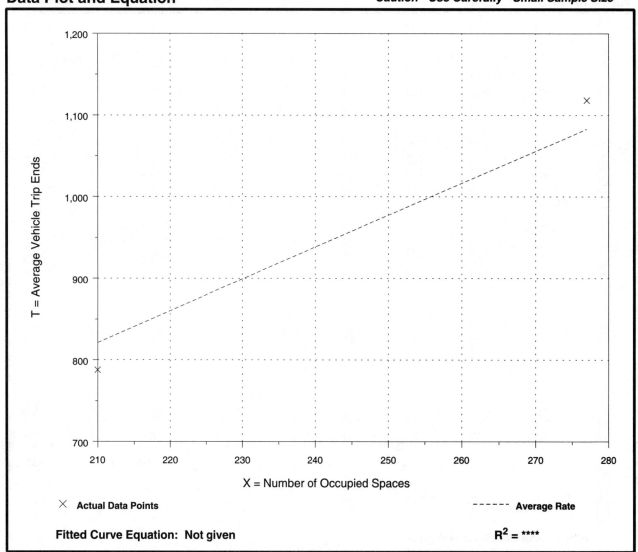

X **Actual Data Points**

- - - - - **Average Rate**

Fitted Curve Equation: Not given

$R^2 = ****$

Land Use: 110
General Light Industrial

Description

Light industrial facilities are free-standing facilities devoted to a single use. The facilities have an emphasis on activities other than manufacturing and typically have minimal office space. Typical light industrial activities include printing, material testing and assembly of data processing equipment. General heavy industrial (Land Use 120), industrial park (Land Use 130) and manufacturing (Land Use 140) are related uses.

Additional Data

No vehicle occupancy data were available specifically for general light industrial, but the average was approximately 1.3 persons per automobile for all industrial uses.

The peak hour of the generator typically coincided with the peak hour of the adjacent street traffic.

Facilities with employees on shift work may peak at other hours.

The sites were surveyed in the early 1970s, the mid- to late 1980s and the 2000s throughout the United States.

Source Numbers

7, 9, 10, 11, 15, 17, 88, 174, 179, 184, 191, 192, 251, 253, 286, 300, 611

General Light Industrial
(110)

Average Vehicle Trip Ends vs: **Employees**
On a: **Weekday**

Number of Studies: 18
Avg. Number of Employees: 469
Directional Distribution: 50% entering, 50% exiting

Trip Generation per Employee

Average Rate	Range of Rates	Standard Deviation
3.02	1.53 - 4.48	1.86

Data Plot and Equation

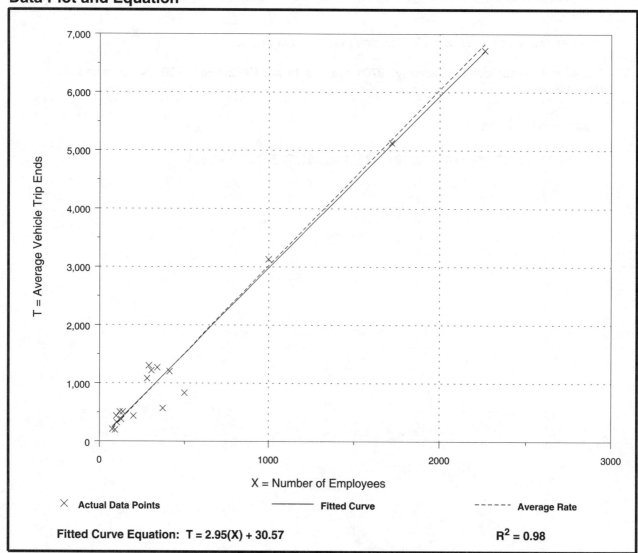

X **Actual Data Points**   ——— **Fitted Curve**   - - - - - **Average Rate**

Fitted Curve Equation: T = 2.95(X) + 30.57 $R^2 = 0.98$

General Light Industrial
(110)

Average Vehicle Trip Ends vs: **Employees**
On a: **Weekday,**
Peak Hour of Adjacent Street Traffic,
One Hour Between 7 and 9 a.m.

Number of Studies: 21
Avg. Number of Employees: 428
Directional Distribution: 83% entering, 17% exiting

Trip Generation per Employee

Average Rate	Range of Rates	Standard Deviation
0.44	0.08 - 1.02	0.69

Data Plot and Equation

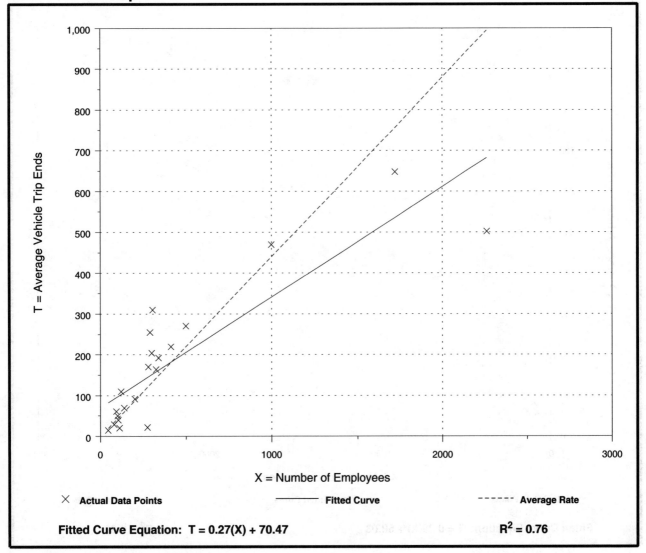

Fitted Curve Equation: T = 0.27(X) + 70.47 $R^2 = 0.76$

General Light Industrial
(110)

Average Vehicle Trip Ends vs: **Employees**
On a: **Weekday,**
Peak Hour of Adjacent Street Traffic,
One Hour Between 4 and 6 p.m.

Number of Studies: 19
Avg. Number of Employees: 451
Directional Distribution: 21% entering, 79% exiting

Trip Generation per Employee

Average Rate	Range of Rates	Standard Deviation
0.42	0.04 - 0.95	0.67

Data Plot and Equation

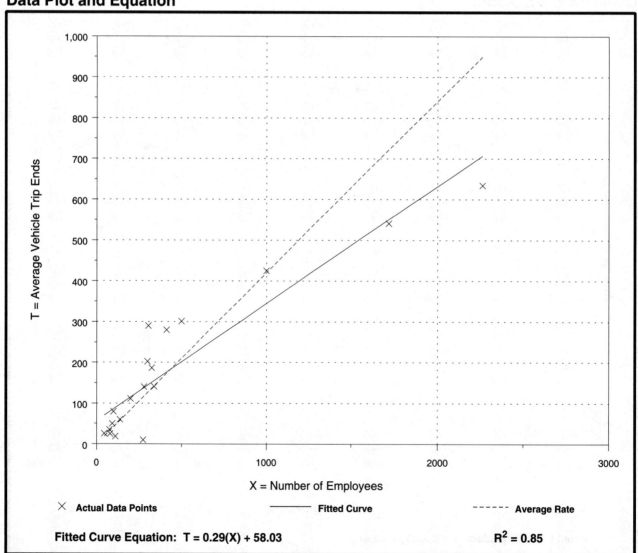

X **Actual Data Points**   ——— **Fitted Curve**   - - - - - **Average Rate**

Fitted Curve Equation: T = 0.29(X) + 58.03 $R^2 = 0.85$

General Light Industrial
(110)

Average Vehicle Trip Ends vs: **Employees**
On a: **Weekday,**
A.M. Peak Hour of Generator

Number of Studies: 21
Avg. Number of Employees: 421
Directional Distribution: 87% entering, 13% exiting

Trip Generation per Employee

Average Rate	Range of Rates	Standard Deviation
0.48	0.25 - 1.02	0.72

Data Plot and Equation

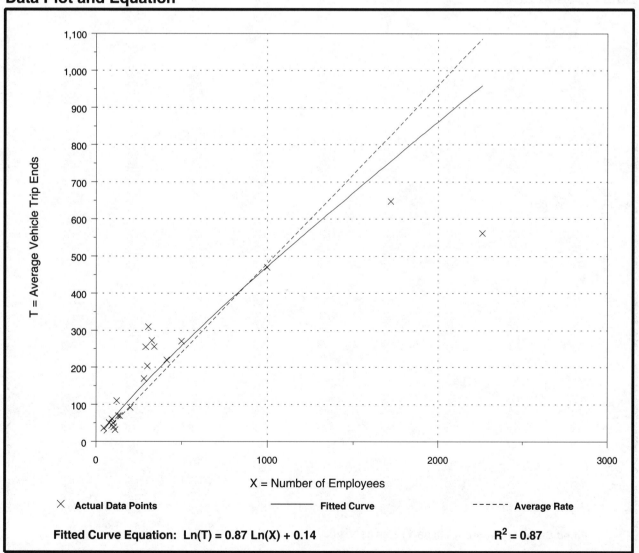

Fitted Curve Equation: $Ln(T) = 0.87 \, Ln(X) + 0.14$ $R^2 = 0.87$

General Light Industrial
(110)

Average Vehicle Trip Ends vs: Employees
On a: Weekday,
P.M. Peak Hour of Generator

Number of Studies: 21
Avg. Number of Employees: 421
Directional Distribution: 29% entering, 71% exiting

Trip Generation per Employee

Average Rate	Range of Rates	Standard Deviation
0.51	0.36 - 1.18	0.75

Data Plot and Equation

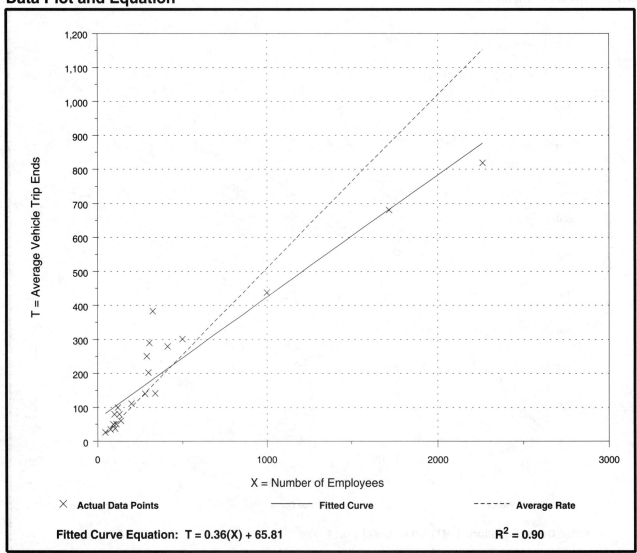

Fitted Curve Equation: T = 0.36(X) + 65.81 $R^2 = 0.90$

General Light Industrial
(110)

Average Vehicle Trip Ends vs: Employees
On a: Saturday

Number of Studies: 6
Avg. Number of Employees: 969
Directional Distribution: 50% entering, 50% exiting

Trip Generation per Employee

Average Rate	Range of Rates	Standard Deviation
0.48	0.29 - 1.32	0.72

Data Plot and Equation

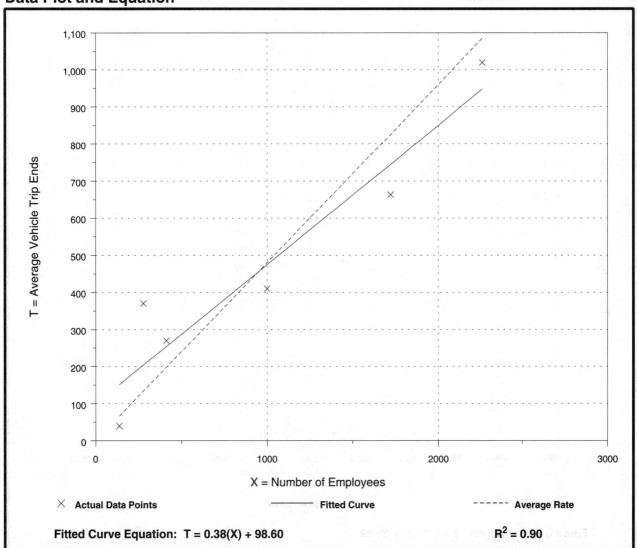

X Actual Data Points   —————— Fitted Curve   ------ Average Rate

Fitted Curve Equation: T = 0.38(X) + 98.60 $R^2 = 0.90$

General Light Industrial
(110)

Average Vehicle Trip Ends vs: **Employees**
On a: **Saturday,**
Peak Hour of Generator

Number of Studies: 5
Avg. Number of Employees: 1,134
Directional Distribution: 47% entering, 53% exiting

Trip Generation per Employee

Average Rate	Range of Rates	Standard Deviation
0.05	0.04 - 0.21	0.23

Data Plot and Equation

Caution - Use Carefully - Small Sample Size

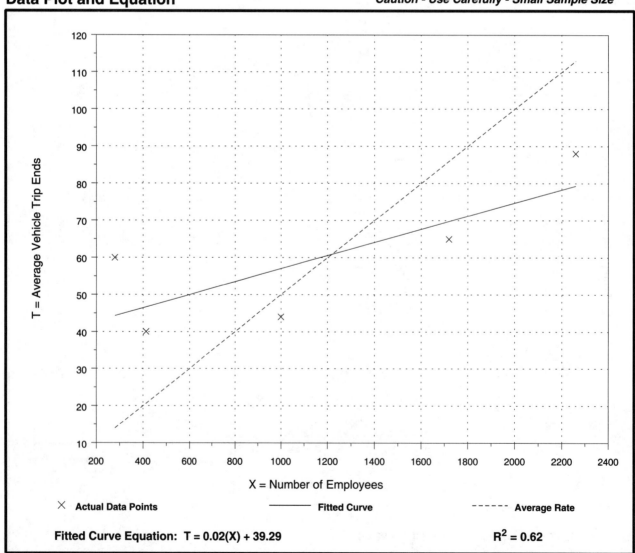

X = Number of Employees

✕ **Actual Data Points** —— **Fitted Curve** - - - - - **Average Rate**

Fitted Curve Equation: T = 0.02(X) + 39.29 $R^2 = 0.62$

General Light Industrial
(110)

Average Vehicle Trip Ends vs: Employees
On a: Sunday

Number of Studies: 4
Avg. Number of Employees: 1,280
Directional Distribution: 50% entering, 50% exiting

Trip Generation per Employee

Average Rate	Range of Rates	Standard Deviation
0.26	0.12 - 2.09	0.60

Data Plot and Equation

Caution - Use Carefully - Small Sample Size

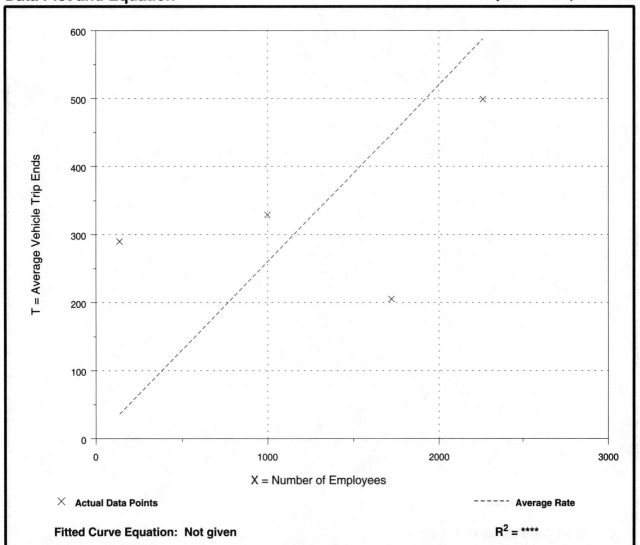

X **Actual Data Points**   - - - - - **Average Rate**

Fitted Curve Equation: Not given $R^2 = ****$

General Light Industrial
(110)

Average Vehicle Trip Ends vs: Employees
On a: Sunday,
Peak Hour of Generator

Number of Studies: 4
Avg. Number of Employees: 1,280
Directional Distribution: 48% entering, 52% exiting

Trip Generation per Employee

Average Rate	Range of Rates	Standard Deviation
0.04	0.02 - 0.29	0.20

Data Plot and Equation

Caution - Use Carefully - Small Sample Size

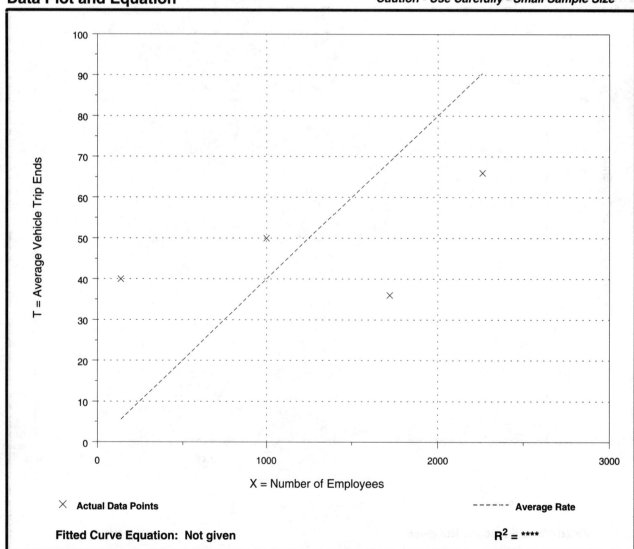

X **Actual Data Points**

------ **Average Rate**

Fitted Curve Equation: Not given $R^2 = ****$

General Light Industrial
(110)

Average Vehicle Trip Ends vs: **1000 Sq. Feet Gross Floor Area**
On a: **Weekday**

Number of Studies: 18
Average 1000 Sq. Feet GFA: 203
Directional Distribution: 50% entering, 50% exiting

Trip Generation per 1000 Sq. Feet Gross Floor Area

Average Rate	Range of Rates	Standard Deviation
6.97	1.58 - 16.88	4.24

Data Plot and Equation

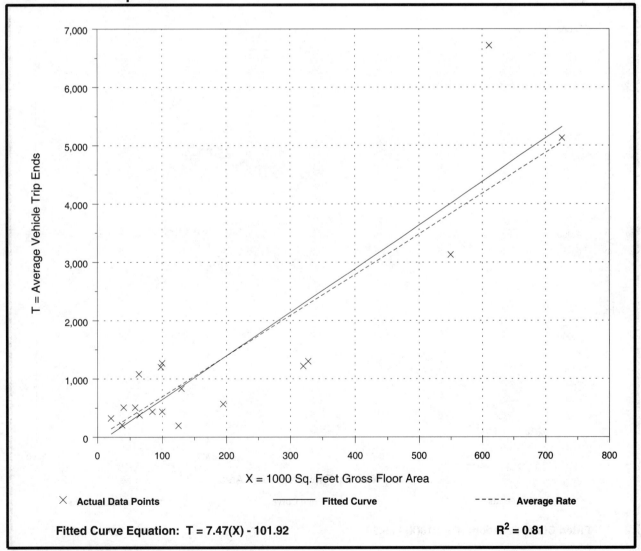

X   **Actual Data Points**   ————— **Fitted Curve**   - - - - - **Average Rate**

Fitted Curve Equation: T = 7.47(X) - 101.92 $R^2 = 0.81$

General Light Industrial
(110)

Average Vehicle Trip Ends vs: 1000 Sq. Feet Gross Floor Area
On a: Weekday,
Peak Hour of Adjacent Street Traffic,
One Hour Between 7 and 9 a.m.

Number of Studies: 29
Average 1000 Sq. Feet GFA: 336
Directional Distribution: 88% entering, 12% exiting

Trip Generation per 1000 Sq. Feet Gross Floor Area

Average Rate	Range of Rates	Standard Deviation
0.92	0.17 - 4.00	1.07

Data Plot and Equation

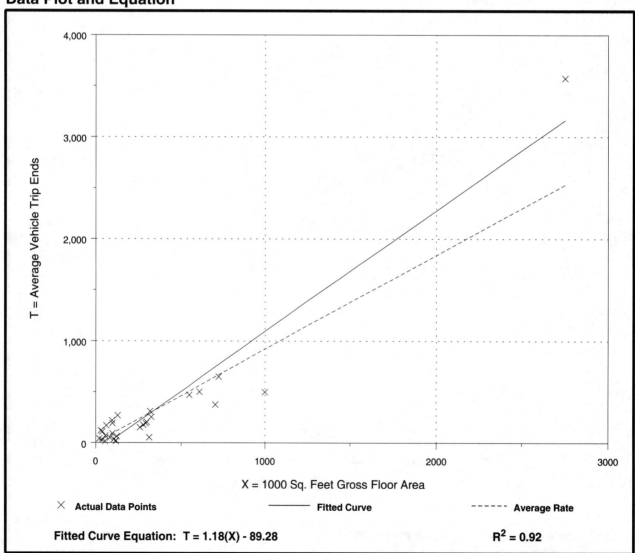

Fitted Curve Equation: T = 1.18(X) - 89.28 $R^2 = 0.92$

General Light Industrial
(110)

Average Vehicle Trip Ends vs: **1000 Sq. Feet Gross Floor Area**
On a: **Weekday,**
  Peak Hour of Adjacent Street Traffic,
  One Hour Between 4 and 6 p.m.

Number of Studies: 27
Average 1000 Sq. Feet GFA: 345
Directional Distribution: 12% entering, 88% exiting

Trip Generation per 1000 Sq. Feet Gross Floor Area

Average Rate	Range of Rates	Standard Deviation
0.97	0.08 - 4.50	1.16

Data Plot and Equation

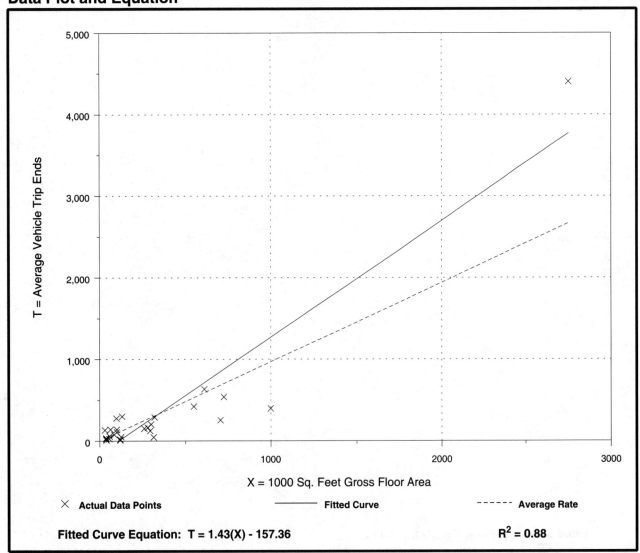

Fitted Curve Equation: T = 1.43(X) - 157.36 $R^2 = 0.88$

General Light Industrial
(110)

Average Vehicle Trip Ends vs: 1000 Sq. Feet Gross Floor Area
On a: Weekday,
A.M. Peak Hour of Generator

Number of Studies: 27
Average 1000 Sq. Feet GFA: 358
Directional Distribution: 90% entering, 10% exiting

Trip Generation per 1000 Sq. Feet Gross Floor Area

Average Rate	Range of Rates	Standard Deviation
1.01	0.27 - 4.00	1.10

Data Plot and Equation

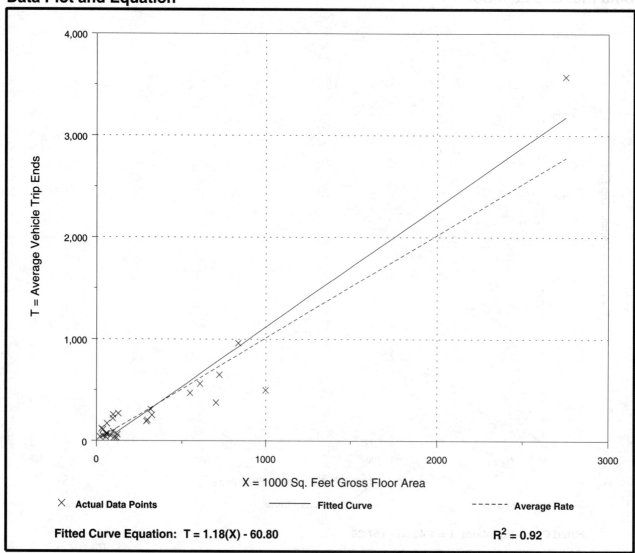

X = 1000 Sq. Feet Gross Floor Area

✕ Actual Data Points   ———— Fitted Curve   ----- Average Rate

Fitted Curve Equation: T = 1.18(X) - 60.80 $R^2 = 0.92$

General Light Industrial
(110)

Average Vehicle Trip Ends vs: **1000 Sq. Feet Gross Floor Area**
On a: **Weekday,**
P.M. Peak Hour of Generator

Number of Studies: 27
Average 1000 Sq. Feet GFA: 364
Directional Distribution: 14% entering, 86% exiting

Trip Generation per 1000 Sq. Feet Gross Floor Area

Average Rate	Range of Rates	Standard Deviation
1.08	0.36 - 4.50	1.18

Data Plot and Equation

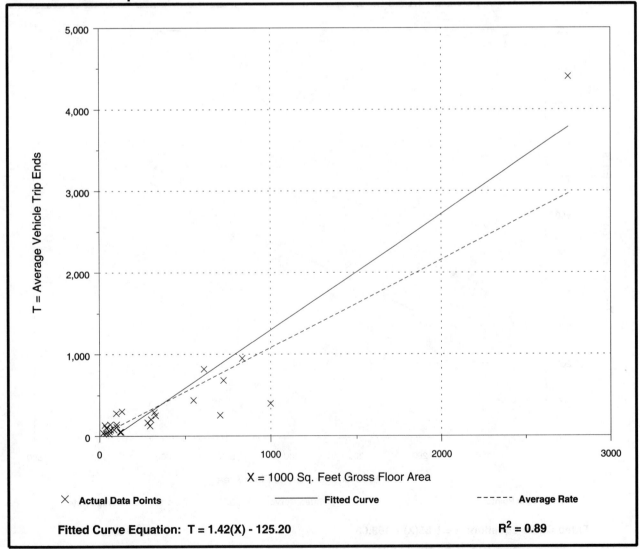

Fitted Curve Equation: T = 1.42(X) - 125.20 $R^2 = 0.89$

General Light Industrial
(110)

Average Vehicle Trip Ends vs: 1000 Sq. Feet Gross Floor Area
On a: Saturday

Number of Studies: 6
Average 1000 Sq. Feet GFA: 351
Directional Distribution: 50% entering, 50% exiting

Trip Generation per 1000 Sq. Feet Gross Floor Area

Average Rate	Range of Rates	Standard Deviation
1.32	0.69 - 5.78	1.48

Data Plot and Equation

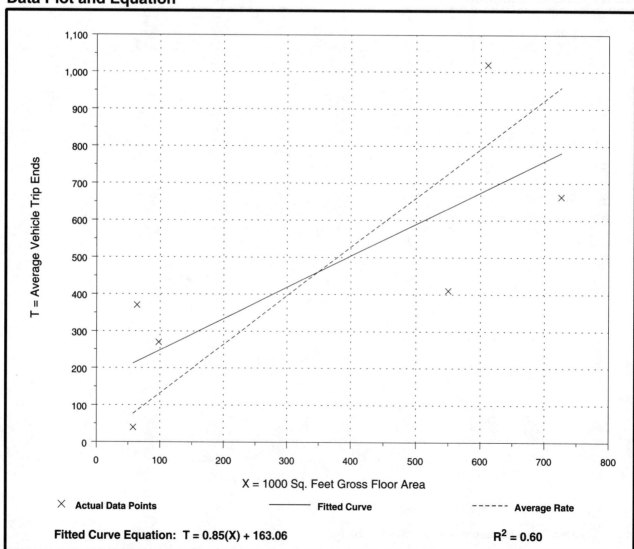

Fitted Curve Equation: T = 0.85(X) + 163.06   **R^2 = 0.60**

General Light Industrial
(110)

Average Vehicle Trip Ends vs: **1000 Sq. Feet Gross Floor Area**
            On a: **Saturday,**
                       Peak Hour of Generator

Number of Studies: 5
Average 1000 Sq. Feet GFA: 410
Directional Distribution: 47% entering, 53% exiting

Trip Generation per 1000 Sq. Feet Gross Floor Area

Average Rate	Range of Rates	Standard Deviation
0.14	0.08 - 0.94	0.41

Data Plot and Equation

Caution - Use Carefully - Small Sample Size

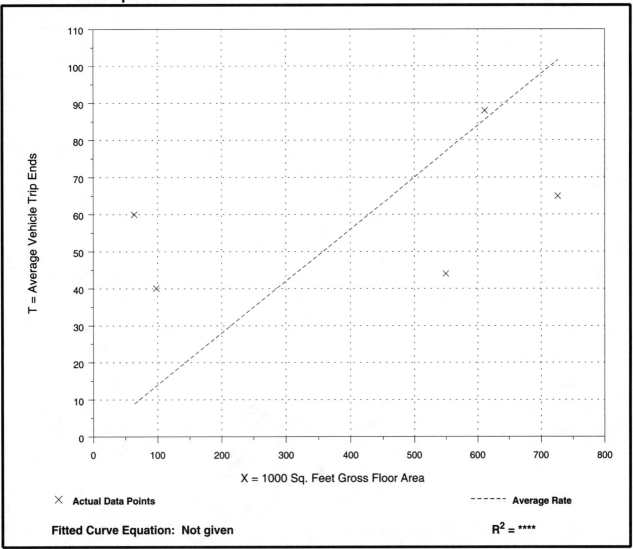

X   **Actual Data Points**   - - - - -   **Average Rate**

Fitted Curve Equation: Not given $R^2 =$ ****

General Light Industrial
(110)

Average Vehicle Trip Ends vs: 1000 Sq. Feet Gross Floor Area
On a: Sunday

Number of Studies: 4
Average 1000 Sq. Feet GFA: 486
Directional Distribution: 50% entering, 50% exiting

Trip Generation per 1000 Sq. Feet Gross Floor Area

Average Rate	Range of Rates	Standard Deviation
0.68	0.28 - 5.00	1.14

Data Plot and Equation

Caution - Use Carefully - Small Sample Size

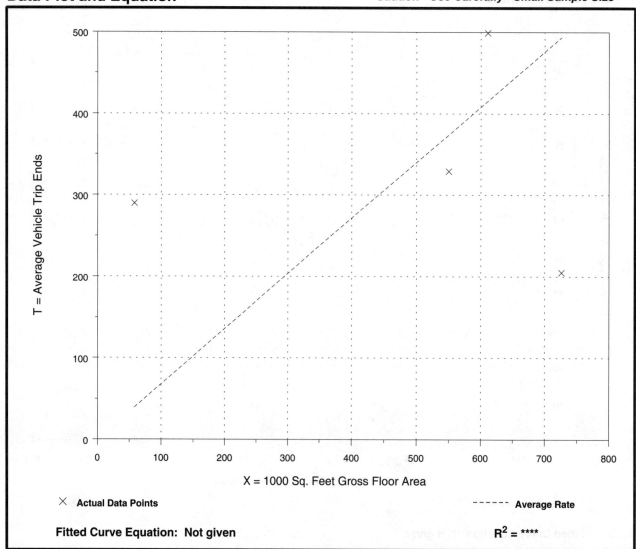

X **Actual Data Points**

- - - - - **Average Rate**

Fitted Curve Equation: Not given $R^2 = ****$

General Light Industrial
(110)

Average Vehicle Trip Ends vs: 1000 Sq. Feet Gross Floor Area
On a: Sunday,
Peak Hour of Generator

Number of Studies: 4
Average 1000 Sq. Feet GFA: 486
Directional Distribution: 48% entering, 52% exiting

Trip Generation per 1000 Sq. Feet Gross Floor Area

Average Rate	Range of Rates	Standard Deviation
0.10	0.05 - 0.69	0.33

Data Plot and Equation

Caution - Use Carefully - Small Sample Size

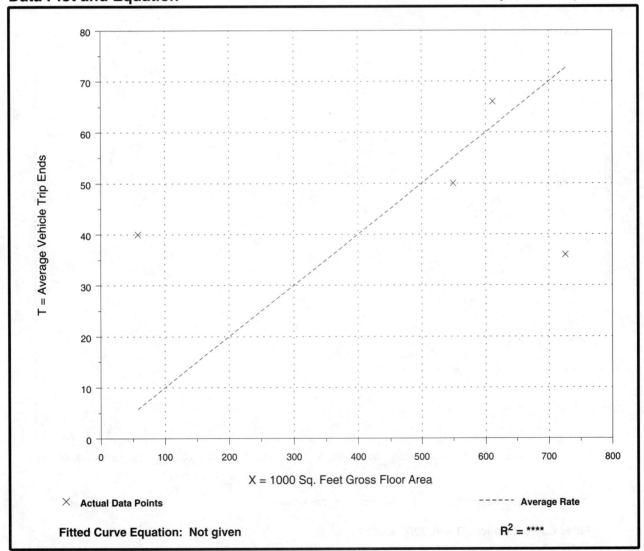

X = 1000 Sq. Feet Gross Floor Area

✕ **Actual Data Points**   - - - - - **Average Rate**

Fitted Curve Equation: Not given $R^2 =$ ****

General Light Industrial
(110)

Average Vehicle Trip Ends vs: Acres
On a: Weekday

Number of Studies: 17
Average Number of Acres: 27
Directional Distribution: 50% entering, 50% exiting

Trip Generation per Acre

Average Rate	Range of Rates	Standard Deviation
51.80	5.21 - 159.38	32.69

Data Plot and Equation

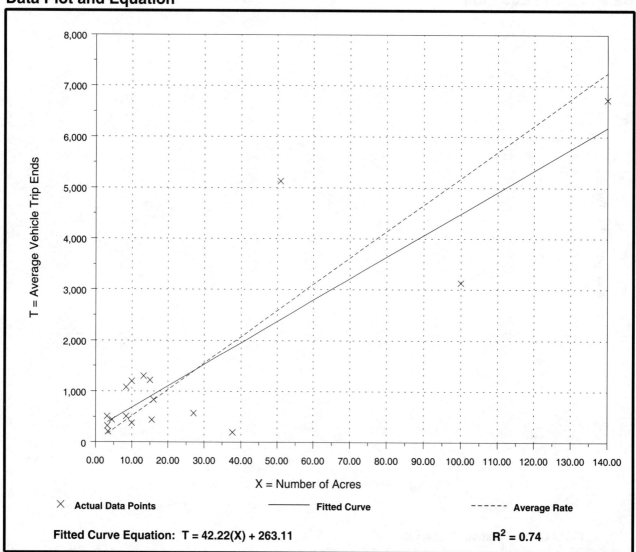

X   **Actual Data Points** ———— **Fitted Curve** - - - - - **Average Rate**

Fitted Curve Equation: T = 42.22(X) + 263.11 $R^2 = 0.74$

General Light Industrial
(110)

Average Vehicle Trip Ends vs: **Acres**
On a: **Weekday,**
Peak Hour of Adjacent Street Traffic,
One Hour Between 7 and 9 a.m.

Number of Studies: 18
Average Number of Acres: 30
Directional Distribution: 83% entering, 17% exiting

Trip Generation per Acre

Average Rate	Range of Rates	Standard Deviation
7.51	1.61 - 34.38	6.51

Data Plot and Equation

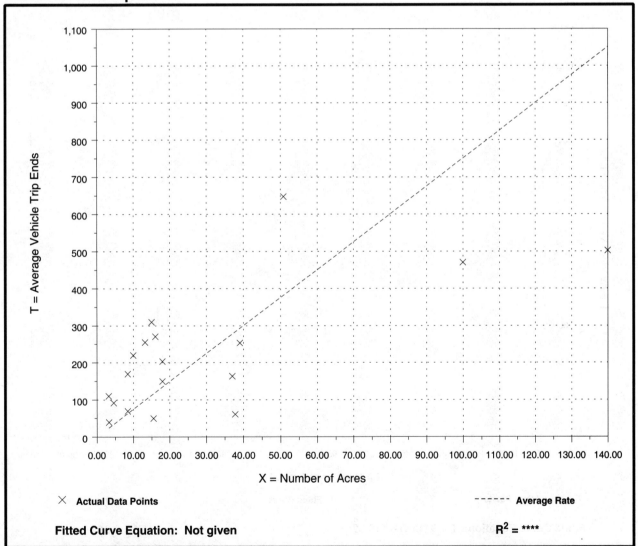

X   **Actual Data Points**   ----- **Average Rate**

Fitted Curve Equation: Not given $R^2 =$ ****

General Light Industrial
(110)

Average Vehicle Trip Ends vs: **Acres**
                           On a: **Weekday,**
                                     Peak Hour of Adjacent Street Traffic,
                                     One Hour Between 4 and 6 p.m.

Number of Studies: 16
Average Number of Acres: 33
Directional Distribution: 22% entering, 78% exiting

Trip Generation per Acre

Average Rate	Range of Rates	Standard Deviation
7.26	1.32 - 28.00	5.99

Data Plot and Equation

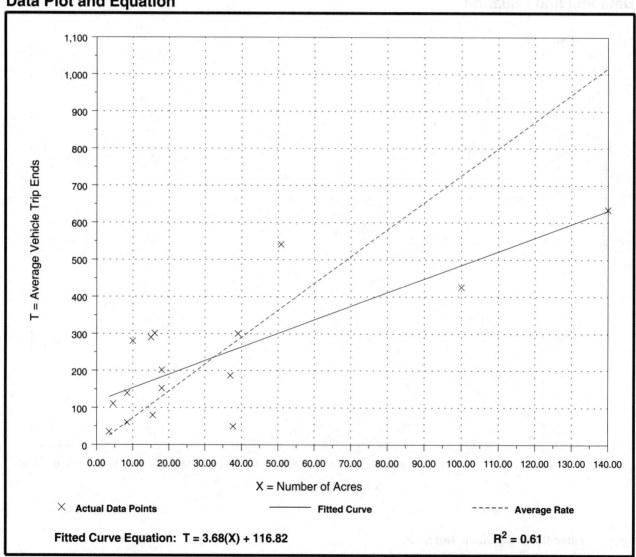

Fitted Curve Equation: T = 3.68(X) + 116.82 $R^2 = 0.61$

General Light Industrial
(110)

Average Vehicle Trip Ends vs: **Acres**
               On a: **Weekday,**
                            A.M. Peak Hour of Generator

Number of Studies: 19
Average Number of Acres: 28
Directional Distribution: 85% entering, 15% exiting

Trip Generation per Acre

Average Rate	Range of Rates	Standard Deviation
7.96	1.61 - 34.38	6.46

Data Plot and Equation

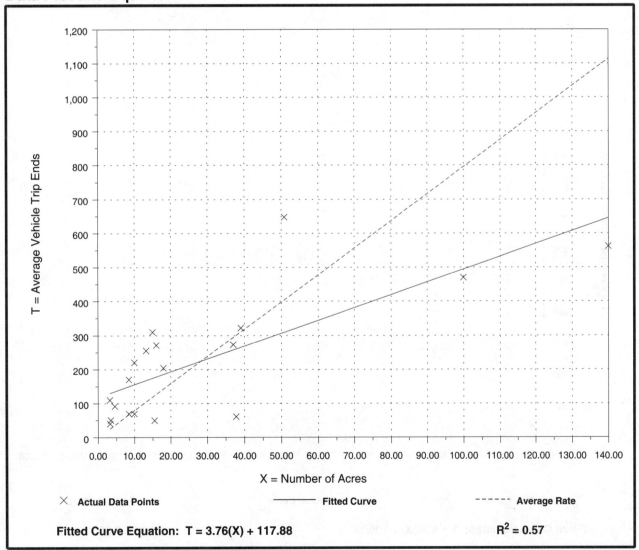

Fitted Curve Equation: $T = 3.76(X) + 117.88$ $R^2 = 0.57$

General Light Industrial
(110)

Average Vehicle Trip Ends vs: **Acres**
On a: **Weekday,**
P.M. Peak Hour of Generator

Number of Studies: 18
Average Number of Acres: 27
Directional Distribution: 30% entering, 70% exiting

Trip Generation per Acre

Average Rate	Range of Rates	Standard Deviation
8.77	1.32 - 31.25	6.74

Data Plot and Equation

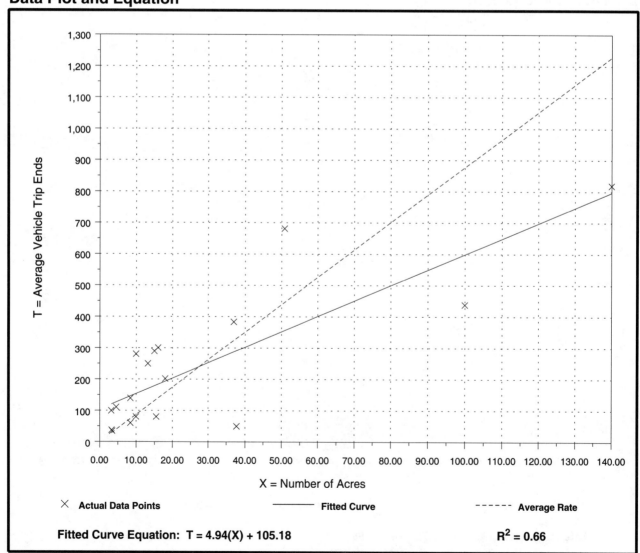

X **Actual Data Points**   ——— **Fitted Curve**   - - - - - **Average Rate**

Fitted Curve Equation: T = 4.94(X) + 105.18 $R^2 = 0.66$

General Light Industrial
(110)

Average Vehicle Trip Ends vs: **Acres**
On a: **Saturday**

Number of Studies: 6
Average Number of Acres: 53
Directional Distribution: 50% entering, 50% exiting

Trip Generation per Acre

Average Rate	Range of Rates	Standard Deviation
8.73	4.10 - 43.53	7.91

Data Plot and Equation

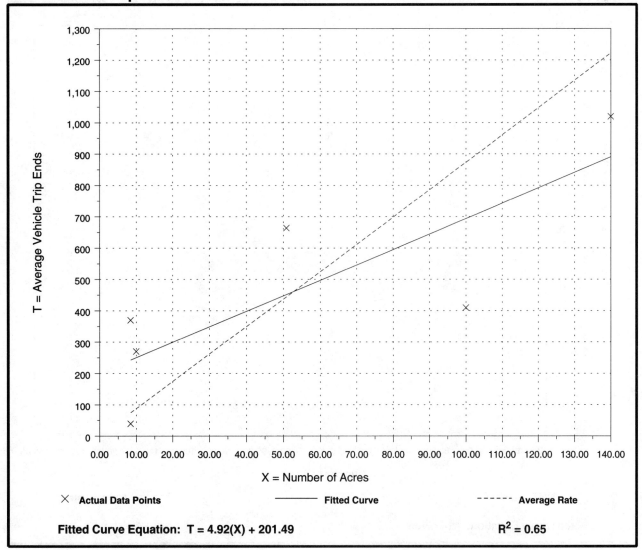

Fitted Curve Equation: $T = 4.92(X) + 201.49$ $R^2 = 0.65$

General Light Industrial
(110)

Average Vehicle Trip Ends vs: **Acres**
On a: **Saturday,**
Peak Hour of Generator

Number of Studies: 5
Average Number of Acres: 62
Directional Distribution: 47% entering, 53% exiting

Trip Generation per Acre

Average Rate	Range of Rates	Standard Deviation
0.96	0.44 - 7.06	1.55

Data Plot and Equation

Caution - Use Carefully - Small Sample Size

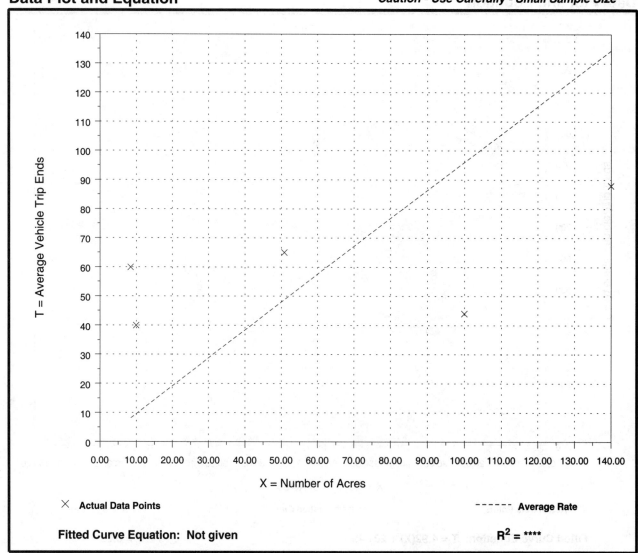

X **Actual Data Points**   - - - - - **Average Rate**

Fitted Curve Equation: Not given $R^2 = ****$

General Light Industrial
(110)

Average Vehicle Trip Ends vs: **Acres**
On a: **Sunday**

Number of Studies: 4
Average Number of Acres: 75
Directional Distribution: 50% entering, 50% exiting

Trip Generation per Acre

Average Rate	Range of Rates	Standard Deviation
4.42	3.29 - 34.12	5.50

Data Plot and Equation

Caution - Use Carefully - Small Sample Size

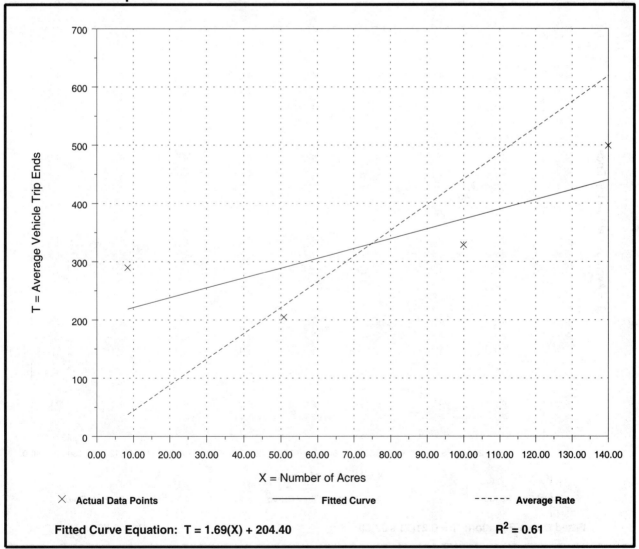

X = Number of Acres

| $\times$ Actual Data Points | —— Fitted Curve | ----- Average Rate |

Fitted Curve Equation: T = 1.69(X) + 204.40 $R^2 = 0.61$

General Light Industrial
(110)

Average Vehicle Trip Ends vs: Acres
On a: Sunday,
Peak Hour of Generator

Number of Studies: 4
Average Number of Acres: 75
Directional Distribution: 48% entering, 52% exiting

Trip Generation per Acre

Average Rate	Range of Rates	Standard Deviation
0.64	0.47 - 4.71	1.06

Data Plot and Equation

Caution - Use Carefully - Small Sample Size

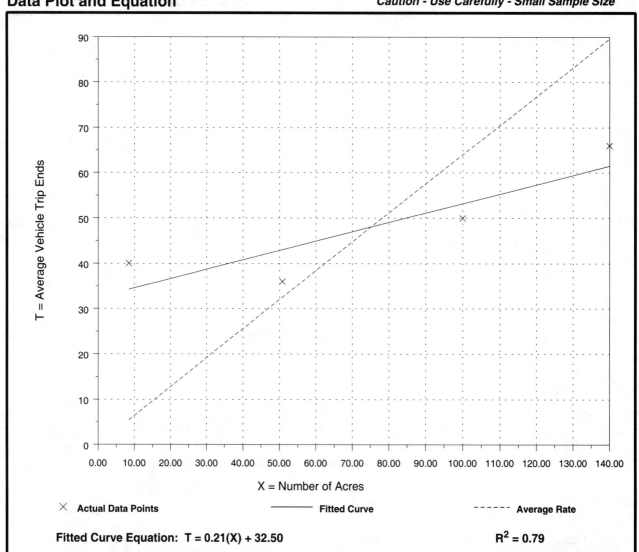

X = Number of Acres

× **Actual Data Points**   ———— **Fitted Curve**   - - - - - **Average Rate**

Fitted Curve Equation: T = 0.21(X) + 32.50   **R² = 0.79**

Land Use: 120
General Heavy Industrial

Description

Heavy industrial facilities usually have a high number of employees per industrial plant and are generally limited to the manufacturing of large items. General light industrial (Land Use 110), industrial park (Land Use 130) and manufacturing (Land Use 140) are related uses.

Additional Data

No vehicle occupancy data were available specifically for general heavy industrial, but the average was approximately 1.3 persons per automobile for all industrial uses.

The peak hour of the generator typically coincided with the peak hour of the adjacent street traffic.

Facilities with employees on shift work may peak at other hours.

The sites were surveyed in the 1970s.

Source Numbers

85, 125

Land Use: 120
General Heavy Industrial
Independent Variables with One Observation

The following trip generation data are for independent variables with only one observation. This information is shown in this table only; there are no related plots for these data.

Users are cautioned to use data with care because of the small sample size.

Day/Time Period	Trip Generation Rate	Size of Independent Variable	Number of Studies	Directional Distribution
1,000 Square Feet Gross Floor Area				
Weekday p.m. Peak Hour of Adjacent Street Traffic	0.19	971	1	Not available
Weekday a.m. Peak Hour of Generator	0.69	2,023	1	Not available

General Heavy Industrial
(120)

Average Vehicle Trip Ends vs: Employees
On a: Weekday

Number of Studies: 3
Avg. Number of Employees: 2,463
Directional Distribution: 50% entering, 50% exiting

Trip Generation per Employee

Average Rate	Range of Rates	Standard Deviation
0.82	0.75 - 1.81	0.93

Data Plot and Equation

Caution - Use Carefully - Small Sample Size

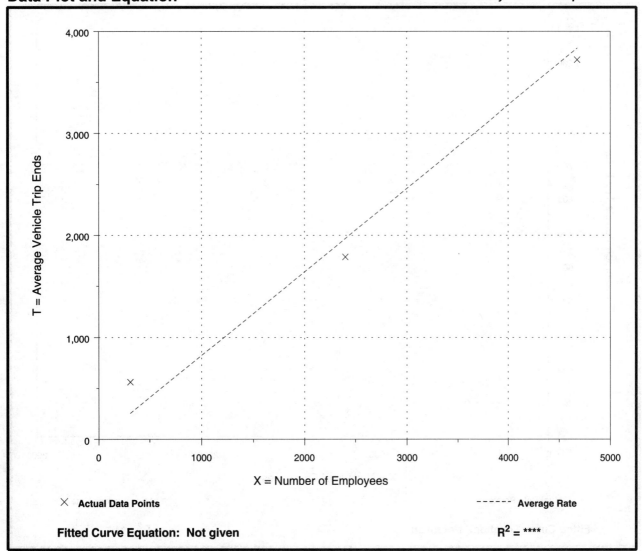

✕ **Actual Data Points**

- - - - - **Average Rate**

Fitted Curve Equation: Not given

$R^2 = ****$

General Heavy Industrial
(120)

Average Vehicle Trip Ends vs: **Employees**
On a: **Weekday,**
Peak Hour of Adjacent Street Traffic,
One Hour Between 7 and 9 a.m.

Number of Studies: 3
Avg. Number of Employees: 1,240
Directional Distribution: Not available

Trip Generation per Employee

Average Rate	Range of Rates	Standard Deviation
0.51	0.36 - 0.84	0.74

Data Plot and Equation

Caution - Use Carefully - Small Sample Size

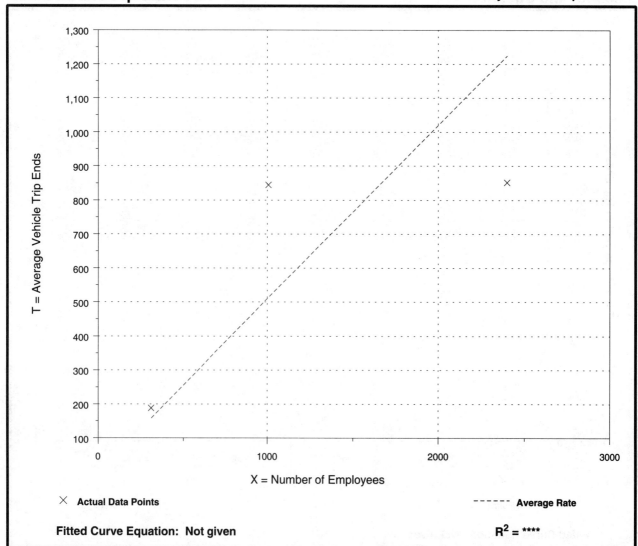

X = Number of Employees

✕ **Actual Data Points**

- - - - - **Average Rate**

Fitted Curve Equation: Not given

$R^2 =$ ****

General Heavy Industrial
(120)

Average Vehicle Trip Ends vs:	Employees
On a:	Weekday,
	Peak Hour of Adjacent Street Traffic,
	One Hour Between 4 and 6 p.m.

Number of Studies: 2
Avg. Number of Employees: 660
Directional Distribution: Not available

Trip Generation per Employee

Average Rate	Range of Rates	Standard Deviation
0.88	0.60 - 0.97	*

Data Plot and Equation

Caution - Use Carefully - Small Sample Size

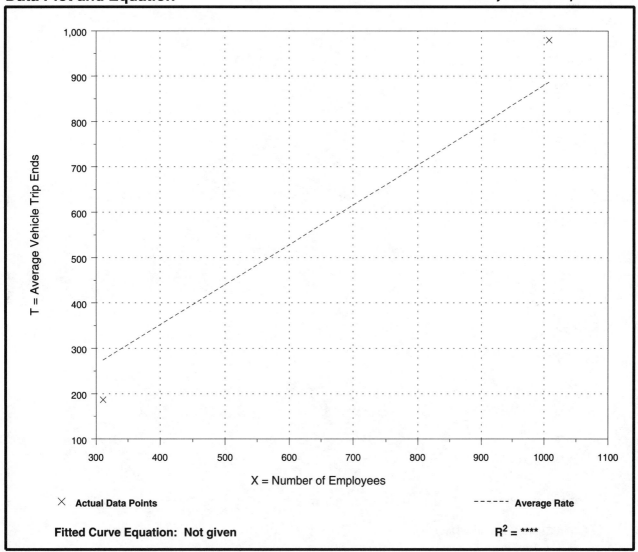

X Actual Data Points   - - - - - Average Rate

Fitted Curve Equation: Not given $R^2 = ****$

General Heavy Industrial
(120)

Average Vehicle Trip Ends vs: **Employees**
On a: **Weekday,**
A.M. Peak Hour of Generator

Number of Studies: 2
Avg. Number of Employees: 2,843
Directional Distribution: Not available

Trip Generation per Employee

Average Rate	Range of Rates	Standard Deviation
0.40	0.30 - 0.84	*

Data Plot and Equation

Caution - Use Carefully - Small Sample Size

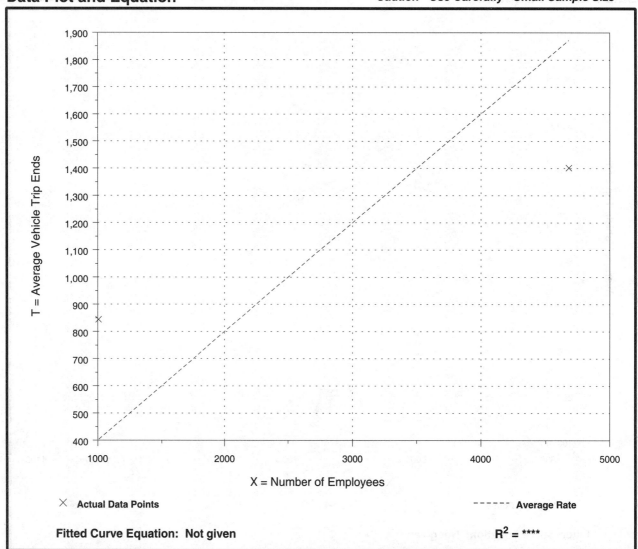

X = Number of Employees

✕ **Actual Data Points**   ----- **Average Rate**

Fitted Curve Equation: Not given $R^2 = ****$

General Heavy Industrial
(120)

Average Vehicle Trip Ends vs: Employees
On a: Weekday,
P.M. Peak Hour of Generator

Number of Studies: 3
Avg. Number of Employees: 2,695
Directional Distribution: Not available

Trip Generation per Employee

Average Rate	Range of Rates	Standard Deviation
0.40	0.22 - 1.10	0.69

Data Plot and Equation

Caution - Use Carefully - Small Sample Size

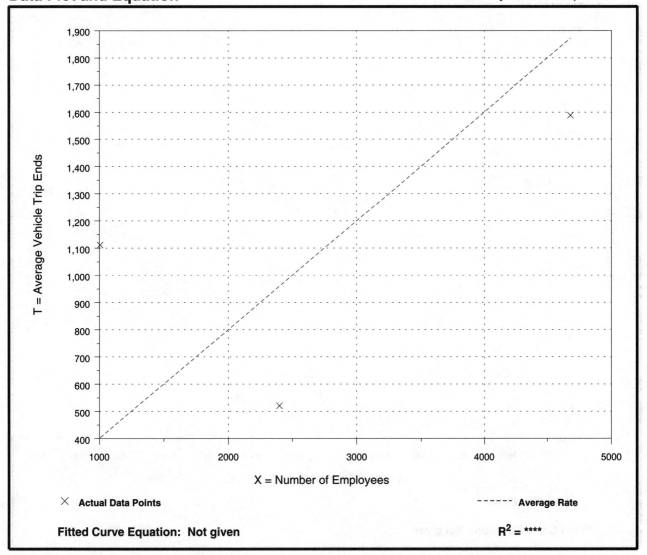

X **Actual Data Points**

- - - - - **Average Rate**

Fitted Curve Equation: Not given

$R^2 = ****$

General Heavy Industrial
(120)

Average Vehicle Trip Ends vs: **1000 Sq. Feet Gross Floor Area**
On a: **Weekday**

Number of Studies: 3
Average 1000 Sq. Feet GFA: 1,353
Directional Distribution: 50% entering, 50% exiting

Trip Generation per 1000 Sq. Feet Gross Floor Area

Average Rate	Range of Rates	Standard Deviation
1.50	0.58 - 1.84	1.33

Data Plot and Equation

Caution - Use Carefully - Small Sample Size

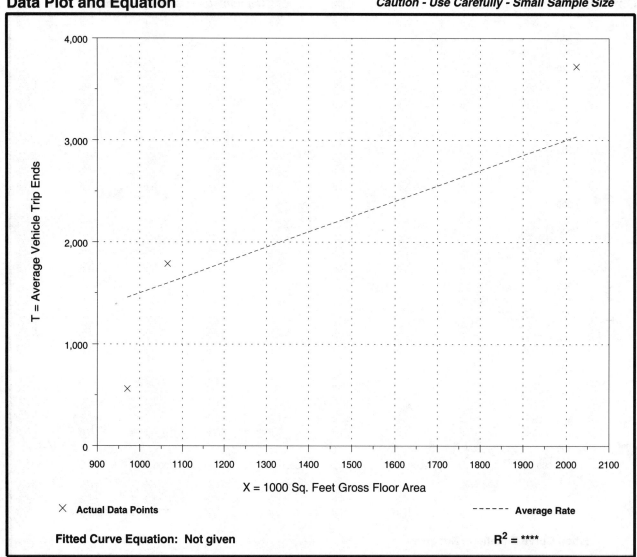

X **Actual Data Points**

- - - - - **Average Rate**

Fitted Curve Equation: Not given $R^2 = ****$

General Heavy Industrial
(120)

Average Vehicle Trip Ends vs: 1000 Sq. Feet Gross Floor Area
On a: Weekday,
Peak Hour of Adjacent Street Traffic,
One Hour Between 7 and 9 a.m.

Number of Studies: 2
Average 1000 Sq. Feet GFA: 1,018
Directional Distribution: Not available

Trip Generation per 1000 Sq. Feet Gross Floor Area

Average Rate	Range of Rates	Standard Deviation
0.51	0.19 - 0.80	*

Data Plot and Equation

Caution - Use Carefully - Small Sample Size

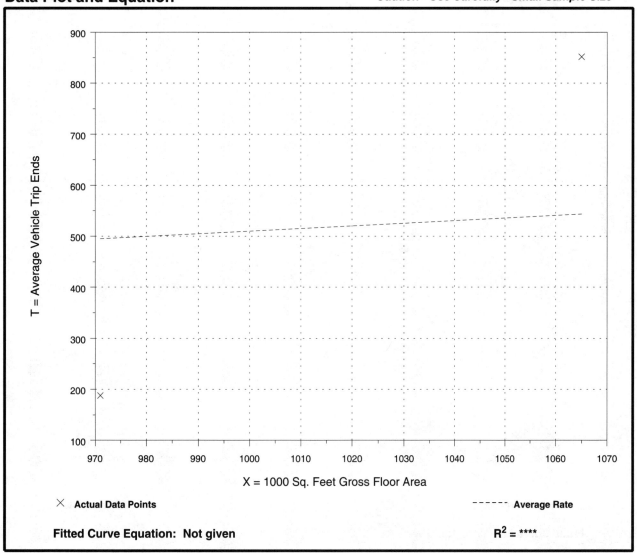

X = 1000 Sq. Feet Gross Floor Area

✕ **Actual Data Points**   ------ **Average Rate**

Fitted Curve Equation: Not given $R^2 = ****$

General Heavy Industrial
(120)

Average Vehicle Trip Ends vs: 1000 Sq. Feet Gross Floor Area
On a: Weekday,
P.M. Peak Hour of Generator

Number of Studies: 2
Average 1000 Sq. Feet GFA: 1,544
Directional Distribution: Not available

Trip Generation per 1000 Sq. Feet Gross Floor Area

Average Rate	Range of Rates	Standard Deviation
0.68	0.49 - 0.78	*

Data Plot and Equation

Caution - Use Carefully - Small Sample Size

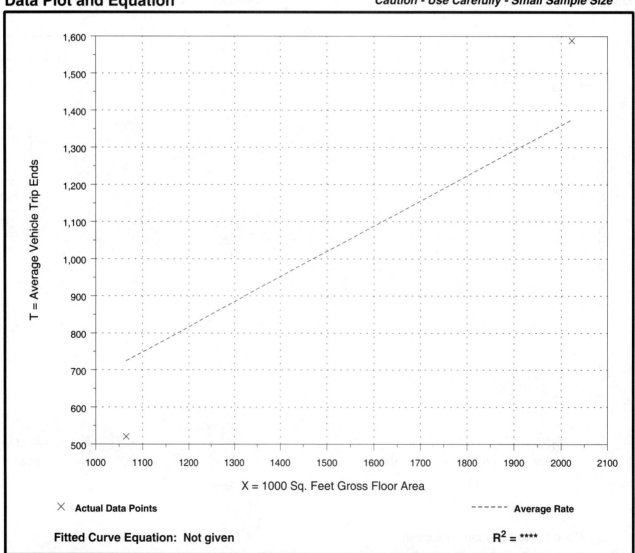

X = 1000 Sq. Feet Gross Floor Area

✕ **Actual Data Points**   - - - - - **Average Rate**

Fitted Curve Equation: Not given $R^2 = ****$

General Heavy Industrial
(120)

Average Vehicle Trip Ends vs: Acres
On a: Weekday

Number of Studies: 3
Average Number of Acres: 300
Directional Distribution: 50% entering, 50% exiting

Trip Generation per Acre

Average Rate	Range of Rates	Standard Deviation
6.75	1.66 - 25.01	8.62

Data Plot and Equation

Caution - Use Carefully - Small Sample Size

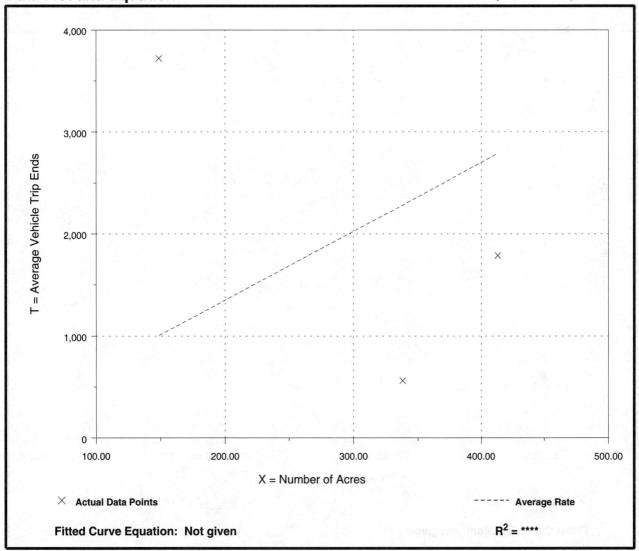

Fitted Curve Equation: Not given $R^2 = ****$

General Heavy Industrial
(120)

Average Vehicle Trip Ends vs: **Acres**
On a: **Weekday,**
Peak Hour of Adjacent Street Traffic,
One Hour Between 7 and 9 a.m.

Number of Studies: 3
Average Number of Acres: 318
Directional Distribution: Not available

Trip Generation per Acre

Average Rate	Range of Rates	Standard Deviation
1.98	0.56 - 4.18	1.93

Data Plot and Equation

Caution - Use Carefully - Small Sample Size

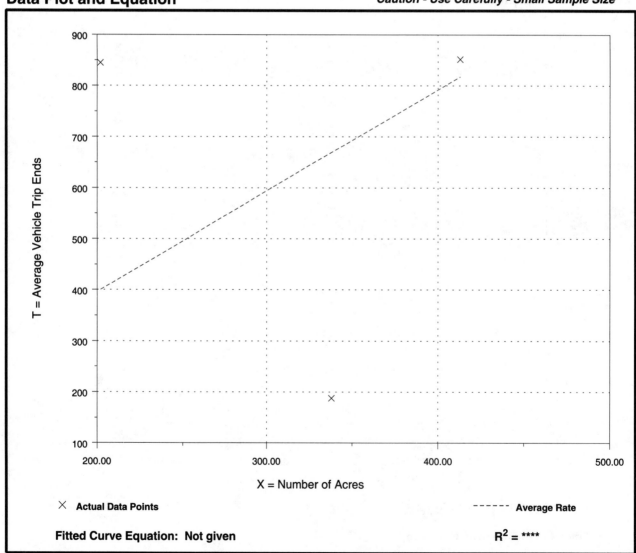

X **Actual Data Points** - - - - - **Average Rate**

Fitted Curve Equation: Not given $R^2 =$ ********

General Heavy Industrial
(120)

Average Vehicle Trip Ends vs: **Acres**
On a: **Weekday,**
Peak Hour of Adjacent Street Traffic,
One Hour Between 4 and 6 p.m.

Number of Studies: 2
Average Number of Acres: 270
Directional Distribution: Not available

Trip Generation per Acre

Average Rate	Range of Rates	Standard Deviation
2.16	0.55 - 4.85	*

Data Plot and Equation

Caution - Use Carefully - Small Sample Size

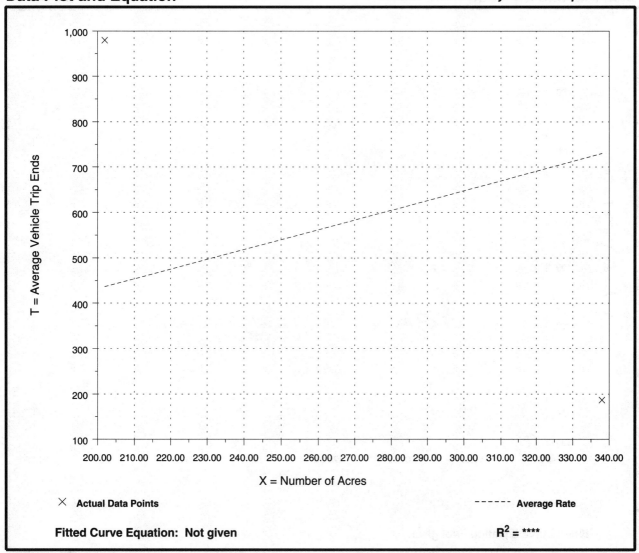

X   **Actual Data Points**   ----- **Average Rate**

Fitted Curve Equation: Not given $R^2 = ****$

General Heavy Industrial
(120)

Average Vehicle Trip Ends vs: Acres
On a: Weekday,
A.M. Peak Hour of Generator

Number of Studies: 2
Average Number of Acres: 175
Directional Distribution: Not available

Trip Generation per Acre

Average Rate	Range of Rates	Standard Deviation
6.41	4.18 - 9.43	*

Data Plot and Equation

Caution - Use Carefully - Small Sample Size

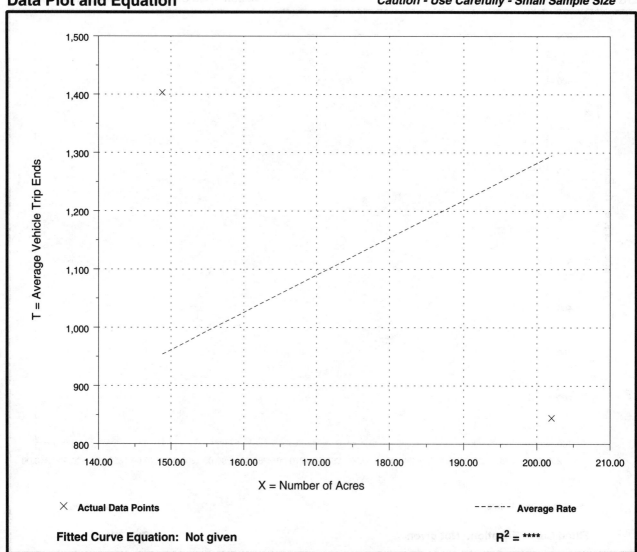

X **Actual Data Points**   ------ **Average Rate**

Fitted Curve Equation: Not given $R^2 =$ ****

General Heavy Industrial
(120)

Average Vehicle Trip Ends vs: **Acres**
On a: **Weekday,**
  P.M. Peak Hour of Generator

Number of Studies: 3
Average Number of Acres: 255
Directional Distribution: Not available

Trip Generation per Acre

Average Rate	Range of Rates	Standard Deviation
4.22	1.26 - 10.67	4.18

Data Plot and Equation

Caution - Use Carefully - Small Sample Size

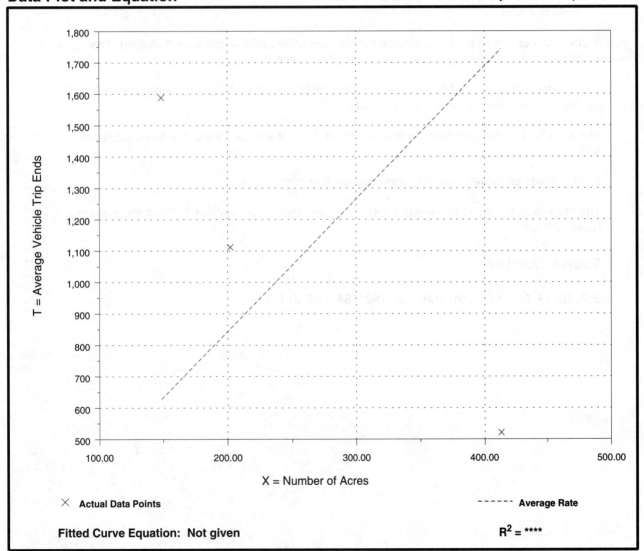

X **Actual Data Points**

- - - - - **Average Rate**

Fitted Curve Equation: Not given

$R^2 = ****$

Land Use: 130
Industrial Park

Description

Industrial parks contain a number of industrial or related facilities. They are characterized by a mix of manufacturing, service and warehouse facilities with a wide variation in the proportion of each type of use from one location to another. Many industrial parks contain highly diversified facilities—some with a large number of small businesses and others with one or two dominant industries. General light industrial (Land Use 110), general heavy industrial (Land Use 120) and manufacturing (Land Use 140) are related uses.

Additional Data

Average weekday transit trip ends:
— 0.03 per employee
— 0.05 per 1,000 square feet gross floor area
— 0.69 per acre

Truck trips accounted for 1 to 22 percent of the weekday traffic at the sites surveyed. The average for all sites surveyed was approximately 8 percent.

Vehicle occupancy ranged from 1.2 to 1.8 persons per automobile on an average weekday. The average for all sites that were surveyed was 1.37.

The peak hour of the generator typically coincided with the peak hour of the adjacent street traffic.

Facilities with employees on shift work may peak at other hours.

The sites were surveyed in the late 1960s, the early 1970s and the mid-1980s throughout the United States.

Source Numbers

3, 7, 10, 14, 68, 74, 85, 91, 100, 146, 162, 184, 251, 277, 422

Industrial Park
(130)

Average Vehicle Trip Ends vs: Employees
On a: Weekday

Number of Studies: 48
Avg. Number of Employees: 840
Directional Distribution: 50% entering, 50% exiting

Trip Generation per Employee

Average Rate	Range of Rates	Standard Deviation
3.34	1.24 - 8.80	2.38

Data Plot and Equation

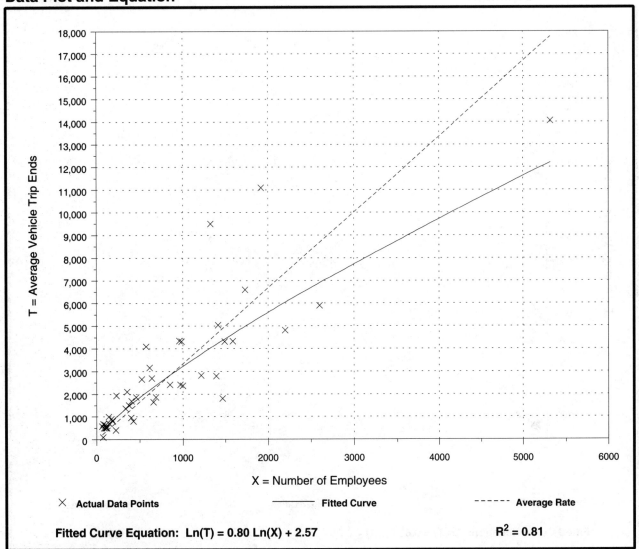

Fitted Curve Equation: Ln(T) = 0.80 Ln(X) + 2.57

$R^2 = 0.81$

Industrial Park
(130)

Average Vehicle Trip Ends vs: **Employees**
On a: **Weekday,**
Peak Hour of Adjacent Street Traffic,
One Hour Between 7 and 9 a.m.

Number of Studies: 34
Avg. Number of Employees: 749
Directional Distribution: 86% entering, 14% exiting

Trip Generation per Employee

Average Rate	Range of Rates	Standard Deviation
0.47	0.28 - 1.13	0.71

Data Plot and Equation

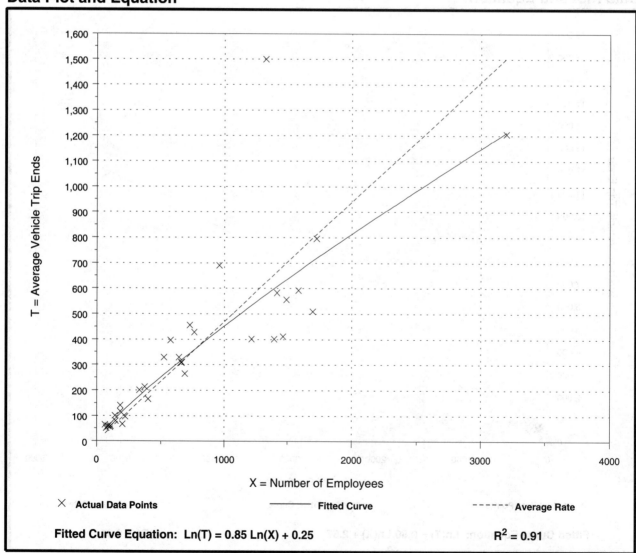

Fitted Curve Equation: Ln(T) = 0.85 Ln(X) + 0.25 $R^2 = 0.91$

Industrial Park
(130)

Average Vehicle Trip Ends vs: **Employees**
On a: **Weekday,**
Peak Hour of Adjacent Street Traffic,
One Hour Between 4 and 6 p.m.

Number of Studies: 34
Avg. Number of Employees: 877
Directional Distribution: 20% entering, 80% exiting

Trip Generation per Employee

Average Rate	Range of Rates	Standard Deviation
0.46	0.26 - 1.36	0.71

Data Plot and Equation

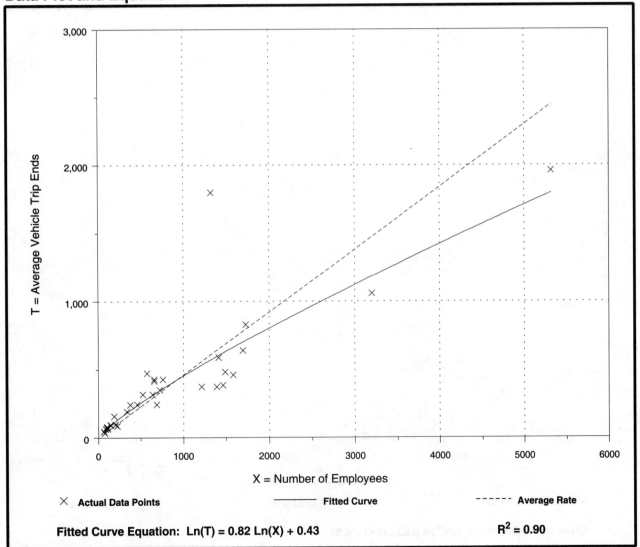

Fitted Curve Equation: $Ln(T) = 0.82 \, Ln(X) + 0.43$ $R^2 = 0.90$

Industrial Park
(130)

Average Vehicle Trip Ends vs: **Employees**
On a: **Weekday,**
A.M. Peak Hour of Generator

Number of Studies: 37
Avg. Number of Employees: 980
Directional Distribution: 87% entering, 13% exiting

Trip Generation per Employee

Average Rate	Range of Rates	Standard Deviation
0.43	0.28 - 1.13	0.68

Data Plot and Equation

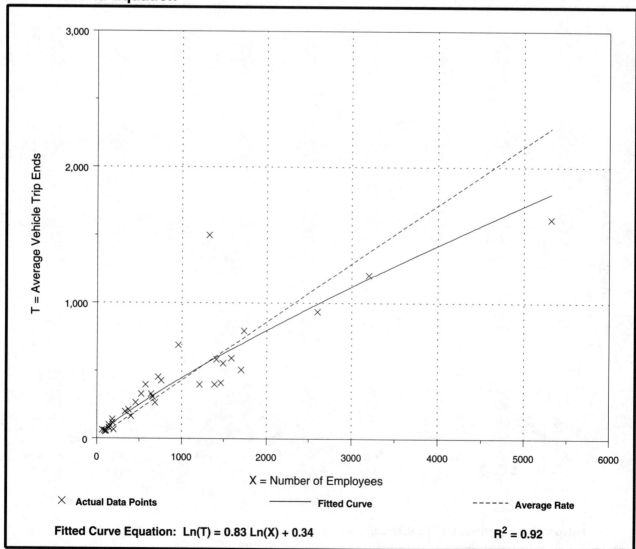

Fitted Curve Equation: Ln(T) = 0.83 Ln(X) + 0.34 $R^2 = 0.92$

Industrial Park
(130)

Average Vehicle Trip Ends vs: **Employees**
On a: **Weekday,**
P.M. Peak Hour of Generator

Number of Studies: 37
Avg. Number of Employees: 980
Directional Distribution: 21% entering, 79% exiting

Trip Generation per Employee

Average Rate	Range of Rates	Standard Deviation
0.45	0.26 - 1.36	0.70

Data Plot and Equation

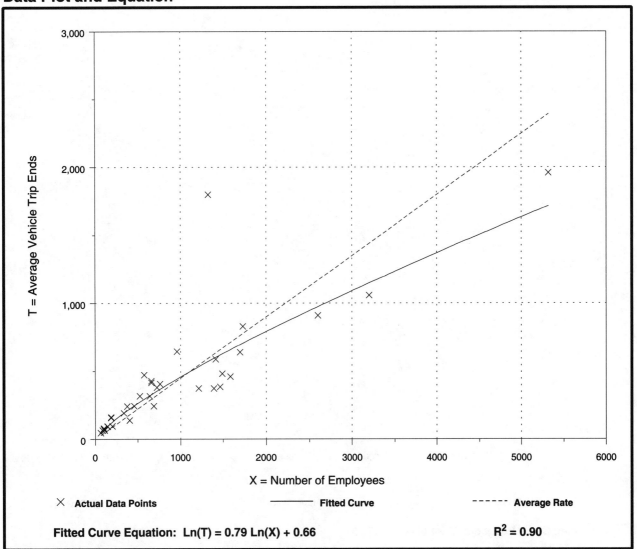

| X | Actual Data Points | ——— Fitted Curve | - - - - Average Rate |

Fitted Curve Equation: Ln(T) = 0.79 Ln(X) + 0.66 $R^2 = 0.90$

Industrial Park
(130)

Average Vehicle Trip Ends vs: **Employees**
On a: **Saturday**

Number of Studies: 14
Avg. Number of Employees: 919
Directional Distribution: 50% entering, 50% exiting

Trip Generation per Employee

Average Rate	Range of Rates	Standard Deviation
1.14	0.35 - 11.03	1.45

Data Plot and Equation

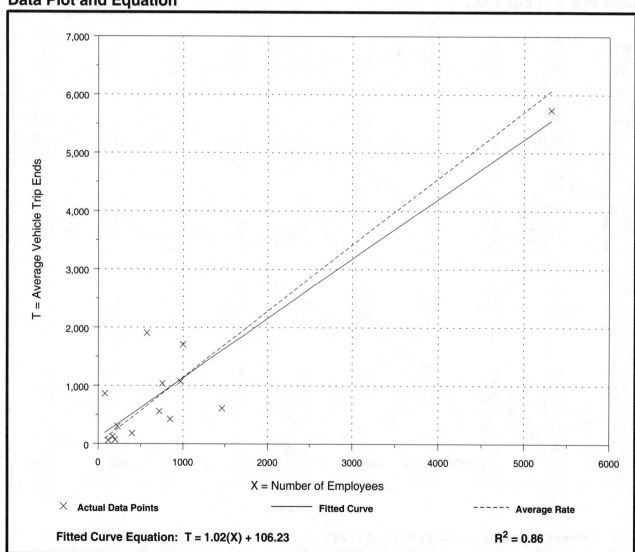

X **Actual Data Points**   ——— **Fitted Curve**   - - - - - **Average Rate**

Fitted Curve Equation: T = 1.02(X) + 106.23 $R^2 = 0.86$

Industrial Park
(130)

Average Vehicle Trip Ends vs: **Employees**
On a: **Saturday,**
Peak Hour of Generator

Number of Studies: 3
Avg. Number of Employees: 2,453
Directional Distribution: 32% entering, 68% exiting

Trip Generation per Employee

Average Rate	Range of Rates	Standard Deviation
0.14	0.07 - 0.31	0.37

Data Plot and Equation

Caution - Use Carefully - Small Sample Size

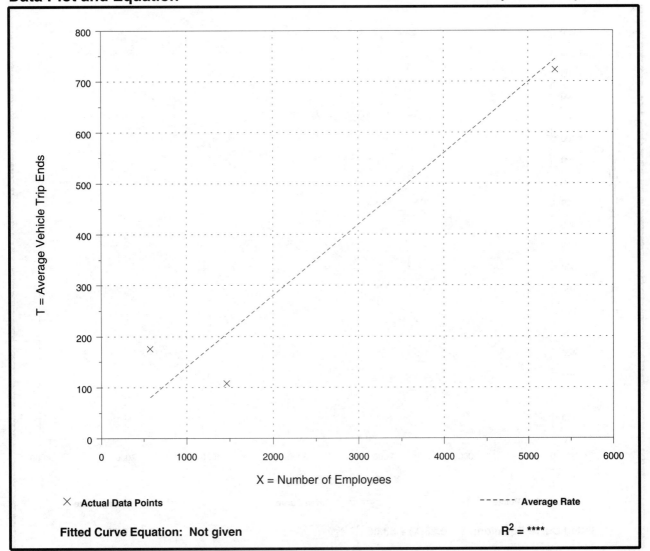

X **Actual Data Points**

- - - - - **Average Rate**

Fitted Curve Equation: Not given

$R^2 = $ ****

Industrial Park
(130)

Average Vehicle Trip Ends vs: Employees
On a: Sunday

Number of Studies: 14
Avg. Number of Employees: 919
Directional Distribution: 50% entering, 50% exiting

Trip Generation per Employee

Average Rate	Range of Rates	Standard Deviation
0.34	0.05 - 1.26	0.64

Data Plot and Equation

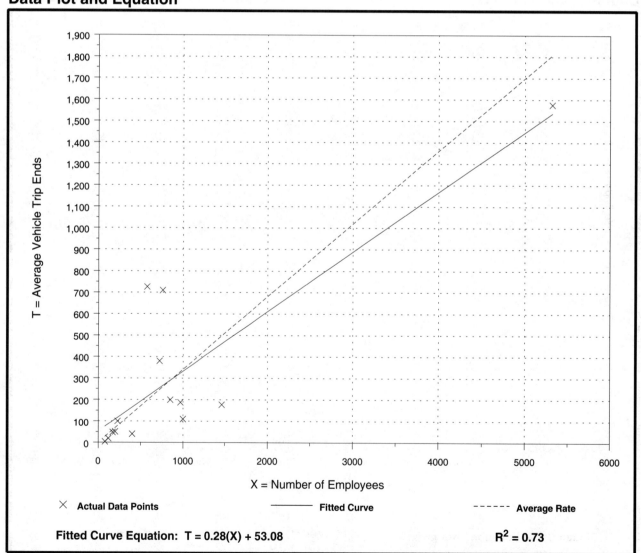

X   Actual Data Points   —————— Fitted Curve   - - - - - Average Rate

Fitted Curve Equation: T = 0.28(X) + 53.08 $R^2 = 0.73$

Industrial Park
(130)

Average Vehicle Trip Ends vs: **Employees**
On a: **Sunday,**
Peak Hour of Generator

Number of Studies: 3
Avg. Number of Employees: 2,453
Directional Distribution: 46% entering, 54% exiting

Trip Generation per Employee

Average Rate	Range of Rates	Standard Deviation
0.03	0.02 - 0.14	0.17

Data Plot and Equation

Caution - Use Carefully - Small Sample Size

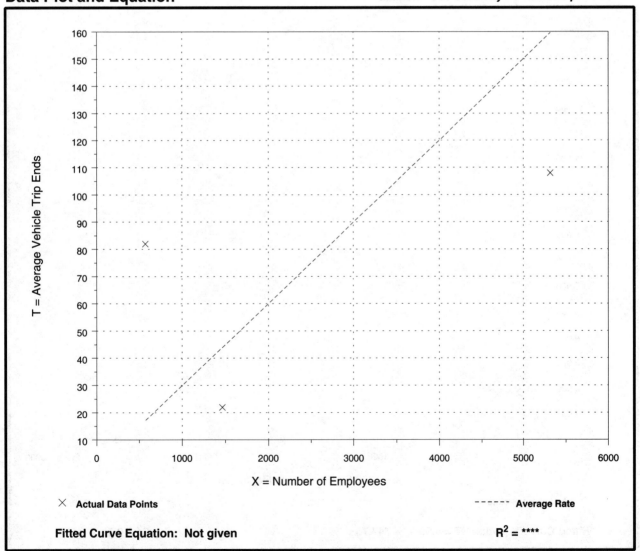

X **Actual Data Points**   - - - - - **Average Rate**

Fitted Curve Equation: Not given $R^2 = $ ****

Industrial Park
(130)

Average Vehicle Trip Ends vs: 1000 Sq. Feet Gross Floor Area
On a: Weekday

Number of Studies: 49
Average 1000 Sq. Feet GFA: 375
Directional Distribution: 50% entering, 50% exiting

Trip Generation per 1000 Sq. Feet Gross Floor Area

Average Rate	Range of Rates	Standard Deviation
6.96	0.91 - 36.97	5.64

Data Plot and Equation

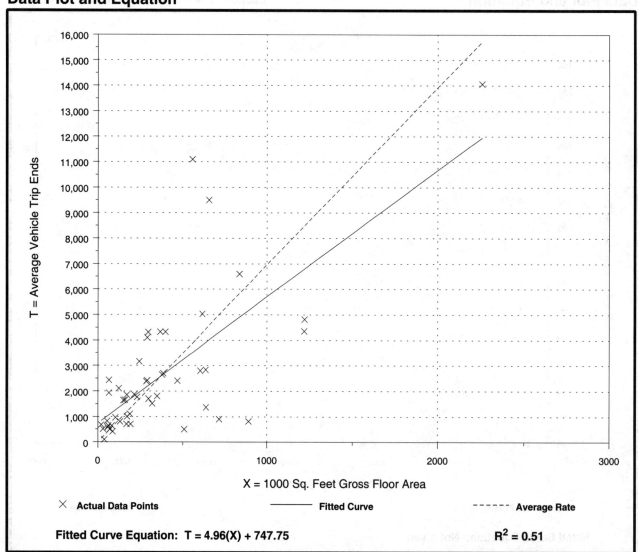

X **Actual Data Points**   ————— **Fitted Curve**   - - - - - **Average Rate**

Fitted Curve Equation: T = 4.96(X) + 747.75 $R^2 = 0.51$

Industrial Park
(130)

Average Vehicle Trip Ends vs: 1000 Sq. Feet Gross Floor Area
On a: Weekday,
Peak Hour of Adjacent Street Traffic,
One Hour Between 7 and 9 a.m.

Number of Studies: 40
Average 1000 Sq. Feet GFA: 439
Directional Distribution: 82% entering, 18% exiting

Trip Generation per 1000 Sq. Feet Gross Floor Area

Average Rate	Range of Rates	Standard Deviation
0.84	0.12 - 2.28	1.03

Data Plot and Equation

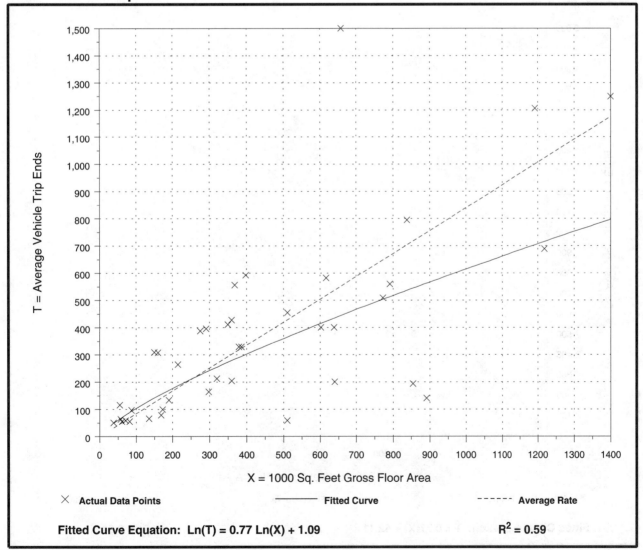

Fitted Curve Equation: $Ln(T) = 0.77 \, Ln(X) + 1.09$ $R^2 = 0.59$

Industrial Park
(130)

Average Vehicle Trip Ends vs:	1000 Sq. Feet Gross Floor Area
On a:	Weekday,
	Peak Hour of Adjacent Street Traffic,
	One Hour Between 4 and 6 p.m.

Number of Studies: 42
Average 1000 Sq. Feet GFA: 447
Directional Distribution: 21% entering, 79% exiting

Trip Generation per 1000 Sq. Feet Gross Floor Area

Average Rate	Range of Rates	Standard Deviation
0.86	0.13 - 2.85	1.07

Data Plot and Equation

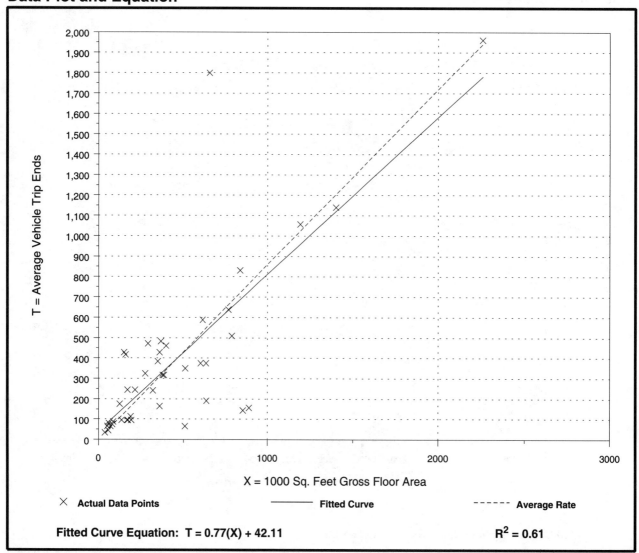

X = 1000 Sq. Feet Gross Floor Area

X **Actual Data Points**	——— **Fitted Curve**	- - - - - **Average Rate**

Fitted Curve Equation: T = 0.77(X) + 42.11 $R^2 = 0.61$

Industrial Park
(130)

Average Vehicle Trip Ends vs: 1000 Sq. Feet Gross Floor Area
On a: Weekday,
A.M. Peak Hour of Generator

Number of Studies: 36
Average 1000 Sq. Feet GFA: 473
Directional Distribution: 86% entering, 14% exiting

Trip Generation per 1000 Sq. Feet Gross Floor Area

Average Rate	Range of Rates	Standard Deviation
0.82	0.12 - 2.28	1.03

Data Plot and Equation

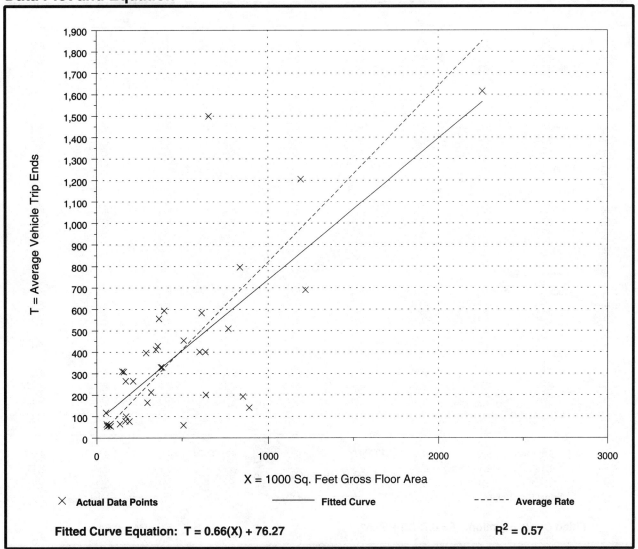

Fitted Curve Equation: $T = 0.66(X) + 76.27$ $R^2 = 0.57$

Industrial Park
(130)

Average Vehicle Trip Ends vs: **1000 Sq. Feet Gross Floor Area**
On a: **Weekday,**
P.M. Peak Hour of Generator

Number of Studies: 36
Average 1000 Sq. Feet GFA: 473
Directional Distribution: 21% entering, 79% exiting

Trip Generation per 1000 Sq. Feet Gross Floor Area

Average Rate	Range of Rates	Standard Deviation
0.86	0.13 - 2.95	1.09

Data Plot and Equation

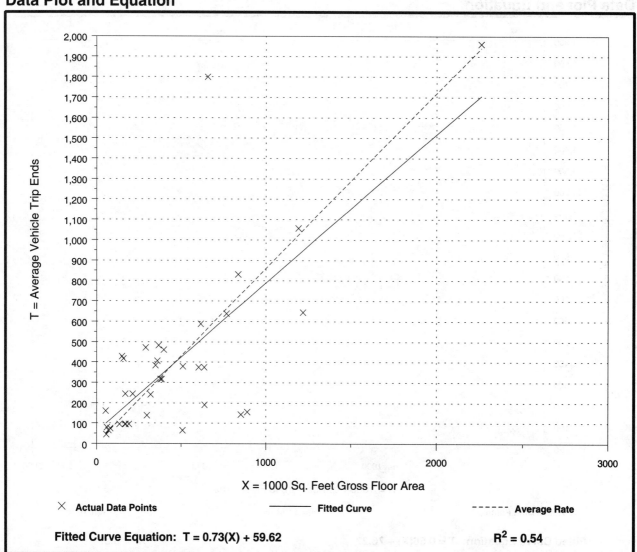

Fitted Curve Equation: T = 0.73(X) + 59.62 $R^2 = 0.54$

Industrial Park
(130)

Average Vehicle Trip Ends vs: 1000 Sq. Feet Gross Floor Area
On a: Saturday

Number of Studies: 14
Average 1000 Sq. Feet GFA: 421
Directional Distribution: 50% entering, 50% exiting

Trip Generation per 1000 Sq. Feet Gross Floor Area

Average Rate	Range of Rates	Standard Deviation
2.49	0.18 - 43.00	3.28

Data Plot and Equation

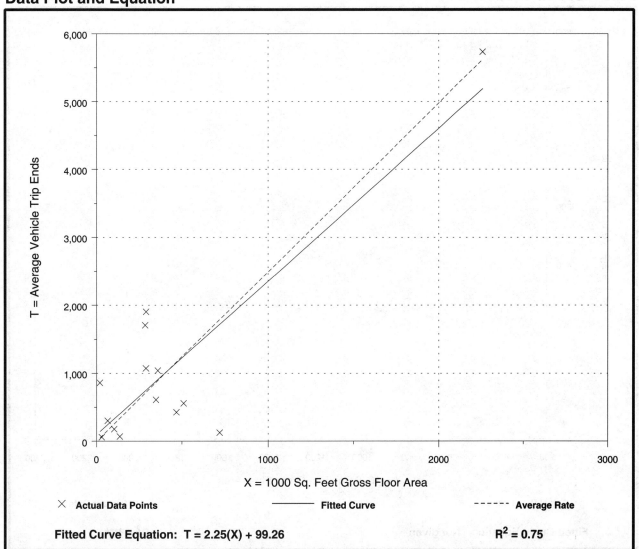

Fitted Curve Equation: T = 2.25(X) + 99.26 $R^2 = 0.75$

Industrial Park
(130)

Average Vehicle Trip Ends vs: **1000 Sq. Feet Gross Floor Area**
On a: **Saturday,**
Peak Hour of Generator

Number of Studies: 3
Average 1000 Sq. Feet GFA: 966
Directional Distribution: 32% entering, 68% exiting

Trip Generation per 1000 Sq. Feet Gross Floor Area

Average Rate	Range of Rates	Standard Deviation
0.35	0.31 - 0.60	0.60

Data Plot and Equation

Caution - Use Carefully - Small Sample Size

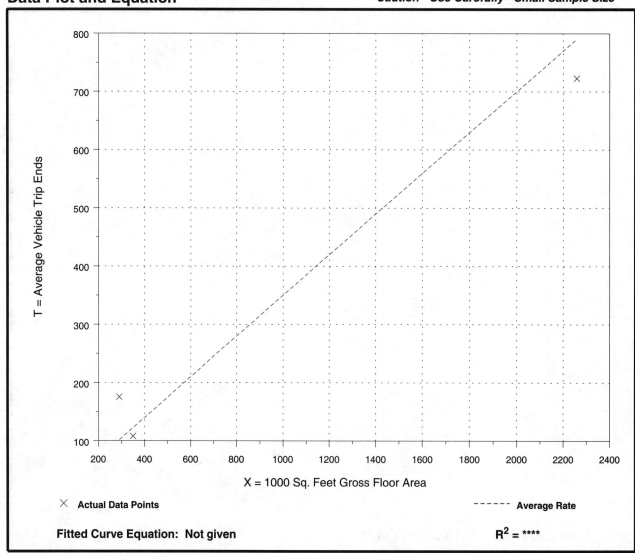

X **Actual Data Points**

‑ ‑ ‑ ‑ ‑ **Average Rate**

Fitted Curve Equation: Not given

$R^2 = ****$

Industrial Park
(130)

Average Vehicle Trip Ends vs: 1000 Sq. Feet Gross Floor Area
On a: Sunday

Number of Studies: 14
Average 1000 Sq. Feet GFA: 421
Directional Distribution: 50% entering, 50% exiting

Trip Generation per 1000 Sq. Feet Gross Floor Area

Average Rate	Range of Rates	Standard Deviation
0.73	0.07 - 2.49	1.03

Data Plot and Equation

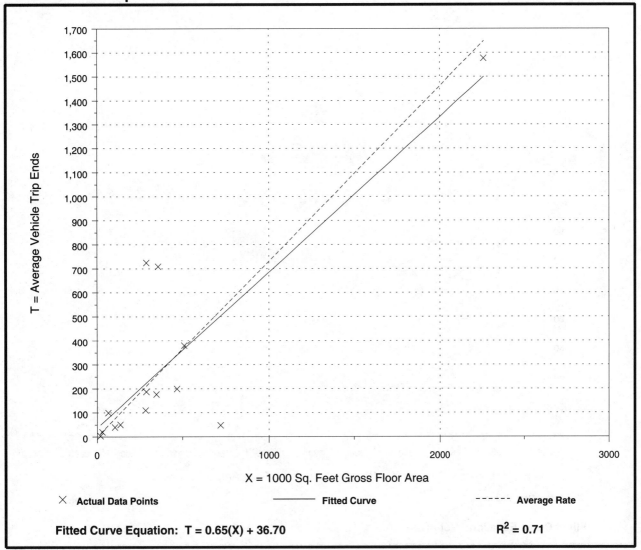

Fitted Curve Equation: T = 0.65(X) + 36.70 $R^2 = 0.71$

Industrial Park
(130)

Average Vehicle Trip Ends vs: 1000 Sq. Feet Gross Floor Area
On a: Sunday,
Peak Hour of Generator

Number of Studies: 3
Average 1000 Sq. Feet GFA: 966
Directional Distribution: 46% entering, 54% exiting

Trip Generation per 1000 Sq. Feet Gross Floor Area

Average Rate	Range of Rates	Standard Deviation
0.07	0.05 - 0.28	0.28

Data Plot and Equation

Caution - Use Carefully - Small Sample Size

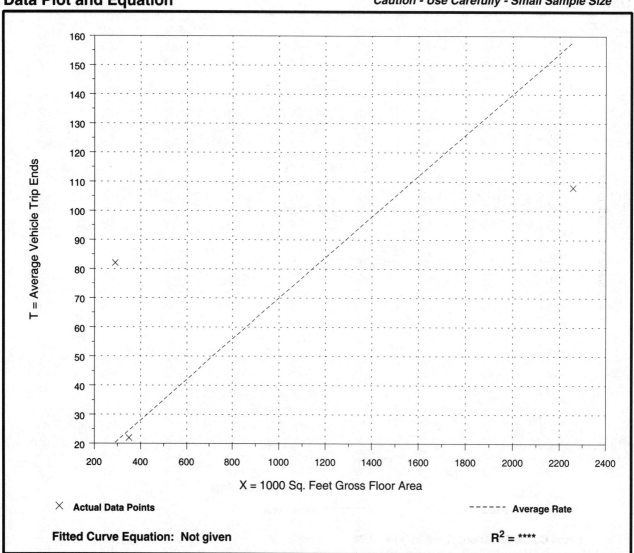

X **Actual Data Points**   - - - - - **Average Rate**

Fitted Curve Equation: Not given $R^2 = ****$

Industrial Park
(130)

Average Vehicle Trip Ends vs: Acres
On a: Weekday

Number of Studies: 43
Average Number of Acres: 39
Directional Distribution: 50% entering, 50% exiting

Trip Generation per Acre

Average Rate	Range of Rates	Standard Deviation
63.11	13.87 - 1272.63	62.04

Data Plot and Equation

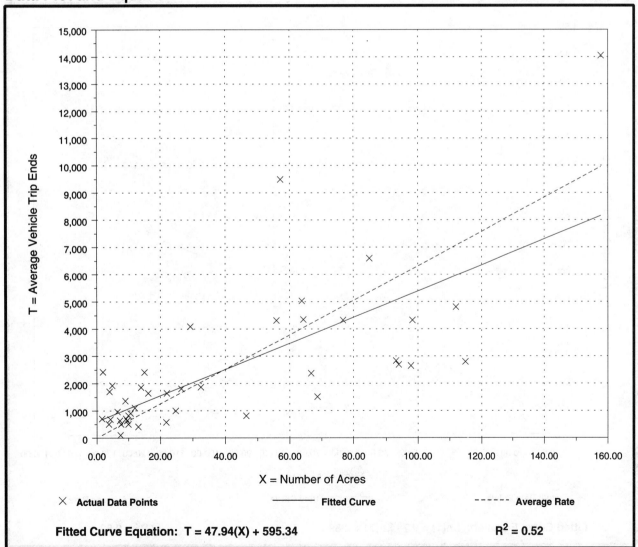

X   **Actual Data Points**   ——— **Fitted Curve**   - - - - - **Average Rate**

Fitted Curve Equation: T = 47.94(X) + 595.34 $R^2 = 0.52$

Industrial Park
(130)

Average Vehicle Trip Ends vs: **Acres**
On a: **Weekday,**
Peak Hour of Adjacent Street Traffic,
One Hour Between 7 and 9 a.m.

Number of Studies: 39
Average Number of Acres: 44
Directional Distribution: 83% entering, 17% exiting

Trip Generation per Acre

Average Rate	Range of Rates	Standard Deviation
8.55	2.94 - 41.25	6.14

Data Plot and Equation

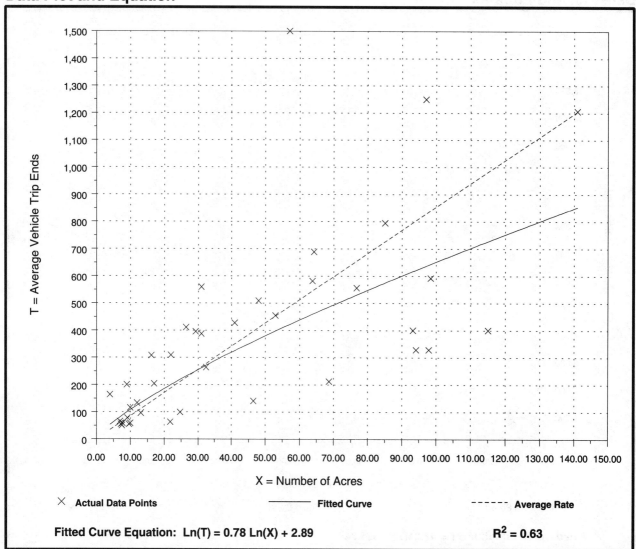

X Actual Data Points   ——— Fitted Curve   - - - - - Average Rate

Fitted Curve Equation: Ln(T) = 0.78 Ln(X) + 2.89 $R^2 = 0.63$

Industrial Park
(130)

Average Vehicle Trip Ends vs: **Acres**
             On a: **Weekday,**
                        Peak Hour of Adjacent Street Traffic,
                        One Hour Between 4 and 6 p.m.

Number of Studies: 39
Average Number of Acres: 46
Directional Distribution: 21% entering, 79% exiting

Trip Generation per Acre

Average Rate	Range of Rates	Standard Deviation
8.84	2.11 - 59.38	6.95

Data Plot and Equation

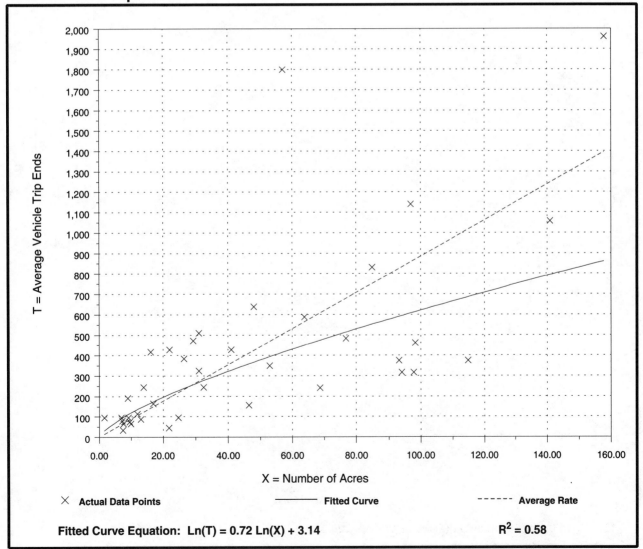

Fitted Curve Equation: $Ln(T) = 0.72 \, Ln(X) + 3.14$ $R^2 = 0.58$

Industrial Park
(130)

Average Vehicle Trip Ends vs: Acres
On a: Weekday,
A.M. Peak Hour of Generator

Number of Studies: 35
Average Number of Acres: 48
Directional Distribution: 87% entering, 13% exiting

Trip Generation per Acre

Average Rate	Range of Rates	Standard Deviation
8.29	2.94 - 48.75	6.12

Data Plot and Equation

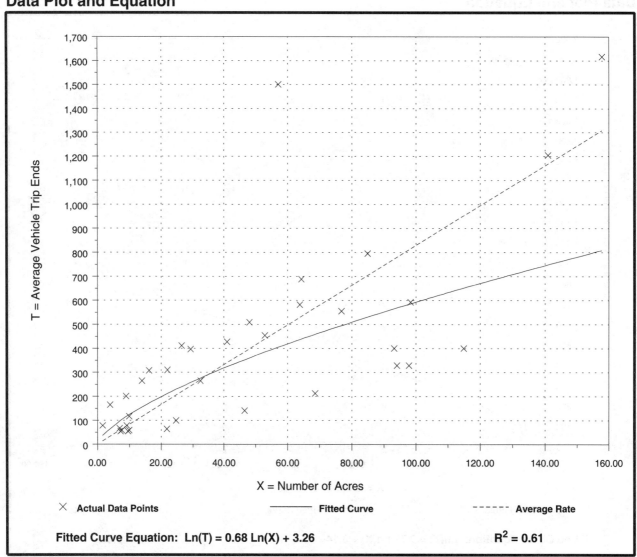

Fitted Curve Equation: Ln(T) = 0.68 Ln(X) + 3.26 $R^2 = 0.61$

Industrial Park
(130)

Average Vehicle Trip Ends vs: **Acres**
On a: **Weekday,**
P.M. Peak Hour of Generator

Number of Studies: 35
Average Number of Acres: 48
Directional Distribution: 21% entering, 79% exiting

Trip Generation per Acre

Average Rate	Range of Rates	Standard Deviation
8.67	2.11 - 59.38	7.16

Data Plot and Equation

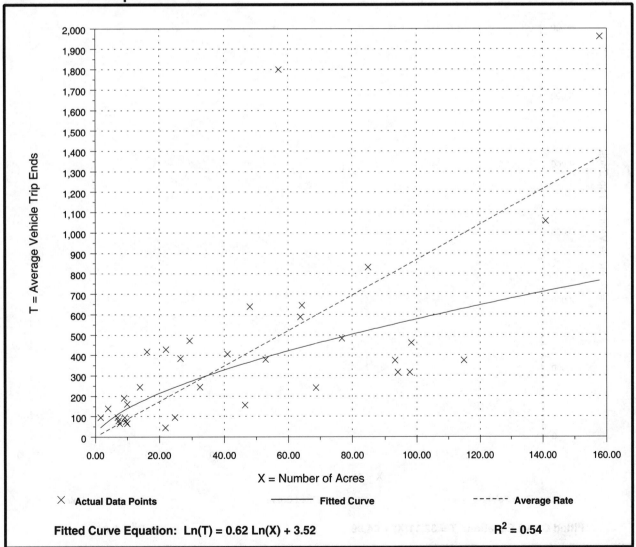

Fitted Curve Equation: Ln(T) = 0.62 Ln(X) + 3.52 $R^2 = 0.54$

Industrial Park
(130)

Average Vehicle Trip Ends vs: Acres
On a: Saturday

Number of Studies: 14
Average Number of Acres: 31
Directional Distribution: 50% entering, 50% exiting

Trip Generation per Acre

Average Rate	Range of Rates	Standard Deviation
34.23	10.00 - 564.21	41.91

Data Plot and Equation

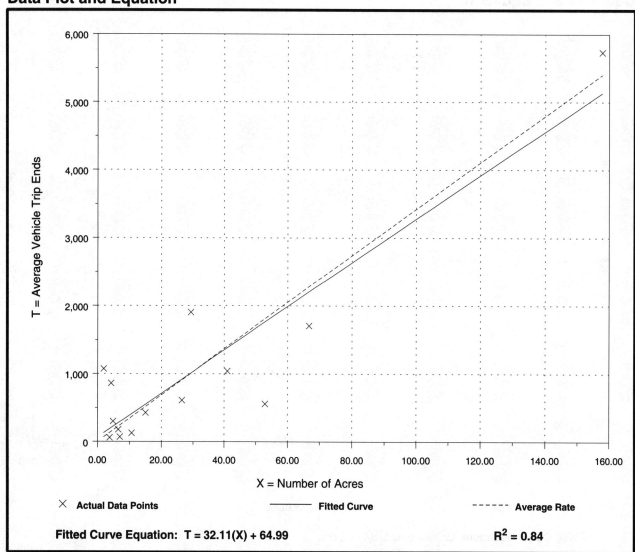

X **Actual Data Points** ——— **Fitted Curve** - - - - **Average Rate**

Fitted Curve Equation: T = 32.11(X) + 64.99 $R^2 = 0.84$

Industrial Park
(130)

Average Vehicle Trip Ends vs: Acres
On a: Saturday,
Peak Hour of Generator

Number of Studies: 3
Average Number of Acres: 71
Directional Distribution: 32% entering, 68% exiting

Trip Generation per Acre

Average Rate	Range of Rates	Standard Deviation
4.71	4.08 - 6.01	2.23

Data Plot and Equation

Caution - Use Carefully - Small Sample Size

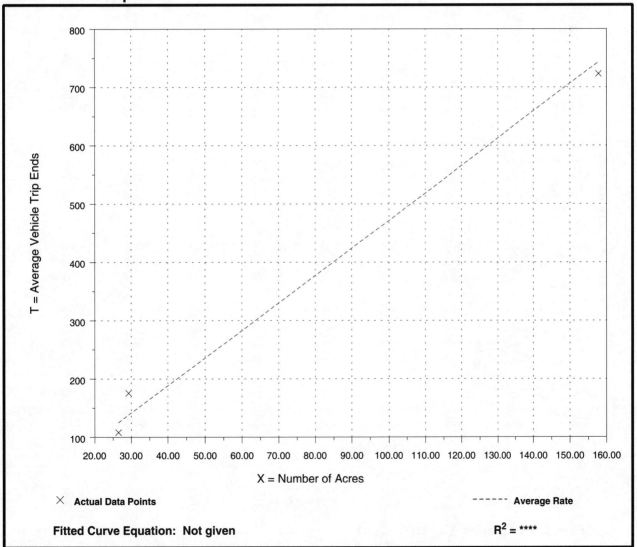

X   **Actual Data Points**   - - - - -   **Average Rate**

Fitted Curve Equation: Not given $R^2 =$ ****

Industrial Park
(130)

Average Vehicle Trip Ends vs: **Acres**
On a: **Sunday**

Number of Studies: 14
Average Number of Acres: 31
Directional Distribution: 50% entering, 50% exiting

Trip Generation per Acre

Average Rate	Range of Rates	Standard Deviation
10.11	0.93 - 98.95	9.02

Data Plot and Equation

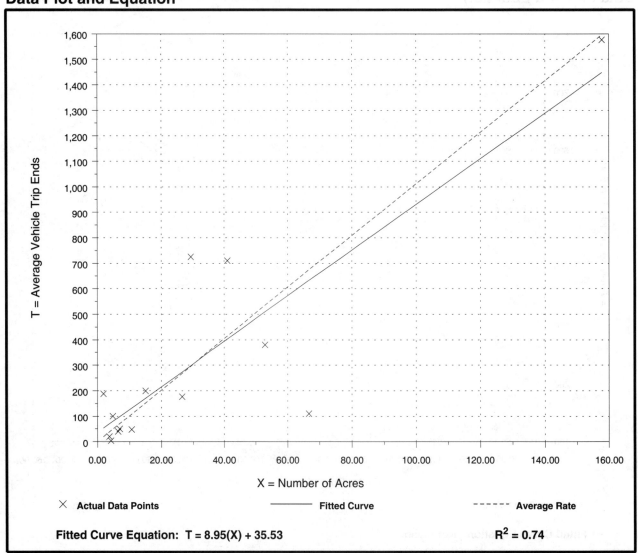

X = Number of Acres

× Actual Data Points ——— Fitted Curve ----- Average Rate

Fitted Curve Equation: T = 8.95(X) + 35.53 $R^2 = 0.74$

Industrial Park
(130)

Average Vehicle Trip Ends vs: **Acres**
On a: **Sunday,**
Peak Hour of Generator

Number of Studies: 3
Average Number of Acres: 71
Directional Distribution: 46% entering, 54% exiting

Trip Generation per Acre

Average Rate	Range of Rates	Standard Deviation
0.99	0.68 - 2.80	1.22

Data Plot and Equation

Caution - Use Carefully - Small Sample Size

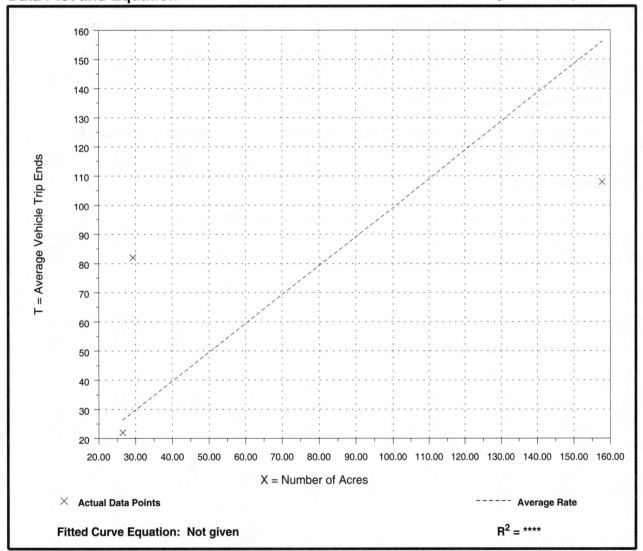

X **Actual Data Points**   - - - - - **Average Rate**

Fitted Curve Equation: Not given $R^2 = ****$

Land Use: 140
Manufacturing

Description

Manufacturing facilities are areas where the primary activity is the conversion of raw materials or parts into finished products. Size and type of activity may vary substantially from one facility to another. In addition to the actual production of goods, manufacturing facilities generally also have office, warehouse, research and associated functions. General light industrial (Land Use 110), general heavy industrial (Land Use 120) and industrial park (Land Use 130) are related uses.

Additional Data

Average weekday transit trip ends:
— 0.09 per employee
— 0.08 per 1,000 square feet gross floor area
— 1.25 per acre

Vehicle occupancy ranged from 1.2 to 1.3 persons per automobile on an average weekday.

The peak hour of the generator typically coincided with the peak hour of the adjacent street traffic.

Facilities with employees on shift work may peak at other hours.

The sites were surveyed in the late 1960s, the early 1970s, the mid-1980s, the 1990s and the 2000s throughout the United States.

Source Numbers

3, 7, 10, 15, 17, 74, 85, 88, 177, 184, 241, 357, 384, 418, 443, 583, 598, 611

Manufacturing
(140)

Average Vehicle Trip Ends vs: Employees
On a: Weekday

Number of Studies: 62
Avg. Number of Employees: 648
Directional Distribution: 50% entering, 50% exiting

Trip Generation per Employee

Average Rate	Range of Rates	Standard Deviation
2.13	0.60 - 6.66	1.66

Data Plot and Equation

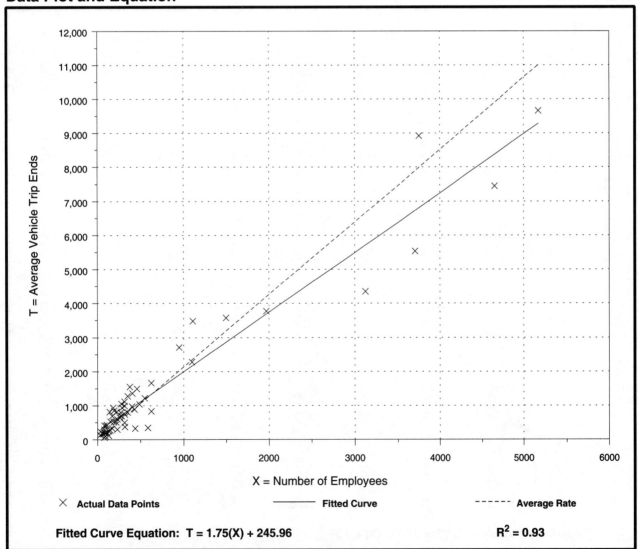

X **Actual Data Points** ———— **Fitted Curve** - - - - - **Average Rate**

Fitted Curve Equation: T = 1.75(X) + 245.96 $R^2 = 0.93$

Manufacturing
(140)

Average Vehicle Trip Ends vs: **Employees**
On a: **Weekday,**
Peak Hour of Adjacent Street Traffic,
One Hour Between 7 and 9 a.m.

Number of Studies: 45
Avg. Number of Employees: 628
Directional Distribution: 73% entering, 27% exiting

Trip Generation per Employee

Average Rate	Range of Rates	Standard Deviation
0.40	0.18 - 0.94	0.65

Data Plot and Equation

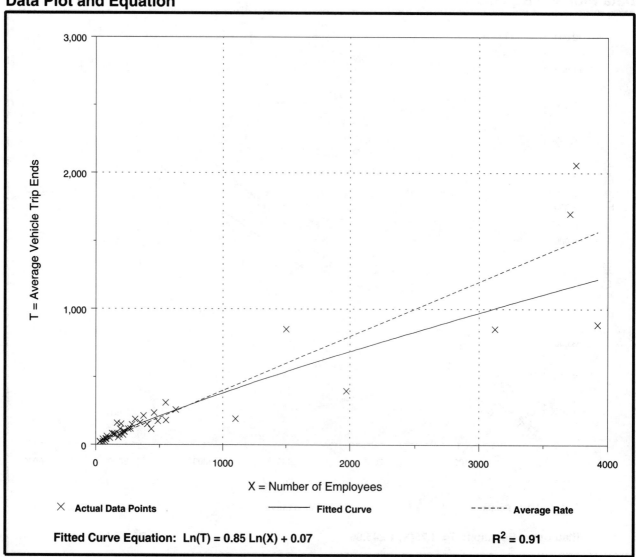

X   Actual Data Points   ———— Fitted Curve   - - - - - Average Rate

Fitted Curve Equation: Ln(T) = 0.85 Ln(X) + 0.07 $R^2 = 0.91$

Manufacturing
(140)

Average Vehicle Trip Ends vs: **Employees**
On a: **Weekday,**
Peak Hour of Adjacent Street Traffic,
One Hour Between 4 and 6 p.m.

Number of Studies: 46
Avg. Number of Employees: 711
Directional Distribution: 44% entering, 56% exiting

Trip Generation per Employee

Average Rate	Range of Rates	Standard Deviation
0.36	0.14 - 0.90	0.62

Data Plot and Equation

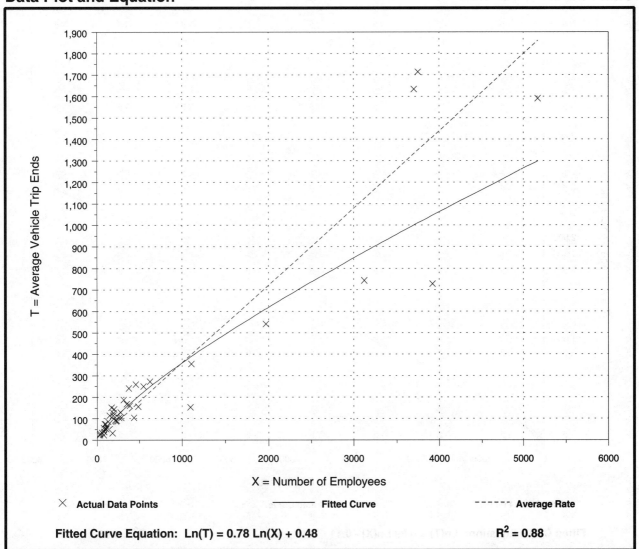

Fitted Curve Equation: Ln(T) = 0.78 Ln(X) + 0.48 $R^2 = 0.88$

Manufacturing
(140)

Average Vehicle Trip Ends vs: Employees
On a: Weekday,
A.M. Peak Hour of Generator

Number of Studies: 52
Avg. Number of Employees: 881
Directional Distribution: 80% entering, 20% exiting

Trip Generation per Employee

Average Rate	Range of Rates	Standard Deviation
0.39	0.20 - 0.94	0.64

Data Plot and Equation

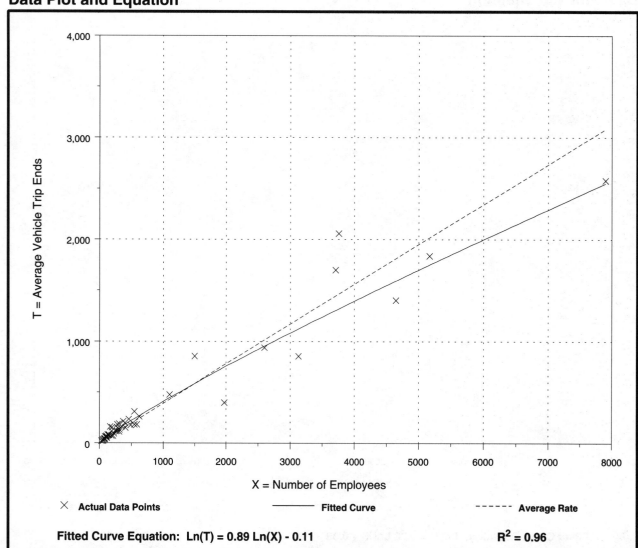

Fitted Curve Equation: Ln(T) = 0.89 Ln(X) - 0.11 $R^2 = 0.96$

Manufacturing
(140)

Average Vehicle Trip Ends vs: **Employees**
On a: **Weekday,**
P.M. Peak Hour of Generator

Number of Studies: 51
Avg. Number of Employees: 744
Directional Distribution: 48% entering, 52% exiting

Trip Generation per Employee

Average Rate	Range of Rates	Standard Deviation
0.40	0.24 - 1.11	0.65

Data Plot and Equation

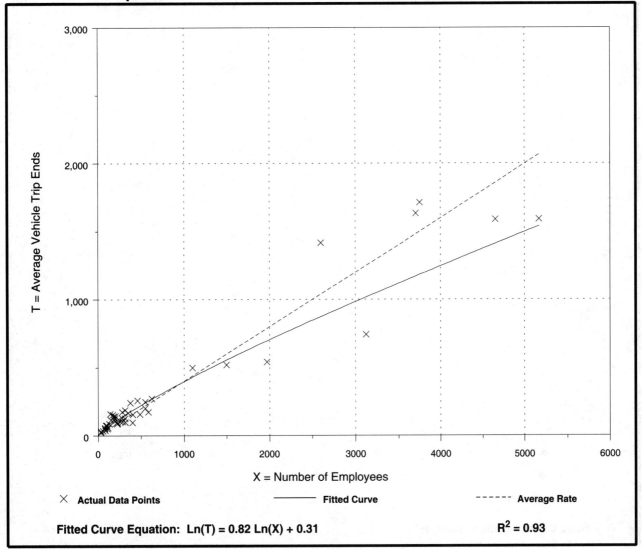

X **Actual Data Points**   ———— **Fitted Curve**   - - - - - **Average Rate**

Fitted Curve Equation: Ln(T) = 0.82 Ln(X) + 0.31 $R^2 = 0.93$

Manufacturing
(140)

Number of Studies: 2
Avg. Number of Employees: 824
Directional Distribution: 50% entering, 50% exiting

Trip Generation per Employee

Average Rate	Range of Rates	Standard Deviation
0.87	0.69 - 1.24	*

Data Plot and Equation

Caution - Use Carefully - Small Sample Size

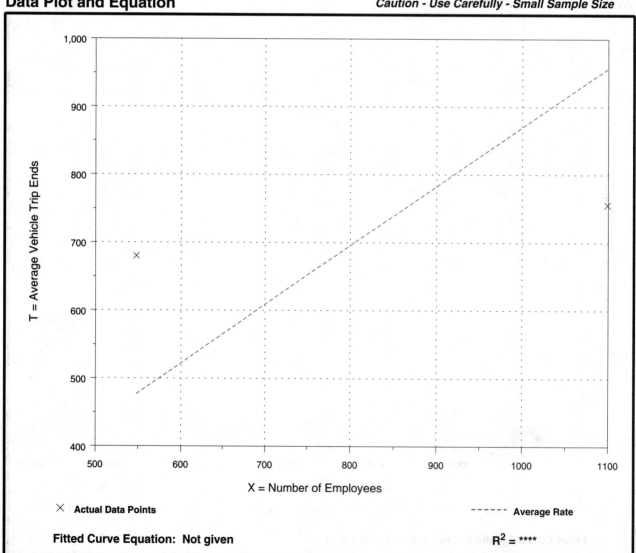

X **Actual Data Points**   - - - - - **Average Rate**

Fitted Curve Equation: Not given $R^2 = $ ****

Manufacturing
(140)

Average Vehicle Trip Ends vs: **Employees**
On a: **Saturday,**
Peak Hour of Generator

Number of Studies: 2
Avg. Number of Employees: 824
Directional Distribution: Not available

Trip Generation per Employee

Average Rate	Range of Rates	Standard Deviation
0.16	0.15 - 0.18	*

Data Plot and Equation

Caution - Use Carefully - Small Sample Size

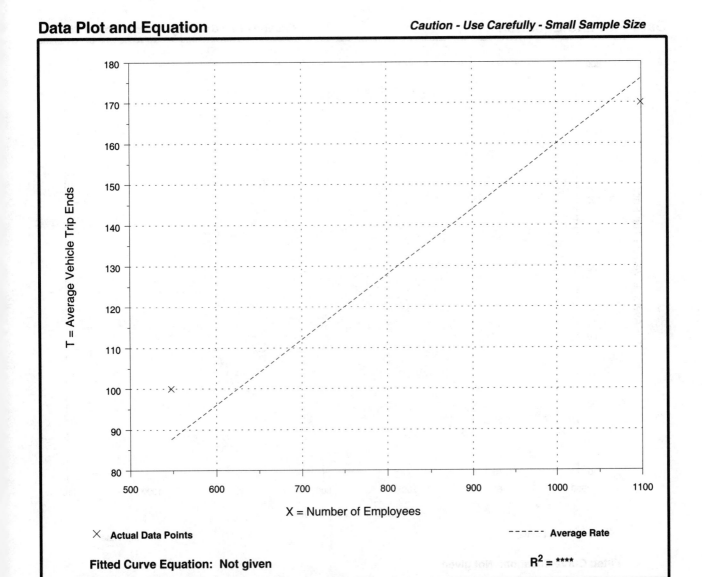

Fitted Curve Equation: Not given   **R² = ******

Manufacturing
(140)

Average Vehicle Trip Ends vs: **Employees**
On a: **Sunday**

Number of Studies: 2
Avg. Number of Employees: 824
Directional Distribution: 50% entering, 50% exiting

Trip Generation per Employee

Average Rate	Range of Rates	Standard Deviation
0.36	0.05 - 0.99	*

Data Plot and Equation

Caution - Use Carefully - Small Sample Size

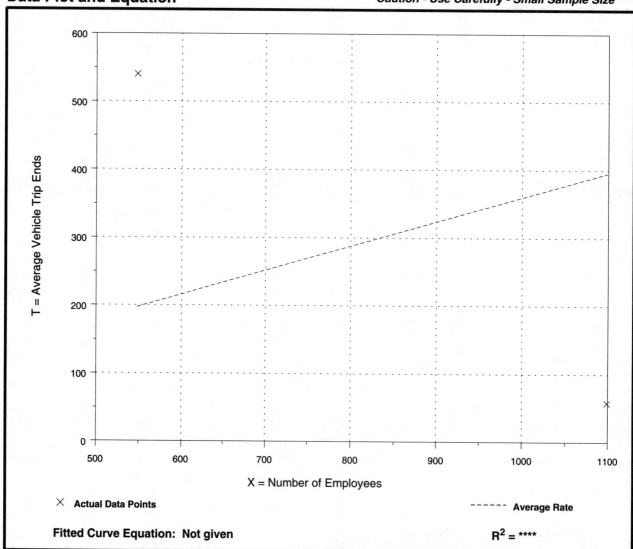

X **Actual Data Points**

- - - - - **Average Rate**

Fitted Curve Equation: Not given $R^2 = ****$

Manufacturing
(140)

Average Vehicle Trip Ends vs: **Employees**
          On a: **Sunday,**
                 Peak Hour of Generator

Number of Studies: 2
Avg. Number of Employees: 824
Directional Distribution: Not available

Trip Generation per Employee

Average Rate	Range of Rates	Standard Deviation
0.05	0.01 - 0.15	*

Data Plot and Equation

Caution - Use Carefully - Small Sample Size

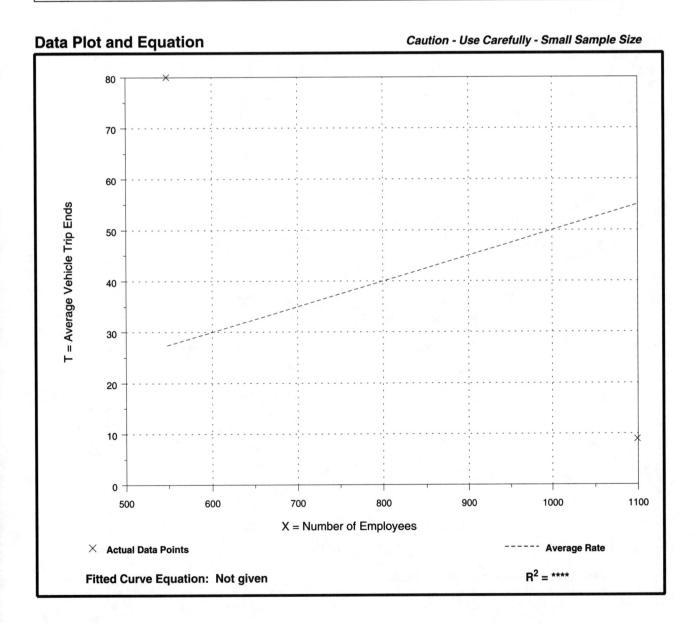

Fitted Curve Equation: Not given　　　　　　$R^2 = ****$

Manufacturing
(140)

Average Vehicle Trip Ends vs: 1000 Sq. Feet Gross Floor Area
On a: Weekday

Number of Studies: 62
Average 1000 Sq. Feet GFA: 349
Directional Distribution: 50% entering, 50% exiting

Trip Generation per 1000 Sq. Feet Gross Floor Area

Average Rate	Range of Rates	Standard Deviation
3.82	0.50 - 52.05	3.07

Data Plot and Equation

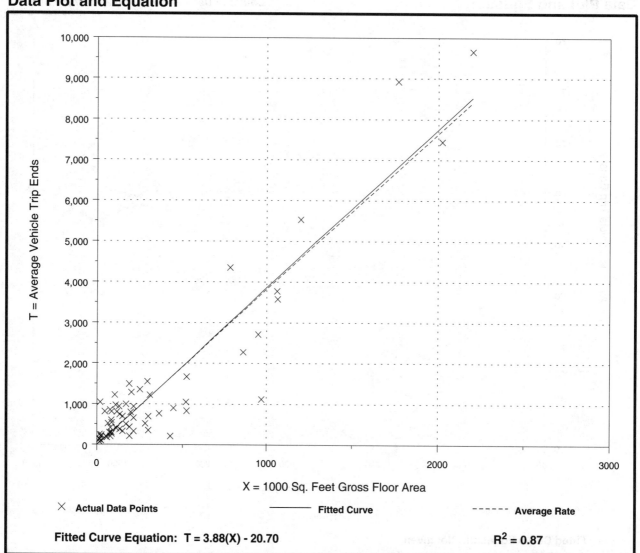

Fitted Curve Equation: T = 3.88(X) - 20.70 $R^2 = 0.87$

Manufacturing
(140)

Average Vehicle Trip Ends vs: 1000 Sq. Feet Gross Floor Area
On a: Weekday,
Peak Hour of Adjacent Street Traffic,
One Hour Between 7 and 9 a.m.

Number of Studies: 51
Average 1000 Sq. Feet GFA: 293
Directional Distribution: 78% entering, 22% exiting

Trip Generation per 1000 Sq. Feet Gross Floor Area

Average Rate	Range of Rates	Standard Deviation
0.73	0.10 - 8.75	1.04

Data Plot and Equation

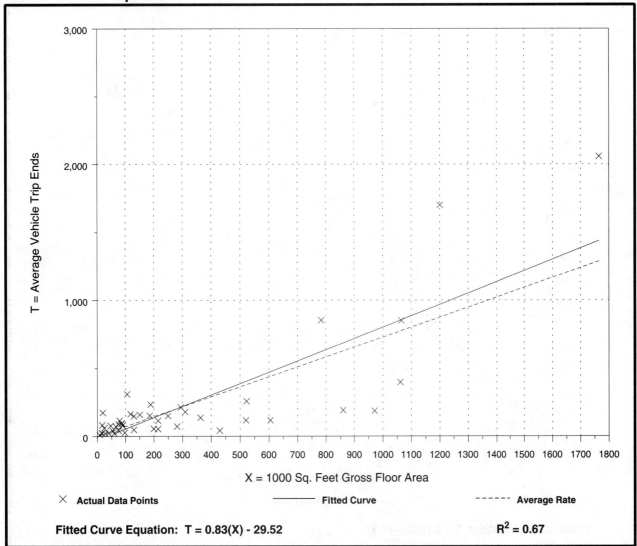

Fitted Curve Equation: $T = 0.83(X) - 29.52$ $\qquad$ $R^2 = 0.67$

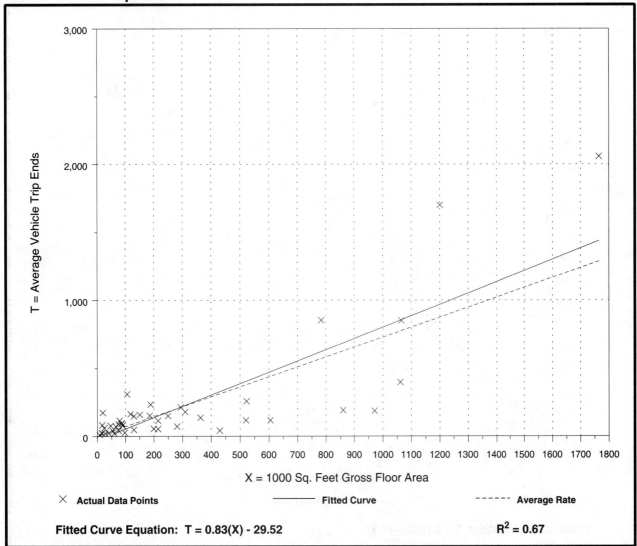

Manufacturing
(140)

Average Vehicle Trip Ends vs: **1000 Sq. Feet Gross Floor Area**
On a: **Weekday,**
Peak Hour of Adjacent Street Traffic,
One Hour Between 4 and 6 p.m.

Number of Studies: 56
Average 1000 Sq. Feet GFA: 318
Directional Distribution: 36% entering, 64% exiting

Trip Generation per 1000 Sq. Feet Gross Floor Area

Average Rate	Range of Rates	Standard Deviation
0.73	0.07 - 7.85	1.01

Data Plot and Equation

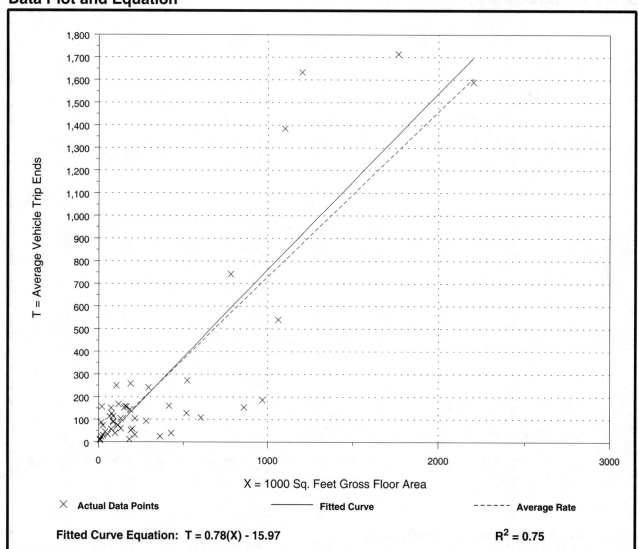

Fitted Curve Equation: $T = 0.78(X) - 15.97$ $R^2 = 0.75$

Manufacturing
(140)

Average Vehicle Trip Ends vs: 1000 Sq. Feet Gross Floor Area
On a: Weekday,
A.M. Peak Hour of Generator

Number of Studies: 50
Average 1000 Sq. Feet GFA: 370
Directional Distribution: 68% entering, 32% exiting

Trip Generation per 1000 Sq. Feet Gross Floor Area

Average Rate	Range of Rates	Standard Deviation
0.78	0.10 - 8.75	1.01

Data Plot and Equation

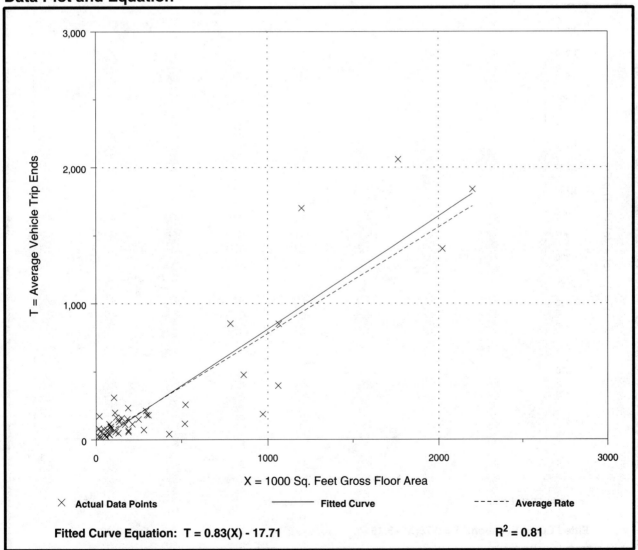

X = 1000 Sq. Feet Gross Floor Area

X   Actual Data Points   —— Fitted Curve   ----- Average Rate

Fitted Curve Equation: T = 0.83(X) - 17.71 $R^2 = 0.81$

Manufacturing
(140)

Average Vehicle Trip Ends vs: **1000 Sq. Feet Gross Floor Area**
On a: **Weekday,**
P.M. Peak Hour of Generator

Number of Studies: 50
Average 1000 Sq. Feet GFA: 370
Directional Distribution: 52% entering, 48% exiting

Trip Generation per 1000 Sq. Feet Gross Floor Area

Average Rate	Range of Rates	Standard Deviation
0.75	0.09 - 7.85	0.98

Data Plot and Equation

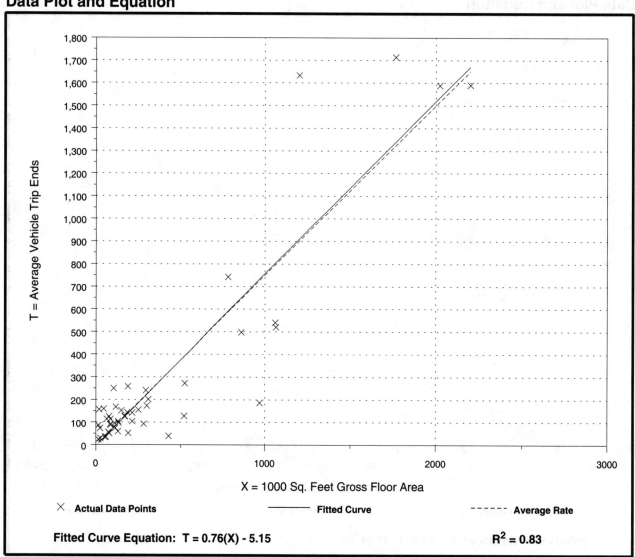

Fitted Curve Equation: T = 0.76(X) - 5.15 $R^2 = 0.83$

Manufacturing
(140)

Average Vehicle Trip Ends vs: 1000 Sq. Feet Gross Floor Area
On a: Saturday

Number of Studies: 2
Average 1000 Sq. Feet GFA: 483
Directional Distribution: 50% entering, 50% exiting

Trip Generation per 1000 Sq. Feet Gross Floor Area

Average Rate	Range of Rates	Standard Deviation
1.49	0.88 - 6.42	*

Data Plot and Equation

Caution - Use Carefully - Small Sample Size

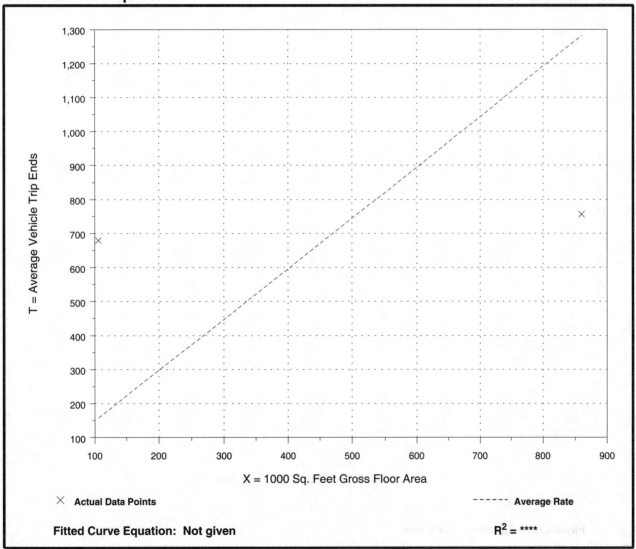

X **Actual Data Points**

- - - - - **Average Rate**

Fitted Curve Equation: Not given $R^2 = ****$

Manufacturing
(140)

Average Vehicle Trip Ends vs: 1000 Sq. Feet Gross Floor Area
On a: Saturday,
Peak Hour of Generator

Number of Studies: 2
Average 1000 Sq. Feet GFA: 483
Directional Distribution: Not available

Trip Generation per 1000 Sq. Feet Gross Floor Area

Average Rate	Range of Rates	Standard Deviation
0.28	0.20 - 0.94	*

Data Plot and Equation

Caution - Use Carefully - Small Sample Size

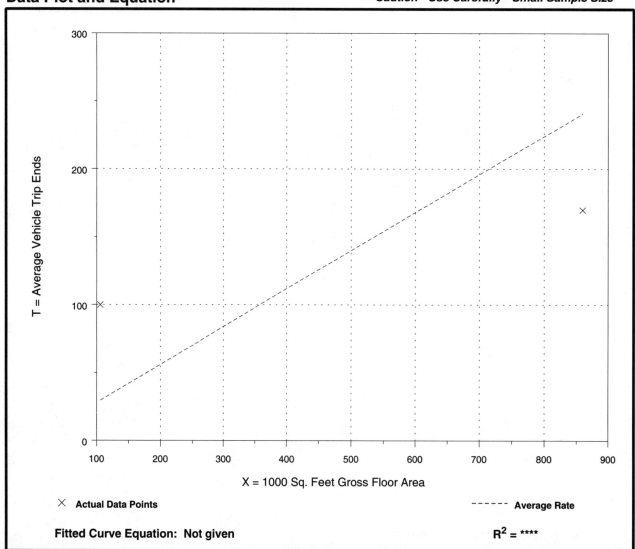

X **Actual Data Points**

- - - - - **Average Rate**

Fitted Curve Equation: Not given $R^2 = ****$

Manufacturing
(140)

Average Vehicle Trip Ends vs: 1000 Sq. Feet Gross Floor Area
On a: Sunday

Number of Studies: 2
Average 1000 Sq. Feet GFA: 483
Directional Distribution: 50% entering, 50% exiting

Trip Generation per 1000 Sq. Feet Gross Floor Area

Average Rate	Range of Rates	Standard Deviation
0.62	0.07 - 5.09	*

Data Plot and Equation

Caution - Use Carefully - Small Sample Size

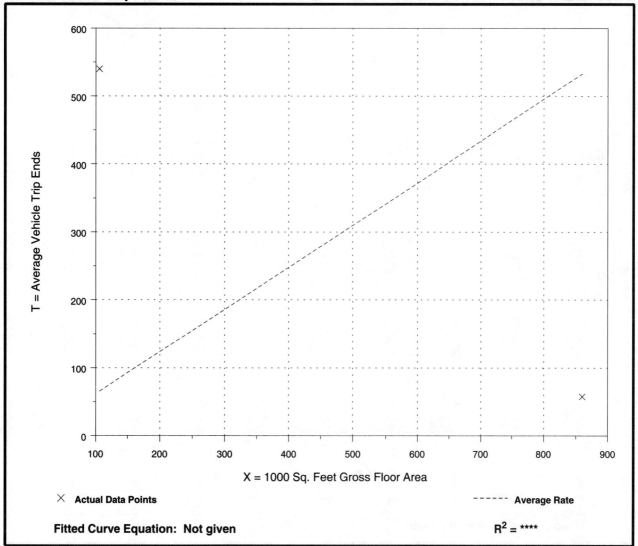

$\times$ **Actual Data Points**

- - - - - **Average Rate**

Fitted Curve Equation: Not given $R^2 = $ ****

Manufacturing
(140)

Average Vehicle Trip Ends vs: 1000 Sq. Feet Gross Floor Area
On a: Sunday,
Peak Hour of Generator

Number of Studies: 2
Average 1000 Sq. Feet GFA: 483
Directional Distribution: Not available

Trip Generation per 1000 Sq. Feet Gross Floor Area

Average Rate	Range of Rates	Standard Deviation
0.09	0.01 - 0.75	*

Data Plot and Equation

Caution - Use Carefully - Small Sample Size

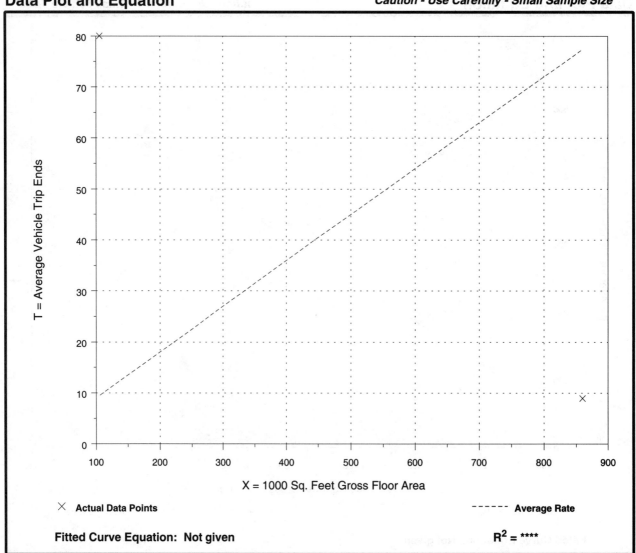

X Actual Data Points

- - - - - Average Rate

Fitted Curve Equation: Not given $R^2 =$ ****

Manufacturing
(140)

Average Vehicle Trip Ends vs: Acres
On a: Weekday

Number of Studies: 56
Average Number of Acres: 35
Directional Distribution: 50% entering, 50% exiting

Trip Generation per Acre

Average Rate	Range of Rates	Standard Deviation
38.88	2.54 - 396.00	41.93

Data Plot and Equation

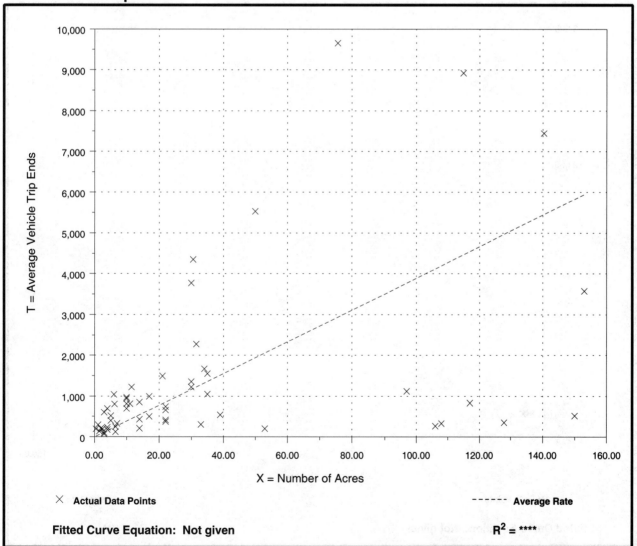

X   **Actual Data Points**   ----- **Average Rate**

Fitted Curve Equation: Not given $R^2 = $ ****

Manufacturing
(140)

Average Vehicle Trip Ends vs: **Acres**
On a: **Weekday,**
Peak Hour of Adjacent Street Traffic,
One Hour Between 7 and 9 a.m.

Number of Studies: 43
Average Number of Acres: 33
Directional Distribution: 93% entering, 7% exiting

Trip Generation per Acre

Average Rate	Range of Rates	Standard Deviation
7.44	0.48 - 124.00	9.45

Data Plot and Equation

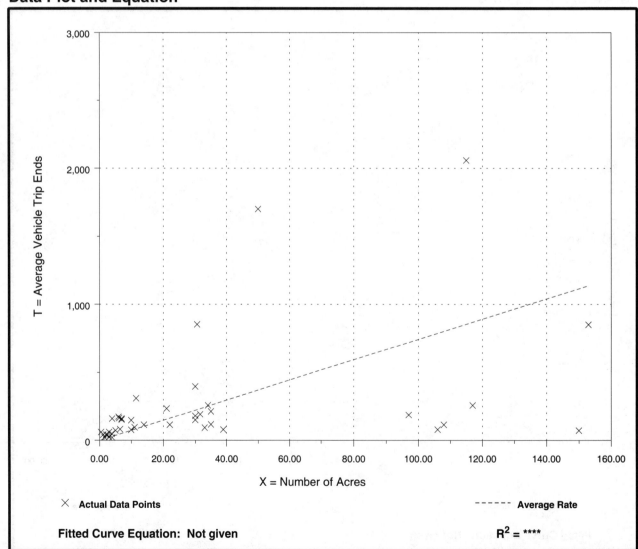

Fitted Curve Equation: Not given $R^2 = ****$

Manufacturing
(140)

Average Vehicle Trip Ends vs: **Acres**
          On a: **Weekday,**
                   Peak Hour of Adjacent Street Traffic,
                   One Hour Between 4 and 6 p.m.

Number of Studies: 43
Average Number of Acres: 30
Directional Distribution: 53% entering, 47% exiting

Trip Generation per Acre

Average Rate	Range of Rates	Standard Deviation
8.35	0.62 - 148.00	10.04

Data Plot and Equation

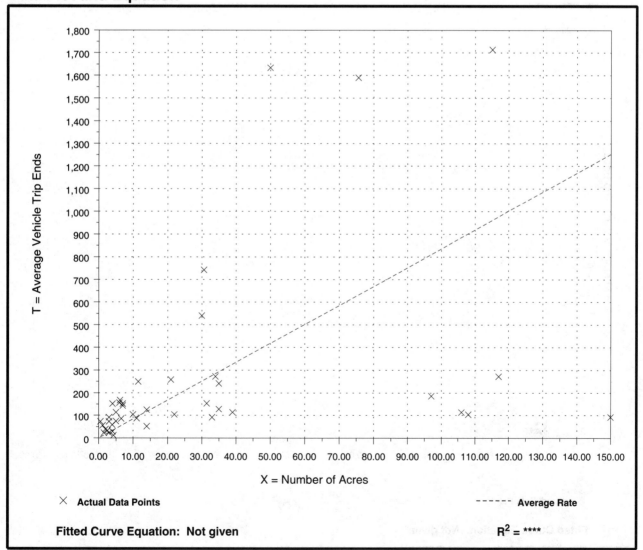

X **Actual Data Points**
‑ ‑ ‑ ‑ ‑ **Average Rate**

Fitted Curve Equation: Not given
$R^2 =$ ********

Manufacturing
(140)

Average Vehicle Trip Ends vs: Acres
On a: Weekday,
A.M. Peak Hour of Generator

Number of Studies: 51
Average Number of Acres: 32
Directional Distribution: 72% entering, 28% exiting

Trip Generation per Acre

Average Rate	Range of Rates	Standard Deviation
9.30	0.48 - 124.00	9.40

Data Plot and Equation

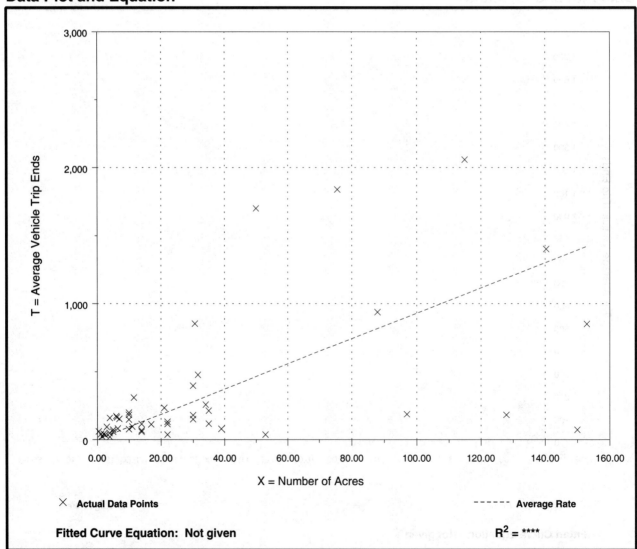

X **Actual Data Points**   ----- **Average Rate**

Fitted Curve Equation: Not given R^2 = ****

Manufacturing
(140)

Average Vehicle Trip Ends vs: **Acres**
On a: **Weekday,**
P.M. Peak Hour of Generator

Number of Studies: 50
Average Number of Acres: 33
Directional Distribution: 48% entering, 52% exiting

Trip Generation per Acre

Average Rate	Range of Rates	Standard Deviation
9.21	0.62 - 148.00	9.12

Data Plot and Equation

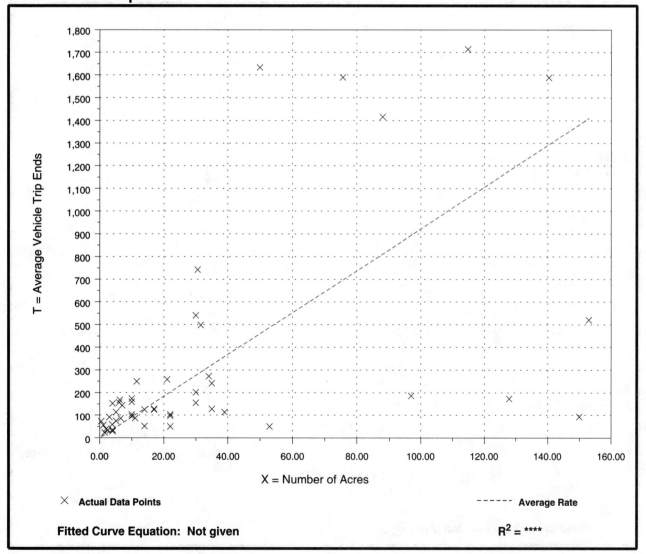

X **Actual Data Points**   ----- **Average Rate**

Fitted Curve Equation: Not given $R^2 = {****}$

Manufacturing
(140)

Average Vehicle Trip Ends vs: Acres
On a: Saturday

Number of Studies: 2
Average Number of Acres: 22
Directional Distribution: 50% entering, 50% exiting

Trip Generation per Acre

Average Rate	Range of Rates	Standard Deviation
33.40	24.00 - 59.13	*

Data Plot and Equation

Caution - Use Carefully - Small Sample Size

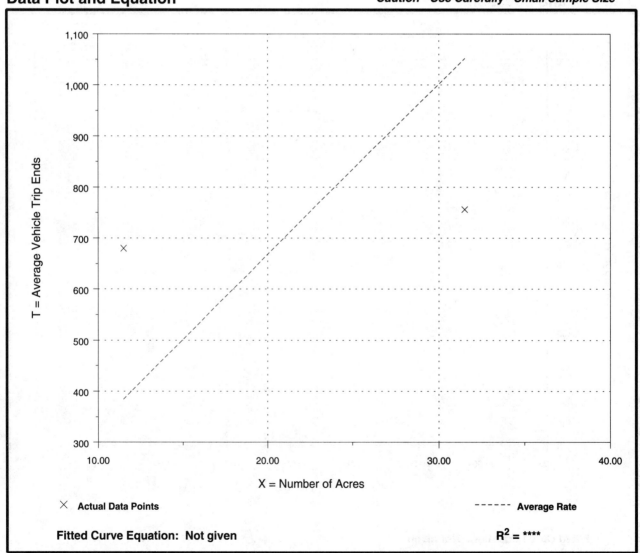

X **Actual Data Points**

- - - - - **Average Rate**

Fitted Curve Equation: Not given $R^2 =$ ****

Manufacturing
(140)

Average Vehicle Trip Ends vs: Acres
On a: Saturday,
Peak Hour of Generator

Number of Studies: 2
Average Number of Acres: 22
Directional Distribution: Not available

Trip Generation per Acre

Average Rate	Range of Rates	Standard Deviation
6.28	5.40 - 8.70	*

Data Plot and Equation

Caution - Use Carefully - Small Sample Size

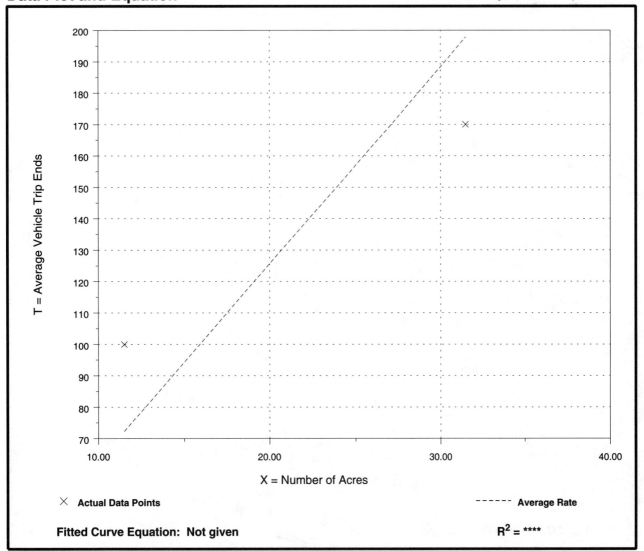

X = Number of Acres

$\times$ **Actual Data Points**   - - - - - **Average Rate**

Fitted Curve Equation: Not given $R^2 = ****$

Manufacturing
(140)

Average Vehicle Trip Ends vs: Acres
On a: Sunday

Number of Studies: 2
Average Number of Acres: 22
Directional Distribution: 50% entering, 50% exiting

Trip Generation per Acre

Average Rate	Range of Rates	Standard Deviation
13.91	1.84 - 46.96	*

Data Plot and Equation

Caution - Use Carefully - Small Sample Size

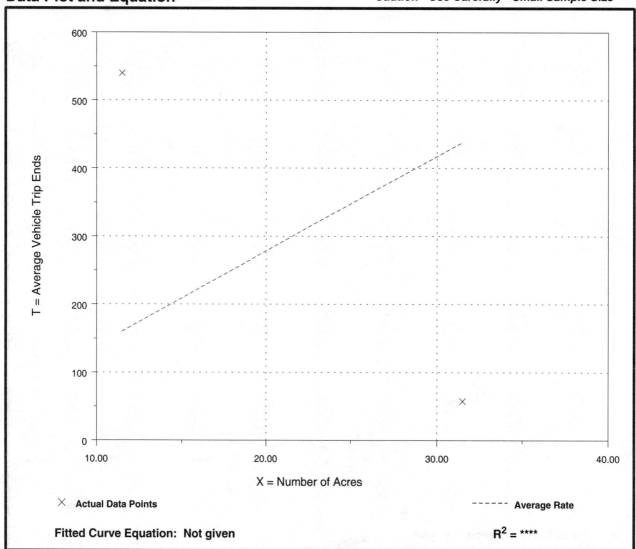

X **Actual Data Points**

----- **Average Rate**

Fitted Curve Equation: Not given

$R^2 = ****$

Manufacturing
(140)

Average Vehicle Trip Ends vs: **Acres**
On a: **Sunday,**
Peak Hour of Generator

Number of Studies: 2
Average Number of Acres: 22
Directional Distribution: Not available

Trip Generation per Acre

Average Rate	Range of Rates	Standard Deviation
2.07	0.29 - 6.96	*

Data Plot and Equation

Caution - Use Carefully - Small Sample Size

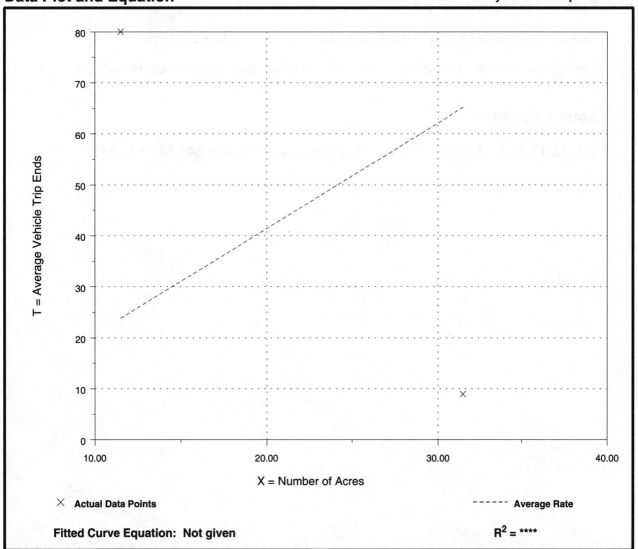

X **Actual Data Points**   ----- **Average Rate**

Fitted Curve Equation: Not given $R^2 =$ ****

Land Use: 150
Warehousing

Description

Warehouses are primarily devoted to the storage of materials, but they may also include office and maintenance areas. High-cube warehouse (Land Use 152) is a related use.

Additional Data

Truck trips accounted for 20 percent of the weekday traffic at one of the sites surveyed. No vehicle occupancy data were available specifically for warehousing, but the average was approximately 1.3 persons per automobile for all industrial uses.

The peak hour of the generator typically coincided with the peak hour of the adjacent street traffic.

Facilities with employees on shift work may peak at other hours.

Two sources indicated that the warehousing sites comprised multiple buildings.

The sites were surveyed between the late 1960s and the 2000s throughout the United States and Canada.

Source Numbers

6, 7, 12, 13, 15, 17, 74, 184, 192, 390, 406, 411, 436, 443, 571, 579, 583, 596, 598, 611

Land Use: 150
Warehousing
Independent Variables with One Observation

The following trip generation data are for independent variables with only one observation. This information is shown in this table only; there are no related plots for these data.

Users are cautioned to use data with care because of the small sample size.

Day/Time Period	Trip Generation Rate	Size of Independent Variable	Number of Studies	Directional Distribution
Loading Bays				
Weekday a.m. Peak Hour of Adjacent Street Traffic	0.69	52	1	61% entering, 39% exiting
Weekday p.m. Peak Hour of Adjacent Street Traffic	0.48	52	1	60% entering, 40% exiting

Warehousing
(150)

Average Vehicle Trip Ends vs: Employees
On a: Weekday

Number of Studies: 15
Avg. Number of Employees: 358
Directional Distribution: 50% entering, 50% exiting

Trip Generation per Employee

Average Rate	Range of Rates	Standard Deviation
3.89	1.47 - 15.71	3.08

Data Plot and Equation

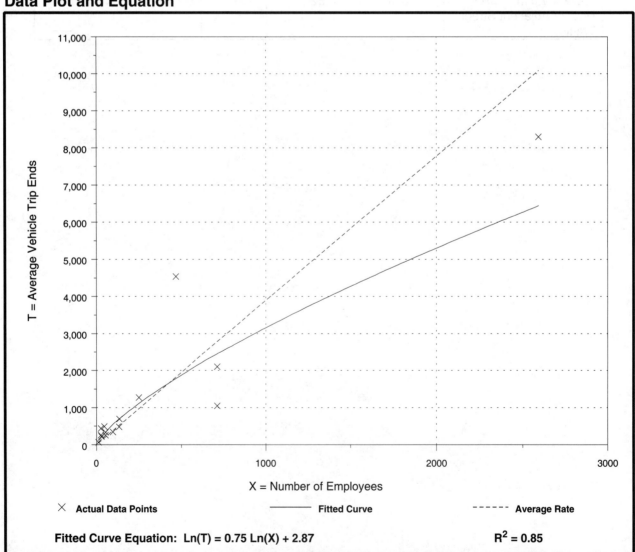

X **Actual Data Points**   ——— **Fitted Curve**   - - - - - **Average Rate**

Fitted Curve Equation: Ln(T) = 0.75 Ln(X) + 2.87 $R^2 = 0.85$

Trip Generation, 8th Edition   190   Institute of Transportation Engineers

Warehousing
(150)

Average Vehicle Trip Ends vs: **Employees**
On a: **Weekday,**
Peak Hour of Adjacent Street Traffic,
One Hour Between 7 and 9 a.m.

Number of Studies: 12
Avg. Number of Employees: 414
Directional Distribution: 72% entering, 28% exiting

Trip Generation per Employee

Average Rate	Range of Rates	Standard Deviation
0.51	0.37 - 2.14	0.74

Data Plot and Equation

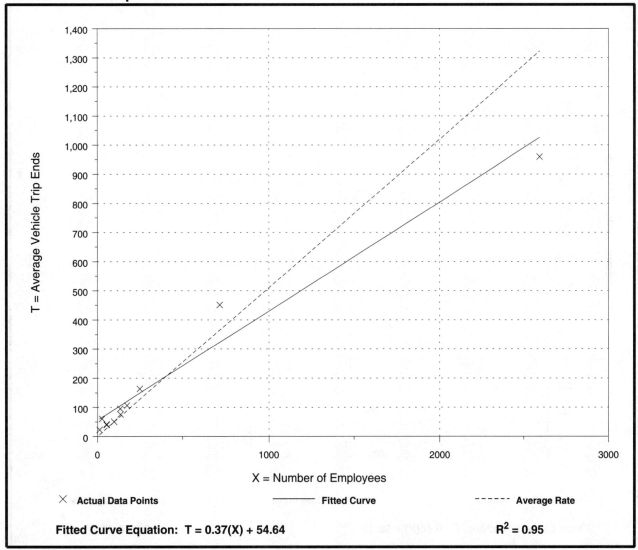

X = Number of Employees

$\times$ Actual Data Points	—— Fitted Curve	- - - Average Rate

Fitted Curve Equation: T = 0.37(X) + 54.64   **R² = 0.95**

Warehousing
(150)

Average Vehicle Trip Ends vs: Employees
On a: Weekday,
Peak Hour of Adjacent Street Traffic,
One Hour Between 4 and 6 p.m.

Number of Studies: 14
Avg. Number of Employees: 392
Directional Distribution: 35% entering, 65% exiting

Trip Generation per Employee

Average Rate	Range of Rates	Standard Deviation
0.59	0.37 - 2.22	0.80

Data Plot and Equation

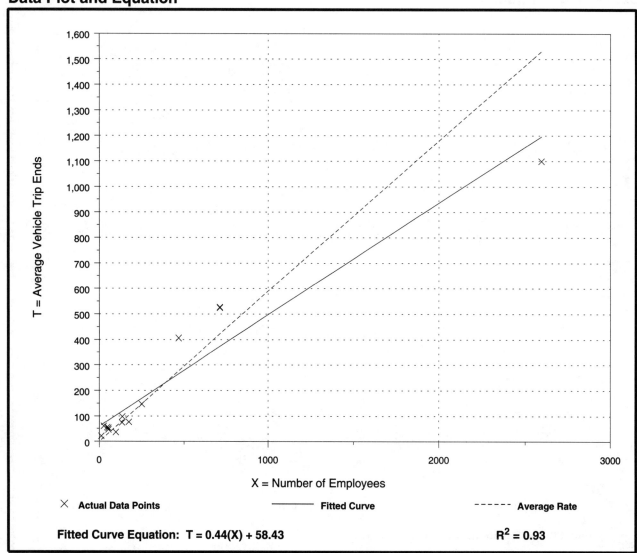

X **Actual Data Points**   ———— **Fitted Curve**   - - - - - **Average Rate**

Fitted Curve Equation: T = 0.44(X) + 58.43 $R^2 = 0.93$

Warehousing
(150)

Average Vehicle Trip Ends vs: Employees
On a: Weekday,
A.M. Peak Hour of Generator

Number of Studies: 15
Avg. Number of Employees: 322
Directional Distribution: 50% entering, 50% exiting

Trip Generation per Employee

Average Rate	Range of Rates	Standard Deviation
0.55	0.37 - 2.14	0.79

Data Plot and Equation

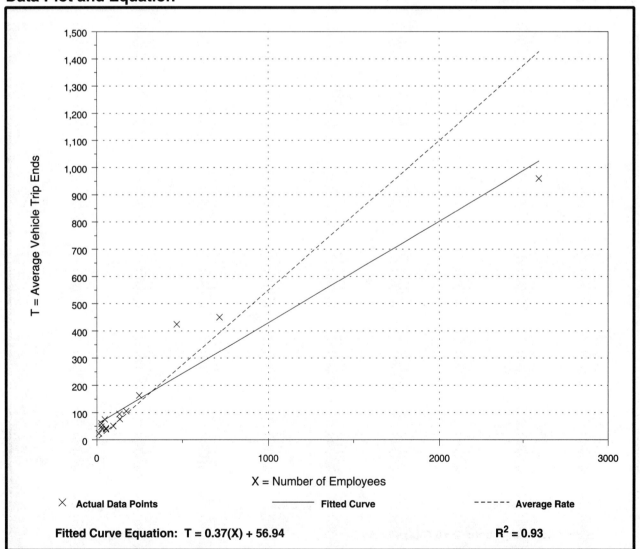

X **Actual Data Points**   —— **Fitted Curve**   - - - - - **Average Rate**

Fitted Curve Equation: T = 0.37(X) + 56.94 $R^2 = 0.93$

Warehousing
(150)

Average Vehicle Trip Ends vs: **Employees**
On a: **Weekday,**
  P.M. Peak Hour of Generator

Number of Studies: 14
Avg. Number of Employees: 335
Directional Distribution: 22% entering, 78% exiting

Trip Generation per Employee

Average Rate	Range of Rates	Standard Deviation
0.58	0.37 - 2.22	0.80

Data Plot and Equation

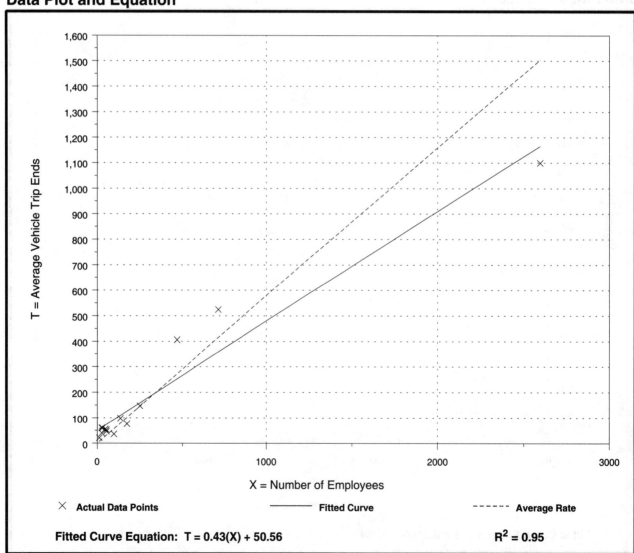

Fitted Curve Equation: T = 0.43(X) + 50.56 $R^2 = 0.95$

Warehousing
(150)

Average Vehicle Trip Ends vs: Employees
On a: Saturday

Number of Studies: 2
Avg. Number of Employees: 1,532
Directional Distribution: 50% entering, 50% exiting

Trip Generation per Employee

Average Rate	Range of Rates	Standard Deviation
1.00	0.51 - 3.70	*

Data Plot and Equation

Caution - Use Carefully - Small Sample Size

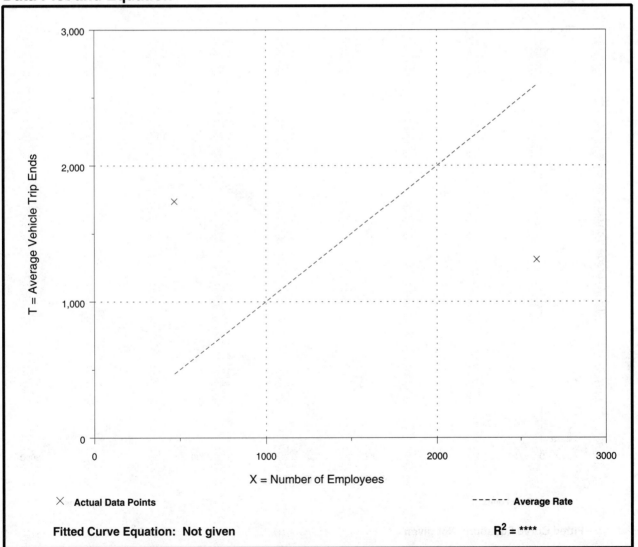

X Actual Data Points

- - - - - Average Rate

Fitted Curve Equation: Not given

$R^2 = ****$

Warehousing
(150)

Average Vehicle Trip Ends vs: **Employees**
On a: **Saturday,**
Peak Hour of Generator

Number of Studies: 2
Avg. Number of Employees: 1,532
Directional Distribution: 64% entering, 36% exiting

Trip Generation per Employee

Average Rate	Range of Rates	Standard Deviation
0.10	0.05 - 0.38	*

Data Plot and Equation

Caution - Use Carefully - Small Sample Size

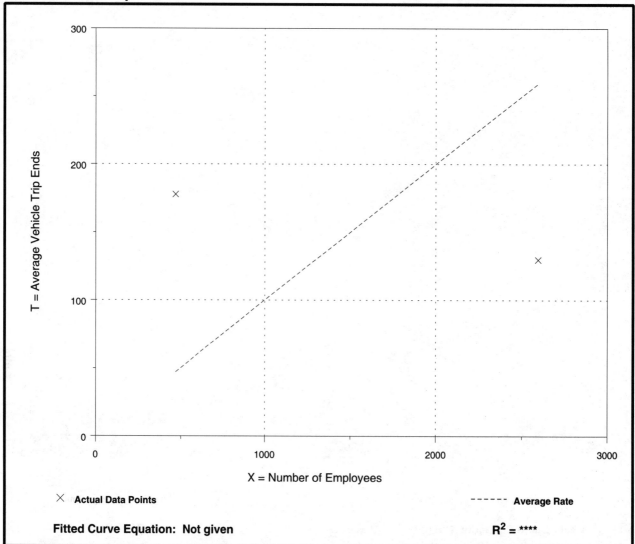

X   **Actual Data Points**

- - - - -   **Average Rate**

Fitted Curve Equation: Not given $R^2 = ****$

Warehousing
(150)

Average Vehicle Trip Ends vs: Employees

On a: Sunday

Number of Studies: 2
Avg. Number of Employees: 1,532
Directional Distribution: 50% entering, 50% exiting

Trip Generation per Employee

Average Rate	Range of Rates	Standard Deviation
0.65	0.23 - 2.94	*

Data Plot and Equation

Caution - Use Carefully - Small Sample Size

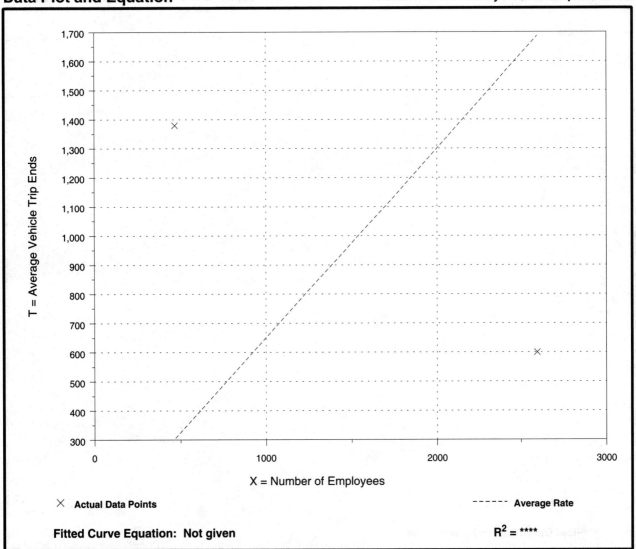

X **Actual Data Points**   - - - - - **Average Rate**

Fitted Curve Equation: Not given $R^2 =$ ****

Warehousing
(150)

Average Vehicle Trip Ends vs: **Employees**
On a: **Sunday,**
Peak Hour of Generator

Number of Studies: 2
Avg. Number of Employees: 1,532
Directional Distribution: 52% entering, 48% exiting

Trip Generation per Employee

Average Rate	Range of Rates	Standard Deviation
0.06	0.02 - 0.24	*

Data Plot and Equation

Caution - Use Carefully - Small Sample Size

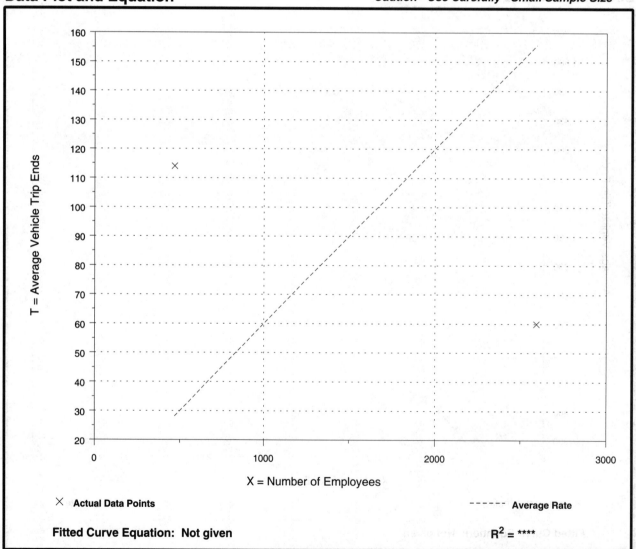

X Actual Data Points

----- **Average Rate**

Fitted Curve Equation: Not given $R^2 = ****$

Warehousing
(150)

Average Vehicle Trip Ends vs: **1000 Sq. Feet Gross Floor Area**
On a: **Weekday**

Number of Studies: 18
Average 1000 Sq. Feet GFA: 431
Directional Distribution: 50% entering, 50% exiting

Trip Generation per 1000 Sq. Feet Gross Floor Area

Average Rate	Range of Rates	Standard Deviation
3.56	1.51 - 17.00	3.58

Data Plot and Equation

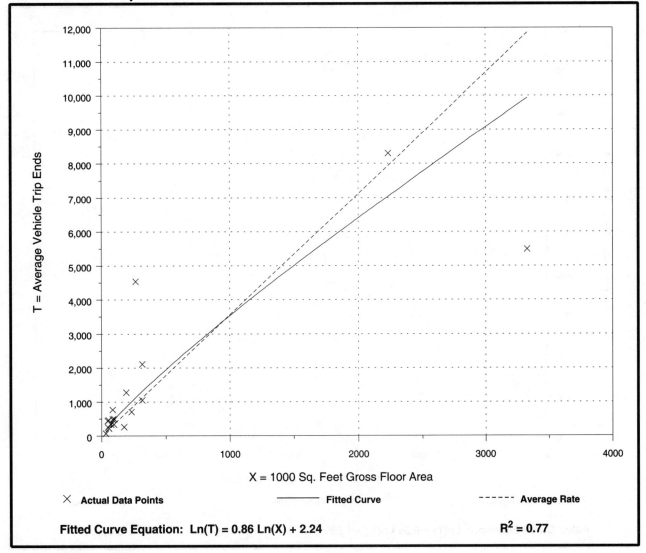

Fitted Curve Equation: Ln(T) = 0.86 Ln(X) + 2.24 $R^2 = 0.77$

Warehousing
(150)

Average Vehicle Trip Ends vs: 1000 Sq. Feet Gross Floor Area
On a: Weekday,
Peak Hour of Adjacent Street Traffic,
One Hour Between 7 and 9 a.m.

Number of Studies: 23
Average 1000 Sq. Feet GFA: 745
Directional Distribution: 79% entering, 21% exiting

Trip Generation per 1000 Sq. Feet Gross Floor Area

Average Rate	Range of Rates	Standard Deviation
0.30	0.08 - 1.93	0.63

Data Plot and Equation

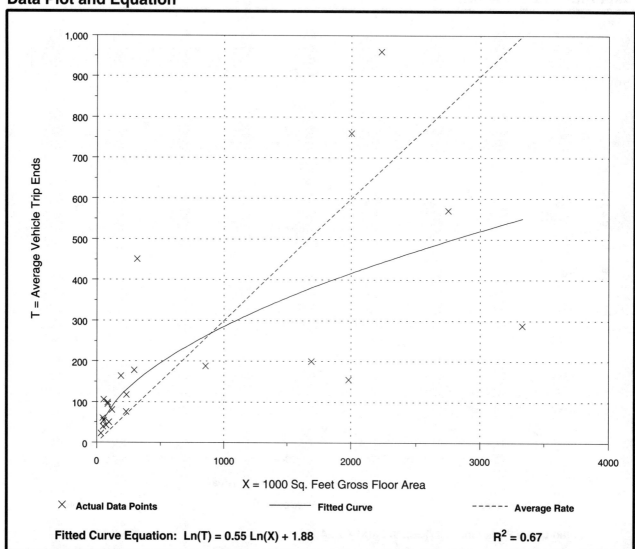

Fitted Curve Equation: $Ln(T) = 0.55 \, Ln(X) + 1.88$ $R^2 = 0.67$

Warehousing
(150)

Average Vehicle Trip Ends vs:	**1000 Sq. Feet Gross Floor Area**
On a:	**Weekday,**
	Peak Hour of Adjacent Street Traffic,
	One Hour Between 4 and 6 p.m.

Number of Studies: 31
Average 1000 Sq. Feet GFA: 572
Directional Distribution: 25% entering, 75% exiting

Trip Generation per 1000 Sq. Feet Gross Floor Area

Average Rate	Range of Rates	Standard Deviation
0.32	0.09 - 1.66	0.67

Data Plot and Equation

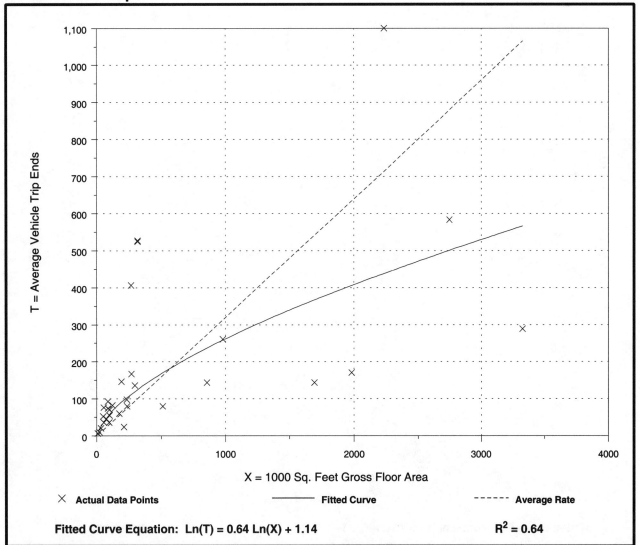

Fitted Curve Equation: $Ln(T) = 0.64\ Ln(X) + 1.14$ $R^2 = 0.64$

Warehousing
(150)

Average Vehicle Trip Ends vs: 1000 Sq. Feet Gross Floor Area
On a: Weekday,
A.M. Peak Hour of Generator

Number of Studies: 20
Average 1000 Sq. Feet GFA: 490
Directional Distribution: 65% entering, 35% exiting

Trip Generation per 1000 Sq. Feet Gross Floor Area

Average Rate	Range of Rates	Standard Deviation
0.42	0.12 - 1.93	0.74

Data Plot and Equation

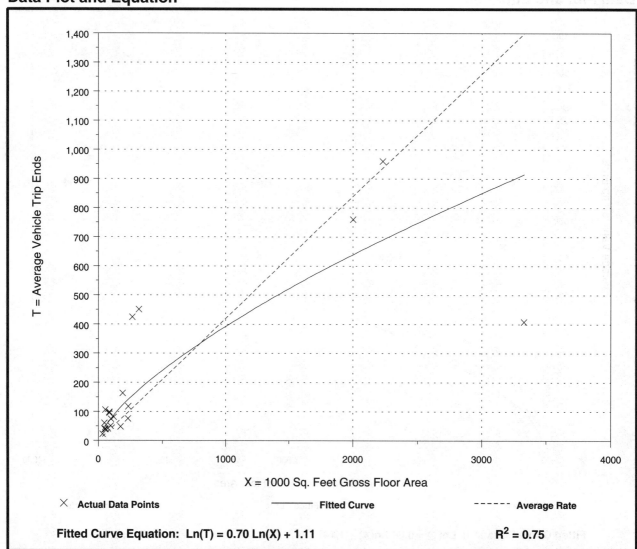

Fitted Curve Equation: $Ln(T) = 0.70 \, Ln(X) + 1.11$ $R^2 = 0.75$

Warehousing
(150)

Average Vehicle Trip Ends vs: **1000 Sq. Feet Gross Floor Area**
On a: **Weekday,**
P.M. Peak Hour of Generator

Number of Studies: 19
Average 1000 Sq. Feet GFA: 511
Directional Distribution: 19% entering, 81% exiting

Trip Generation per 1000 Sq. Feet Gross Floor Area

Average Rate	Range of Rates	Standard Deviation
0.45	0.16 - 1.65	0.76

Data Plot and Equation

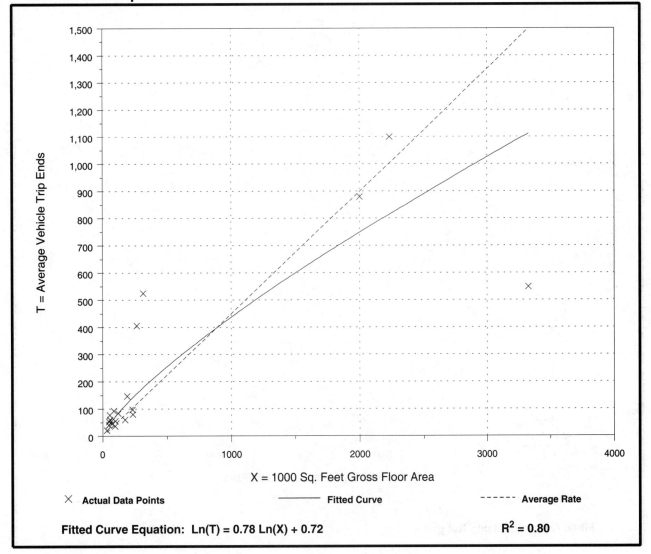

X = 1000 Sq. Feet Gross Floor Area

× **Actual Data Points**   —— **Fitted Curve**   - - - - - **Average Rate**

Fitted Curve Equation: Ln(T) = 0.78 Ln(X) + 0.72 $R^2 = 0.80$

Warehousing
(150)

Average Vehicle Trip Ends vs: 1000 Sq. Feet Gross Floor Area
On a: Saturday

Number of Studies: 3
Average 1000 Sq. Feet GFA: 851
Directional Distribution: 50% entering, 50% exiting

Trip Generation per 1000 Sq. Feet Gross Floor Area

Average Rate	Range of Rates	Standard Deviation
1.23	0.59 - 6.52	2.12

Data Plot and Equation

Caution - Use Carefully - Small Sample Size

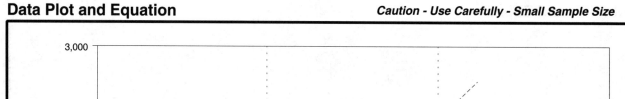

X **Actual Data Points**

- - - - - **Average Rate**

Fitted Curve Equation: Not given $R^2 =$ ****

Warehousing
(150)

Average Vehicle Trip Ends vs: 1000 Sq. Feet Gross Floor Area
On a: Saturday,
Peak Hour of Generator

Number of Studies: 3
Average 1000 Sq. Feet GFA: 851
Directional Distribution: 64% entering, 36% exiting

Trip Generation per 1000 Sq. Feet Gross Floor Area

Average Rate	Range of Rates	Standard Deviation
0.13	0.06 - 0.67	0.40

Data Plot and Equation

Caution - Use Carefully - Small Sample Size

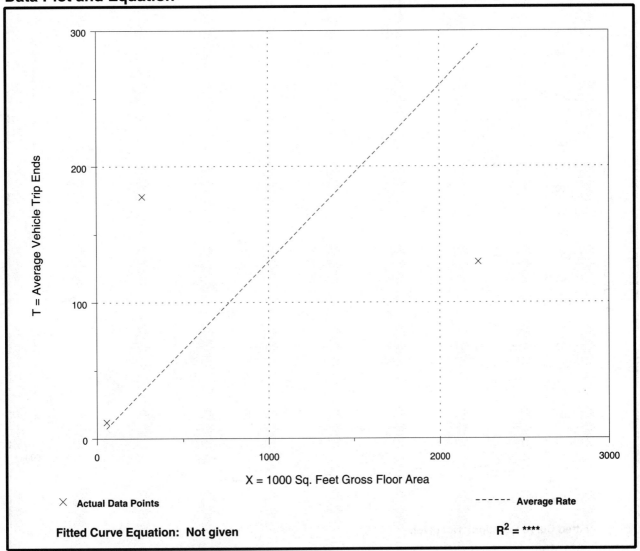

X = 1000 Sq. Feet Gross Floor Area

✕ **Actual Data Points**   - - - - - **Average Rate**

Fitted Curve Equation: Not given $R^2 = ****$

Warehousing
(150)

Average Vehicle Trip Ends vs: **1000 Sq. Feet Gross Floor Area**
On a: **Sunday**

Number of Studies: 3
Average 1000 Sq. Feet GFA: 851
Directional Distribution: 50% entering, 50% exiting

Trip Generation per 1000 Sq. Feet Gross Floor Area

Average Rate	Range of Rates	Standard Deviation
0.78	0.27 - 5.17	1.74

Data Plot and Equation

Caution - Use Carefully - Small Sample Size

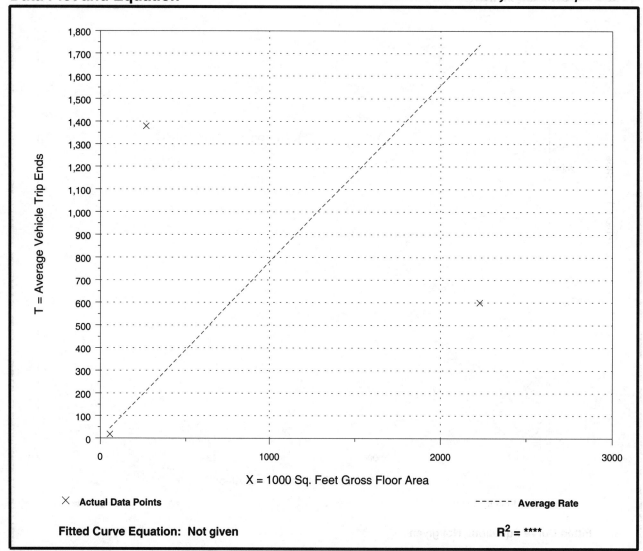

X **Actual Data Points**

----- **Average Rate**

Fitted Curve Equation: Not given

$R^2 = $ ****

Warehousing
(150)

Average Vehicle Trip Ends vs: 1000 Sq. Feet Gross Floor Area
On a: Sunday,
Peak Hour of Generator

Number of Studies: 3
Average 1000 Sq. Feet GFA: 851
Directional Distribution: 52% entering, 48% exiting

Trip Generation per 1000 Sq. Feet Gross Floor Area

Average Rate	Range of Rates	Standard Deviation
0.07	0.03 - 0.43	0.29

Data Plot and Equation

Caution - Use Carefully - Small Sample Size

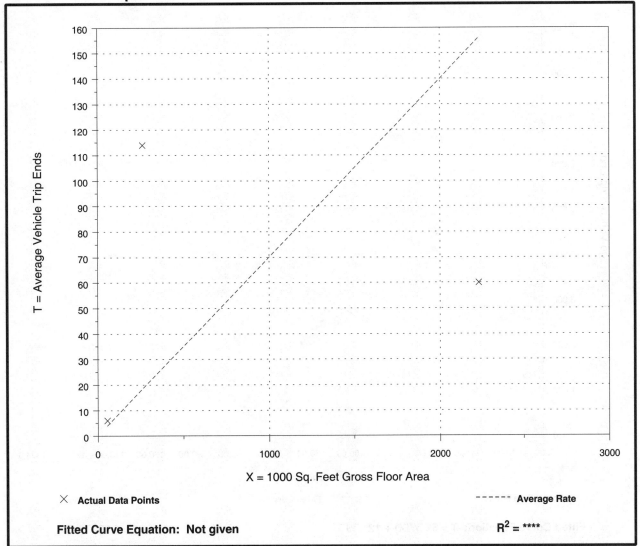

Fitted Curve Equation: Not given $R^2 = ****$

Warehousing
(150)

Average Vehicle Trip Ends vs: Acres
On a: Weekday

Number of Studies: 15
Average Number of Acres: 25
Directional Distribution: 50% entering, 50% exiting

Trip Generation per Acre

Average Rate	Range of Rates	Standard Deviation
57.23	20.23 - 255.80	33.09

Data Plot and Equation

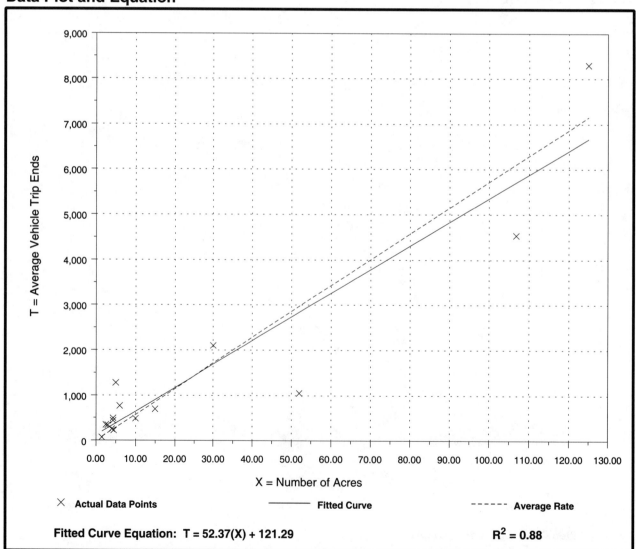

X   **Actual Data Points**   ———— **Fitted Curve**   - - - - - **Average Rate**

Fitted Curve Equation: T = 52.37(X) + 121.29 $R^2 = 0.88$

Warehousing
(150)

Average Vehicle Trip Ends vs: Acres
On a: Weekday,
Peak Hour of Adjacent Street Traffic,
One Hour Between 7 and 9 a.m.

Number of Studies: 13
Average Number of Acres: 20
Directional Distribution: 72% entering, 28% exiting

Trip Generation per Acre

Average Rate	Range of Rates	Standard Deviation
10.03	5.07 - 42.40	6.26

Data Plot and Equation

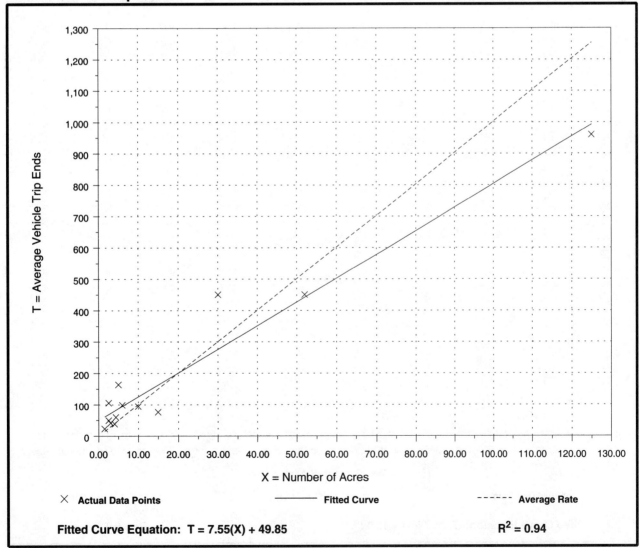

X = Number of Acres

✕ **Actual Data Points** ——— **Fitted Curve** - - - - - **Average Rate**

Fitted Curve Equation: T = 7.55(X) + 49.85 $R^2 = 0.94$

Warehousing
(150)

Average Vehicle Trip Ends vs: **Acres**
On a: **Weekday,**
Peak Hour of Adjacent Street Traffic,
One Hour Between 4 and 6 p.m.

Number of Studies: 15
Average Number of Acres: 25
Directional Distribution: 35% entering, 65% exiting

Trip Generation per Acre

Average Rate	Range of Rates	Standard Deviation
8.69	2.35 - 30.80	5.79

Data Plot and Equation

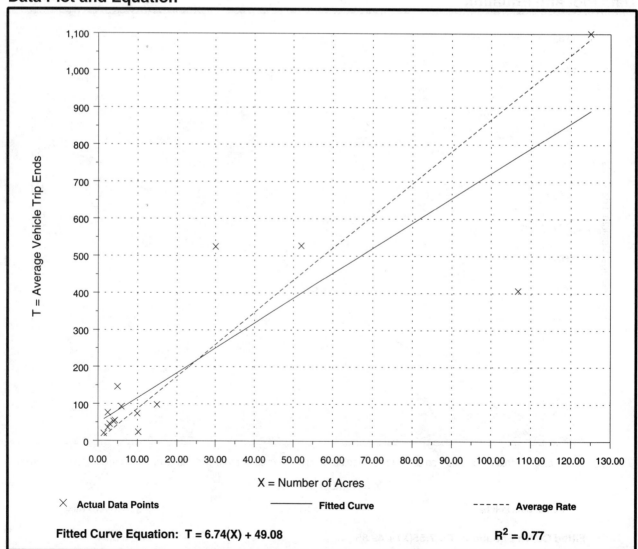

X = Number of Acres

✕ Actual Data Points   —— Fitted Curve   - - - - Average Rate

Fitted Curve Equation: T = 6.74(X) + 49.08 $R^2 = 0.77$

Warehousing
(150)

Average Vehicle Trip Ends vs: **Acres**
On a: **Weekday,**
A.M. Peak Hour of Generator

Number of Studies: 15
Average Number of Acres: 22
Directional Distribution: 50% entering, 50% exiting

Trip Generation per Acre

Average Rate	Range of Rates	Standard Deviation
8.34	3.98 - 42.40	6.43

Data Plot and Equation

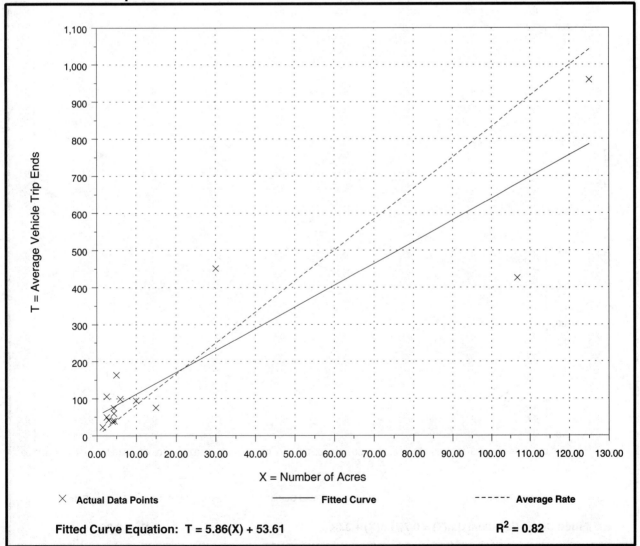

Fitted Curve Equation: $T = 5.86(X) + 53.61$ $R^2 = 0.82$

Warehousing
(150)

Average Vehicle Trip Ends vs: **Acres**
On a: **Weekday,**
P.M. Peak Hour of Generator

Number of Studies: 14
Average Number of Acres: 22
Directional Distribution: 22% entering, 78% exiting

Trip Generation per Acre

Average Rate	Range of Rates	Standard Deviation
8.77	3.80 - 30.80	6.10

Data Plot and Equation

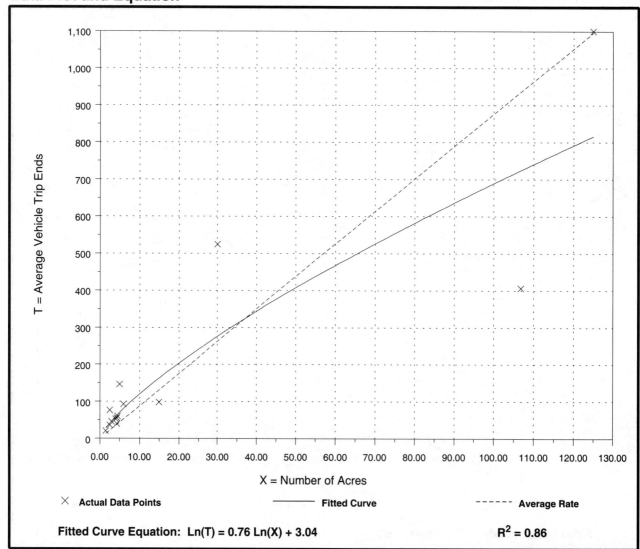

X **Actual Data Points** ——— **Fitted Curve** - - - - - **Average Rate**

Fitted Curve Equation: $Ln(T) = 0.76\ Ln(X) + 3.04$ $R^2 = 0.86$

Warehousing
(150)

Average Vehicle Trip Ends vs: Acres
On a: Saturday

Number of Studies: 2
Average Number of Acres: 116
Directional Distribution: 50% entering, 50% exiting

Trip Generation per Acre

Average Rate	Range of Rates	Standard Deviation
13.16	10.48 - 16.29	*

Data Plot and Equation

Caution - Use Carefully - Small Sample Size

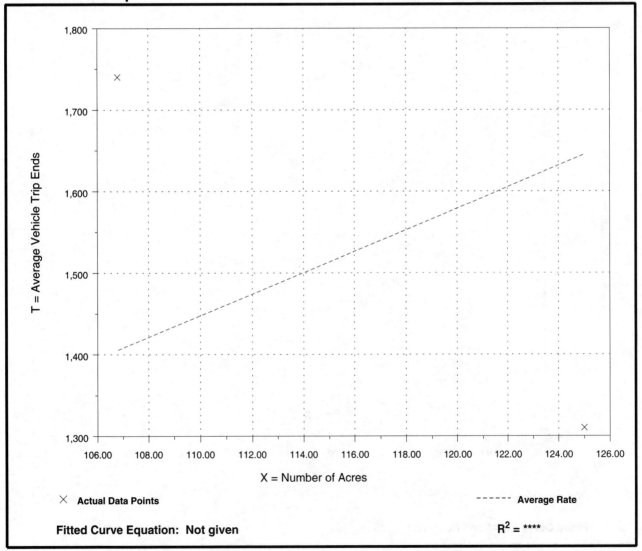

X = Number of Acres

$\times$ **Actual Data Points**   - - - - - **Average Rate**

Fitted Curve Equation: Not given $R^2 =$ ****

Warehousing
(150)

Average Vehicle Trip Ends vs: Acres
On a: Saturday,
Peak Hour of Generator

Number of Studies: 2
Average Number of Acres: 116
Directional Distribution: 64% entering, 36% exiting

Trip Generation per Acre

Average Rate	Range of Rates	Standard Deviation
1.33	1.04 - 1.67	*

Data Plot and Equation

Caution - Use Carefully - Small Sample Size

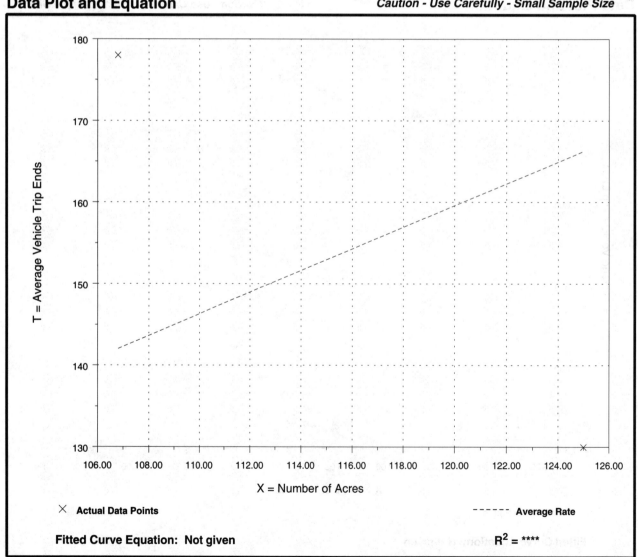

X **Actual Data Points**   - - - - - **Average Rate**

Fitted Curve Equation: Not given $R^2 = ****$

Warehousing
(150)

Average Vehicle Trip Ends vs: **Acres**
On a: **Sunday**

Number of Studies: 2
Average Number of Acres: 116
Directional Distribution: 50% entering, 50% exiting

Trip Generation per Acre

Average Rate	Range of Rates	Standard Deviation
8.54	4.80 - 12.92	*

Data Plot and Equation

Caution - Use Carefully - Small Sample Size

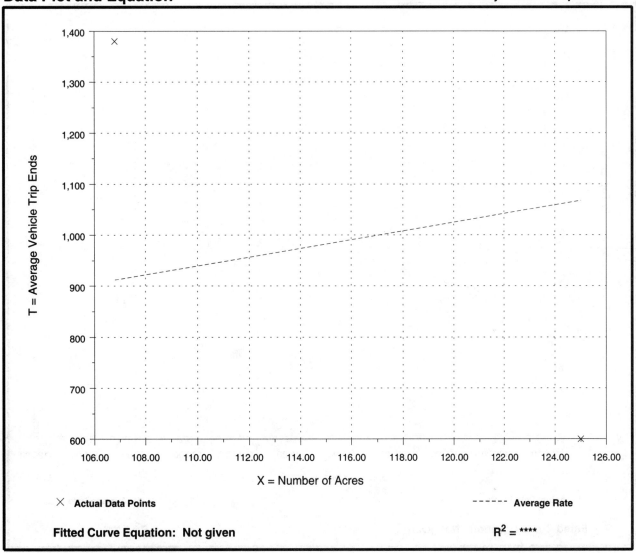

X **Actual Data Points**   ----- **Average Rate**

Fitted Curve Equation: Not given $R^2 = ****$

Warehousing
(150)

Average Vehicle Trip Ends vs: Acres
On a: Sunday,
Peak Hour of Generator

Number of Studies: 2
Average Number of Acres: 116
Directional Distribution: 52% entering, 48% exiting

Trip Generation per Acre

Average Rate	Range of Rates	Standard Deviation
0.75	0.48 - 1.07	*

Data Plot and Equation

Caution - Use Carefully - Small Sample Size

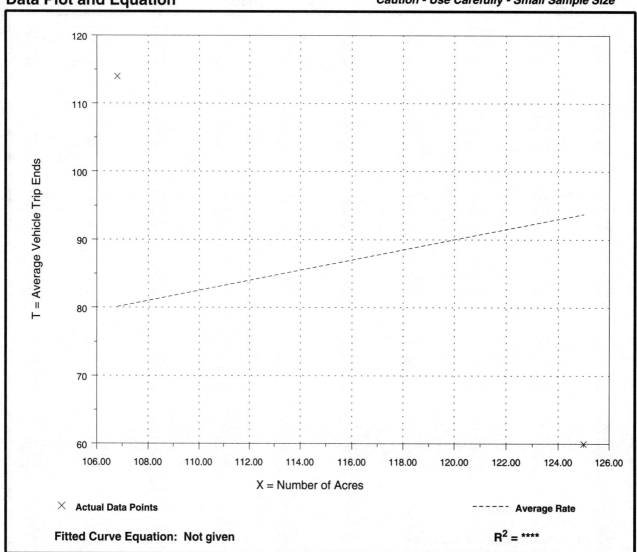

X **Actual Data Points**   - - - - - **Average Rate**

Fitted Curve Equation: Not given $R^2 = $ ****

Land Use: 151
Mini-Warehouse

Description

Mini-warehouses are buildings in which a number of storage units or vaults are rented for the storage of goods. They are typically referred to as "self-storage" facilities. Each unit is physically separated from other units, and access is usually provided through an overhead door or other common access point.

Additional Data

Truck trips accounted for 2 to 15 percent of the weekday traffic at the sites surveyed.

Vehicle occupancy ranged from 1.2 to 1.9 persons per automobile on an average weekday.

Peak hours of the generator —
> The weekday p.m. peak hour was between 1:00 p.m. and 7:00 p.m. The Saturday peak hour was between 10:00 a.m. and 1:00 p.m. The Sunday peak hour was between 1:00 p.m. and 6:00 p.m.

For the purpose of this land use, the independent variable "occupied storage units" is defined as the number of units that have been rented.

The sites were surveyed between 1979 and 2005 in California, Colorado and New Jersey.

Source Numbers

113, 212, 403, 551, 568, 642

Mini-Warehouse
(151)

Average Vehicle Trip Ends vs: Employees
On a: Weekday

Number of Studies: 13
Avg. Number of Employees: 2
Directional Distribution: 50% entering, 50% exiting

Trip Generation per Employee

Average Rate	Range of Rates	Standard Deviation
61.90	17.00 - 194.00	46.28

Data Plot and Equation

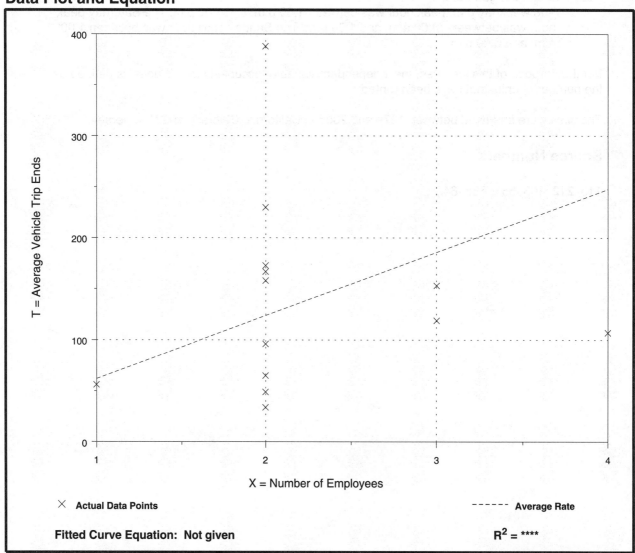

X **Actual Data Points**

- - - - - **Average Rate**

Fitted Curve Equation: Not given

$R^2 = ****$

Mini-Warehouse
(151)

Average Vehicle Trip Ends vs: **Employees**
On a: **Weekday,**
Peak Hour of Adjacent Street Traffic,
One Hour Between 7 and 9 a.m.

Number of Studies: 9
Avg. Number of Employees: 2
Directional Distribution: 67% entering, 33% exiting

Trip Generation per Employee

Average Rate	Range of Rates	Standard Deviation
5.26	1.00 - 12.00	3.96

Data Plot and Equation

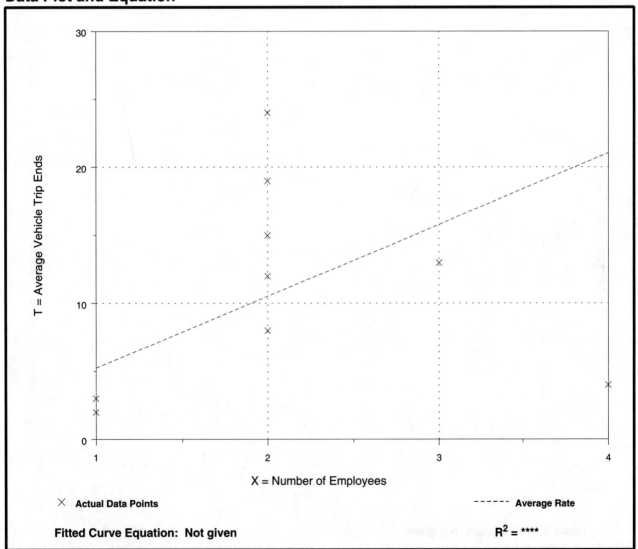

X Actual Data Points

------ Average Rate

Fitted Curve Equation: Not given

$R^2 = ****$

Mini-Warehouse
(151)

Average Vehicle Trip Ends vs: Employees
On a: Weekday,
Peak Hour of Adjacent Street Traffic,
One Hour Between 4 and 6 p.m.

Number of Studies: 13
Avg. Number of Employees: 2
Directional Distribution: 52% entering, 48% exiting

Trip Generation per Employee

Average Rate	Range of Rates	Standard Deviation
6.04	1.00 - 18.50	4.97

Data Plot and Equation

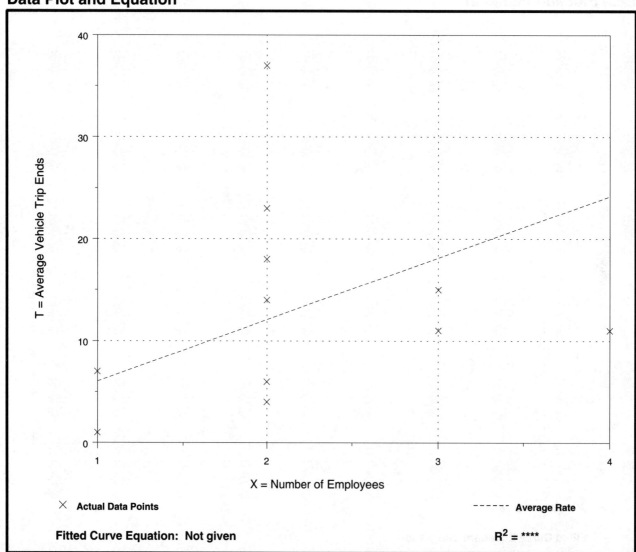

X **Actual Data Points**

------ **Average Rate**

Fitted Curve Equation: Not given

$R^2 = $ ****

Mini-Warehouse
(151)

Average Vehicle Trip Ends vs: **Employees**
On a: **Weekday,**
A.M. Peak Hour of Generator

Number of Studies: 8
Avg. Number of Employees: 2
Directional Distribution: Not available

Trip Generation per Employee

Average Rate	Range of Rates	Standard Deviation
8.00	3.00 - 19.50	5.79

Data Plot and Equation

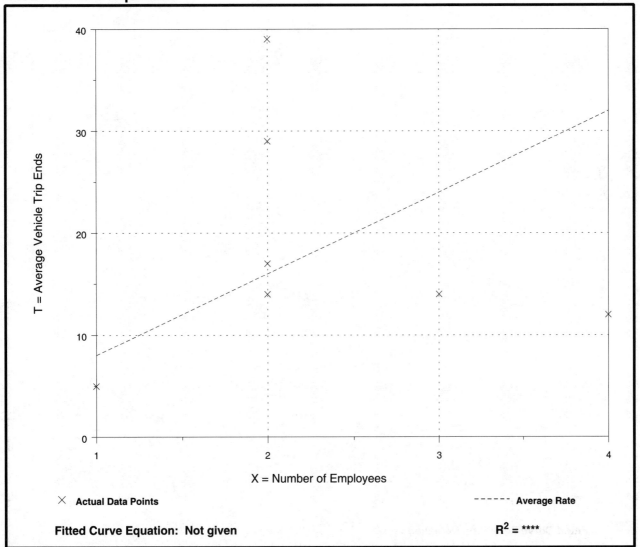

X **Actual Data Points**   ------ **Average Rate**

Fitted Curve Equation: Not given $R^2 = $ ****

Mini-Warehouse
(151)

Average Vehicle Trip Ends vs: Employees
On a: Weekday,
P.M. Peak Hour of Generator

Number of Studies: 13
Avg. Number of Employees: 2
Directional Distribution: 52% entering, 48% exiting

Trip Generation per Employee

Average Rate	Range of Rates	Standard Deviation
6.79	2.00 - 20.50	5.59

Data Plot and Equation

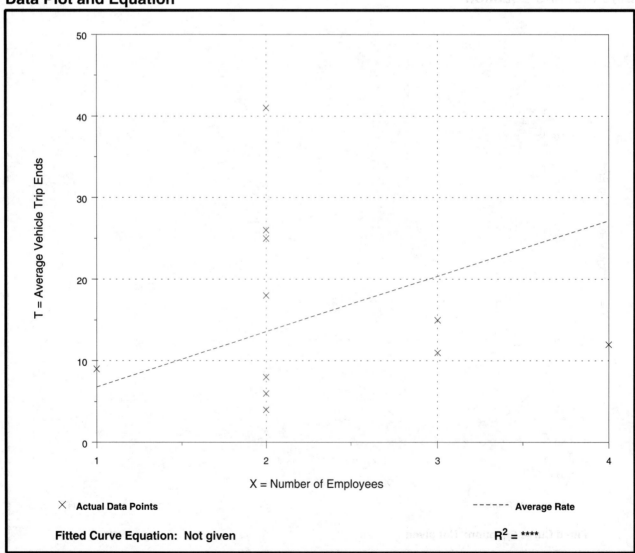

Fitted Curve Equation: Not given $R^2 = ****$

Mini-Warehouse
(151)

Average Vehicle Trip Ends vs: Employees

On a: Saturday

Number of Studies: 13
Avg. Number of Employees: 2
Directional Distribution: 50% entering, 50% exiting

Trip Generation per Employee

Average Rate	Range of Rates	Standard Deviation
54.93	17.00 - 115.00	35.66

Data Plot and Equation

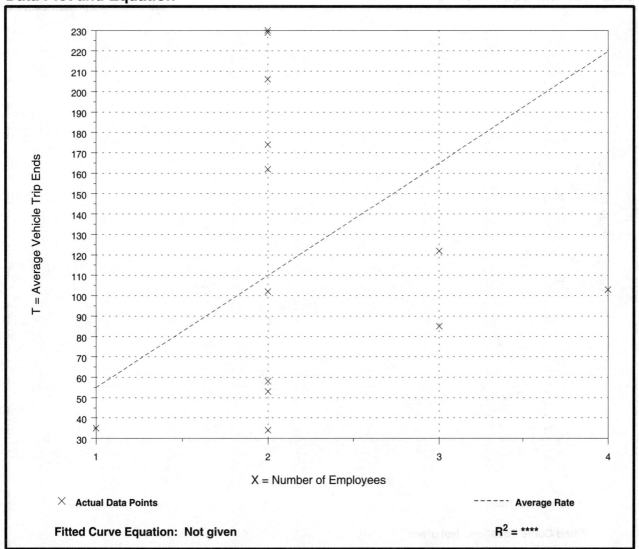

Fitted Curve Equation: Not given $R^2 = ****$

Mini-Warehouse
(151)

Average Vehicle Trip Ends vs: Employees
On a: Saturday,
Peak Hour of Generator

Number of Studies: 8
Avg. Number of Employees: 2
Directional Distribution: Not available

Trip Generation per Employee

Average Rate	Range of Rates	Standard Deviation
11.50	4.25 - 18.50	6.73

Data Plot and Equation

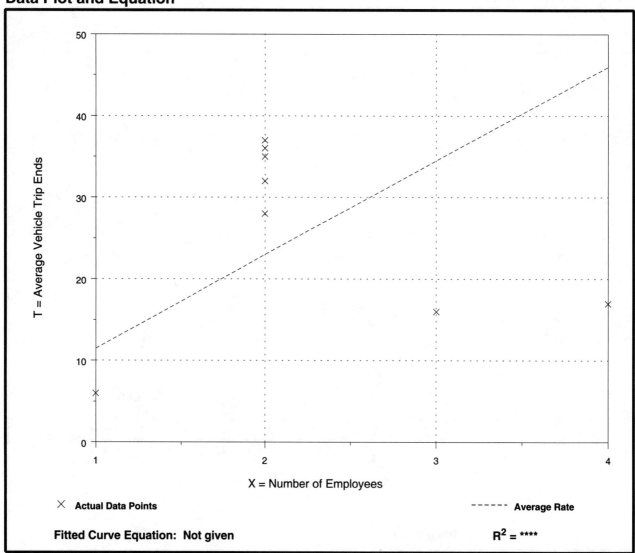

X   **Actual Data Points**   - - - - - -   **Average Rate**

Fitted Curve Equation: Not given $R^2 = ****$

Mini-Warehouse
(151)

Average Vehicle Trip Ends vs: Employees
On a: Sunday

Number of Studies: 12
Avg. Number of Employees: 2
Directional Distribution: 50% entering, 50% exiting

Trip Generation per Employee

Average Rate	Range of Rates	Standard Deviation
41.23	11.00 - 76.00	20.82

Data Plot and Equation

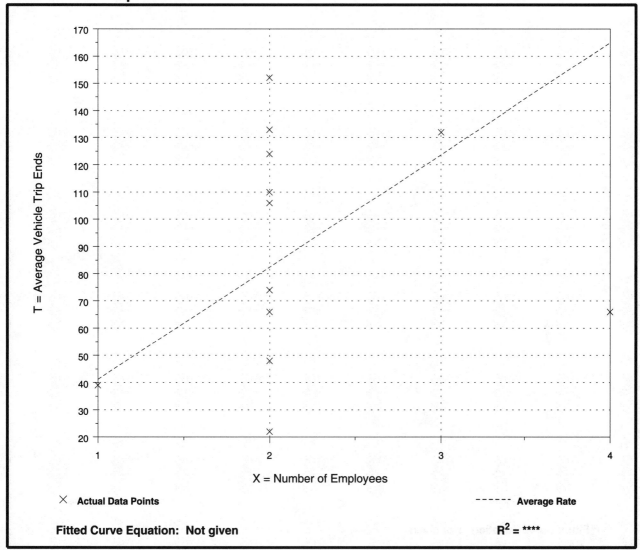

X = Number of Employees

T = Average Vehicle Trip Ends

✕ **Actual Data Points**   ----- **Average Rate**

Fitted Curve Equation: Not given $R^2 = ****$

Mini-Warehouse
(151)

Average Vehicle Trip Ends vs: **Employees**
On a: **Sunday,**
Peak Hour of Generator

Number of Studies: 8
Avg. Number of Employees: 2
Directional Distribution: Not available

Trip Generation per Employee

Average Rate	Range of Rates	Standard Deviation
8.50	3.00 - 15.50	4.56

Data Plot and Equation

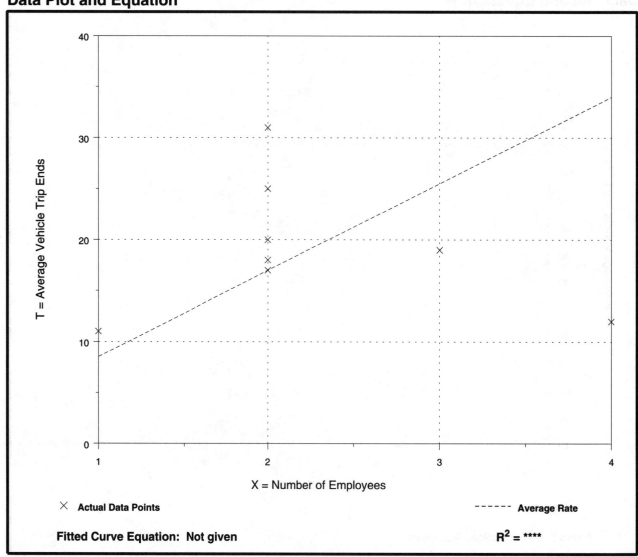

X = Number of Employees

✕ **Actual Data Points**   - - - - - - **Average Rate**

Fitted Curve Equation: Not given $R^2 =$ ****

Mini-Warehouse
(151)

Average Vehicle Trip Ends vs: 1000 Sq. Feet Gross Floor Area
On a: Weekday

Number of Studies: 14
Average 1000 Sq. Feet GFA: 56
Directional Distribution: 50% entering, 50% exiting

Trip Generation per 1000 Sq. Feet Gross Floor Area

Average Rate	Range of Rates	Standard Deviation
2.50	1.21 - 4.36	1.78

Data Plot and Equation

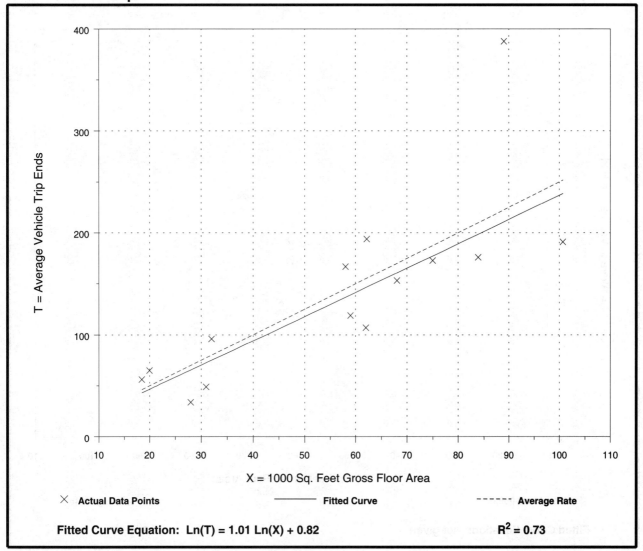

Fitted Curve Equation: Ln(T) = 1.01 Ln(X) + 0.82 $R^2 = 0.73$

Mini-Warehouse
(151)

Average Vehicle Trip Ends vs: **1000 Sq. Feet Gross Floor Area**
On a: **Weekday,**
Peak Hour of Adjacent Street Traffic,
One Hour Between 7 and 9 a.m.

Number of Studies: 9
Average 1000 Sq. Feet GFA: 69
Directional Distribution: 59% entering, 41% exiting

Trip Generation per 1000 Sq. Feet Gross Floor Area

Average Rate	Range of Rates	Standard Deviation
0.15	0.04 - 0.27	0.39

Data Plot and Equation

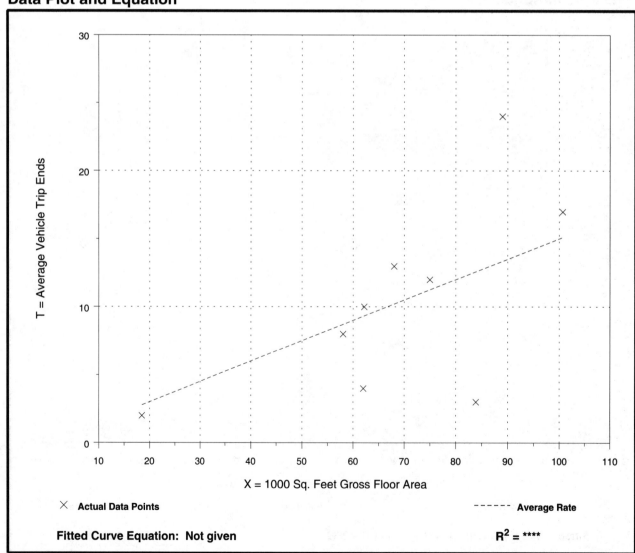

Fitted Curve Equation: Not given $R^2 = ****$

Mini-Warehouse
(151)

Average Vehicle Trip Ends vs: 1000 Sq. Feet Gross Floor Area
On a: Weekday,
Peak Hour of Adjacent Street Traffic,
One Hour Between 4 and 6 p.m.

Number of Studies: 13
Average 1000 Sq. Feet GFA: 58
Directional Distribution: 51% entering, 49% exiting

Trip Generation per 1000 Sq. Feet Gross Floor Area

Average Rate	Range of Rates	Standard Deviation
0.26	0.13 - 0.48	0.52

Data Plot and Equation

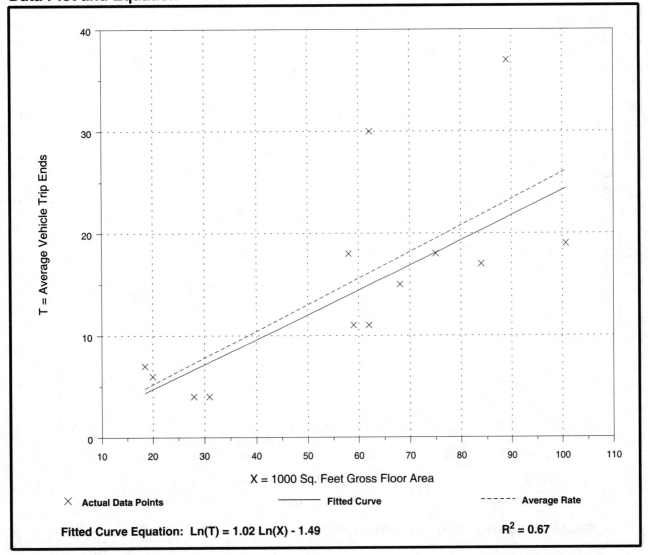

Fitted Curve Equation: $Ln(T) = 1.02 \, Ln(X) - 1.49$ $R^2 = 0.67$

Mini-Warehouse
(151)

Average Vehicle Trip Ends vs: 1000 Sq. Feet Gross Floor Area
On a: Weekday,
A.M. Peak Hour of Generator

Number of Studies: 9
Average 1000 Sq. Feet GFA: 69
Directional Distribution: 48% entering, 52% exiting

Trip Generation per 1000 Sq. Feet Gross Floor Area

Average Rate	Range of Rates	Standard Deviation
0.28	0.17 - 0.58	0.54

Data Plot and Equation

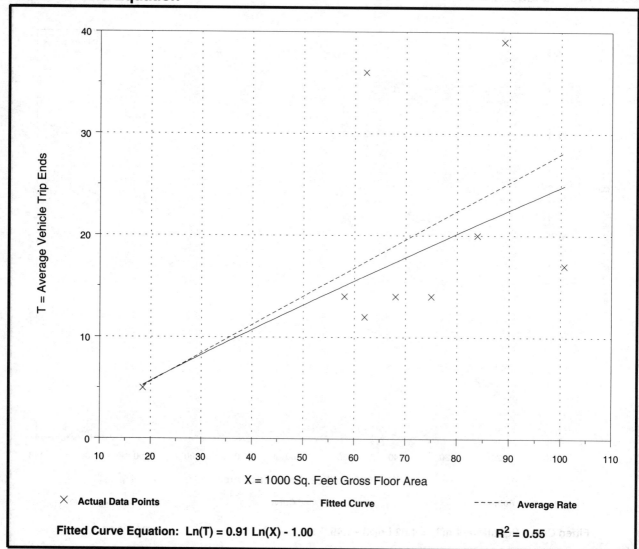

X Actual Data Points ——— Fitted Curve ----- Average Rate

Fitted Curve Equation: Ln(T) = 0.91 Ln(X) - 1.00 $R^2 = 0.55$

Mini-Warehouse
(151)

Average Vehicle Trip Ends vs: 1000 Sq. Feet Gross Floor Area
On a: Weekday,
P.M. Peak Hour of Generator

Number of Studies: 14
Average 1000 Sq. Feet GFA: 56
Directional Distribution: 53% entering, 47% exiting

Trip Generation per 1000 Sq. Feet Gross Floor Area

Average Rate	Range of Rates	Standard Deviation
0.29	0.13 - 0.50	0.54

Data Plot and Equation

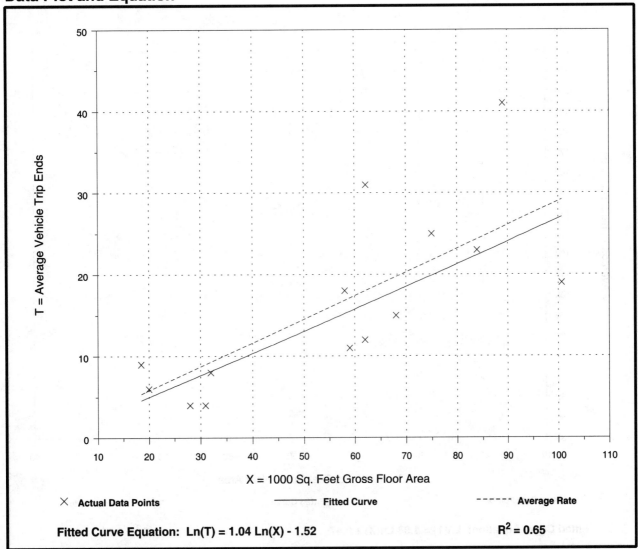

Fitted Curve Equation: Ln(T) = 1.04 Ln(X) - 1.52 $R^2 = 0.65$

Mini-Warehouse
(151)

Average Vehicle Trip Ends vs: 1000 Sq. Feet Gross Floor Area
On a: Saturday

Number of Studies: 11
Average 1000 Sq. Feet GFA: 49
Directional Distribution: 50% entering, 50% exiting

Trip Generation per 1000 Sq. Feet Gross Floor Area

Average Rate	Range of Rates	Standard Deviation
2.33	1.21 - 3.55	1.69

Data Plot and Equation

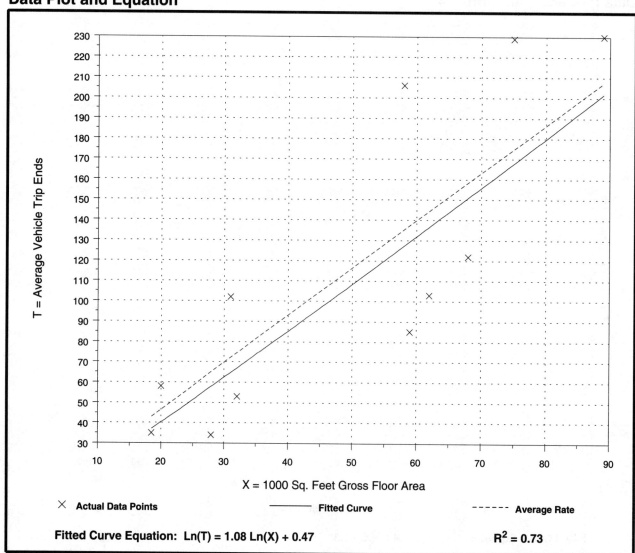

X   **Actual Data Points**   —— **Fitted Curve**   - - - - - **Average Rate**

Fitted Curve Equation: Ln(T) = 1.08 Ln(X) + 0.47 $R^2 = 0.73$

Mini-Warehouse
(151)

Average Vehicle Trip Ends vs: **1000 Sq. Feet Gross Floor Area**
On a: **Saturday,**
  Peak Hour of Generator

Number of Studies:	6
Average 1000 Sq. Feet GFA:	62
Directional Distribution:	Not available

Trip Generation per 1000 Sq. Feet Gross Floor Area

Average Rate	Range of Rates	Standard Deviation
0.40	0.24 - 0.60	0.64

Data Plot and Equation

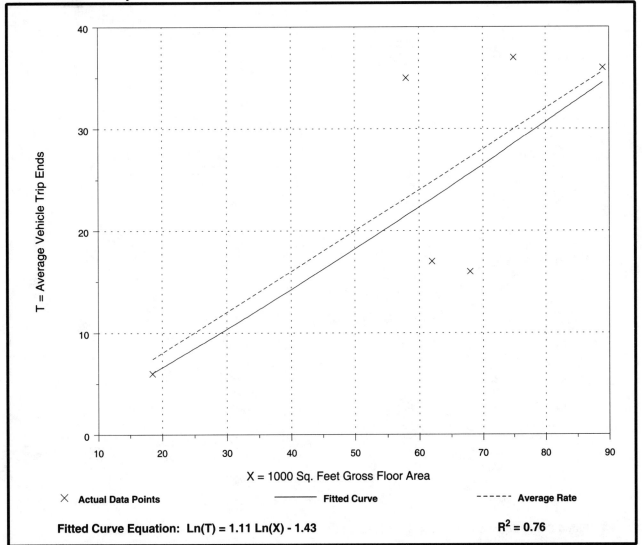

X = 1000 Sq. Feet Gross Floor Area

✕ **Actual Data Points**   —— **Fitted Curve**   - - - - - **Average Rate**

Fitted Curve Equation: $Ln(T) = 1.11\ Ln(X) - 1.43$ $R^2 = 0.76$

Mini-Warehouse
(151)

Average Vehicle Trip Ends vs: 1000 Sq. Feet Gross Floor Area
On a: Sunday

Number of Studies: 10
Average 1000 Sq. Feet GFA: 48
Directional Distribution: 50% entering, 50% exiting

Trip Generation per 1000 Sq. Feet Gross Floor Area

Average Rate	Range of Rates	Standard Deviation
1.78	0.69 - 3.70	1.46

Data Plot and Equation

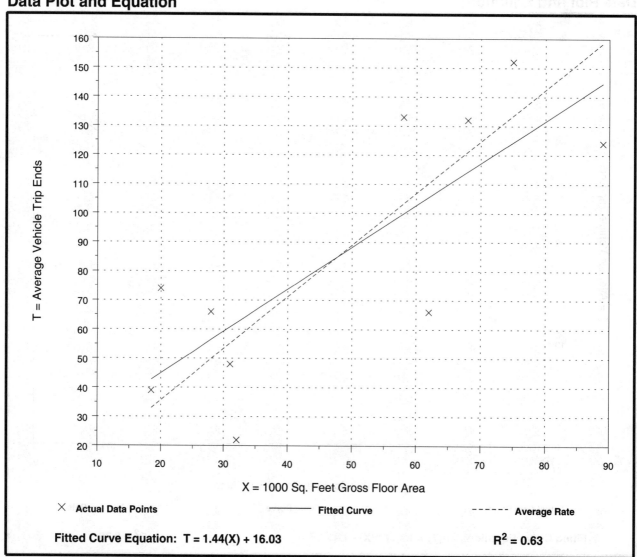

Fitted Curve Equation: T = 1.44(X) + 16.03 $R^2 = 0.63$

Mini-Warehouse
(151)

Average Vehicle Trip Ends vs: **1000 Sq. Feet Gross Floor Area**
             On a: **Sunday,**
                    Peak Hour of Generator

        Number of Studies: 6
Average 1000 Sq. Feet GFA: 62
   Directional Distribution: Not available

Trip Generation per 1000 Sq. Feet Gross Floor Area

Average Rate	Range of Rates	Standard Deviation
0.30	0.19 - 0.59	0.55

Data Plot and Equation

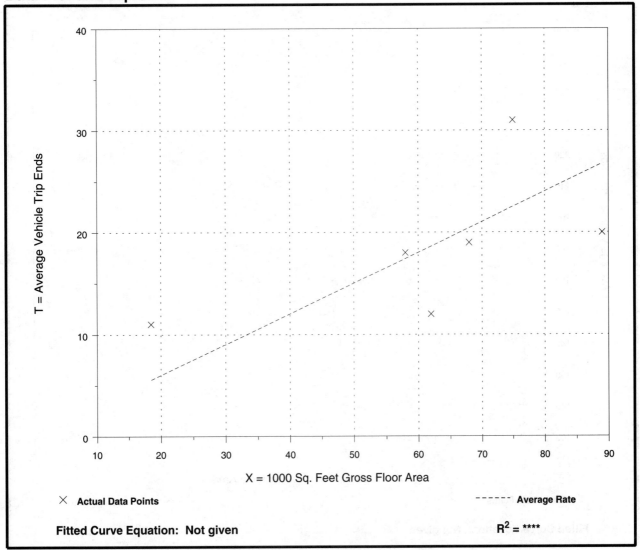

Fitted Curve Equation: Not given $R^2 = ****$

Mini-Warehouse
(151)

Average Vehicle Trip Ends vs: **1000 Sq. Feet Net Rentable Area**
On a: **Weekday**

Number of Studies: 4
Average 1000 Sq. Feet NRA: 114
Directional Distribution: 50% entering, 50% exiting

Trip Generation per 1000 Sq. Feet Net Rentable Area

Average Rate	Range of Rates	Standard Deviation
1.65	1.19 - 2.17	1.34

Data Plot and Equation

Caution - Use Carefully - Small Sample Size

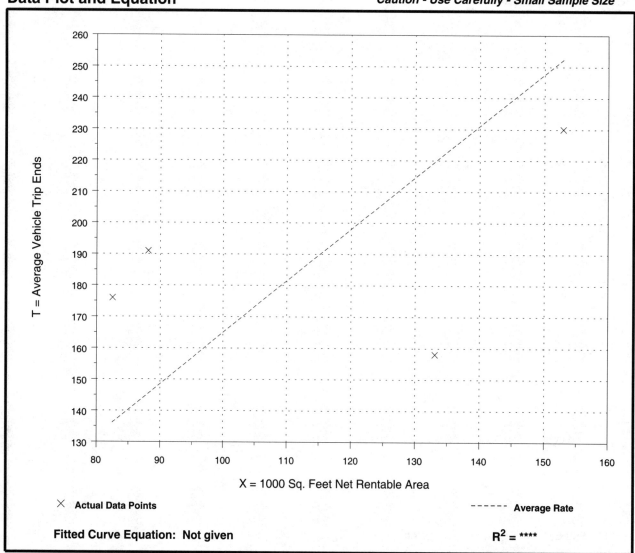

$\times$ **Actual Data Points**   - - - - - **Average Rate**

Fitted Curve Equation: Not given $R^2 = ****$

Mini-Warehouse
(151)

Average Vehicle Trip Ends vs: **1000 Sq. Feet Net Rentable Area**
On a: **Weekday,**
Peak Hour of Adjacent Street Traffic,
One Hour Between 7 and 9 a.m.

Number of Studies: 6
Average 1000 Sq. Feet NRA: 94
Directional Distribution: 54% entering, 46% exiting

Trip Generation per 1000 Sq. Feet Net Rentable Area

Average Rate	Range of Rates	Standard Deviation
0.11	0.04 - 0.19	0.34

Data Plot and Equation

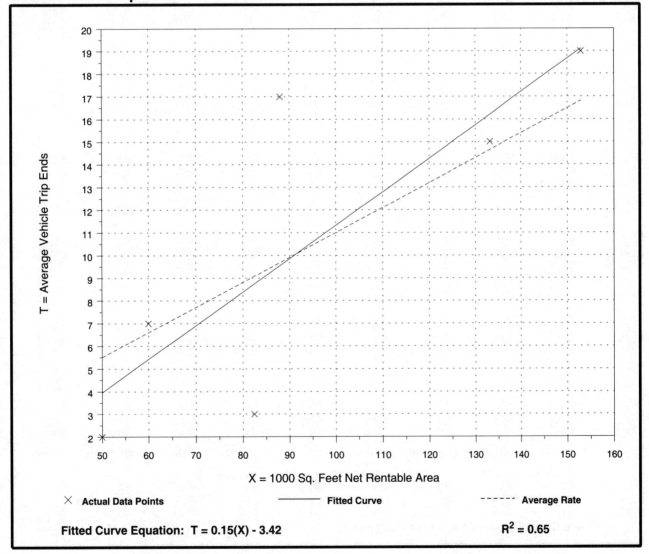

X Actual Data Points ——— **Fitted Curve** - - - - - **Average Rate**

Fitted Curve Equation: T = 0.15(X) - 3.42 $R^2 = 0.65$

Mini-Warehouse
(151)

Average Vehicle Trip Ends vs: **1000 Sq. Feet Net Rentable Area**
On a: **Weekday,**
Peak Hour of Adjacent Street Traffic,
One Hour Between 4 and 6 p.m.

Number of Studies: 6
Average 1000 Sq. Feet NRA: 94
Directional Distribution: 55% entering, 45% exiting

Trip Generation per 1000 Sq. Feet Net Rentable Area

Average Rate	Range of Rates	Standard Deviation
0.17	0.11 - 0.24	0.41

Data Plot and Equation

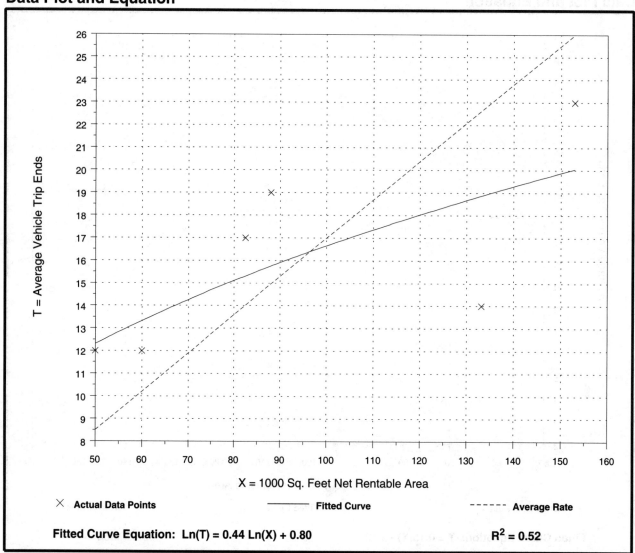

Fitted Curve Equation: $Ln(T) = 0.44\ Ln(X) + 0.80$ $\qquad$ $R^2 = 0.52$

Mini-Warehouse
(151)

Average Vehicle Trip Ends vs: **1000 Sq. Feet Net Rentable Area**
On a: **Weekday,**
        A.M. Peak Hour of Generator

Number of Studies: 6
Average 1000 Sq. Feet NRA: 94
Directional Distribution: 50% entering, 50% exiting

Trip Generation per 1000 Sq. Feet Net Rentable Area

Average Rate	Range of Rates	Standard Deviation
0.19	0.13 - 0.24	0.43

Data Plot and Equation

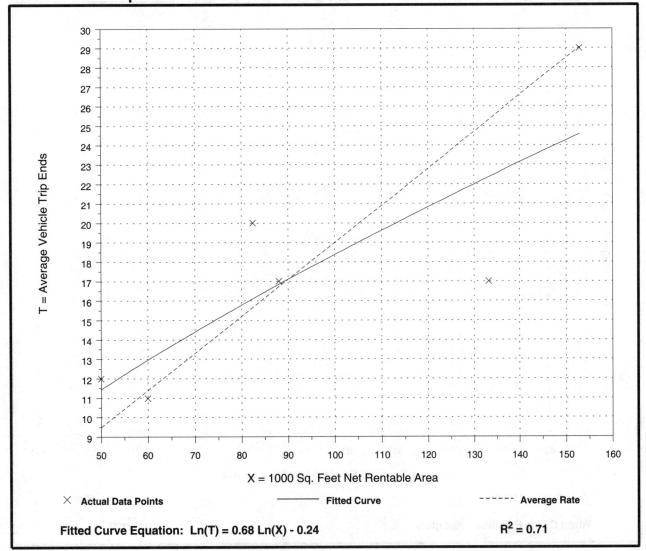

X = 1000 Sq. Feet Net Rentable Area

✕ **Actual Data Points**   ——— **Fitted Curve**   - - - - - **Average Rate**

Fitted Curve Equation: $Ln(T) = 0.68 \, Ln(X) - 0.24$ $R^2 = 0.71$

Mini-Warehouse
(151)

Average Vehicle Trip Ends vs: **1000 Sq. Feet Net Rentable Area**
On a: **Weekday,**
P.M. Peak Hour of Generator

Number of Studies: 5
Average 1000 Sq. Feet NRA: 103
Directional Distribution: 50% entering, 50% exiting

Trip Generation per 1000 Sq. Feet Net Rentable Area

Average Rate	Range of Rates	Standard Deviation
0.21	0.14 - 0.33	0.46

Data Plot and Equation

Caution - Use Carefully - Small Sample Size

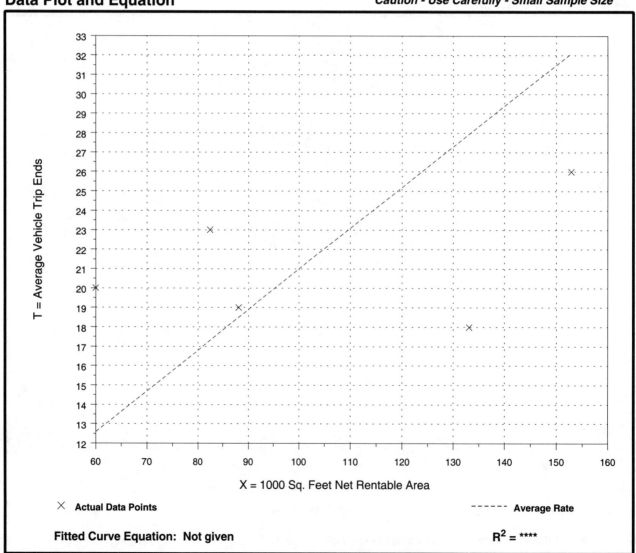

X   **Actual Data Points**

-----   **Average Rate**

Fitted Curve Equation: Not given $R^2 = ****$

Mini-Warehouse
(151)

Average Vehicle Trip Ends vs: 1000 Sq. Feet Net Rentable Area
On a: Saturday

Number of Studies: 2
Average 1000 Sq. Feet NRA: 143
Directional Distribution: 50% entering, 50% exiting

Trip Generation per 1000 Sq. Feet Net Rentable Area

Average Rate	Range of Rates	Standard Deviation
1.17	1.14 - 1.22	*

Data Plot and Equation

Caution - Use Carefully - Small Sample Size

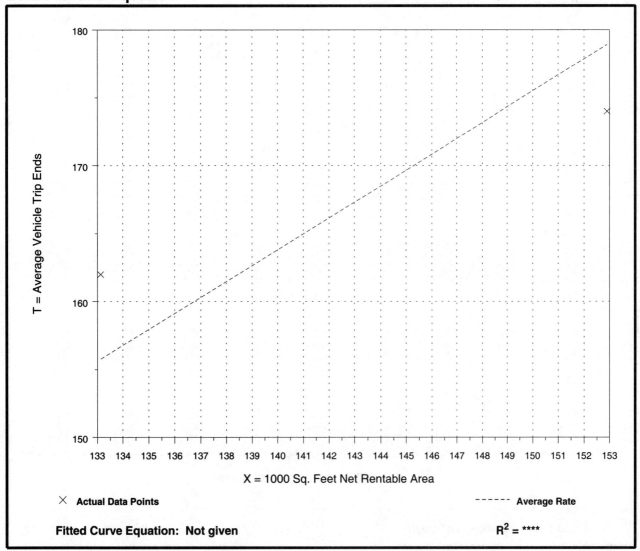

X **Actual Data Points**

----- **Average Rate**

Fitted Curve Equation: Not given

$R^2 = ****$

Mini-Warehouse
(151)

Average Vehicle Trip Ends vs: **1000 Sq. Feet Net Rentable Area**
On a: **Saturday,**
Peak Hour of Generator

Number of Studies: 2
Average 1000 Sq. Feet NRA: 143
Directional Distribution: Not available

Trip Generation per 1000 Sq. Feet Net Rentable Area

Average Rate	Range of Rates	Standard Deviation
0.21	0.21 - 0.21	*

Data Plot and Equation

Caution - Use Carefully - Small Sample Size

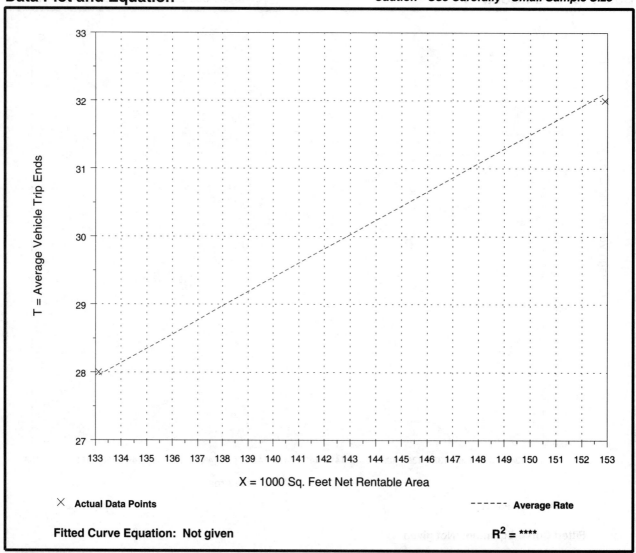

X = 1000 Sq. Feet Net Rentable Area

✕ **Actual Data Points**　　　　　　　　　　　　- - - - - **Average Rate**

Fitted Curve Equation: Not given　　　　　　$R^2 = {}^{****}$

Mini-Warehouse
(151)

Average Vehicle Trip Ends vs: 1000 Sq. Feet Net Rentable Area
On a: Sunday

Number of Studies: 2
Average 1000 Sq. Feet NRA: 143
Directional Distribution: 50% entering, 50% exiting

Trip Generation per 1000 Sq. Feet Net Rentable Area

Average Rate	Range of Rates	Standard Deviation
0.76	0.69 - 0.83	*

Data Plot and Equation

Caution - Use Carefully - Small Sample Size

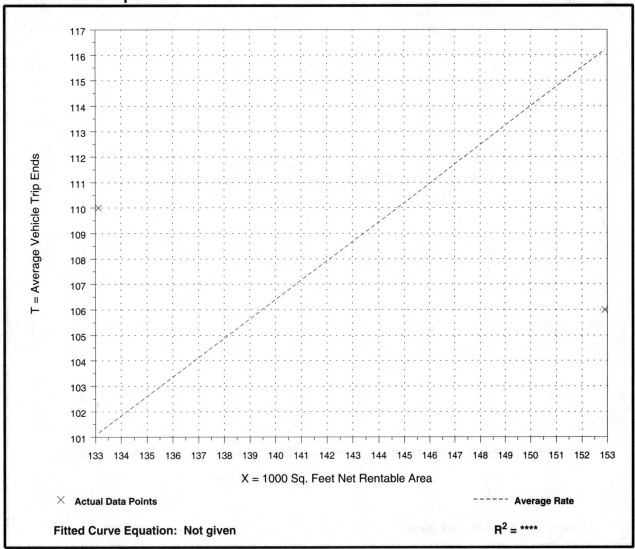

X   **Actual Data Points**   - - - - - - **Average Rate**

Fitted Curve Equation: Not given $R^2 = ****$

Mini-Warehouse
(151)

Average Vehicle Trip Ends vs: **1000 Sq. Feet Net Rentable Area**
On a: **Sunday,**
Peak Hour of Generator

Number of Studies: 2
Average 1000 Sq. Feet NRA: 143
Directional Distribution: Not available

Trip Generation per 1000 Sq. Feet Net Rentable Area

Average Rate	Range of Rates	Standard Deviation
0.15	0.13 - 0.16	*

Data Plot and Equation

Caution - Use Carefully - Small Sample Size

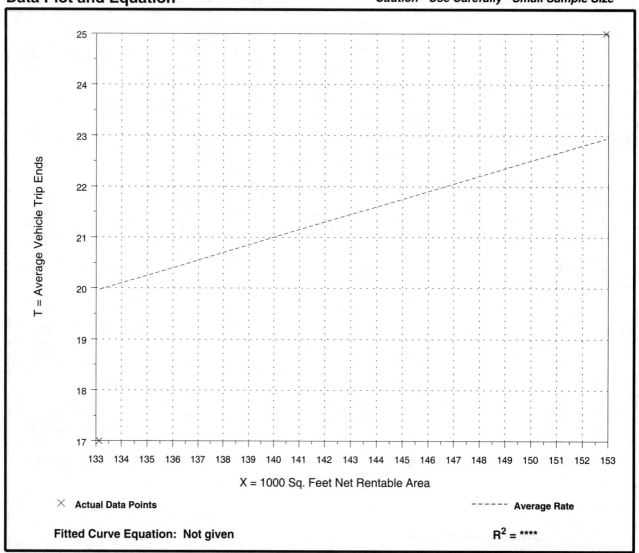

X **Actual Data Points**

----- **Average Rate**

Fitted Curve Equation: Not given $R^2 =$ ****

Mini-Warehouse
(151)

Average Vehicle Trip Ends vs: Storage Units
On a: Weekday

Number of Studies: 8
Average Number of Storage Units: 717
Directional Distribution: 50% entering, 50% exiting

Trip Generation per Storage Unit

Average Rate	Range of Rates	Standard Deviation
0.25	0.15 - 0.46	0.51

Data Plot and Equation

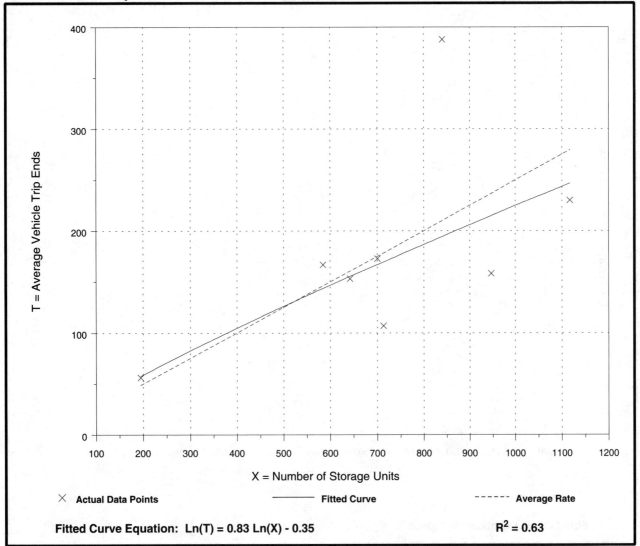

X **Actual Data Points**　　　——— **Fitted Curve**　　　----- **Average Rate**

Fitted Curve Equation: Ln(T) = 0.83 Ln(X) - 0.35　　　　$R^2 = 0.63$

Mini-Warehouse
(151)

Average Vehicle Trip Ends vs: **Storage Units**
On a: **Weekday,**
Peak Hour of Adjacent Street Traffic,
One Hour Between 7 and 9 a.m.

Number of Studies: 9
Average Number of Storage Units: 668
Directional Distribution: 67% entering, 33% exiting

Trip Generation per Storage Unit

Average Rate	Range of Rates	Standard Deviation
0.02	0.01 - 0.03	0.13

Data Plot and Equation

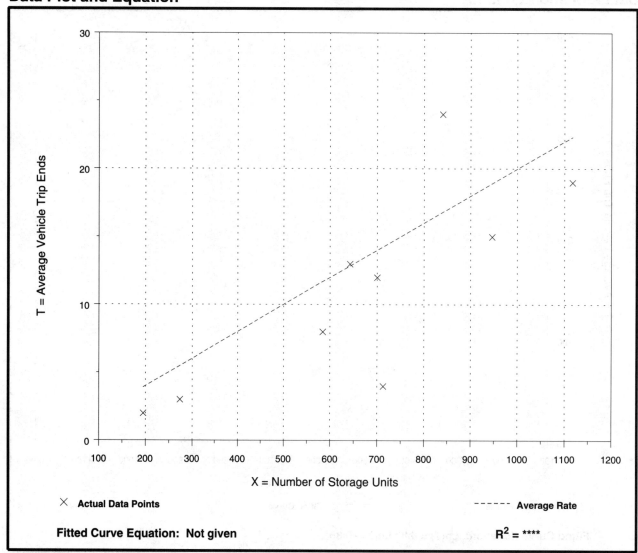

Fitted Curve Equation: Not given　　　　　　　　　　　$R^2 = ****$

Mini-Warehouse
(151)

Average Vehicle Trip Ends vs: Storage Units
On a: Weekday,
Peak Hour of Adjacent Street Traffic,
One Hour Between 4 and 6 p.m.

Number of Studies: 8
Average Number of Storage Units: 717
Directional Distribution: Not available

Trip Generation per Storage Unit

Average Rate	Range of Rates	Standard Deviation
0.02	0.01 - 0.04	0.16

Data Plot and Equation

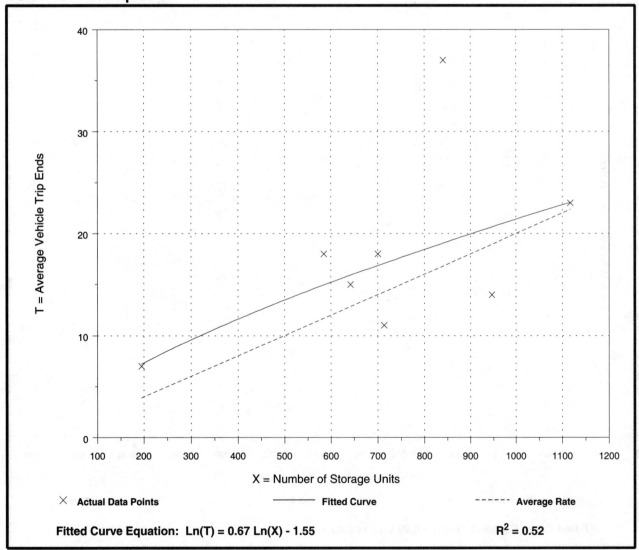

Fitted Curve Equation: $Ln(T) = 0.67 \, Ln(X) - 1.55$ **$R^2 = 0.52$**

Mini-Warehouse
(151)

Average Vehicle Trip Ends vs: Storage Units
On a: Weekday,
A.M. Peak Hour of Generator

Number of Studies: 8
Average Number of Storage Units: 717
Directional Distribution: Not available

Trip Generation per Storage Unit

Average Rate	Range of Rates	Standard Deviation
0.03	0.02 - 0.05	0.16

Data Plot and Equation

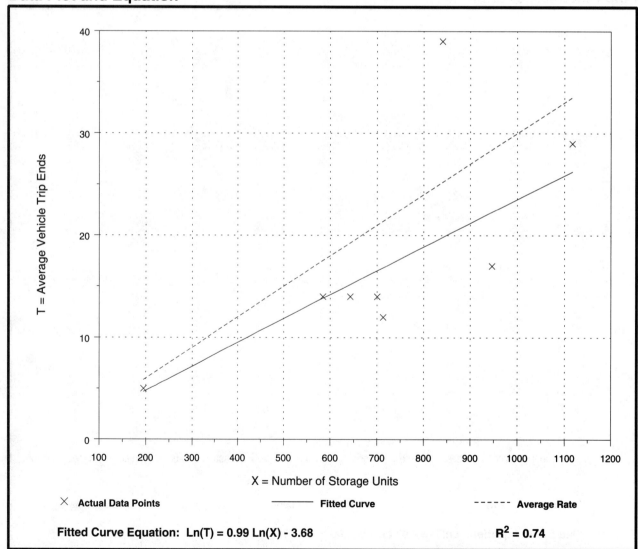

Fitted Curve Equation: Ln(T) = 0.99 Ln(X) - 3.68 $R^2 = 0.74$

Mini-Warehouse
(151)

Average Vehicle Trip Ends vs: **Storage Units**
On a: **Weekday,**
P.M. Peak Hour of Generator

Number of Studies: 8
Average Number of Storage Units: 717
Directional Distribution: Not available

Trip Generation per Storage Unit

Average Rate	Range of Rates	Standard Deviation
0.03	0.02 - 0.05	0.17

Data Plot and Equation

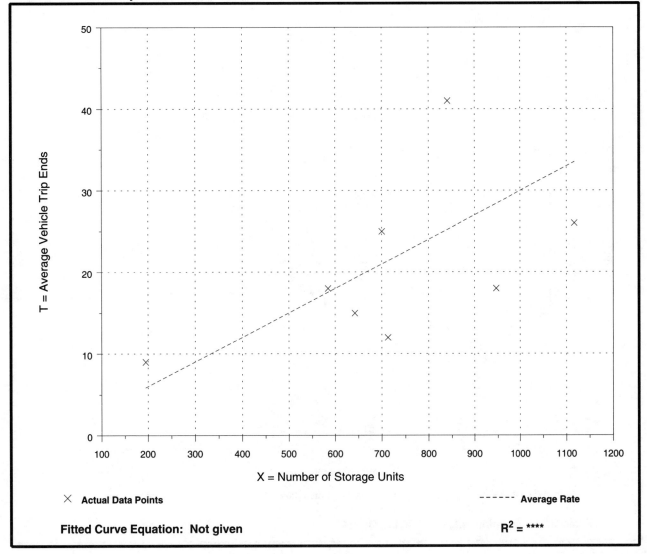

Fitted Curve Equation: Not given $R^2 = ****$

Mini-Warehouse
(151)

Average Vehicle Trip Ends vs: **Storage Units**
On a: **Saturday**

Number of Studies: 8
Average Number of Storage Units: 717
Directional Distribution: 50% entering, 50% exiting

Trip Generation per Storage Unit

Average Rate	Range of Rates	Standard Deviation
0.22	0.14 - 0.35	0.47

Data Plot and Equation

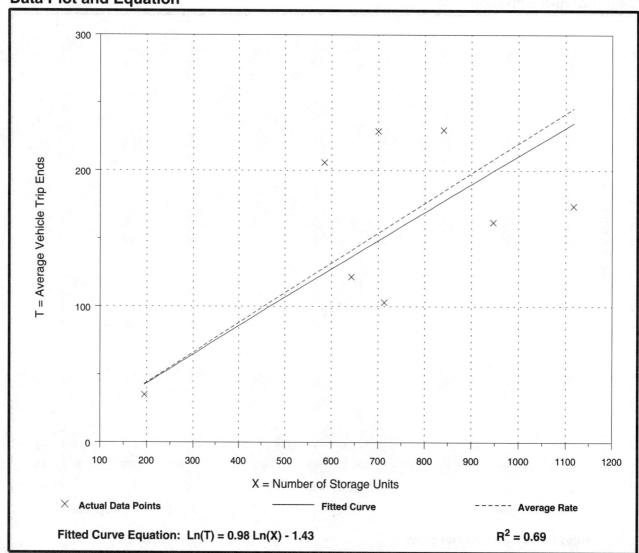

X = Number of Storage Units

✕ **Actual Data Points** ——— **Fitted Curve** ----- **Average Rate**

Fitted Curve Equation: $\text{Ln}(T) = 0.98\,\text{Ln}(X) - 1.43$ $R^2 = 0.69$

Mini-Warehouse
(151)

Average Vehicle Trip Ends vs: **Storage Units**
On a: **Saturday,**
Peak Hour of Generator

Number of Studies: 8
Average Number of Storage Units: 717
Directional Distribution: Not available

Trip Generation per Storage Unit

Average Rate	Range of Rates	Standard Deviation
0.04	0.02 - 0.06	0.19

Data Plot and Equation

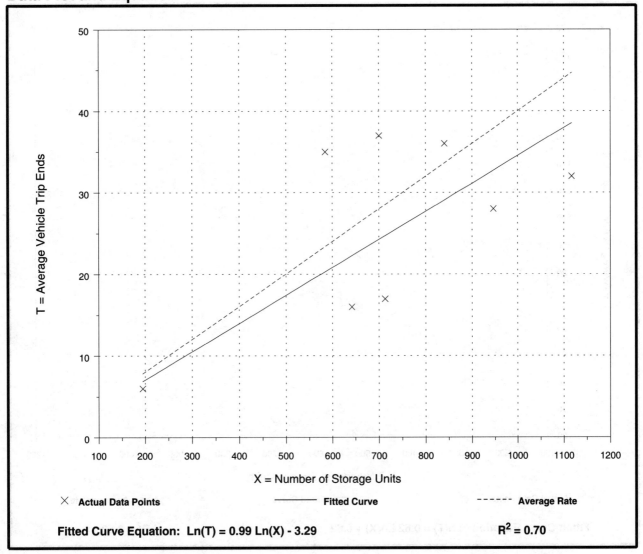

Fitted Curve Equation: Ln(T) = 0.99 Ln(X) - 3.29   **R² = 0.70**

Mini-Warehouse
(151)

Average Vehicle Trip Ends vs: Storage Units
On a: Sunday

Number of Studies: 8
Average Number of Storage Units: 717
Directional Distribution: 50% entering, 50% exiting

Trip Generation per Storage Unit

Average Rate	Range of Rates	Standard Deviation
0.15	0.09 - 0.23	0.39

Data Plot and Equation

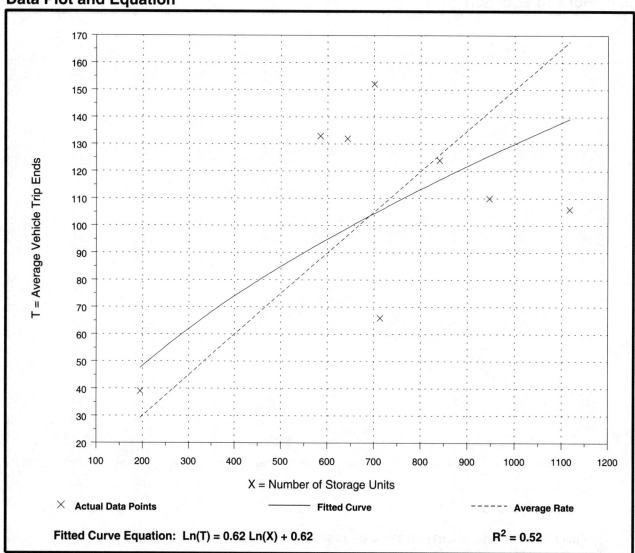

X = Number of Storage Units

X Actual Data Points   ———— Fitted Curve   ----- Average Rate

Fitted Curve Equation: Ln(T) = 0.62 Ln(X) + 0.62 $R^2 = 0.52$

Mini-Warehouse
(151)

Average Vehicle Trip Ends vs: **Storage Units**
On a: **Sunday,**
Peak Hour of Generator

Number of Studies: 8
Average Number of Storage Units: 717
Directional Distribution: Not available

Trip Generation per Storage Unit

Average Rate	Range of Rates	Standard Deviation
0.03	0.02 - 0.06	0.16

Data Plot and Equation

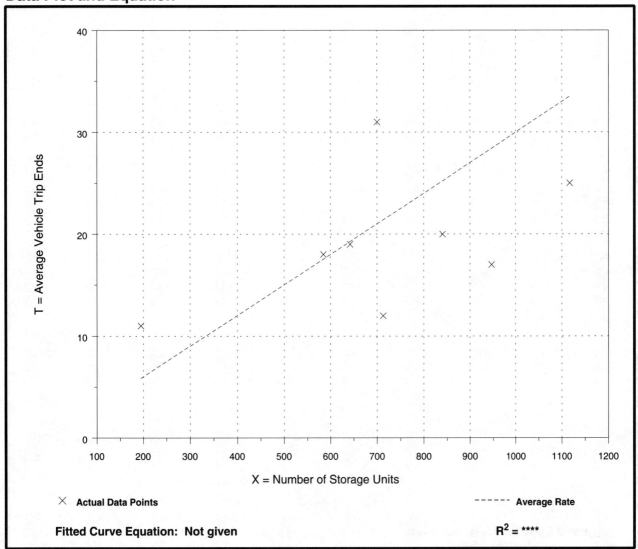

X **Actual Data Points**   ----- **Average Rate**

Fitted Curve Equation: Not given $R^2 = $ ****

Mini-Warehouse
(151)

Average Vehicle Trip Ends vs: Occupied Storage Units
On a: Weekday

Number of Studies: 3
Avg. Num. of Occupied Storage Units: 1,029
Directional Distribution: 50% entering, 50% exiting

Trip Generation per Occupied Storage Unit

Average Rate	Range of Rates	Standard Deviation
0.20	0.18 - 0.21	0.45

Data Plot and Equation

Caution - Use Carefully - Small Sample Size

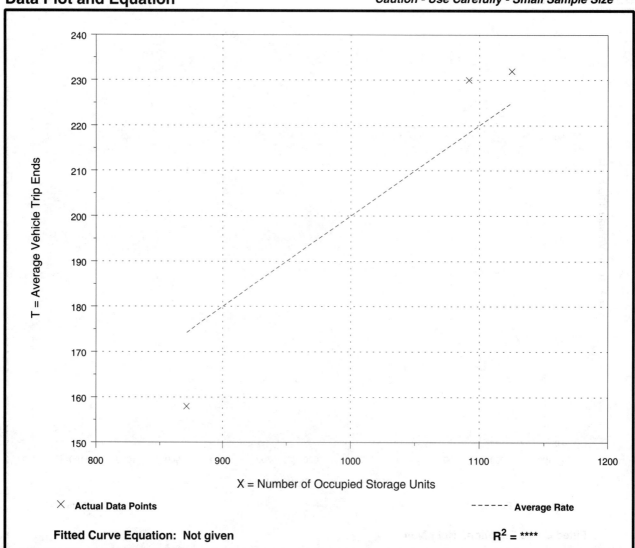

X **Actual Data Points**   - - - - - **Average Rate**

Fitted Curve Equation: Not given $R^2 = ****$

Mini-Warehouse
(151)

Average Vehicle Trip Ends vs: Occupied Storage Units
On a: Weekday,
Peak Hour of Adjacent Street Traffic,
One Hour Between 7 and 9 a.m.

Number of Studies: 3
Avg. Num. of Occupied Storage Units: 1,029
Directional Distribution: Not available

Trip Generation per Occupied Storage Unit

Average Rate	Range of Rates	Standard Deviation
0.02	0.01 - 0.02	0.13

Data Plot and Equation

Caution - Use Carefully - Small Sample Size

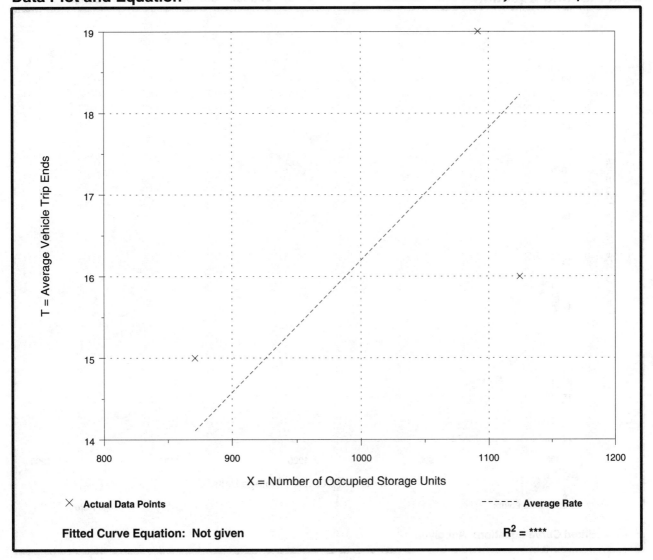

X **Actual Data Points**   ----- **Average Rate**

Fitted Curve Equation: Not given $R^2 = ****$

Mini-Warehouse
(151)

Average Vehicle Trip Ends vs: **Occupied Storage Units**
On a: **Weekday,**
Peak Hour of Adjacent Street Traffic,
One Hour Between 4 and 6 p.m.

Number of Studies: 3
Avg. Num. of Occupied Storage Units: 1,029
Directional Distribution: Not available

Trip Generation per Occupied Storage Unit

Average Rate	Range of Rates	Standard Deviation
0.02	0.02 - 0.02	0.14

Data Plot and Equation

Caution - Use Carefully - Small Sample Size

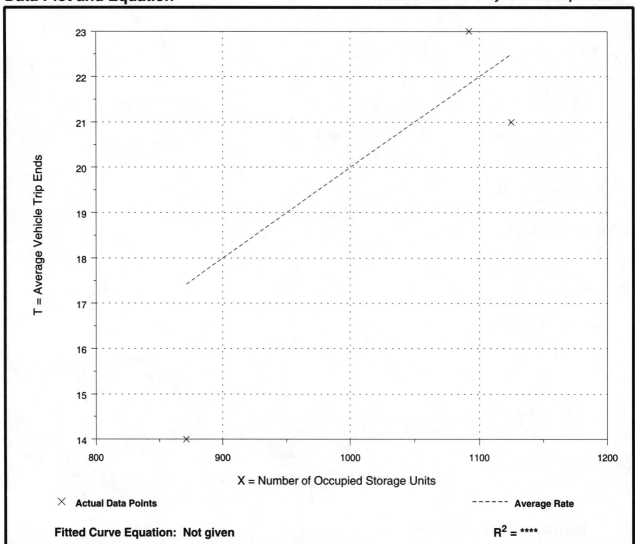

X **Actual Data Points**

- - - - - - **Average Rate**

Fitted Curve Equation: Not given $R^2 = ****$

Mini-Warehouse
(151)

Average Vehicle Trip Ends vs: Occupied Storage Units
On a: Weekday,
A.M. Peak Hour of Generator

Number of Studies: 3
Avg. Num. of Occupied Storage Units: 1,029
Directional Distribution: Not available

Trip Generation per Occupied Storage Unit

Average Rate	Range of Rates	Standard Deviation
0.02	0.02 - 0.03	0.15

Data Plot and Equation

Caution - Use Carefully - Small Sample Size

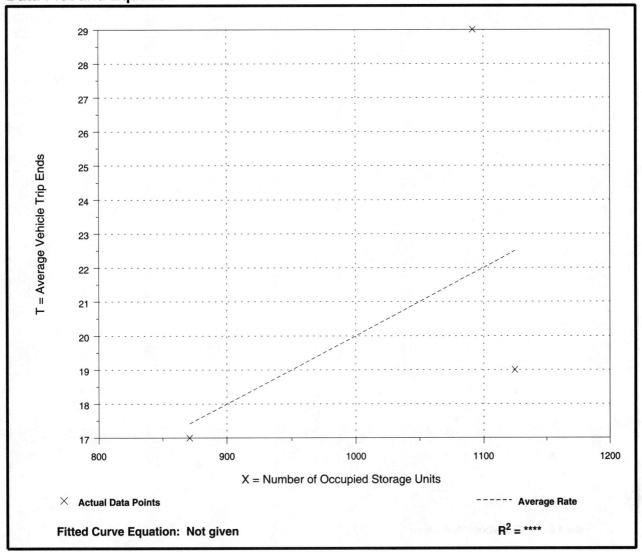

X   **Actual Data Points** — — — — **Average Rate**

Fitted Curve Equation: Not given $R^2 = ****$

Mini-Warehouse
(151)

Average Vehicle Trip Ends vs: **Occupied Storage Units**
On a: **Weekday,**
P.M. Peak Hour of Generator

Number of Studies: 3
Avg. Num. of Occupied Storage Units: 1,029
Directional Distribution: Not available

Trip Generation per Occupied Storage Unit

Average Rate	Range of Rates	Standard Deviation
0.02	0.02 - 0.02	0.15

Data Plot and Equation

Caution - Use Carefully - Small Sample Size

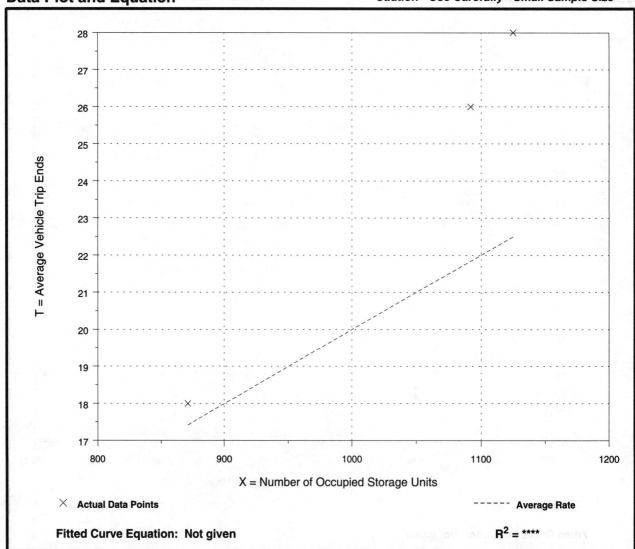

X = Number of Occupied Storage Units

✕ **Actual Data Points** - - - - - **Average Rate**

Fitted Curve Equation: Not given $R^2 = ****$

Mini-Warehouse
(151)

Average Vehicle Trip Ends vs: Occupied Storage Units
On a: Saturday

Number of Studies: 3
Avg. Num. of Occupied Storage Units: 1,029
Directional Distribution: 50% entering, 50% exiting

Trip Generation per Occupied Storage Unit

Average Rate	Range of Rates	Standard Deviation
0.19	0.16 - 0.22	0.43

Data Plot and Equation

Caution - Use Carefully - Small Sample Size

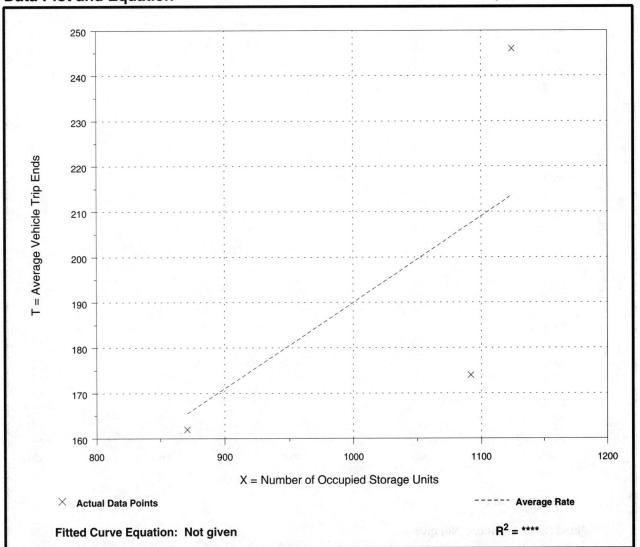

X = Number of Occupied Storage Units

$\times$ **Actual Data Points**   - - - - - **Average Rate**

Fitted Curve Equation: Not given $R^2 = ****$

Mini-Warehouse
(151)

Average Vehicle Trip Ends vs: Occupied Storage Units
On a: Saturday,
Peak Hour of Generator

Number of Studies: 3
Avg. Num. of Occupied Storage Units: 1,029
Directional Distribution: Not available

Trip Generation per Occupied Storage Unit

Average Rate	Range of Rates	Standard Deviation
0.03	0.03 - 0.03	0.18

Data Plot and Equation

Caution - Use Carefully - Small Sample Size

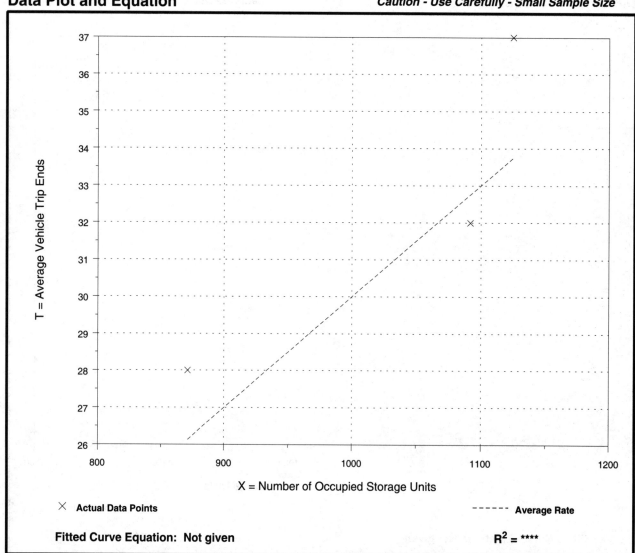

X **Actual Data Points**

------ **Average Rate**

Fitted Curve Equation: Not given $R^2 = ****$

Mini-Warehouse
(151)

Average Vehicle Trip Ends vs: Occupied Storage Units
On a: Sunday

Number of Studies: 3
Avg. Num. of Occupied Storage Units: 1,029
Directional Distribution: 50% entering, 50% exiting

Trip Generation per Occupied Storage Unit

Average Rate	Range of Rates	Standard Deviation
0.15	0.10 - 0.23	0.40

Data Plot and Equation

Caution - Use Carefully - Small Sample Size

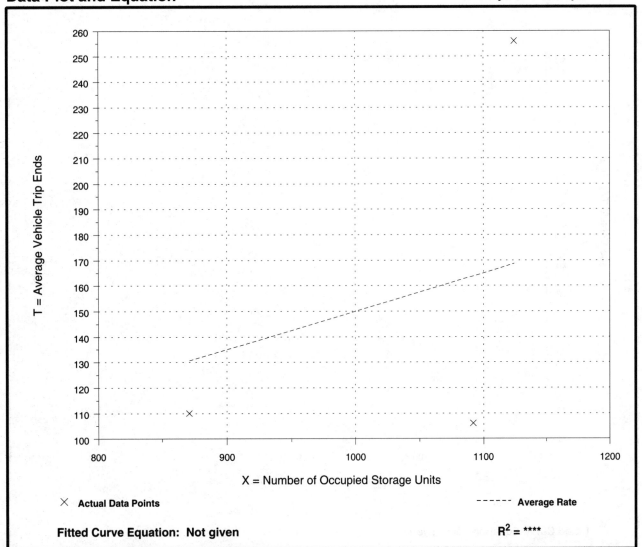

X **Actual Data Points**   - - - - - **Average Rate**

Fitted Curve Equation: Not given R^2 = ****

Mini-Warehouse
(151)

Average Vehicle Trip Ends vs: **Occupied Storage Units**
On a: **Sunday,**
Peak Hour of Generator

Number of Studies: 3
Avg. Num. of Occupied Storage Units: 1,029
Directional Distribution: Not available

Trip Generation per Occupied Storage Unit

Average Rate	Range of Rates	Standard Deviation
0.02	0.02 - 0.03	0.15

Data Plot and Equation

Caution - Use Carefully - Small Sample Size

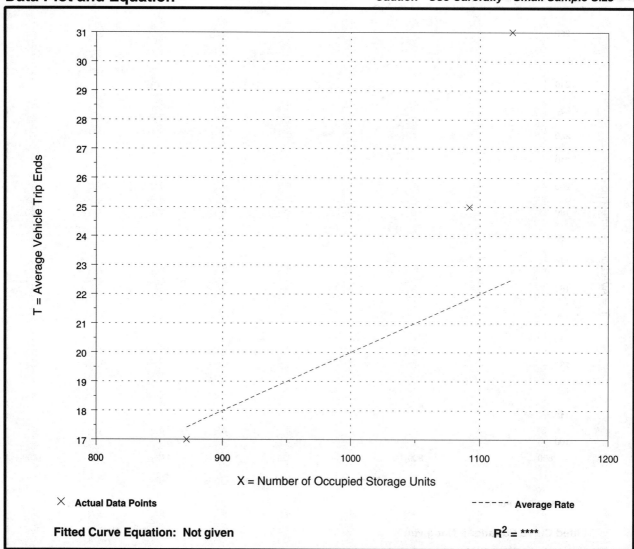

X **Actual Data Points**   - - - - - **Average Rate**

Fitted Curve Equation: Not given $R^2 = ****$

Mini-Warehouse
(151)

Average Vehicle Trip Ends vs: **Acres**
On a: **Weekday**

Number of Studies: 13
Average Number of Acres: 4
Directional Distribution: 50% entering, 50% exiting

Trip Generation per Acre

Average Rate	Range of Rates	Standard Deviation
35.43	14.78 - 64.67	15.63

Data Plot and Equation

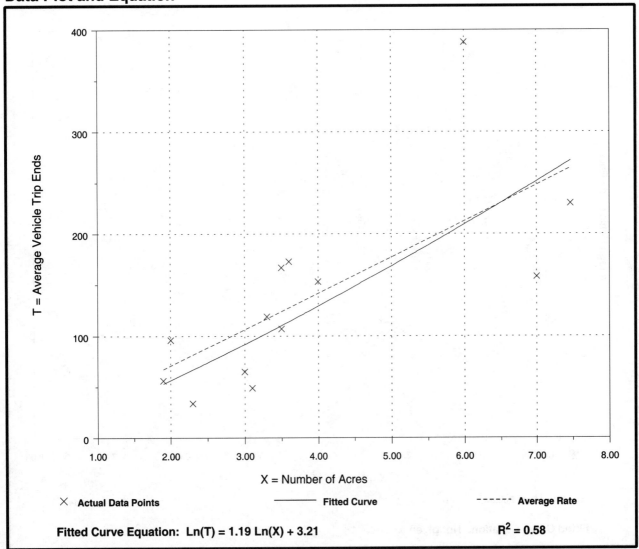

X = Number of Acres

$\times$ **Actual Data Points** ——— **Fitted Curve** - - - - - **Average Rate**

Fitted Curve Equation: $Ln(T) = 1.19 \, Ln(X) + 3.21$ $R^2 = 0.58$

Mini-Warehouse
(151)

Average Vehicle Trip Ends vs: **Acres**
On a: **Weekday,**
Peak Hour of Adjacent Street Traffic,
One Hour Between 7 and 9 a.m.

Number of Studies: 8
Average Number of Acres: 5
Directional Distribution: Not available

Trip Generation per Acre

Average Rate	Range of Rates	Standard Deviation
2.62	1.05 - 4.00	1.72

Data Plot and Equation

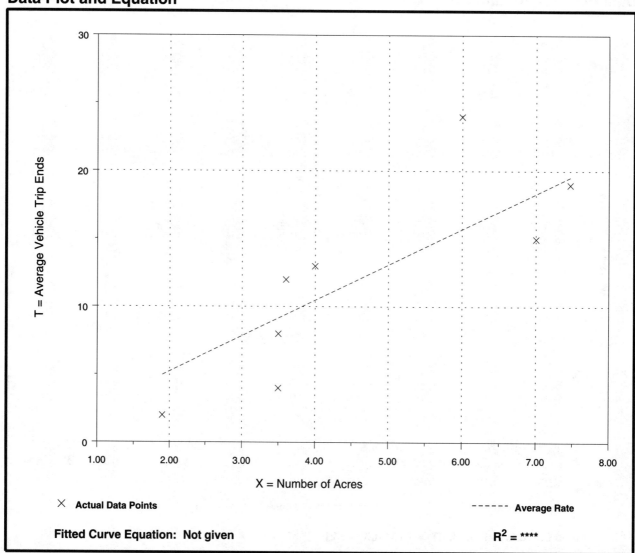

X **Actual Data Points**

- - - - - **Average Rate**

Fitted Curve Equation: Not given $R^2 = ****$

Mini-Warehouse
(151)

Average Vehicle Trip Ends vs: **Acres**
On a: **Weekday,**
Peak Hour of Adjacent Street Traffic,
One Hour Between 4 and 6 p.m.

Number of Studies: 12
Average Number of Acres: 4
Directional Distribution: 52% entering, 48% exiting

Trip Generation per Acre

Average Rate	Range of Rates	Standard Deviation
3.45	1.29 - 6.17	2.22

Data Plot and Equation

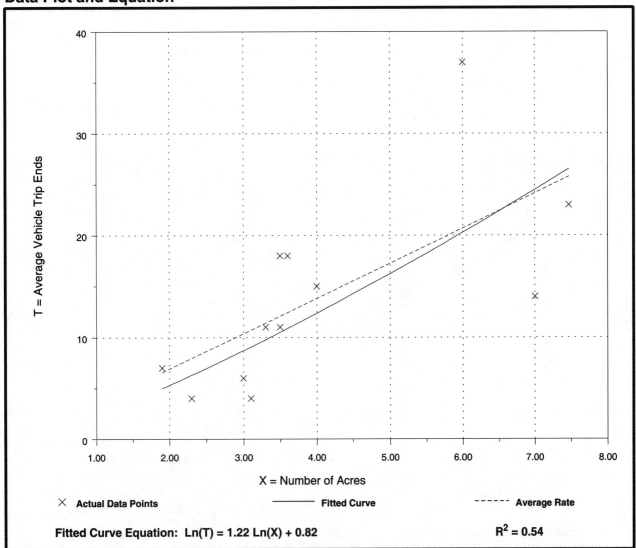

X **Actual Data Points**   ———— **Fitted Curve**   - - - - - **Average Rate**

Fitted Curve Equation: Ln(T) = 1.22 Ln(X) + 0.82 $R^2 = 0.54$

Mini-Warehouse
(151)

Average Vehicle Trip Ends vs: **Acres**
On a: **Weekday,**
A.M. Peak Hour of Generator

Number of Studies: 8
Average Number of Acres: 5
Directional Distribution: Not available

Trip Generation per Acre

Average Rate	Range of Rates	Standard Deviation
3.90	2.43 - 6.50	2.20

Data Plot and Equation

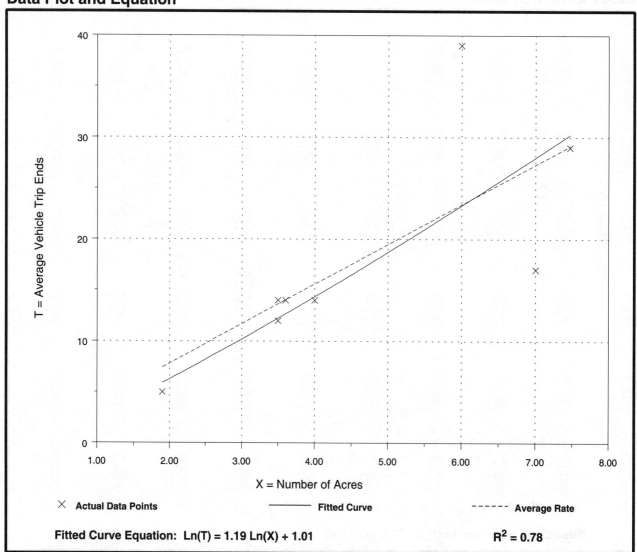

X **Actual Data Points**   —— **Fitted Curve**   - - - - **Average Rate**

Fitted Curve Equation: Ln(T) = 1.19 Ln(X) + 1.01 $R^2 = 0.78$

Mini-Warehouse
(151)

Average Vehicle Trip Ends vs: **Acres**
On a: **Weekday,**
P.M. Peak Hour of Generator

Number of Studies: 13
Average Number of Acres: 4
Directional Distribution: 52% entering, 48% exiting

Trip Generation per Acre

Average Rate	Range of Rates	Standard Deviation
3.89	1.29 - 6.94	2.45

Data Plot and Equation

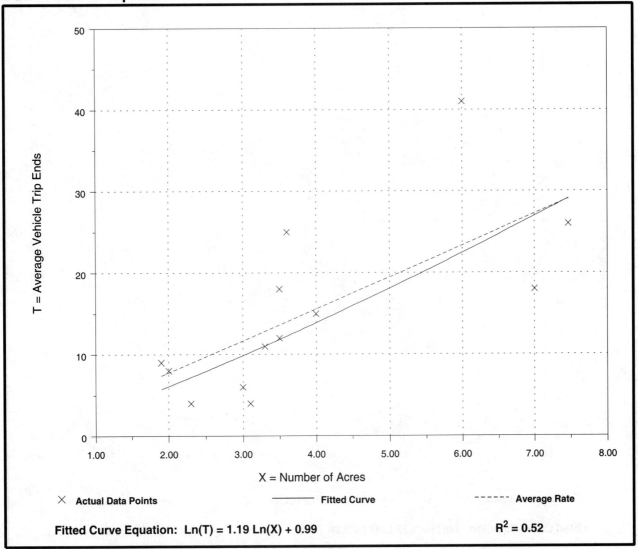

X **Actual Data Points**　　　　——— **Fitted Curve**　　　- - - - - **Average Rate**

Fitted Curve Equation: Ln(T) = 1.19 Ln(X) + 0.99　　　$R^2 = 0.52$

Mini-Warehouse
(151)

Average Vehicle Trip Ends vs: Acres
On a: Saturday

Number of Studies: 13
Average Number of Acres: 4
Directional Distribution: 50% entering, 50% exiting

Trip Generation per Acre

Average Rate	Range of Rates	Standard Deviation
31.44	14.78 - 63.61	14.46

Data Plot and Equation

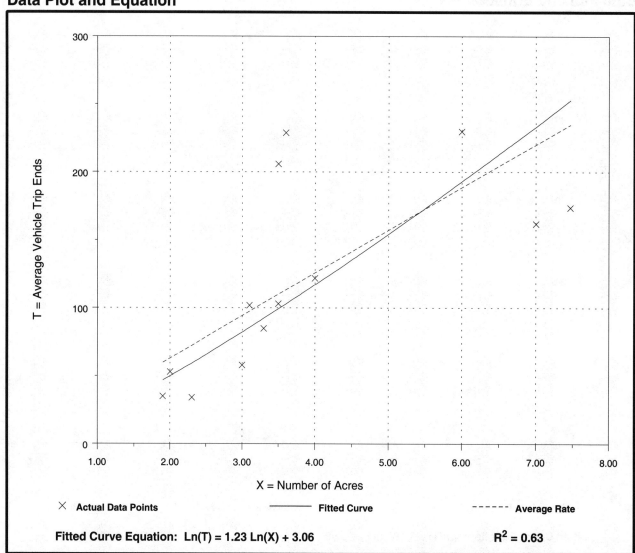

X = Number of Acres

✕ **Actual Data Points**   ———— **Fitted Curve**   - - - - **Average Rate**

Fitted Curve Equation: Ln(T) = 1.23 Ln(X) + 3.06 $R^2 = 0.63$

Mini-Warehouse
(151)

Average Vehicle Trip Ends vs: Acres
On a: Saturday,
Peak Hour of Generator

Number of Studies: 8
Average Number of Acres: 5
Directional Distribution: Not available

Trip Generation per Acre

Average Rate	Range of Rates	Standard Deviation
5.60	3.16 - 10.28	3.17

Data Plot and Equation

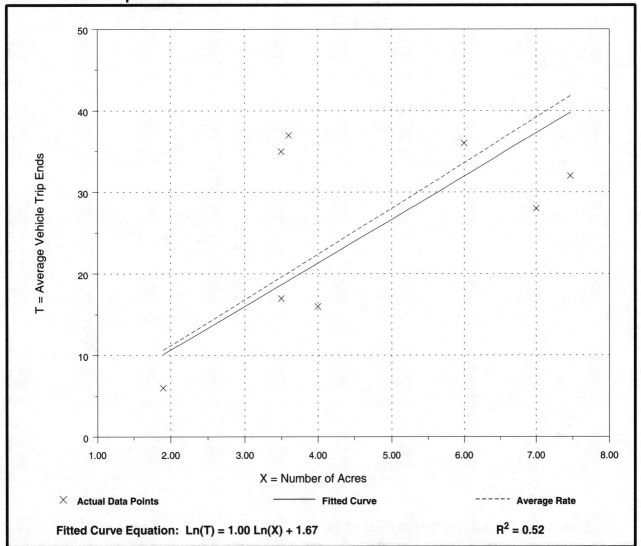

X **Actual Data Points**   —— **Fitted Curve**   - - - - **Average Rate**

Fitted Curve Equation: Ln(T) = 1.00 Ln(X) + 1.67 $R^2 = 0.52$

Mini-Warehouse
(151)

Average Vehicle Trip Ends vs: Acres
On a: Sunday

Number of Studies: 12
Average Number of Acres: 4
Directional Distribution: 50% entering, 50% exiting

Trip Generation per Acre

Average Rate	Range of Rates	Standard Deviation
22.63	11.00 - 42.22	10.28

Data Plot and Equation

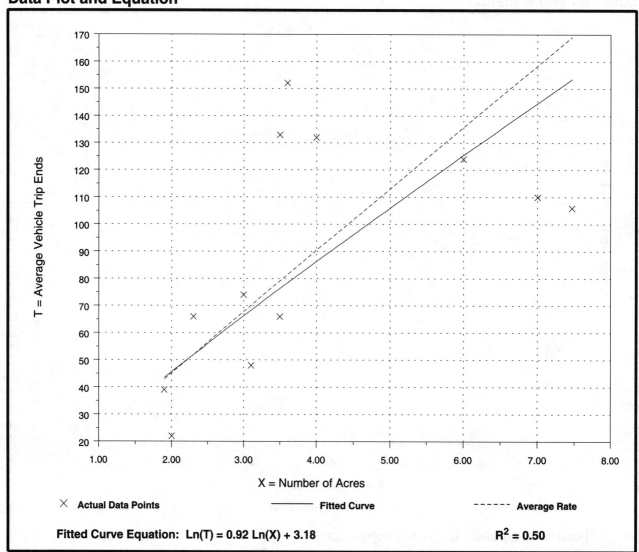

X Actual Data Points   —— Fitted Curve   - - - - - Average Rate

Fitted Curve Equation: Ln(T) = 0.92 Ln(X) + 3.18 $R^2 = 0.50$

Mini-Warehouse
(151)

Average Vehicle Trip Ends vs: **Acres**
On a: **Sunday,**
Peak Hour of Generator

Number of Studies: 8
Average Number of Acres: 5
Directional Distribution: Not available

Trip Generation per Acre

Average Rate	Range of Rates	Standard Deviation
4.14	2.43 - 8.61	2.52

Data Plot and Equation

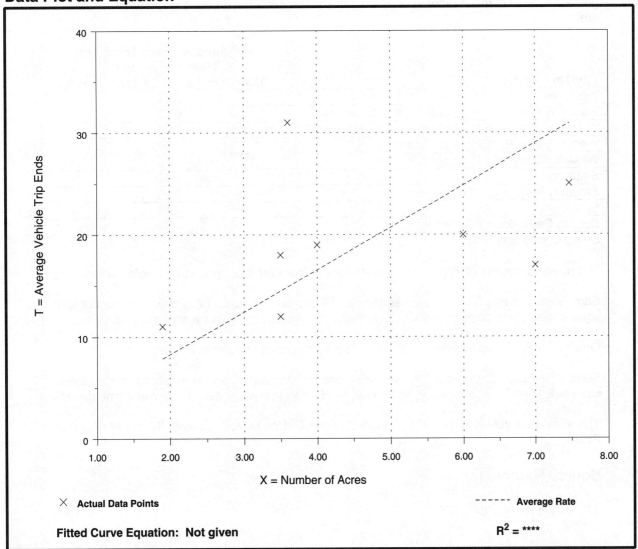

X Actual Data Points

------ Average Rate

Fitted Curve Equation: Not given

$R^2 = ****$

Land Use: 152
High-Cube Warehouse

Description

High-cube warehouses are used for the storage of manufactured goods prior to their distribution to retail outlets. These facilities consist of large shells of steel buildings and large halls, often subdivided for individual tenants, with a typical ceiling height of 24 to 30 feet. They are also characterized by a small employment count due to a high level of mechanization, truck activities frequently outside of the peak hour of the adjacent street system and good freeway access. Warehousing (Land Use 150) is a related use.

Additional Data

Truck trips accounted for 9 to 29 percent of the peak hour traffic at the sites surveyed.

Average truck trip generation rates for five sites are summarized in the table below. The average gross floor area of these facilities is 1,020,238 square feet. These sites are located in a rural area.

Day/Time Period	Weighted Average Truck Trip Generation Rate (trip ends per 1,000 square feet)
Weekday	0.64
Weekday a.m. Peak Hour of Adjacent Street Traffic	0.02
Weekday p.m. Peak Hour of Adjacent Street Traffic	0.02
Weekday a.m. Peak Hour of Generator	0.02
Weekday p.m. Peak Hour of Generator	0.03
Saturday	0.49
Saturday Peak Hour of Generator	0.03
Sunday	0.48
Sunday Peak Hour of Generator	0.03

Sources: 605, 642, 649

The average number of truck docks was 46 for the four sites that provided this information.

Some sites surveyed for this land use indicated that a small amount (less than 5 percent of total square footage) of office space was included in the overall gross floor areas reported.

One source indicated that the warehousing sites comprised multiple buildings.

Some of the sites surveyed in this land use were in full operation on the weekends while others were not. Therefore, caution should be exercised when applying rates for weekend time periods.

The sites were surveyed in 1989 and the 2000s in California, New Jersey, Texas, Michigan and Florida.

Source Numbers

331, 605, 619, 642, 645, 649

High-Cube Warehouse
(152)

Average Vehicle Trip Ends vs: **1000 Sq. Feet Gross Floor Area**
On a: **Weekday**

Number of Studies: 35
Average 1000 Sq. Feet GFA: 509
Directional Distribution: 50% entering, 50% exiting

Trip Generation per 1000 Sq. Feet Gross Floor Area

Average Rate	Range of Rates	Standard Deviation
1.44	0.20 - 2.88	1.39

Data Plot and Equation

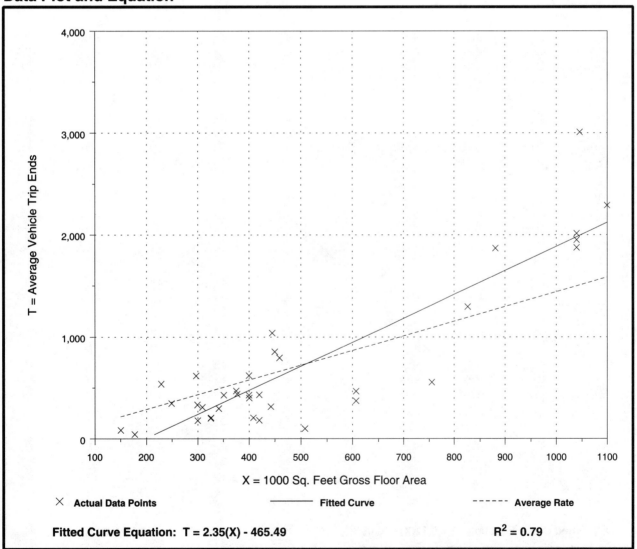

Fitted Curve Equation: T = 2.35(X) - 465.49 $R^2 = 0.79$

High-Cube Warehouse
(152)

Average Vehicle Trip Ends vs: 1000 Sq. Feet Gross Floor Area
On a: Weekday,
Peak Hour of Adjacent Street Traffic,
One Hour Between 7 and 9 a.m.

Number of Studies: 41
Average 1000 Sq. Feet GFA: 567
Directional Distribution: 65% entering, 35% exiting

Trip Generation per 1000 Sq. Feet Gross Floor Area

Average Rate	Range of Rates	Standard Deviation
0.09	0.01 - 0.23	0.30

Data Plot and Equation

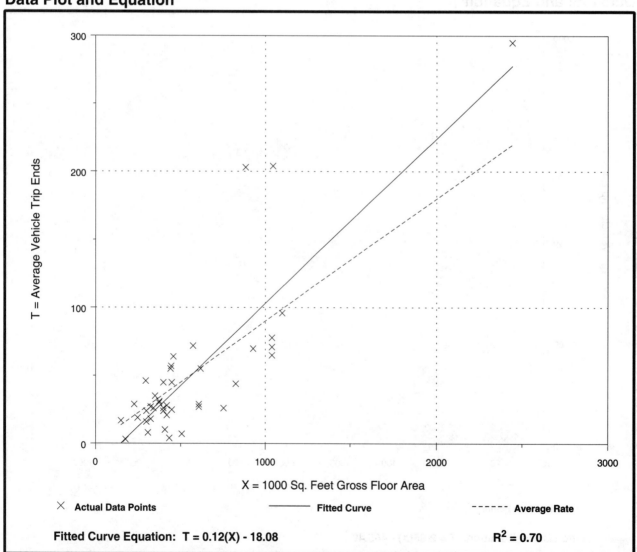

X Actual Data Points ———— Fitted Curve - - - - - Average Rate

Fitted Curve Equation: T = 0.12(X) - 18.08 $R^2 = 0.70$

High-Cube Warehouse
(152)

Average Vehicle Trip Ends vs: **1000 Sq. Feet Gross Floor Area**
On a: **Weekday,**
Peak Hour of Adjacent Street Traffic,
One Hour Between 4 and 6 p.m.

Number of Studies: 44
Average 1000 Sq. Feet GFA: 549
Directional Distribution: 33% entering, 67% exiting

Trip Generation per 1000 Sq. Feet Gross Floor Area

Average Rate	Range of Rates	Standard Deviation
0.10	0.00 - 0.21	0.32

Data Plot and Equation

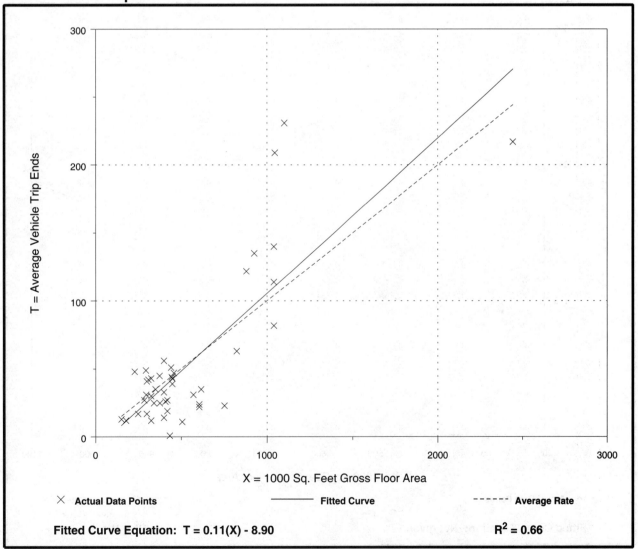

Fitted Curve Equation: $T = 0.11(X) - 8.90$ $\qquad$ $R^2 = 0.66$

High-Cube Warehouse
(152)

Average Vehicle Trip Ends vs: 1000 Sq. Feet Gross Floor Area
On a: Weekday,
A.M. Peak Hour of Generator

Number of Studies: 9
Average 1000 Sq. Feet GFA: 810
Directional Distribution: 80% entering, 20% exiting

Trip Generation per 1000 Sq. Feet Gross Floor Area

Average Rate	Range of Rates	Standard Deviation
0.17	0.08 - 0.24	0.41

Data Plot and Equation

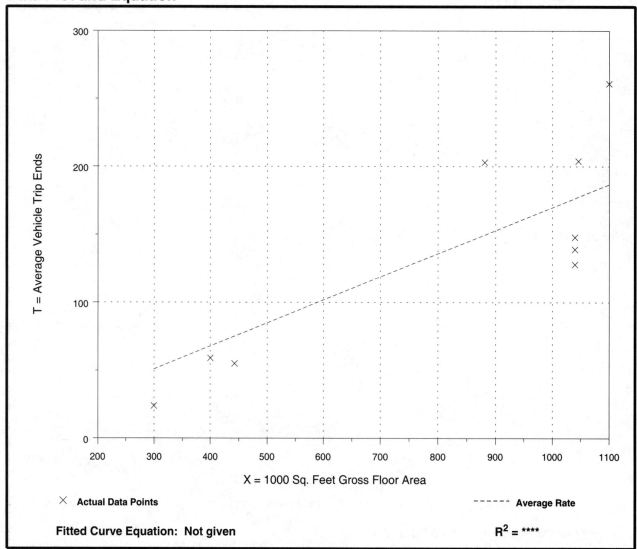

Fitted Curve Equation: Not given $R^2 = ****$

High-Cube Warehouse
(152)

Average Vehicle Trip Ends vs: **1000 Sq. Feet Gross Floor Area**
On a: **Weekday,**
P.M. Peak Hour of Generator

Number of Studies: 12
Average 1000 Sq. Feet GFA: 683
Directional Distribution: 40% entering, 60% exiting

Trip Generation per 1000 Sq. Feet Gross Floor Area

Average Rate	Range of Rates	Standard Deviation
0.18	0.09 - 0.26	0.43

Data Plot and Equation

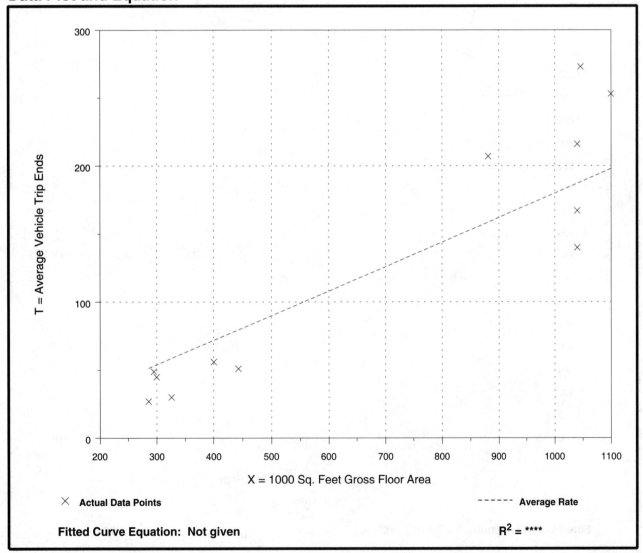

Fitted Curve Equation: Not given $R^2 = ****$

High-Cube Warehouse
(152)

Average Vehicle Trip Ends vs: 1000 Sq. Feet Gross Floor Area
On a: Saturday

Number of Studies: 9
Average 1000 Sq. Feet GFA: 732
Directional Distribution: 50% entering, 50% exiting

Trip Generation per 1000 Sq. Feet Gross Floor Area

Average Rate	Range of Rates	Standard Deviation
1.05	0.01 - 1.65	1.21

Data Plot and Equation

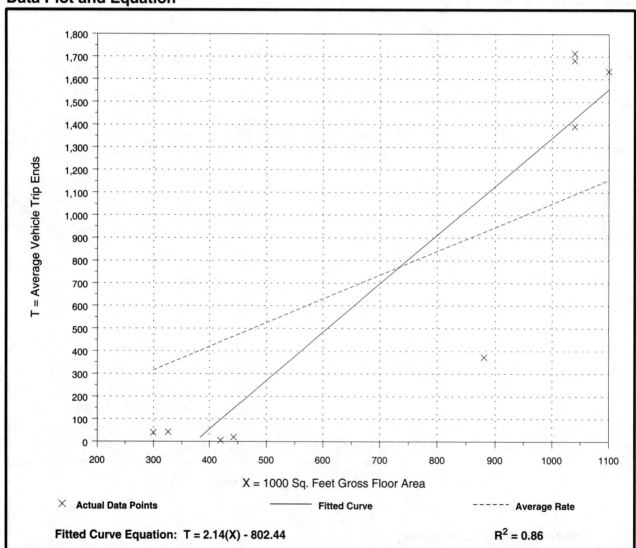

Fitted Curve Equation: T = 2.14(X) - 802.44   **$R^2 = 0.86$**

High-Cube Warehouse
(152)

Average Vehicle Trip Ends vs: 1000 Sq. Feet Gross Floor Area
On a: Saturday,
Peak Hour of Generator

Number of Studies: 7
Average 1000 Sq. Feet GFA: 835
Directional Distribution: 60% entering, 40% exiting

Trip Generation per 1000 Sq. Feet Gross Floor Area

Average Rate	Range of Rates	Standard Deviation
0.14	0.01 - 0.23	0.38

Data Plot and Equation

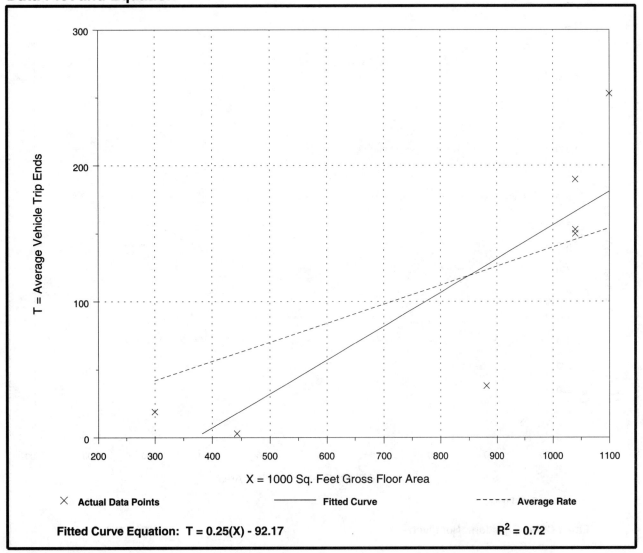

Fitted Curve Equation: T = 0.25(X) - 92.17 $R^2 = 0.72$

High-Cube Warehouse
(152)

Average Vehicle Trip Ends vs: 1000 Sq. Feet Gross Floor Area
On a: Sunday

Number of Studies: 9
Average 1000 Sq. Feet GFA: 732
Directional Distribution: 50% entering, 50% exiting

Trip Generation per 1000 Sq. Feet Gross Floor Area

Average Rate	Range of Rates	Standard Deviation
0.98	0.01 - 1.49	1.16

Data Plot and Equation

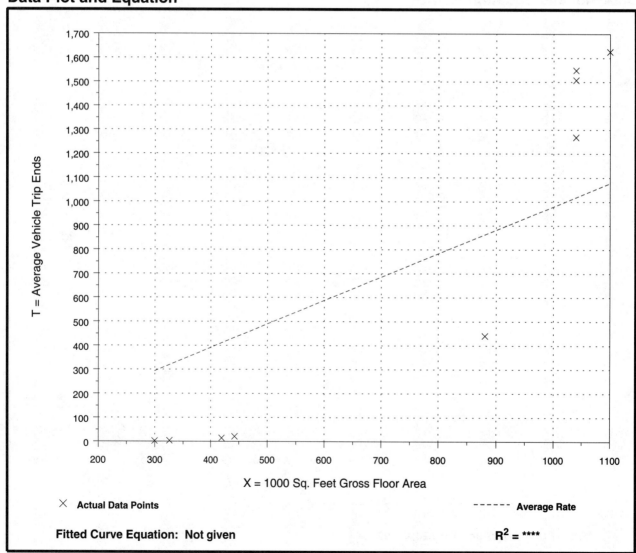

X Actual Data Points

----- Average Rate

Fitted Curve Equation: Not given

$R^2 = ****$

High-Cube Warehouse
(152)

Average Vehicle Trip Ends vs: 1000 Sq. Feet Gross Floor Area
On a: Sunday,
Peak Hour of Generator

Number of Studies: 7
Average 1000 Sq. Feet GFA: 835
Directional Distribution: 66% entering, 34% exiting

Trip Generation per 1000 Sq. Feet Gross Floor Area

Average Rate	Range of Rates	Standard Deviation
0.14	0.01 - 0.21	0.38

Data Plot and Equation

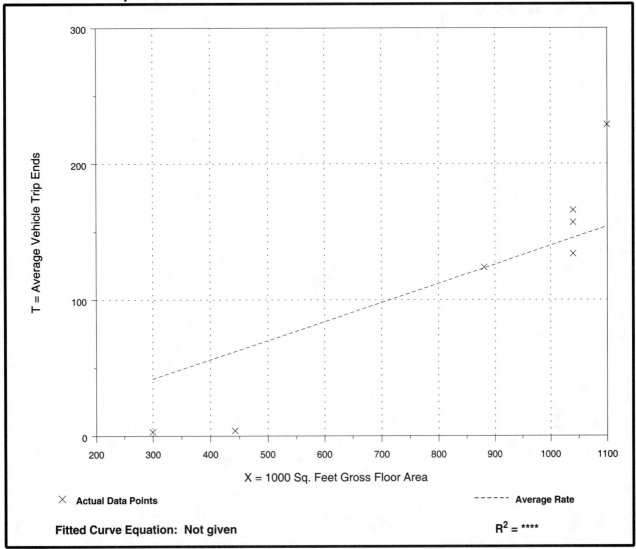

X Actual Data Points

----- Average Rate

Fitted Curve Equation: Not given

$R^2 = ****$

Land Use: 170
Utilities

Description

Utilities are free-standing buildings that contain electromechanical or industrial space/equipment. These facilities may also have storage areas and office space.

Additional Data

One of the sites surveyed was identified as a telephone company headquarters building.

The sites were surveyed between the late 1970s and the 2000s in California, Delaware, New York, Oregon and Washington.

Source Numbers

107, 192, 422, 443, 538

Land Use: 170
Utilities
Independent Variables with One Observation

The following trip generation data are for independent variables with only one observation. This information is shown in this table only; there are no related plots for these data.

Users are cautioned to use data with care because of the small sample size.

Day/Time Period	Trip Generation Rate	Size of Independent Variable	Number of Studies	Directional Distribution
Acres				
Weekday a.m. Peak Hour of Generator	6.93	8	1	63% entering, 37% exiting
Weekday p.m. Peak Hour of Adjacent Street Traffic	1.32	38	1	Not available

Utilities
(170)

Average Vehicle Trip Ends vs: **Employees**
On a: **Weekday,**
Peak Hour of Adjacent Street Traffic,
One Hour Between 7 and 9 a.m.

Number of Studies: 3
Avg. Number of Employees: 298
Directional Distribution: 90% entering, 10% exiting

Trip Generation per Employee

Average Rate	Range of Rates	Standard Deviation
0.76	0.66 - 0.94	0.87

Data Plot and Equation

Caution - Use Carefully - Small Sample Size

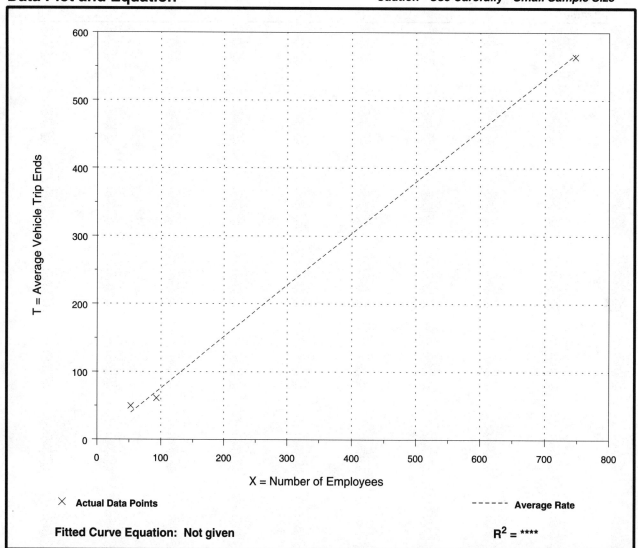

X **Actual Data Points**

- - - - - **Average Rate**

Fitted Curve Equation: Not given $R^2 = ****$

Utilities
(170)

Average Vehicle Trip Ends vs: **Employees**
On a: **Weekday,**
Peak Hour of Adjacent Street Traffic,
One Hour Between 4 and 6 p.m.

Number of Studies: 4
Avg. Number of Employees: 378
Directional Distribution: 15% entering, 85% exiting

Trip Generation per Employee

Average Rate	Range of Rates	Standard Deviation
0.76	0.54 - 0.91	0.88

Data Plot and Equation

Caution - Use Carefully - Small Sample Size

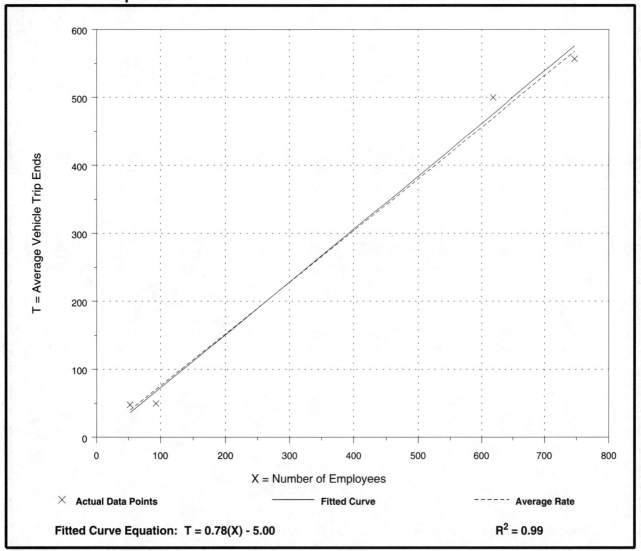

X = Number of Employees

✕ **Actual Data Points** ——— **Fitted Curve** - - - - - **Average Rate**

Fitted Curve Equation: T = 0.78(X) - 5.00 $R^2 = 0.99$

Utilities
(170)

Average Vehicle Trip Ends vs: **1000 Sq. Feet Gross Floor Area**
On a: **Weekday,**
Peak Hour of Adjacent Street Traffic,
One Hour Between 7 and 9 a.m.

Number of Studies: 2
Average 1000 Sq. Feet GFA: 69
Directional Distribution: Not available

Trip Generation per 1000 Sq. Feet Gross Floor Area

Average Rate	Range of Rates	Standard Deviation
0.80	0.49 - 3.65	*

Data Plot and Equation

Caution - Use Carefully - Small Sample Size

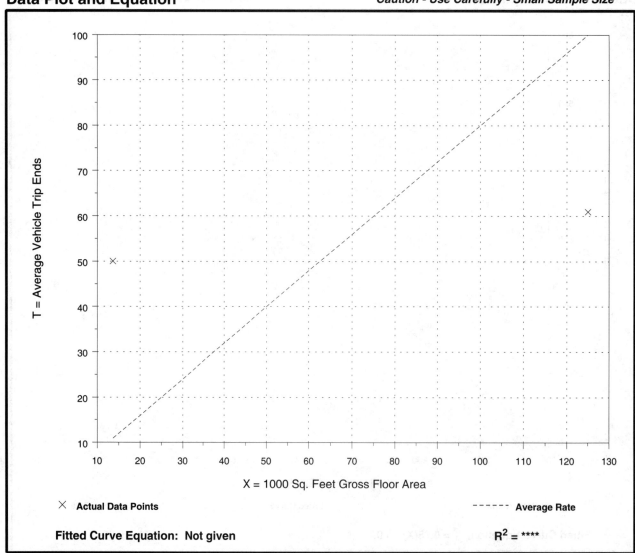

X **Actual Data Points**

----- **Average Rate**

Fitted Curve Equation: Not given $R^2 = ****$

Utilities
(170)

Average Vehicle Trip Ends vs: **1000 Sq. Feet Gross Floor Area**
On a: **Weekday,**
Peak Hour of Adjacent Street Traffic,
One Hour Between 4 and 6 p.m.

Number of Studies: 3
Average 1000 Sq. Feet GFA: 52
Directional Distribution: 45% entering, 55% exiting

Trip Generation per 1000 Sq. Feet Gross Floor Area

Average Rate	Range of Rates	Standard Deviation
0.76	0.40 - 3.50	1.23

Data Plot and Equation

Caution - Use Carefully - Small Sample Size

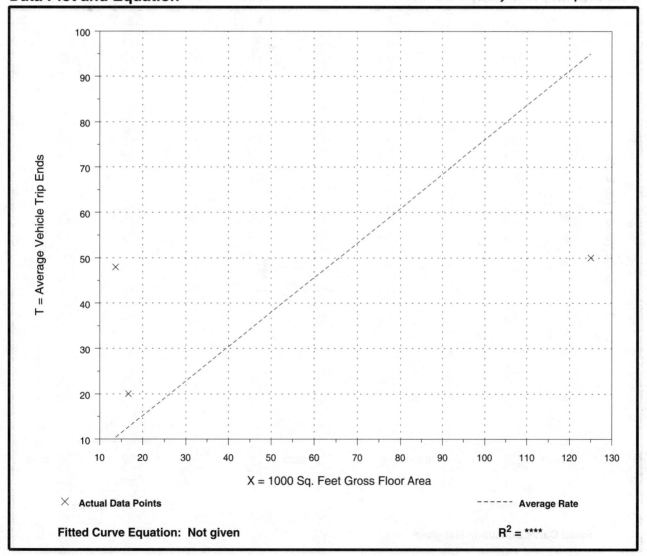

Fitted Curve Equation: Not given $R^2 = ****$

Utilities
(170)

Average Vehicle Trip Ends vs: **Acres**
On a: **Weekday,**
Peak Hour of Adjacent Street Traffic,
One Hour Between 7 and 9 a.m.

Number of Studies: 2
Average Number of Acres: 23
Directional Distribution: 63% entering, 37% exiting

Trip Generation per Acre

Average Rate	Range of Rates	Standard Deviation
2.49	1.61 - 6.93	*

Data Plot and Equation

Caution - Use Carefully - Small Sample Size

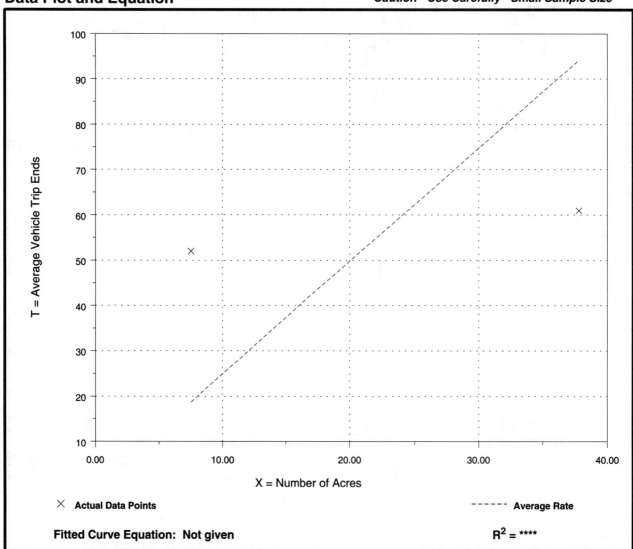

X **Actual Data Points**   - - - - - - **Average Rate**

Fitted Curve Equation: Not given $R^2 = ****$

Land Use: 210
Single-Family Detached Housing

Description

Single-family detached housing includes all single-family detached homes on individual lots. A typical site surveyed is a suburban subdivision.

Additional Data

The number of vehicles and residents had a high correlation with average weekday vehicle trip ends. The use of these variables was limited, however, because the number of vehicles and residents was often difficult to obtain or predict. The number of dwelling units was generally used as the independent variable of choice because it was usually readily available, easy to project and had a high correlation with average weekday vehicle trip ends.

This land use included data from a wide variety of units with different sizes, price ranges, locations and ages. Consequently, there was a wide variation in trips generated within this category. As expected, dwelling units that were larger in size, more expensive, or farther away from the central business district (CBD) had a higher rate of trip generation per unit than those smaller in size, less expensive, or closer to the CBD. Other factors, such as geographic location and type of adjacent and nearby development, may also have had an effect on the site trip generation.

Single-family detached units had the highest trip generation rate per dwelling unit of all residential uses because they were the largest units in size and had more residents and more vehicles per unit than other residential land uses; they were generally located farther away from shopping centers, employment areas and other trip attractors than other residential land uses; and they generally had fewer alternate modes of transportation available because they were typically not as concentrated as other residential land uses.

The peak hour of the generator typically coincided with the peak hour of the adjacent street traffic.

The sites were surveyed between the late 1960s and the 2000s throughout the United States and Canada.

Source Numbers

1, 4, 5, 6, 7, 8, 11, 12, 13, 14, 16, 19, 20, 21, 26, 34, 35, 36, 38, 40, 71, 72, 84, 91, 98, 100, 105, 108, 110, 114, 117, 119, 157, 167, 177, 187, 192, 207, 211, 246, 275, 283, 293, 300, 319, 320, 357, 384, 435, 550, 552, 579, 598, 601, 603, 611, 614, 637

Single-Family Detached Housing
(210)

Average Vehicle Trip Ends vs: Dwelling Units
On a: Weekday

Number of Studies: 351
Avg. Number of Dwelling Units: 197
Directional Distribution: 50% entering, 50% exiting

Trip Generation per Dwelling Unit

Average Rate	Range of Rates	Standard Deviation
9.57	4.31 - 21.85	3.69

Data Plot and Equation

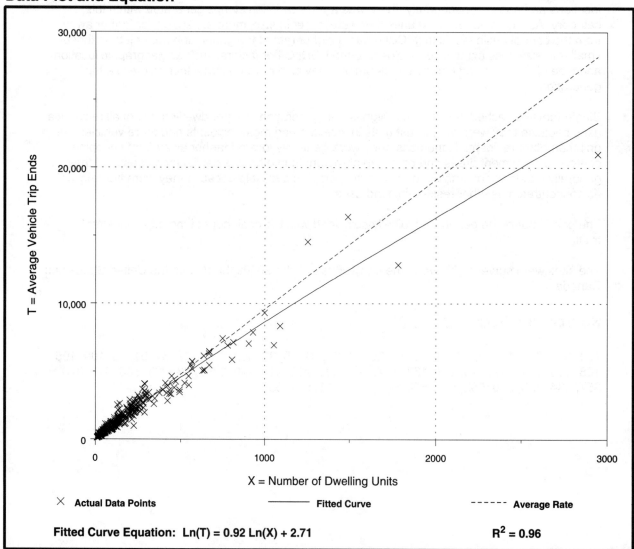

X **Actual Data Points**   ——— **Fitted Curve**   - - - - - **Average Rate**

Fitted Curve Equation: Ln(T) = 0.92 Ln(X) + 2.71 $R^2 = 0.96$

Single-Family Detached Housing
(210)

Average Vehicle Trip Ends vs: **Dwelling Units**
On a: **Weekday,**
Peak Hour of Adjacent Street Traffic,
One Hour Between 7 and 9 a.m.

Number of Studies: 286
Avg. Number of Dwelling Units: 194
Directional Distribution: 25% entering, 75% exiting

Trip Generation per Dwelling Unit

Average Rate	Range of Rates	Standard Deviation
0.75	0.33 - 2.27	0.90

Data Plot and Equation

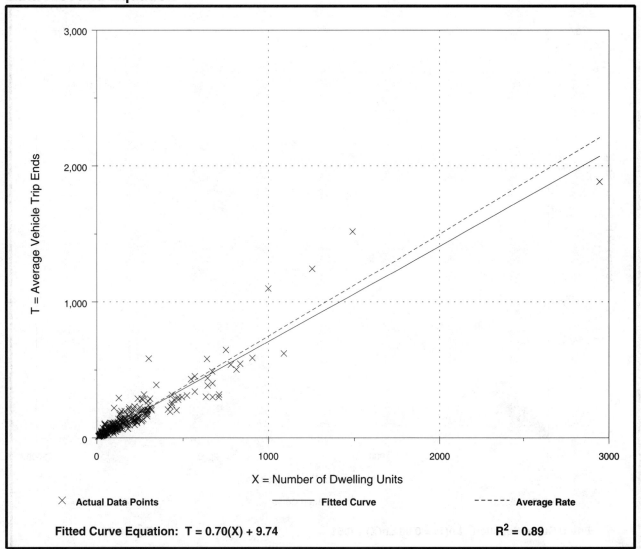

Fitted Curve Equation: T = 0.70(X) + 9.74 $R^2 = 0.89$

Single-Family Detached Housing
(210)

Average Vehicle Trip Ends vs:	**Dwelling Units**	
On a:	**Weekday,**	
	Peak Hour of Adjacent Street Traffic,	
	One Hour Between 4 and 6 p.m.	

Number of Studies: 314
Avg. Number of Dwelling Units: 208
Directional Distribution: 63% entering, 37% exiting

Trip Generation per Dwelling Unit

Average Rate	Range of Rates	Standard Deviation
1.01	0.42 - 2.98	1.05

Data Plot and Equation

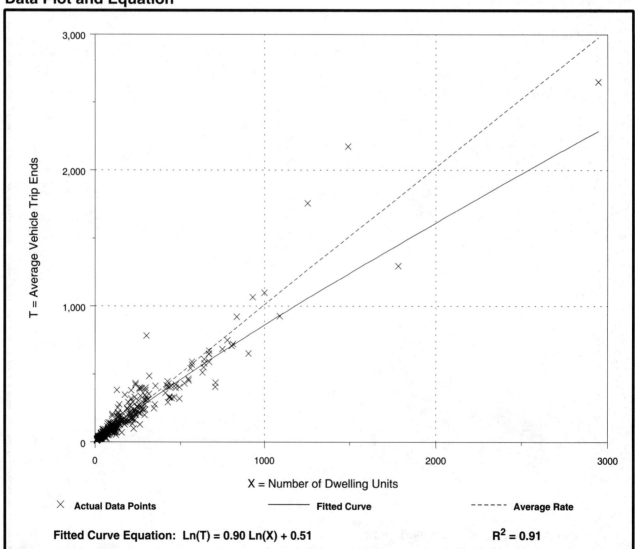

Fitted Curve Equation: $Ln(T) = 0.90\ Ln(X) + 0.51$ $R^2 = 0.91$

Single-Family Detached Housing
(210)

Average Vehicle Trip Ends vs: Dwelling Units
On a: Weekday,
A.M. Peak Hour of Generator

Number of Studies: 341
Avg. Number of Dwelling Units: 181
Directional Distribution: 26% entering, 74% exiting

Trip Generation per Dwelling Unit

Average Rate	Range of Rates	Standard Deviation
0.77	0.33 - 2.27	0.91

Data Plot and Equation

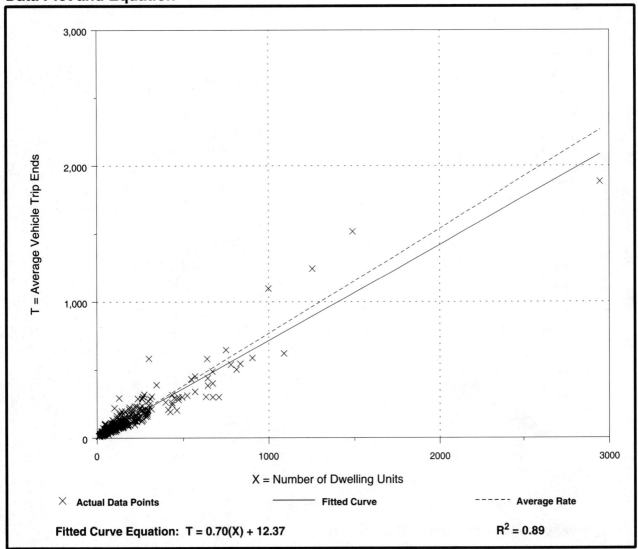

Fitted Curve Equation: T = 0.70(X) + 12.37 $R^2 = 0.89$

Single-Family Detached Housing
(210)

Average Vehicle Trip Ends vs:	**Dwelling Units**
On a:	**Weekday,**
	P.M. Peak Hour of Generator

Number of Studies: 360
Avg. Number of Dwelling Units: 174
Directional Distribution: 64% entering, 36% exiting

Trip Generation per Dwelling Unit

Average Rate	Range of Rates	Standard Deviation
1.02	0.42 - 2.98	1.05

Data Plot and Equation

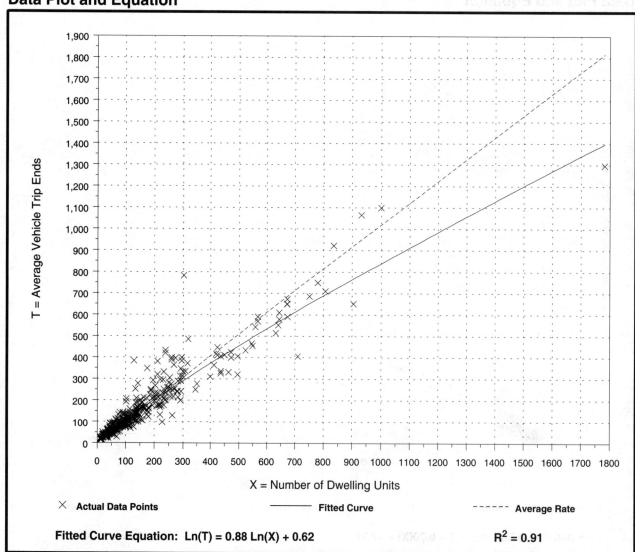

X **Actual Data Points**   ——— **Fitted Curve**   - - - - **Average Rate**

Fitted Curve Equation: Ln(T) = 0.88 Ln(X) + 0.62 $R^2 = 0.91$

Single-Family Detached Housing
(210)

Average Vehicle Trip Ends vs: **Dwelling Units**
On a: **Saturday**

Number of Studies: 74
Avg. Number of Dwelling Units: 213
Directional Distribution: 50% entering, 50% exiting

Trip Generation per Dwelling Unit

Average Rate	Range of Rates	Standard Deviation
10.08	5.32 - 15.25	3.68

Data Plot and Equation

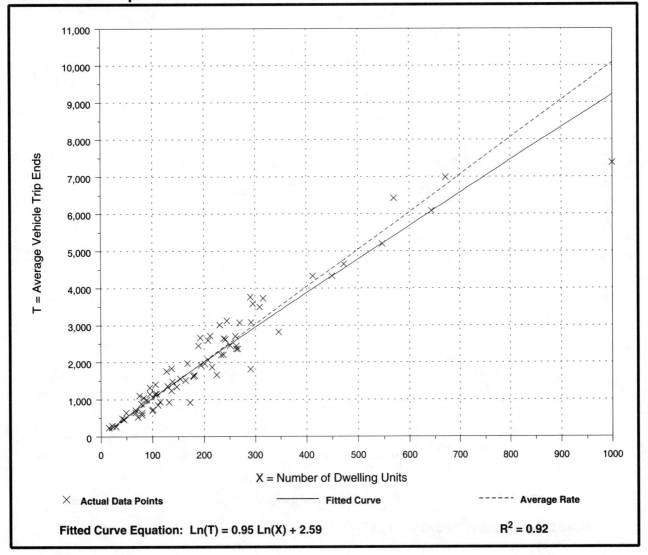

X Actual Data Points   ——— Fitted Curve   - - - - - Average Rate

Fitted Curve Equation: $Ln(T) = 0.95 \, Ln(X) + 2.59$ $R^2 = 0.92$

Single-Family Detached Housing
(210)

Average Vehicle Trip Ends vs: **Dwelling Units**
On a: **Saturday,**
Peak Hour of Generator

Number of Studies: 53
Avg. Number of Dwelling Units: 217
Directional Distribution: 53% entering, 47% exiting

Trip Generation per Dwelling Unit

Average Rate	Range of Rates	Standard Deviation
0.93	0.50 - 1.75	0.99

Data Plot and Equation

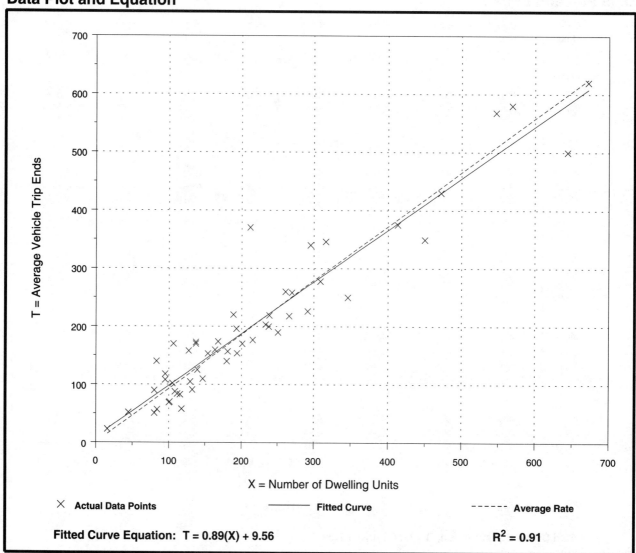

X   **Actual Data Points**   ——— **Fitted Curve**   - - - - - **Average Rate**

Fitted Curve Equation: T = 0.89(X) + 9.56 $R^2 = 0.91$

Single-Family Detached Housing
(210)

Average Vehicle Trip Ends vs: Dwelling Units
On a: Sunday

Number of Studies: 70
Avg. Number of Dwelling Units: 216
Directional Distribution: 50% entering, 50% exiting

Trip Generation per Dwelling Unit

Average Rate	Range of Rates	Standard Deviation
8.77	4.74 - 12.31	3.33

Data Plot and Equation

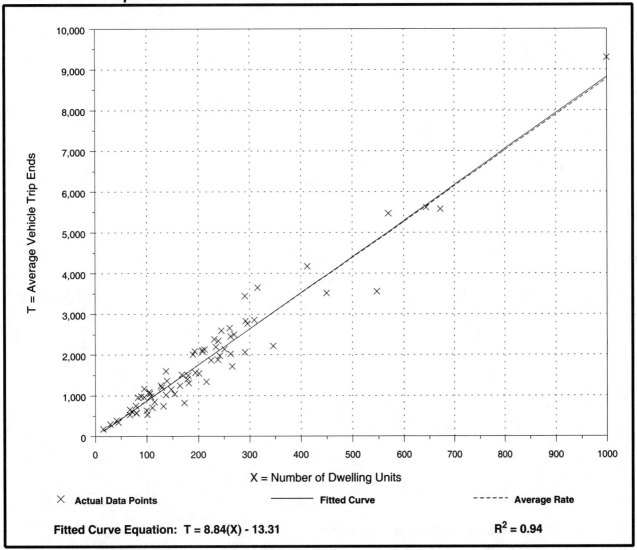

X = Number of Dwelling Units

$\times$ **Actual Data Points**   —— **Fitted Curve**   - - - - - **Average Rate**

Fitted Curve Equation: T = 8.84(X) - 13.31 $R^2 = 0.94$

Single-Family Detached Housing
(210)

Average Vehicle Trip Ends vs: **Dwelling Units**
On a: **Sunday,**
Peak Hour of Generator

Number of Studies: 52
Avg. Number of Dwelling Units: 215
Directional Distribution: 53% entering, 47% exiting

Trip Generation per Dwelling Unit

Average Rate	Range of Rates	Standard Deviation
0.86	0.55 - 1.48	0.95

Data Plot and Equation

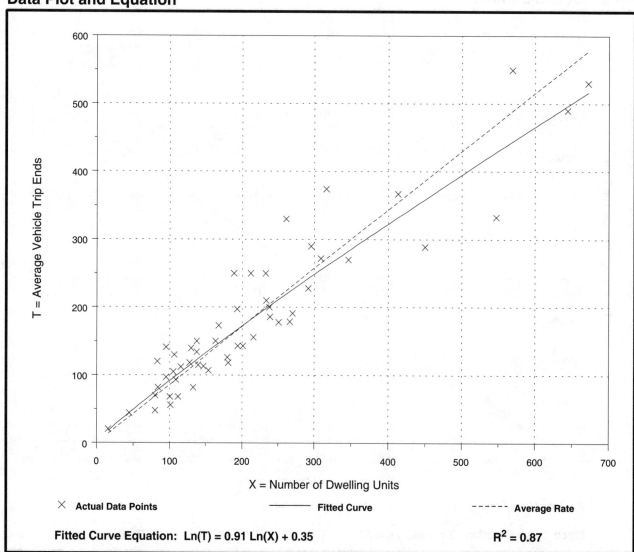

X   **Actual Data Points**   ——— **Fitted Curve**   - - - - - **Average Rate**

Fitted Curve Equation: $Ln(T) = 0.91 \, Ln(X) + 0.35$ $R^2 = 0.87$

Single-Family Detached Housing
(210)

Average Vehicle Trip Ends vs: **Persons**
On a: **Weekday**

Number of Studies: 185
Average Number of Persons: 557
Directional Distribution: 50% entering, 50% exiting

Trip Generation per Person

Average Rate	Range of Rates	Standard Deviation
2.55	1.16 - 5.62	1.69

Data Plot and Equation

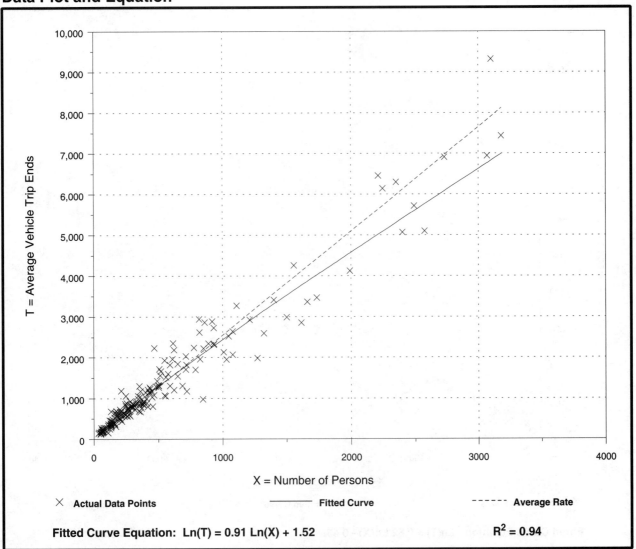

Fitted Curve Equation: Ln(T) = 0.91 Ln(X) + 1.52 $R^2 = 0.94$

Single-Family Detached Housing
(210)

Average Vehicle Trip Ends vs: Persons
On a: Weekday,
Peak Hour of Adjacent Street Traffic,
One Hour Between 7 and 9 a.m.

Number of Studies: 111
Average Number of Persons: 632
Directional Distribution: 31% entering, 69% exiting

Trip Generation per Person

Average Rate	Range of Rates	Standard Deviation
0.21	0.10 - 0.56	0.46

Data Plot and Equation

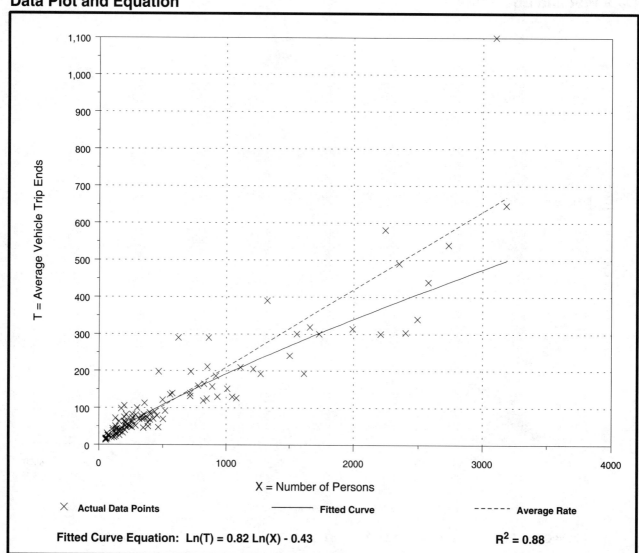

X Actual Data Points   **—— Fitted Curve**   **- - - - - Average Rate**

Fitted Curve Equation: Ln(T) = 0.82 Ln(X) - 0.43 $R^2 = 0.88$

Single-Family Detached Housing
(210)

Average Vehicle Trip Ends vs: **Persons**
On a: **Weekday,**
Peak Hour of Adjacent Street Traffic,
One Hour Between 4 and 6 p.m.

Number of Studies: 111
Average Number of Persons: 629
Directional Distribution: 66% entering, 34% exiting

Trip Generation per Person

Average Rate	Range of Rates	Standard Deviation
0.28	0.12 - 0.68	0.53

Data Plot and Equation

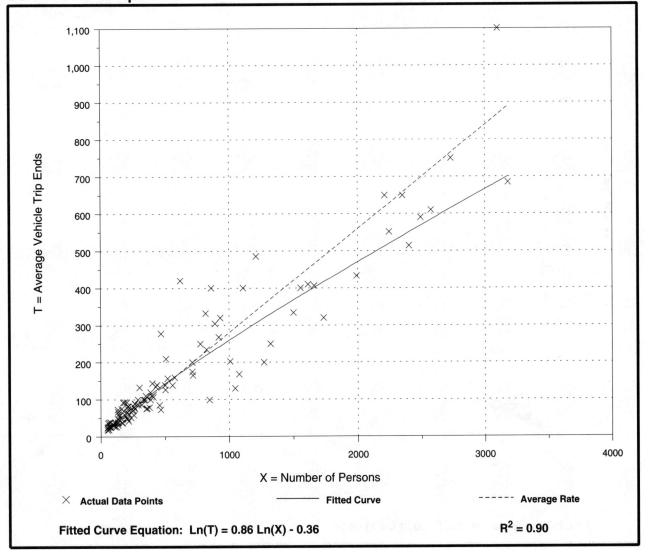

Fitted Curve Equation: $Ln(T) = 0.86\ Ln(X) - 0.36$ $R^2 = 0.90$

Single-Family Detached Housing
(210)

Average Vehicle Trip Ends vs: Persons
On a: Weekday,
A.M. Peak Hour of Generator

Number of Studies: 175
Average Number of Persons: 559
Directional Distribution: 30% entering, 70% exiting

Trip Generation per Person

Average Rate	Range of Rates	Standard Deviation
0.21	0.11 - 0.56	0.46

Data Plot and Equation

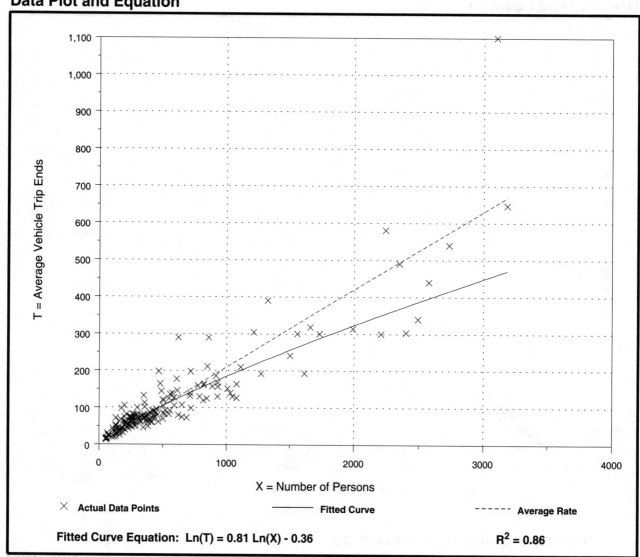

Fitted Curve Equation: $Ln(T) = 0.81\ Ln(X) - 0.36$ $R^2 = 0.86$

Single-Family Detached Housing
(210)

Average Vehicle Trip Ends vs: Persons
On a: Weekday,
P.M. Peak Hour of Generator

Number of Studies: 174
Average Number of Persons: 557
Directional Distribution: 66% entering, 34% exiting

Trip Generation per Person

Average Rate	Range of Rates	Standard Deviation
0.27	0.12 - 0.68	0.53

Data Plot and Equation

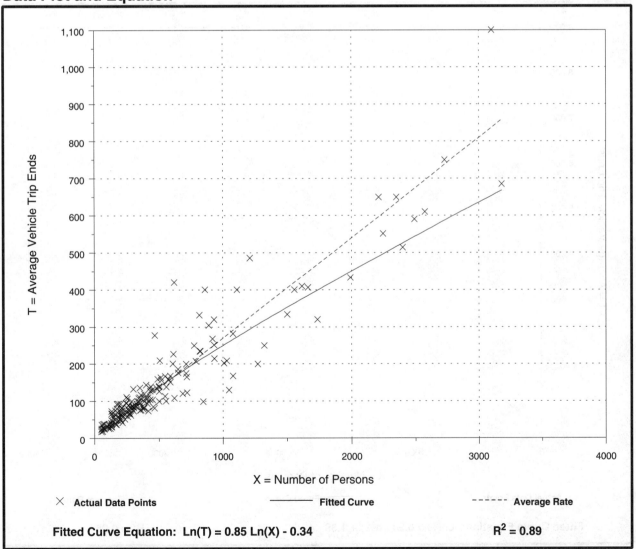

X = Number of Persons

| × Actual Data Points | —— Fitted Curve | ----- Average Rate |

Fitted Curve Equation: Ln(T) = 0.85 Ln(X) - 0.34 $R^2 = 0.89$

Single-Family Detached Housing
(210)

Average Vehicle Trip Ends vs: Persons
On a: Saturday

Number of Studies: 23
Average Number of Persons: 1,028
Directional Distribution: 50% entering, 50% exiting

Trip Generation per Person

Average Rate	Range of Rates	Standard Deviation
2.66	1.43 - 3.68	1.70

Data Plot and Equation

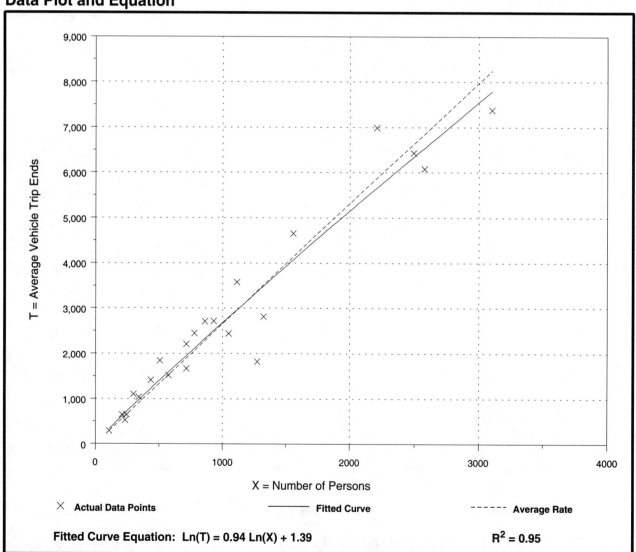

Fitted Curve Equation: $Ln(T) = 0.94 Ln(X) + 1.39$ $\qquad$ $R^2 = 0.95$

Single-Family Detached Housing
(210)

Average Vehicle Trip Ends vs: **Persons**
On a: **Saturday,**
Peak Hour of Generator

Number of Studies: 17
Average Number of Persons: 1,027
Directional Distribution: 54% entering, 46% exiting

Trip Generation per Person

Average Rate	Range of Rates	Standard Deviation
0.27	0.19 - 0.41	0.52

Data Plot and Equation

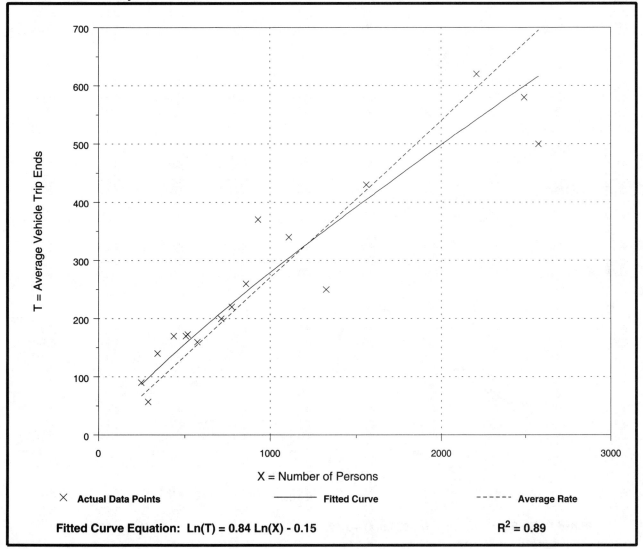

Fitted Curve Equation: Ln(T) = 0.84 Ln(X) - 0.15 $R^2 = 0.89$

Single-Family Detached Housing
(210)

Average Vehicle Trip Ends vs: Persons
On a: Sunday

Number of Studies: 19
Average Number of Persons: 1,130
Directional Distribution: 50% entering, 50% exiting

Trip Generation per Person

Average Rate	Range of Rates	Standard Deviation
2.42	1.62 - 3.16	1.61

Data Plot and Equation

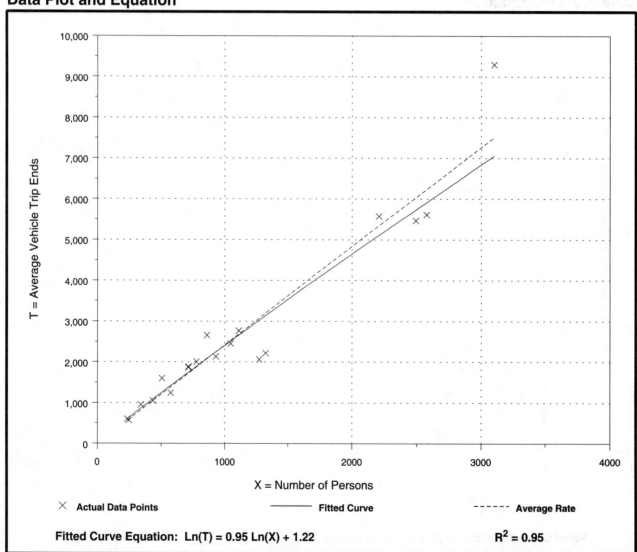

Fitted Curve Equation: Ln(T) = 0.95 Ln(X) + 1.22 $R^2 = 0.95$

Single-Family Detached Housing
(210)

Average Vehicle Trip Ends vs: **Persons**
On a: **Sunday,**
Peak Hour of Generator

Number of Studies: 17
Average Number of Persons: 984
Directional Distribution: 50% entering, 50% exiting

Trip Generation per Person

Average Rate	Range of Rates	Standard Deviation
0.25	0.19 - 0.38	0.51

Data Plot and Equation

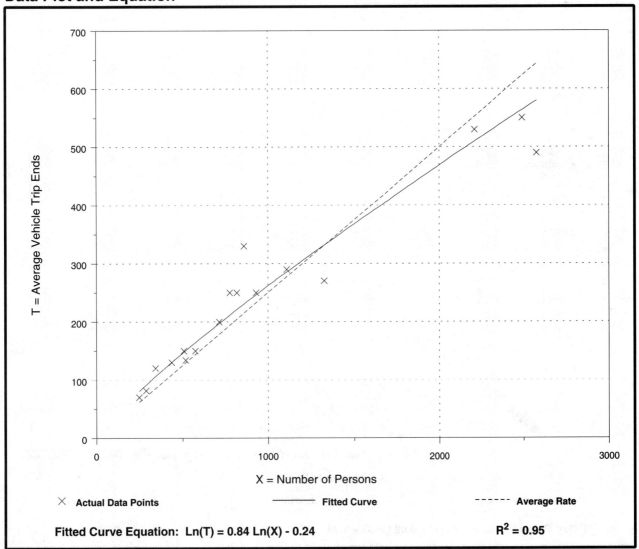

X   **Actual Data Points**   ——— **Fitted Curve**   - - - - **Average Rate**

Fitted Curve Equation: Ln(T) = 0.84 Ln(X) - 0.24 $R^2 = 0.95$

Single-Family Detached Housing
(210)

Average Vehicle Trip Ends vs: Vehicles
On a: Weekday

Number of Studies: 120
Average Number of Vehicles: 257
Directional Distribution: 50% entering, 50% exiting

Trip Generation per Vehicle

Average Rate	Range of Rates	Standard Deviation
6.02	2.69 - 9.38	2.77

Data Plot and Equation

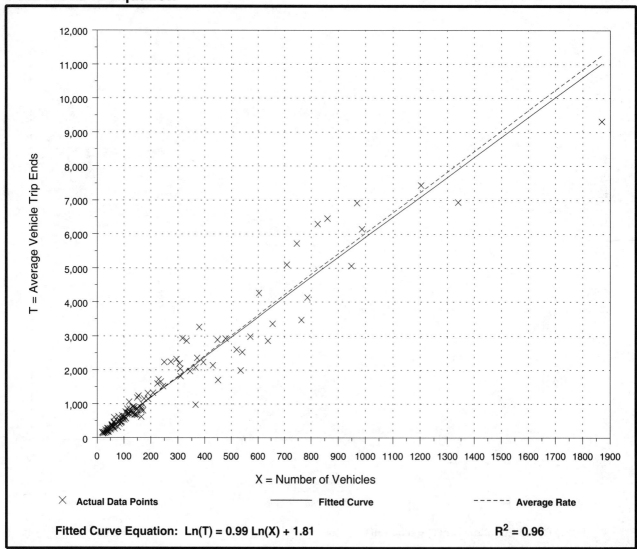

Fitted Curve Equation: Ln(T) = 0.99 Ln(X) + 1.81 $R^2 = 0.96$

Single-Family Detached Housing
(210)

Average Vehicle Trip Ends vs: Vehicles
On a: Weekday,
Peak Hour of Adjacent Street Traffic,
One Hour Between 7 and 9 a.m.

Number of Studies: 110
Average Number of Vehicles: 262
Directional Distribution: 31% entering, 69% exiting

Trip Generation per Vehicle

Average Rate	Range of Rates	Standard Deviation
0.51	0.24 - 1.38	0.73

Data Plot and Equation

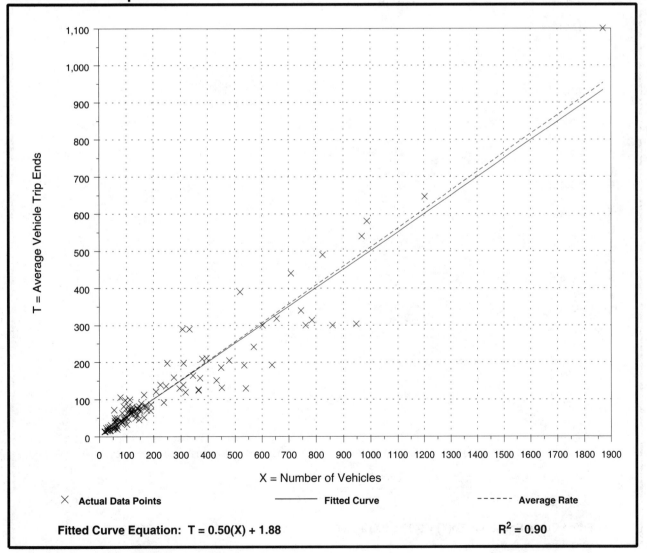

Fitted Curve Equation: T = 0.50(X) + 1.88 $R^2 = 0.90$

Single-Family Detached Housing
(210)

Average Vehicle Trip Ends vs:	Vehicles
On a:	Weekday,
	Peak Hour of Adjacent Street Traffic,
	One Hour Between 4 and 6 p.m.

Number of Studies: 110
Average Number of Vehicles: 260
Directional Distribution: 66% entering, 34% exiting

Trip Generation per Vehicle

Average Rate	Range of Rates	Standard Deviation
0.67	0.24 - 1.37	0.84

Data Plot and Equation

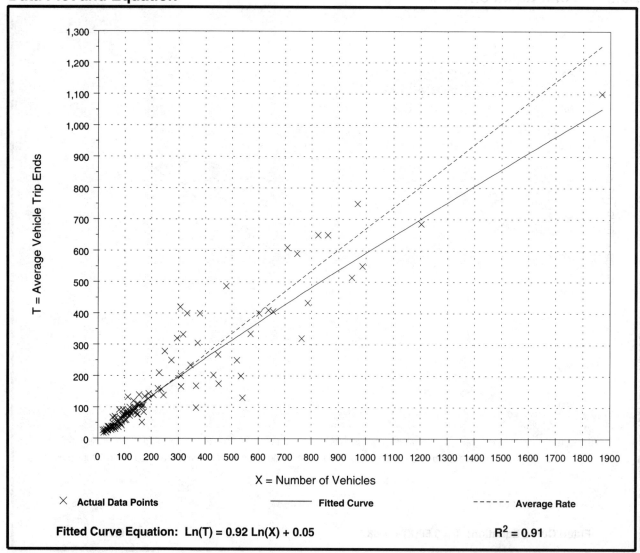

X = Number of Vehicles

✕ Actual Data Points ———— Fitted Curve - - - - - Average Rate

Fitted Curve Equation: Ln(T) = 0.92 Ln(X) + 0.05 $R^2 = 0.91$

Single-Family Detached Housing
(210)

Average Vehicle Trip Ends vs: **Vehicles**
On a: **Weekday,**
A.M. Peak Hour of Generator

Number of Studies: 111
Average Number of Vehicles: 261
Directional Distribution: 30% entering, 70% exiting

Trip Generation per Vehicle

Average Rate	Range of Rates	Standard Deviation
0.51	0.24 - 1.38	0.73

Data Plot and Equation

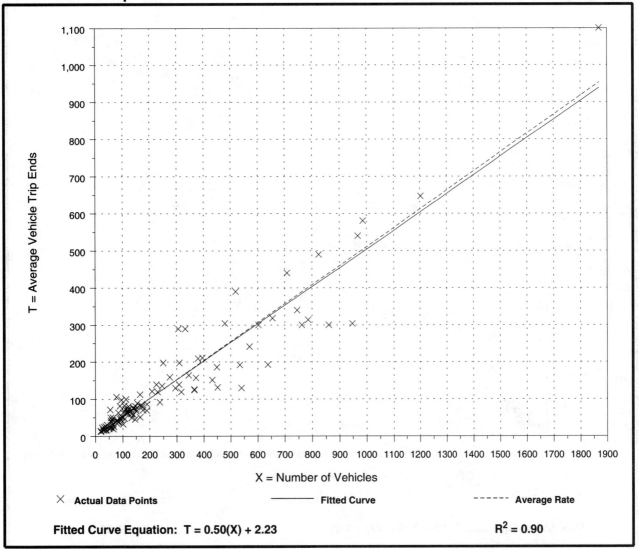

Fitted Curve Equation: $T = 0.50(X) + 2.23$ $R^2 = 0.90$

Single-Family Detached Housing
(210)

Average Vehicle Trip Ends vs: **Vehicles**
On a: **Weekday,**
P.M. Peak Hour of Generator

Number of Studies: 110
Average Number of Vehicles: 260
Directional Distribution: 66% entering, 34% exiting

Trip Generation per Vehicle

Average Rate	Range of Rates	Standard Deviation
0.67	0.24 - 1.37	0.84

Data Plot and Equation

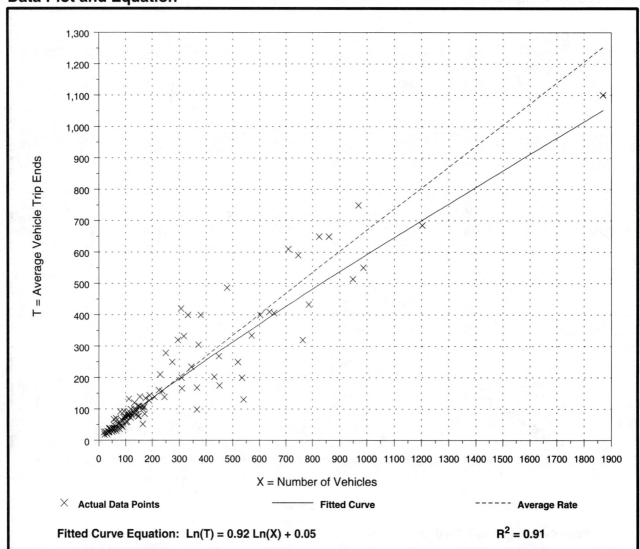

X **Actual Data Points**   ——— **Fitted Curve**   - - - - - **Average Rate**

Fitted Curve Equation: $Ln(T) = 0.92 \, Ln(X) + 0.05$ $R^2 = 0.91$

Single-Family Detached Housing
(210)

Average Vehicle Trip Ends vs: **Vehicles**
On a: **Saturday**

Number of Studies: 23
Average Number of Vehicles: 418
Directional Distribution: 50% entering, 50% exiting

Trip Generation per Vehicle

Average Rate	Range of Rates	Standard Deviation
6.55	3.20 - 11.60	3.40

Data Plot and Equation

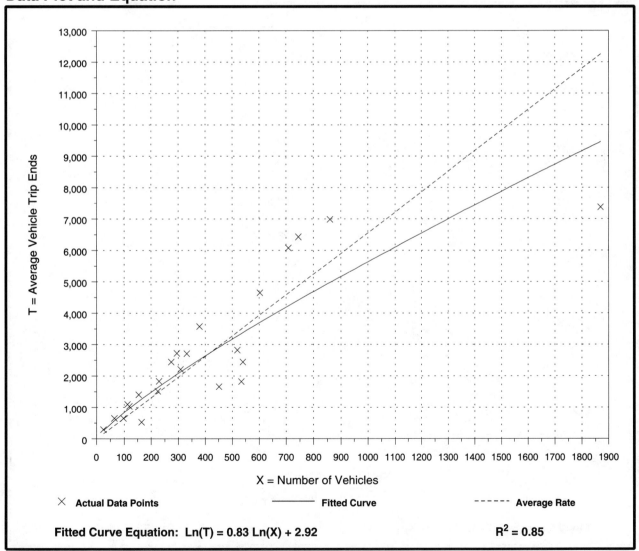

X = Number of Vehicles

$\times$ **Actual Data Points** ——— **Fitted Curve** ----- **Average Rate**

Fitted Curve Equation: Ln(T) = 0.83 Ln(X) + 2.92 $R^2 = 0.85$

Single-Family Detached Housing
(210)

Average Vehicle Trip Ends vs: Vehicles
On a: Saturday,
Peak Hour of Generator

Number of Studies: 17
Average Number of Vehicles: 366
Directional Distribution: 54% entering, 46% exiting

Trip Generation per Vehicle

Average Rate	Range of Rates	Standard Deviation
0.76	0.35 - 1.41	0.89

Data Plot and Equation

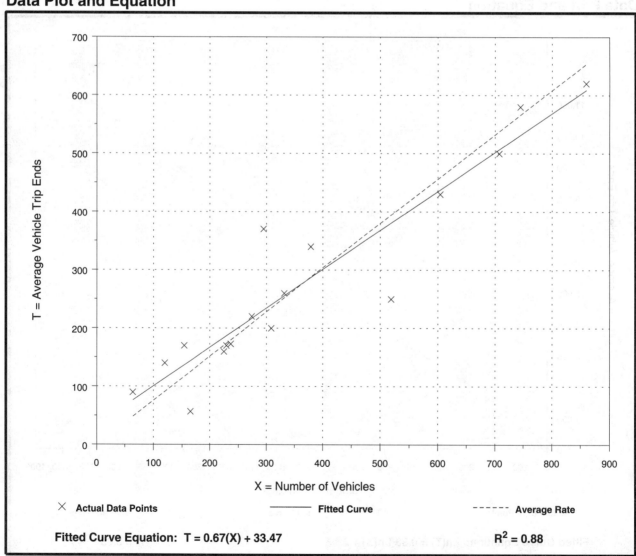

X **Actual Data Points**   ———— **Fitted Curve**   - - - - - **Average Rate**

Fitted Curve Equation: T = 0.67(X) + 33.47 $R^2 = 0.88$

Single-Family Detached Housing
(210)

Average Vehicle Trip Ends vs: **Vehicles**
On a: **Sunday**

Number of Studies: 19
Average Number of Vehicles: 462
Directional Distribution: 50% entering, 50% exiting

Trip Generation per Vehicle

Average Rate	Range of Rates	Standard Deviation
5.93	3.67 - 8.91	2.82

Data Plot and Equation

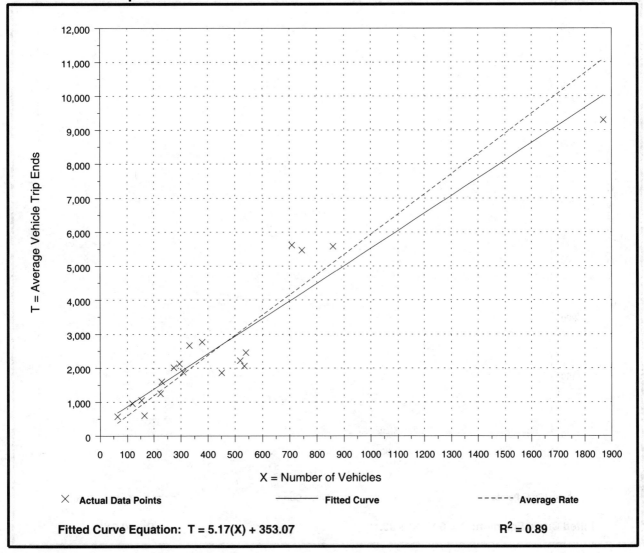

Fitted Curve Equation: $T = 5.17(X) + 353.07$ $R^2 = 0.89$

Single-Family Detached Housing
(210)

Average Vehicle Trip Ends vs: **Vehicles**
On a: **Sunday,**
Peak Hour of Generator

Number of Studies: 17
Average Number of Vehicles: 349
Directional Distribution: 50% entering, 50% exiting

Trip Generation per Vehicle

Average Rate	Range of Rates	Standard Deviation
0.72	0.50 - 1.09	0.86

Data Plot and Equation

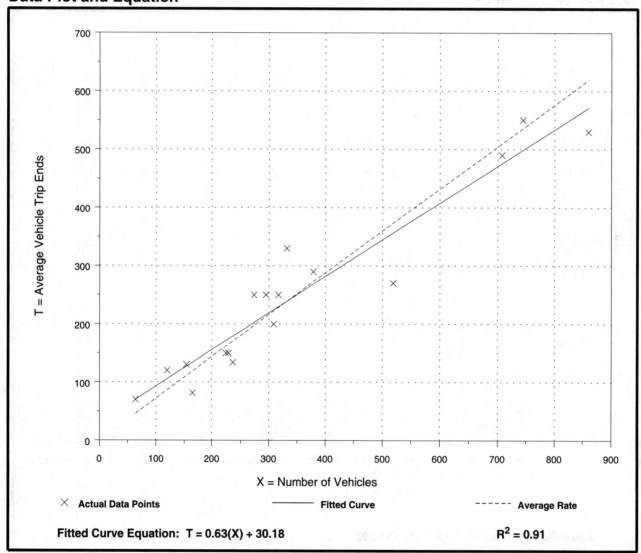

✕ Actual Data Points	—— Fitted Curve	- - - - Average Rate

Fitted Curve Equation: T = 0.63(X) + 30.18 $R^2 = 0.91$

Single-Family Detached Housing
(210)

Average Vehicle Trip Ends vs: **Acres**
On a: **Weekday**

Number of Studies: 144
Average Number of Acres: 70
Directional Distribution: 50% entering, 50% exiting

Trip Generation per Acre

Average Rate	Range of Rates	Standard Deviation
26.04	3.17 - 84.94	19.62

Data Plot and Equation

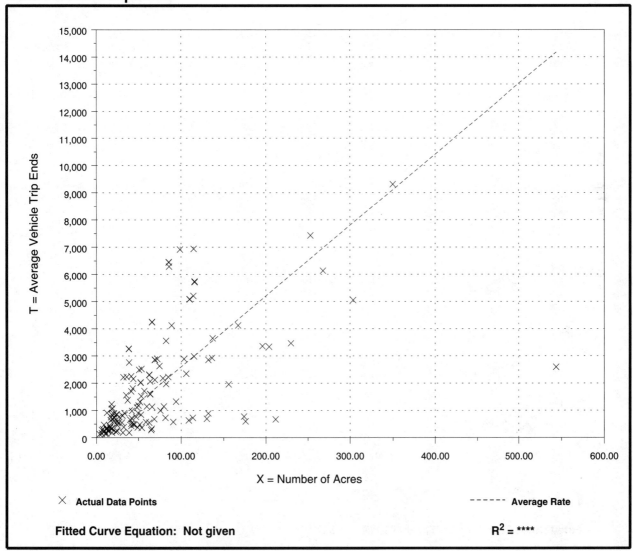

X **Actual Data Points**   - - - - - **Average Rate**

Fitted Curve Equation: Not given R^2 = ****

Single-Family Detached Housing
(210)

Average Vehicle Trip Ends vs: **Acres**
On a: **Weekday,**
Peak Hour of Adjacent Street Traffic,
One Hour Between 7 and 9 a.m.

Number of Studies: 123
Average Number of Acres: 71
Directional Distribution: 31% entering, 69% exiting

Trip Generation per Acre

Average Rate	Range of Rates	Standard Deviation
2.06	0.28 - 6.59	1.97

Data Plot and Equation

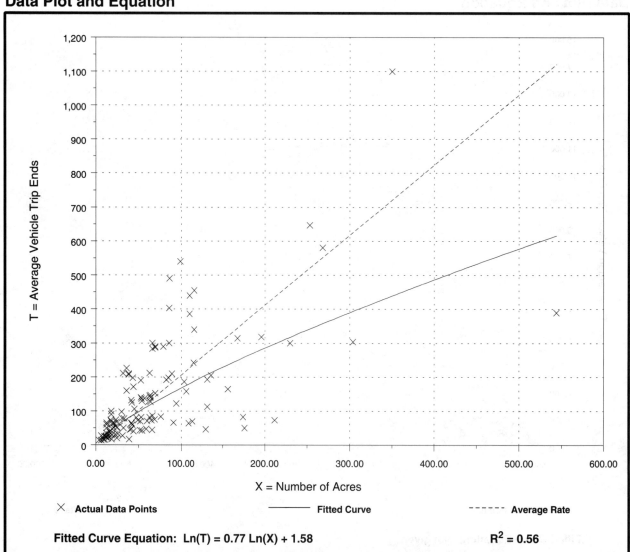

Fitted Curve Equation: $Ln(T) = 0.77 \, Ln(X) + 1.58$ $R^2 = 0.56$

Single-Family Detached Housing
(210)

Average Vehicle Trip Ends vs: **Acres**
On a: **Weekday,**
Peak Hour of Adjacent Street Traffic,
One Hour Between 4 and 6 p.m.

Number of Studies: 124
Average Number of Acres: 70
Directional Distribution: 66% entering, 34% exiting

Trip Generation per Acre

Average Rate	Range of Rates	Standard Deviation
2.74	0.36 - 10.39	2.65

Data Plot and Equation

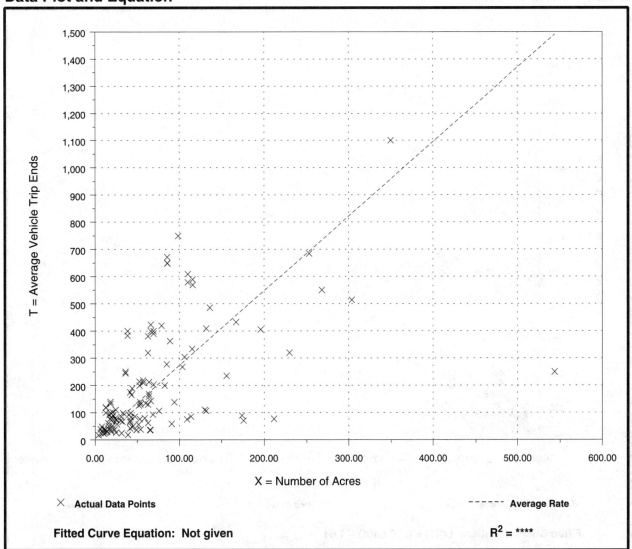

Fitted Curve Equation: Not given $R^2 = ****$

Single-Family Detached Housing
(210)

Average Vehicle Trip Ends vs: **Acres**
On a: **Weekday,**
A.M. Peak Hour of Generator

Number of Studies: 132
Average Number of Acres: 69
Directional Distribution: 30% entering, 70% exiting

Trip Generation per Acre

Average Rate	Range of Rates	Standard Deviation
2.08	0.28 - 6.59	1.99

Data Plot and Equation

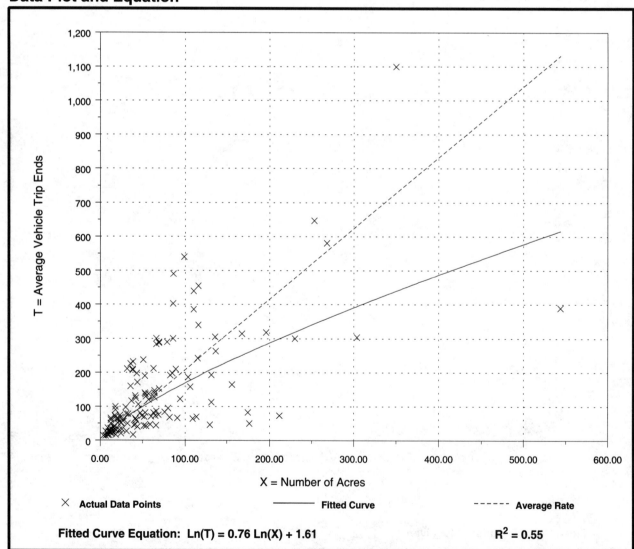

X = Number of Acres

✕ **Actual Data Points**   ——— **Fitted Curve**   - - - - - **Average Rate**

Fitted Curve Equation: Ln(T) = 0.76 Ln(X) + 1.61   **$R^2 = 0.55$**

Single-Family Detached Housing
(210)

Average Vehicle Trip Ends vs: **Acres**
On a: **Weekday,**
P.M. Peak Hour of Generator

Number of Studies: 132
Average Number of Acres: 69
Directional Distribution: 66% entering, 34% exiting

Trip Generation per Acre

Average Rate	Range of Rates	Standard Deviation
2.73	0.36 - 10.39	2.64

Data Plot and Equation

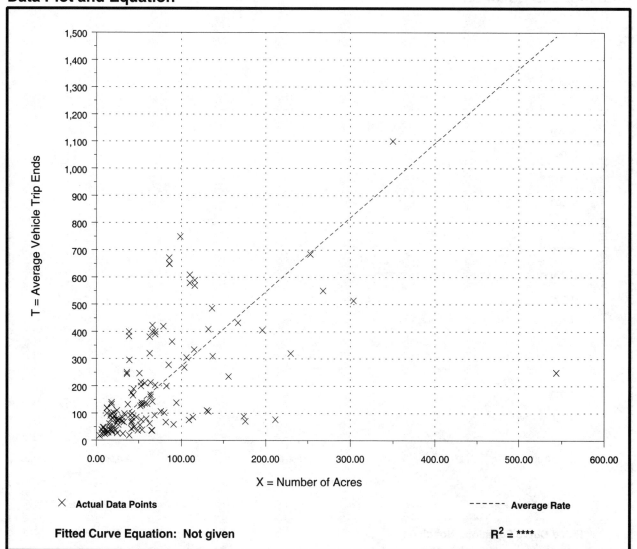

X **Actual Data Points**   - - - - - **Average Rate**

Fitted Curve Equation: Not given $R^2 =$ ****

Single-Family Detached Housing
(210)

Average Vehicle Trip Ends vs: **Acres**
On a: **Saturday**

Number of Studies: 37
Average Number of Acres: 75
Directional Distribution: 50% entering, 50% exiting

Trip Generation per Acre

Average Rate	Range of Rates	Standard Deviation
31.02	3.69 - 92.99	24.43

Data Plot and Equation

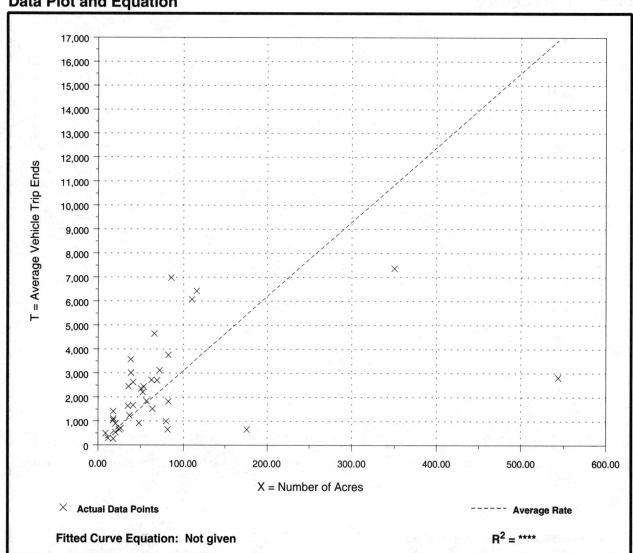

X **Actual Data Points**   - - - - - **Average Rate**

Fitted Curve Equation: Not given $R^2 = ****$

Single-Family Detached Housing
(210)

Average Vehicle Trip Ends vs: **Acres**
On a: **Saturday,**
Peak Hour of Generator

Number of Studies: 15
Average Number of Acres: 101
Directional Distribution: 54% entering, 46% exiting

Trip Generation per Acre

Average Rate	Range of Rates	Standard Deviation
2.97	0.46 - 9.44	3.20

Data Plot and Equation

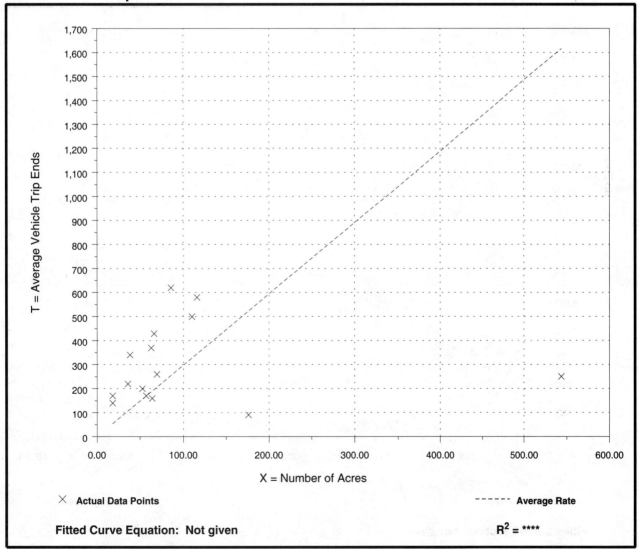

Fitted Curve Equation: Not given $R^2 = ****$

Single-Family Detached Housing
(210)

Average Vehicle Trip Ends vs: Acres
On a: Sunday

Number of Studies: 33
Average Number of Acres: 80
Directional Distribution: 50% entering, 50% exiting

Trip Generation per Acre

Average Rate	Range of Rates	Standard Deviation
27.02	3.24 - 71.95	19.90

Data Plot and Equation

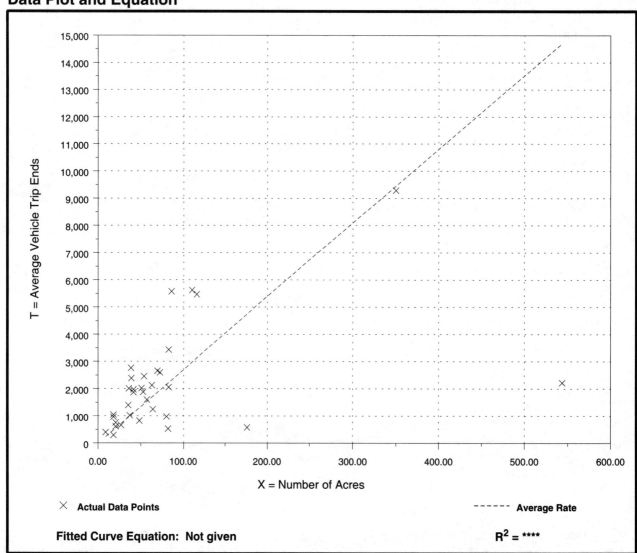

X **Actual Data Points**   - - - - - **Average Rate**

Fitted Curve Equation: Not given $R^2 = ****$

Single-Family Detached Housing
(210)

Average Vehicle Trip Ends vs: **Acres**
On a: **Sunday,**
Peak Hour of Generator

Number of Studies: 14
Average Number of Acres: 103
Directional Distribution: 50% entering, 50% exiting

Trip Generation per Acre

Average Rate	Range of Rates	Standard Deviation
2.61	0.40 - 7.53	2.86

Data Plot and Equation

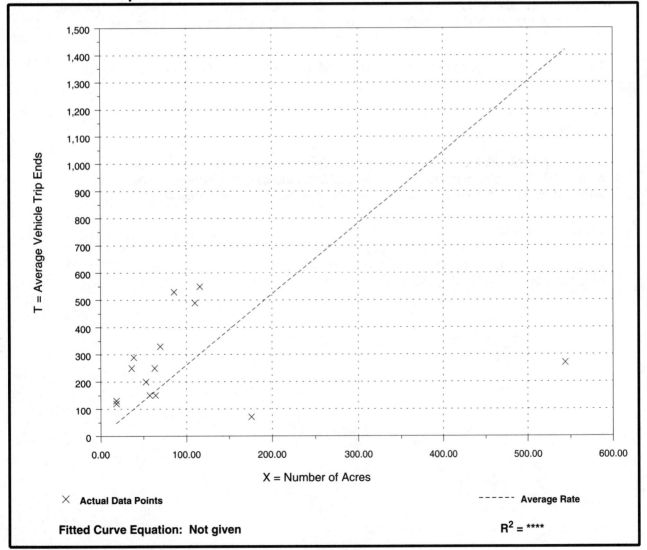

X **Actual Data Points**   - - - - - **Average Rate**

Fitted Curve Equation: Not given $R^2 = ****$

Land Use: 220
Apartment

Description

Apartments are rental dwelling units located within the same building with at least three other dwelling units, for example, quadraplexes and all types of apartment buildings. The studies included in this land use did not identify whether the apartments were low-rise, mid-rise, or high-rise. Low-rise apartment (Land Use 221), high-rise apartment (Land Use 222) and mid-rise apartment (Land Use 223) are related uses.

Additional Data

This land use included data from a wide variety of units with different sizes, price ranges, locations and ages. Consequently, there was a wide variation in trips generated within this category. As expected, dwelling units that were larger in size, more expensive, or farther away from the central business district (CBD) had a higher rate of trip generation per unit than those smaller in size, less expensive, or closer to the CBD. Other factors, such as geographic location and type of adjacent and nearby development, may also have had an effect on the site trip generation.

The peak hour of the generator typically coincided with the peak hour of the adjacent street traffic.

The sites were surveyed between the late 1960s and the 2000s throughout the United States and Canada.

Many of the studies included in this land use did not indicate the total number of bedrooms. To assist in the future analysis of this land use, it is important that this information be collected and included in trip generation data submissions.

Source Numbers

2, 4, 5, 6, 9, 10, 11, 12, 13, 14, 16, 19, 20, 34, 35, 40, 72, 91, 100, 108, 188, 192, 204, 211, 253, 283, 357, 436, 525, 530, 579, 583, 638

Apartment
(220)

Average Vehicle Trip Ends vs: Dwelling Units
On a: Weekday

Number of Studies: 88
Avg. Number of Dwelling Units: 210
Directional Distribution: 50% entering, 50% exiting

Trip Generation per Dwelling Unit

Average Rate	Range of Rates	Standard Deviation
6.65	1.27 - 12.50	3.07

Data Plot and Equation

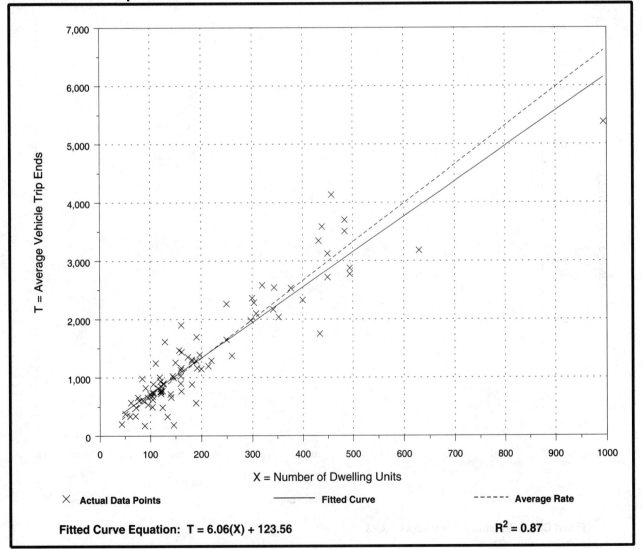

X Actual Data Points   ——— **Fitted Curve**   - - - - - **Average Rate**

Fitted Curve Equation: T = 6.06(X) + 123.56 $R^2 = 0.87$

Apartment
(220)

Average Vehicle Trip Ends vs: **Dwelling Units**
On a: **Weekday,**
Peak Hour of Adjacent Street Traffic,
One Hour Between 7 and 9 a.m.

Number of Studies: 78
Avg. Number of Dwelling Units: 235
Directional Distribution: 20% entering, 80% exiting

Trip Generation per Dwelling Unit

Average Rate	Range of Rates	Standard Deviation
0.51	0.10 - 1.02	0.73

Data Plot and Equation

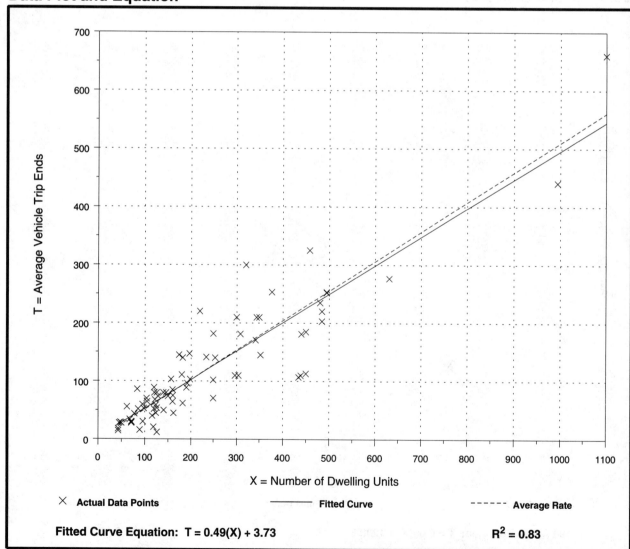

X   **Actual Data Points**   ——— **Fitted Curve**   - - - - - **Average Rate**

Fitted Curve Equation: T = 0.49(X) + 3.73 $R^2 = 0.83$

Apartment
(220)

Average Vehicle Trip Ends vs:	**Dwelling Units**	
On a:	**Weekday,**	
	Peak Hour of Adjacent Street Traffic,	
	One Hour Between 4 and 6 p.m.	

Number of Studies: 90
Avg. Number of Dwelling Units: 233
Directional Distribution: 65% entering, 35% exiting

Trip Generation per Dwelling Unit

Average Rate	Range of Rates	Standard Deviation
0.62	0.10 - 1.64	0.82

Data Plot and Equation

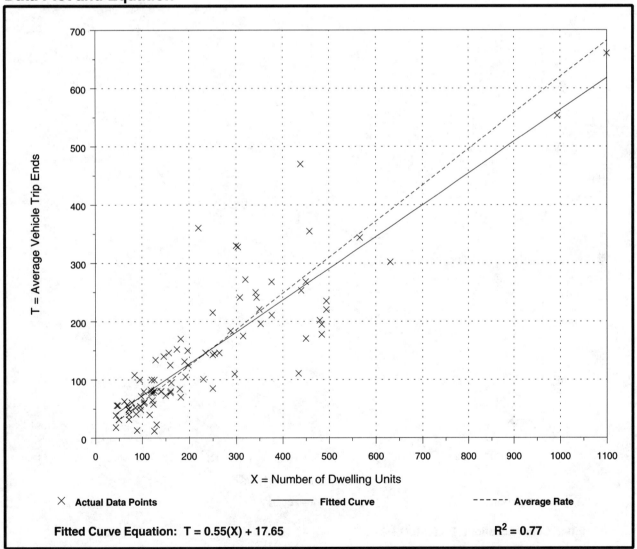

X **Actual Data Points**   ——— **Fitted Curve**   - - - - - **Average Rate**

Fitted Curve Equation: T = 0.55(X) + 17.65 $R^2 = 0.77$

Apartment
(220)

Average Vehicle Trip Ends vs: Dwelling Units
On a: Weekday,
A.M. Peak Hour of Generator

Number of Studies: 83
Avg. Number of Dwelling Units: 230
Directional Distribution: 29% entering, 71% exiting

Trip Generation per Dwelling Unit

Average Rate	Range of Rates	Standard Deviation
0.55	0.10 - 1.08	0.76

Data Plot and Equation

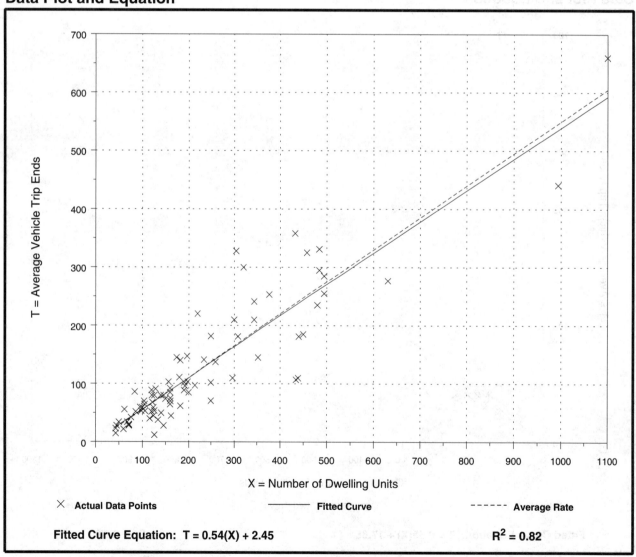

X **Actual Data Points** ———— **Fitted Curve** ----- **Average Rate**

Fitted Curve Equation: T = 0.54(X) + 2.45 $R^2 = 0.82$

Apartment
(220)

Average Vehicle Trip Ends vs: Dwelling Units
On a: Weekday,
P.M. Peak Hour of Generator

Number of Studies: 85
Avg. Number of Dwelling Units: 229
Directional Distribution: 61% entering, 39% exiting

Trip Generation per Dwelling Unit

Average Rate	Range of Rates	Standard Deviation
0.67	0.10 - 1.64	0.85

Data Plot and Equation

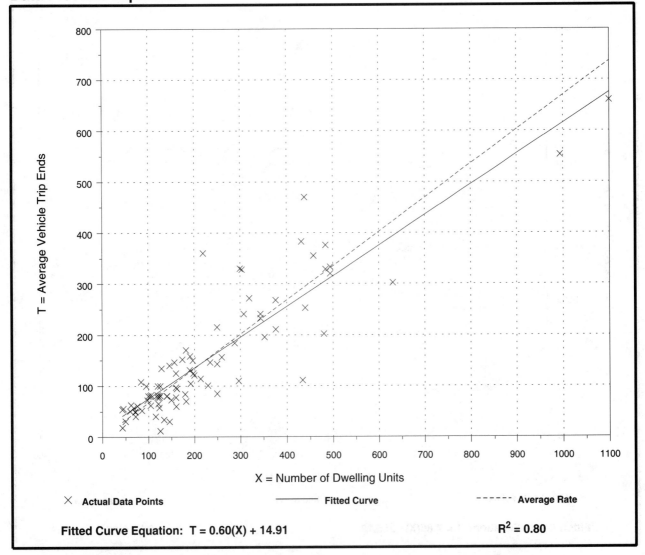

X Actual Data Points   ——— Fitted Curve   - - - - - Average Rate

Fitted Curve Equation: T = 0.60(X) + 14.91 $R^2 = 0.80$

Apartment
(220)

Average Vehicle Trip Ends vs: Dwelling Units
On a: Saturday

Number of Studies: 15
Avg. Number of Dwelling Units: 175
Directional Distribution: 50% entering, 50% exiting

Trip Generation per Dwelling Unit

Average Rate	Range of Rates	Standard Deviation
6.39	2.84 - 8.40	2.99

Data Plot and Equation

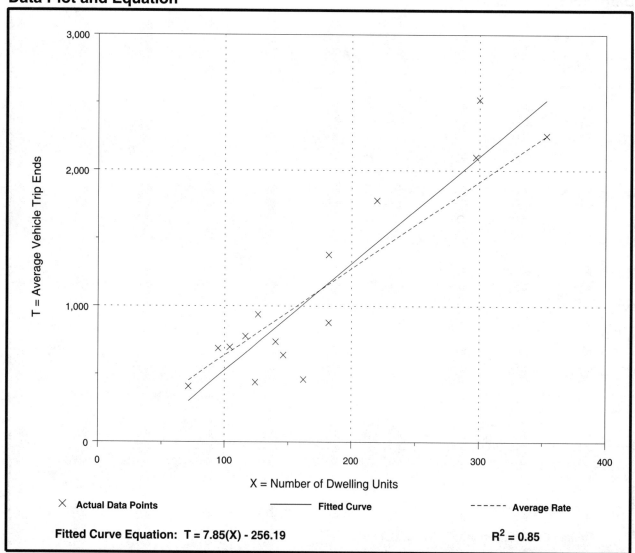

X   **Actual Data Points** ——— **Fitted Curve** - - - - - **Average Rate**

Fitted Curve Equation: T = 7.85(X) - 256.19 $R^2 = 0.85$

Apartment
(220)

Average Vehicle Trip Ends vs: Dwelling Units
On a: Saturday,
Peak Hour of Generator

Number of Studies: 14
Avg. Number of Dwelling Units: 178
Directional Distribution: Not available

Trip Generation per Dwelling Unit

Average Rate	Range of Rates	Standard Deviation
0.52	0.26 - 1.05	0.74

Data Plot and Equation

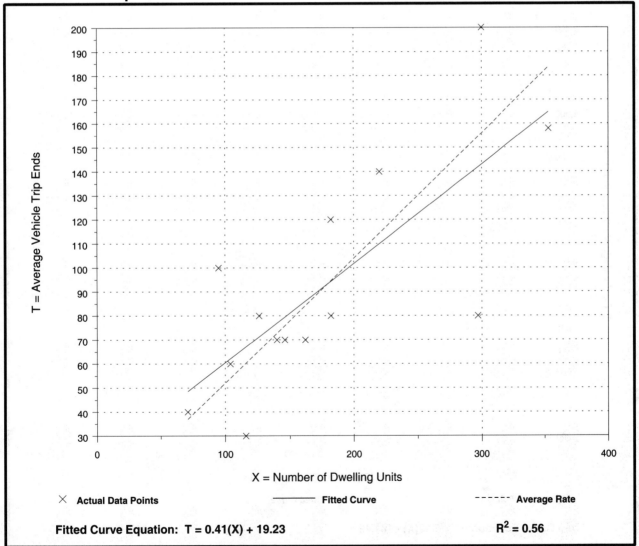

X **Actual Data Points**   ———— **Fitted Curve**   - - - - - **Average Rate**

Fitted Curve Equation: T = 0.41(X) + 19.23 $R^2 = 0.56$

Apartment
(220)

Average Vehicle Trip Ends vs: Dwelling Units
On a: Sunday

Number of Studies: 14
Avg. Number of Dwelling Units: 182
Directional Distribution: 50% entering, 50% exiting

Trip Generation per Dwelling Unit

Average Rate	Range of Rates	Standard Deviation
5.86	3.21 - 7.53	2.73

Data Plot and Equation

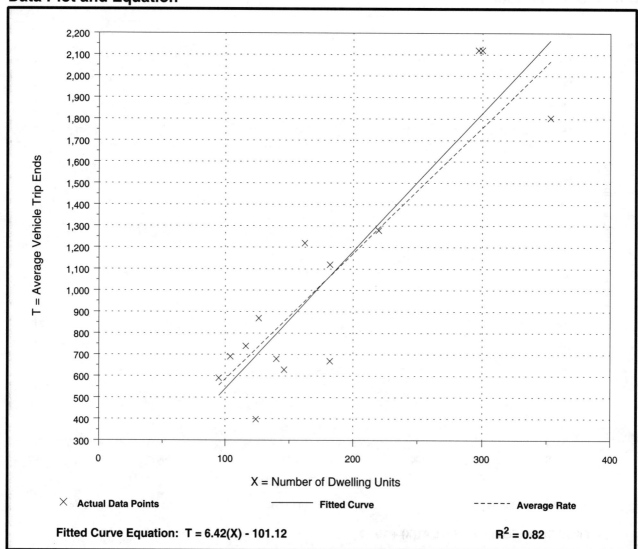

X = Number of Dwelling Units

✕ Actual Data Points	—— Fitted Curve	- - - - Average Rate

Fitted Curve Equation: T = 6.42(X) - 101.12 $R^2 = 0.82$

Apartment
(220)

Average Vehicle Trip Ends vs: **Dwelling Units**
On a: **Sunday,**
Peak Hour of Generator

Number of Studies: 13
Avg. Number of Dwelling Units: 186
Directional Distribution: Not available

Trip Generation per Dwelling Unit

Average Rate	Range of Rates	Standard Deviation
0.51	0.26 - 1.43	0.75

Data Plot and Equation

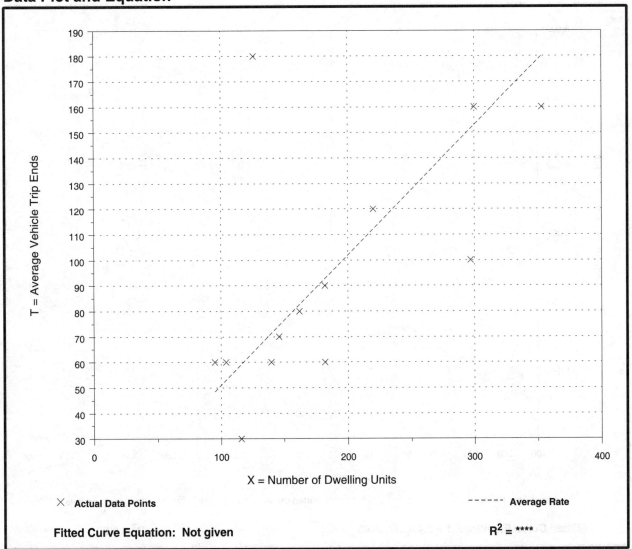

Fitted Curve Equation: Not given $R^2 = ****$

Apartment
(220)

Average Vehicle Trip Ends vs: Persons
On a: Weekday

Number of Studies: 37
Average Number of Persons: 397
Directional Distribution: 50% entering, 50% exiting

Trip Generation per Person

Average Rate	Range of Rates	Standard Deviation
3.31	1.16 - 5.85	1.99

Data Plot and Equation

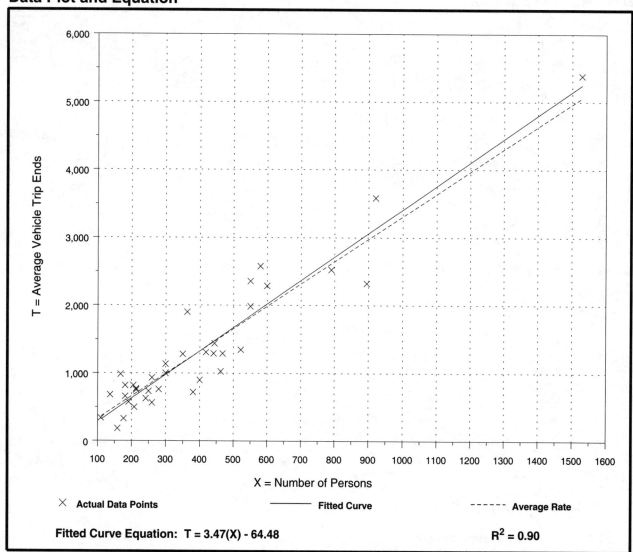

Fitted Curve Equation: T = 3.47(X) - 64.48 $R^2 = 0.90$

Apartment
(220)

Average Vehicle Trip Ends vs: **Persons**
On a: **Weekday,**
Peak Hour of Adjacent Street Traffic,
One Hour Between 7 and 9 a.m.

Number of Studies: 26
Average Number of Persons: 427
Directional Distribution: Not available

Trip Generation per Person

Average Rate	Range of Rates	Standard Deviation
0.28	0.10 - 0.52	0.54

Data Plot and Equation

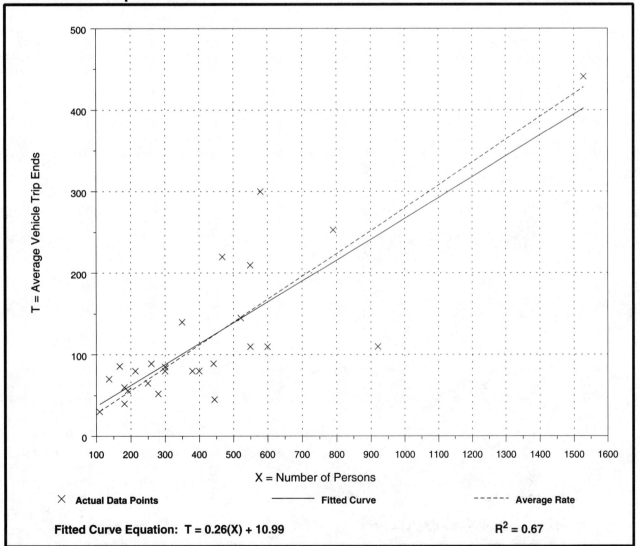

Fitted Curve Equation: T = 0.26(X) + 10.99 $R^2 = 0.67$

Apartment
(220)

Average Vehicle Trip Ends vs: **Persons**
On a: **Weekday,**
Peak Hour of Adjacent Street Traffic,
One Hour Between 4 and 6 p.m.

Number of Studies: 28
Average Number of Persons: 412
Directional Distribution: Not available

Trip Generation per Person

Average Rate	Range of Rates	Standard Deviation
0.40	0.20 - 0.77	0.65

Data Plot and Equation

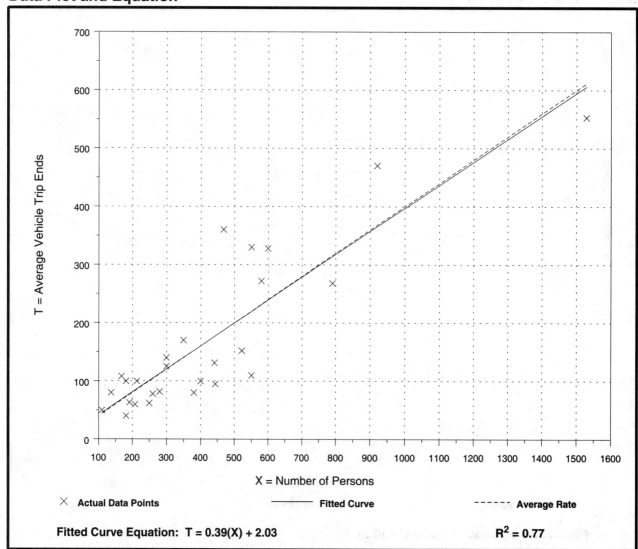

X **Actual Data Points**   ———— **Fitted Curve**   - - - - - **Average Rate**

Fitted Curve Equation: T = 0.39(X) + 2.03   **$R^2 = 0.77$**

Apartment
(220)

Average Vehicle Trip Ends vs: **Persons**
On a: **Weekday,**
A.M. Peak Hour of Generator

Number of Studies: 28
Average Number of Persons: 408
Directional Distribution: 48% entering, 52% exiting

Trip Generation per Person

Average Rate	Range of Rates	Standard Deviation
0.30	0.10 - 0.55	0.56

Data Plot and Equation

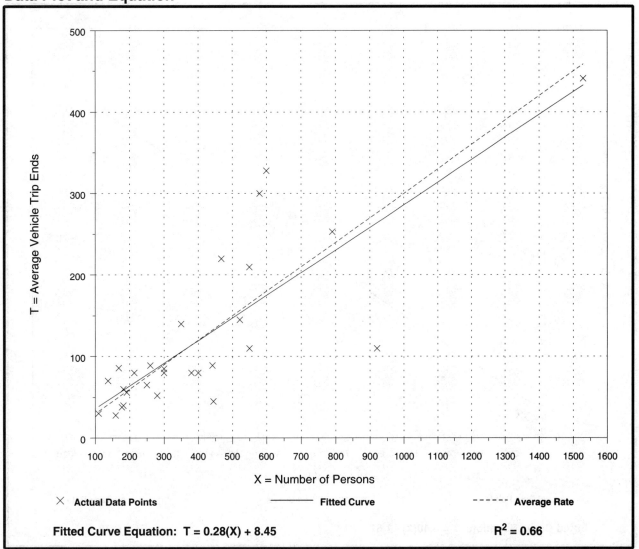

X = Number of Persons

| ✕ **Actual Data Points** | —— **Fitted Curve** | - - - - **Average Rate** |

Fitted Curve Equation: $T = 0.28(X) + 8.45$ $R^2 = 0.66$

Apartment
(220)

Average Vehicle Trip Ends vs: Persons
On a: Weekday,
P.M. Peak Hour of Generator

Number of Studies: 29
Average Number of Persons: 402
Directional Distribution: 59% entering, 41% exiting

Trip Generation per Person

Average Rate	Range of Rates	Standard Deviation
0.40	0.19 - 0.77	0.64

Data Plot and Equation

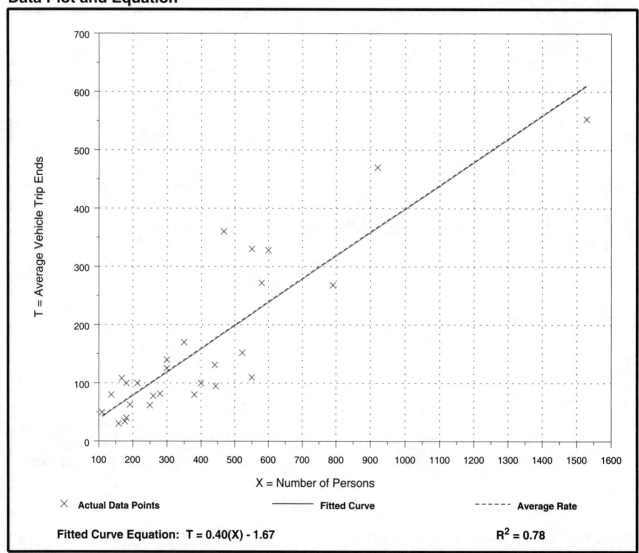

Fitted Curve Equation: T = 0.40(X) - 1.67 $R^2 = 0.78$

Apartment
(220)

Average Vehicle Trip Ends vs: Persons
On a: Saturday

Number of Studies: 12
Average Number of Persons: 338
Directional Distribution: 50% entering, 50% exiting

Trip Generation per Person

Average Rate	Range of Rates	Standard Deviation
3.24	1.03 - 5.11	2.16

Data Plot and Equation

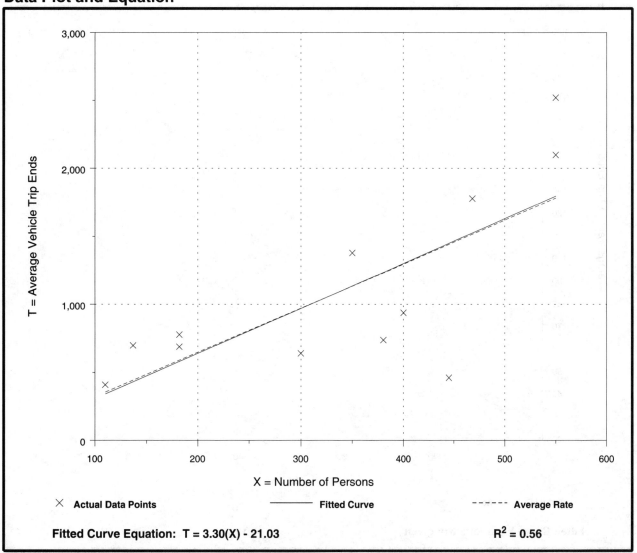

Fitted Curve Equation: T = 3.30(X) - 21.03 $R^2 = 0.56$

Apartment
(220)

Average Vehicle Trip Ends vs: Persons
On a: Saturday,
Peak Hour of Generator

Number of Studies: 12
Average Number of Persons: 338
Directional Distribution: Not available

Trip Generation per Person

Average Rate	Range of Rates	Standard Deviation
0.26	0.15 - 0.55	0.52

Data Plot and Equation

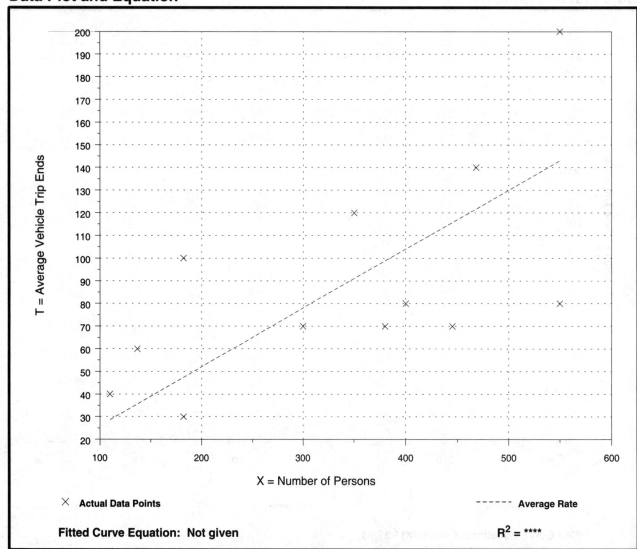

X = Number of Persons

× **Actual Data Points**   - - - - - **Average Rate**

Fitted Curve Equation: Not given $R^2 = ****$

Apartment
(220)

Average Vehicle Trip Ends vs: Persons
On a: Sunday

Number of Studies: 11
Average Number of Persons: 359
Directional Distribution: 50% entering, 50% exiting

Trip Generation per Person

Average Rate	Range of Rates	Standard Deviation
3.06	1.79 - 5.04	1.93

Data Plot and Equation

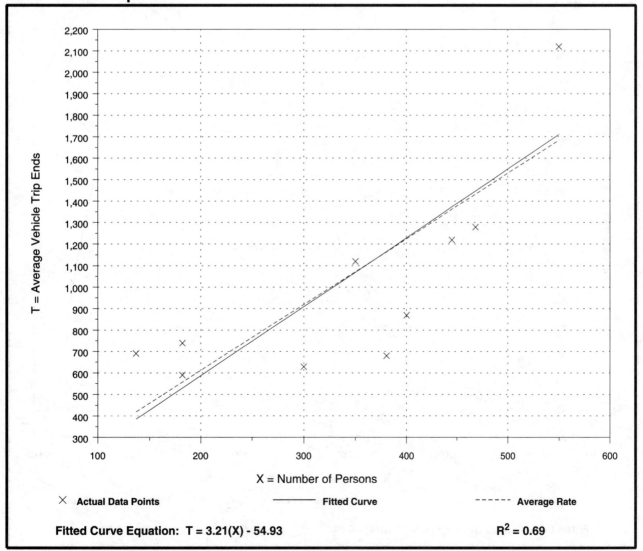

X = Number of Persons

$\times$ **Actual Data Points**   —— **Fitted Curve**   ----- **Average Rate**

Fitted Curve Equation: T = 3.21(X) - 54.93 $R^2 = 0.69$

Apartment
(220)

Average Vehicle Trip Ends vs: **Persons**
On a: **Sunday,**
Peak Hour of Generator

Number of Studies: 11
Average Number of Persons: 359
Directional Distribution: Not available

Trip Generation per Person

Average Rate	Range of Rates	Standard Deviation
0.26	0.16 - 0.45	0.51

Data Plot and Equation

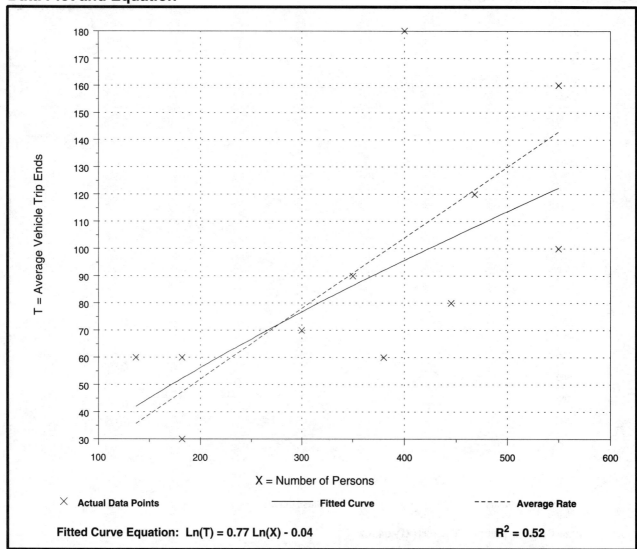

X = Number of Persons

✕ **Actual Data Points** ——— **Fitted Curve** - - - - - **Average Rate**

Fitted Curve Equation: $Ln(T) = 0.77 \, Ln(X) - 0.04$ $R^2 = 0.52$

Apartment
(220)

Average Vehicle Trip Ends vs: **Vehicles**
On a: **Weekday**

Number of Studies: 29
Average Number of Vehicles: 252
Directional Distribution: 50% entering, 50% exiting

Trip Generation per Vehicle

Average Rate	Range of Rates	Standard Deviation
5.10	2.91 - 8.57	2.73

Data Plot and Equation

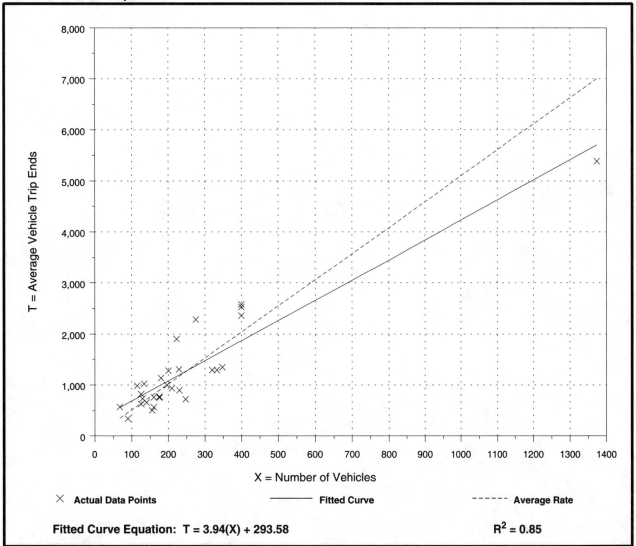

Fitted Curve Equation: T = 3.94(X) + 293.58   **R^2 = 0.85**

Apartment
(220)

Average Vehicle Trip Ends vs: Vehicles
On a: Weekday,
Peak Hour of Adjacent Street Traffic,
One Hour Between 7 and 9 a.m.

Number of Studies: 21
Average Number of Vehicles: 285
Directional Distribution: Not available

Trip Generation per Vehicle

Average Rate	Range of Rates	Standard Deviation
0.46	0.27 - 0.82	0.69

Data Plot and Equation

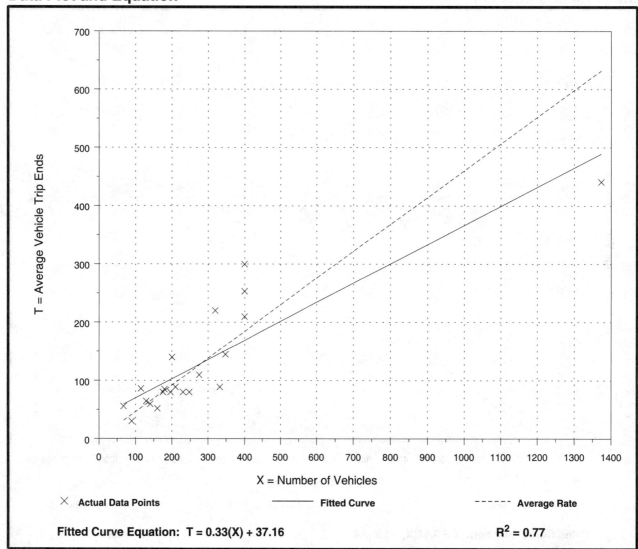

X = Number of Vehicles

Fitted Curve Equation: T = 0.33(X) + 37.16 $R^2 = 0.77$

Apartment
(220)

Average Vehicle Trip Ends vs: **Vehicles**
On a: **Weekday,**
Peak Hour of Adjacent Street Traffic,
One Hour Between 4 and 6 p.m.

Number of Studies: 23
Average Number of Vehicles: 275
Directional Distribution: Not available

Trip Generation per Vehicle

Average Rate	Range of Rates	Standard Deviation
0.60	0.32 - 1.19	0.81

Data Plot and Equation

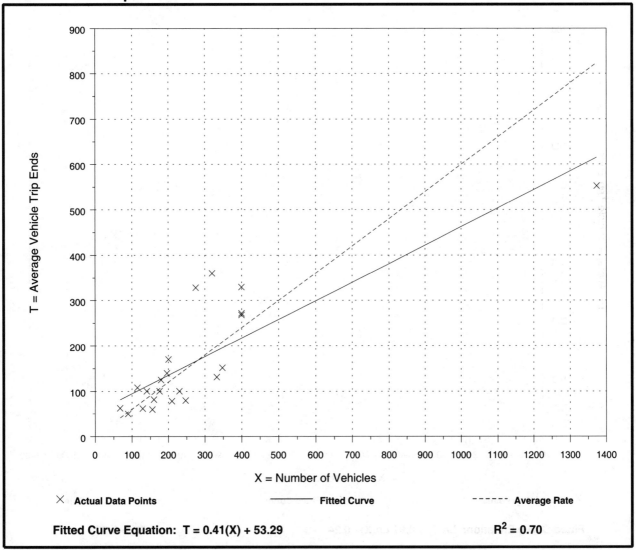

Fitted Curve Equation: T = 0.41(X) + 53.29 $R^2 = 0.70$

Apartment
(220)

Average Vehicle Trip Ends vs: Vehicles
On a: Weekday,
A.M. Peak Hour of Generator

Number of Studies: 21
Average Number of Vehicles: 285
Directional Distribution: Not available

Trip Generation per Vehicle

Average Rate	Range of Rates	Standard Deviation
0.50	0.27 - 1.19	0.74

Data Plot and Equation

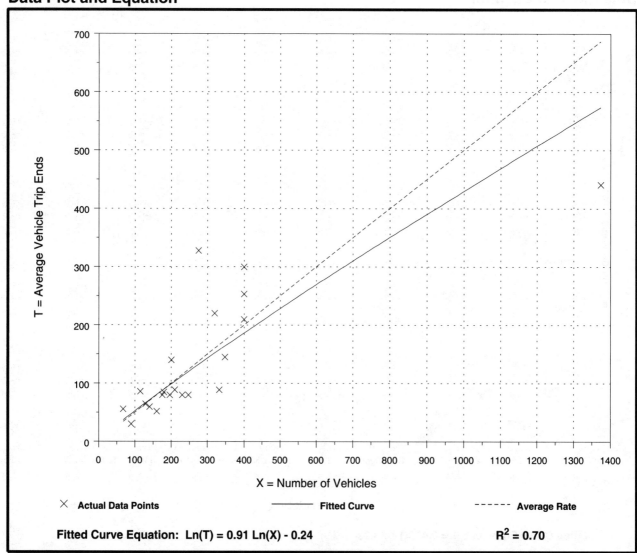

X = Number of Vehicles

✕ **Actual Data Points**	—— **Fitted Curve**	----- **Average Rate**

Fitted Curve Equation: Ln(T) = 0.91 Ln(X) - 0.24 $R^2 = 0.70$

Apartment
(220)

Average Vehicle Trip Ends vs: **Vehicles**
On a: **Weekday,**
P.M. Peak Hour of Generator

Number of Studies: 22
Average Number of Vehicles: 280
Directional Distribution: Not available

Trip Generation per Vehicle

Average Rate	Range of Rates	Standard Deviation
0.61	0.32 - 1.19	0.82

Data Plot and Equation

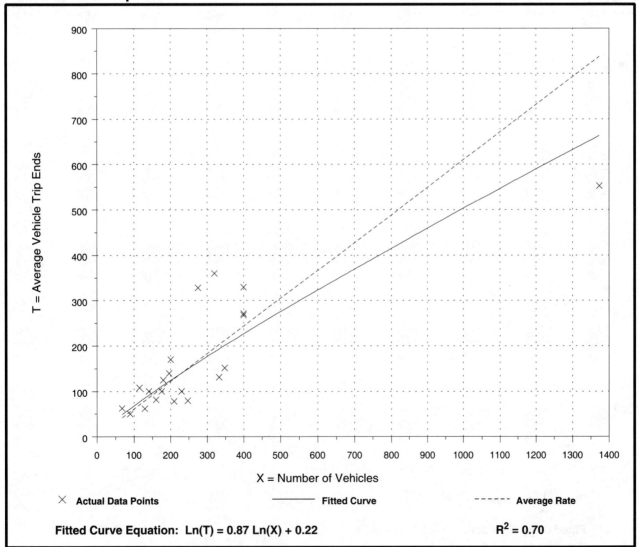

X Actual Data Points   —— Fitted Curve   ----- Average Rate

Fitted Curve Equation: $Ln(T) = 0.87\ Ln(X) + 0.22$ $R^2 = 0.70$

Apartment
(220)

Average Vehicle Trip Ends vs: Vehicles
On a: Saturday

Number of Studies: 8
Average Number of Vehicles: 228
Directional Distribution: 50% entering, 50% exiting

Trip Generation per Vehicle

Average Rate	Range of Rates	Standard Deviation
4.99	3.00 - 6.90	2.60

Data Plot and Equation

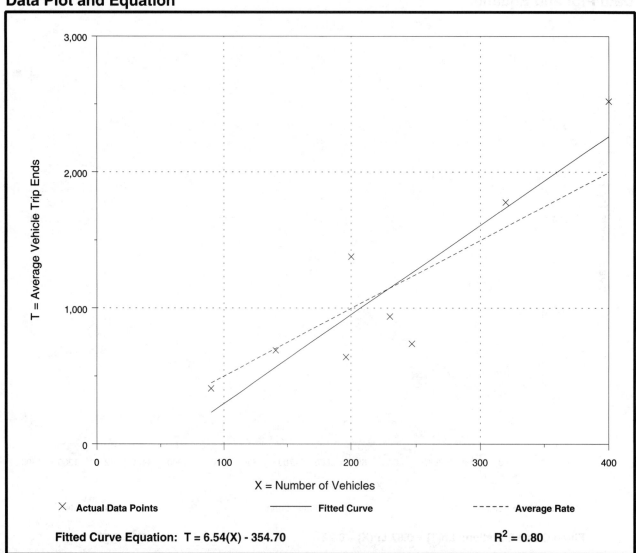

Fitted Curve Equation: T = 6.54(X) - 354.70 $R^2 = 0.80$

Apartment
(220)

Average Vehicle Trip Ends vs: **Vehicles**
On a: **Saturday,**
Peak Hour of Generator

Number of Studies: 8
Average Number of Vehicles: 228
Directional Distribution: Not available

Trip Generation per Vehicle

Average Rate	Range of Rates	Standard Deviation
0.45	0.28 - 0.71	0.68

Data Plot and Equation

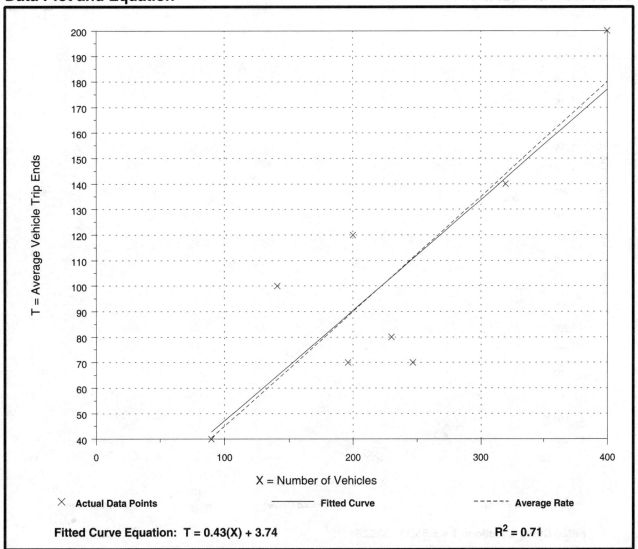

X = Number of Vehicles

$\times$ **Actual Data Points** ——— **Fitted Curve** ----- **Average Rate**

Fitted Curve Equation: T = 0.43(X) + 3.74 $R^2 = 0.71$

Apartment
(220)

Average Vehicle Trip Ends vs: Vehicles
On a: Sunday

Number of Studies: 7
Average Number of Vehicles: 248
Directional Distribution: 50% entering, 50% exiting

Trip Generation per Vehicle

Average Rate	Range of Rates	Standard Deviation
4.20	2.75 - 5.60	2.27

Data Plot and Equation

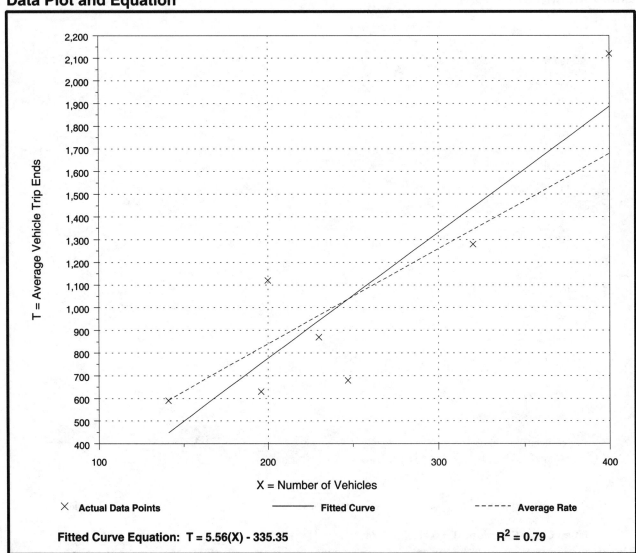

X = Number of Vehicles

✕ **Actual Data Points**	—— **Fitted Curve**	- - - - - **Average Rate**

Fitted Curve Equation: T = 5.56(X) - 335.35 $R^2 = 0.79$

Apartment
(220)

Average Vehicle Trip Ends vs: Vehicles
On a: Sunday,
Peak Hour of Generator

Number of Studies: 7
Average Number of Vehicles: 248
Directional Distribution: Not available

Trip Generation per Vehicle

Average Rate	Range of Rates	Standard Deviation
0.43	0.24 - 0.78	0.67

Data Plot and Equation

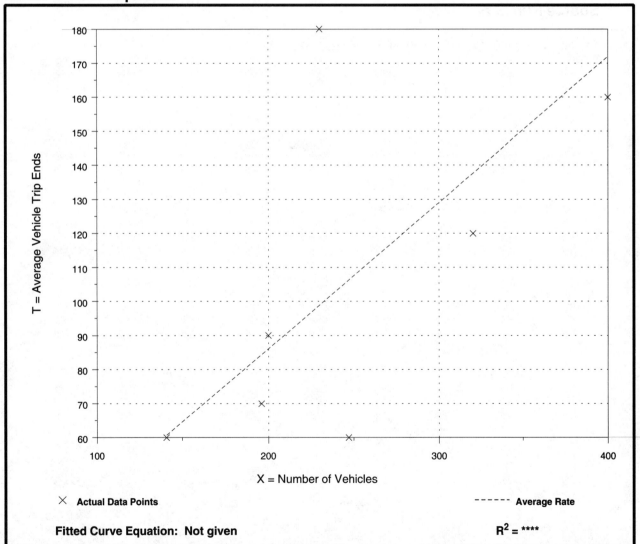

X **Actual Data Points**   - - - - - **Average Rate**

Fitted Curve Equation: Not given $R^2 = ****$

Land Use: 221
Low-Rise Apartment

Description

Low-rise apartments (rental dwelling units) are units located in rental buildings that have one or two levels (floors), such as garden apartments. Apartment (Land Use 220), high-rise apartment (Land Use 222) and mid-rise apartment (Land Use 223) are related uses.

Additional Data

The peak hour of the generator typically coincided with the peak hour of the adjacent street traffic.

The sites were surveyed between the early 1970s and the late 1990s throughout the United States and Canada.

Source Numbers

11, 21, 71, 98, 110, 177, 192, 300, 305, 306, 320, 321, 525

Land Use: 221
Low-Rise Apartment
Independent Variables with One Observation

The following trip generation data are for independent variables with only one observation. This information is shown in this table only; there are no related plots for these data.

Users are cautioned to use data with care because of the small sample size.

Independent Variable	Trip Generation Rate	Size of Independent Variable	Number of Studies	Directional Distribution
Persons				
Weekday a.m. Peak Hour of Adjacent Street Traffic	0.24	211	1	Not available
Weekday p.m. Peak Hour of Adjacent Street Traffic	0.38	211	1	Not available

Low-Rise Apartment
(221)

Average Vehicle Trip Ends vs: Occupied Dwelling Units
On a: Weekday

Number of Studies: 22
Avg. Num. of Occupied Dwelling Units: 264
Directional Distribution: 50% entering, 50% exiting

Trip Generation per Occupied Dwelling Unit

Average Rate	Range of Rates	Standard Deviation
6.59	5.10 - 9.24	2.84

Data Plot and Equation

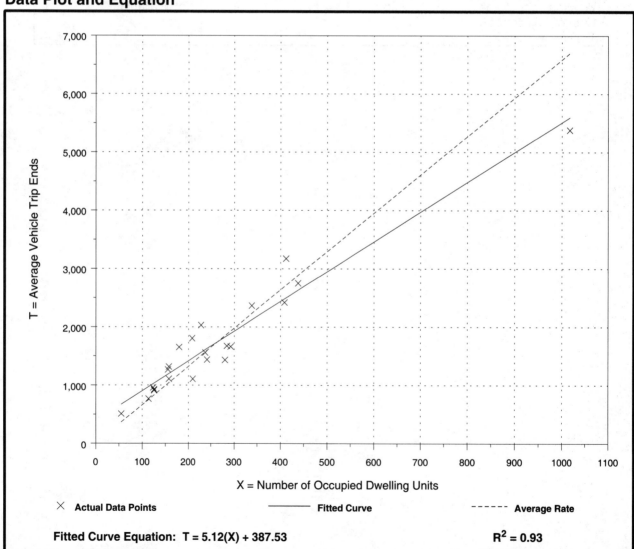

Fitted Curve Equation: T = 5.12(X) + 387.53 $R^2 = 0.93$

Low-Rise Apartment
(221)

Average Vehicle Trip Ends vs: **Occupied Dwelling Units**
On a: **Weekday,**
Peak Hour of Adjacent Street Traffic,
One Hour Between 7 and 9 a.m.

Number of Studies: 27
Avg. Num. of Occupied Dwelling Units: 257
Directional Distribution: 21% entering, 79% exiting

Trip Generation per Occupied Dwelling Unit

Average Rate	Range of Rates	Standard Deviation
0.46	0.25 - 0.86	0.70

Data Plot and Equation

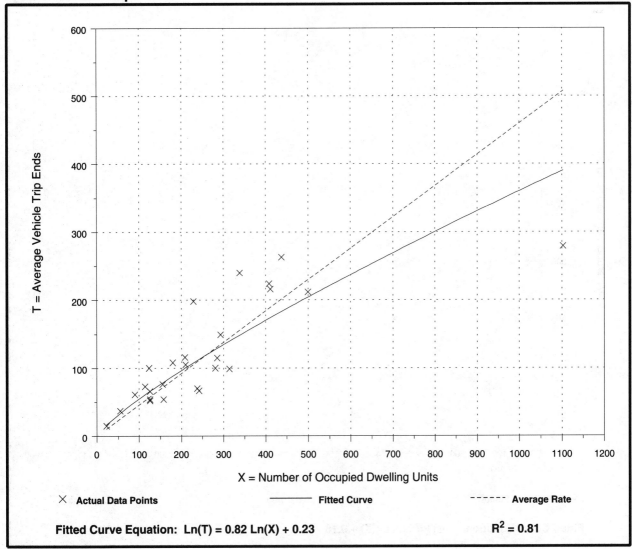

X **Actual Data Points**   —— **Fitted Curve**   - - - - - **Average Rate**

Fitted Curve Equation: Ln(T) = 0.82 Ln(X) + 0.23 $R^2 = 0.81$

Low-Rise Apartment
(221)

Average Vehicle Trip Ends vs: **Occupied Dwelling Units**
On a: **Weekday,**
Peak Hour of Adjacent Street Traffic,
One Hour Between 4 and 6 p.m.

Number of Studies: 27
Avg. Num. of Occupied Dwelling Units: 257
Directional Distribution: 65% entering, 35% exiting

Trip Generation per Occupied Dwelling Unit

Average Rate	Range of Rates	Standard Deviation
0.58	0.38 - 0.93	0.77

Data Plot and Equation

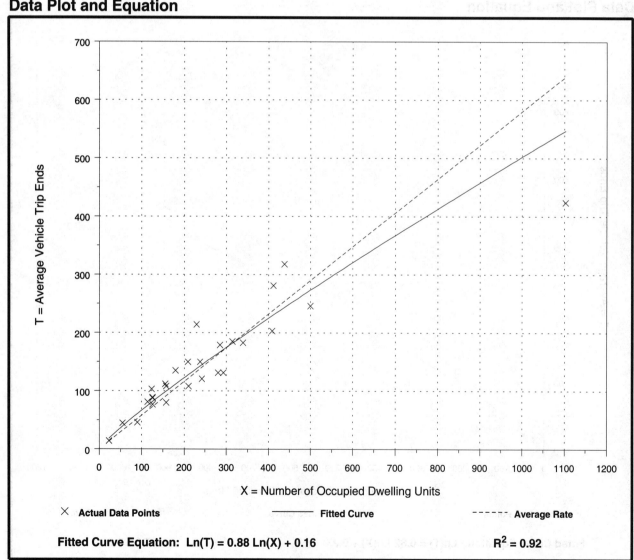

Fitted Curve Equation: Ln(T) = 0.88 Ln(X) + 0.16 $R^2 = 0.92$

Low-Rise Apartment
(221)

Average Vehicle Trip Ends vs: **Occupied Dwelling Units**
On a: **Weekday,**
A.M. Peak Hour of Generator

Number of Studies: 36
Avg. Num. of Occupied Dwelling Units: 264
Directional Distribution: 20% entering, 80% exiting

Trip Generation per Occupied Dwelling Unit

Average Rate	Range of Rates	Standard Deviation
0.51	0.25 - 0.98	0.73

Data Plot and Equation

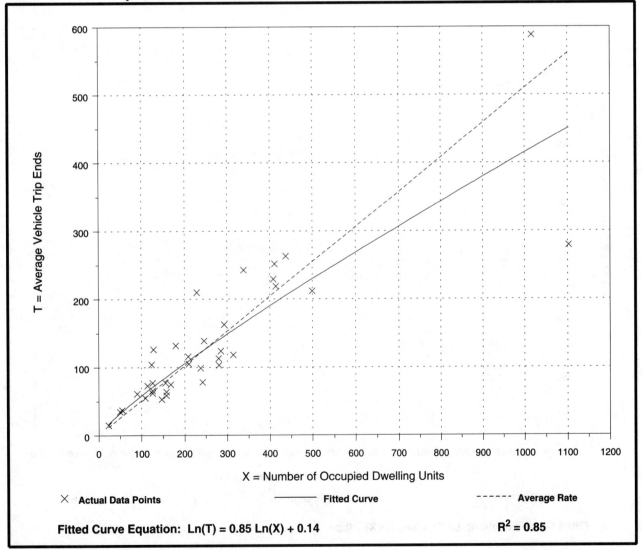

Fitted Curve Equation: $Ln(T) = 0.85 \, Ln(X) + 0.14$ $\qquad$ $R^2 = 0.85$

Low-Rise Apartment
(221)

Average Vehicle Trip Ends vs: **Occupied Dwelling Units**
On a: **Weekday,**
P.M. Peak Hour of Generator

Number of Studies: 33
Avg. Num. of Occupied Dwelling Units: 250
Directional Distribution: 64% entering, 36% exiting

Trip Generation per Occupied Dwelling Unit

Average Rate	Range of Rates	Standard Deviation
0.62	0.38 - 1.23	0.80

Data Plot and Equation

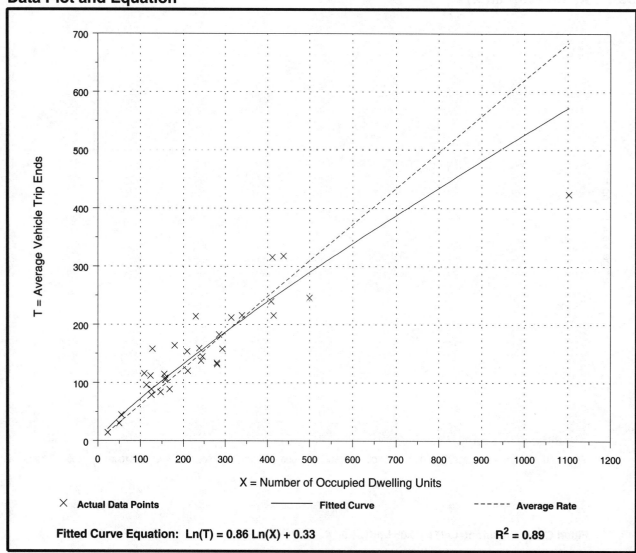

X   **Actual Data Points**   ——— **Fitted Curve**   - - - - - **Average Rate**

Fitted Curve Equation: Ln(T) = 0.86 Ln(X) + 0.33 $R^2 = 0.89$

Low-Rise Apartment
(221)

Average Vehicle Trip Ends vs: Occupied Dwelling Units
On a: Saturday

Number of Studies: 21
Avg. Num. of Occupied Dwelling Units: 228
Directional Distribution: 50% entering, 50% exiting

Trip Generation per Occupied Dwelling Unit

Average Rate	Range of Rates	Standard Deviation
7.16	4.41 - 9.20	2.96

Data Plot and Equation

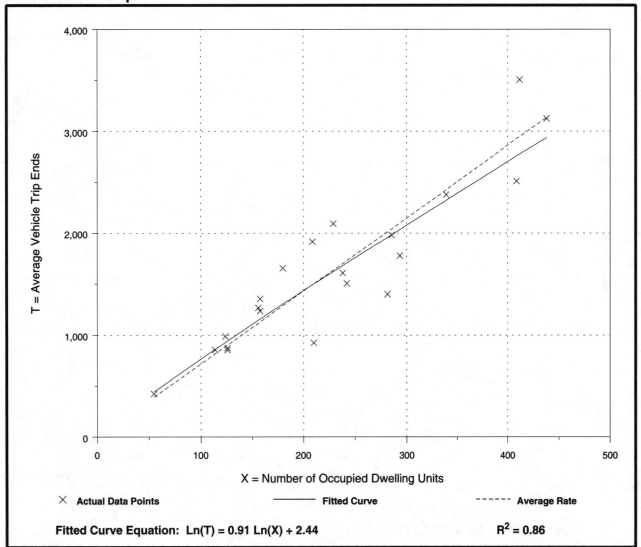

X Actual Data Points   —— Fitted Curve   - - - - - Average Rate

Fitted Curve Equation: Ln(T) = 0.91 Ln(X) + 2.44 $R^2 = 0.86$

Low-Rise Apartment
(221)

Average Vehicle Trip Ends vs: Occupied Dwelling Units
On a: Saturday,
Peak Hour of Generator

Number of Studies: 21
Avg. Num. of Occupied Dwelling Units: 228
Directional Distribution: 54% entering, 46% exiting

Trip Generation per Occupied Dwelling Unit

Average Rate	Range of Rates	Standard Deviation
0.58	0.34 - 0.75	0.77

Data Plot and Equation

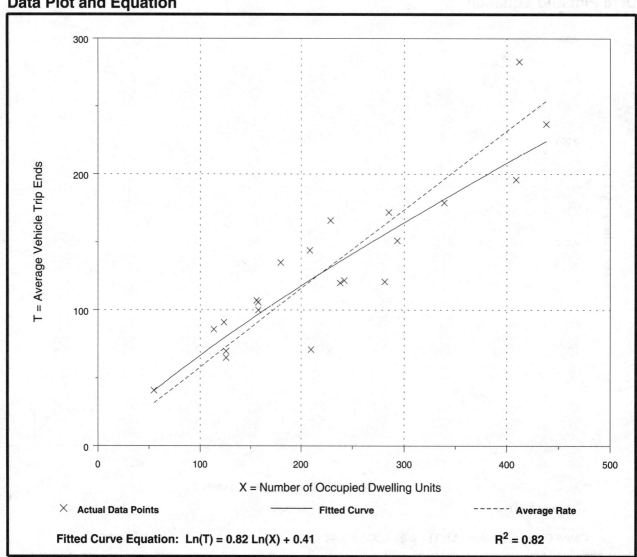

X = Number of Occupied Dwelling Units

| X | Actual Data Points | —— Fitted Curve | - - - - - Average Rate |

Fitted Curve Equation: Ln(T) = 0.82 Ln(X) + 0.41 $R^2 = 0.82$

Low-Rise Apartment
(221)

Average Vehicle Trip Ends vs: Occupied Dwelling Units
On a: Sunday

Number of Studies: 21
Avg. Num. of Occupied Dwelling Units: 228
Directional Distribution: 50% entering, 50% exiting

Trip Generation per Occupied Dwelling Unit

Average Rate	Range of Rates	Standard Deviation
6.07	4.20 - 8.77	2.71

Data Plot and Equation

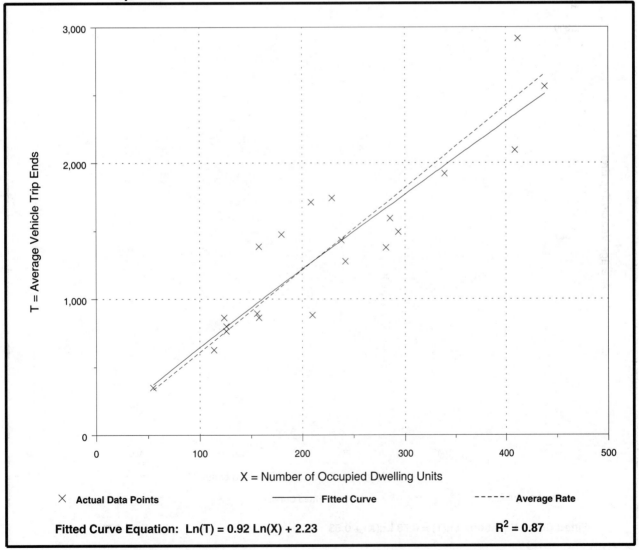

X   **Actual Data Points**   ———— **Fitted Curve**   − − − − − **Average Rate**

Fitted Curve Equation: Ln(T) = 0.92 Ln(X) + 2.23 $R^2 = 0.87$

Low-Rise Apartment
(221)

Average Vehicle Trip Ends vs: **Occupied Dwelling Units**
On a: **Sunday,**
Peak Hour of Generator

Number of Studies: 20
Avg. Num. of Occupied Dwelling Units: 227
Directional Distribution: 53% entering, 47% exiting

Trip Generation per Occupied Dwelling Unit

Average Rate	Range of Rates	Standard Deviation
0.56	0.35 - 1.17	0.76

Data Plot and Equation

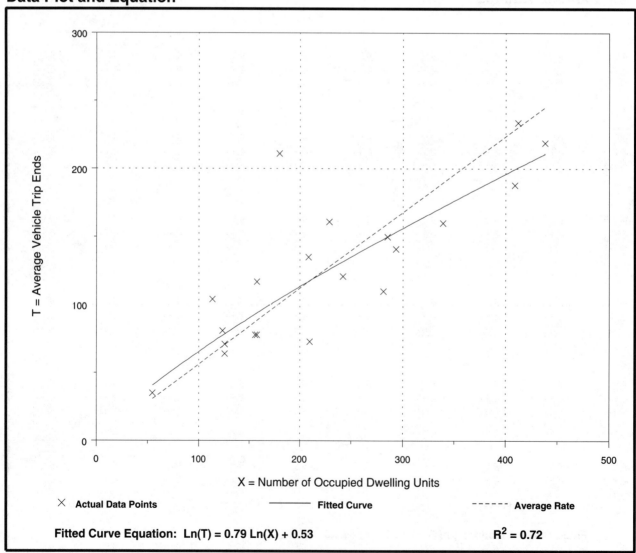

Fitted Curve Equation: Ln(T) = 0.79 Ln(X) + 0.53 $R^2 = 0.72$

Low-Rise Apartment
(221)

Average Vehicle Trip Ends vs: Persons
On a: Weekday,
A.M. Peak Hour of Generator

Number of Studies: 7
Average Number of Persons: 392
Directional Distribution: 17% entering, 83% exiting

Trip Generation per Person

Average Rate	Range of Rates	Standard Deviation
0.28	0.19 - 0.52	0.54

Data Plot and Equation

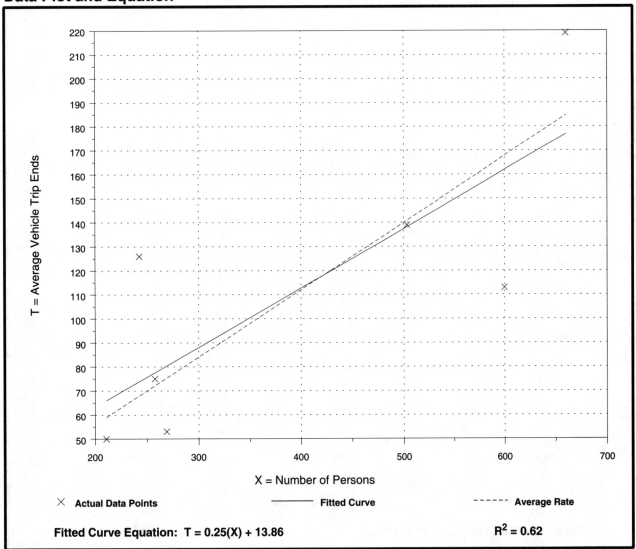

X = Number of Persons

✕ Actual Data Points	——— Fitted Curve	- - - - - Average Rate

Fitted Curve Equation: T = 0.25(X) + 13.86 $R^2 = 0.62$

Low-Rise Apartment
(221)

Average Vehicle Trip Ends vs: **Persons**
On a: **Weekday,**
P.M. Peak Hour of Generator

Number of Studies: 7
Average Number of Persons: 392
Directional Distribution: 63% entering, 37% exiting

Trip Generation per Person

Average Rate	Range of Rates	Standard Deviation
0.33	0.22 - 0.65	0.58

Data Plot and Equation

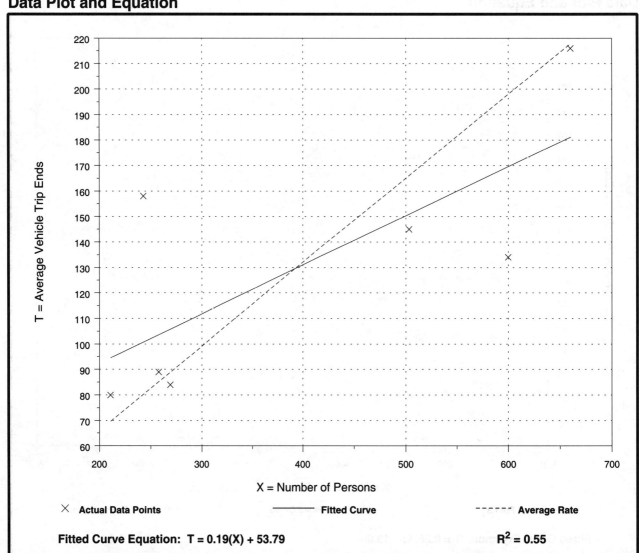

X = Number of Persons

$\times$ Actual Data Points	——— Fitted Curve	----- Average Rate

Fitted Curve Equation: T = 0.19(X) + 53.79 **$R^2 = 0.55$**

Land Use: 222
High-Rise Apartment

Description

High-rise apartments (rental dwelling units) are units located in rental buildings that have more than 10 levels (floors) and most likely have one or more elevators. Apartment (Land Use 220), low-rise apartment (Land Use 221) and mid-rise apartment (Land Use 223) are related uses.

Additional Data

The peak hour of the generator typically coincided with the peak hour of the adjacent street traffic.

The sites were surveyed between the late 1960s and the late 1980s throughout the United States.

Source Numbers

35, 38, 98, 105, 169, 171, 187, 305, 321

Land Use: 222
High-Rise Apartment
Independent Variables with One Observation

The following trip generation data are for independent variables with only one observation. This information is shown in this table only; there are no related plots for these data.

Users are cautioned to use data with care because of the small sample size.

Independent Variable	Trip Generation Rate	Size of Independent Variable	Number of Studies	Directional Distribution
Persons				
Weekday	1.78	1,580	1	50% entering, 50% exiting
Weekday a.m. Peak Hour of Adjacent Street Traffic	0.17	1,580	1	39% entering, 61% exiting
Weekday p.m. Peak Hour of Adjacent Street Traffic	0.18	1,580	1	61% entering, 39% exiting

High-Rise Apartment
(222)

Average Vehicle Trip Ends vs: **Dwelling Units**
On a: **Weekday**

Number of Studies: 9
Avg. Number of Dwelling Units: 435
Directional Distribution: 50% entering, 50% exiting

Trip Generation per Dwelling Unit

Average Rate	Range of Rates	Standard Deviation
4.20	3.00 - 6.45	2.32

Data Plot and Equation

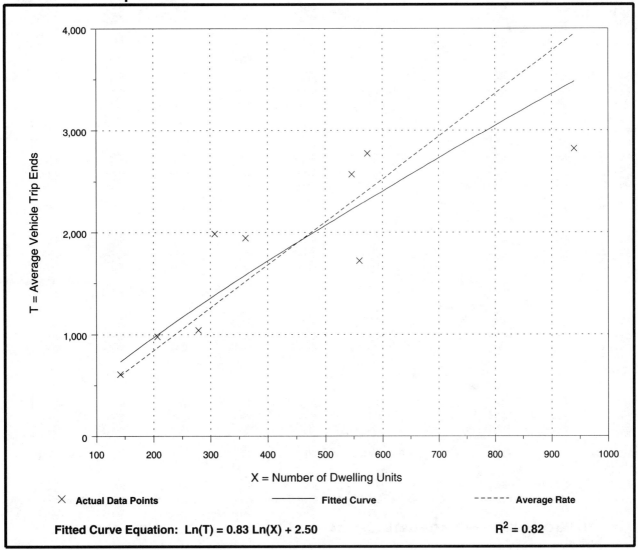

Fitted Curve Equation: $Ln(T) = 0.83\ Ln(X) + 2.50$ $R^2 = 0.82$

High-Rise Apartment
(222)

Average Vehicle Trip Ends vs: Dwelling Units
On a: Weekday,
Peak Hour of Adjacent Street Traffic,
One Hour Between 7 and 9 a.m.

Number of Studies: 17
Avg. Number of Dwelling Units: 420
Directional Distribution: 25% entering, 75% exiting

Trip Generation per Dwelling Unit

Average Rate	Range of Rates	Standard Deviation
0.30	0.18 - 0.47	0.55

Data Plot and Equation

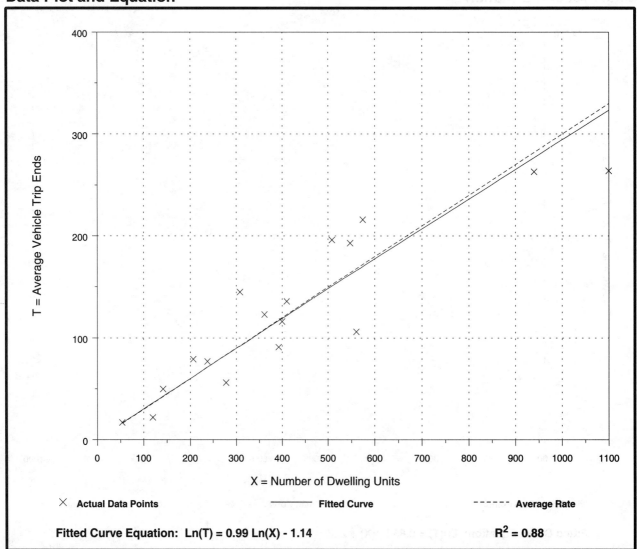

Fitted Curve Equation: Ln(T) = 0.99 Ln(X) - 1.14 $R^2 = 0.88$

High-Rise Apartment
(222)

Average Vehicle Trip Ends vs: **Dwelling Units**
On a: **Weekday,**
Peak Hour of Adjacent Street Traffic,
One Hour Between 4 and 6 p.m.

Number of Studies: 17
Avg. Number of Dwelling Units: 420
Directional Distribution: 61% entering, 39% exiting

Trip Generation per Dwelling Unit

Average Rate	Range of Rates	Standard Deviation
0.35	0.23 - 0.50	0.59

Data Plot and Equation

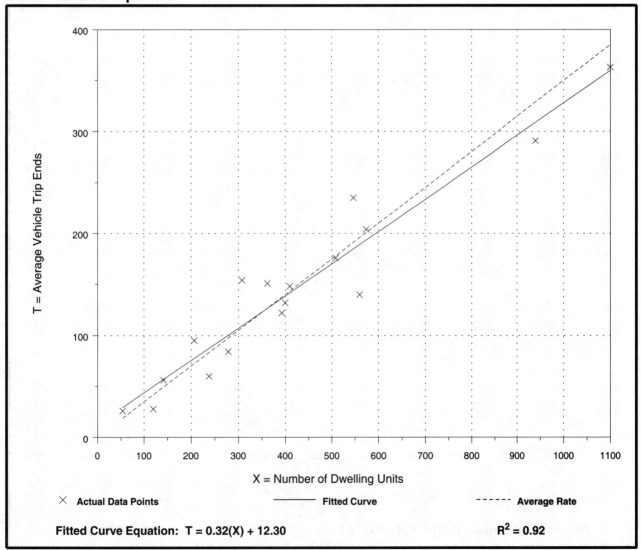

X **Actual Data Points**   ———— **Fitted Curve**   - - - - - **Average Rate**

Fitted Curve Equation: T = 0.32(X) + 12.30 $R^2 = 0.92$

High-Rise Apartment
(222)

Average Vehicle Trip Ends vs: Dwelling Units
On a: Weekday,
A.M. Peak Hour of Generator

Number of Studies: 18
Avg. Number of Dwelling Units: 399
Directional Distribution: 22% entering, 78% exiting

Trip Generation per Dwelling Unit

Average Rate	Range of Rates	Standard Deviation
0.34	0.19 - 0.47	0.59

Data Plot and Equation

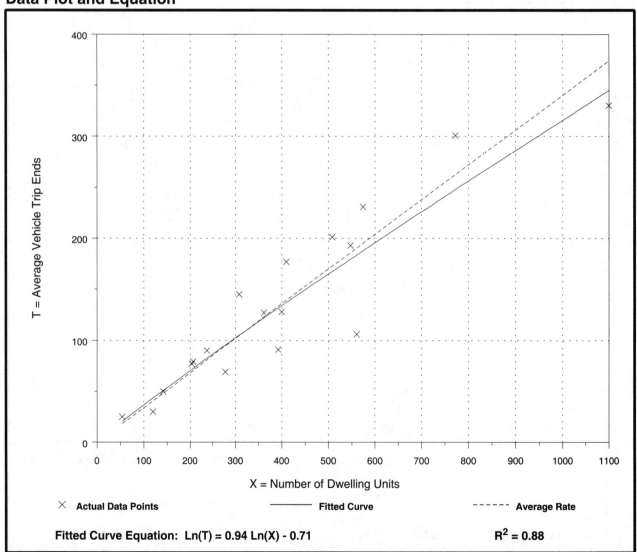

X = Number of Dwelling Units

X **Actual Data Points** ————— **Fitted Curve** - - - - - **Average Rate**

Fitted Curve Equation: Ln(T) = 0.94 Ln(X) - 0.71 $R^2 = 0.88$

High-Rise Apartment
(222)

Average Vehicle Trip Ends vs: Dwelling Units
On a: Weekday,
P.M. Peak Hour of Generator

Number of Studies: 17
Avg. Number of Dwelling Units: 389
Directional Distribution: 62% entering, 38% exiting

Trip Generation per Dwelling Unit

Average Rate	Range of Rates	Standard Deviation
0.40	0.30 - 0.59	0.63

Data Plot and Equation

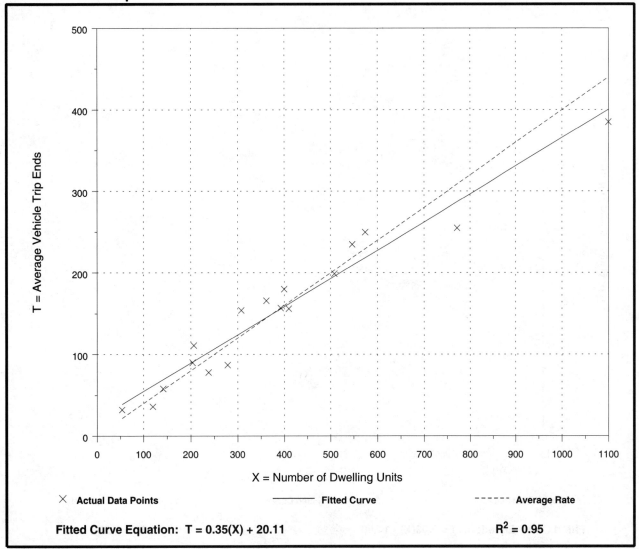

X = Number of Dwelling Units

✕ Actual Data Points	——— Fitted Curve	- - - - - Average Rate

Fitted Curve Equation: T = 0.35(X) + 20.11 $R^2 = 0.95$

High-Rise Apartment
(222)

Average Vehicle Trip Ends vs: Dwelling Units
On a: Saturday

Number of Studies: 5
Avg. Number of Dwelling Units: 313
Directional Distribution: 50% entering, 50% exiting

Trip Generation per Dwelling Unit

Average Rate	Range of Rates	Standard Deviation
4.98	3.63 - 6.00	2.36

Data Plot and Equation

Caution - Use Carefully - Small Sample Size

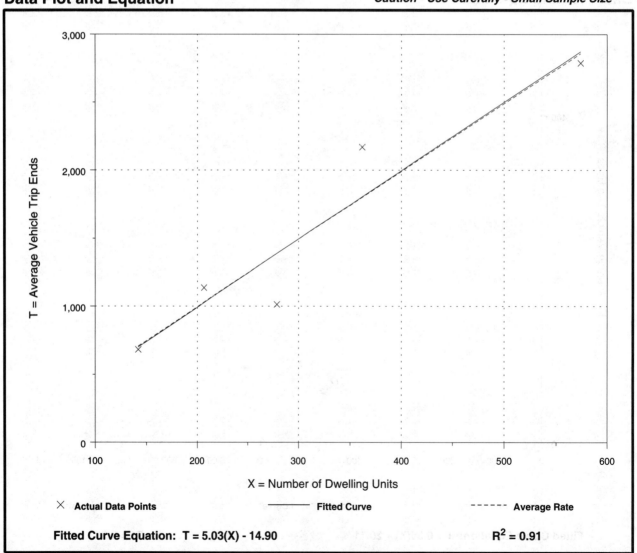

X **Actual Data Points**   —— **Fitted Curve**   - - - - - **Average Rate**

Fitted Curve Equation: T = 5.03(X) - 14.90 $R^2 = 0.91$

High-Rise Apartment
(222)

Average Vehicle Trip Ends vs: **Dwelling Units**
On a: **Saturday,**
Peak Hour of Generator

Number of Studies: 5
Avg. Number of Dwelling Units: 313
Directional Distribution: 57% entering, 43% exiting

Trip Generation per Dwelling Unit

Average Rate	Range of Rates	Standard Deviation
0.40	0.35 - 0.46	0.63

Data Plot and Equation

Caution - Use Carefully - Small Sample Size

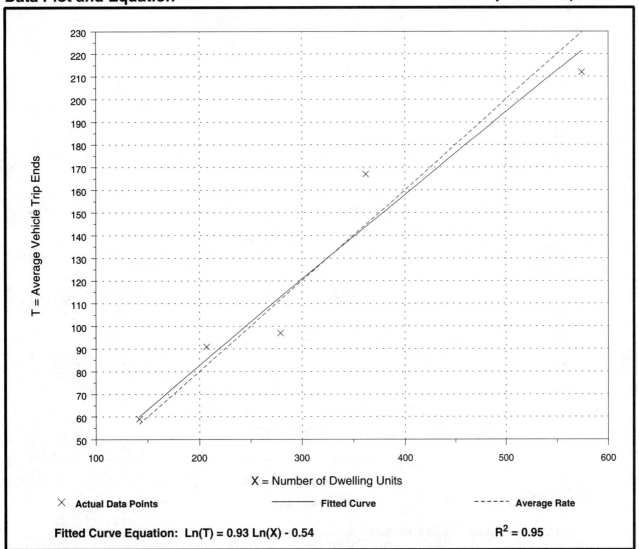

X   **Actual Data Points**   ———— **Fitted Curve**   ----- **Average Rate**

Fitted Curve Equation: Ln(T) = 0.93 Ln(X) - 0.54 $R^2 = 0.95$

High-Rise Apartment
(222)

Average Vehicle Trip Ends vs: Dwelling Units
On a: Sunday

Number of Studies: 5
Avg. Number of Dwelling Units: 313
Directional Distribution: 50% entering, 50% exiting

Trip Generation per Dwelling Unit

Average Rate	Range of Rates	Standard Deviation
3.65	2.78 - 4.17	1.96

Data Plot and Equation

Caution - Use Carefully - Small Sample Size

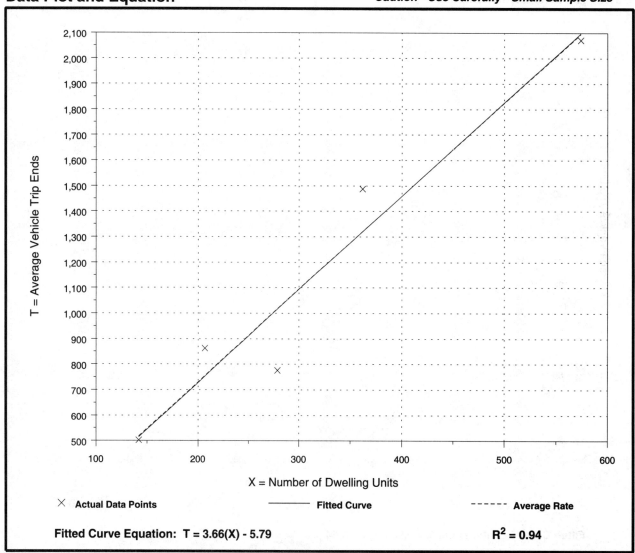

X **Actual Data Points**   —— **Fitted Curve**   - - - - - **Average Rate**

Fitted Curve Equation: T = 3.66(X) - 5.79 $R^2 = 0.94$

High-Rise Apartment
(222)

Average Vehicle Trip Ends vs: **Dwelling Units**
On a: **Sunday,**
Peak Hour of Generator

Number of Studies: 5
Avg. Number of Dwelling Units: 313
Directional Distribution: 53% entering, 47% exiting

Trip Generation per Dwelling Unit

Average Rate	Range of Rates	Standard Deviation
0.31	0.29 - 0.34	0.56

Data Plot and Equation

Caution - Use Carefully - Small Sample Size

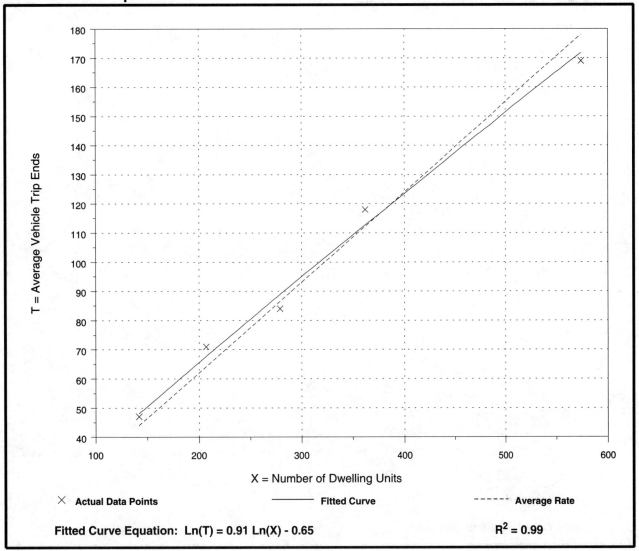

X = Number of Dwelling Units

✕ **Actual Data Points**   ――― **Fitted Curve**   - - - - - **Average Rate**

Fitted Curve Equation: $Ln(T) = 0.91 \ Ln(X) - 0.65$ $R^2 = 0.99$

High-Rise Apartment
(222)

Average Vehicle Trip Ends vs: Persons
On a: Weekday,
A.M. Peak Hour of Generator

Number of Studies: 2
Average Number of Persons: 869
Directional Distribution: 16% entering, 84% exiting

Trip Generation per Person

Average Rate	Range of Rates	Standard Deviation
0.22	0.22 - 0.22	*

Data Plot and Equation

Caution - Use Carefully - Small Sample Size

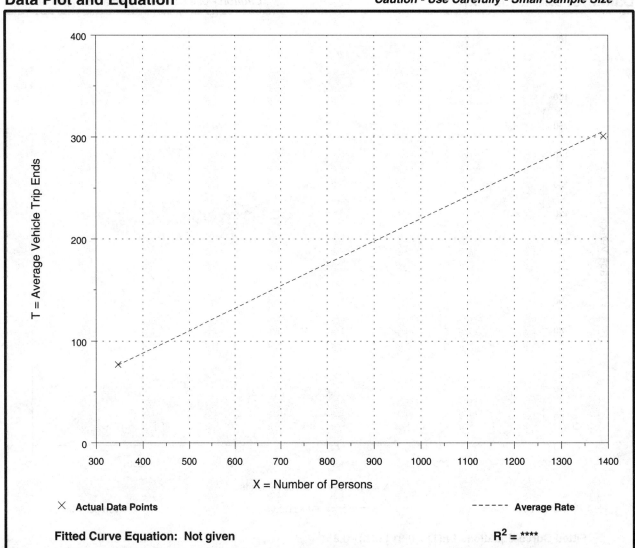

Fitted Curve Equation: Not given

$R^2 = ****$

High-Rise Apartment
(222)

Average Vehicle Trip Ends vs: Persons
On a: Weekday,
P.M. Peak Hour of Generator

Number of Studies: 2
Average Number of Persons: 869
Directional Distribution: 73% entering, 27% exiting

Trip Generation per Person

Average Rate	Range of Rates	Standard Deviation
0.20	0.18 - 0.26	*

Data Plot and Equation

Caution - Use Carefully - Small Sample Size

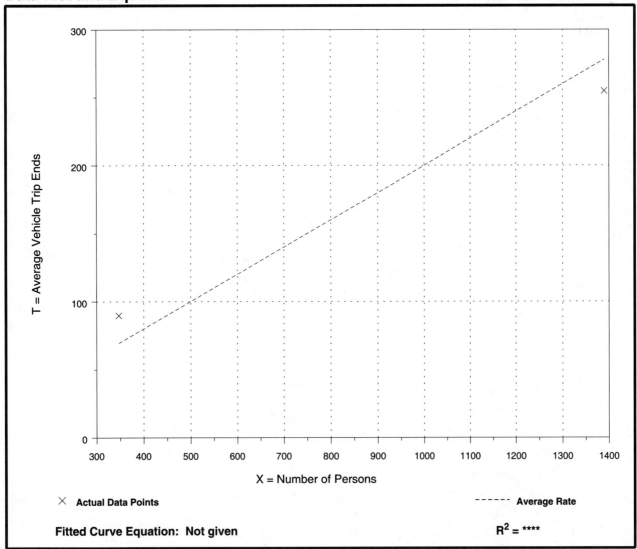

X **Actual Data Points**

------ **Average Rate**

Fitted Curve Equation: Not given

$R^2 = ****$

Land Use: 223
Mid-Rise Apartment

Description

Mid-rise apartments are apartments (rental dwelling units) in rental buildings that have between three and 10 levels (floors). Apartment (Land Use 220), low-rise apartment (Land Use 221) and high-rise apartment (Land Use 222) are related uses.

Additional Data

The peak hour of the generator typically coincided with the peak hour of the adjacent street traffic.

The sites were surveyed in the late 1980s in Montgomery County, Maryland.

Source Number

321

Mid-Rise Apartment
(223)

Average Vehicle Trip Ends vs: **Dwelling Units**

On a: **Weekday,**
Peak Hour of Adjacent Street Traffic,
One Hour Between 7 and 9 a.m.

Number of Studies: 7
Avg. Number of Dwelling Units: 120
Directional Distribution: 31% entering, 69% exiting

Trip Generation per Dwelling Unit

Average Rate	Range of Rates	Standard Deviation
0.30	0.06 - 0.46	0.56

Data Plot and Equation

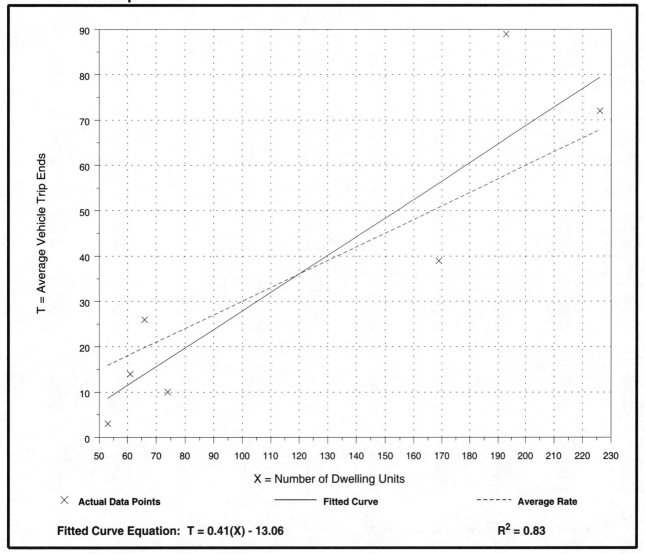

Fitted Curve Equation: T = 0.41(X) - 13.06　　　　　　$R^2 = 0.83$

Mid-Rise Apartment
(223)

Average Vehicle Trip Ends vs: **Dwelling Units**
On a: **Weekday,**
Peak Hour of Adjacent Street Traffic,
One Hour Between 4 and 6 p.m.

Number of Studies: 7
Avg. Number of Dwelling Units: 120
Directional Distribution: 58% entering, 42% exiting

Trip Generation per Dwelling Unit

Average Rate	Range of Rates	Standard Deviation
0.39	0.15 - 0.54	0.63

Data Plot and Equation

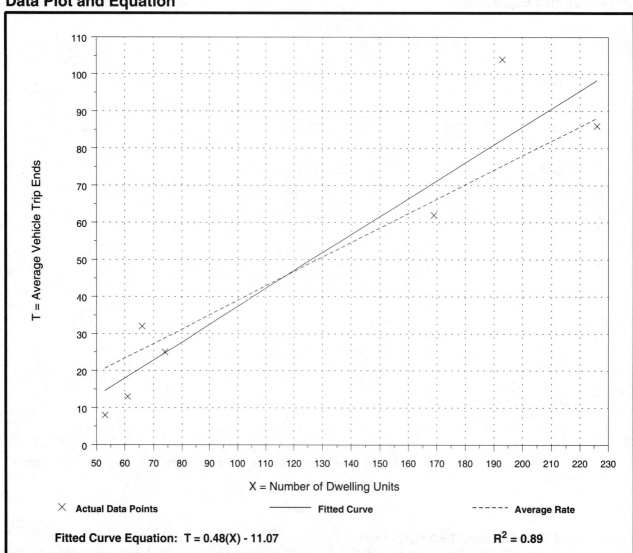

X **Actual Data Points** ——— **Fitted Curve** - - - - - **Average Rate**

Fitted Curve Equation: T = 0.48(X) - 11.07 **R² = 0.89**

Mid-Rise Apartment
(223)

Average Vehicle Trip Ends vs: Dwelling Units
On a: Weekday,
A.M. Peak Hour of Generator

Number of Studies: 7
Avg. Number of Dwelling Units: 120
Directional Distribution: 29% entering, 71% exiting

Trip Generation per Dwelling Unit

Average Rate	Range of Rates	Standard Deviation
0.35	0.19 - 0.47	0.60

Data Plot and Equation

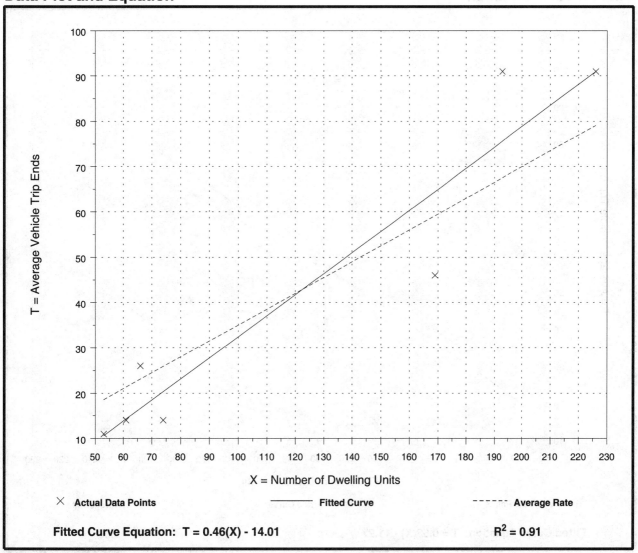

Fitted Curve Equation: T = 0.46(X) - 14.01 $R^2 = 0.91$

Mid-Rise Apartment
(223)

Average Vehicle Trip Ends vs: Dwelling Units
On a: Weekday,
P.M. Peak Hour of Generator

Number of Studies: 7
Avg. Number of Dwelling Units: 120
Directional Distribution: 59% entering, 41% exiting

Trip Generation per Dwelling Unit

Average Rate	Range of Rates	Standard Deviation
0.44	0.19 - 0.60	0.67

Data Plot and Equation

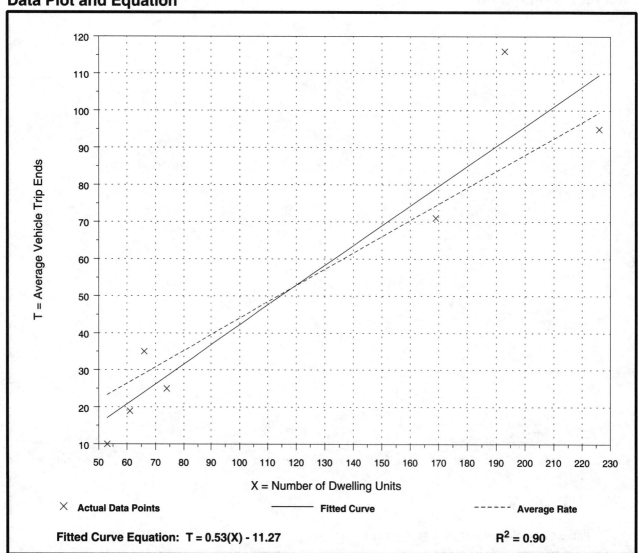

X = Number of Dwelling Units

× **Actual Data Points** ——— **Fitted Curve** - - - - - **Average Rate**

Fitted Curve Equation: T = 0.53(X) - 11.27 $R^2 = 0.90$

Land Use: 224
Rental Townhouse

Description

Rental townhouses are townhouse developments with rented rather than owned units and a minimum of two attached units per building structure. Units are not stacked on top of one another.

Additional Data

The peak hour of the generator typically coincided with the peak hour of the adjacent street traffic.

The site was surveyed in the late 1980s in Montgomery County, Maryland.

Source Number

321

Land Use: 224
Rental Townhouse
Independent Variables with One Observation

The following trip generation data are for independent variables with only one observation. This information is shown in this table only; there are no related plots for these data.

Users are cautioned to use data with care because of the small sample size.

Dwelling Units

Independent Variable	Trip Generation Rate	Size of Independent Variable	Number of Studies	Directional Distribution
Weekday a.m. Peak Hour of Adjacent Street Traffic	0.70	103	1	33% entering, 67% exiting
Weekday p.m. Peak Hour of Adjacent Street Traffic	0.72	103	1	51% entering, 49% exiting
Weekday a.m. Peak Hour of Generator	0.73	103	1	35% entering, 65% exiting
Weekday p.m. Peak Hour of Generator	0.73	103	1	55% entering, 45% exiting

Land Use: 230
Residential Condominium/Townhouse

Description

Residential condominiums/townhouses are defined as <u>ownership</u> units that have at least one other owned unit within the same building structure. **Both condominiums and townhouses are included in this land use.** The studies in this land use did not identify whether the condominiums/townhouses were low-rise or high-rise. Low-rise residential condominium/townhouse (Land Use 231), high-rise residential condominium/townhouse (Land Use 232) and luxury condominium/townhouse (Land Use 233) are related uses.

Additional Data

The number of vehicles and the number of residents had a high correlation with average weekday vehicle trip ends. The use of these variables was limited, however, because the number of vehicles and residents was often difficult to obtain or predict. The number of dwelling units was generally used as the independent variable of choice because it is usually readily available, easy to project and had a high correlation with average weekday vehicle trip ends.

The peak hour of the generator typically coincided with the peak hour of the adjacent street traffic.

The sites were surveyed between the mid-1970s and the 2000s throughout the United States and Canada.

Source Numbers

4, 92, 94, 95, 97, 100, 105, 106, 114, 168, 186, 204, 237, 253, 293, 319, 320, 321, 390, 412, 418, 561, 562, 583, 638

Residential Condominium/Townhouse
(230)

Average Vehicle Trip Ends vs: Dwelling Units
On a: Weekday

Number of Studies: 56
Avg. Number of Dwelling Units: 179
Directional Distribution: 50% entering, 50% exiting

Trip Generation per Dwelling Unit

Average Rate	Range of Rates	Standard Deviation
5.81	1.53 - 11.79	3.11

Data Plot and Equation

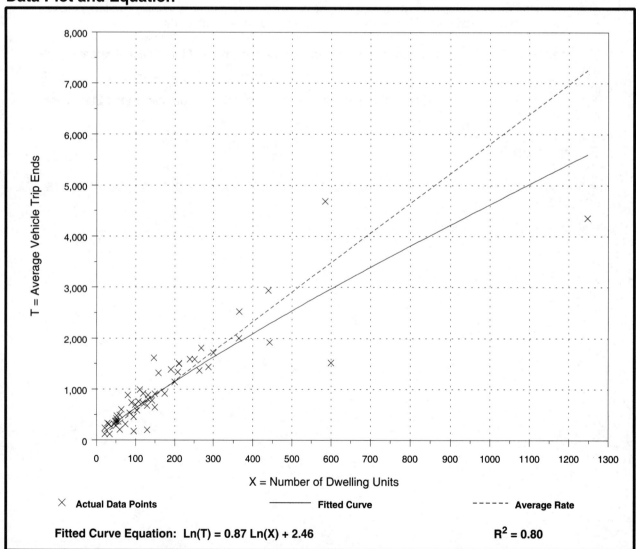

Fitted Curve Equation: Ln(T) = 0.87 Ln(X) + 2.46 $R^2 = 0.80$

Residential Condominium/Townhouse
(230)

Average Vehicle Trip Ends vs: **Dwelling Units**
On a: **Weekday,**
Peak Hour of Adjacent Street Traffic,
One Hour Between 7 and 9 a.m.

Number of Studies: 59
Avg. Number of Dwelling Units: 213
Directional Distribution: 17% entering, 83% exiting

Trip Generation per Dwelling Unit

Average Rate	Range of Rates	Standard Deviation
0.44	0.15 - 1.61	0.69

Data Plot and Equation

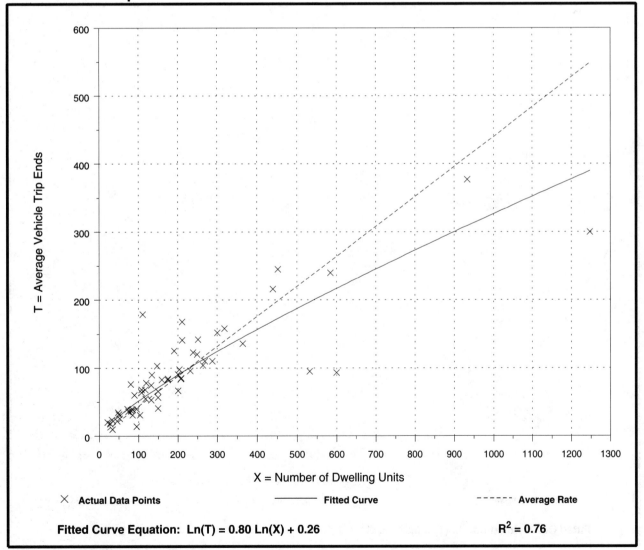

Fitted Curve Equation: Ln(T) = 0.80 Ln(X) + 0.26 $R^2 = 0.76$

Residential Condominium/Townhouse
(230)

Average Vehicle Trip Ends vs: **Dwelling Units**
On a: **Weekday,**
Peak Hour of Adjacent Street Traffic,
One Hour Between 4 and 6 p.m.

Number of Studies: 62
Avg. Number of Dwelling Units: 205
Directional Distribution: 67% entering, 33% exiting

Trip Generation per Dwelling Unit

Average Rate	Range of Rates	Standard Deviation
0.52	0.18 - 1.24	0.75

Data Plot and Equation

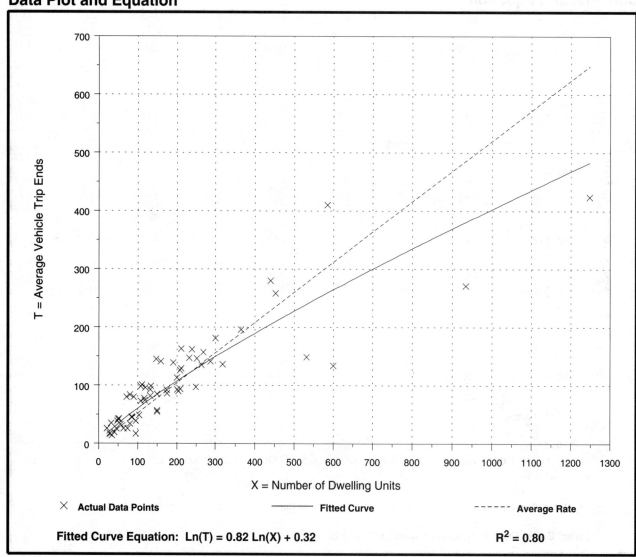

X Actual Data Points ——— Fitted Curve - - - - Average Rate

Fitted Curve Equation: Ln(T) = 0.82 Ln(X) + 0.32 $R^2 = 0.80$

Residential Condominium/Townhouse
(230)

Average Vehicle Trip Ends vs: **Dwelling Units**
On a: **Weekday,**
A.M. Peak Hour of Generator

Number of Studies: 54
Avg. Number of Dwelling Units: 196
Directional Distribution: 19% entering, 81% exiting

Trip Generation per Dwelling Unit

Average Rate	Range of Rates	Standard Deviation
0.44	0.15 - 0.97	0.68

Data Plot and Equation

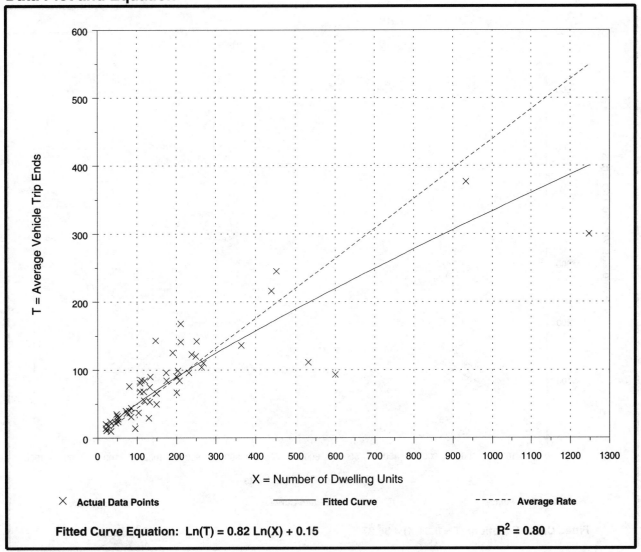

Fitted Curve Equation: $Ln(T) = 0.82\ Ln(X) + 0.15$

$R^2 = 0.80$

Residential Condominium/Townhouse
(230)

Average Vehicle Trip Ends vs: **Dwelling Units**
On a: **Weekday,**
P.M. Peak Hour of Generator

Number of Studies: 52
Avg. Number of Dwelling Units: 199
Directional Distribution: 64% entering, 36% exiting

Trip Generation per Dwelling Unit

Average Rate	Range of Rates	Standard Deviation
0.52	0.18 - 1.24	0.75

Data Plot and Equation

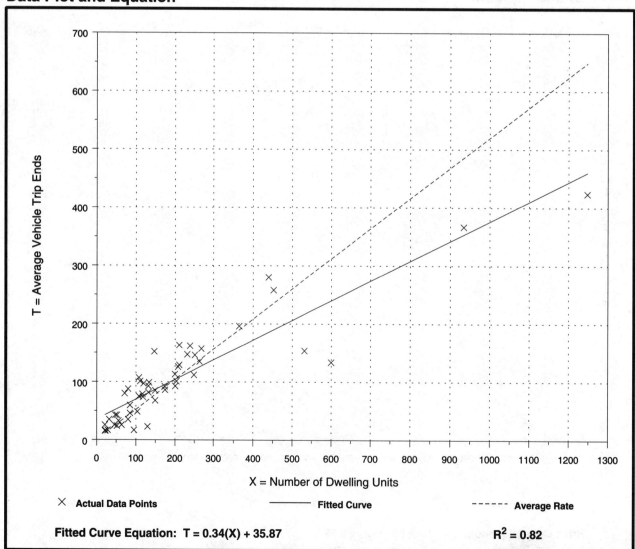

X   **Actual Data Points** ——— **Fitted Curve** - - - - - **Average Rate**

Fitted Curve Equation: T = 0.34(X) + 35.87   **R² = 0.82**

Residential Condominium/Townhouse
(230)

Average Vehicle Trip Ends vs: **Dwelling Units**
On a: **Saturday**

Number of Studies: 30
Avg. Number of Dwelling Units: 209
Directional Distribution: 50% entering, 50% exiting

Trip Generation per Dwelling Unit

Average Rate	Range of Rates	Standard Deviation
5.67	1.17 - 11.40	3.10

Data Plot and Equation

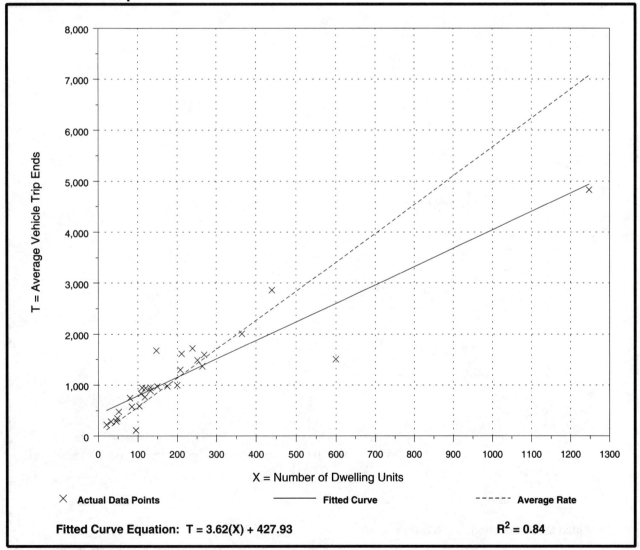

Fitted Curve Equation: T = 3.62(X) + 427.93 $R^2 = 0.84$

Residential Condominium/Townhouse
(230)

Average Vehicle Trip Ends vs: Dwelling Units
On a: Saturday,
Peak Hour of Generator

Number of Studies: 27
Avg. Number of Dwelling Units: 228
Directional Distribution: 54% entering, 46% exiting

Trip Generation per Dwelling Unit

Average Rate	Range of Rates	Standard Deviation
0.47	0.14 - 0.93	0.71

Data Plot and Equation

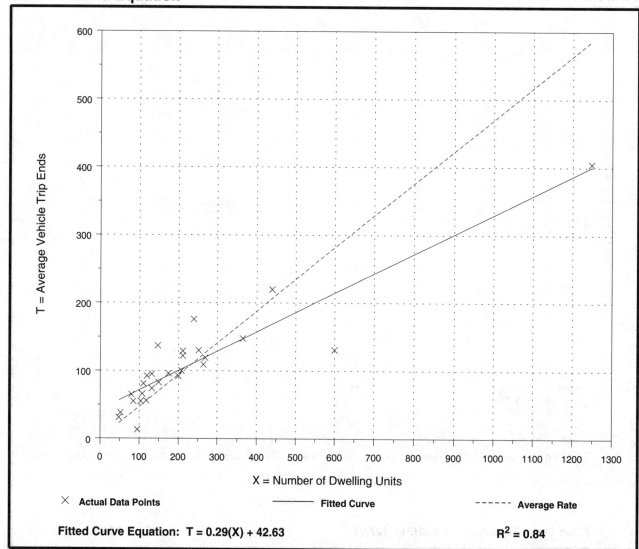

X **Actual Data Points**   —— **Fitted Curve**   - - - - - **Average Rate**

Fitted Curve Equation: T = 0.29(X) + 42.63 $R^2 = 0.84$

Residential Condominium/Townhouse
(230)

Average Vehicle Trip Ends vs: Dwelling Units
On a: Sunday

Number of Studies: 30
Avg. Number of Dwelling Units: 209
Directional Distribution: 50% entering, 50% exiting

Trip Generation per Dwelling Unit

Average Rate	Range of Rates	Standard Deviation
4.84	1.36 - 8.56	2.71

Data Plot and Equation

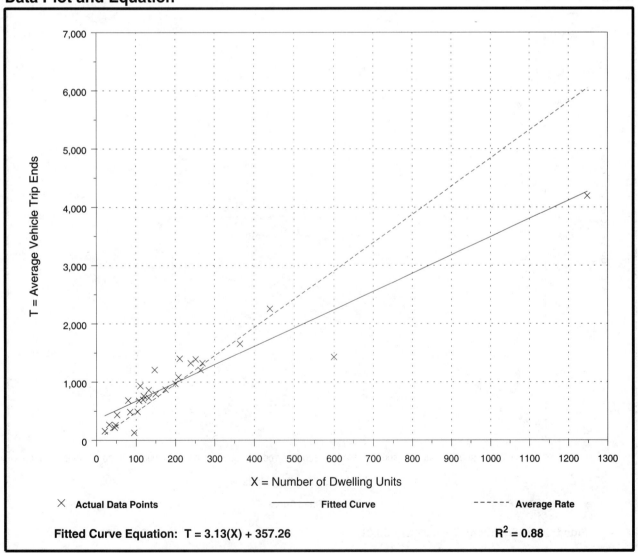

Fitted Curve Equation: $T = 3.13(X) + 357.26$ $R^2 = 0.88$

Residential Condominium/Townhouse
(230)

Average Vehicle Trip Ends vs: **Dwelling Units**
On a: **Sunday,**
Peak Hour of Generator

Number of Studies: 27
Avg. Number of Dwelling Units: 228
Directional Distribution: 49% entering, 51% exiting

Trip Generation per Dwelling Unit

Average Rate	Range of Rates	Standard Deviation
0.45	0.16 - 1.07	0.70

Data Plot and Equation

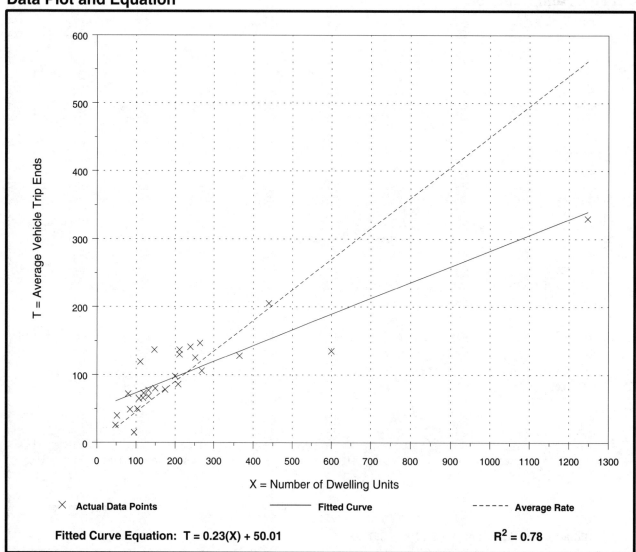

X **Actual Data Points**   ——— **Fitted Curve**   - - - - - **Average Rate**

Fitted Curve Equation: T = 0.23(X) + 50.01 $R^2 = 0.78$

Residential Condominium/Townhouse
(230)

Average Vehicle Trip Ends vs: Persons
On a: Weekday

Number of Studies: 27
Average Number of Persons: 388
Directional Distribution: 50% entering, 50% exiting

Trip Generation per Person

Average Rate	Range of Rates	Standard Deviation
2.49	1.10 - 6.73	1.80

Data Plot and Equation

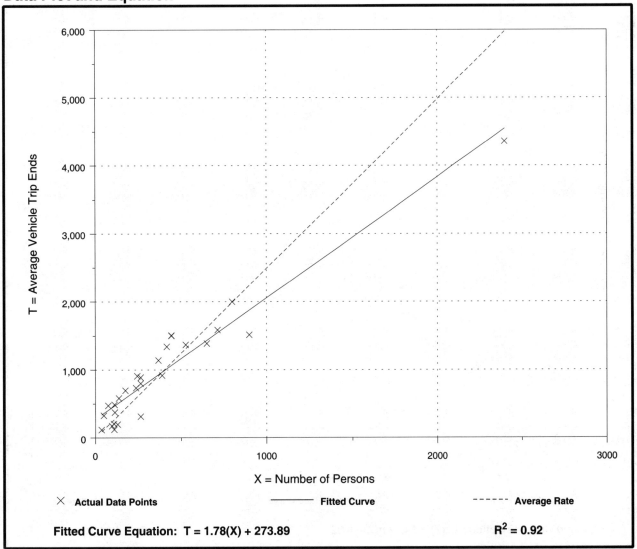

X = Number of Persons

$\times$ **Actual Data Points**   —— **Fitted Curve**   ----- **Average Rate**

Fitted Curve Equation: T = 1.78(X) + 273.89 $R^2 = 0.92$

Residential Condominium/Townhouse
(230)

Average Vehicle Trip Ends vs: **Persons**
On a: **Weekday,**
Peak Hour of Adjacent Street Traffic,
One Hour Between 7 and 9 a.m.

Number of Studies: 21
Average Number of Persons: 469
Directional Distribution: 16% entering, 84% exiting

Trip Generation per Person

Average Rate	Range of Rates	Standard Deviation
0.19	0.09 - 0.38	0.44

Data Plot and Equation

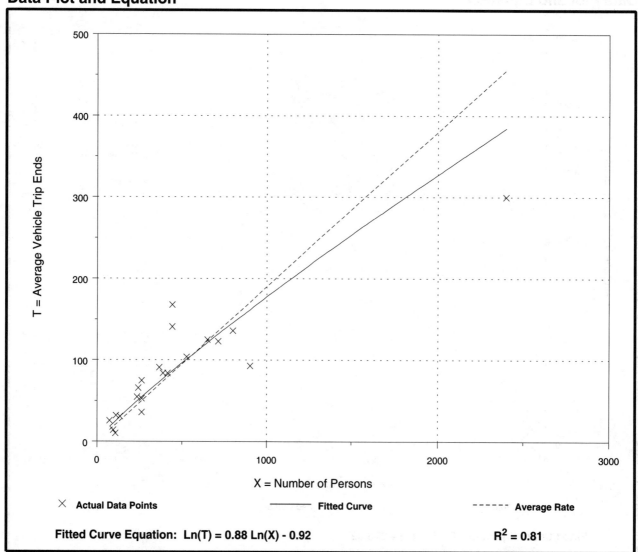

X Actual Data Points — **Fitted Curve** — - - - - **Average Rate**

Fitted Curve Equation: Ln(T) = 0.88 Ln(X) - 0.92 $R^2 = 0.81$

Residential Condominium/Townhouse
(230)

Average Vehicle Trip Ends vs: Persons
On a: Weekday,
Peak Hour of Adjacent Street Traffic,
One Hour Between 4 and 6 p.m.

Number of Studies: 21
Average Number of Persons: 469
Directional Distribution: 67% entering, 33% exiting

Trip Generation per Person

Average Rate	Range of Rates	Standard Deviation
0.24	0.10 - 0.57	0.49

Data Plot and Equation

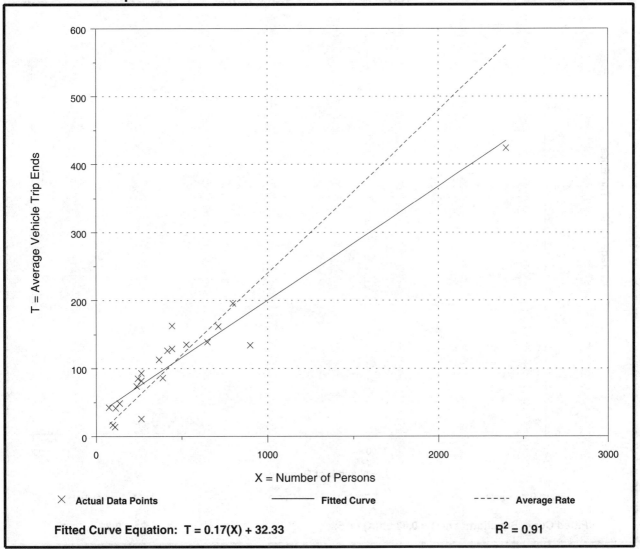

Fitted Curve Equation: T = 0.17(X) + 32.33 $R^2 = 0.91$

Residential Condominium/Townhouse
(230)

Average Vehicle Trip Ends vs: **Persons**
On a: **Weekday,**
A.M. Peak Hour of Generator

Number of Studies: 23
Average Number of Persons: 436
Directional Distribution: 16% entering, 84% exiting

Trip Generation per Person

Average Rate	Range of Rates	Standard Deviation
0.19	0.09 - 0.39	0.44

Data Plot and Equation

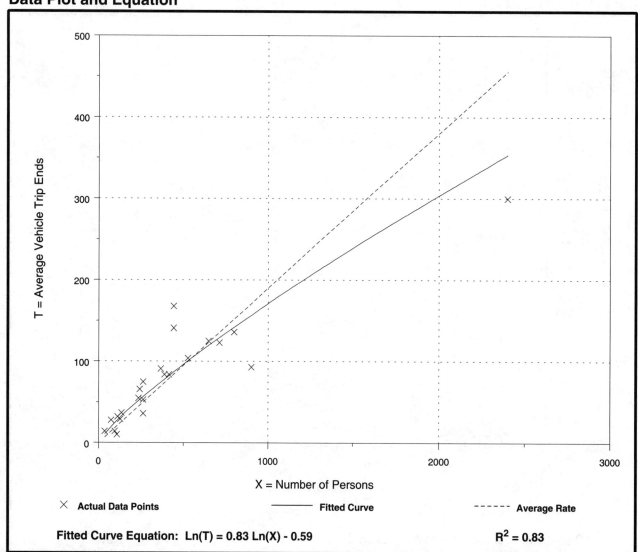

Fitted Curve Equation: Ln(T) = 0.83 Ln(X) - 0.59 $R^2 = 0.83$

Residential Condominium/Townhouse
(230)

Average Vehicle Trip Ends vs: **Persons**
On a: **Weekday,**
P.M. Peak Hour of Generator

Number of Studies: 19
Average Number of Persons: 468
Directional Distribution: 67% entering, 33% exiting

Trip Generation per Person

Average Rate	Range of Rates	Standard Deviation
0.24	0.15 - 0.57	0.50

Data Plot and Equation

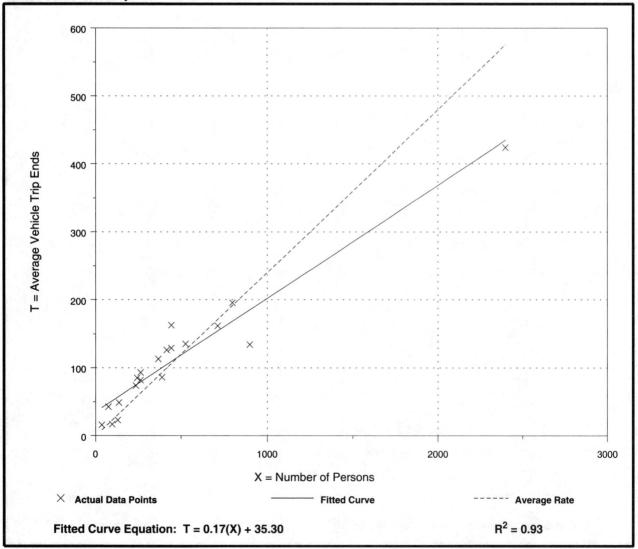

Fitted Curve Equation: T = 0.17(X) + 35.30 $R^2 = 0.93$

Residential Condominium/Townhouse
(230)

Average Vehicle Trip Ends vs: Persons
On a: Saturday

Number of Studies: 17
Average Number of Persons: 513
Directional Distribution: 50% entering, 50% exiting

Trip Generation per Person

Average Rate	Range of Rates	Standard Deviation
2.60	1.16 - 6.35	1.79

Data Plot and Equation

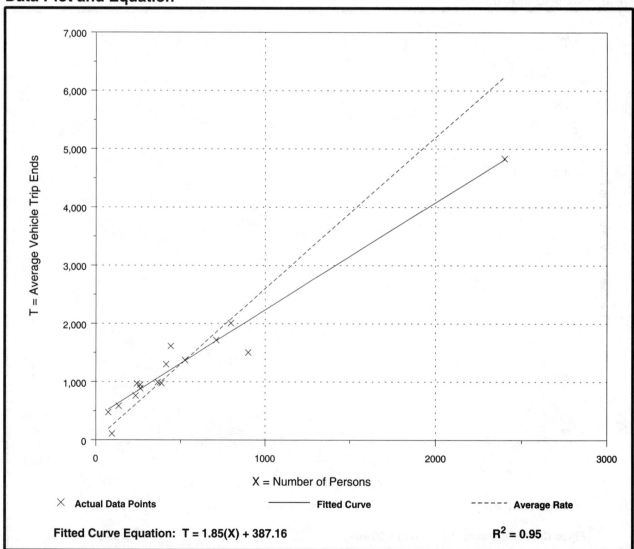

Fitted Curve Equation: T = 1.85(X) + 387.16 $R^2 = 0.95$

Residential Condominium/Townhouse
(230)

Average Vehicle Trip Ends vs: **Persons**
On a: **Saturday,**
Peak Hour of Generator

Number of Studies: 17
Average Number of Persons: 513
Directional Distribution: 55% entering, 45% exiting

Trip Generation per Person

Average Rate	Range of Rates	Standard Deviation
0.22	0.14 - 0.51	0.47

Data Plot and Equation

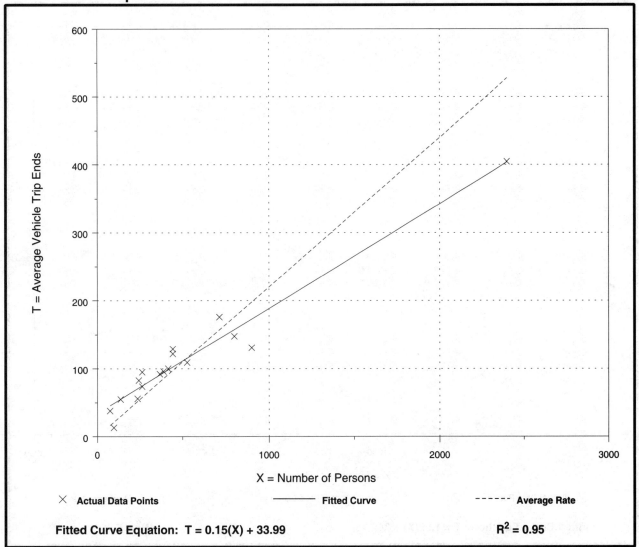

Fitted Curve Equation: T = 0.15(X) + 33.99   **R² = 0.95**

Residential Condominium/Townhouse
(230)

Average Vehicle Trip Ends vs: Persons
On a: Sunday

Number of Studies: 17
Average Number of Persons: 513
Directional Distribution: 50% entering, 50% exiting

Trip Generation per Person

Average Rate	Range of Rates	Standard Deviation
2.26	1.34 - 5.84	1.65

Data Plot and Equation

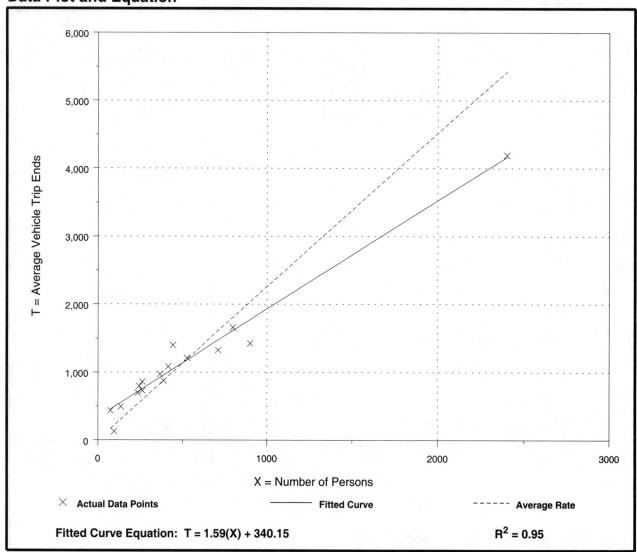

Fitted Curve Equation: T = 1.59(X) + 340.15 $R^2 = 0.95$

Residential Condominium/Townhouse
(230)

Average Vehicle Trip Ends vs: **Persons**
On a: **Sunday,**
Peak Hour of Generator

Number of Studies: 17
Average Number of Persons: 513
Directional Distribution: 49% entering, 51% exiting

Trip Generation per Person

Average Rate	Range of Rates	Standard Deviation
0.21	0.14 - 0.53	0.46

Data Plot and Equation

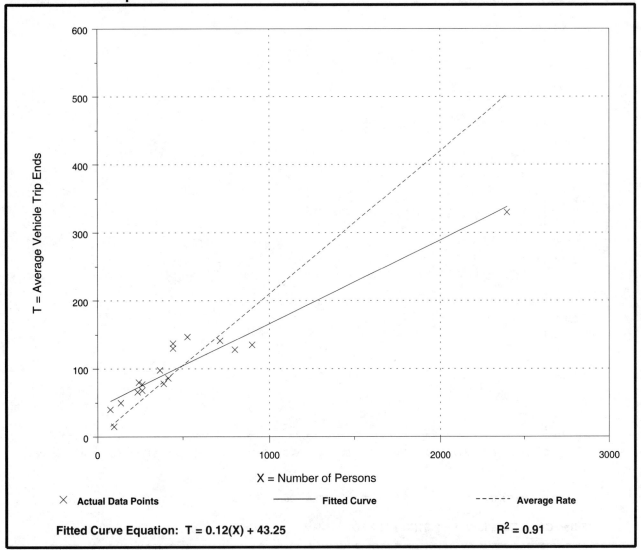

Fitted Curve Equation: T = 0.12(X) + 43.25 $R^2 = 0.91$

Residential Condominium/Townhouse
(230)

Average Vehicle Trip Ends vs: Vehicles
On a: Weekday

Number of Studies: 25
Average Number of Vehicles: 300
Directional Distribution: 50% entering, 50% exiting

Trip Generation per Vehicle

Average Rate	Range of Rates	Standard Deviation
3.34	1.90 - 7.34	2.07

Data Plot and Equation

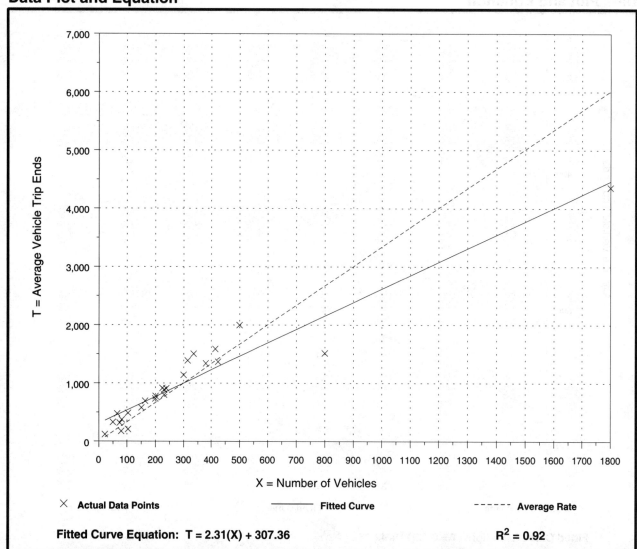

Fitted Curve Equation: T = 2.31(X) + 307.36 $R^2 = 0.92$

Residential Condominium/Townhouse
(230)

Average Vehicle Trip Ends vs:	**Vehicles**
On a:	**Weekday,**
	Peak Hour of Adjacent Street Traffic,
	One Hour Between 7 and 9 a.m.

Number of Studies: 20
Average Number of Vehicles: 343
Directional Distribution: 16% entering, 84% exiting

Trip Generation per Vehicle

Average Rate	Range of Rates	Standard Deviation
0.24	0.12 - 0.49	0.50

Data Plot and Equation

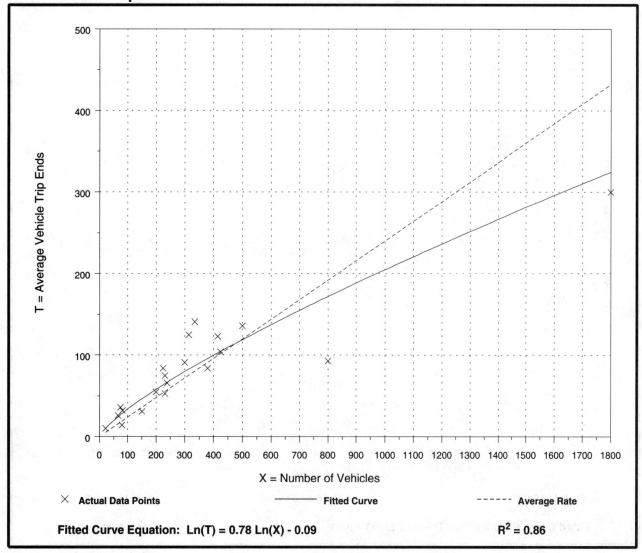

X = Number of Vehicles

× **Actual Data Points**   —— **Fitted Curve**   - - - - - **Average Rate**

Fitted Curve Equation: $Ln(T) = 0.78\ Ln(X) - 0.09$ $R^2 = 0.86$

Residential Condominium/Townhouse
(230)

Average Vehicle Trip Ends vs: **Vehicles**
On a: **Weekday,**
Peak Hour of Adjacent Street Traffic,
One Hour Between 4 and 6 p.m.

Number of Studies: 20
Average Number of Vehicles: 343
Directional Distribution: 66% entering, 34% exiting

Trip Generation per Vehicle

Average Rate	Range of Rates	Standard Deviation
0.32	0.17 - 0.66	0.57

Data Plot and Equation

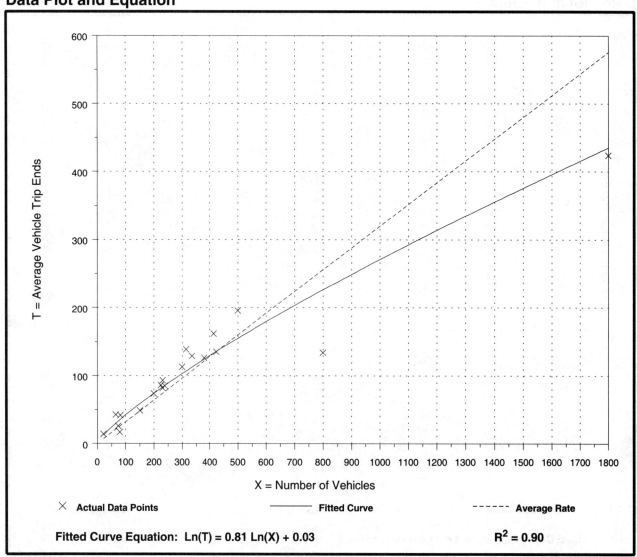

Fitted Curve Equation: $Ln(T) = 0.81 \, Ln(X) + 0.03$ $R^2 = 0.90$

Residential Condominium/Townhouse
(230)

Average Vehicle Trip Ends vs: **Vehicles**
On a: **Weekday,**
A.M. Peak Hour of Generator

Number of Studies: 20
Average Number of Vehicles: 343
Directional Distribution: 17% entering, 83% exiting

Trip Generation per Vehicle

Average Rate	Range of Rates	Standard Deviation
0.25	0.12 - 0.49	0.50

Data Plot and Equation

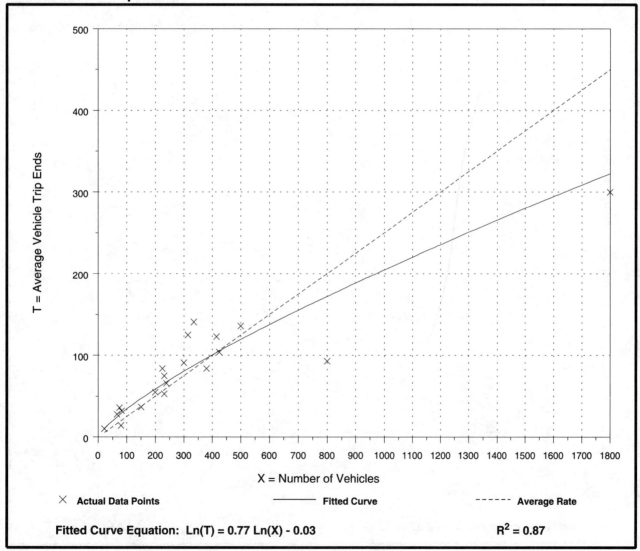

Fitted Curve Equation: $\text{Ln}(T) = 0.77 \, \text{Ln}(X) - 0.03$ $R^2 = 0.87$

Residential Condominium/Townhouse
(230)

Average Vehicle Trip Ends vs: Vehicles
On a: Weekday,
P.M. Peak Hour of Generator

Number of Studies: 16
Average Number of Vehicles: 399
Directional Distribution: 66% entering, 34% exiting

Trip Generation per Vehicle

Average Rate	Range of Rates	Standard Deviation
0.31	0.17 - 0.66	0.56

Data Plot and Equation

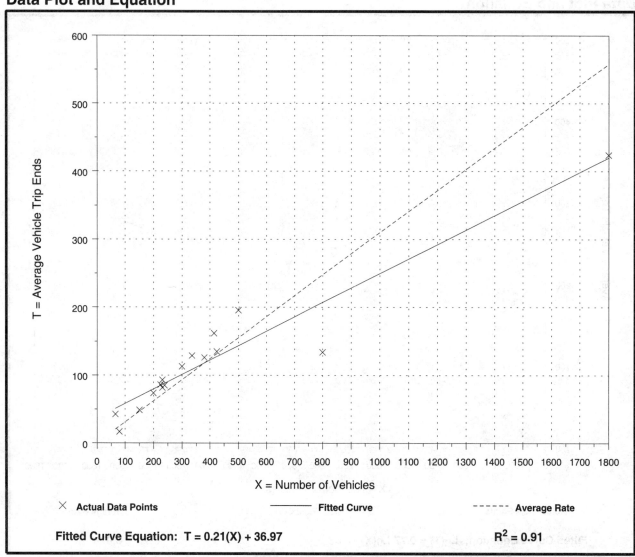

X **Actual Data Points**　　　　——— **Fitted Curve**　　　　- - - - - **Average Rate**

Fitted Curve Equation: T = 0.21(X) + 36.97　　　　$R^2 = 0.91$

Residential Condominium/Townhouse
(230)

Average Vehicle Trip Ends vs: **Vehicles**
On a: **Saturday**

Number of Studies: 16
Average Number of Vehicles: 399
Directional Distribution: 50% entering, 50% exiting

Trip Generation per Vehicle

Average Rate	Range of Rates	Standard Deviation
3.31	1.39 - 7.32	2.05

Data Plot and Equation

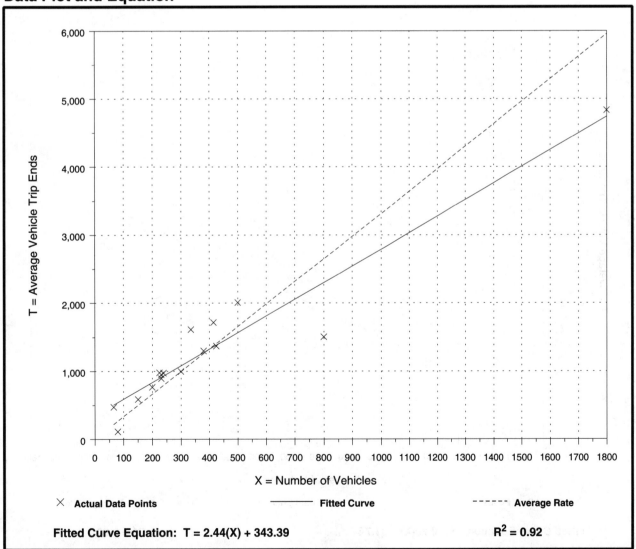

X = Number of Vehicles

✕ **Actual Data Points** — **Fitted Curve** ----- **Average Rate**

Fitted Curve Equation: T = 2.44(X) + 343.39　　　　$R^2 = 0.92$

Residential Condominium/Townhouse
(230)

Average Vehicle Trip Ends vs: Vehicles
On a: Saturday,
Peak Hour of Generator

Number of Studies: 16
Average Number of Vehicles: 399
Directional Distribution: 56% entering, 44% exiting

Trip Generation per Vehicle

Average Rate	Range of Rates	Standard Deviation
0.28	0.16 - 0.58	0.54

Data Plot and Equation

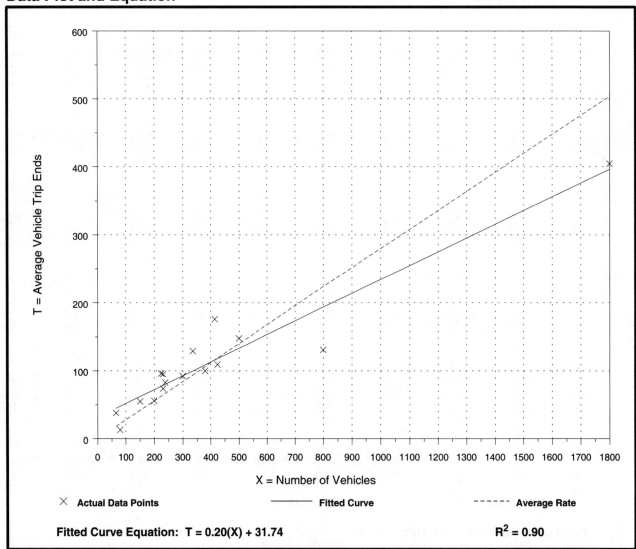

Fitted Curve Equation: T = 0.20(X) + 31.74 $R^2 = 0.90$

Residential Condominium/Townhouse
(230)

Average Vehicle Trip Ends vs: Vehicles
On a: Sunday

Number of Studies: 16
Average Number of Vehicles: 399
Directional Distribution: 50% entering, 50% exiting

Trip Generation per Vehicle

Average Rate	Range of Rates	Standard Deviation
2.87	1.61 - 6.74	1.86

Data Plot and Equation

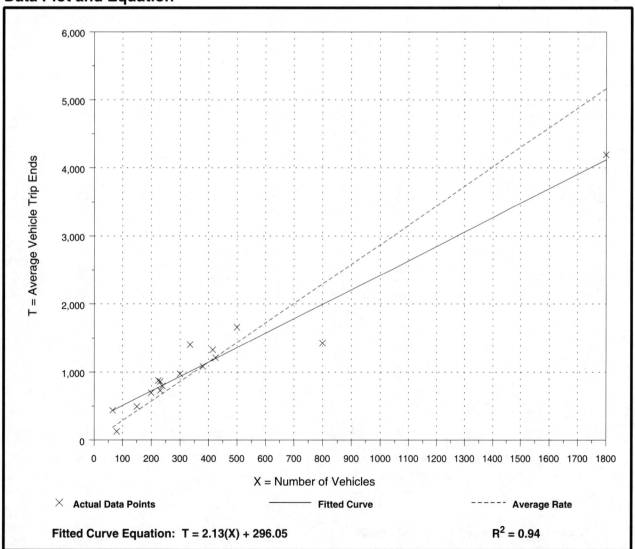

X Actual Data Points　　　　　**——— Fitted Curve**　　　　　**- - - - - Average Rate**

Fitted Curve Equation: T = 2.13(X) + 296.05　　　　　**R^2 = 0.94**

Residential Condominium/Townhouse
(230)

Average Vehicle Trip Ends vs: **Vehicles**
On a: **Sunday,**
Peak Hour of Generator

Number of Studies: 16
Average Number of Vehicles: 399
Directional Distribution: 48% entering, 52% exiting

Trip Generation per Vehicle

Average Rate	Range of Rates	Standard Deviation
0.26	0.17 - 0.62	0.52

Data Plot and Equation

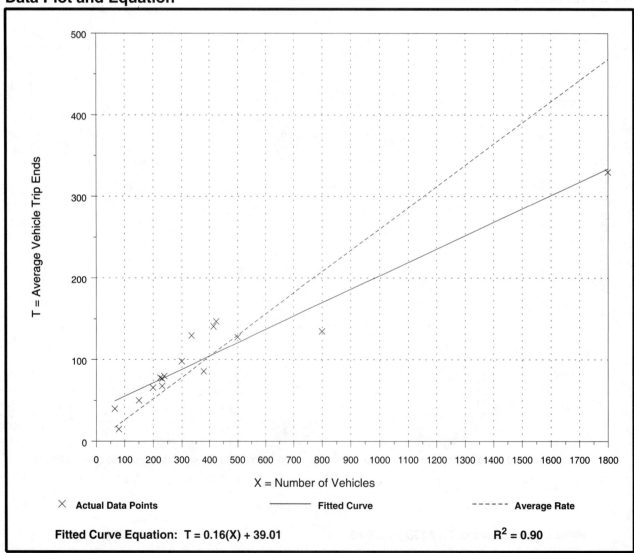

Fitted Curve Equation: T = 0.16(X) + 39.01 $R^2 = 0.90$

Land Use: 231
Low-Rise Residential Condominium/Townhouse

Description

Low-rise residential condominiums/townhouses are units located in buildings that have one or two levels (floors). **Both condominiums and townhouses are included in this land use.** Residential condominium/townhouse (Land Use 230), high-rise residential condominium/townhouse (Land Use 232) and luxury condominium/townhouse (Land Use 233) are related uses.

Additional Data

The peak hour of the generator typically coincided with the peak hour of the adjacent street traffic.

The sites were surveyed between the late 1970s and the 2000s throughout the United States.

Source Numbers

187, 192, 305, 306, 571

Low-Rise Residential Condominium/Townhouse
(231)

Average Vehicle Trip Ends vs: **Dwelling Units**
On a: **Weekday,**
Peak Hour of Adjacent Street Traffic,
One Hour Between 7 and 9 a.m.

Number of Studies: 5
Avg. Number of Dwelling Units: 234
Directional Distribution: 25% entering, 75% exiting

Trip Generation per Dwelling Unit

Average Rate	Range of Rates	Standard Deviation
0.67	0.33 - 0.82	0.83

Data Plot and Equation

Caution - Use Carefully - Small Sample Size

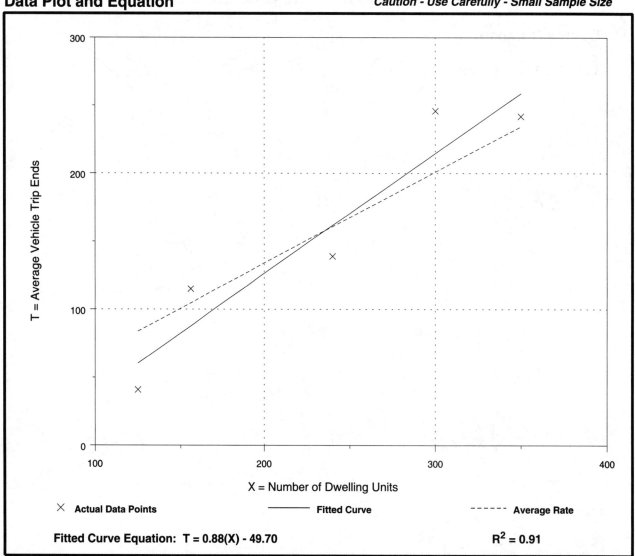

X Actual Data Points — Fitted Curve ----- Average Rate

Fitted Curve Equation: T = 0.88(X) - 49.70 $R^2 = 0.91$

Low-Rise Residential Condominium/Townhouse
(231)

Average Vehicle Trip Ends vs: **Dwelling Units**
On a: **Weekday,**
Peak Hour of Adjacent Street Traffic,
One Hour Between 4 and 6 p.m.

Number of Studies: 5
Avg. Number of Dwelling Units: 234
Directional Distribution: 58% entering, 42% exiting

Trip Generation per Dwelling Unit

Average Rate	Range of Rates	Standard Deviation
0.78	0.38 - 1.11	0.93

Data Plot and Equation

Caution - Use Carefully - Small Sample Size

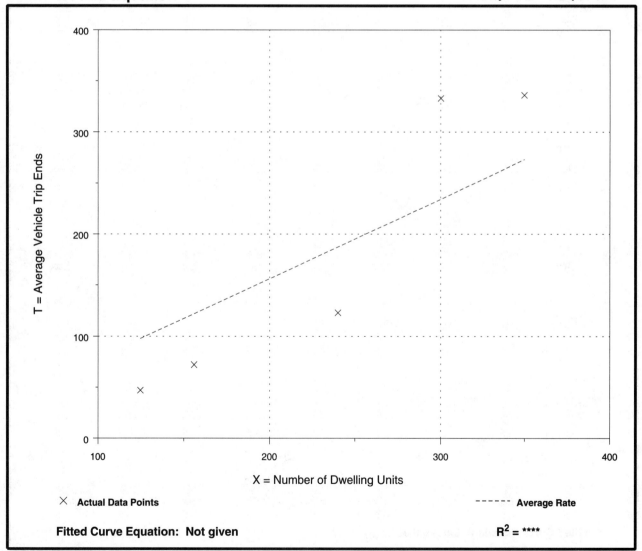

X **Actual Data Points**   - - - - - **Average Rate**

Fitted Curve Equation: Not given $R^2 = ****$

Low-Rise Residential Condominium/Townhouse
(231)

Average Vehicle Trip Ends vs: Dwelling Units
On a: Weekday,
A.M. Peak Hour of Generator

Number of Studies: 7
Avg. Number of Dwelling Units: 155
Directional Distribution: 18% entering, 82% exiting

Trip Generation per Dwelling Unit

Average Rate	Range of Rates	Standard Deviation
0.54	0.34 - 0.82	0.76

Data Plot and Equation

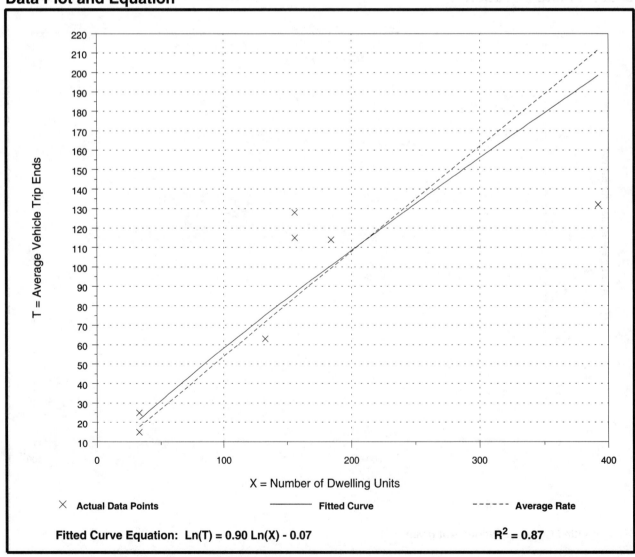

X = Number of Dwelling Units

✕ **Actual Data Points**   —— **Fitted Curve**   - - - - - **Average Rate**

Fitted Curve Equation: Ln(T) = 0.90 Ln(X) - 0.07 $R^2 = 0.87$

Low-Rise Residential Condominium/Townhouse
(231)

Average Vehicle Trip Ends vs: **Dwelling Units**
On a: **Weekday,**
P.M. Peak Hour of Generator

Number of Studies: 6
Avg. Number of Dwelling Units: 151
Directional Distribution: 55% entering, 45% exiting

Trip Generation per Dwelling Unit

Average Rate	Range of Rates	Standard Deviation
0.52	0.37 - 0.79	0.74

Data Plot and Equation

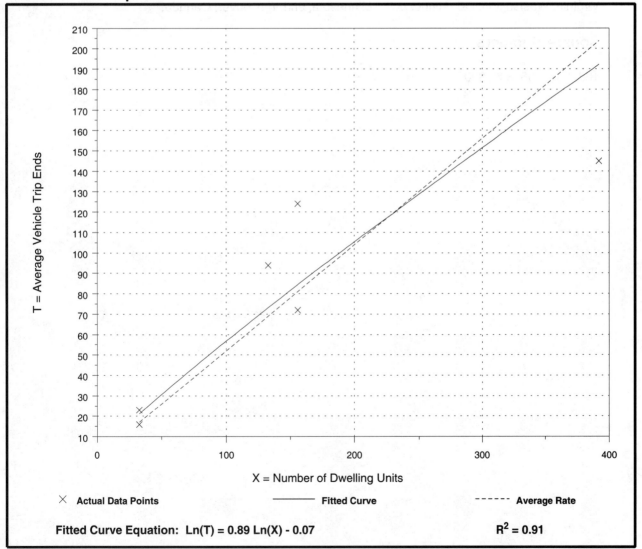

X **Actual Data Points** ——— **Fitted Curve** - - - - - **Average Rate**

Fitted Curve Equation: Ln(T) = 0.89 Ln(X) - 0.07 $R^2 = 0.91$

Land Use: 232
High-Rise Residential Condominium/Townhouse

Description

High-rise residential condominiums/townhouses are units located in buildings that have three or more levels (floors). **Both condominiums and townhouses are included in this land use.** Residential condominium/townhouse (Land Use 230), low-rise residential condominium/townhouse (Land Use 231) and luxury condominium/townhouse (Land Use 233) are related uses.

Additional Data

The peak hour of the generator typically coincided with the peak hour of the adjacent street traffic.

The sites were surveyed in the 1980s and the 1990s in the metropolitan areas of Richmond, Virginia; Washington, DC; Minneapolis, Minnesota; and Vancouver, Canada.

Source Numbers

168, 237, 305, 306, 390

High-Rise Residential Condominium/Townhouse
(232)

Average Vehicle Trip Ends vs: Dwelling Units
On a: Weekday

Number of Studies: 4
Avg. Number of Dwelling Units: 543
Directional Distribution: 50% entering, 50% exiting

Trip Generation per Dwelling Unit

Average Rate	Range of Rates	Standard Deviation
4.18	3.91 - 4.93	2.08

Data Plot and Equation

Caution - Use Carefully - Small Sample Size

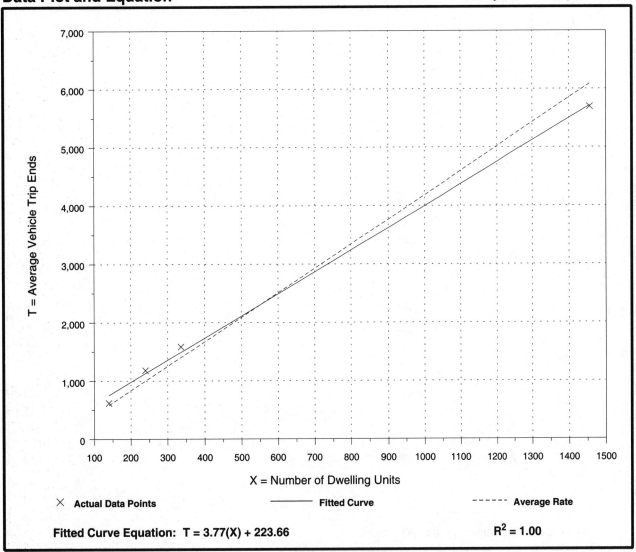

X **Actual Data Points** ——————— **Fitted Curve** - - - - - **Average Rate**

Fitted Curve Equation: T = 3.77(X) + 223.66 $R^2 = 1.00$

High-Rise Residential Condominium/Townhouse
(232)

Average Vehicle Trip Ends vs: **Dwelling Units**
On a: **Weekday,**
Peak Hour of Adjacent Street Traffic,
One Hour Between 7 and 9 a.m.

Number of Studies: 4
Avg. Number of Dwelling Units: 543
Directional Distribution: 19% entering, 81% exiting

Trip Generation per Dwelling Unit

Average Rate	Range of Rates	Standard Deviation
0.34	0.31 - 0.48	0.59

Data Plot and Equation

Caution - Use Carefully - Small Sample Size

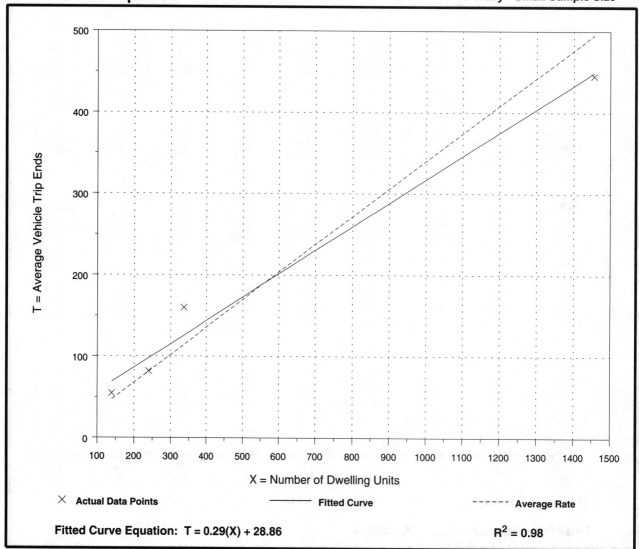

X   **Actual Data Points**   ———— **Fitted Curve**   - - - - - **Average Rate**

Fitted Curve Equation: T = 0.29(X) + 28.86 $R^2 = 0.98$

High-Rise Residential Condominium/Townhouse
(232)

Average Vehicle Trip Ends vs: **Dwelling Units**
On a: **Weekday,**
Peak Hour of Adjacent Street Traffic,
One Hour Between 4 and 6 p.m.

Number of Studies: 5
Avg. Number of Dwelling Units: 444
Directional Distribution: 62% entering, 38% exiting

Trip Generation per Dwelling Unit

Average Rate	Range of Rates	Standard Deviation
0.38	0.34 - 0.49	0.62

Data Plot and Equation

Caution - Use Carefully - Small Sample Size

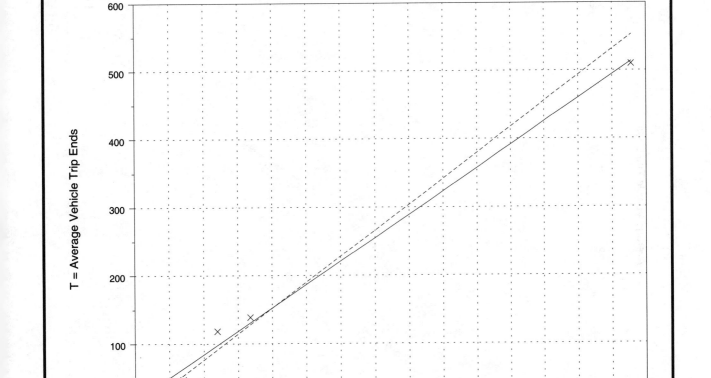

Fitted Curve Equation: T = 0.34(X) + 15.47 $R^2 = 0.99$

High-Rise Residential Condominium/Townhouse
(232)

Average Vehicle Trip Ends vs: **Dwelling Units**
On a: **Weekday,**
A.M. Peak Hour of Generator

Number of Studies: 7
Avg. Number of Dwelling Units: 588
Directional Distribution: 17% entering, 83% exiting

Trip Generation per Dwelling Unit

Average Rate	Range of Rates	Standard Deviation
0.34	0.23 - 0.54	0.59

Data Plot and Equation

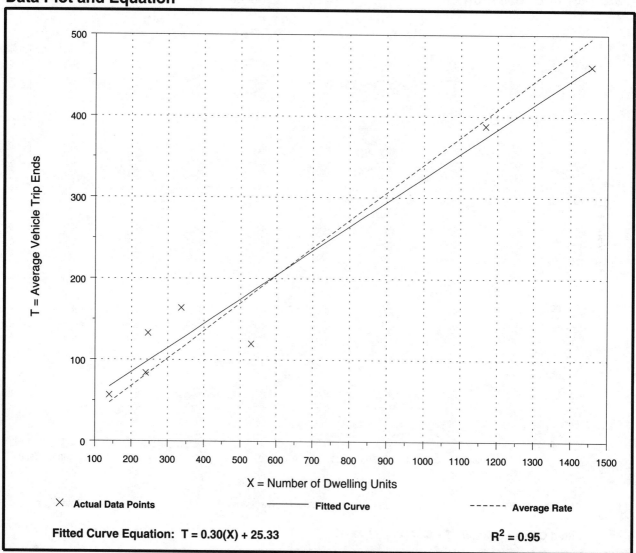

X **Actual Data Points**   ——— **Fitted Curve**   - - - - - **Average Rate**

Fitted Curve Equation: T = 0.30(X) + 25.33   **R² = 0.95**

High-Rise Residential Condominium/Townhouse
(232)

Average Vehicle Trip Ends vs: **Dwelling Units**
On a: **Weekday,**
P.M. Peak Hour of Generator

Number of Studies: 6
Avg. Number of Dwelling Units: 598
Directional Distribution: 68% entering, 32% exiting

Trip Generation per Dwelling Unit

Average Rate	Range of Rates	Standard Deviation
0.38	0.33 - 0.50	0.62

Data Plot and Equation

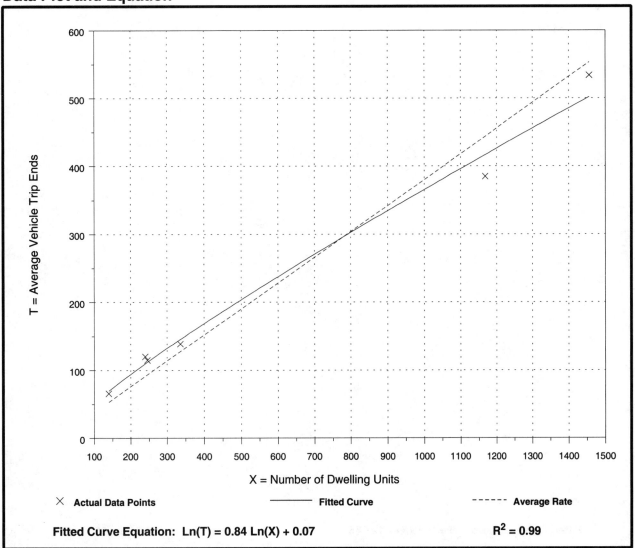

Fitted Curve Equation: Ln(T) = 0.84 Ln(X) + 0.07 $R^2 = 0.99$

High-Rise Residential Condominium/Townhouse
(232)

Average Vehicle Trip Ends vs: **Dwelling Units**
On a: **Saturday**

Number of Studies: 4
Avg. Number of Dwelling Units: 543
Directional Distribution: 50% entering, 50% exiting

Trip Generation per Dwelling Unit

Average Rate	Range of Rates	Standard Deviation
4.31	4.07 - 5.31	2.11

Data Plot and Equation

Caution - Use Carefully - Small Sample Size

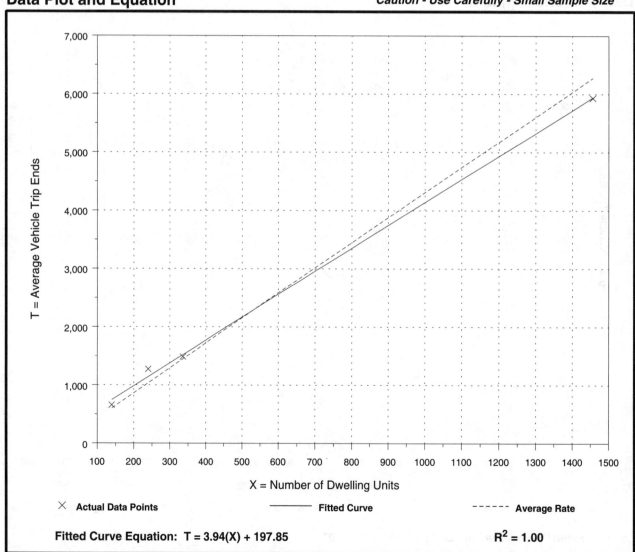

X = Number of Dwelling Units

× Actual Data Points	—— Fitted Curve	----- Average Rate

Fitted Curve Equation: T = 3.94(X) + 197.85 $R^2 = 1.00$

High-Rise Residential Condominium/Townhouse
(232)

Average Vehicle Trip Ends vs: **Dwelling Units**
On a: **Saturday,**
Peak Hour of Generator

Number of Studies: 4
Avg. Number of Dwelling Units: 543
Directional Distribution: 43% entering, 57% exiting

Trip Generation per Dwelling Unit

Average Rate	Range of Rates	Standard Deviation
0.35	0.32 - 0.43	0.59

Data Plot and Equation

Caution - Use Carefully - Small Sample Size

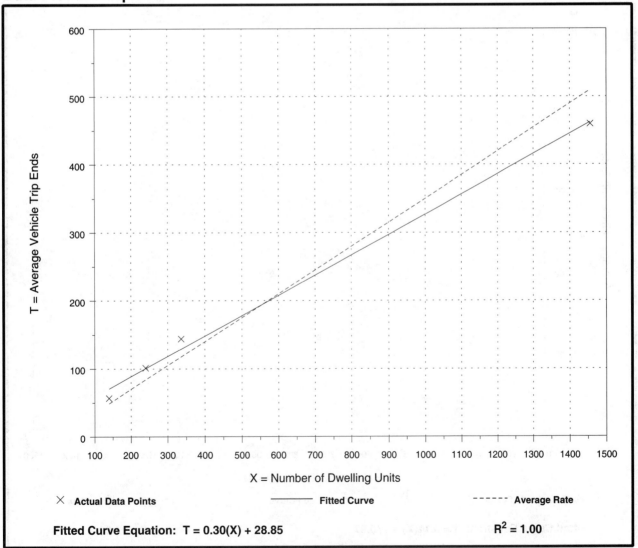

X = Number of Dwelling Units

$\times$ **Actual Data Points**   —— **Fitted Curve**   - - - - - **Average Rate**

Fitted Curve Equation: T = 0.30(X) + 28.85 $R^2 = 1.00$

High-Rise Residential Condominium/Townhouse
(232)

Average Vehicle Trip Ends vs: **Dwelling Units**
On a: **Sunday**

Number of Studies: 4
Avg. Number of Dwelling Units: 543
Directional Distribution: 50% entering, 50% exiting

Trip Generation per Dwelling Unit

Average Rate	Range of Rates	Standard Deviation
3.43	3.23 - 4.24	1.88

Data Plot and Equation

Caution - Use Carefully - Small Sample Size

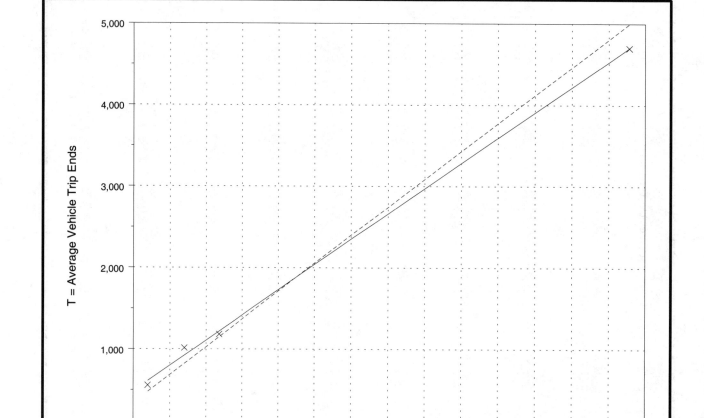

X **Actual Data Points** ———— **Fitted Curve** - - - - - **Average Rate**

Fitted Curve Equation: T = 3.11(X) + 176.97 $R^2 = 1.00$

High-Rise Residential Condominium/Townhouse
(232)

Average Vehicle Trip Ends vs: **Dwelling Units**
On a: **Sunday,**
Peak Hour of Generator

Number of Studies: 4
Avg. Number of Dwelling Units: 543
Directional Distribution: 54% entering, 46% exiting

Trip Generation per Dwelling Unit

Average Rate	Range of Rates	Standard Deviation
0.30	0.28 - 0.42	0.55

Data Plot and Equation

Caution - Use Carefully - Small Sample Size

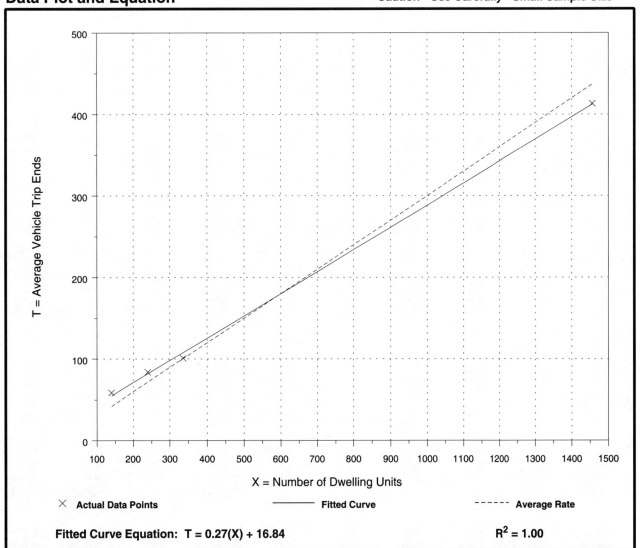

X Actual Data Points   —— Fitted Curve   - - - - - Average Rate

Fitted Curve Equation: T = 0.27(X) + 16.84 $R^2 = 1.00$

Land Use: 233
Luxury Condominium/Townhouse

Description

Luxury condominiums/townhouses are units in buildings with luxury facilities or services. **Both condominiums and townhouses are included in this land use.** Residential condominium/townhouse (Land Use 230), low-rise residential condominium/townhouse (Land Use 231) and high-rise residential condominium/townhouse (Land Use 232) are related uses.

Additional Data

The sites were surveyed in the 1980s and the 1990s in Indiana and New Jersey.

Source Numbers

260, 407

Luxury Condominium/Townhouse
(233)

Average Vehicle Trip Ends vs: **Occupied Dwelling Units**
On a: **Weekday,**
Peak Hour of Adjacent Street Traffic,
One Hour Between 7 and 9 a.m.

Number of Studies: 4
Avg. Num. of Occupied Dwelling Units: 110
Directional Distribution: 23% entering, 77% exiting

Trip Generation per Occupied Dwelling Unit

Average Rate	Range of Rates	Standard Deviation
0.56	0.50 - 0.62	0.75

Data Plot and Equation

Caution - Use Carefully - Small Sample Size

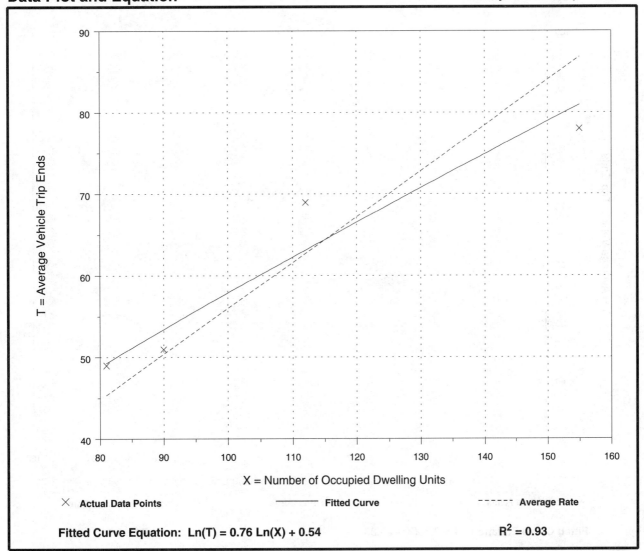

X = Number of Occupied Dwelling Units

✕ **Actual Data Points**   —— **Fitted Curve**   - - - - - **Average Rate**

Fitted Curve Equation: Ln(T) = 0.76 Ln(X) + 0.54 $R^2 = 0.93$

Luxury Condominium/Townhouse
(233)

Average Vehicle Trip Ends vs: Occupied Dwelling Units

On a: Weekday,
Peak Hour of Adjacent Street Traffic,
One Hour Between 4 and 6 p.m.

Number of Studies: 4
Avg. Num. of Occupied Dwelling Units: 110
Directional Distribution: 63% entering, 37% exiting

Trip Generation per Occupied Dwelling Unit

Average Rate	Range of Rates	Standard Deviation
0.55	0.48 - 0.63	0.74

Data Plot and Equation

Caution - Use Carefully - Small Sample Size

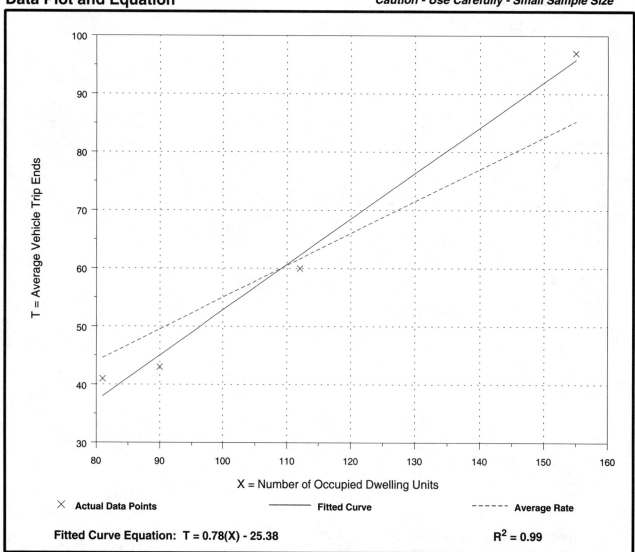

X **Actual Data Points**   —————— **Fitted Curve**   - - - - - **Average Rate**

Fitted Curve Equation: T = 0.78(X) - 25.38 $R^2 = 0.99$

Luxury Condominium/Townhouse
(233)

Average Vehicle Trip Ends vs: Occupied Dwelling Units
On a: Weekday,
A.M. Peak Hour of Generator

Number of Studies: 4
Avg. Num. of Occupied Dwelling Units: 110
Directional Distribution: 32% entering, 68% exiting

Trip Generation per Occupied Dwelling Unit

Average Rate	Range of Rates	Standard Deviation
0.65	0.58 - 0.69	0.81

Data Plot and Equation

Caution - Use Carefully - Small Sample Size

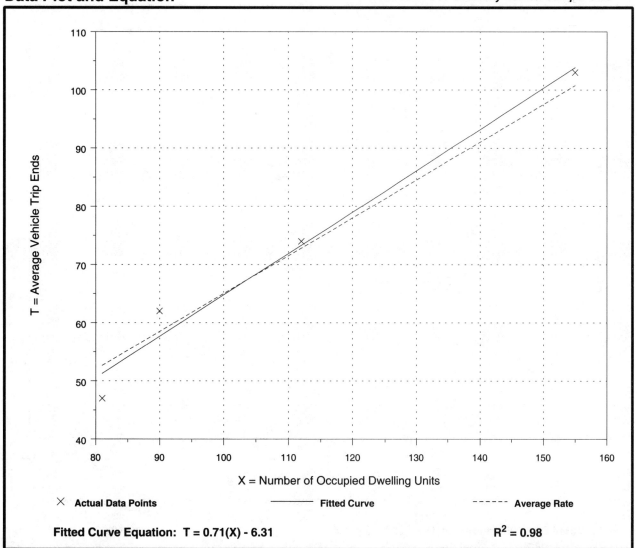

X = Number of Occupied Dwelling Units

× **Actual Data Points** ———— **Fitted Curve** - - - - - **Average Rate**

Fitted Curve Equation: T = 0.71(X) - 6.31 $R^2 = 0.98$

Luxury Condominium/Townhouse
(233)

Average Vehicle Trip Ends vs: Occupied Dwelling Units
On a: Weekday,
P.M. Peak Hour of Generator

Number of Studies: 4
Avg. Num. of Occupied Dwelling Units: 110
Directional Distribution: 60% entering, 40% exiting

Trip Generation per Occupied Dwelling Unit

Average Rate	Range of Rates	Standard Deviation
0.65	0.60 - 0.72	0.81

Data Plot and Equation

Caution - Use Carefully - Small Sample Size

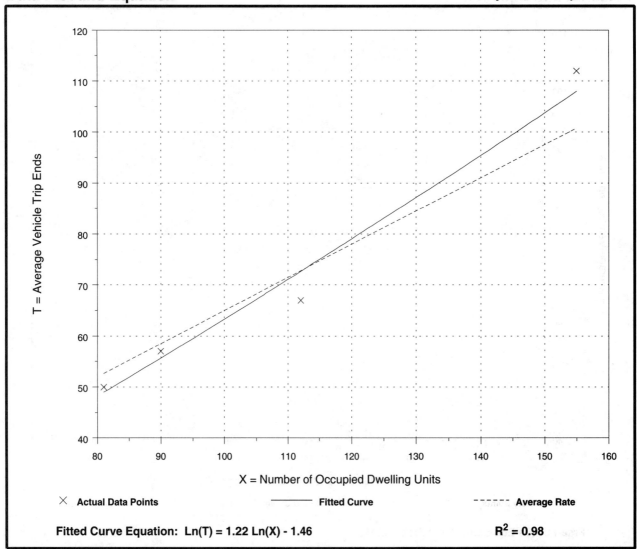

X   **Actual Data Points**   ———— **Fitted Curve**   - - - - - **Average Rate**

Fitted Curve Equation: Ln(T) = 1.22 Ln(X) - 1.46 $R^2 = 0.98$

Land Use: 240
Mobile Home Park

Description

Mobile home parks generally consist of manufactured homes that are sited and installed on permanent foundations and typically have community facilities such as recreation rooms, swimming pools and laundry facilities. Many mobile home parks restrict occupancy to adults.

Additional Data

The sites were surveyed between the late 1960s and the 1980s throughout the United States.

Source Numbers

9, 10, 11, 100, 155, 169, 252, 273

Mobile Home Park
(240)

Average Vehicle Trip Ends vs: Occupied Dwelling Units
On a: Weekday

Number of Studies: 35
Avg. Num. of Occupied Dwelling Units: 188
Directional Distribution: 50% entering, 50% exiting

Trip Generation per Occupied Dwelling Unit

Average Rate	Range of Rates	Standard Deviation
4.99	2.29 - 10.42	2.59

Data Plot and Equation

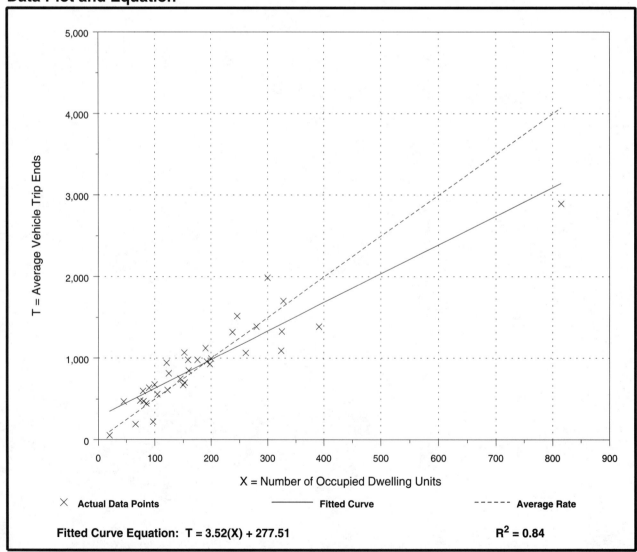

Fitted Curve Equation: T = 3.52(X) + 277.51 $R^2 = 0.84$

Mobile Home Park
(240)

Average Vehicle Trip Ends vs: **Occupied Dwelling Units**
On a: **Weekday,**
Peak Hour of Adjacent Street Traffic,
One Hour Between 7 and 9 a.m.

Number of Studies: 18
Avg. Num. of Occupied Dwelling Units: 165
Directional Distribution: 20% entering, 80% exiting

Trip Generation per Occupied Dwelling Unit

Average Rate	Range of Rates	Standard Deviation
0.44	0.20 - 1.00	0.68

Data Plot and Equation

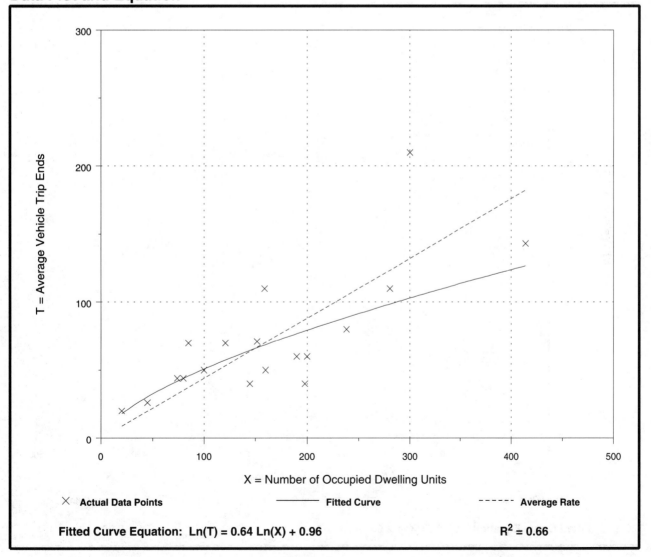

Fitted Curve Equation: $Ln(T) = 0.64 \, Ln(X) + 0.96$ $R^2 = 0.66$

Mobile Home Park
(240)

Average Vehicle Trip Ends vs: Occupied Dwelling Units
On a: Weekday,
Peak Hour of Adjacent Street Traffic,
One Hour Between 4 and 6 p.m.

Number of Studies: 23
Avg. Num. of Occupied Dwelling Units: 168
Directional Distribution: 62% entering, 38% exiting

Trip Generation per Occupied Dwelling Unit

Average Rate	Range of Rates	Standard Deviation
0.59	0.33 - 1.04	0.77

Data Plot and Equation

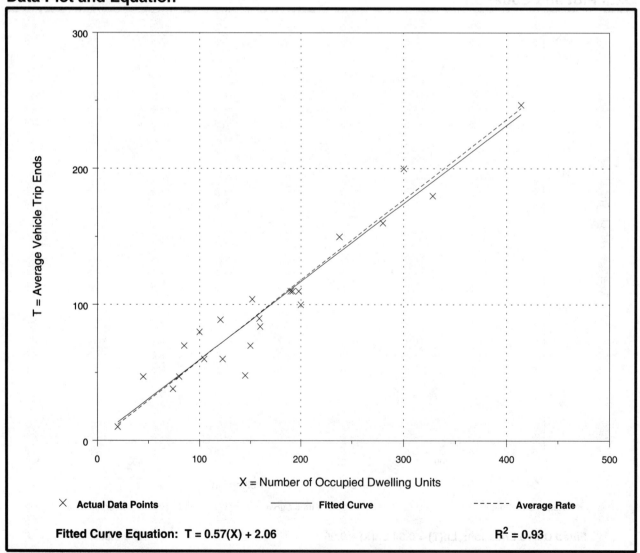

Fitted Curve Equation: T = 0.57(X) + 2.06 $R^2 = 0.93$

Mobile Home Park
(240)

Average Vehicle Trip Ends vs: **Occupied Dwelling Units**
On a: **Weekday,**
A.M. Peak Hour of Generator

Number of Studies: 25
Avg. Num. of Occupied Dwelling Units: 167
Directional Distribution: 25% entering, 75% exiting

Trip Generation per Occupied Dwelling Unit

Average Rate	Range of Rates	Standard Deviation
0.44	0.30 - 1.00	0.68

Data Plot and Equation

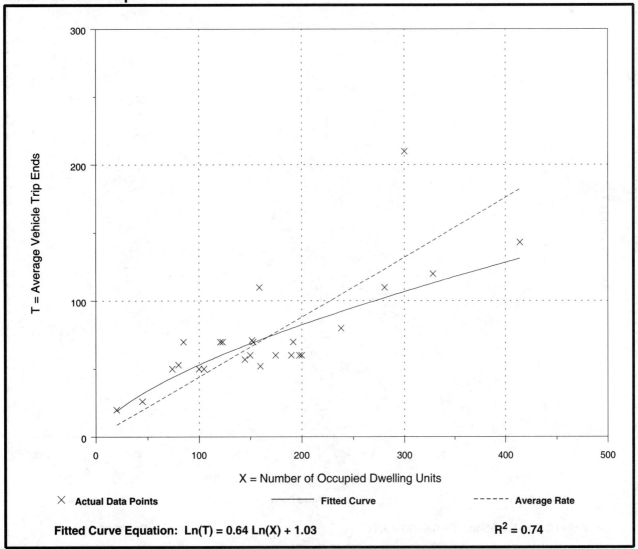

X **Actual Data Points**   ———— **Fitted Curve**   ----- **Average Rate**

Fitted Curve Equation: Ln(T) = 0.64 Ln(X) + 1.03 $R^2 = 0.74$

Mobile Home Park
(240)

Average Vehicle Trip Ends vs: Occupied Dwelling Units
On a: Weekday,
P.M. Peak Hour of Generator

Number of Studies: 25
Avg. Num. of Occupied Dwelling Units: 167
Directional Distribution: 61% entering, 39% exiting

Trip Generation per Occupied Dwelling Unit

Average Rate	Range of Rates	Standard Deviation
0.60	0.39 - 1.07	0.78

Data Plot and Equation

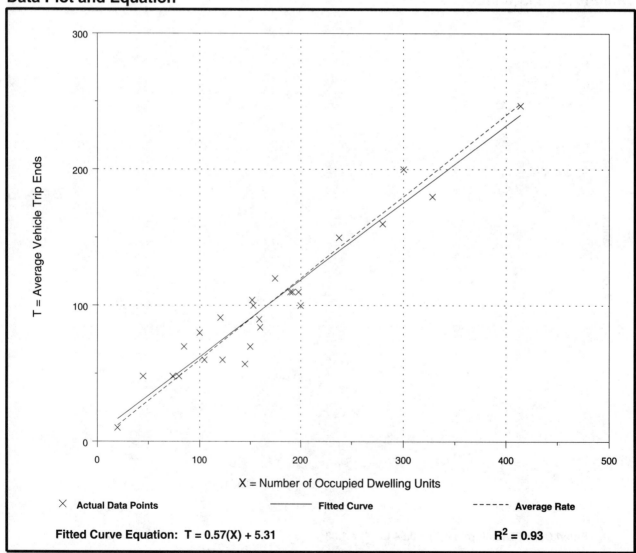

Fitted Curve Equation: T = 0.57(X) + 5.31 $R^2 = 0.93$

Mobile Home Park
(240)

Average Vehicle Trip Ends vs: Occupied Dwelling Units
On a: Saturday

Number of Studies: 31
Avg. Num. of Occupied Dwelling Units: 190
Directional Distribution: 50% entering, 50% exiting

Trip Generation per Occupied Dwelling Unit

Average Rate	Range of Rates	Standard Deviation
5.00	2.12 - 10.93	2.75

Data Plot and Equation

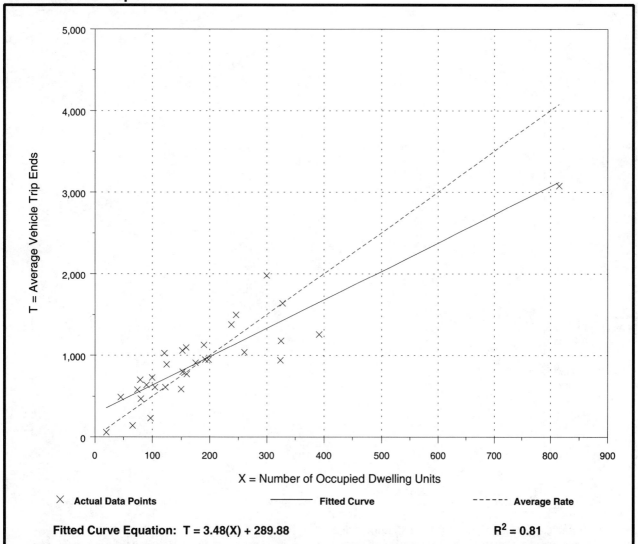

Fitted Curve Equation: T = 3.48(X) + 289.88 $R^2 = 0.81$

Mobile Home Park
(240)

Average Vehicle Trip Ends vs: Occupied Dwelling Units
On a: Saturday,
Peak Hour of Generator

Number of Studies: 20
Avg. Num. of Occupied Dwelling Units: 153
Directional Distribution: 53% entering, 47% exiting

Trip Generation per Occupied Dwelling Unit

Average Rate	Range of Rates	Standard Deviation
0.54	0.38 - 1.13	0.74

Data Plot and Equation

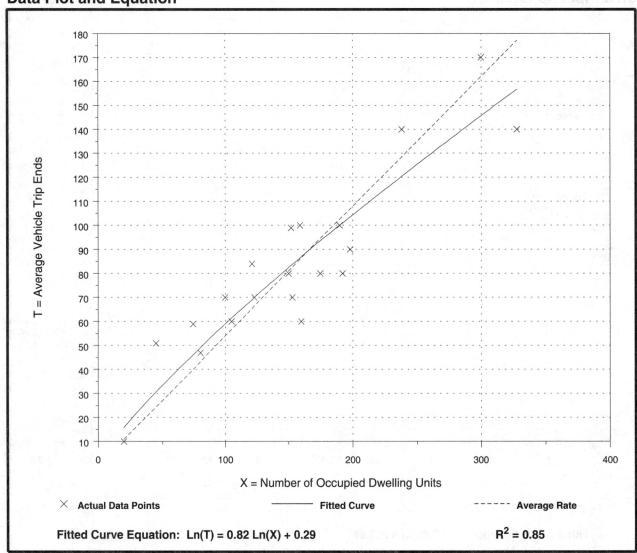

X = Number of Occupied Dwelling Units

$\times$ **Actual Data Points** ———— **Fitted Curve** ----- **Average Rate**

Fitted Curve Equation: $\text{Ln}(T) = 0.82 \text{ Ln}(X) + 0.29$ $R^2 = 0.85$

Mobile Home Park
(240)

Average Vehicle Trip Ends vs: Occupied Dwelling Units
On a: Sunday

Number of Studies: 32
Avg. Num. of Occupied Dwelling Units: 193
Directional Distribution: 50% entering, 50% exiting

Trip Generation per Occupied Dwelling Unit

Average Rate	Range of Rates	Standard Deviation
4.36	1.86 - 8.98	2.49

Data Plot and Equation

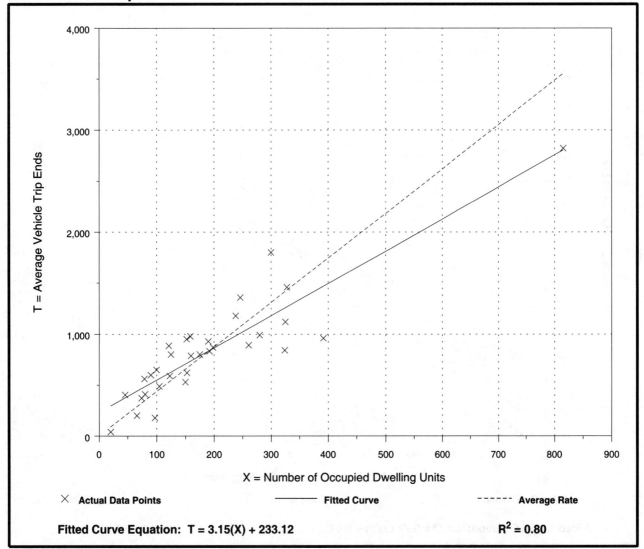

Fitted Curve Equation: T = 3.15(X) + 233.12 $R^2 = 0.80$

Mobile Home Park
(240)

Average Vehicle Trip Ends vs: **Occupied Dwelling Units**
On a: **Sunday,**
Peak Hour of Generator

Number of Studies: 21
Avg. Num. of Occupied Dwelling Units: 159
Directional Distribution: 50% entering, 50% exiting

Trip Generation per Occupied Dwelling Unit

Average Rate	Range of Rates	Standard Deviation
0.50	0.29 - 1.47	0.72

Data Plot and Equation

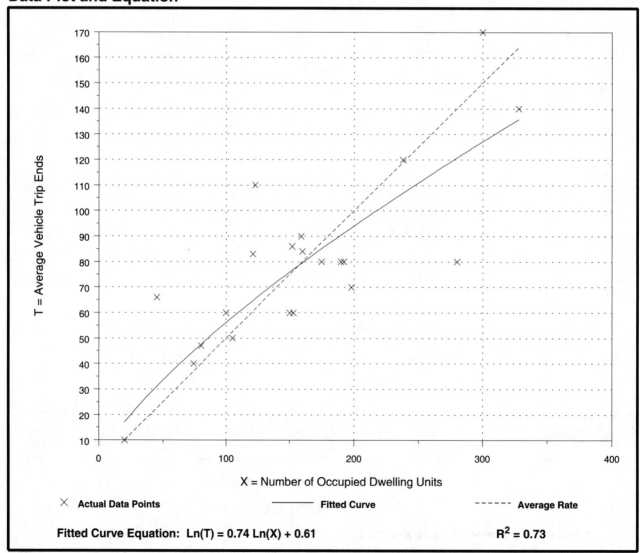

Fitted Curve Equation: $Ln(T) = 0.74 \, Ln(X) + 0.61$ $R^2 = 0.73$

Mobile Home Park
(240)

Average Vehicle Trip Ends vs: Persons
On a: Weekday

Number of Studies: 28
Average Number of Persons: 405
Directional Distribution: 50% entering, 50% exiting

Trip Generation per Person

Average Rate	Range of Rates	Standard Deviation
2.46	1.23 - 3.63	1.67

Data Plot and Equation

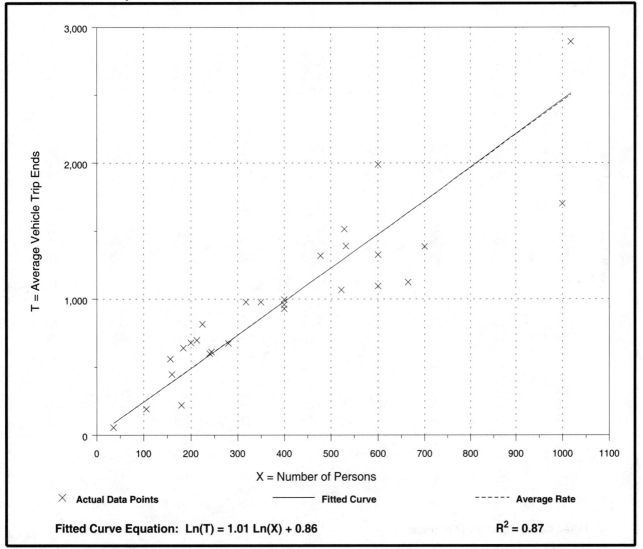

X = Number of Persons

| ✕ | **Actual Data Points** | ——— | **Fitted Curve** | - - - - - | **Average Rate** |

Fitted Curve Equation: Ln(T) = 1.01 Ln(X) + 0.86 $R^2 = 0.87$

Mobile Home Park
(240)

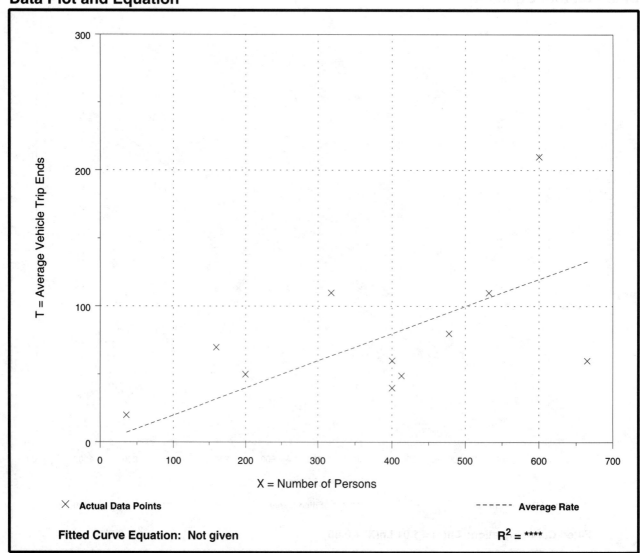

Average Vehicle Trip Ends vs: **Persons**
           On a: **Weekday,**
                     Peak Hour of Adjacent Street Traffic,
                     One Hour Between 7 and 9 a.m.

Number of Studies: 11
Average Number of Persons: 382
Directional Distribution: 18% entering, 82% exiting

Trip Generation per Person

Average Rate	Range of Rates	Standard Deviation
0.20	0.09 - 0.56	0.46

Data Plot and Equation

Fitted Curve Equation: Not given   **R^2 = ******

Mobile Home Park
(240)

Average Vehicle Trip Ends vs: **Persons**

On a: **Weekday,**
Peak Hour of Adjacent Street Traffic,
One Hour Between 4 and 6 p.m.

Number of Studies: 16
Average Number of Persons: 393
Directional Distribution: 63% entering, 37% exiting

Trip Generation per Person

Average Rate	Range of Rates	Standard Deviation
0.26	0.14 - 0.44	0.51

Data Plot and Equation

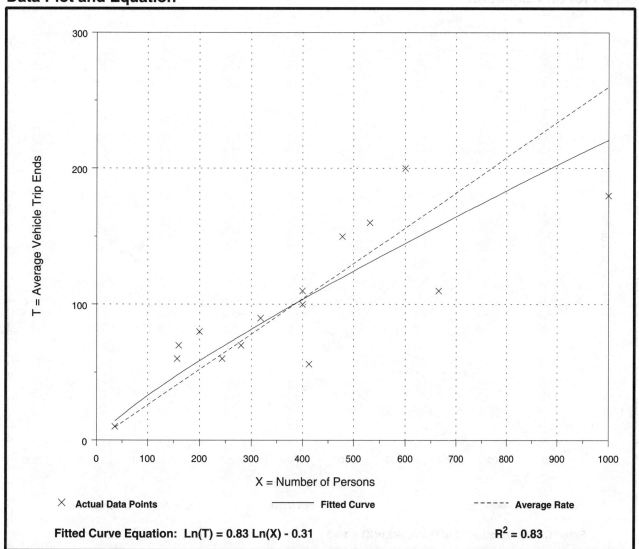

X = Number of Persons

✕ **Actual Data Points** ———— **Fitted Curve** - - - - **Average Rate**

Fitted Curve Equation: Ln(T) = 0.83 Ln(X) - 0.31 $R^2 = 0.83$

Mobile Home Park
(240)

Average Vehicle Trip Ends vs: **Persons**
On a: **Weekday,**
  A.M. Peak Hour of Generator

Number of Studies: 18
Average Number of Persons: 380
Directional Distribution: 25% entering, 75% exiting

Trip Generation per Person

Average Rate	Range of Rates	Standard Deviation
0.20	0.09 - 0.56	0.46

Data Plot and Equation

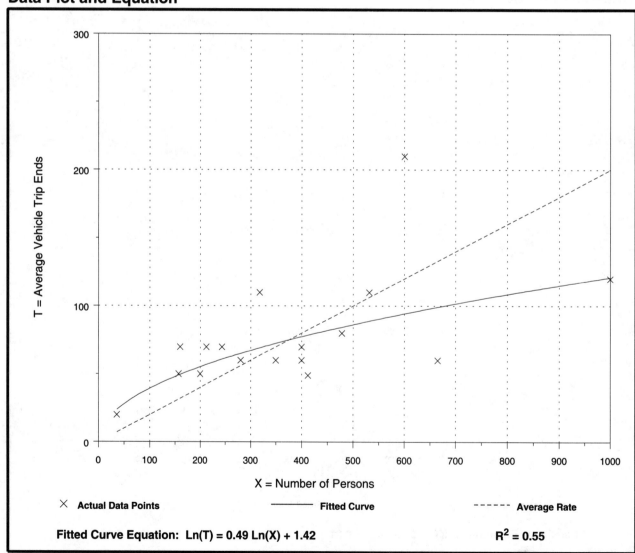

Fitted Curve Equation: Ln(T) = 0.49 Ln(X) + 1.42 $R^2 = 0.55$

Mobile Home Park
(240)

Average Vehicle Trip Ends vs: Persons
On a: Weekday,
P.M. Peak Hour of Generator

Number of Studies: 18
Average Number of Persons: 380
Directional Distribution: 63% entering, 37% exiting

Trip Generation per Person

Average Rate	Range of Rates	Standard Deviation
0.27	0.14 - 0.47	0.52

Data Plot and Equation

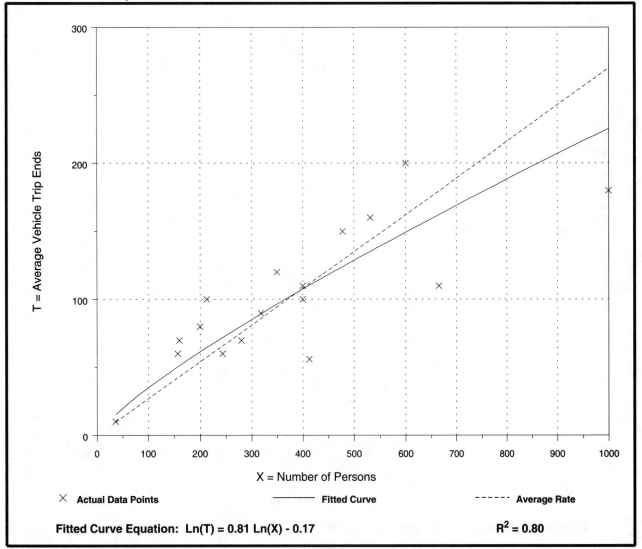

X = Number of Persons

✕ **Actual Data Points**   ——— **Fitted Curve**   - - - - - **Average Rate**

Fitted Curve Equation: Ln(T) = 0.81 Ln(X) - 0.17 $R^2 = 0.80$

Mobile Home Park
(240)

Average Vehicle Trip Ends vs: Persons
On a: Saturday

Number of Studies: 27
Average Number of Persons: 414
Directional Distribution: 50% entering, 50% exiting

Trip Generation per Person

Average Rate	Range of Rates	Standard Deviation
2.38	1.28 - 3.96	1.71

Data Plot and Equation

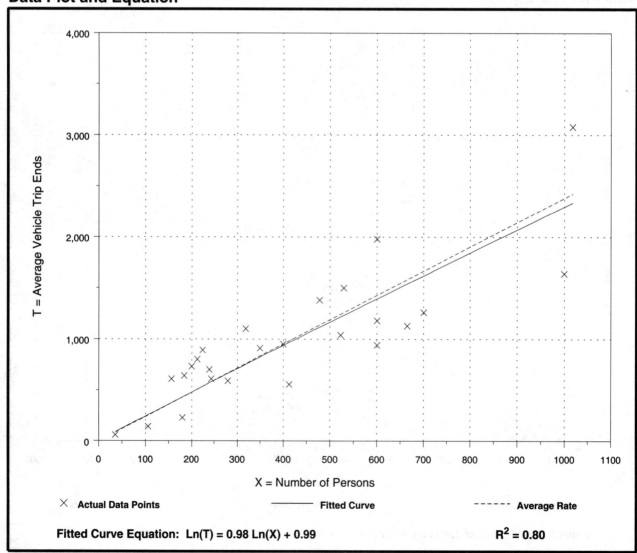

X Actual Data Points   ———— Fitted Curve   - - - - - Average Rate

Fitted Curve Equation: Ln(T) = 0.98 Ln(X) + 0.99 $R^2 = 0.80$

Mobile Home Park
(240)

Average Vehicle Trip Ends vs: **Persons**
On a: **Saturday,**
Peak Hour of Generator

Number of Studies: 14
Average Number of Persons: 382
Directional Distribution: 54% entering, 46% exiting

Trip Generation per Person

Average Rate	Range of Rates	Standard Deviation
0.24	0.14 - 0.38	0.49

Data Plot and Equation

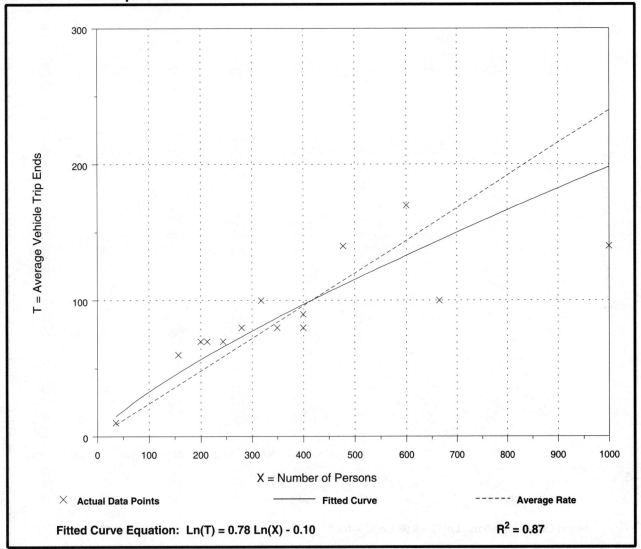

Fitted Curve Equation: $Ln(T) = 0.78 \, Ln(X) - 0.10$ $R^2 = 0.87$

Mobile Home Park
(240)

Average Vehicle Trip Ends vs: Persons
On a: Sunday

Number of Studies: 28
Average Number of Persons: 418
Directional Distribution: 50% entering, 50% exiting

Trip Generation per Person

Average Rate	Range of Rates	Standard Deviation
2.08	0.87 - 3.56	1.59

Data Plot and Equation

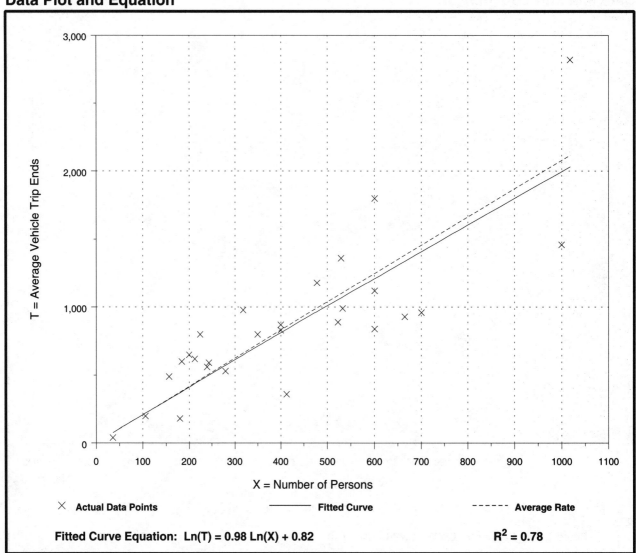

Fitted Curve Equation: Ln(T) = 0.98 Ln(X) + 0.82 $R^2 = 0.78$

Mobile Home Park
(240)

Average Vehicle Trip Ends vs: **Persons**
On a: **Sunday,**
Peak Hour of Generator

Number of Studies: 15
Average Number of Persons: 392
Directional Distribution: 51% entering, 49% exiting

Trip Generation per Person

Average Rate	Range of Rates	Standard Deviation
0.21	0.12 - 0.45	0.47

Data Plot and Equation

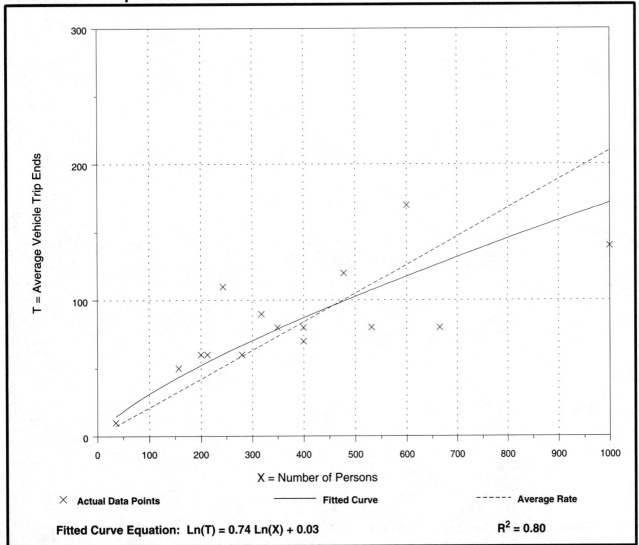

X = Number of Persons

✕ **Actual Data Points** —— **Fitted Curve** - - - - **Average Rate**

Fitted Curve Equation: Ln(T) = 0.74 Ln(X) + 0.03 $R^2 = 0.80$

Mobile Home Park
(240)

Average Vehicle Trip Ends vs: **Vehicles**
On a: **Weekday**

Number of Studies: 17
Average Number of Vehicles: 280
Directional Distribution: 50% entering, 50% exiting

Trip Generation per Vehicle

Average Rate	Range of Rates	Standard Deviation
3.38	1.93 - 4.80	1.91

Data Plot and Equation

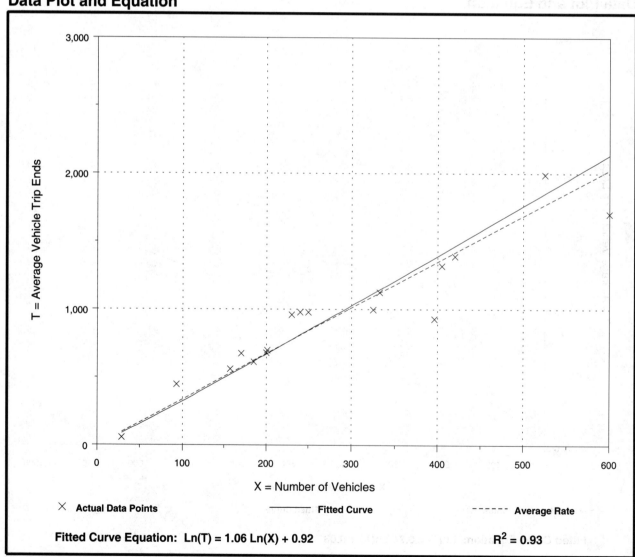

X **Actual Data Points**   ——— **Fitted Curve**   - - - - - **Average Rate**

Fitted Curve Equation: Ln(T) = 1.06 Ln(X) + 0.92 $R^2 = 0.93$

Mobile Home Park
(240)

Average Vehicle Trip Ends vs: Vehicles
On a: Weekday,
Peak Hour of Adjacent Street Traffic,
One Hour Between 7 and 9 a.m.

Number of Studies: 10
Average Number of Vehicles: 297
Directional Distribution: 16% entering, 84% exiting

Trip Generation per Vehicle

Average Rate	Range of Rates	Standard Deviation
0.27	0.10 - 0.75	0.54

Data Plot and Equation

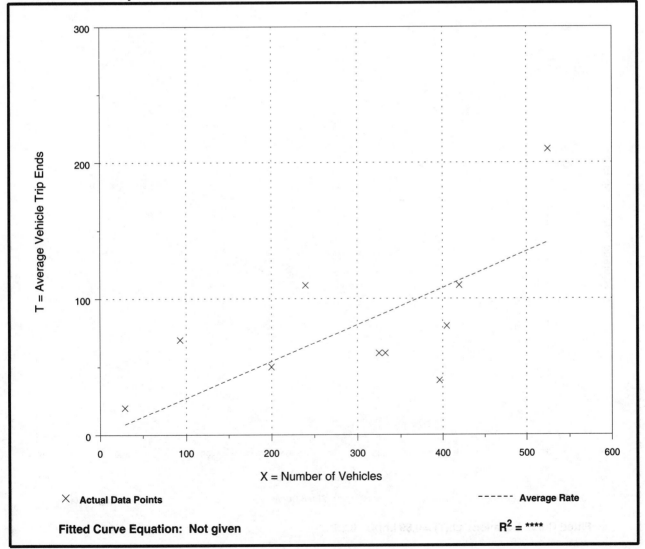

Fitted Curve Equation: Not given $R^2 = ****$

Mobile Home Park
(240)

Average Vehicle Trip Ends vs: **Vehicles**
On a: **Weekday,**
Peak Hour of Adjacent Street Traffic,
One Hour Between 4 and 6 p.m.

Number of Studies: 15
Average Number of Vehicles: 287
Directional Distribution: 63% entering, 37% exiting

Trip Generation per Vehicle

Average Rate	Range of Rates	Standard Deviation
0.36	0.28 - 0.75	0.61

Data Plot and Equation

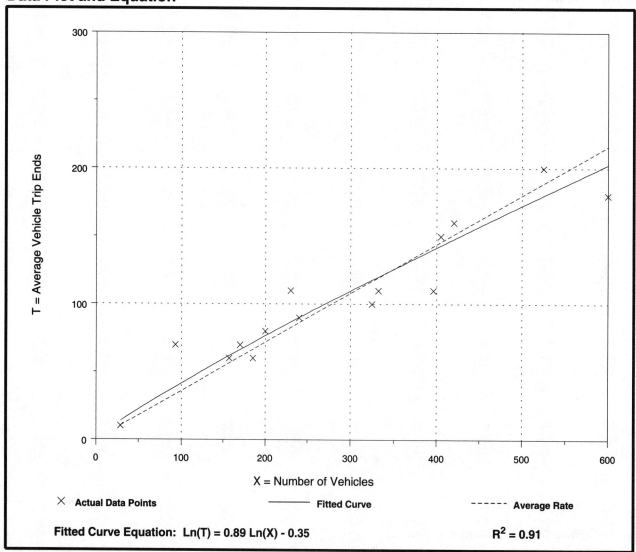

X = Number of Vehicles

X **Actual Data Points** ——— **Fitted Curve** - - - - - **Average Rate**

Fitted Curve Equation: Ln(T) = 0.89 Ln(X) - 0.35 $R^2 = 0.91$

Mobile Home Park
(240)

Average Vehicle Trip Ends vs: **Vehicles**
On a: **Weekday,**
A.M. Peak Hour of Generator

Number of Studies: 17
Average Number of Vehicles: 280
Directional Distribution: 25% entering, 75% exiting

Trip Generation per Vehicle

Average Rate	Range of Rates	Standard Deviation
0.28	0.15 - 0.75	0.54

Data Plot and Equation

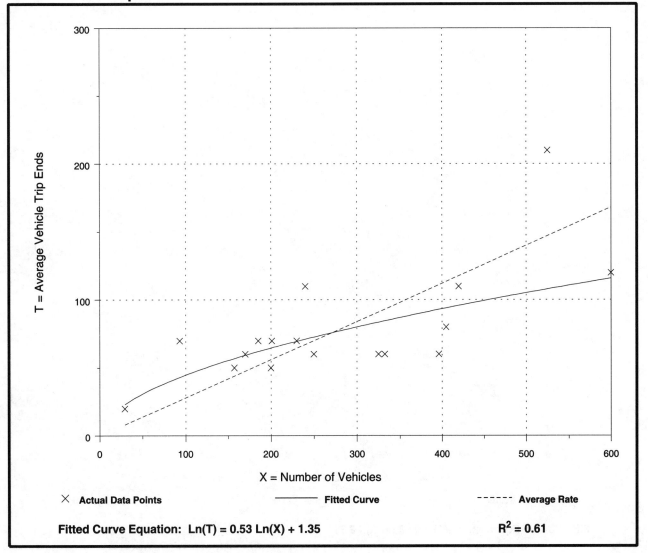

Fitted Curve Equation: $Ln(T) = 0.53\ Ln(X) + 1.35$ $R^2 = 0.61$

Mobile Home Park
(240)

Average Vehicle Trip Ends vs: **Vehicles**
On a: **Weekday,**
P.M. Peak Hour of Generator

Number of Studies: 17
Average Number of Vehicles: 280
Directional Distribution: 63% entering, 37% exiting

Trip Generation per Vehicle

Average Rate	Range of Rates	Standard Deviation
0.37	0.28 - 0.75	0.62

Data Plot and Equation

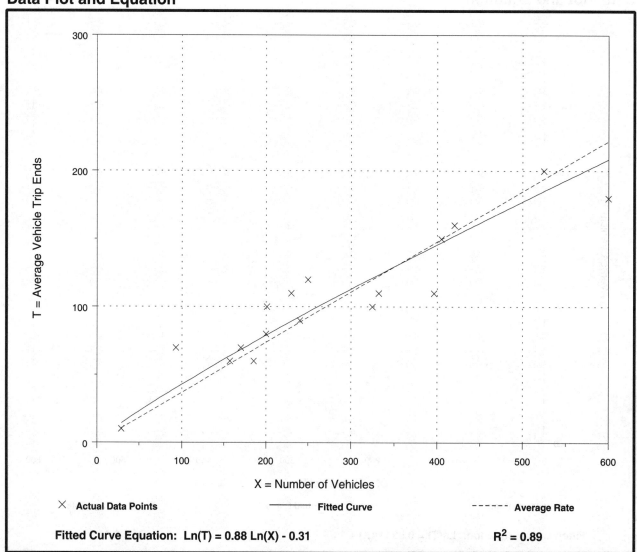

X   **Actual Data Points** ———— **Fitted Curve** - - - - - **Average Rate**

Fitted Curve Equation: Ln(T) = 0.88 Ln(X) - 0.31 $R^2 = 0.89$

Mobile Home Park
(240)

Average Vehicle Trip Ends vs: Vehicles
On a: Saturday

Number of Studies: 14
Average Number of Vehicles: 280
Directional Distribution: 50% entering, 50% exiting

Trip Generation per Vehicle

Average Rate	Range of Rates	Standard Deviation
3.43	2.07 - 4.58	1.94

Data Plot and Equation

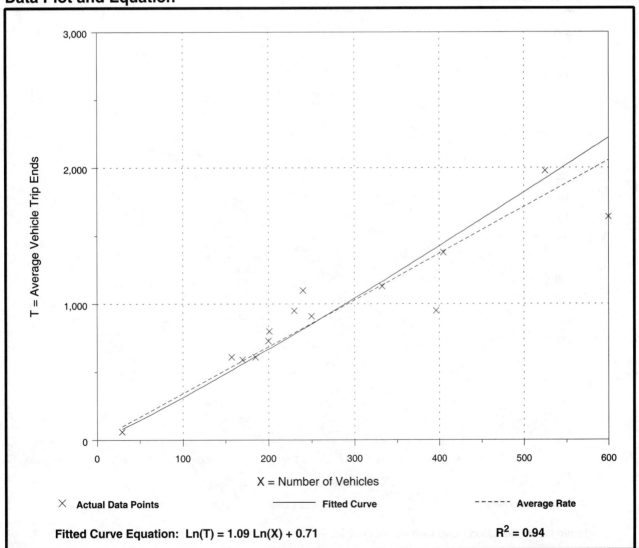

X = Number of Vehicles

$\times$ **Actual Data Points**   —— **Fitted Curve**   - - - - - **Average Rate**

Fitted Curve Equation: Ln(T) = 1.09 Ln(X) + 0.71 $R^2 = 0.94$

Mobile Home Park
(240)

Average Vehicle Trip Ends vs: **Vehicles**
On a: **Saturday,**
Peak Hour of Generator

Number of Studies: 14
Average Number of Vehicles: 280
Directional Distribution: 54% entering, 46% exiting

Trip Generation per Vehicle

Average Rate	Range of Rates	Standard Deviation
0.32	0.23 - 0.47	0.57

Data Plot and Equation

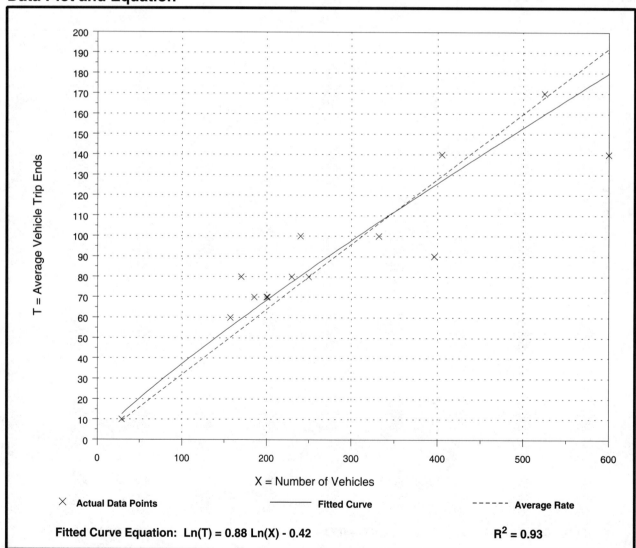

Fitted Curve Equation: $Ln(T) = 0.88 \ Ln(X) - 0.42$ $R^2 = 0.93$

Mobile Home Park
(240)

Average Vehicle Trip Ends vs: Vehicles
On a: Sunday

Number of Studies: 15
Average Number of Vehicles: 289
Directional Distribution: 50% entering, 50% exiting

Trip Generation per Vehicle

Average Rate	Range of Rates	Standard Deviation
2.94	1.38 - 4.08	1.79

Data Plot and Equation

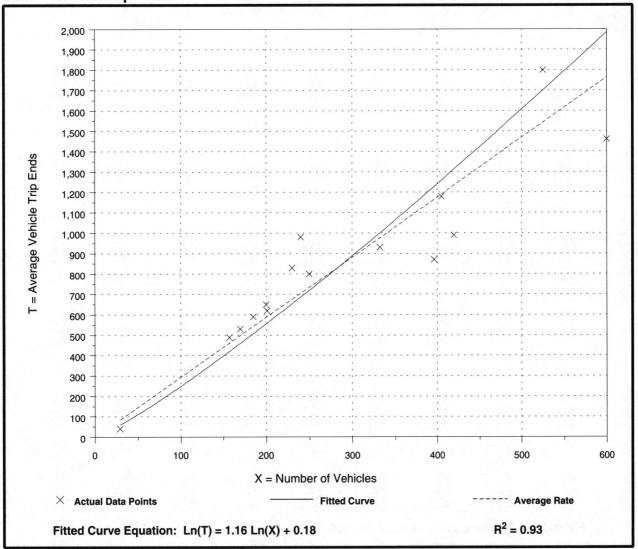

X = Number of Vehicles

✕ Actual Data Points	——— Fitted Curve	- - - - - Average Rate

Fitted Curve Equation: Ln(T) = 1.16 Ln(X) + 0.18 $R^2 = 0.93$

Mobile Home Park
(240)

Average Vehicle Trip Ends vs: Vehicles
On a: Sunday,
Peak Hour of Generator

Number of Studies: 15
Average Number of Vehicles: 289
Directional Distribution: 51% entering, 49% exiting

Trip Generation per Vehicle

Average Rate	Range of Rates	Standard Deviation
0.29	0.18 - 0.59	0.54

Data Plot and Equation

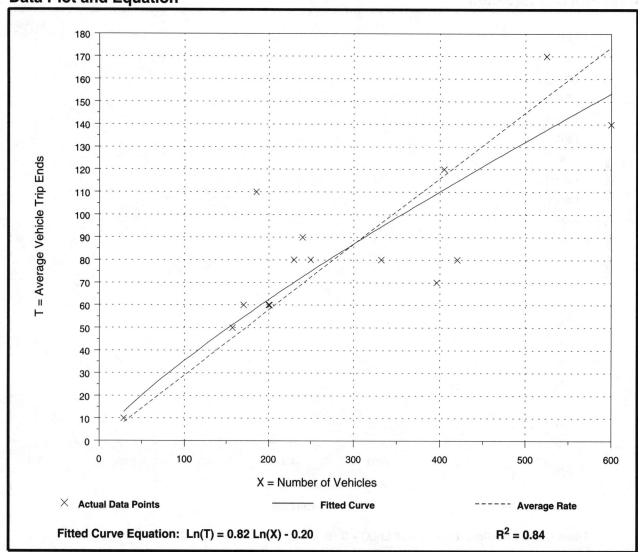

Fitted Curve Equation: Ln(T) = 0.82 Ln(X) - 0.20 $R^2 = 0.84$

Mobile Home Park
(240)

Average Vehicle Trip Ends vs: **Acres**
On a: **Weekday**

Number of Studies: 28
Average Number of Acres: 25
Directional Distribution: 50% entering, 50% exiting

Trip Generation per Acre

Average Rate	Range of Rates	Standard Deviation
39.61	15.86 - 85.89	15.29

Data Plot and Equation

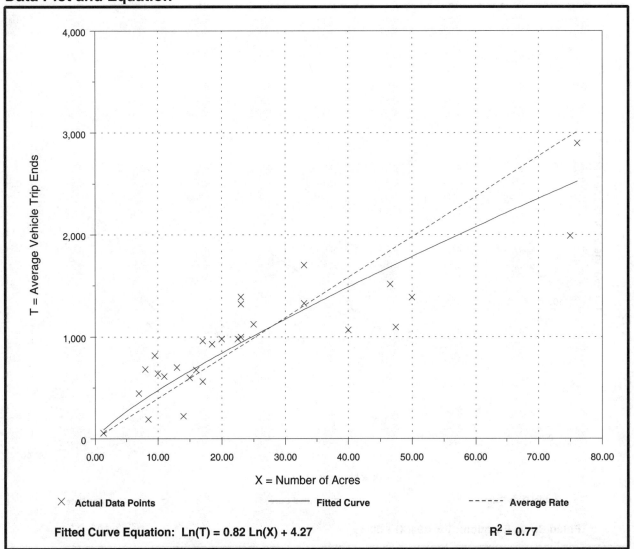

X = Number of Acres

✕ **Actual Data Points** ——— **Fitted Curve** - - - - - **Average Rate**

Fitted Curve Equation: Ln(T) = 0.82 Ln(X) + 4.27 $R^2 = 0.77$

Mobile Home Park
(240)

Average Vehicle Trip Ends vs: **Acres**
On a: **Weekday,**
Peak Hour of Adjacent Street Traffic,
One Hour Between 7 and 9 a.m.

Number of Studies: 11
Average Number of Acres: 24
Directional Distribution: 18% entering, 82% exiting

Trip Generation per Acre

Average Rate	Range of Rates	Standard Deviation
3.20	1.09 - 15.38	2.60

Data Plot and Equation

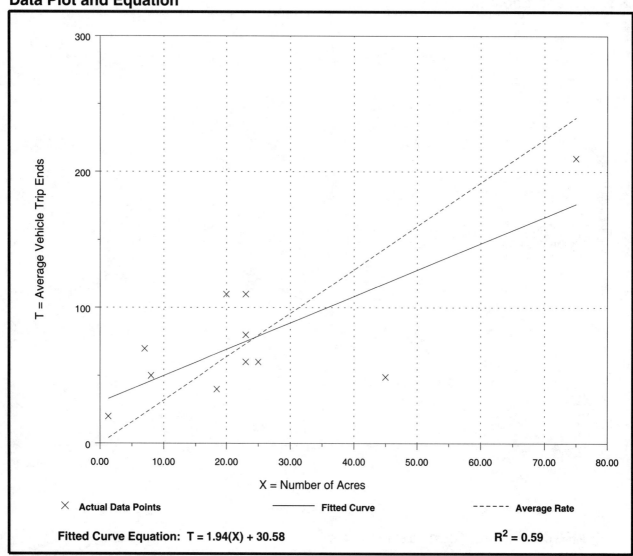

Fitted Curve Equation: T = 1.94(X) + 30.58 $R^2 = 0.59$

Mobile Home Park
(240)

Average Vehicle Trip Ends vs: **Acres**
On a: **Weekday,**
Peak Hour of Adjacent Street Traffic,
One Hour Between 4 and 6 p.m.

Number of Studies: 16
Average Number of Acres: 23
Directional Distribution: 63% entering, 37% exiting

Trip Generation per Acre

Average Rate	Range of Rates	Standard Deviation
4.45	1.24 - 10.00	2.93

Data Plot and Equation

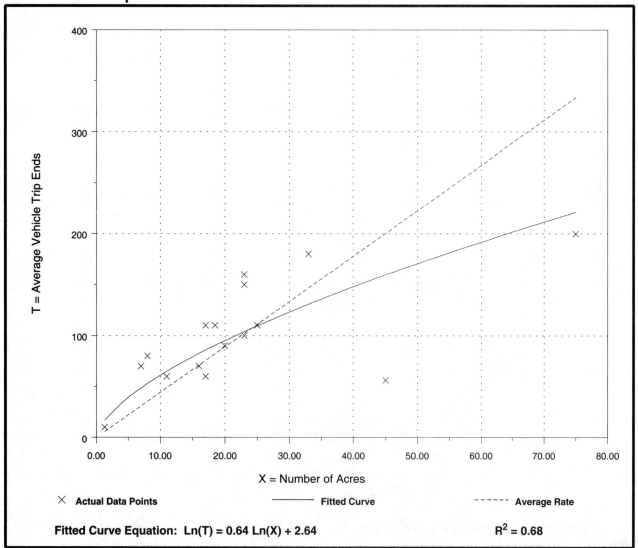

Fitted Curve Equation: $\text{Ln}(T) = 0.64\ \text{Ln}(X) + 2.64$ $R^2 = 0.68$

Mobile Home Park
(240)

Average Vehicle Trip Ends vs: Acres
On a: Weekday,
A.M. Peak Hour of Generator

Number of Studies: 18
Average Number of Acres: 22
Directional Distribution: 25% entering, 75% exiting

Trip Generation per Acre

Average Rate	Range of Rates	Standard Deviation
3.46	1.09 - 15.38	2.49

Data Plot and Equation

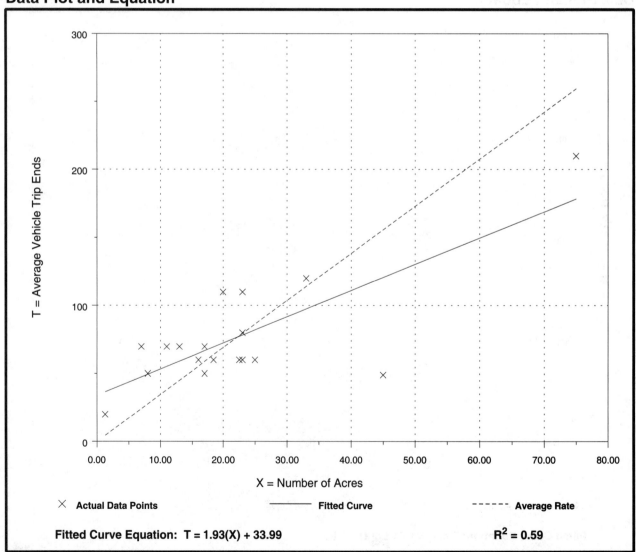

Fitted Curve Equation: T = 1.93(X) + 33.99 $R^2 = 0.59$

Mobile Home Park
(240)

Average Vehicle Trip Ends vs: Acres
On a: Weekday,
P.M. Peak Hour of Generator

Number of Studies: 18
Average Number of Acres: 22
Directional Distribution: 63% entering, 37% exiting

Trip Generation per Acre

Average Rate	Range of Rates	Standard Deviation
4.61	1.24 - 10.00	2.95

Data Plot and Equation

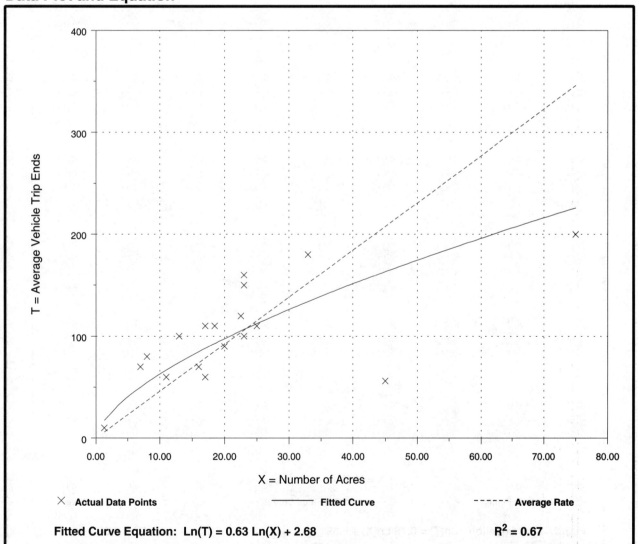

X **Actual Data Points**   ——— **Fitted Curve**   - - - - - **Average Rate**

Fitted Curve Equation: Ln(T) = 0.63 Ln(X) + 2.68 $R^2 = 0.67$

Mobile Home Park
(240)

Average Vehicle Trip Ends vs: Acres
On a: Saturday

Number of Studies: 27
Average Number of Acres: 27
Directional Distribution: 50% entering, 50% exiting

Trip Generation per Acre

Average Rate	Range of Rates	Standard Deviation
36.21	12.36 - 93.68	17.04

Data Plot and Equation

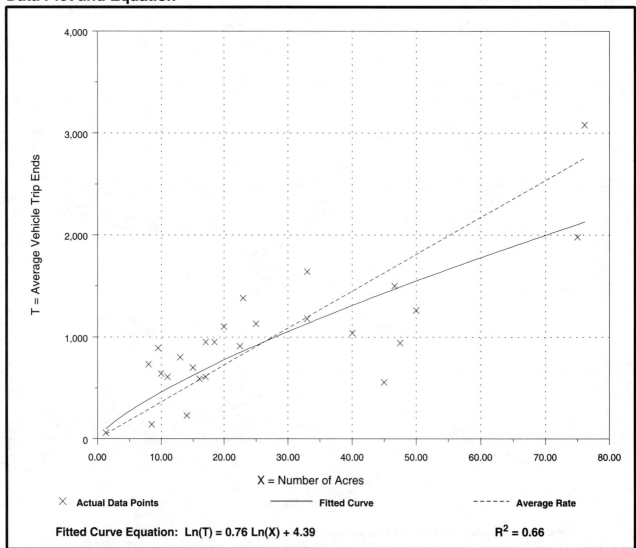

X = Number of Acres

✕ Actual Data Points   —— Fitted Curve   ----- Average Rate

Fitted Curve Equation: Ln(T) = 0.76 Ln(X) + 4.39 $R^2 = 0.66$

Mobile Home Park
(240)

Average Vehicle Trip Ends vs: Acres
On a: Saturday,
Peak Hour of Generator

Number of Studies: 14
Average Number of Acres: 21
Directional Distribution: 54% entering, 46% exiting

Trip Generation per Acre

Average Rate	Range of Rates	Standard Deviation
4.20	2.27 - 8.75	2.49

Data Plot and Equation

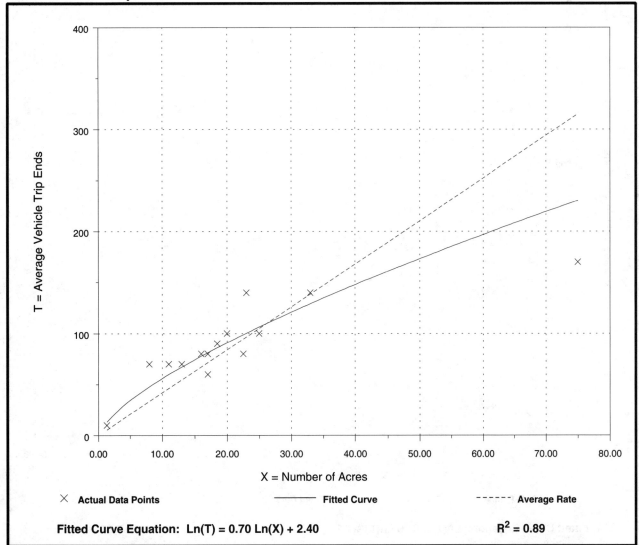

Fitted Curve Equation: $Ln(T) = 0.70 \ Ln(X) + 2.40$ $R^2 = 0.89$

Mobile Home Park
(240)

Average Vehicle Trip Ends vs: Acres
On a: Sunday

Number of Studies: 28
Average Number of Acres: 27
Directional Distribution: 50% entering, 50% exiting

Trip Generation per Acre

Average Rate	Range of Rates	Standard Deviation
32.09	8.02 - 84.21	15.49

Data Plot and Equation

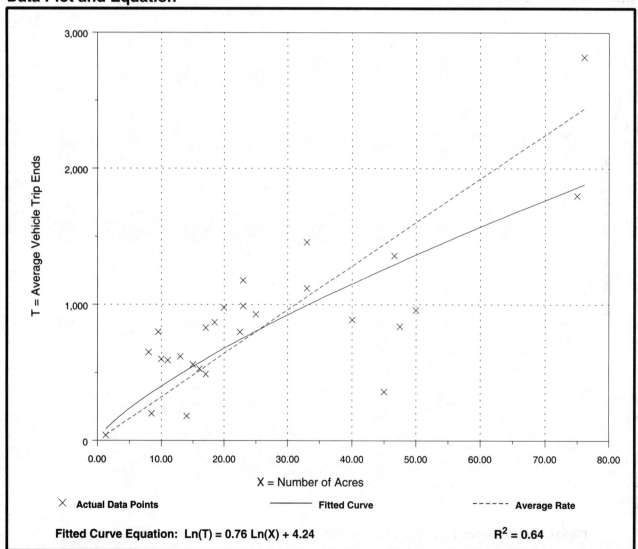

X = Number of Acres

× **Actual Data Points**　　　　—— **Fitted Curve**　　　- - - - - **Average Rate**

Fitted Curve Equation: Ln(T) = 0.76 Ln(X) + 4.24　　　　$R^2 = 0.64$

Mobile Home Park
(240)

Average Vehicle Trip Ends vs: **Acres**
On a: **Sunday,**
Peak Hour of Generator

Number of Studies: 15
Average Number of Acres: 22
Directional Distribution: 51% entering, 49% exiting

Trip Generation per Acre

Average Rate	Range of Rates	Standard Deviation
3.90	2.27 - 10.00	2.51

Data Plot and Equation

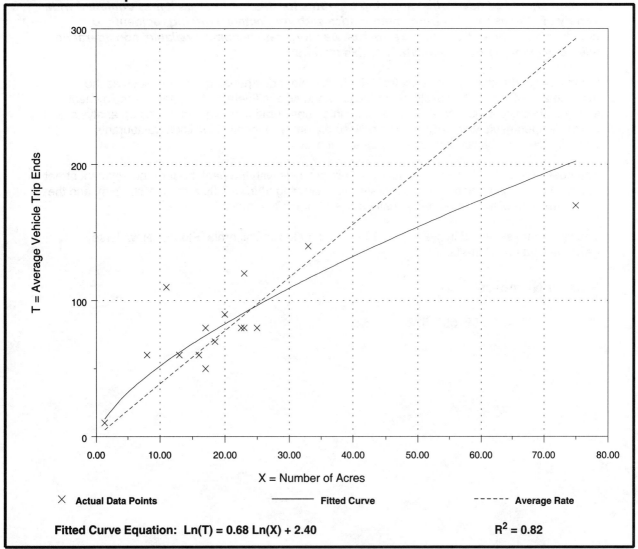

Fitted Curve Equation: Ln(T) = 0.68 Ln(X) + 2.40 $R^2 = 0.82$

Land Use: 251
Senior Adult Housing—Detached

Description

Senior adult housing consists of detached independent living developments, including retirement communities, age-restricted housing and active adult communities. These developments may include amenities such as golf courses, swimming pools, 24-hour security, transportation and common recreational facilities. However, they generally lack centralized dining and on-site health facilities. Detached senior adult housing communities may or may not be gated. Residents in these communities are typically active (requiring little to no medical supervision). The percentage of retired residents varies by development. Senior adult housing—attached (Land Use 252), congregate care facility (Land Use 253) and continuing care retirement community (Land Use 255) are related uses.

Additional Data

Caution should be used when applying trip rates for this land use as it may contain a wide variety of studies ranging from communities with very active, working residents to communities with older, retired residents. As more data become available, consideration will be given to future stratification of this land use.

Many factors affected the trip rates for detached senior adult housing. Factors such as the average age of residents, development location and size, affluence of residents, employment status and vehicular access should be taken into consideration when conducting an analysis. Some developments were located within close proximity to medical facilities, restaurants, shopping centers, banks and recreational activities.

The peak hour of the generator typically did not coincide with the peak hour of the adjacent street traffic. The a.m. peak hour of the generator typically ranged from 7:00 a.m. to 12:00 p.m. and the p.m. peak hour of the generator typically ranged from 1:00 p.m. to 6:00 p.m.

The sites were surveyed in the 1980s, 1990s and 2000s in California, Florida, New Jersey, Pennsylvania and Canada.

Source Numbers

221, 289, 398, 421, 500, 550, 598, 601, 629

Land Use: 251
Senior Adult Housing—Detached
Independent Variables with One Observation

The following trip generation data are for independent variables with only one observation. This information is shown in this table only; there are no related plots for these data.

Users are cautioned to use data with care because of the small sample size.

Independent Variable	Trip Generation Rate	Size of Independent Variable	Number of Studies	Directional Distribution
Dwelling Units				
Sunday Peak Hour of Generator	0.21	2,136	1	51% entering, 49% exiting

Senior Adult Housing - Detached
(251)

Average Vehicle Trip Ends vs: **Dwelling Units**
On a: **Weekday**

Number of Studies: 7
Avg. Number of Dwelling Units: 862
Directional Distribution: 50% entering, 50% exiting

Trip Generation per Dwelling Unit

Average Rate	Range of Rates	Standard Deviation
3.71	2.90 - 5.70	2.04

Data Plot and Equation

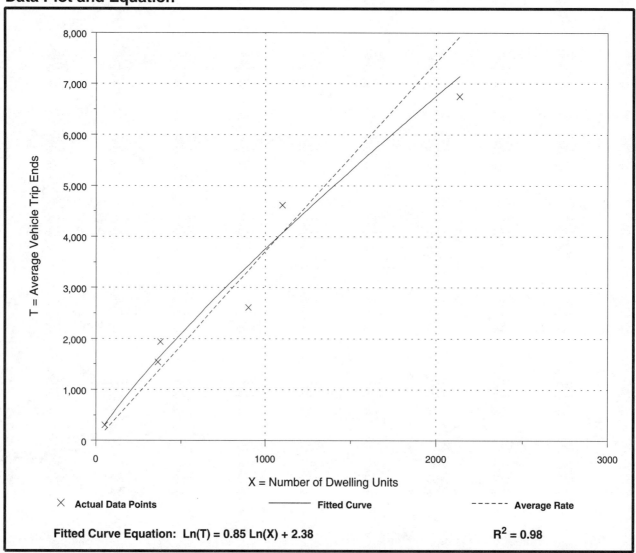

Fitted Curve Equation: $\text{Ln}(T) = 0.85\,\text{Ln}(X) + 2.38$ $R^2 = 0.98$

Senior Adult Housing - Detached
(251)

Average Vehicle Trip Ends vs: **Dwelling Units**
On a: **Weekday,**
Peak Hour of Adjacent Street Traffic,
One Hour Between 7 and 9 a.m.

Number of Studies: 23
Avg. Number of Dwelling Units: 607
Directional Distribution: 35% entering, 65% exiting

Trip Generation per Dwelling Unit

Average Rate	Range of Rates	Standard Deviation
0.22	0.13 - 0.84	0.47

Data Plot and Equation

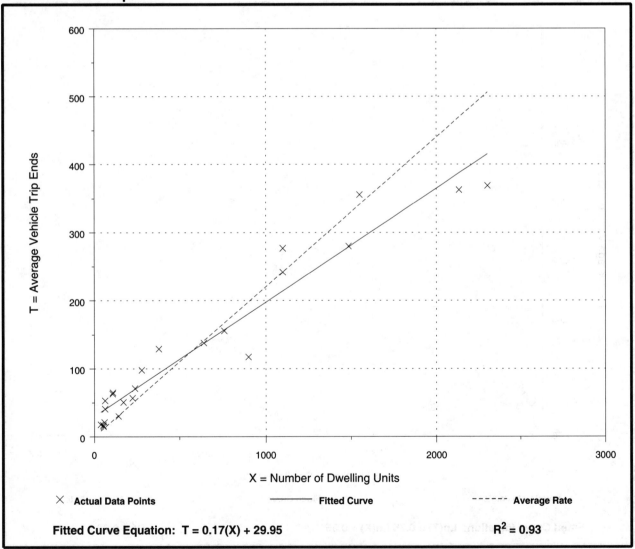

Fitted Curve Equation: T = 0.17(X) + 29.95   **R² = 0.93**

Senior Adult Housing - Detached
(251)

Average Vehicle Trip Ends vs: **Dwelling Units**
On a: **Weekday,**
Peak Hour of Adjacent Street Traffic,
One Hour Between 4 and 6 p.m.

Number of Studies: 24
Avg. Number of Dwelling Units: 605
Directional Distribution: 61% entering, 39% exiting

Trip Generation per Dwelling Unit

Average Rate	Range of Rates	Standard Deviation
0.27	0.17 - 0.95	0.53

Data Plot and Equation

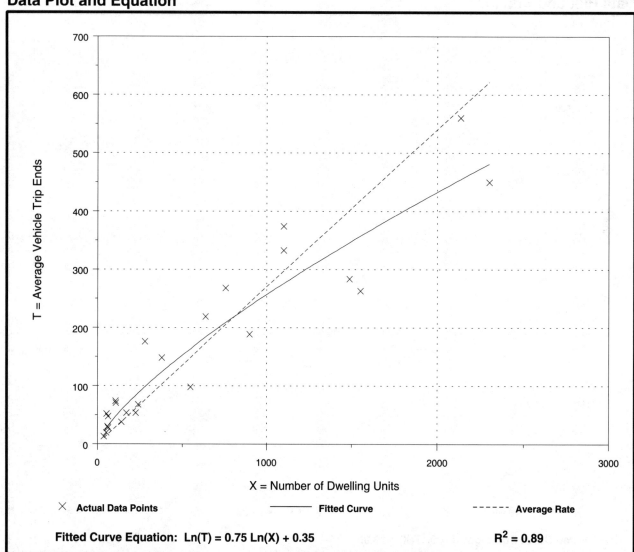

X = Number of Dwelling Units

✕ Actual Data Points ──── Fitted Curve ------ Average Rate

Fitted Curve Equation: $Ln(T) = 0.75 \, Ln(X) + 0.35$ $R^2 = 0.89$

Senior Adult Housing - Detached
(251)

Average Vehicle Trip Ends vs: **Dwelling Units**
On a: **Weekday,**
     A.M. Peak Hour of Generator

Number of Studies: 15
Avg. Number of Dwelling Units: 442
Directional Distribution: 43% entering, 57% exiting

Trip Generation per Dwelling Unit

Average Rate	Range of Rates	Standard Deviation
0.29	0.21 - 0.90	0.56

Data Plot and Equation

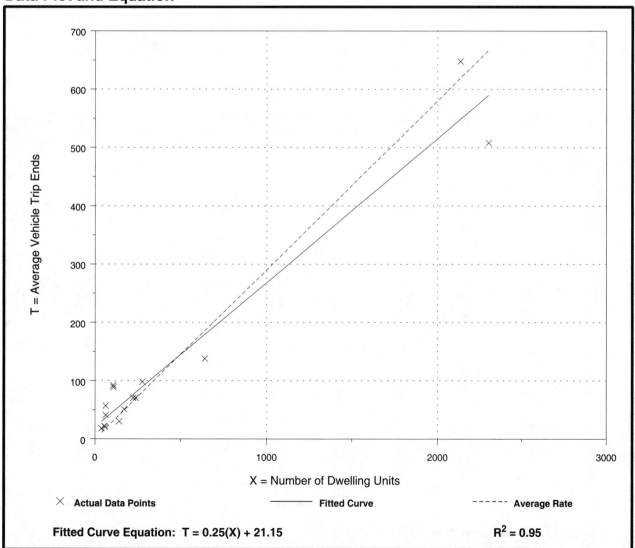

X = Number of Dwelling Units

✕ **Actual Data Points**   ——— **Fitted Curve**   ----- **Average Rate**

Fitted Curve Equation: T = 0.25(X) + 21.15 $R^2 = 0.95$

Senior Adult Housing - Detached
(251)

Average Vehicle Trip Ends vs: **Dwelling Units**
On a: **Weekday,**
P.M. Peak Hour of Generator

Number of Studies: 15
Avg. Number of Dwelling Units: 442
Directional Distribution: 56% entering, 44% exiting

Trip Generation per Dwelling Unit

Average Rate	Range of Rates	Standard Deviation
0.34	0.20 - 1.01	0.61

Data Plot and Equation

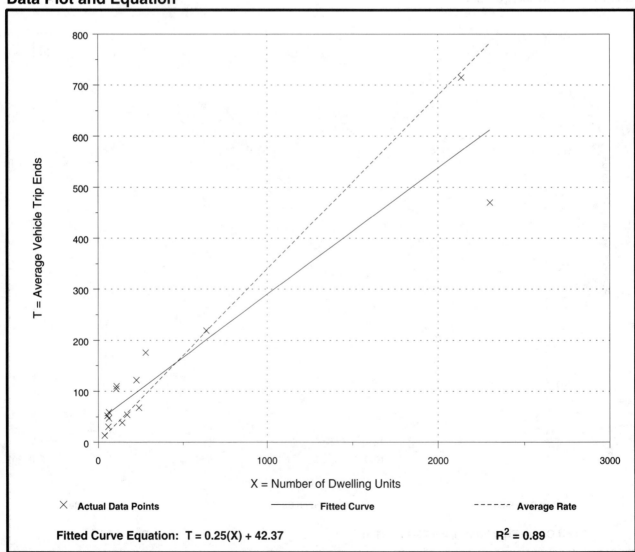

X **Actual Data Points**   ———— **Fitted Curve**   - - - - - **Average Rate**

Fitted Curve Equation: T = 0.25(X) + 42.37 $R^2 = 0.89$

Senior Adult Housing - Detached
(251)

Average Vehicle Trip Ends vs: **Dwelling Units**
On a: **Saturday**

Number of Studies: 2
Avg. Number of Dwelling Units: 1,095
Directional Distribution: 50% entering, 50% exiting

Trip Generation per Dwelling Unit

Average Rate	Range of Rates	Standard Deviation
2.77	2.70 - 5.53	*

Data Plot and Equation

Caution - Use Carefully - Small Sample Size

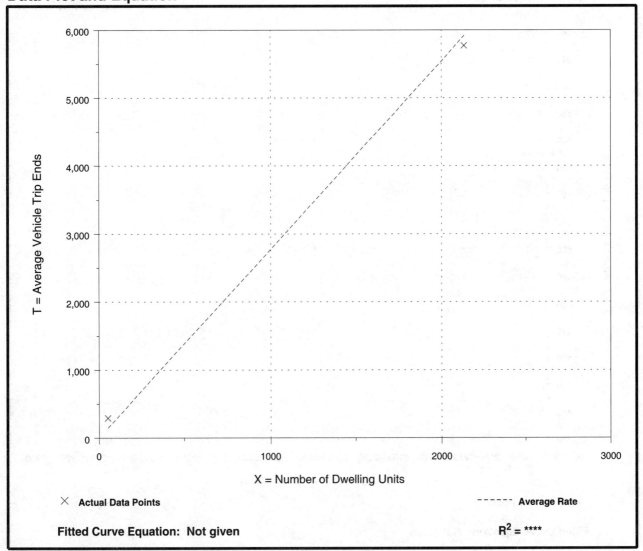

X **Actual Data Points**   ------ **Average Rate**

Fitted Curve Equation: Not given $R^2 = ****$

Senior Adult Housing - Detached
(251)

Average Vehicle Trip Ends vs: **Dwelling Units**
On a: **Saturday,**
Peak Hour of Generator

Number of Studies: 2
Avg. Number of Dwelling Units: 2,218
Directional Distribution: 48% entering, 52% exiting

Trip Generation per Dwelling Unit

Average Rate	Range of Rates	Standard Deviation
0.23	0.19 - 0.27	*

Data Plot and Equation

Caution - Use Carefully - Small Sample Size

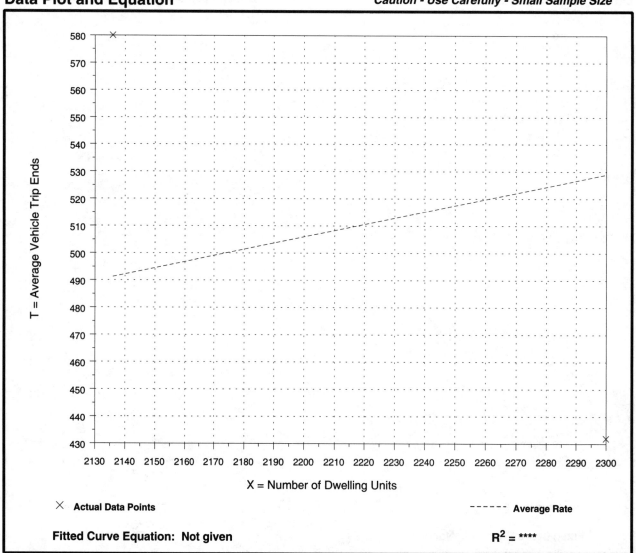

X **Actual Data Points**

- - - - - **Average Rate**

Fitted Curve Equation: Not given

$R^2 = ****$

Senior Adult Housing - Detached
(251)

Average Vehicle Trip Ends vs: **Dwelling Units**
On a: **Sunday**

Number of Studies: 2
Avg. Number of Dwelling Units: 1,095
Directional Distribution: 50% entering, 50% exiting

Trip Generation per Dwelling Unit

Average Rate	Range of Rates	Standard Deviation
2.33	2.27 - 4.77	*

Data Plot and Equation

Caution - Use Carefully - Small Sample Size

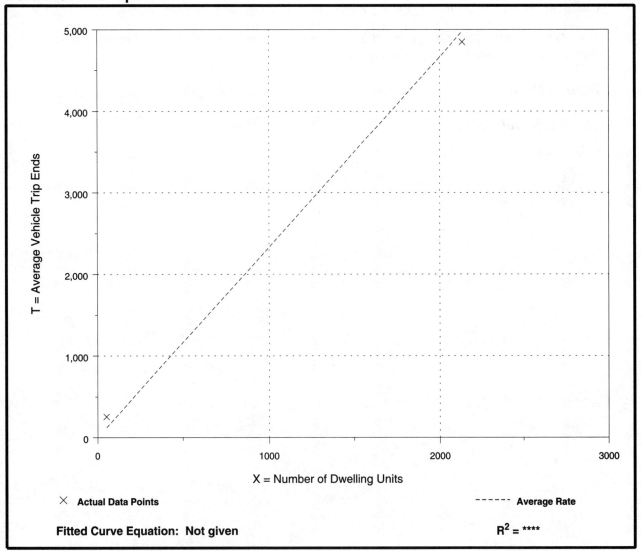

X **Actual Data Points**   - - - - - **Average Rate**

Fitted Curve Equation: Not given $R^2 = ****$

Land Use: 252
Senior Adult Housing—Attached

Description

Senior adult housing consists of attached independent living developments, including retirement communities, age-restricted housing and active adult communities. These developments may include limited social or recreational services. However, they generally lack centralized dining and on-site medical facilities. Residents in these communities live independently, are typically active (requiring little to no medical supervision) and may or may not be retired. Senior adult housing—detached (Land Use 251), congregate care facility (Land Use 253) and continuing care retirement community (Land Use 255) are related uses.

Additional Data

The peak hour of the generator typically did not coincide with the peak hour of the adjacent street traffic. The a.m. peak hour of the generator typically ranged from 8:30 a.m. to 12:00 p.m. and the p.m. peak hour of the generator typically ranged from 1:00 p.m. to 6:00 p.m.

The sites were surveyed between the 1980s and the 2000s in California, Illinois, Pennsylvania, New Jersey and Canada.

Source Numbers

237, 272, 501, 576, 602

Land Use: 252
Senior Adult Housing—Attached
Independent Variables with One Observation

The following trip generation data are for independent variables with only one observation. This information is shown in this table only; there are no related plots for these data.

Users are cautioned to use data with care because of the small sample size.

Independent Variable	Trip Generation Rate	Size of Independent Variable	Number of Studies	Directional Distribution
Occupied Dwelling Units				
Weekday	3.48	67	1	50% entering, 50% exiting
Saturday	2.51	67	1	50% entering, 50% exiting
Saturday Peak Hour of Generator	0.30	67	1	Not available
Sunday	2.70	67	1	50% entering, 50% exiting
Sunday Peak Hour of Generator	0.55	67	1	Not available

Senior Adult Housing - Attached
(252)

Average Vehicle Trip Ends vs: **Occupied Dwelling Units**
On a: **Weekday,**
Peak Hour of Adjacent Street Traffic,
One Hour Between 7 and 9 a.m.

Number of Studies: 8
Avg. Num. of Occupied Dwelling Units: 214
Directional Distribution: 36% entering, 64% exiting

Trip Generation per Occupied Dwelling Unit

Average Rate	Range of Rates	Standard Deviation
0.13	0.02 - 0.27	0.37

Data Plot and Equation

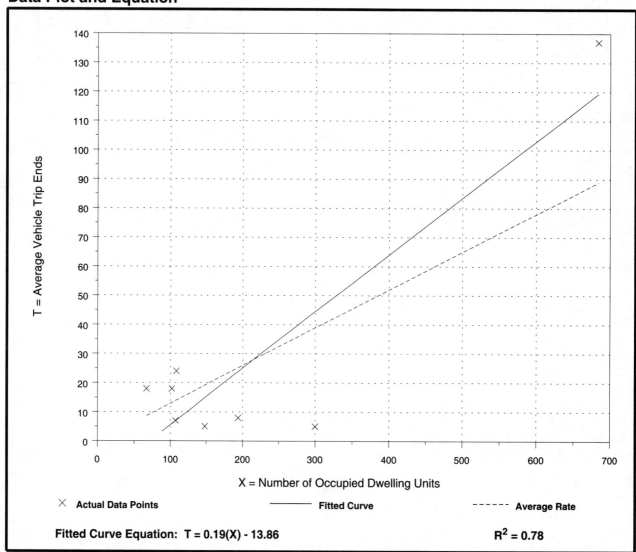

Fitted Curve Equation: T = 0.19(X) - 13.86 $R^2 = 0.78$

Senior Adult Housing - Attached
(252)

Average Vehicle Trip Ends vs: **Occupied Dwelling Units**
On a: **Weekday,**
Peak Hour of Adjacent Street Traffic,
One Hour Between 4 and 6 p.m.

Number of Studies: 8
Avg. Num. of Occupied Dwelling Units: 214
Directional Distribution: 60% entering, 40% exiting

Trip Generation per Occupied Dwelling Unit

Average Rate	Range of Rates	Standard Deviation
0.16	0.03 - 0.31	0.41

Data Plot and Equation

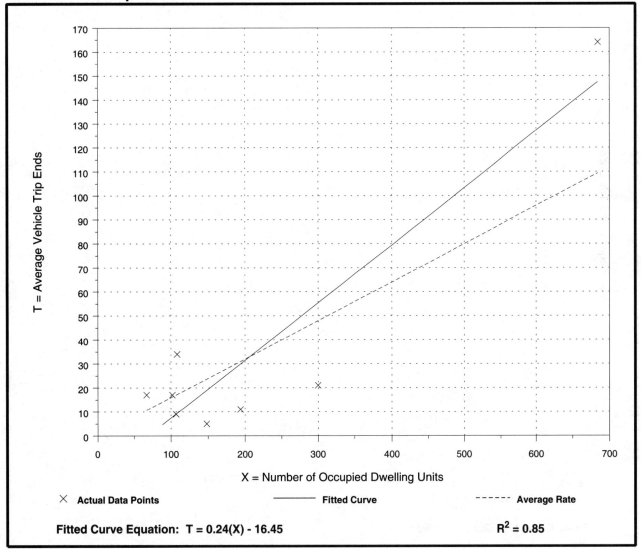

Fitted Curve Equation: T = 0.24(X) - 16.45 $R^2 = 0.85$

Senior Adult Housing - Attached
(252)

Average Vehicle Trip Ends vs: **Occupied Dwelling Units**
On a: **Weekday,**
A.M. Peak Hour of Generator

Number of Studies: 4
Avg. Num. of Occupied Dwelling Units: 177
Directional Distribution: 50% entering, 50% exiting

Trip Generation per Occupied Dwelling Unit

Average Rate	Range of Rates	Standard Deviation
0.06	0.02 - 0.37	0.27

Data Plot and Equation

Caution - Use Carefully - Small Sample Size

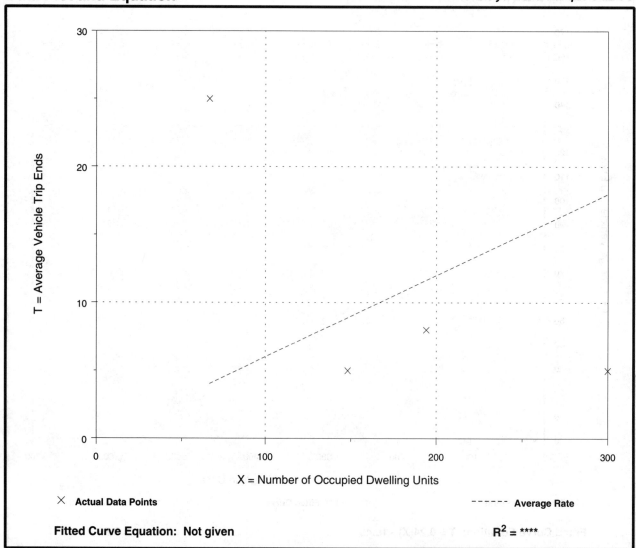

X Actual Data Points

----- **Average Rate**

Fitted Curve Equation: Not given

$R^2 = ****$

Senior Adult Housing - Attached
(252)

Average Vehicle Trip Ends vs: **Occupied Dwelling Units**
On a: **Weekday,**
P.M. Peak Hour of Generator

Number of Studies: 4
Avg. Num. of Occupied Dwelling Units: 177
Directional Distribution: 53% entering, 47% exiting

Trip Generation per Occupied Dwelling Unit

Average Rate	Range of Rates	Standard Deviation
0.11	0.03 - 0.25	0.33

Data Plot and Equation

Caution - Use Carefully - Small Sample Size

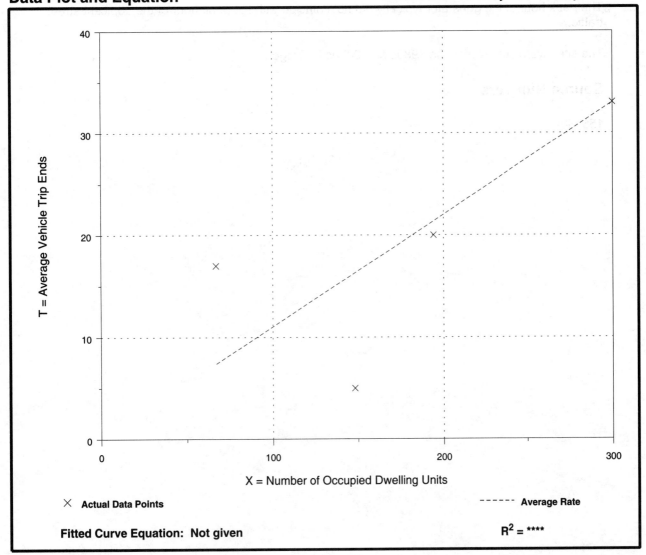

X   **Actual Data Points**

--- **Average Rate**

Fitted Curve Equation: Not given $R^2 = ****$

Land Use: 253
Congregate Care Facility

Description

Congregate care facilities are independent living developments that provide centralized amenities such as dining, housekeeping, transportation and organized social/recreational activities. Limited medical services (such as nursing and dental) may or may not be provided. The resident may contract additional medical services or personal assistance. Senior adult housing—detached (Land Use 251), senior adult housing—attached (Land Use 252) and continuing care retirement community (Land Use 255) are related uses.

Additional Data

Vehicle ownership levels were very low at congregate care facilities; the facilities' employees or services provided to the residents generated the majority of the trips to the sites.

The peak hour of the generator typically did not coincide with the peak hour of the adjacent street traffic.

The sites were surveyed in the 1980s and 2000s in Oregon.

Source Numbers

155, 584

Congregate Care Facility
(253)

Average Vehicle Trip Ends vs: **Dwelling Units**
On a: **Weekday**

Number of Studies: 2
Avg. Number of Dwelling Units: 194
Directional Distribution: 50% entering, 50% exiting

Trip Generation per Dwelling Unit

Average Rate	Range of Rates	Standard Deviation
2.02	1.63 - 2.15	*

Data Plot and Equation

Caution - Use Carefully - Small Sample Size

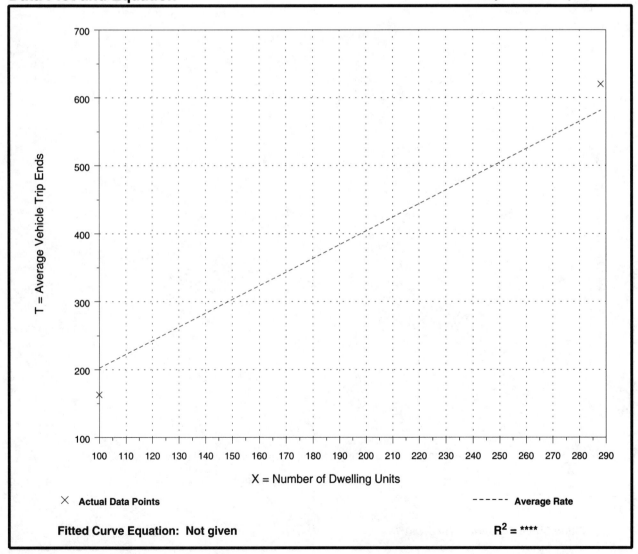

X = Number of Dwelling Units

✕ Actual Data Points   ----- Average Rate

Fitted Curve Equation: Not given $R^2 = ****$

Congregate Care Facility
(253)

Average Vehicle Trip Ends vs: **Dwelling Units**
On a: **Weekday,**
Peak Hour of Adjacent Street Traffic,
One Hour Between 7 and 9 a.m.

Number of Studies: 3
Avg. Number of Dwelling Units: 164
Directional Distribution: 59% entering, 41% exiting

Trip Generation per Dwelling Unit

Average Rate	Range of Rates	Standard Deviation
0.06	0.05 - 0.06	0.24

Data Plot and Equation

Caution - Use Carefully - Small Sample Size

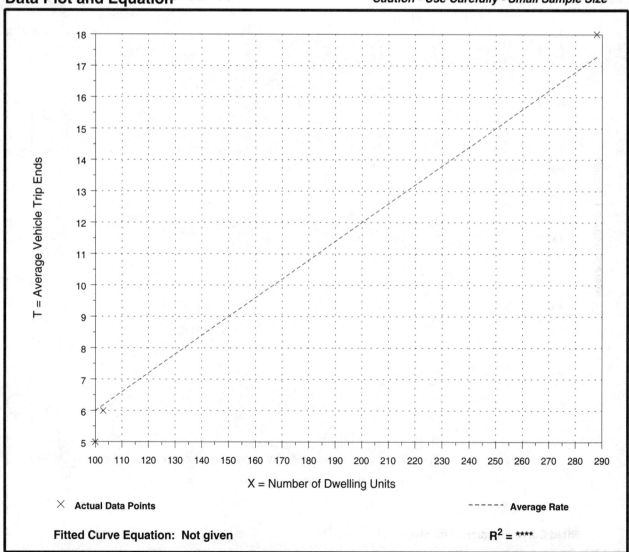

$\times$ **Actual Data Points** — — — — **Average Rate**

Fitted Curve Equation: Not given $R^2 = ****$

Congregate Care Facility
(253)

Average Vehicle Trip Ends vs: Dwelling Units
On a: Weekday,
Peak Hour of Adjacent Street Traffic,
One Hour Between 4 and 6 p.m.

Number of Studies: 3
Avg. Number of Dwelling Units: 164
Directional Distribution: 55% entering, 45% exiting

Trip Generation per Dwelling Unit

Average Rate	Range of Rates	Standard Deviation
0.17	0.16 - 0.19	0.41

Data Plot and Equation

Caution - Use Carefully - Small Sample Size

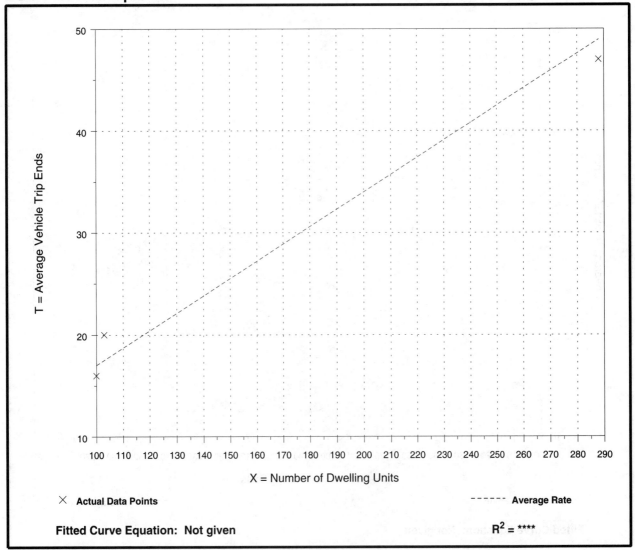

X = Number of Dwelling Units

✕ **Actual Data Points**   ----- **Average Rate**

Fitted Curve Equation: Not given $R^2 = ****$

Congregate Care Facility
(253)

Average Vehicle Trip Ends vs: Dwelling Units
On a: Weekday,
A.M. Peak Hour of Generator

Number of Studies: 2
Avg. Number of Dwelling Units: 194
Directional Distribution: 50% entering, 50% exiting

Trip Generation per Dwelling Unit

Average Rate	Range of Rates	Standard Deviation
0.14	0.10 - 0.16	*

Data Plot and Equation

Caution - Use Carefully - Small Sample Size

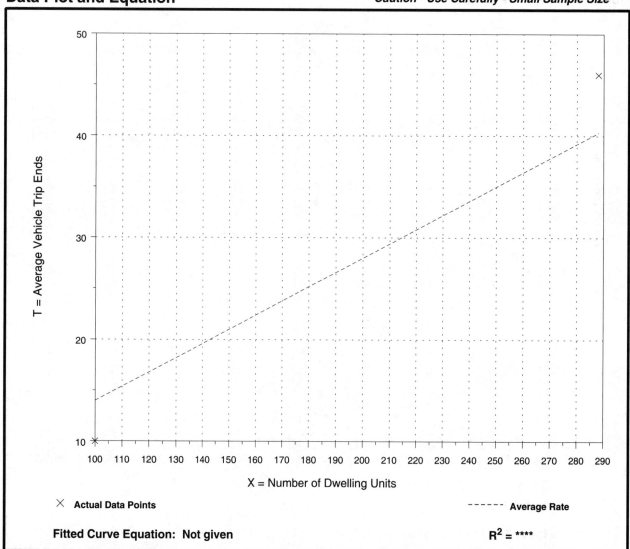

X **Actual Data Points**

- - - - - **Average Rate**

Fitted Curve Equation: Not given $R^2 = ****$

Congregate Care Facility
(253)

Average Vehicle Trip Ends vs: Dwelling Units
On a: Weekday,
P.M. Peak Hour of Generator

Number of Studies: 2
Avg. Number of Dwelling Units: 194
Directional Distribution: 60% entering, 40% exiting

Trip Generation per Dwelling Unit

Average Rate	Range of Rates	Standard Deviation
0.20	0.16 - 0.21	*

Data Plot and Equation

Caution - Use Carefully - Small Sample Size

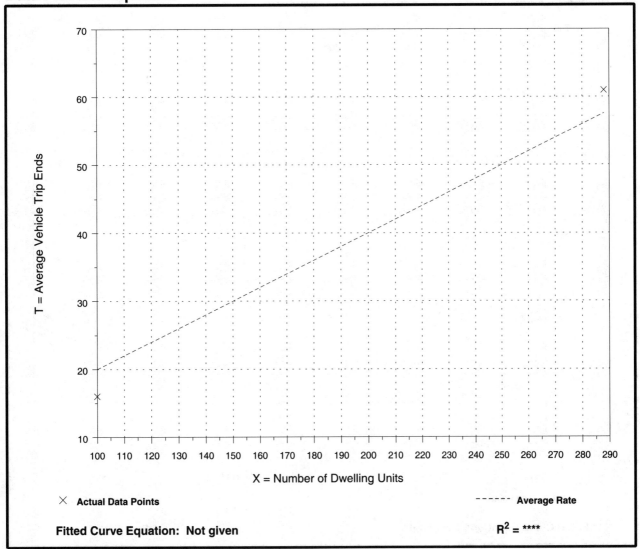

X = Number of Dwelling Units

× **Actual Data Points**

----- **Average Rate**

Fitted Curve Equation: Not given

R^2 = ****

Congregate Care Facility
(253)

Average Vehicle Trip Ends vs: Occupied Dwelling Units
On a: Weekday

Number of Studies: 2
Avg. Num. of Occupied Dwelling Units: 183
Directional Distribution: 50% entering, 50% exiting

Trip Generation per Occupied Dwelling Unit

Average Rate	Range of Rates	Standard Deviation
2.15	2.12 - 2.15	*

Data Plot and Equation

Caution - Use Carefully - Small Sample Size

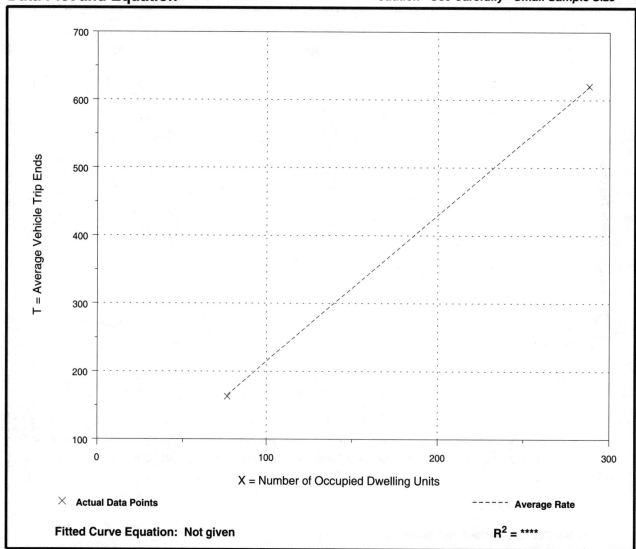

X **Actual Data Points**   - - - - - **Average Rate**

Fitted Curve Equation: Not given $R^2 = ****$

Congregate Care Facility
(253)

Average Vehicle Trip Ends vs: **Occupied Dwelling Units**
On a: **Weekday,**
Peak Hour of Adjacent Street Traffic,
One Hour Between 7 and 9 a.m.

Number of Studies: 2
Avg. Num. of Occupied Dwelling Units: 183
Directional Distribution: 61% entering, 39% exiting

Trip Generation per Occupied Dwelling Unit

Average Rate	Range of Rates	Standard Deviation
0.06	0.06 - 0.06	*

Data Plot and Equation

Caution - Use Carefully - Small Sample Size

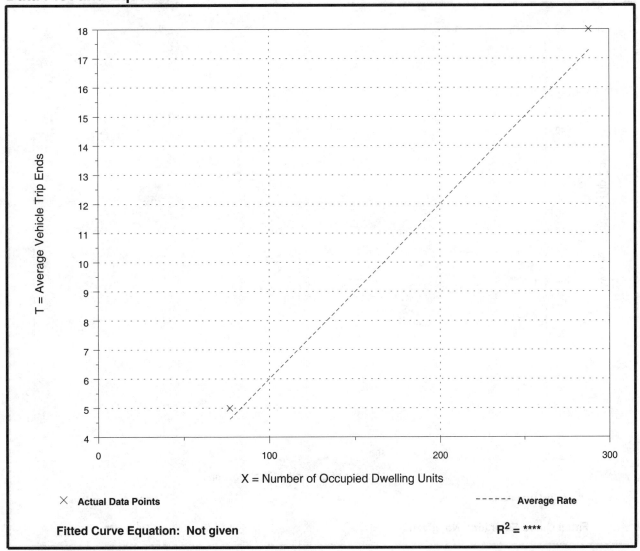

X Actual Data Points

- - - - - Average Rate

Fitted Curve Equation: Not given

$R^2 = ****$

Congregate Care Facility
(253)

Average Vehicle Trip Ends vs: **Occupied Dwelling Units**
On a: **Weekday,**
Peak Hour of Adjacent Street Traffic,
One Hour Between 4 and 6 p.m.

Number of Studies: 2
Avg. Num. of Occupied Dwelling Units: 183
Directional Distribution: 56% entering, 44% exiting

Trip Generation per Occupied Dwelling Unit

Average Rate	Range of Rates	Standard Deviation
0.17	0.16 - 0.21	*

Data Plot and Equation

Caution - Use Carefully - Small Sample Size

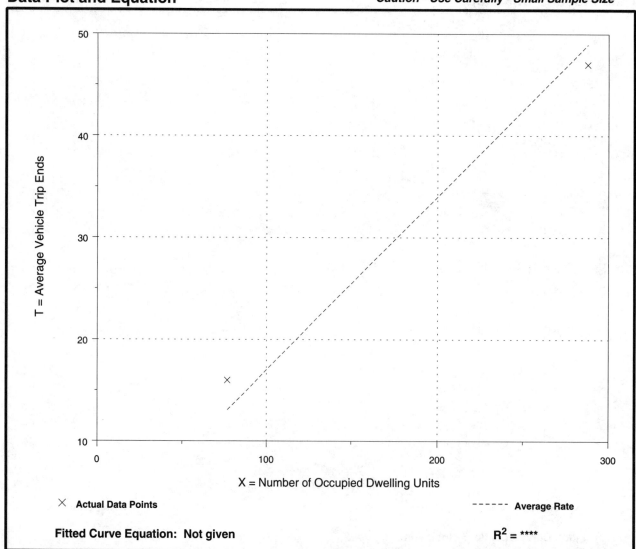

X Actual Data Points

- - - - - **Average Rate**

Fitted Curve Equation: Not given

$R^2 = ****$

Congregate Care Facility
(253)

Average Vehicle Trip Ends vs: **Occupied Dwelling Units**
On a: **Weekday,**
A.M. Peak Hour of Generator

Number of Studies: 2
Avg. Num. of Occupied Dwelling Units: 183
Directional Distribution: 50% entering, 50% exiting

Trip Generation per Occupied Dwelling Unit

Average Rate	Range of Rates	Standard Deviation
0.15	0.13 - 0.16	*

Data Plot and Equation

Caution - Use Carefully - Small Sample Size

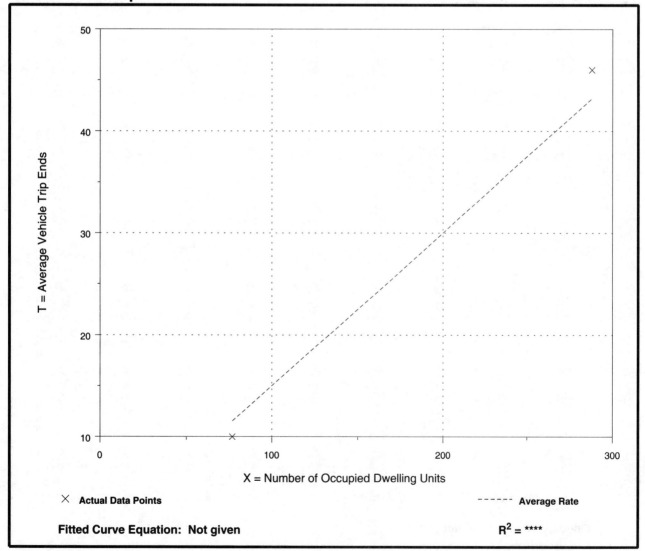

X   **Actual Data Points**   ----- **Average Rate**

Fitted Curve Equation: Not given $R^2 = ****$

Congregate Care Facility
(253)

Average Vehicle Trip Ends vs: **Occupied Dwelling Units**
On a: **Weekday,**
P.M. Peak Hour of Generator

Number of Studies: 2
Avg. Num. of Occupied Dwelling Units: 183
Directional Distribution: 60% entering, 40% exiting

Trip Generation per Occupied Dwelling Unit

Average Rate	Range of Rates	Standard Deviation
0.21	0.21 - 0.21	*

Data Plot and Equation

Caution - Use Carefully - Small Sample Size

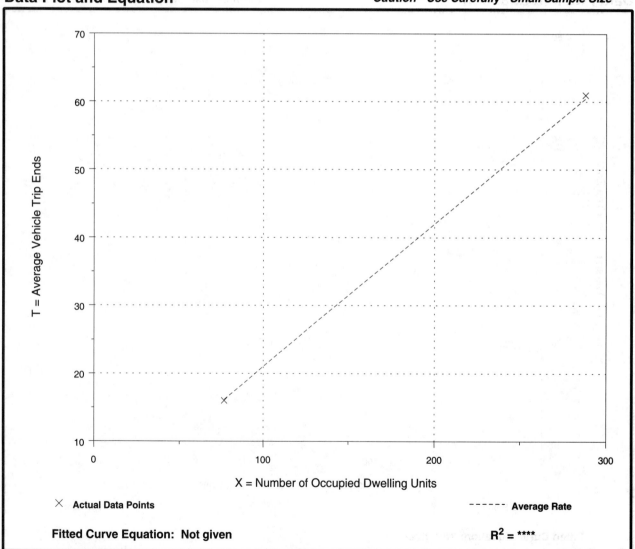

X = Number of Occupied Dwelling Units

✕ **Actual Data Points**   - - - - - **Average Rate**

Fitted Curve Equation: Not given $R^2 = ****$

Land Use: 254
Assisted Living

Description

Assisted living complexes are residential settings that provide either routine general protective oversight or assistance with activities necessary for independent living to mentally or physically limited persons. They commonly have separate living quarters for residents, and services include dining, housekeeping, social and physical activities, medication administration and transportation. Alzheimer's and ALS care are commonly offered by these facilities, though the living quarters for these patients may be located separately from the other residents. Assisted care commonly bridges the gap between independent living and nursing homes. In some areas of the country, assisted living residences may be called personal care, residential care, or domiciliary care. Staff may be available at an assisted care facility 24 hours a day, but skilled medical care—which is limited in nature—is not required. Continuing care retirement community (Land Use 255) and nursing home (Land Use 620) are related uses.

Additional Data

The rooms in these facilities may be private or shared accommodations, consisting of either a single room or a small apartment-style unit with a kitchenette and living space.

One study reported that according to national and local data, less than 5 percent of the residents owned cars, which were rarely driven. Employees, visitors and delivery trucks made most of the trips to these facilities.

Truck traffic was captured for some studies in this land use and is presented in the table below. Although truck traffic was very low overall, most trips occurred during the mid-day period on a weekday.

The peak hour of the generator typically did not coincide with the peak hour of the adjacent street traffic, primarily because of the shifts of the employees. For the data collected in this land use, shifts typically began at 7:00 a.m., 3:00 p.m. and 11:00 p.m. The a.m. peak hour of the generator typically occurred between 6:00 a.m. and 7:00 a.m., while the p.m. peak hour of the generator typically occurred between 3:00 p.m. and 4:00 p.m.

Time Period	% Trucks
Weekday Morning (6:30 a.m.–9:30 a.m.)	1
Weekday Mid-Day (11:00 a.m.–1:30 p.m.)	9
Weekday Evening (2:45 p.m.–6:45 p.m.)	2
Saturday Mid-Day (11:00 a.m.–2:00 p.m.)	4
Saturday Evening (3:00 p.m.–6:00 p.m.)	0
Sunday Mid-Day (11:00 a.m.–2:00 p.m.)	1
Sunday Evening (3:00 p.m.–6:00 p.m.)	0

The sites were surveyed in the late 1980s, the late 1990s and the 2000s in Connecticut, New Jersey, New York, Pennsylvania and Oregon.

Source Numbers

91, 244, 573, 581, 611

Land Use: 254
Assisted Living
Independent Variables with One Observation

The following trip generation data are for independent variables with only one observation. This information is shown in this table only; there are no related plots for these data.

Users are cautioned to use data with care because of the small sample size.

Independent Variable	Trip Generation Rate	Size of Independent Variable	Number of Studies	Directional Distribution
Occupied Beds				
Weekday a.m. Peak Hour of Adjacent Street Traffic	0.17	87	1	73% entering, 27% exiting
Weekday p.m. Peak Hour of Adjacent Street Traffic	0.29	87	1	52% entering, 48% exiting
Weekday a.m. Peak Hour of Generator	0.25	87	1	77% entering, 23% exiting

Assisted Living
(254)

Average Vehicle Trip Ends vs: Occupied Beds
On a: Weekday

Number of Studies: 15
Average Number of Occupied Beds: 117
Directional Distribution: 50% entering, 50% exiting

Trip Generation per Occupied Bed

Average Rate	Range of Rates	Standard Deviation
2.74	1.88 - 4.14	1.75

Data Plot and Equation

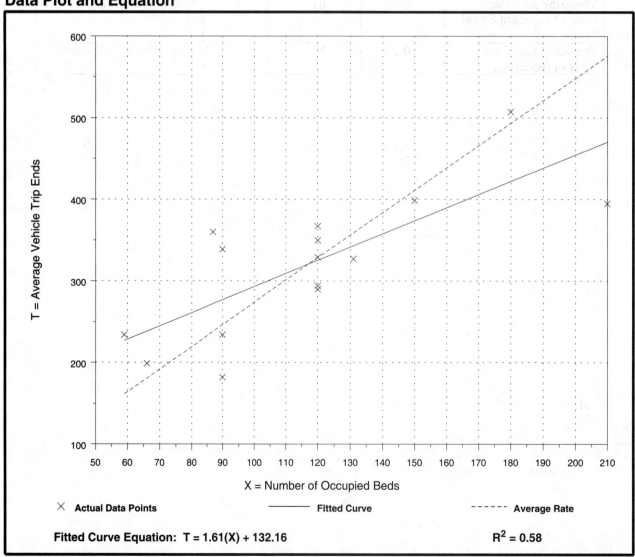

X **Actual Data Points**   —— **Fitted Curve**   - - - - - **Average Rate**

Fitted Curve Equation: T = 1.61(X) + 132.16 $R^2 = 0.58$

Assisted Living
(254)

Average Vehicle Trip Ends vs: Occupied Beds
On a: Weekday,
P.M. Peak Hour of Generator

Number of Studies: 15
Average Number of Occupied Beds: 117
Directional Distribution: 36% entering, 64% exiting

Trip Generation per Occupied Bed

Average Rate	Range of Rates	Standard Deviation
0.38	0.28 - 0.53	0.61

Data Plot and Equation

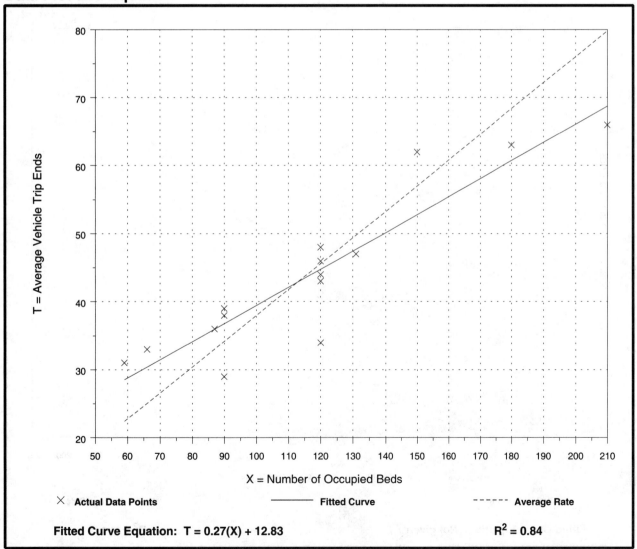

X Actual Data Points ———— Fitted Curve - - - - - Average Rate

Fitted Curve Equation: T = 0.27(X) + 12.83 $R^2 = 0.84$

Assisted Living
(254)

Average Vehicle Trip Ends vs: Occupied Beds
On a: Saturday

Number of Studies: 15
Average Number of Occupied Beds: 117
Directional Distribution: 50% entering, 50% exiting

Trip Generation per Occupied Bed

Average Rate	Range of Rates	Standard Deviation
2.20	1.45 - 3.53	1.57

Data Plot and Equation

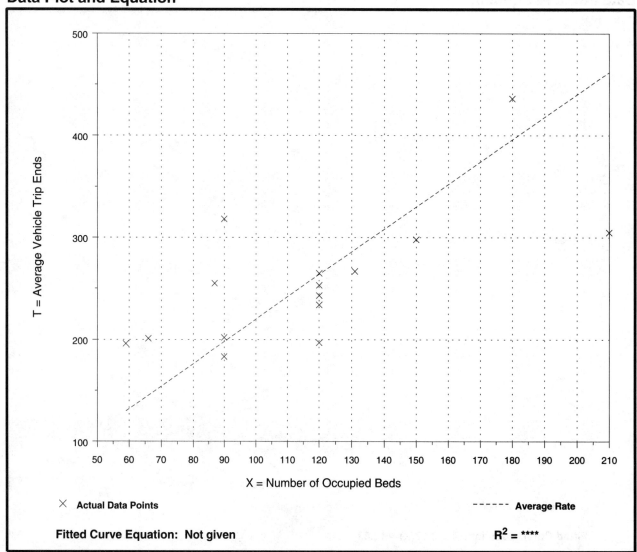

Fitted Curve Equation: Not given $R^2 = ****$

Assisted Living
(254)

Average Vehicle Trip Ends vs: **Occupied Beds**
On a: **Saturday,**
Peak Hour of Generator

Number of Studies: 15
Average Number of Occupied Beds: 117
Directional Distribution: 51% entering, 49% exiting

Trip Generation per Occupied Bed

Average Rate	Range of Rates	Standard Deviation
0.36	0.28 - 0.46	0.60

Data Plot and Equation

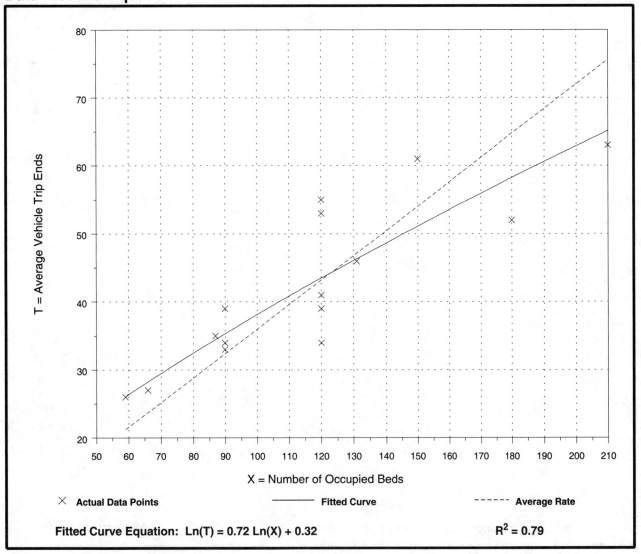

X **Actual Data Points**   ———— **Fitted Curve**   - - - - **Average Rate**

Fitted Curve Equation: Ln(T) = 0.72 Ln(X) + 0.32 $R^2 = 0.79$

Assisted Living
(254)

Average Vehicle Trip Ends vs: Occupied Beds
On a: Sunday

Number of Studies: 15
Average Number of Occupied Beds: 117
Directional Distribution: 50% entering, 50% exiting

Trip Generation per Occupied Bed

Average Rate	Range of Rates	Standard Deviation
2.44	1.67 - 3.73	1.65

Data Plot and Equation

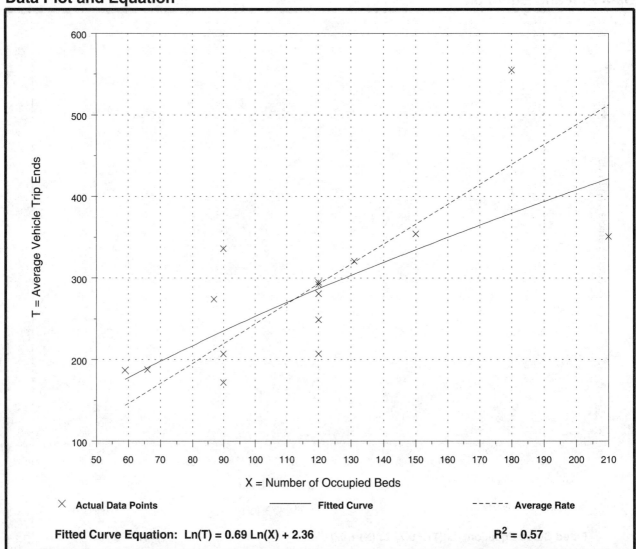

X **Actual Data Points**   ———— **Fitted Curve**   - - - - - **Average Rate**

Fitted Curve Equation: Ln(T) = 0.69 Ln(X) + 2.36 $R^2 = 0.57$

Assisted Living
(254)

Average Vehicle Trip Ends vs: **Occupied Beds**
On a: **Sunday,**
Peak Hour of Generator

Number of Studies: 15
Average Number of Occupied Beds: 117
Directional Distribution: 45% entering, 55% exiting

Trip Generation per Occupied Bed

Average Rate	Range of Rates	Standard Deviation
0.42	0.27 - 0.58	0.65

Data Plot and Equation

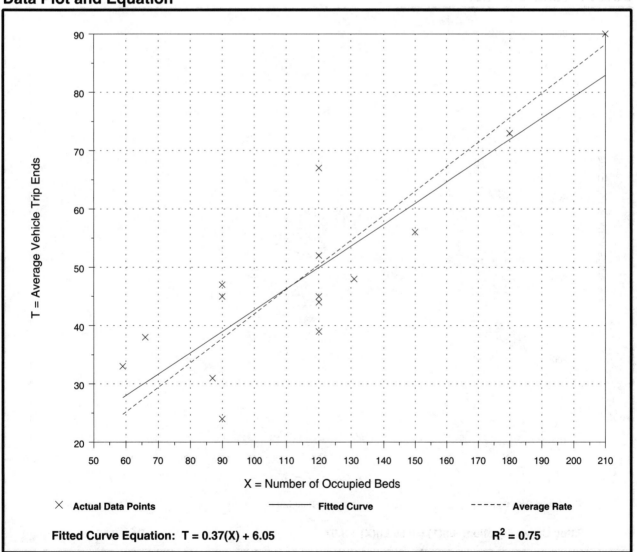

Fitted Curve Equation: T = 0.37(X) + 6.05 $R^2 = 0.75$

Assisted Living
(254)

Average Vehicle Trip Ends vs: **Beds**
On a: **Weekday**

Number of Studies: 16
Average Number of Beds: 121
Directional Distribution: 50% entering, 50% exiting

Trip Generation per Bed

Average Rate	Range of Rates	Standard Deviation
2.66	1.86 - 4.14	1.74

Data Plot and Equation

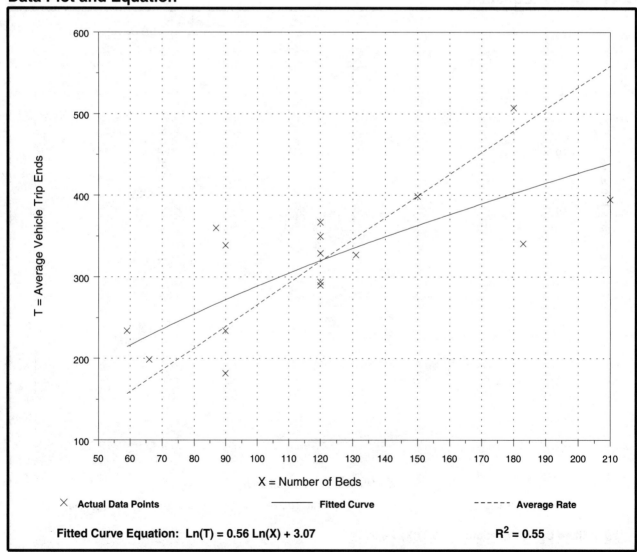

Fitted Curve Equation: Ln(T) = 0.56 Ln(X) + 3.07 $R^2 = 0.55$

Assisted Living
(254)

Average Vehicle Trip Ends vs: **Beds**
On a: **Weekday,**
Peak Hour of Adjacent Street Traffic,
One Hour Between 7 and 9 a.m.

Number of Studies: 7
Average Number of Beds: 121
Directional Distribution: 65% entering, 35% exiting

Trip Generation per Bed

Average Rate	Range of Rates	Standard Deviation
0.14	0.08 - 0.28	0.37

Data Plot and Equation

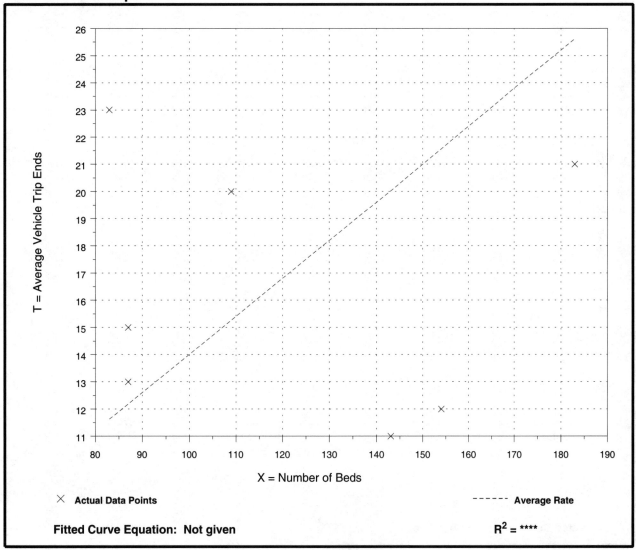

X **Actual Data Points**   - - - - - **Average Rate**

Fitted Curve Equation: Not given $R^2 =$ ****

Assisted Living
(254)

Average Vehicle Trip Ends vs: **Beds**
On a: **Weekday,**
Peak Hour of Adjacent Street Traffic,
One Hour Between 4 and 6 p.m.

Number of Studies: 7
Average Number of Beds: 121
Directional Distribution: 44% entering, 56% exiting

Trip Generation per Bed

Average Rate	Range of Rates	Standard Deviation
0.22	0.11 - 0.30	0.47

Data Plot and Equation

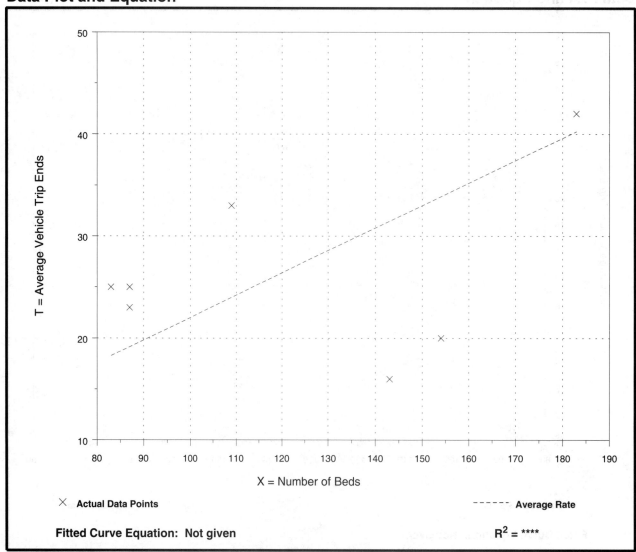

Fitted Curve Equation: Not given $R^2 = ****$

Assisted Living
(254)

Average Vehicle Trip Ends vs: Beds

On a: Weekday,

A.M. Peak Hour of Generator

Number of Studies: 7

Average Number of Beds: 121

Directional Distribution: 67% entering, 33% exiting

Trip Generation per Bed

Average Rate	Range of Rates	Standard Deviation
0.18	0.13 - 0.34	0.43

Data Plot and Equation

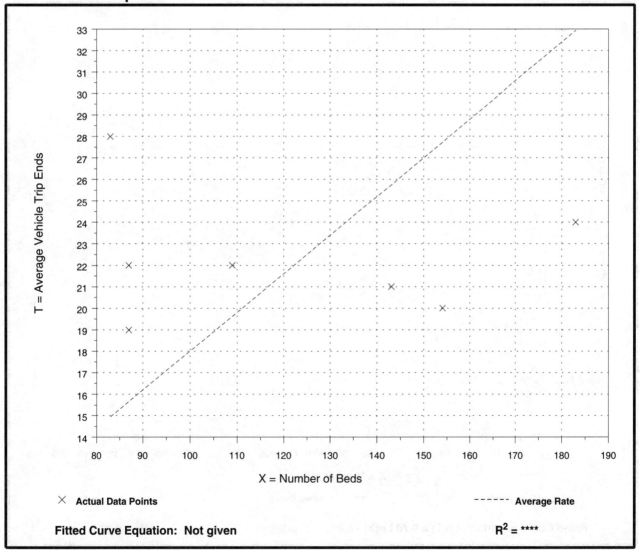

Fitted Curve Equation: Not given

$R^2 = $ ****

Assisted Living
(254)

Average Vehicle Trip Ends vs: **Beds**
On a: **Weekday,**
P.M. Peak Hour of Generator

Number of Studies: 24
Average Number of Beds: 107
Directional Distribution: 47% entering, 53% exiting

Trip Generation per Bed

Average Rate	Range of Rates	Standard Deviation
0.35	0.16 - 0.87	0.59

Data Plot and Equation

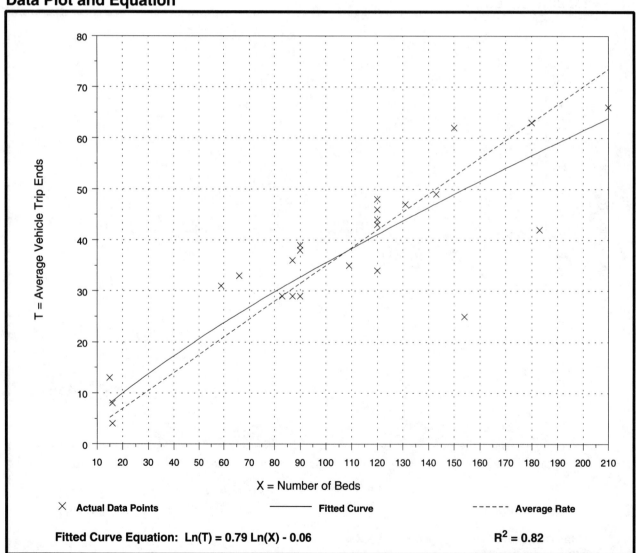

Fitted Curve Equation: $\text{Ln}(T) = 0.79 \, \text{Ln}(X) - 0.06$ $R^2 = 0.82$

Assisted Living
(254)

Average Vehicle Trip Ends vs: Beds
On a: Saturday

Number of Studies: 15
Average Number of Beds: 117
Directional Distribution: 50% entering, 50% exiting

Trip Generation per Bed

Average Rate	Range of Rates	Standard Deviation
2.20	1.45 - 3.53	1.57

Data Plot and Equation

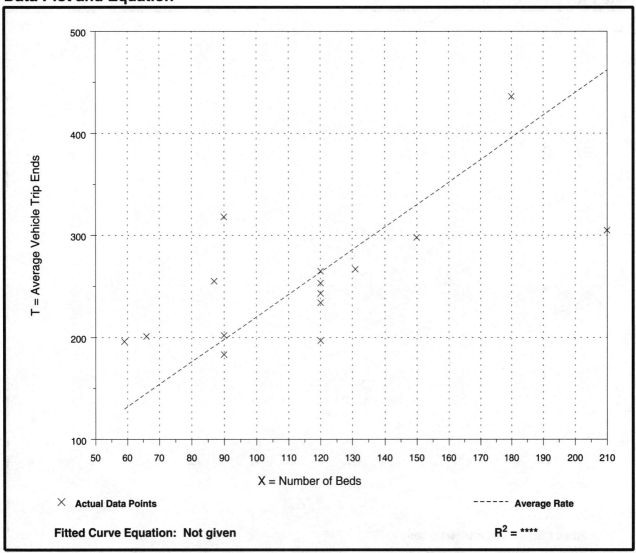

X Actual Data Points   - - - - - Average Rate

Fitted Curve Equation: Not given $R^2 = ****$

Assisted Living
(254)

Average Vehicle Trip Ends vs: **Beds**
On a: **Saturday,**
Peak Hour of Generator

Number of Studies: 20
Average Number of Beds: 116
Directional Distribution: 46% entering, 54% exiting

Trip Generation per Bed

Average Rate	Range of Rates	Standard Deviation
0.33	0.17 - 0.46	0.58

Data Plot and Equation

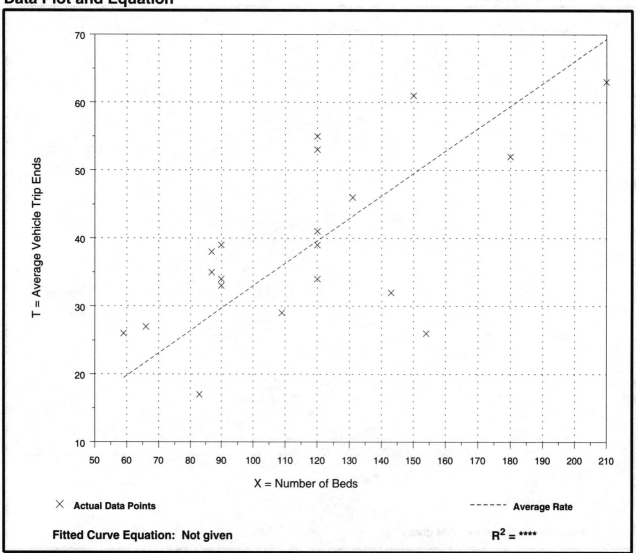

Fitted Curve Equation: Not given $R^2 = ****$

Assisted Living
(254)

Average Vehicle Trip Ends vs: Beds
On a: Sunday

Number of Studies: 15
Average Number of Beds: 117
Directional Distribution: 50% entering, 50% exiting

Trip Generation per Bed

Average Rate	Range of Rates	Standard Deviation
2.44	1.67 - 3.73	1.65

Data Plot and Equation

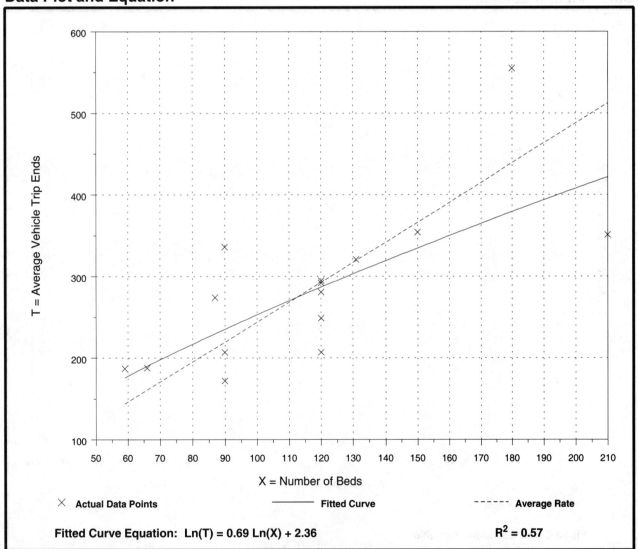

Fitted Curve Equation: Ln(T) = 0.69 Ln(X) + 2.36 $R^2 = 0.57$

Assisted Living
(254)

Average Vehicle Trip Ends vs: Beds
On a: Sunday,
Peak Hour of Generator

Number of Studies: 20
Average Number of Beds: 116
Directional Distribution: 43% entering, 57% exiting

Trip Generation per Bed

Average Rate	Range of Rates	Standard Deviation
0.38	0.13 - 0.58	0.62

Data Plot and Equation

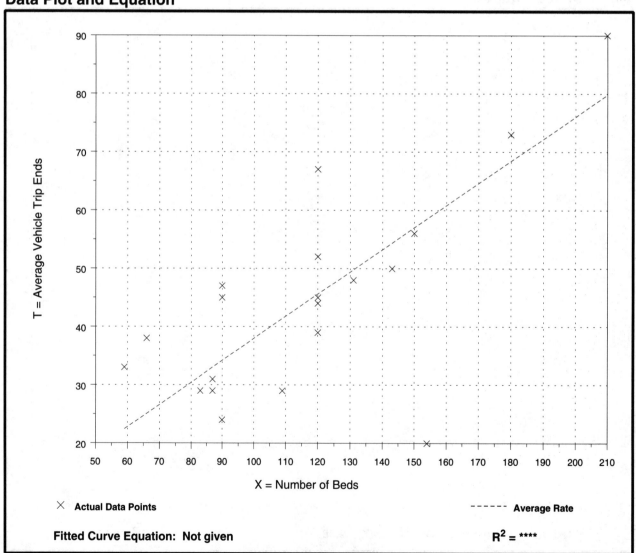

X **Actual Data Points**

- - - - - **Average Rate**

Fitted Curve Equation: Not given $R^2 = ****$

Assisted Living
(254)

Average Vehicle Trip Ends vs: Employees
On a: Weekday

Number of Studies: 14
Avg. Number of Employees: 81
Directional Distribution: 50% entering, 50% exiting

Trip Generation per Employee

Average Rate	Range of Rates	Standard Deviation
3.93	2.53 - 9.69	2.43

Data Plot and Equation

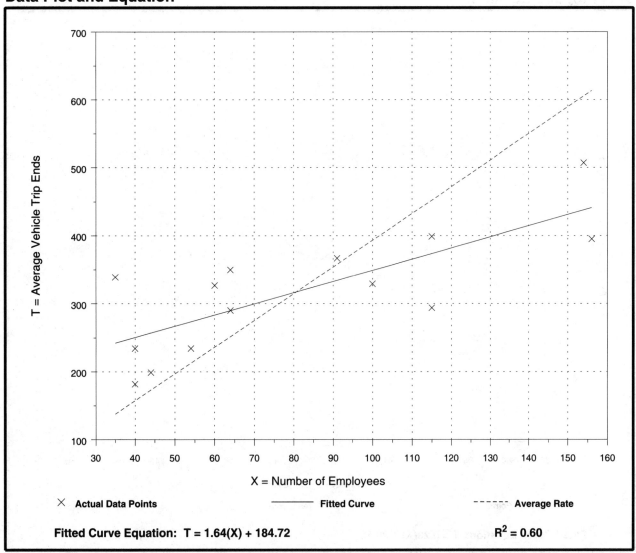

Fitted Curve Equation: T = 1.64(X) + 184.72 $R^2 = 0.60$

Assisted Living
(254)

Average Vehicle Trip Ends vs: **Employees**
On a: **Weekday,**
P.M. Peak Hour of Generator

Number of Studies: 14
Avg. Number of Employees: 81
Directional Distribution: Not available

Trip Generation per Employee

Average Rate	Range of Rates	Standard Deviation
0.55	0.30 - 1.09	0.76

Data Plot and Equation

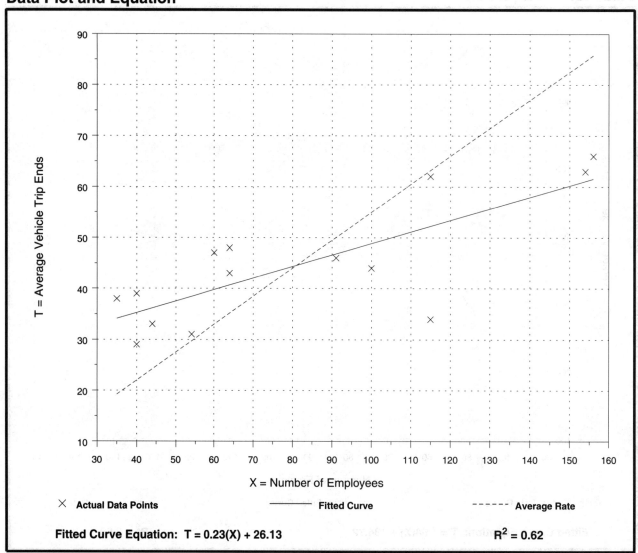

Fitted Curve Equation: T = 0.23(X) + 26.13 $R^2 = 0.62$

Assisted Living
(254)

Average Vehicle Trip Ends vs: Employees
On a: Saturday

Number of Studies: 14
Avg. Number of Employees: 81
Directional Distribution: 50% entering, 50% exiting

Trip Generation per Employee

Average Rate	Range of Rates	Standard Deviation
3.18	1.96 - 9.09	2.27

Data Plot and Equation

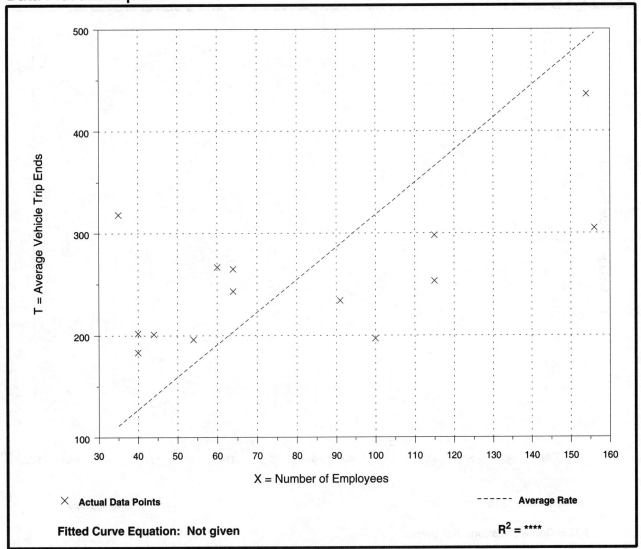

X **Actual Data Points**   - - - - - **Average Rate**

Fitted Curve Equation: Not given $R^2 = $ ********

Assisted Living
(254)

Average Vehicle Trip Ends vs: Employees
On a: Saturday,
Peak Hour of Generator

Number of Studies: 14
Avg. Number of Employees: 81
Directional Distribution: Not available

Trip Generation per Employee

Average Rate	Range of Rates	Standard Deviation
0.53	0.34 - 1.11	0.76

Data Plot and Equation

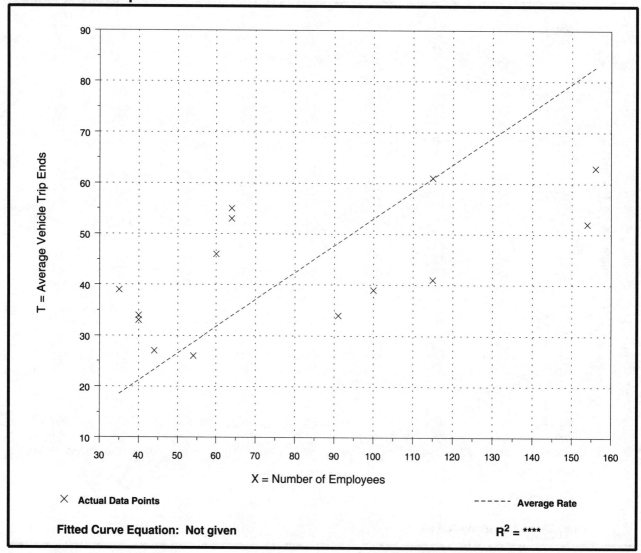

X **Actual Data Points**

- - - - - **Average Rate**

Fitted Curve Equation: Not given

$R^2 = ****$

Assisted Living
(254)

Average Vehicle Trip Ends vs: Employees
On a: Sunday

Number of Studies: 14
Avg. Number of Employees: 81
Directional Distribution: 50% entering, 50% exiting

Trip Generation per Employee

Average Rate	Range of Rates	Standard Deviation
3.53	2.07 - 9.60	2.36

Data Plot and Equation

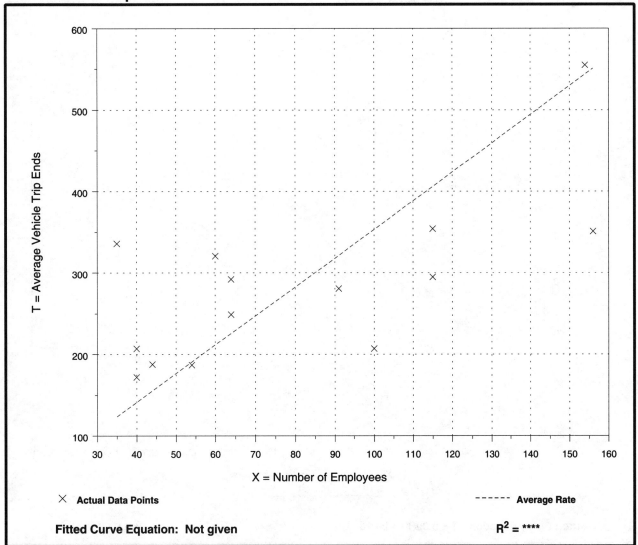

X **Actual Data Points**   - - - - - **Average Rate**

Fitted Curve Equation: Not given $R^2 = ****$

Assisted Living
(254)

Average Vehicle Trip Ends vs: **Employees**
On a: **Sunday,**
Peak Hour of Generator

Number of Studies: 14
Avg. Number of Employees: 81
Directional Distribution: Not available

Trip Generation per Employee

Average Rate	Range of Rates	Standard Deviation
0.62	0.34 - 1.34	0.82

Data Plot and Equation

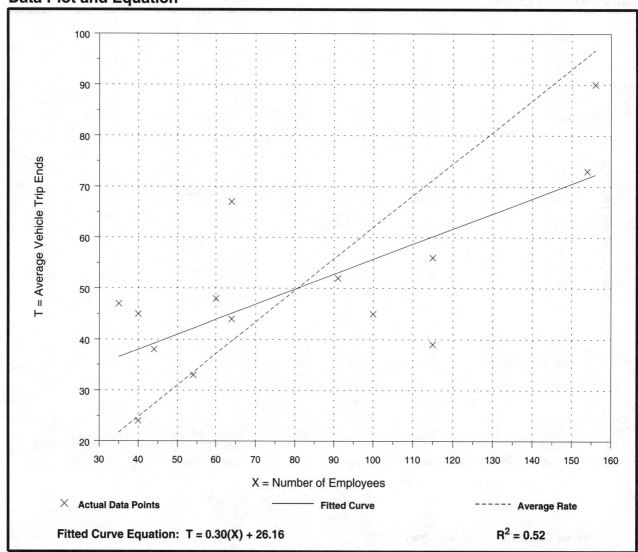

X **Actual Data Points**   ——— **Fitted Curve**   - - - - - **Average Rate**

Fitted Curve Equation: T = 0.30(X) + 26.16 $R^2 = 0.52$

Land Use: 255
Continuing Care Retirement Community (CCRC)

Description

Continuing care retirement communities (CCRCs) are land uses that provide multiple elements of senior adult living. CCRCs combine aspects of independent living with increased care, as lifestyle needs change with time. Housing options may include various combinations of senior adult (detached), senior adult (attached), congregate care, assisted living and skilled nursing care—aimed at allowing the residents to live in one community as their medical needs change. The communities may also contain special services such as medical, dining, recreational and some limited, supporting retail facilities. CCRCs are usually self-contained villages. Senior adult housing—detached (Land Use 251), senior adult housing—attached (Land Use 252), congregate care facility (Land Use 253), assisted living (Land Use 254) and nursing home (Land Use 620) are related uses.

Additional Data

Caution should be used when applying these data. CCRCs are relatively new and unique land uses. These developments consist of various housing components (dwelling units, rooms and beds[1]) that often exist in varying proportions. Therefore, the use of a single housing component does not fully describe the trip generation characteristics of these communities. Based upon the limited data submitted for this land use, it was determined that a comprehensive independent variable, occupied units, was the most appropriate descriptor of the characteristics. This variable is defined as an aggregate of all living accommodations common to these communities.

To illustrate the varying proportions of housing options that exist and to provide a more complete description of the data contained in this land use, the following table is provided for the nine CCRCs included in this land use. Users are strongly cautioned to exercise proper engineering judgment in applying these data.

Living Accommodations at CCRCs		
Occupied Dwelling Units/Rooms[2]	Occupied Beds	Total Occupied Units
215	46	261
220	151	371
620	100	720
312	166	478
210	37	247
323	120[3]	443
233	121[3]	354
209	33	242
234	94	328

---

[1] Dwelling units, rooms and beds are the independent variables typically used to represent independent housing (detached/attached/congregate care), assisted living facilities and nursing homes, respectively. Occupied dwelling units/rooms may be private or shared accommodations.
[2] Total number of combined dwelling units and rooms available within a community.
[3] For analysis purposes, an assumption was made that the total number of beds equaled the total number of occupied beds.

Peak hours of the generator—
        The weekday a.m. peak hour varied between 9:00 a.m. and 12:00 p.m. The weekday
        p.m. peak hour varied between 12:00 p.m. and 4:00 p.m.

The sites were surveyed in the mid-1980s and early 1990s in Illinois, Pennsylvania and Virginia.

A complete study of CCRCs requires future analysis of their various components. Therefore, it is important to collect as much information as possible. At the very least, the total numbers of dwelling units, rooms and beds should be obtained; if possible, the number of corresponding occupied units should be recorded as well.

Source Numbers

244, 253, 388, 501, 576

Land Use: 255
Continuing Care Retirement Community (CCRC)
Independent Variables with One Observation

The following trip generation data are for independent variables with only one observation. This information is shown in this table only; there are no related plots for these data.

Users are cautioned to use data with care because of the small sample size.

Independent Variable	Trip Generation Rate	Size of Independent Variable	Number of Studies	Directional Distribution
Occupied Units				
Saturday	3.00	242	1	50% entering, 50% exiting
Saturday Peak Hour of Generator	0.39	242	1	54% entering, 46% exiting
Sunday	2.79	242	1	50% entering, 50% exiting
Sunday Peak Hour of Generator	0.32	242	1	54% entering, 46% exiting

Continuing Care Retirement Community (CCRC)
(255)

Average Vehicle Trip Ends vs: Occupied Units
On a: Weekday

Number of Studies: 5
Average Number of Occupied Units: 323
Directional Distribution: 50% entering, 50% exiting

Trip Generation per Occupied Unit

Average Rate	Range of Rates	Standard Deviation
2.81	1.98 - 4.71	1.99

Data Plot and Equation

Caution - Use Carefully - Small Sample Size

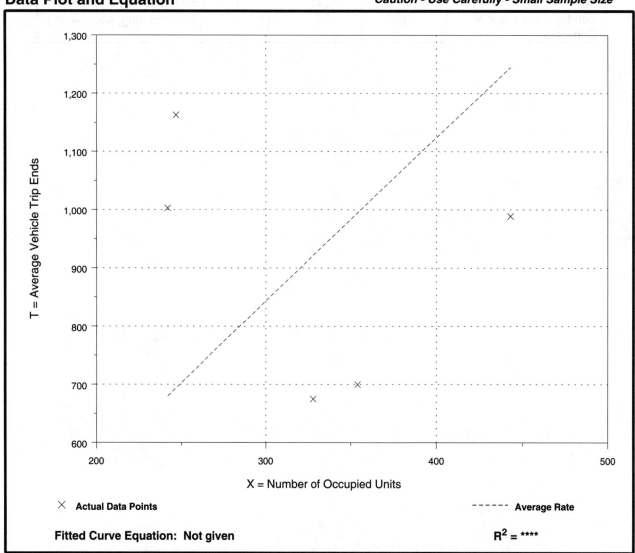

X   **Actual Data Points**   ----- **Average Rate**

Fitted Curve Equation: Not given $R^2 = ****$

Continuing Care Retirement Community (CCRC)
(255)

Average Vehicle Trip Ends vs: **Occupied Units**
On a: **Weekday,**
Peak Hour of Adjacent Street Traffic,
One Hour Between 7 and 9 a.m.

Number of Studies: 9
Average Number of Occupied Units: 383
Directional Distribution: 64% entering, 36% exiting

Trip Generation per Occupied Unit

Average Rate	Range of Rates	Standard Deviation
0.18	0.10 - 0.32	0.43

Data Plot and Equation

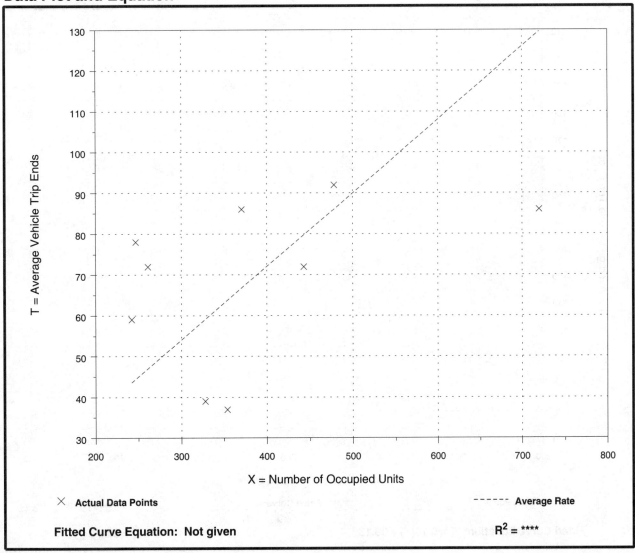

X **Actual Data Points**

---- **Average Rate**

Fitted Curve Equation: Not given $R^2 = ****$

Continuing Care Retirement Community (CCRC)
(255)

Average Vehicle Trip Ends vs: **Occupied Units**
On a: **Weekday,**
Peak Hour of Adjacent Street Traffic,
One Hour Between 4 and 6 p.m.

Number of Studies: 9
Average Number of Occupied Units: 383
Directional Distribution: 48% entering, 52% exiting

Trip Generation per Occupied Unit

Average Rate	Range of Rates	Standard Deviation
0.29	0.20 - 0.45	0.54

Data Plot and Equation

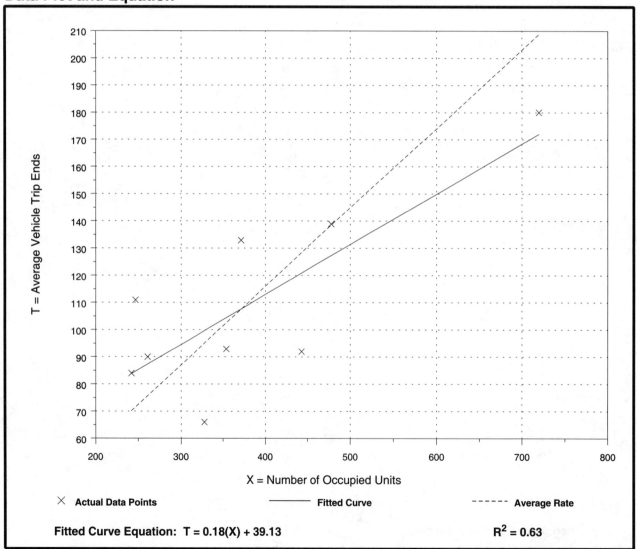

X = Number of Occupied Units

× **Actual Data Points**   ———— **Fitted Curve**   - - - - - **Average Rate**

Fitted Curve Equation: T = 0.18(X) + 39.13 $R^2 = 0.63$

Land Use: 260
Recreational Homes

Description

Recreational homes are usually located in a resort containing local services and complete recreational facilities. These dwellings are often second homes used by the owner periodically or rented on a seasonal basis. Timeshare (Land Use 265) is a related use.

Additional Data

A large number of internal trips were made for recreational purposes in resort communities containing recreational homes.

The sites were surveyed between the late 1970s and the mid-1980s.

Source Numbers

95, 187

Recreational Homes
(260)

Average Vehicle Trip Ends vs: Dwelling Units
On a: Weekday

Number of Studies: 2
Avg. Number of Dwelling Units: 1,091
Directional Distribution: 50% entering, 50% exiting

Trip Generation per Dwelling Unit

Average Rate	Range of Rates	Standard Deviation
3.16	3.00 - 3.24	*

Data Plot and Equation

Caution - Use Carefully - Small Sample Size

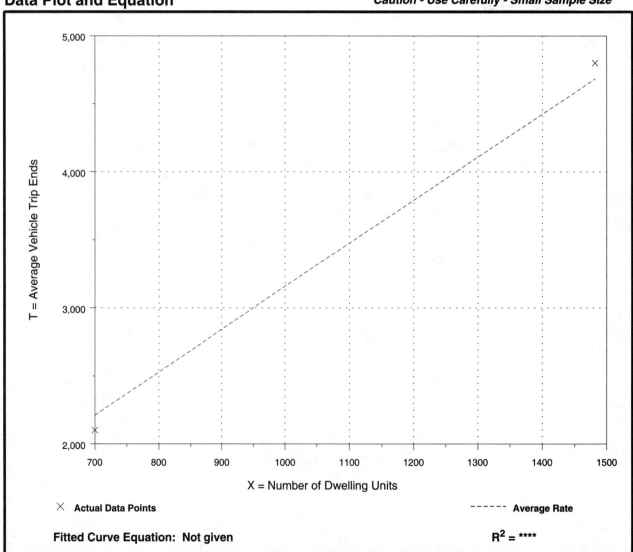

X **Actual Data Points**

----- **Average Rate**

Fitted Curve Equation: Not given

$R^2 = ****$

Recreational Homes
(260)

Average Vehicle Trip Ends vs:	Dwelling Units
On a:	**Weekday,**
	Peak Hour of Adjacent Street Traffic,
	One Hour Between 7 and 9 a.m.

Number of Studies: 2
Avg. Number of Dwelling Units: 1,091
Directional Distribution: 67% entering, 33% exiting

Trip Generation per Dwelling Unit

Average Rate	Range of Rates	Standard Deviation
0.16	0.11 - 0.19	*

Data Plot and Equation

Caution - Use Carefully - Small Sample Size

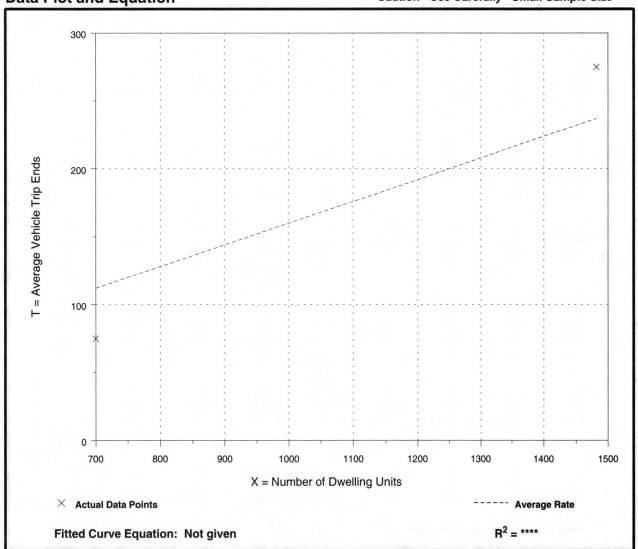

X   **Actual Data Points**

- - - - - **Average Rate**

Fitted Curve Equation: Not given

R^2 = ****

Recreational Homes
(260)

Average Vehicle Trip Ends vs: Dwelling Units
On a: Weekday,
Peak Hour of Adjacent Street Traffic,
One Hour Between 4 and 6 p.m.

Number of Studies: 2
Avg. Number of Dwelling Units: 1,091
Directional Distribution: 41% entering, 59% exiting

Trip Generation per Dwelling Unit

Average Rate	Range of Rates	Standard Deviation
0.26	0.24 - 0.27	*

Data Plot and Equation

Caution - Use Carefully - Small Sample Size

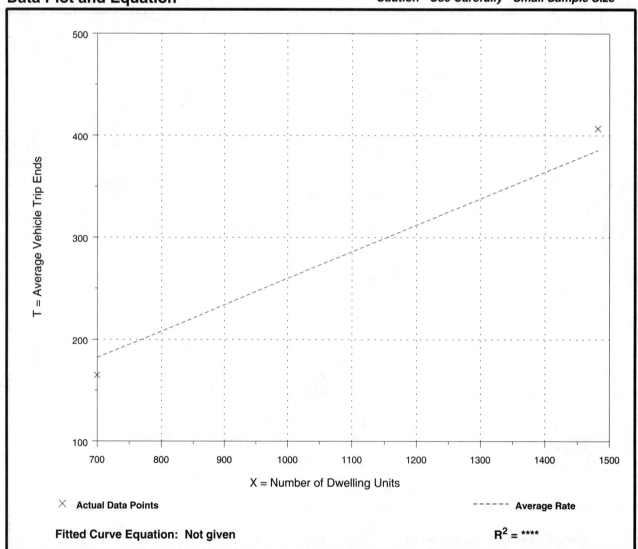

X **Actual Data Points**

----- **Average Rate**

Fitted Curve Equation: Not given $R^2 = ****$

Recreational Homes
(260)

Average Vehicle Trip Ends vs: Dwelling Units
On a: Weekday,
A.M. Peak Hour of Generator

Number of Studies: 8
Avg. Number of Dwelling Units: 331
Directional Distribution: 49% entering, 51% exiting

Trip Generation per Dwelling Unit

Average Rate	Range of Rates	Standard Deviation
0.30	0.21 - 1.33	0.57

Data Plot and Equation

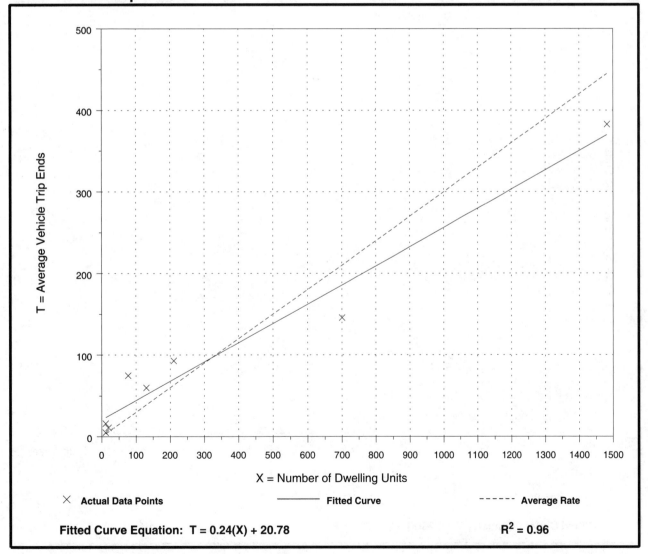

X = Number of Dwelling Units

✕ **Actual Data Points** ——— **Fitted Curve** - - - - **Average Rate**

Fitted Curve Equation: T = 0.24(X) + 20.78 $R^2 = 0.96$

Recreational Homes
(260)

Average Vehicle Trip Ends vs: **Dwelling Units**
On a: **Weekday,**
P.M. Peak Hour of Generator

Number of Studies: 8
Avg. Number of Dwelling Units: 331
Directional Distribution: 44% entering, 56% exiting

Trip Generation per Dwelling Unit

Average Rate	Range of Rates	Standard Deviation
0.31	0.25 - 1.33	0.56

Data Plot and Equation

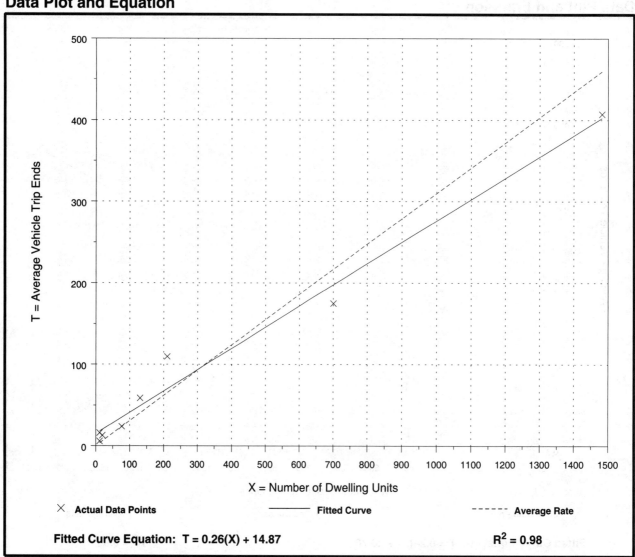

Fitted Curve Equation: T = 0.26(X) + 14.87 $R^2 = 0.98$

Recreational Homes
(260)

Average Vehicle Trip Ends vs: Dwelling Units
On a: Saturday

Number of Studies: 2
Avg. Number of Dwelling Units: 1,091
Directional Distribution: 50% entering, 50% exiting

Trip Generation per Dwelling Unit

Average Rate	Range of Rates	Standard Deviation
3.07	2.99 - 3.23	*

Data Plot and Equation

Caution - Use Carefully - Small Sample Size

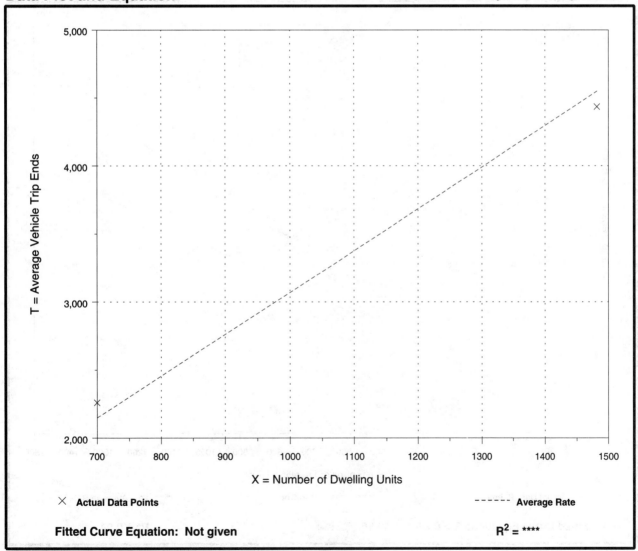

X **Actual Data Points**   - - - - - **Average Rate**

Fitted Curve Equation: Not given $R^2 = ****$

Recreational Homes
(260)

Average Vehicle Trip Ends vs: **Dwelling Units**
On a: **Saturday,**
Peak Hour of Generator

Number of Studies: 8
Avg. Number of Dwelling Units: 331
Directional Distribution: 48% entering, 52% exiting

Trip Generation per Dwelling Unit

Average Rate	Range of Rates	Standard Deviation
0.36	0.26 - 1.70	0.64

Data Plot and Equation

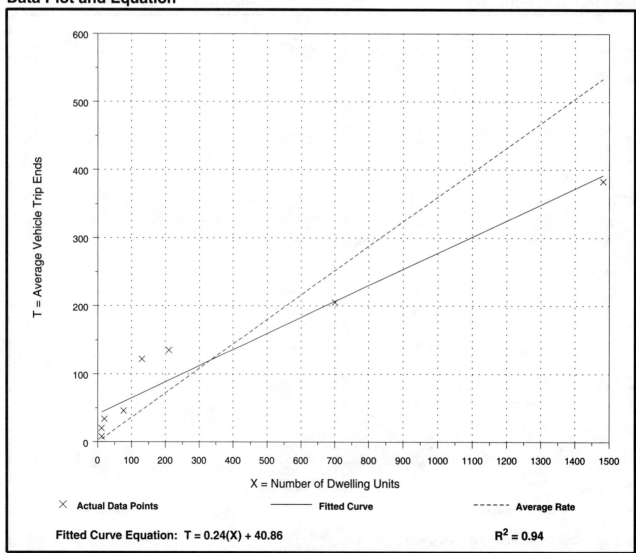

Fitted Curve Equation: T = 0.24(X) + 40.86 $R^2 = 0.94$

Recreational Homes
(260)

Average Vehicle Trip Ends vs: Dwelling Units
On a: Sunday

Number of Studies: 2
Avg. Number of Dwelling Units: 1,091
Directional Distribution: 50% entering, 50% exiting

Trip Generation per Dwelling Unit

Average Rate	Range of Rates	Standard Deviation
2.93	2.82 - 3.17	*

Data Plot and Equation

Caution - Use Carefully - Small Sample Size

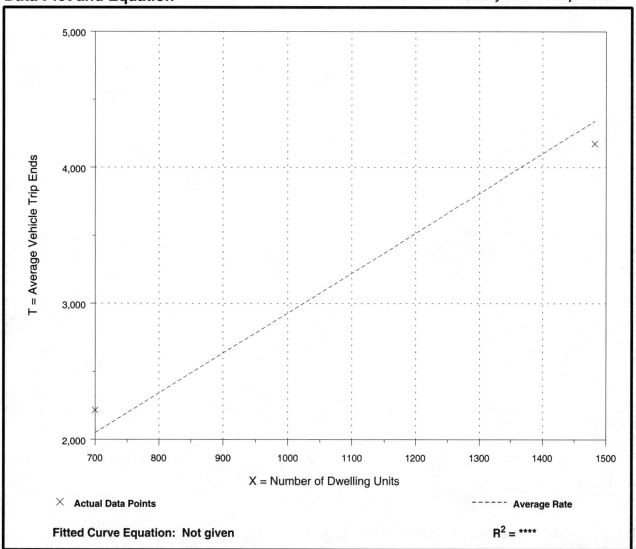

Fitted Curve Equation: Not given $R^2 = $ ****

Recreational Homes
(260)

Average Vehicle Trip Ends vs: **Dwelling Units**
On a: **Sunday,**
Peak Hour of Generator

Number of Studies: 8
Avg. Number of Dwelling Units: 331
Directional Distribution: 46% entering, 54% exiting

Trip Generation per Dwelling Unit

Average Rate	Range of Rates	Standard Deviation
0.36	0.25 - 1.92	0.63

Data Plot and Equation

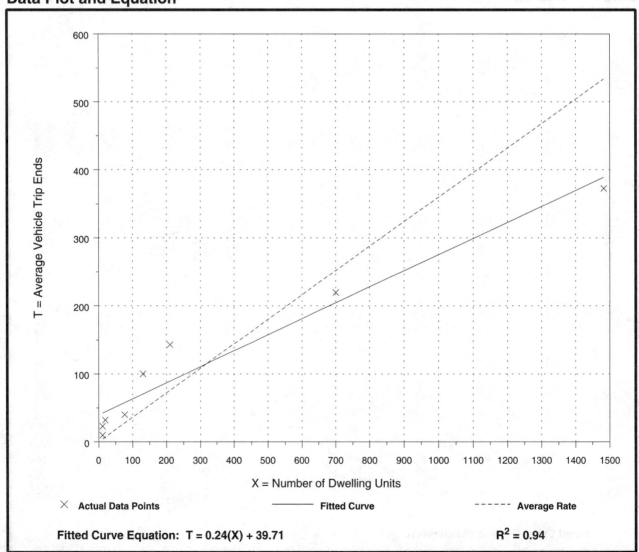

Fitted Curve Equation: T = 0.24(X) + 39.71 $R^2 = 0.94$

Recreational Homes
(260)

Average Vehicle Trip Ends vs: **Acres**
On a: **Weekday**

Number of Studies: 2
Average Number of Acres: 2,587
Directional Distribution: 50% entering, 50% exiting

Trip Generation per Acre

Average Rate	Range of Rates	Standard Deviation
1.33	1.17 - 1.42	*

Data Plot and Equation

Caution - Use Carefully - Small Sample Size

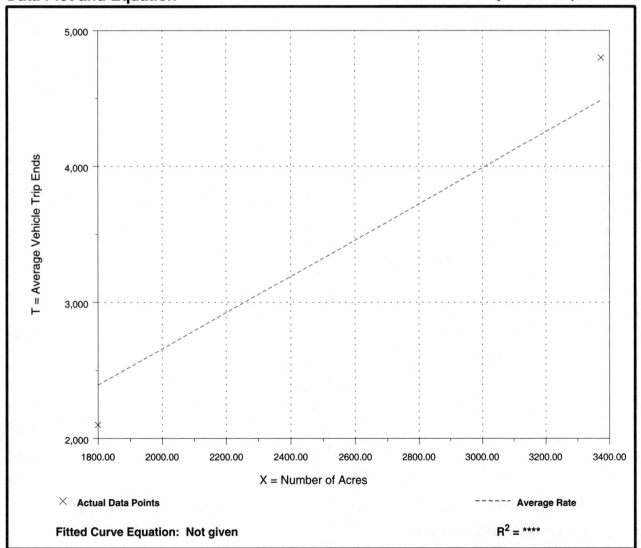

X **Actual Data Points**   - - - - - **Average Rate**

Fitted Curve Equation: Not given $R^2 = ****$

Recreational Homes
(260)

Average Vehicle Trip Ends vs: **Acres**
On a: **Weekday,**
Peak Hour of Adjacent Street Traffic,
One Hour Between 7 and 9 a.m.

Number of Studies: 2
Average Number of Acres: 2,587
Directional Distribution: 67% entering, 33% exiting

Trip Generation per Acre

Average Rate	Range of Rates	Standard Deviation
0.07	0.04 - 0.08	*

Data Plot and Equation

Caution - Use Carefully - Small Sample Size

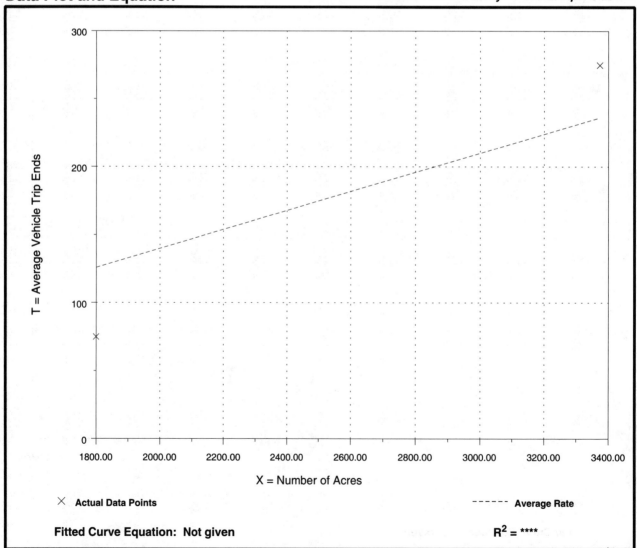

X Actual Data Points

- - - - - Average Rate

Fitted Curve Equation: Not given

$R^2 = ****$

Recreational Homes
(260)

Average Vehicle Trip Ends vs: **Acres**
On a: **Weekday,**
Peak Hour of Adjacent Street Traffic,
One Hour Between 4 and 6 p.m.

Number of Studies: 2
Average Number of Acres: 2,587
Directional Distribution: 41% entering, 59% exiting

Trip Generation per Acre

Average Rate	Range of Rates	Standard Deviation
0.11	0.09 - 0.12	*

Data Plot and Equation

Caution - Use Carefully - Small Sample Size

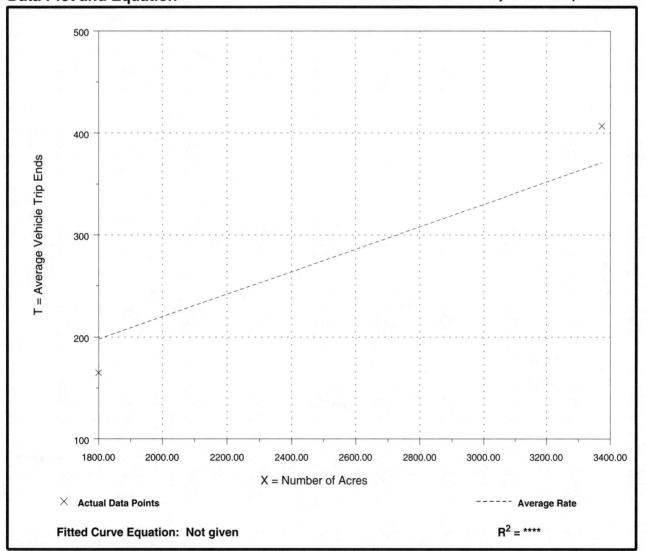

Fitted Curve Equation: Not given $R^2 =$ ****

Recreational Homes
(260)

Average Vehicle Trip Ends vs: **Acres**
On a: **Weekday,**
A.M. Peak Hour of Generator

Number of Studies: 8
Average Number of Acres: 723
Directional Distribution: 49% entering, 51% exiting

Trip Generation per Acre

Average Rate	Range of Rates	Standard Deviation
0.14	0.08 - 1.12	0.40

Data Plot and Equation

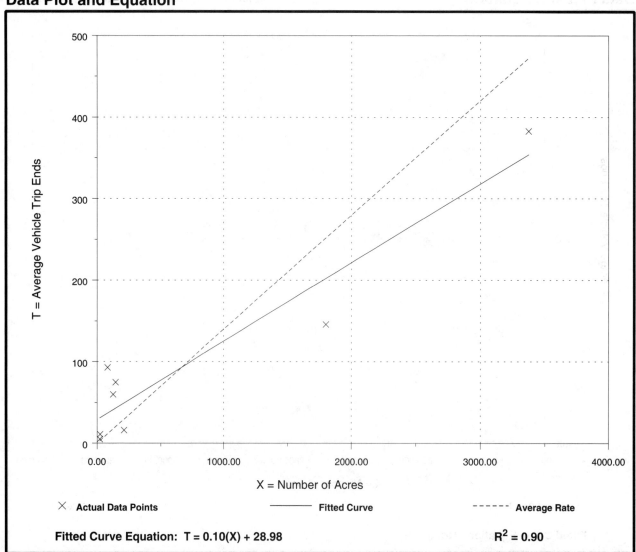

Fitted Curve Equation: T = 0.10(X) + 28.98 $R^2 = 0.90$

Recreational Homes
(260)

Average Vehicle Trip Ends vs: **Acres**
On a: **Weekday,**
P.M. Peak Hour of Generator

Number of Studies: 8
Average Number of Acres: 723
Directional Distribution: 44% entering, 56% exiting

Trip Generation per Acre

Average Rate	Range of Rates	Standard Deviation
0.14	0.08 - 1.33	0.40

Data Plot and Equation

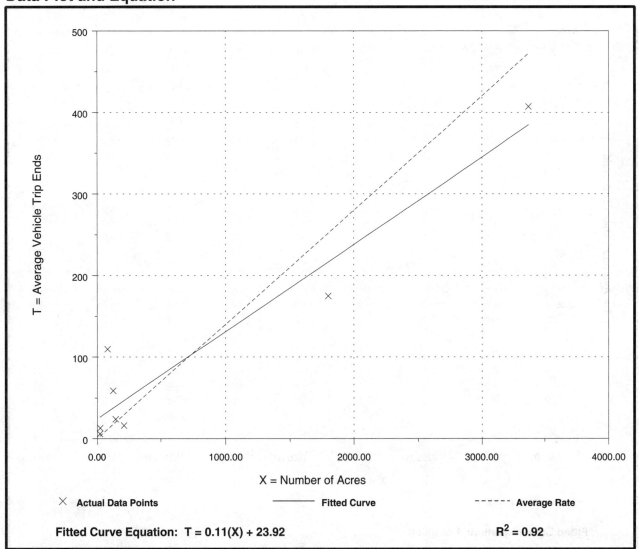

Fitted Curve Equation: T = 0.11(X) + 23.92 $R^2 = 0.92$

Recreational Homes
(260)

Average Vehicle Trip Ends vs: Acres
On a: Saturday

Number of Studies: 2
Average Number of Acres: 2,587
Directional Distribution: 50% entering, 50% exiting

Trip Generation per Acre

Average Rate	Range of Rates	Standard Deviation
1.29	1.26 - 1.31	*

Data Plot and Equation

Caution - Use Carefully - Small Sample Size

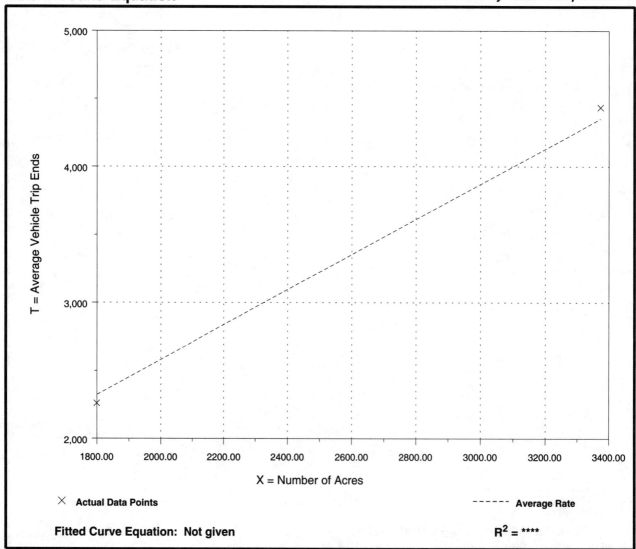

X = Number of Acres

✕ **Actual Data Points**

- - - - - **Average Rate**

Fitted Curve Equation: Not given

$R^2 = $ ****

Recreational Homes
(260)

Average Vehicle Trip Ends vs: **Acres**
On a: **Saturday,**
Peak Hour of Generator

Number of Studies: 8
Average Number of Acres: 723
Directional Distribution: 48% entering, 52% exiting

Trip Generation per Acre

Average Rate	Range of Rates	Standard Deviation
0.16	0.09 - 1.63	0.47

Data Plot and Equation

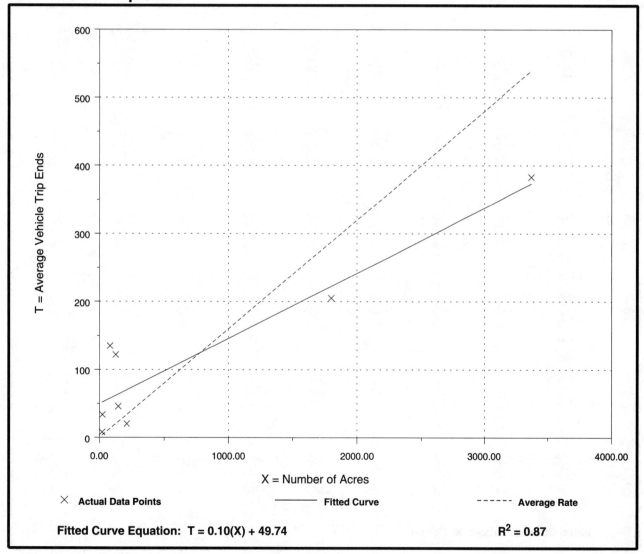

X **Actual Data Points**   ———— **Fitted Curve**   - - - - - **Average Rate**

Fitted Curve Equation: T = 0.10(X) + 49.74 $R^2 = 0.87$

Recreational Homes
(260)

Average Vehicle Trip Ends vs: Acres
On a: Sunday

Number of Studies: 2
Average Number of Acres: 2,587
Directional Distribution: 50% entering, 50% exiting

Trip Generation per Acre

Average Rate	Range of Rates	Standard Deviation
1.24	1.23 - 1.24	*

Data Plot and Equation

Caution - Use Carefully - Small Sample Size

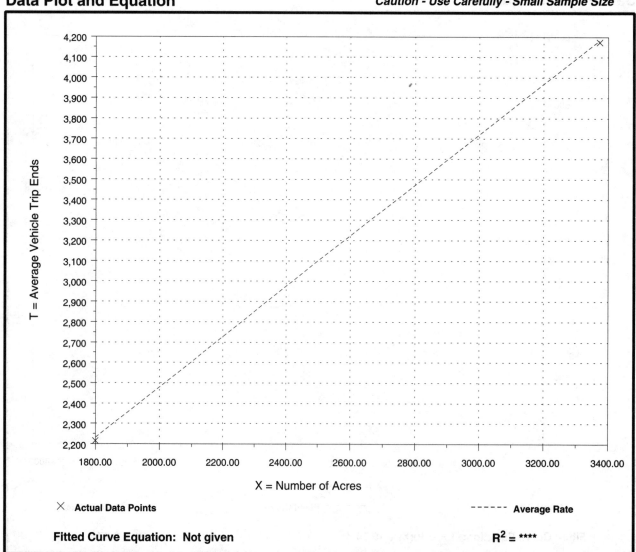

X = Number of Acres

⛌ **Actual Data Points** ----- **Average Rate**

Fitted Curve Equation: Not given $R^2 = ****$

Recreational Homes
(260)

Average Vehicle Trip Ends vs: **Acres**
On a: **Sunday,**
Peak Hour of Generator

Number of Studies: 8
Average Number of Acres: 723
Directional Distribution: 46% entering, 54% exiting

Trip Generation per Acre

Average Rate	Range of Rates	Standard Deviation
0.16	0.11 - 1.72	0.46

Data Plot and Equation

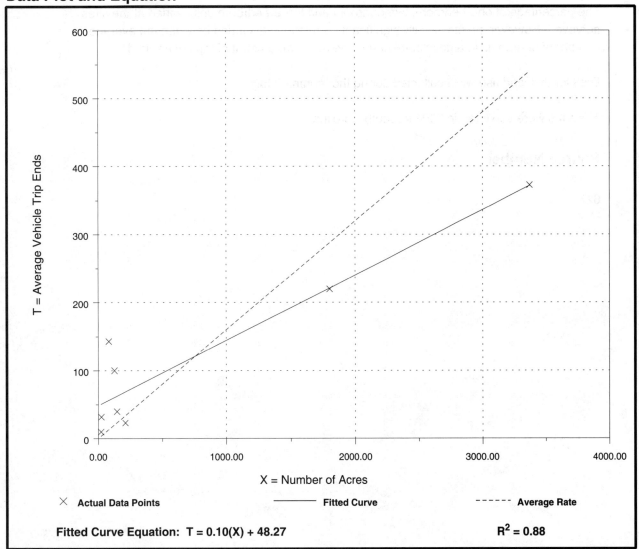

Fitted Curve Equation: T = 0.10(X) + 48.27 $R^2 = 0.88$

Land Use: 265
Timeshare

Description

Timeshares are developments where multiple purchasers buy interests in the same property and each purchaser receives the right to use the facility for a period of time each year. The shared property is commonly a vacation or recreational condominium. Recreational homes (Land Use 260) is a related use.

Additional Data

Occupancy rates for the sites surveyed ranged from 86 percent to 100 percent.

For the purpose of this land use, the independent variable "occupied dwelling units" is defined as the total number of units that were occupied at the time of the survey.

The percentage of one-bedroom, two-bedroom and three-bedroom units varied at the sites surveyed. However, no statistically significant correlation was found between the average number of bedrooms in a development and the resultant amount of trips generated.

Data for this land use were collected during the month of July.

The sites were surveyed in 2004 in South Carolina.

Source Number

627

Timeshare
(265)

Average Vehicle Trip Ends vs: **Occupied Dwelling Units**
On a: **Weekday**

Number of Studies: 12
Avg. Num. of Occupied Dwelling Units: 66
Directional Distribution: 50% entering, 50% exiting

Trip Generation per Occupied Dwelling Unit

Average Rate	Range of Rates	Standard Deviation
10.56	5.91 - 18.08	4.63

Data Plot and Equation

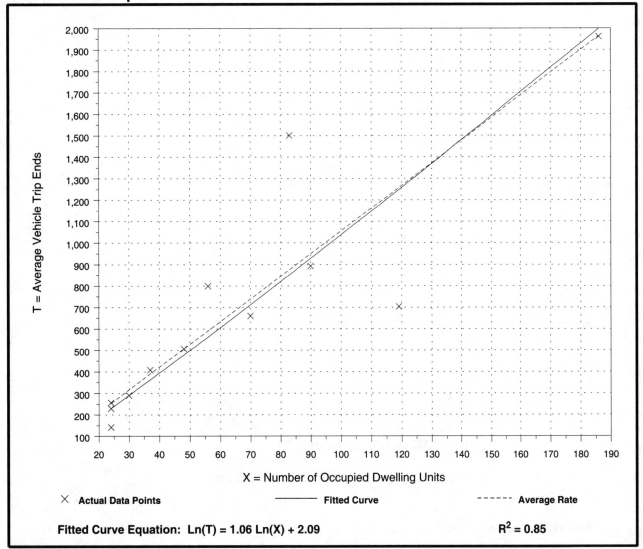

Fitted Curve Equation: Ln(T) = 1.06 Ln(X) + 2.09 $R^2 = 0.85$

Timeshare
(265)

Average Vehicle Trip Ends vs: **Occupied Dwelling Units**
On a: **Weekday,**
Peak Hour of Adjacent Street Traffic,
One Hour Between 7 and 9 a.m.

Number of Studies: 12
Avg. Num. of Occupied Dwelling Units: 66
Directional Distribution: Not available

Trip Generation per Occupied Dwelling Unit

Average Rate	Range of Rates	Standard Deviation
0.51	0.24 - 0.89	0.73

Data Plot and Equation

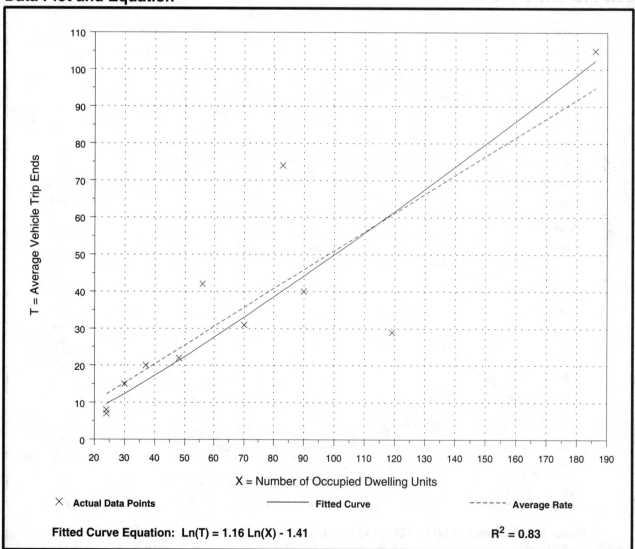

T = Average Vehicle Trip Ends

X = Number of Occupied Dwelling Units

$\times$ **Actual Data Points** —— **Fitted Curve** ----- **Average Rate**

Fitted Curve Equation: Ln(T) = 1.16 Ln(X) - 1.41 $R^2 = 0.83$

Timeshare
(265)

Average Vehicle Trip Ends vs: **Occupied Dwelling Units**
On a: **Weekday,**
Peak Hour of Adjacent Street Traffic,
One Hour Between 4 and 6 p.m.

Number of Studies: 12
Avg. Num. of Occupied Dwelling Units: 66
Directional Distribution: Not available

Trip Generation per Occupied Dwelling Unit

Average Rate	Range of Rates	Standard Deviation
0.79	0.47 - 1.20	0.91

Data Plot and Equation

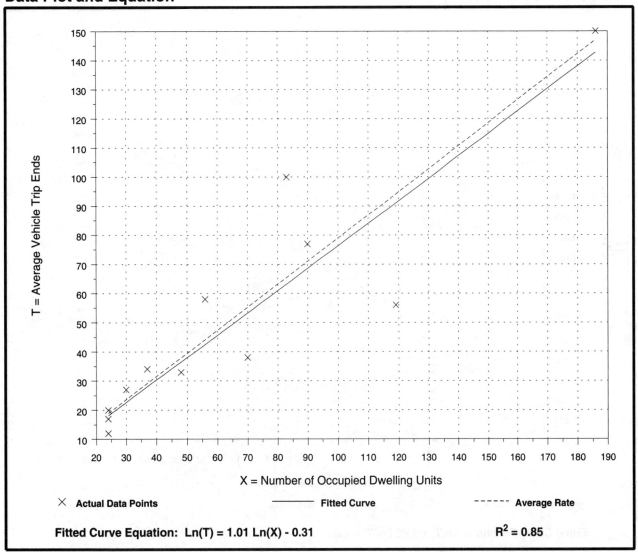

X = Number of Occupied Dwelling Units

$\times$ **Actual Data Points**   —— **Fitted Curve**   - - - - - **Average Rate**

Fitted Curve Equation: Ln(T) = 1.01 Ln(X) - 0.31 $R^2 = 0.85$

Timeshare
(265)

Average Vehicle Trip Ends vs: Dwelling Units
On a: Weekday

Number of Studies: 12
Avg. Number of Dwelling Units: 69
Directional Distribution: 50% entering, 50% exiting

Trip Generation per Dwelling Unit

Average Rate	Range of Rates	Standard Deviation
10.03	5.76 - 17.06	4.38

Data Plot and Equation

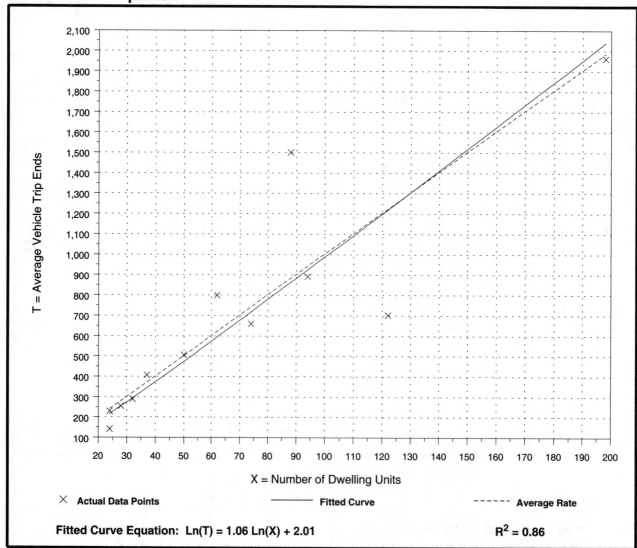

X = Number of Dwelling Units

X **Actual Data Points**   ———— **Fitted Curve**   - - - - - **Average Rate**

Fitted Curve Equation: Ln(T) = 1.06 Ln(X) + 2.01 $R^2 = 0.86$

Timeshare
(265)

Average Vehicle Trip Ends vs: Dwelling Units
On a: Weekday,
Peak Hour of Adjacent Street Traffic,
One Hour Between 7 and 9 a.m.

Number of Studies: 12
Avg. Number of Dwelling Units: 69
Directional Distribution: Not available

Trip Generation per Dwelling Unit

Average Rate	Range of Rates	Standard Deviation
0.48	0.24 - 0.84	0.71

Data Plot and Equation

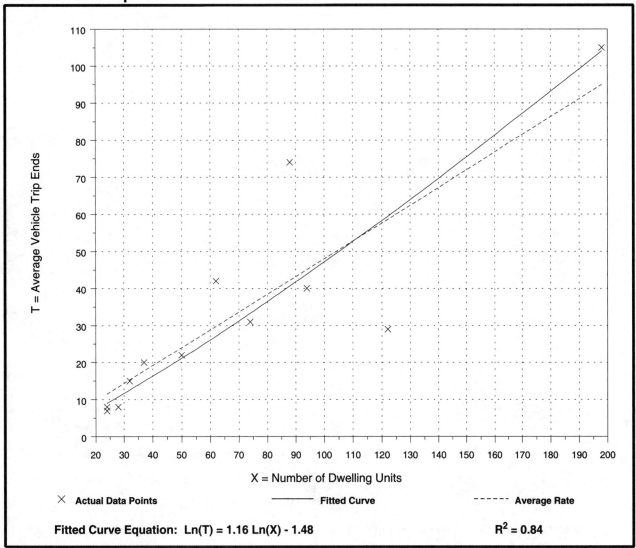

Fitted Curve Equation: $\text{Ln}(T) = 1.16 \, \text{Ln}(X) - 1.48$ $R^2 = 0.84$

Timeshare
(265)

Average Vehicle Trip Ends vs: Dwelling Units
On a: Weekday,
Peak Hour of Adjacent Street Traffic,
One Hour Between 4 and 6 p.m.

Number of Studies: 12
Avg. Number of Dwelling Units: 69
Directional Distribution: Not available

Trip Generation per Dwelling Unit

Average Rate	Range of Rates	Standard Deviation
0.75	0.46 - 1.14	0.88

Data Plot and Equation

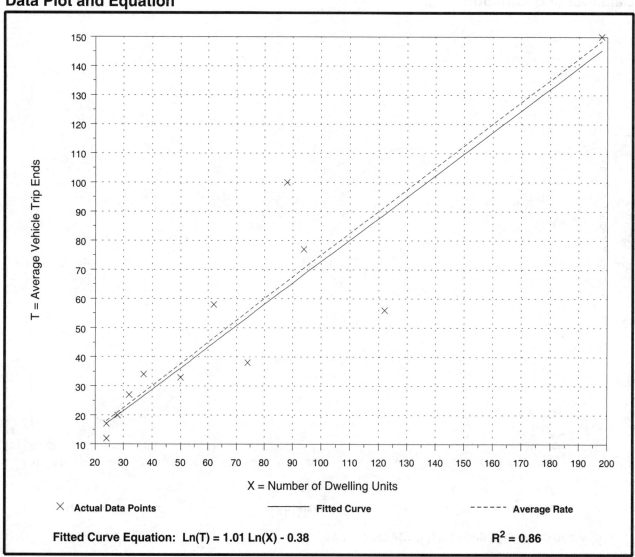

Fitted Curve Equation: Ln(T) = 1.01 Ln(X) - 0.38 $R^2 = 0.86$

Land Use: 270
Residential Planned Unit Development (PUD)

Description

Residential planned unit developments (PUD), for the purposes of trip generation, are defined as containing any combination of residential land uses. These developments might also contain supporting services such as limited retail and recreational facilities.

Additional Data

Caution—The description of a PUD is general in nature because these developments vary by density and type of dwelling. It is therefore recommended that when information on the number and type of dwellings is known, trip generation should be calculated on the basis of the known type of dwellings rather than on the basis of Land Use 270. Data for Land Use 270 are provided as general information and would be applicable only when the number of dwellings is known.

The sites were surveyed between the late 1970s and the mid-1990s throughout the United States.

Source Numbers

6, 11, 13, 16, 26, 95, 110, 111, 119, 165, 169, 192, 193, 357

Residential Planned Unit Development (PUD)
(270)

Average Vehicle Trip Ends vs: Dwelling Units
On a: Weekday

Number of Studies: 13
Avg. Number of Dwelling Units: 664
Directional Distribution: 50% entering, 50% exiting

Trip Generation per Dwelling Unit

Average Rate	Range of Rates	Standard Deviation
7.50	5.79 - 14.38	3.32

Data Plot and Equation

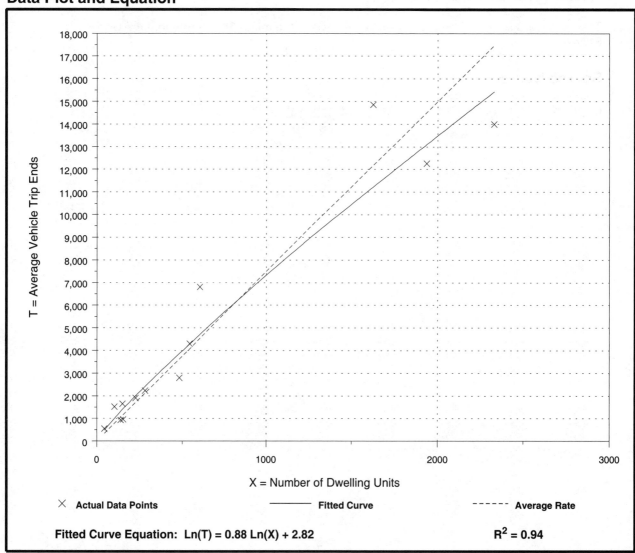

X = Number of Dwelling Units

✕ Actual Data Points ——— Fitted Curve ----- Average Rate

Fitted Curve Equation: Ln(T) = 0.88 Ln(X) + 2.82 $R^2 = 0.94$

Residential Planned Unit Development (PUD)
(270)

Average Vehicle Trip Ends vs: **Dwelling Units**
On a: **Weekday,**
Peak Hour of Adjacent Street Traffic,
One Hour Between 7 and 9 a.m.

Number of Studies: 17
Avg. Number of Dwelling Units: 771
Directional Distribution: 22% entering, 78% exiting

Trip Generation per Dwelling Unit

Average Rate	Range of Rates	Standard Deviation
0.51	0.20 - 0.77	0.72

Data Plot and Equation

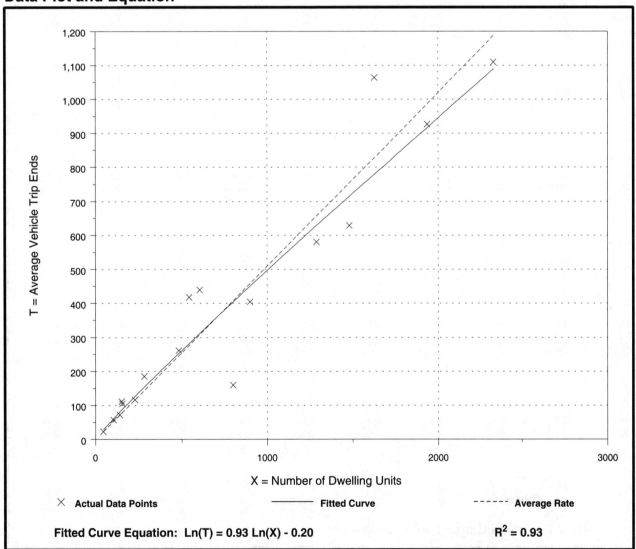

Fitted Curve Equation: $Ln(T) = 0.93 \, Ln(X) - 0.20$ $R^2 = 0.93$

Residential Planned Unit Development (PUD)
(270)

Average Vehicle Trip Ends vs: **Dwelling Units**
On a: **Weekday,**
  Peak Hour of Adjacent Street Traffic,
  One Hour Between 4 and 6 p.m.

Number of Studies: 18
Avg. Number of Dwelling Units: 945
Directional Distribution: 65% entering, 35% exiting

Trip Generation per Dwelling Unit

Average Rate	Range of Rates	Standard Deviation
0.62	0.43 - 1.13	0.80

Data Plot and Equation

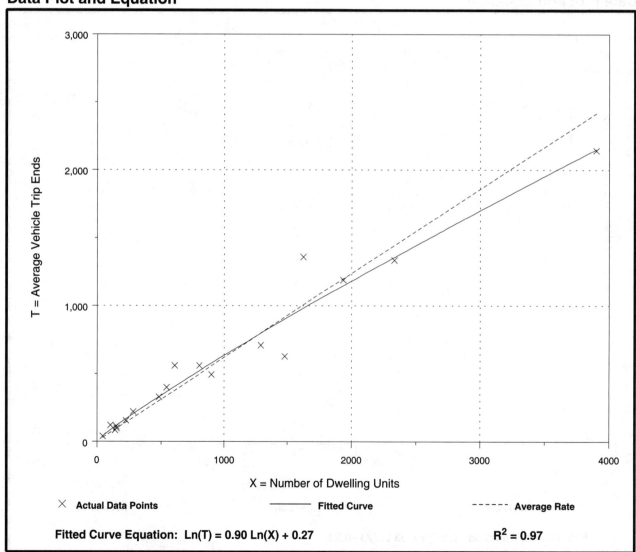

Fitted Curve Equation: $Ln(T) = 0.90 \, Ln(X) + 0.27$ $R^2 = 0.97$

Residential Planned Unit Development (PUD)
(270)

Average Vehicle Trip Ends vs: **Dwelling Units**
On a: **Weekday,**
A.M. Peak Hour of Generator

Number of Studies: 11
Avg. Number of Dwelling Units: 757
Directional Distribution: 23% entering, 77% exiting

Trip Generation per Dwelling Unit

Average Rate	Range of Rates	Standard Deviation
0.58	0.49 - 0.98	0.77

Data Plot and Equation

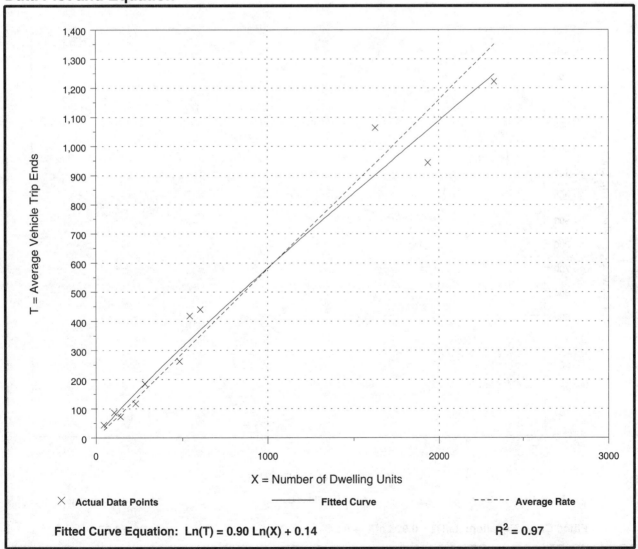

X = Number of Dwelling Units

✕ **Actual Data Points**   —— **Fitted Curve**   - - - - - **Average Rate**

Fitted Curve Equation: Ln(T) = 0.90 Ln(X) + 0.14 $R^2 = 0.97$

Residential Planned Unit Development (PUD)
(270)

Average Vehicle Trip Ends vs: **Dwelling Units**
On a: **Weekday,**
P.M. Peak Hour of Generator

Number of Studies: 11
Avg. Number of Dwelling Units: 757
Directional Distribution: 64% entering, 36% exiting

Trip Generation per Dwelling Unit

Average Rate	Range of Rates	Standard Deviation
0.72	0.59 - 1.17	0.86

Data Plot and Equation

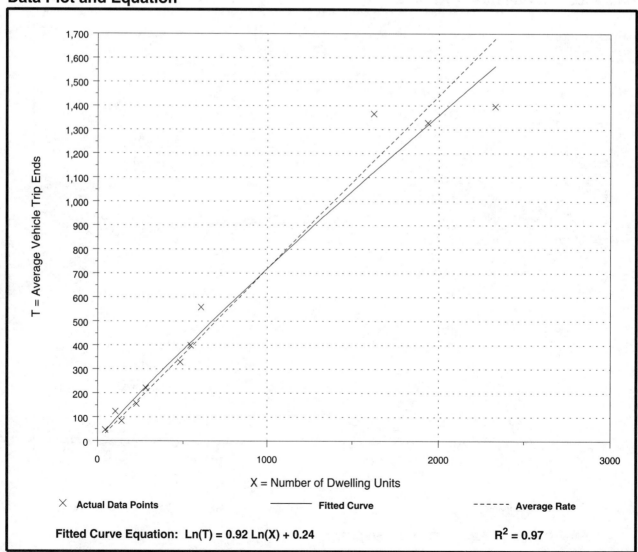

Fitted Curve Equation: $Ln(T) = 0.92 \, Ln(X) + 0.24$ $R^2 = 0.97$

Residential Planned Unit Development (PUD)
(270)

Average Vehicle Trip Ends vs: **Dwelling Units**
On a: **Saturday**

Number of Studies: 5
Avg. Number of Dwelling Units: 1,408
Directional Distribution: 50% entering, 50% exiting

Trip Generation per Dwelling Unit

Average Rate	Range of Rates	Standard Deviation
6.82	6.11 - 7.47	2.66

Data Plot and Equation

Caution - Use Carefully - Small Sample Size

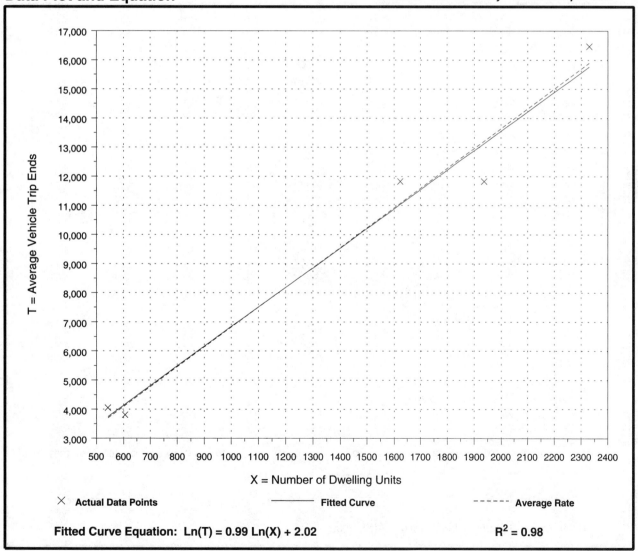

X = Number of Dwelling Units

X **Actual Data Points** ———— **Fitted Curve** - - - - - **Average Rate**

Fitted Curve Equation: $\mathrm{Ln}(T) = 0.99\,\mathrm{Ln}(X) + 2.02$ $R^2 = 0.98$

Residential Planned Unit Development (PUD)
(270)

Average Vehicle Trip Ends vs: **Dwelling Units**
On a: **Saturday,**
Peak Hour of Generator

Number of Studies: 5
Avg. Number of Dwelling Units: 1,408
Directional Distribution: 49% entering, 51% exiting

Trip Generation per Dwelling Unit

Average Rate	Range of Rates	Standard Deviation
0.56	0.47 - 0.60	0.75

Data Plot and Equation

Caution - Use Carefully - Small Sample Size

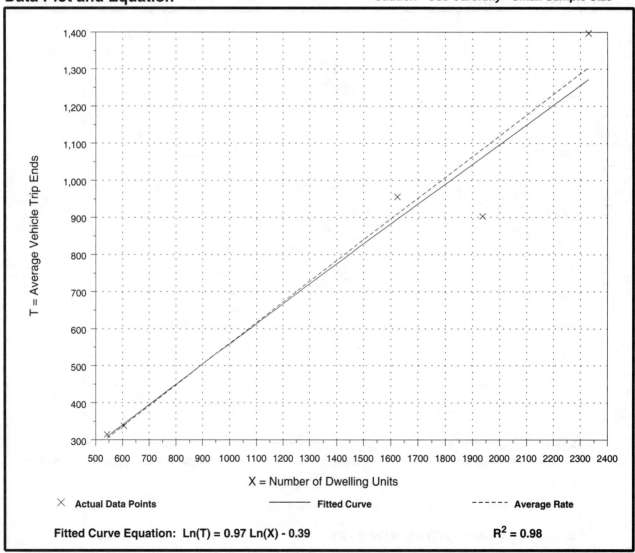

X = Number of Dwelling Units

✕ **Actual Data Points**   ——— **Fitted Curve**   - - - - - **Average Rate**

Fitted Curve Equation: Ln(T) = 0.97 Ln(X) - 0.39 $R^2 = 0.98$

Residential Planned Unit Development (PUD)
(270)

Average Vehicle Trip Ends vs: Dwelling Units
On a: Sunday

Number of Studies: 5
Avg. Number of Dwelling Units: 1,408
Directional Distribution: 50% entering, 50% exiting

Trip Generation per Dwelling Unit

Average Rate	Range of Rates	Standard Deviation
5.09	4.24 - 6.35	2.36

Data Plot and Equation

Caution - Use Carefully - Small Sample Size

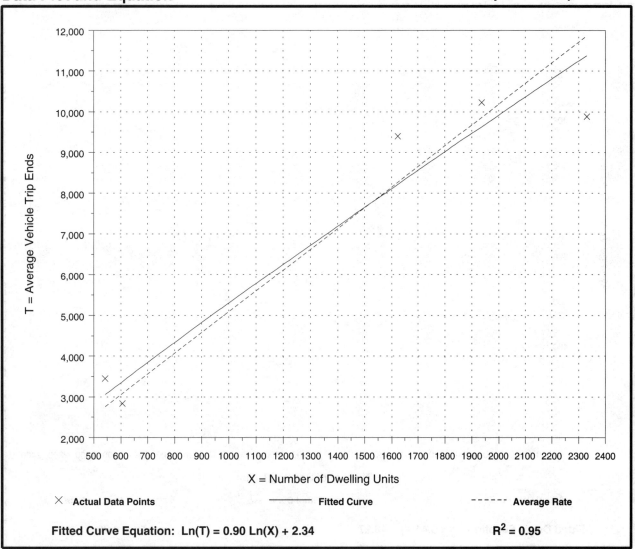

X **Actual Data Points**   ———— **Fitted Curve**   - - - - - **Average Rate**

Fitted Curve Equation: Ln(T) = 0.90 Ln(X) + 2.34 $R^2 = 0.95$

Residential Planned Unit Development (PUD)
(270)

Average Vehicle Trip Ends vs: **Dwelling Units**
On a: **Sunday,**
Peak Hour of Generator

Number of Studies: 5
Avg. Number of Dwelling Units: 1,408
Directional Distribution: 52% entering, 48% exiting

Trip Generation per Dwelling Unit

Average Rate	Range of Rates	Standard Deviation
0.44	0.38 - 0.55	0.66

Data Plot and Equation

Caution - Use Carefully - Small Sample Size

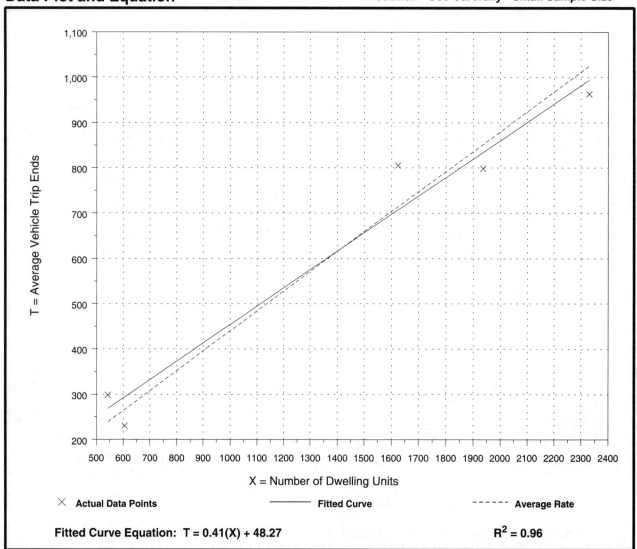

X = Number of Dwelling Units

$\times$ **Actual Data Points** ——— **Fitted Curve** - - - - - **Average Rate**

Fitted Curve Equation: T = 0.41(X) + 48.27 $R^2 = 0.96$

Residential Planned Unit Development (PUD)
(270)

Average Vehicle Trip Ends vs: **Acres**
On a: **Weekday**

Number of Studies: 4
Average Number of Acres: 33
Directional Distribution: 50% entering, 50% exiting

Trip Generation per Acre

Average Rate	Range of Rates	Standard Deviation
46.78	41.85 - 50.80	7.82

Data Plot and Equation

Caution - Use Carefully - Small Sample Size

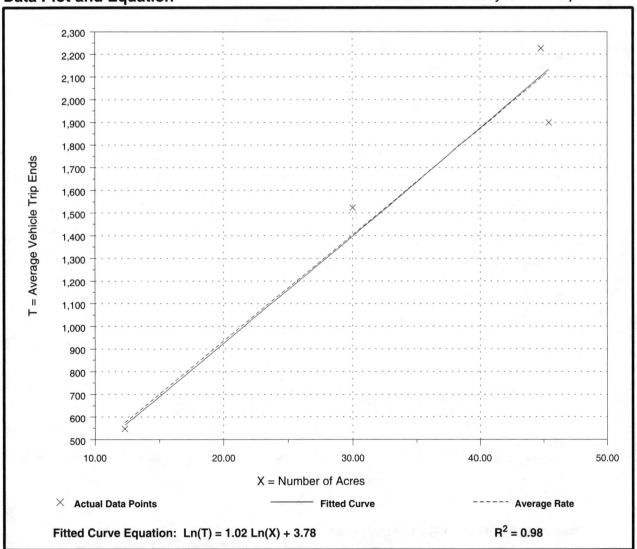

X = Number of Acres

✕ **Actual Data Points**   ——— **Fitted Curve**   - - - - - **Average Rate**

Fitted Curve Equation: $Ln(T) = 1.02\ Ln(X) + 3.78$ $R^2 = 0.98$

Residential Planned Unit Development (PUD)
(270)

Average Vehicle Trip Ends vs: **Acres**
On a: **Weekday,**
Peak Hour of Adjacent Street Traffic,
One Hour Between 7 and 9 a.m.

Number of Studies: 4
Average Number of Acres: 33
Directional Distribution: Not available

Trip Generation per Acre

Average Rate	Range of Rates	Standard Deviation
2.88	1.87 - 4.13	1.92

Data Plot and Equation

Caution - Use Carefully - Small Sample Size

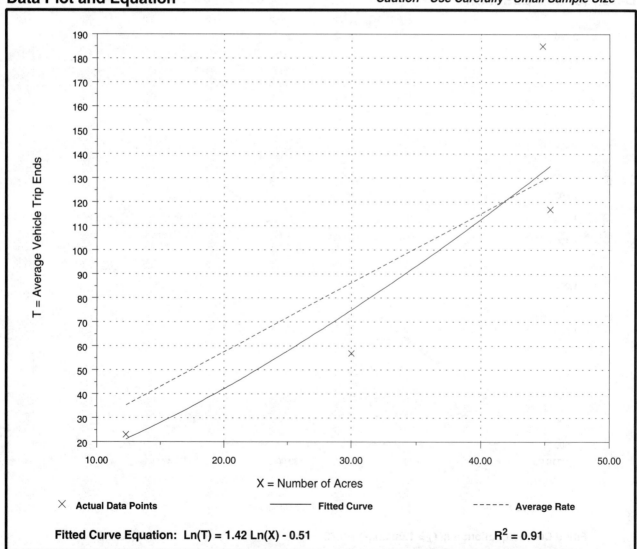

X Actual Data Points   —— Fitted Curve   - - - - - Average Rate

Fitted Curve Equation: Ln(T) = 1.42 Ln(X) - 0.51 $R^2 = 0.91$

Residential Planned Unit Development (PUD)
(270)

Average Vehicle Trip Ends vs:	**Acres**
On a:	**Weekday,**
	Peak Hour of Adjacent Street Traffic,
	One Hour Between 4 and 6 p.m.

Number of Studies: 4
Average Number of Acres: 33
Directional Distribution: Not available

Trip Generation per Acre

Average Rate	Range of Rates	Standard Deviation
4.05	3.25 - 4.93	2.10

Data Plot and Equation

Caution - Use Carefully - Small Sample Size

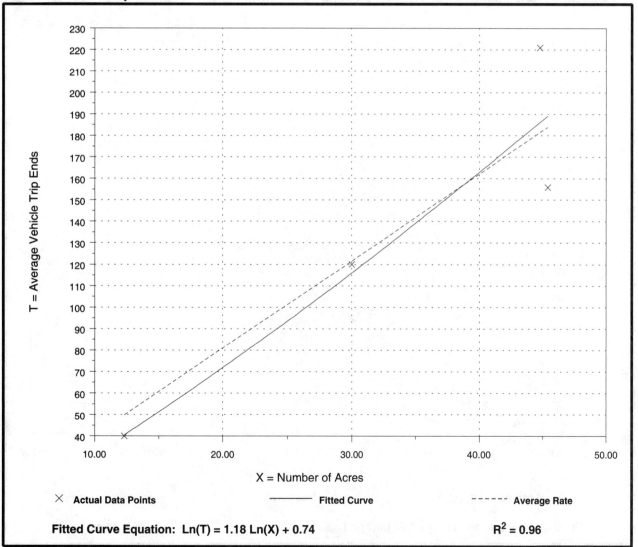

Fitted Curve Equation: $Ln(T) = 1.18 \ Ln(X) + 0.74$ $R^2 = 0.96$

Residential Planned Unit Development (PUD)
(270)

Average Vehicle Trip Ends vs: Acres
On a: Weekday,
A.M. Peak Hour of Generator

Number of Studies: 4
Average Number of Acres: 33
Directional Distribution: Not available

Trip Generation per Acre

Average Rate	Range of Rates	Standard Deviation
3.27	2.58 - 4.13	1.91

Data Plot and Equation

Caution - Use Carefully - Small Sample Size

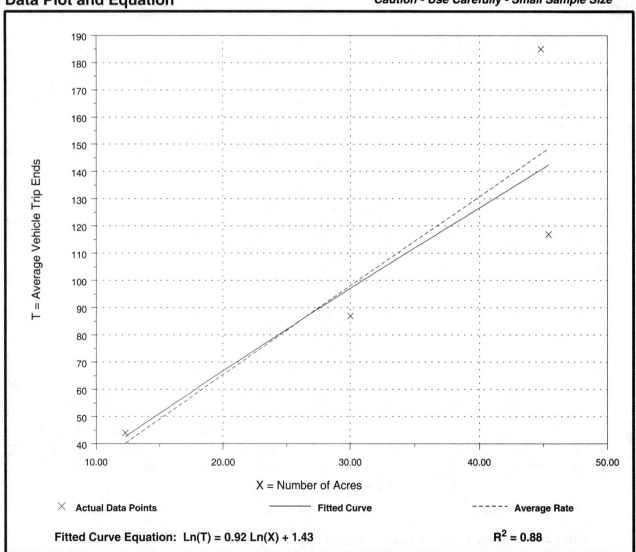

X = Number of Acres

✕ Actual Data Points   —— Fitted Curve   - - - - Average Rate

Fitted Curve Equation: Ln(T) = 0.92 Ln(X) + 1.43 $R^2 = 0.88$

Residential Planned Unit Development (PUD)
(270)

Average Vehicle Trip Ends vs: **Acres**
On a: **Weekday,**
P.M. Peak Hour of Generator

Number of Studies: **4**
Average Number of Acres: **33**
Directional Distribution: **Not available**

Trip Generation per Acre

Average Rate	Range of Rates	Standard Deviation
4.13	3.44 - 4.93	2.11

Data Plot and Equation

Caution - Use Carefully - Small Sample Size

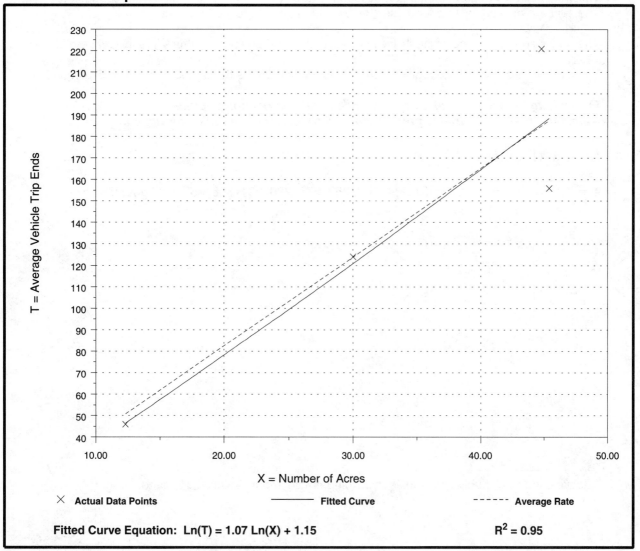

Fitted Curve Equation: $Ln(T) = 1.07\ Ln(X) + 1.15$ $R^2 = 0.95$

Land Use: 310
Hotel

Description

Hotels are places of lodging that provide sleeping accommodations and supporting facilities such as restaurants; cocktail lounges; meeting and banquet rooms or convention facilities; limited recreational facilities (pool, fitness room); and/or other retail and service shops. Some of the sites included in this land use category are actually large motels providing the hotel facilities noted above. All suites hotel (Land Use 311), business hotel (Land Use 312), motel (Land Use 320) and resort hotel (Land Use 330) are related uses.

Additional Data

Studies of hotel employment density indicate that, on the average, a hotel will employ 0.9 employees per room.[1]

Thirty studies provided information on occupancy rates at the time the studies were conducted. The average occupancy rate for these studies was approximately 83 percent.

The hotels surveyed were primarily located outside central business districts in suburban areas.

The sites were surveyed between the late 1960s and the 2000s throughout the United States.

For all lodging uses, it is important to collect data on occupied rooms as well as total rooms in order to accurately predict trip generation characteristics for the site.

Source Numbers

4, 5, 12, 13, 18, 55, 72, 170, 187, 254, 260, 262, 277, 280, 301, 306, 357, 422, 436, 507, 577

---

[1] Buttke, Carl H. Unpublished studies of building employment densities, Portland, Oregon.

Hotel
(310)

Average Vehicle Trip Ends vs: Occupied Rooms
On a: Weekday

Number of Studies: 4
Average Number of Occupied Rooms: 216
Directional Distribution: 50% entering, 50% exiting

Trip Generation per Occupied Room

Average Rate	Range of Rates	Standard Deviation
8.92	4.14 - 17.44	6.04

Data Plot and Equation

Caution - Use Carefully - Small Sample Size

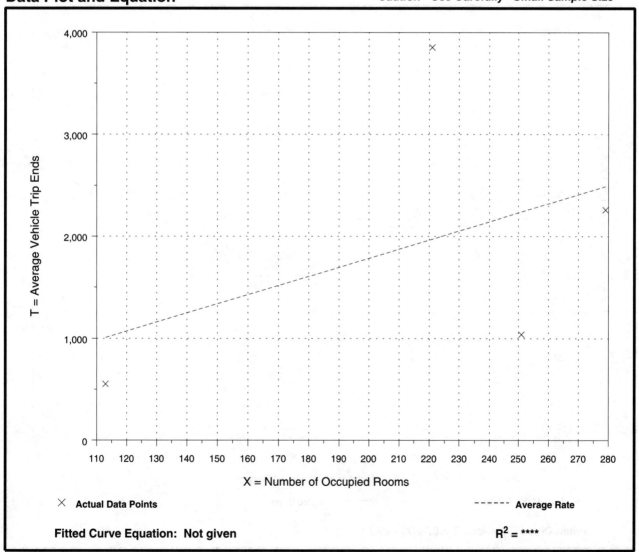

X **Actual Data Points**   - - - - **Average Rate**

Fitted Curve Equation: Not given $R^2 =$ ****

Hotel
(310)

Average Vehicle Trip Ends vs: Occupied Rooms
On a: Weekday,
Peak Hour of Adjacent Street Traffic,
One Hour Between 7 and 9 a.m.

Number of Studies: 17
Average Number of Occupied Rooms: 256
Directional Distribution: 58% entering, 42% exiting

Trip Generation per Occupied Room

Average Rate	Range of Rates	Standard Deviation
0.67	0.35 - 1.10	0.84

Data Plot and Equation

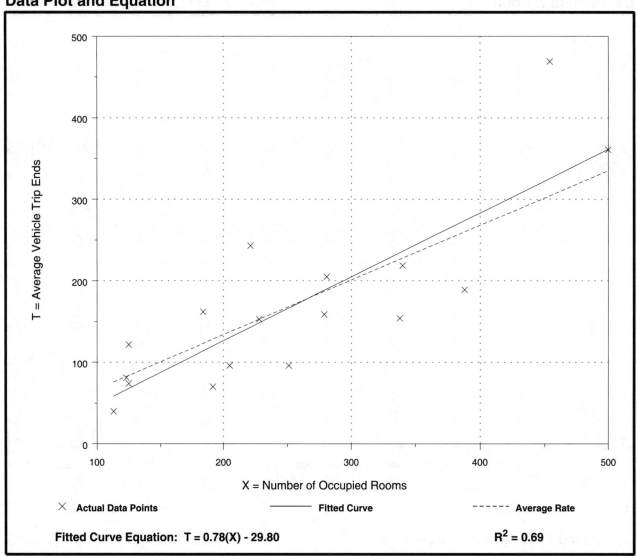

X **Actual Data Points**   ——— **Fitted Curve**   - - - - - **Average Rate**

Fitted Curve Equation: T = 0.78(X) - 29.80 $R^2 = 0.69$

Hotel
(310)

Average Vehicle Trip Ends vs: **Occupied Rooms**
On a: **Weekday,**
Peak Hour of Adjacent Street Traffic,
One Hour Between 4 and 6 p.m.

Number of Studies: 20
Average Number of Occupied Rooms: 243
Directional Distribution: 49% entering, 51% exiting

Trip Generation per Occupied Room

Average Rate	Range of Rates	Standard Deviation
0.70	0.25 - 1.11	0.87

Data Plot and Equation

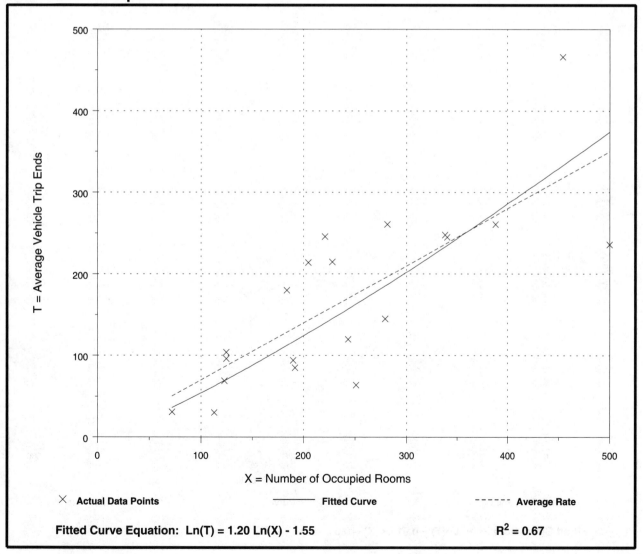

Fitted Curve Equation: $Ln(T) = 1.20 \, Ln(X) - 1.55$ $R^2 = 0.67$

Hotel
(310)

Average Vehicle Trip Ends vs: Occupied Rooms
On a: Weekday,
A.M. Peak Hour of Generator

Number of Studies: 26
Average Number of Occupied Rooms: 259
Directional Distribution: 55% entering, 45% exiting

Trip Generation per Occupied Room

Average Rate	Range of Rates	Standard Deviation
0.64	0.27 - 1.51	0.84

Data Plot and Equation

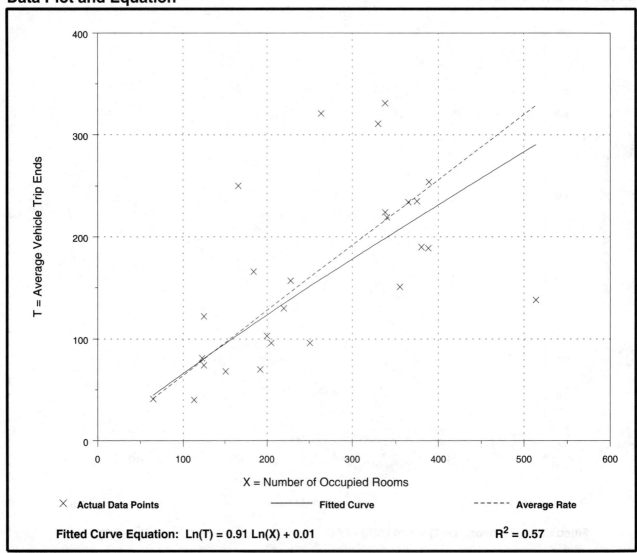

Fitted Curve Equation: $Ln(T) = 0.91 \, Ln(X) + 0.01$ $R^2 = 0.57$

Hotel
(310)

Average Vehicle Trip Ends vs: Occupied Rooms
On a: Weekday,
P.M. Peak Hour of Generator

Number of Studies: 28
Average Number of Occupied Rooms: 274
Directional Distribution: 57% entering, 43% exiting

Trip Generation per Occupied Room

Average Rate	Range of Rates	Standard Deviation
0.74	0.25 - 1.23	0.89

Data Plot and Equation

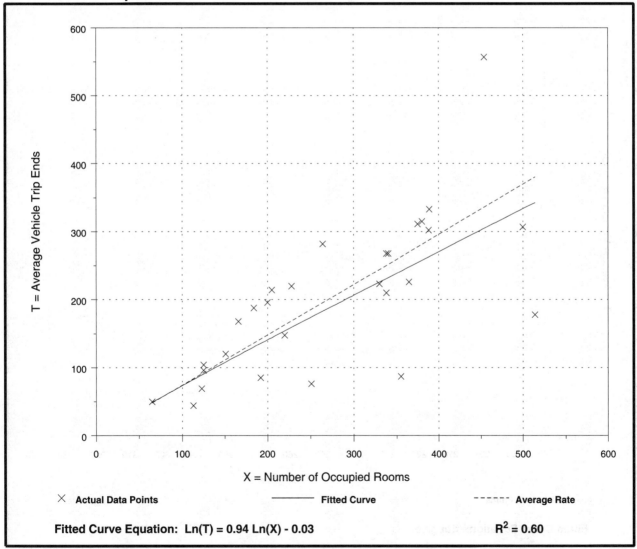

X = Number of Occupied Rooms

✕ Actual Data Points   —— Fitted Curve   ----- Average Rate

Fitted Curve Equation: Ln(T) = 0.94 Ln(X) - 0.03 $R^2 = 0.60$

Hotel
(310)

Average Vehicle Trip Ends vs: Occupied Rooms
On a: Saturday

Number of Studies: 3
Average Number of Occupied Rooms: 250
Directional Distribution: 50% entering, 50% exiting

Trip Generation per Occupied Room

Average Rate	Range of Rates	Standard Deviation
10.50	7.07 - 13.86	4.11

Data Plot and Equation

Caution - Use Carefully - Small Sample Size

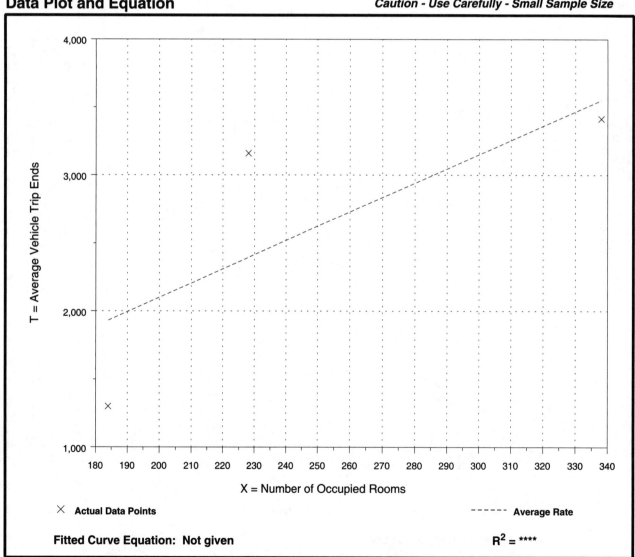

X **Actual Data Points**

- - - - - **Average Rate**

Fitted Curve Equation: Not given $R^2 = ****$

Hotel
(310)

Average Vehicle Trip Ends vs: Occupied Rooms
On a: Saturday,
Peak Hour of Generator

Number of Studies: 3
Average Number of Occupied Rooms: 250
Directional Distribution: Not available

Trip Generation per Occupied Room

Average Rate	Range of Rates	Standard Deviation
0.87	0.65 - 1.05	0.94

Data Plot and Equation

Caution - Use Carefully - Small Sample Size

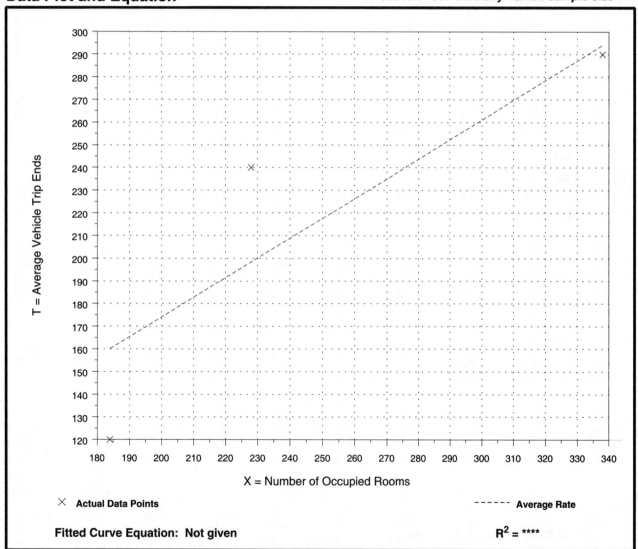

X **Actual Data Points**

- - - - - **Average Rate**

Fitted Curve Equation: Not given

$R^2 = ****$

Hotel
(310)

Average Vehicle Trip Ends vs: Occupied Rooms
On a: Sunday

Number of Studies: 3
Average Number of Occupied Rooms: 250
Directional Distribution: 50% entering, 50% exiting

Trip Generation per Occupied Room

Average Rate	Range of Rates	Standard Deviation
8.48	5.60 - 10.40	3.42

Data Plot and Equation

Caution - Use Carefully - Small Sample Size

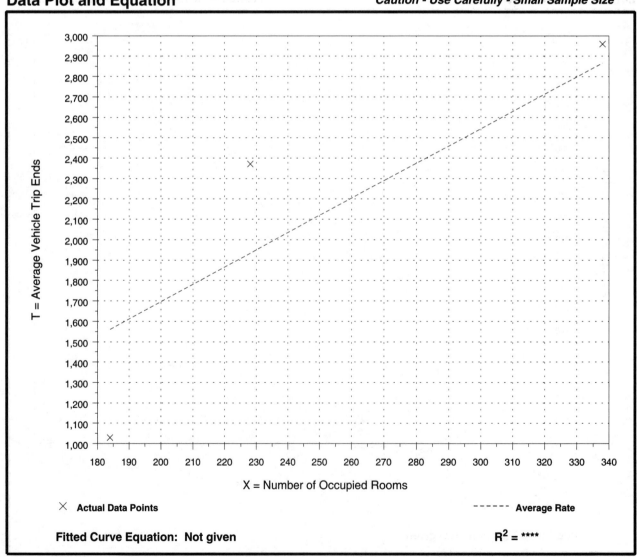

X **Actual Data Points**

----- **Average Rate**

Fitted Curve Equation: Not given $R^2 = ****$

Hotel
(310)

Average Vehicle Trip Ends vs: **Occupied Rooms**
On a: **Sunday,**
Peak Hour of Generator

Number of Studies: 3
Average Number of Occupied Rooms: 250
Directional Distribution: Not available

Trip Generation per Occupied Room

Average Rate	Range of Rates	Standard Deviation
0.75	0.49 - 0.98	0.88

Data Plot and Equation

Caution - Use Carefully - Small Sample Size

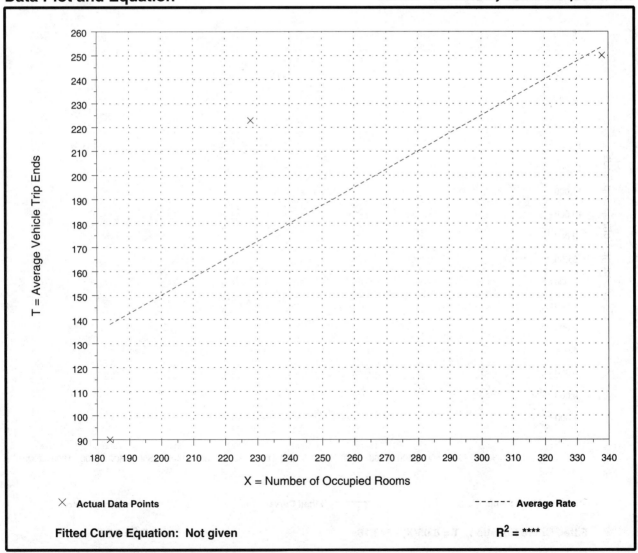

X **Actual Data Points**   - - - - - **Average Rate**

Fitted Curve Equation: Not given $R^2 = $ ****

Hotel
(310)

Average Vehicle Trip Ends vs: Rooms
On a: Weekday

Number of Studies: 10
Average Number of Rooms: 476
Directional Distribution: 50% entering, 50% exiting

Trip Generation per Room

Average Rate	Range of Rates	Standard Deviation
8.17	3.47 - 9.58	3.38

Data Plot and Equation

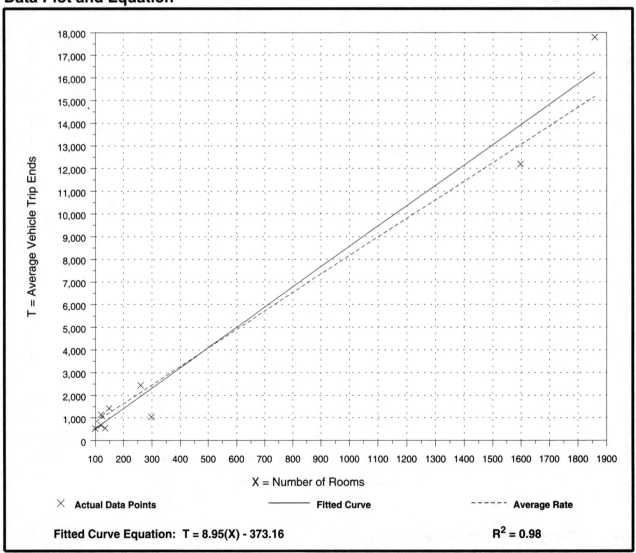

X **Actual Data Points**   ——— **Fitted Curve**   - - - - **Average Rate**

Fitted Curve Equation: T = 8.95(X) - 373.16 $R^2 = 0.98$

Hotel
(310)

Average Vehicle Trip Ends vs: Rooms
On a: Weekday,
Peak Hour of Adjacent Street Traffic,
One Hour Between 7 and 9 a.m.

Number of Studies: 20
Average Number of Rooms: 240
Directional Distribution: 61% entering, 39% exiting

Trip Generation per Room

Average Rate	Range of Rates	Standard Deviation
0.56	0.20 - 1.03	0.78

Data Plot and Equation

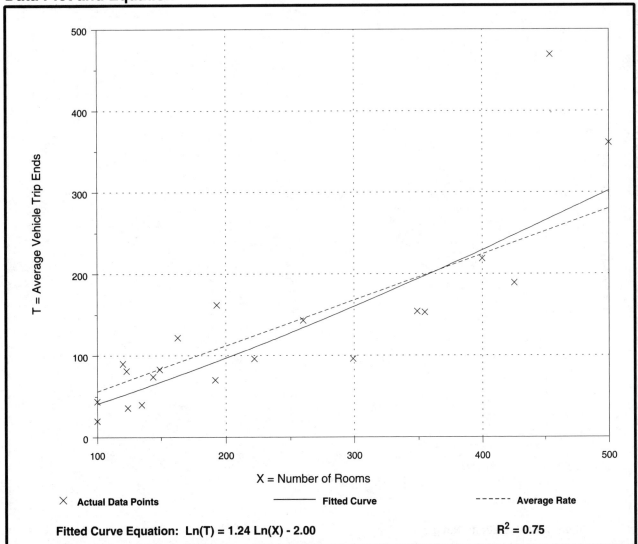

Fitted Curve Equation: Ln(T) = 1.24 Ln(X) - 2.00 $R^2 = 0.75$

Hotel
(310)

Average Vehicle Trip Ends vs: Rooms
On a: Weekday,
Peak Hour of Adjacent Street Traffic,
One Hour Between 4 and 6 p.m.

Number of Studies: 25
Average Number of Rooms: 224
Directional Distribution: 53% entering, 47% exiting

Trip Generation per Room

Average Rate	Range of Rates	Standard Deviation
0.59	0.21 - 1.03	0.80

Data Plot and Equation

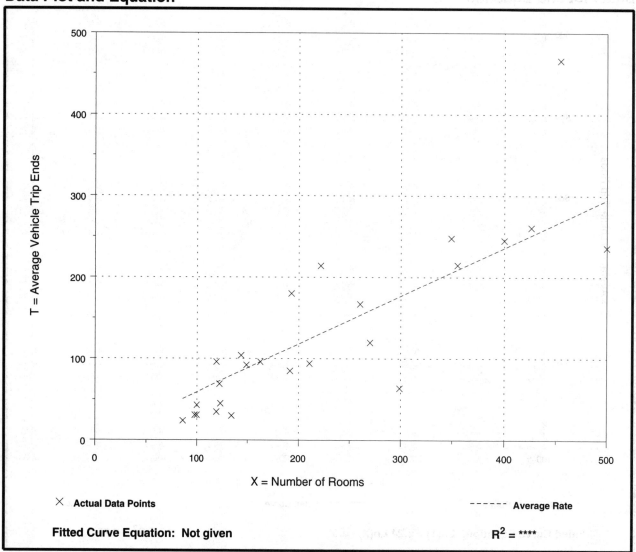

Fitted Curve Equation: Not given R^2 = ****

Hotel
(310)

Average Vehicle Trip Ends vs: Rooms
On a: Weekday,
A.M. Peak Hour of Generator

Number of Studies: 32
Average Number of Rooms: 289
Directional Distribution: 55% entering, 45% exiting

Trip Generation per Room

Average Rate	Range of Rates	Standard Deviation
0.52	0.16 - 1.42	0.75

Data Plot and Equation

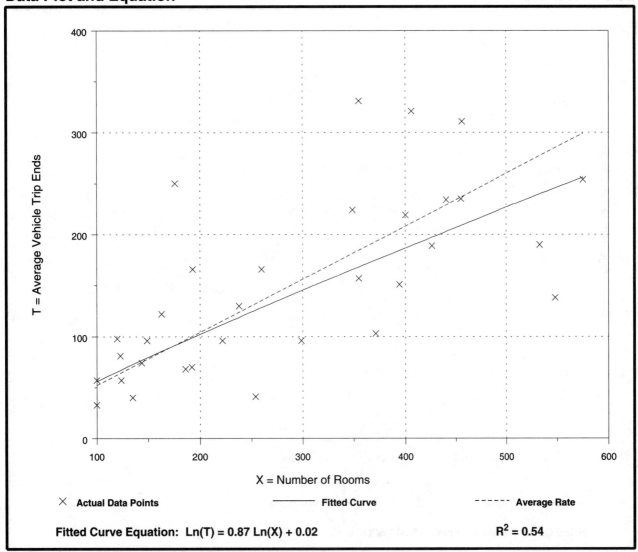

X = Number of Rooms

✕ **Actual Data Points** ——— **Fitted Curve** - - - - - **Average Rate**

Fitted Curve Equation: Ln(T) = 0.87 Ln(X) + 0.02 $R^2 = 0.54$

Hotel
(310)

Average Vehicle Trip Ends vs: Rooms
On a: Weekday,
P.M. Peak Hour of Generator

Number of Studies: 35
Average Number of Rooms: 294
Directional Distribution: 58% entering, 42% exiting

Trip Generation per Room

Average Rate	Range of Rates	Standard Deviation
0.61	0.20 - 1.23	0.81

Data Plot and Equation

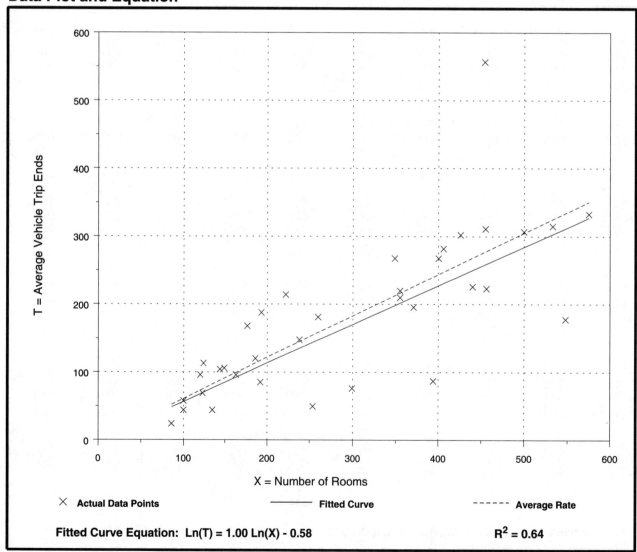

Fitted Curve Equation: Ln(T) = 1.00 Ln(X) - 0.58 $R^2 = 0.64$

Hotel
(310)

Average Vehicle Trip Ends vs: Rooms
On a: Saturday

Number of Studies: 8
Average Number of Rooms: 206
Directional Distribution: 50% entering, 50% exiting

Trip Generation per Room

Average Rate	Range of Rates	Standard Deviation
8.19	6.35 - 9.79	3.13

Data Plot and Equation

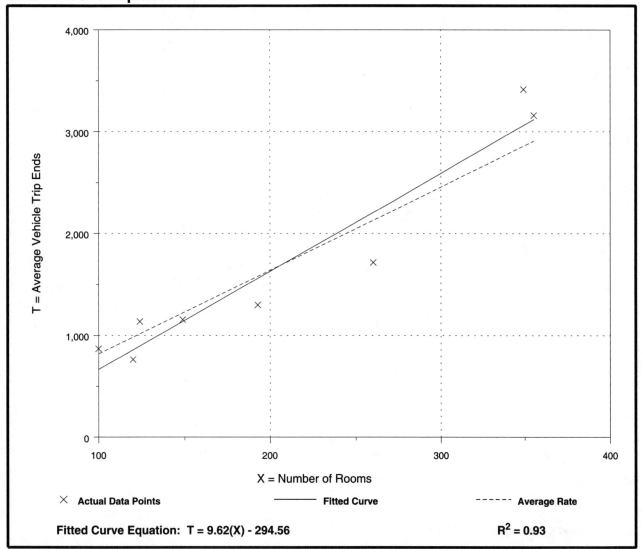

Fitted Curve Equation: T = 9.62(X) - 294.56 $R^2 = 0.93$

Hotel
(310)

Average Vehicle Trip Ends vs: Rooms
On a: Saturday,
Peak Hour of Generator

Number of Studies: 9
Average Number of Rooms: 194
Directional Distribution: 56% entering, 44% exiting

Trip Generation per Room

Average Rate	Range of Rates	Standard Deviation
0.72	0.49 - 1.23	0.87

Data Plot and Equation

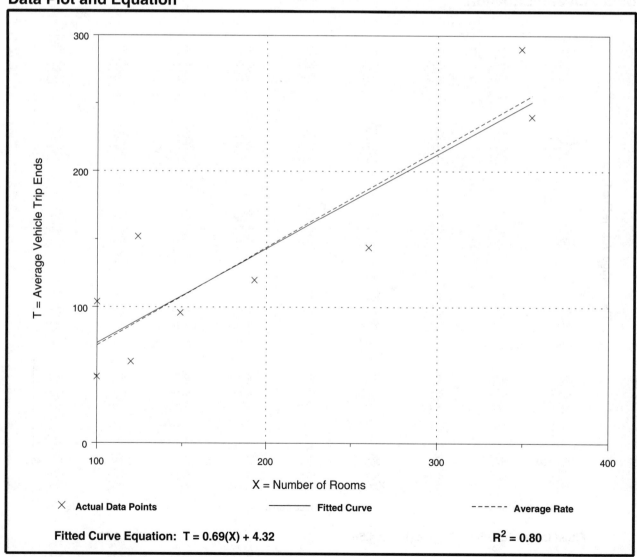

X Actual Data Points   —— **Fitted Curve**   - - - - - **Average Rate**

Fitted Curve Equation: T = 0.69(X) + 4.32 $R^2 = 0.80$

Hotel
(310)

Average Vehicle Trip Ends vs: Rooms
On a: Sunday

Number of Studies: 8
Average Number of Rooms: 206
Directional Distribution: 50% entering, 50% exiting

Trip Generation per Room

Average Rate	Range of Rates	Standard Deviation
5.95	4.01 - 8.48	2.89

Data Plot and Equation

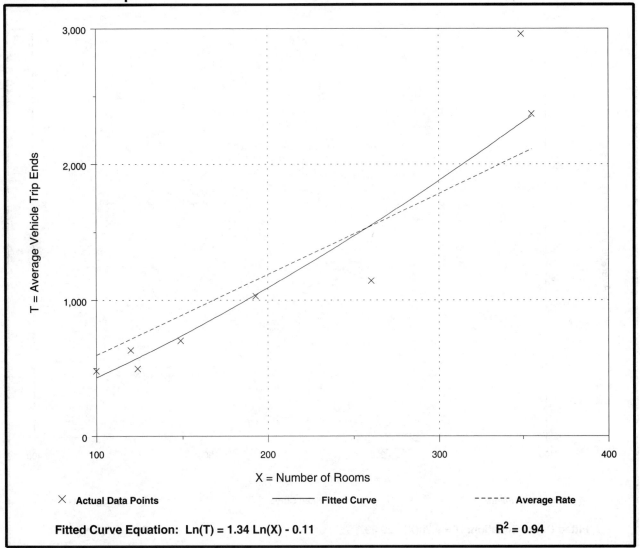

Fitted Curve Equation: $Ln(T) = 1.34 \, Ln(X) - 0.11$ $R^2 = 0.94$

Hotel
(310)

Average Vehicle Trip Ends vs: Rooms
On a: Sunday,
Peak Hour of Generator

Number of Studies: 8
Average Number of Rooms: 206
Directional Distribution: 46% entering, 54% exiting

Trip Generation per Room

Average Rate	Range of Rates	Standard Deviation
0.56	0.39 - 0.72	0.75

Data Plot and Equation

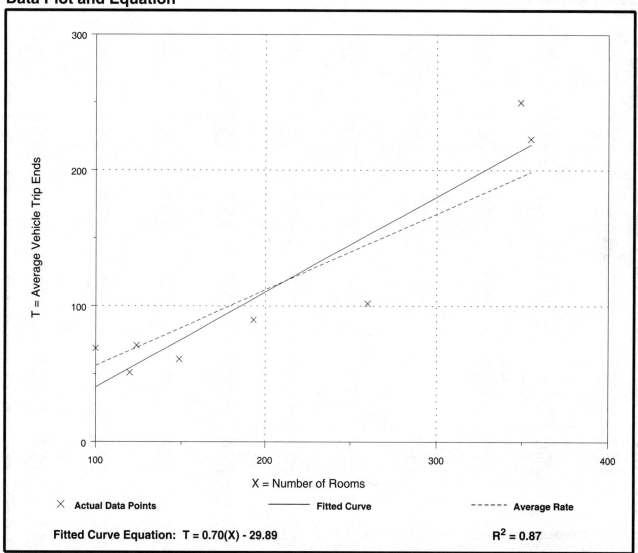

Fitted Curve Equation: T = 0.70(X) - 29.89 $R^2 = 0.87$

Hotel
(310)

Average Vehicle Trip Ends vs: Employees
On a: Weekday

Number of Studies: 5
Avg. Number of Employees: 92
Directional Distribution: 50% entering, 50% exiting

Trip Generation per Employee

Average Rate	Range of Rates	Standard Deviation
14.34	8.85 - 24.47	6.73

Data Plot and Equation

Caution - Use Carefully - Small Sample Size

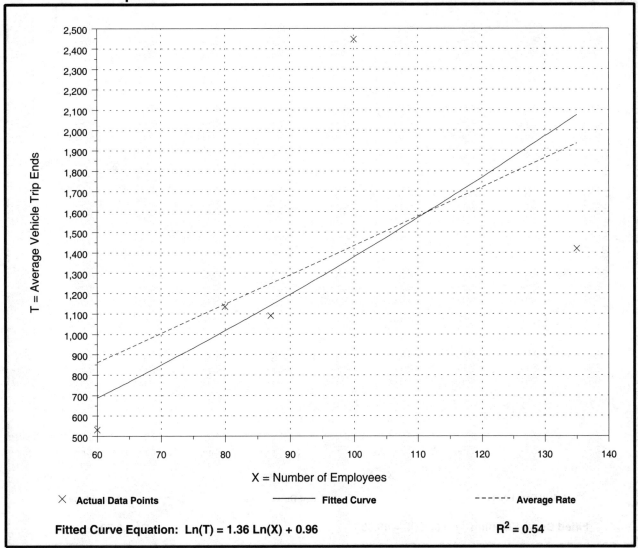

X **Actual Data Points**　　　　——— **Fitted Curve**　　　- - - - - **Average Rate**

Fitted Curve Equation: Ln(T) = 1.36 Ln(X) + 0.96　　　　$R^2 = 0.54$

Hotel
(310)

Average Vehicle Trip Ends vs: Employees
On a: Weekday,
Peak Hour of Adjacent Street Traffic,
One Hour Between 7 and 9 a.m.

Number of Studies: 13
Avg. Number of Employees: 205
Directional Distribution: 60% entering, 40% exiting

Trip Generation per Employee

Average Rate	Range of Rates	Standard Deviation
0.69	0.33 - 2.49	0.90

Data Plot and Equation

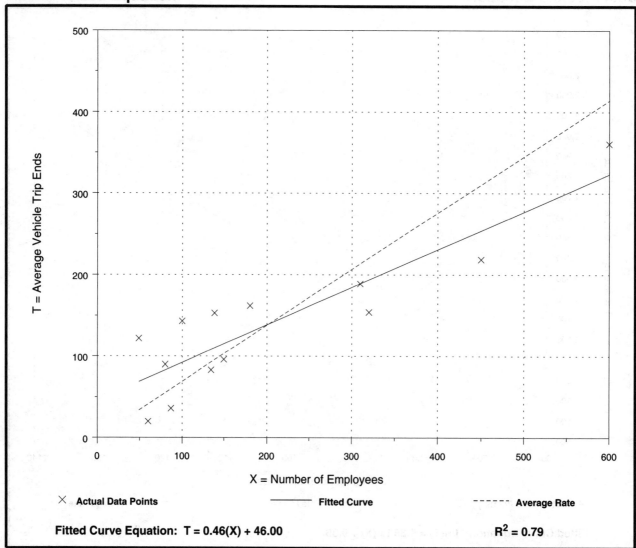

Fitted Curve Equation: T = 0.46(X) + 46.00 $R^2 = 0.79$

Hotel
(310)

Average Vehicle Trip Ends vs: **Employees**
On a: **Weekday,**
Peak Hour of Adjacent Street Traffic,
One Hour Between 4 and 6 p.m.

Number of Studies: 13
Avg. Number of Employees: 205
Directional Distribution: 54% entering, 46% exiting

Trip Generation per Employee

Average Rate	Range of Rates	Standard Deviation
0.80	0.39 - 1.96	0.98

Data Plot and Equation

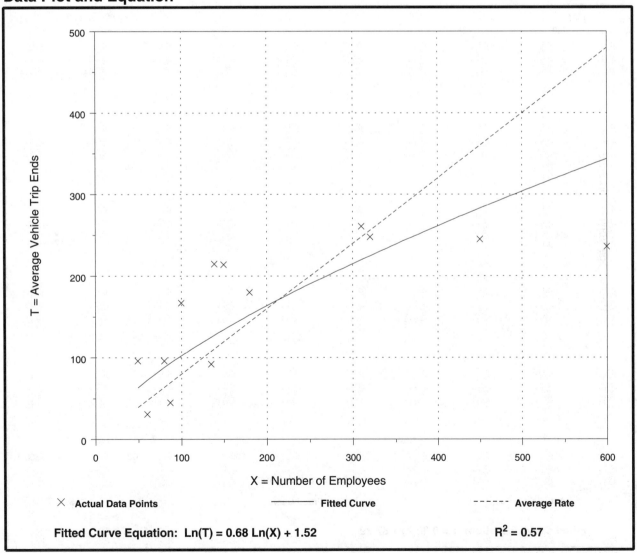

X = Number of Employees

× **Actual Data Points**	——— **Fitted Curve**	- - - - **Average Rate**

Fitted Curve Equation: Ln(T) = 0.68 Ln(X) + 1.52 $R^2 = 0.57$

Hotel
(310)

Average Vehicle Trip Ends vs: Employees
On a: Weekday,
A.M. Peak Hour of Generator

Number of Studies: 12
Avg. Number of Employees: 172
Directional Distribution: 57% entering, 43% exiting

Trip Generation per Employee

Average Rate	Range of Rates	Standard Deviation
0.79	0.49 - 2.49	0.97

Data Plot and Equation

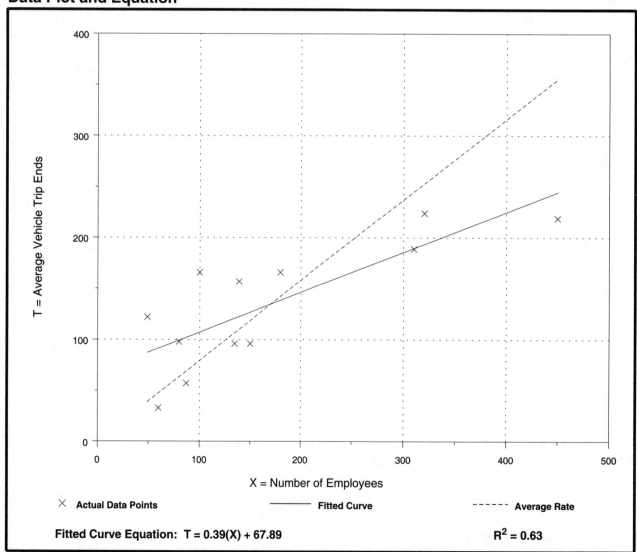

X = Number of Employees

× Actual Data Points	—— Fitted Curve	- - - - Average Rate

Fitted Curve Equation: T = 0.39(X) + 67.89 $R^2 = 0.63$

Hotel
(310)

Average Vehicle Trip Ends vs: Employees
On a: Weekday,
P.M. Peak Hour of Generator

Number of Studies: 13
Avg. Number of Employees: 205
Directional Distribution: 59% entering, 41% exiting

Trip Generation per Employee

Average Rate	Range of Rates	Standard Deviation
0.90	0.51 - 1.96	1.03

Data Plot and Equation

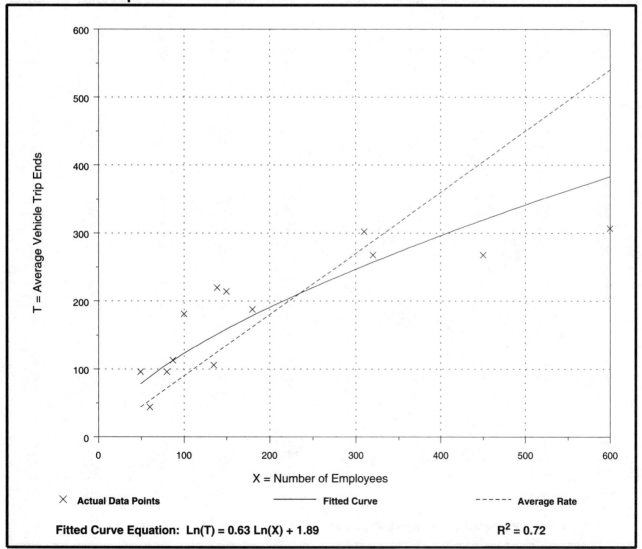

Fitted Curve Equation: Ln(T) = 0.63 Ln(X) + 1.89 $R^2 = 0.72$

Hotel
(310)

Average Vehicle Trip Ends vs: Employees
On a: Saturday

Number of Studies: 8
Avg. Number of Employees: 138
Directional Distribution: 50% entering, 50% exiting

Trip Generation per Employee

Average Rate	Range of Rates	Standard Deviation
12.27	7.22 - 22.73	5.97

Data Plot and Equation

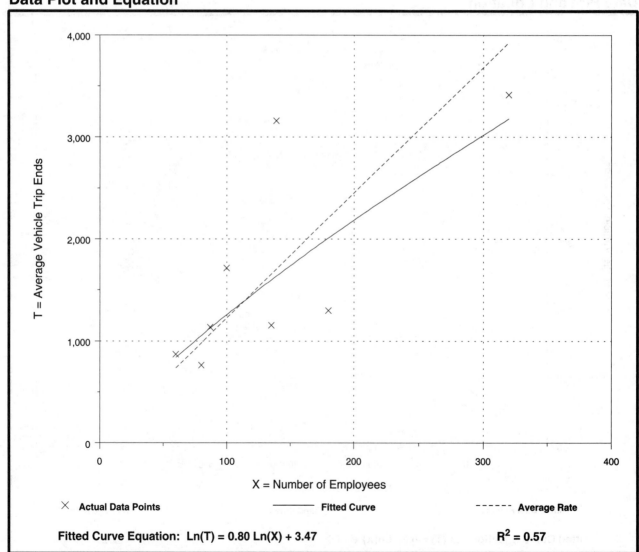

X **Actual Data Points** —— **Fitted Curve** - - - - **Average Rate**

Fitted Curve Equation: Ln(T) = 0.80 Ln(X) + 3.47 $R^2 = 0.57$

Hotel
(310)

Average Vehicle Trip Ends vs: Employees
On a: Saturday,
Peak Hour of Generator

Number of Studies: 8
Avg. Number of Employees: 138
Directional Distribution: 56% entering, 44% exiting

Trip Generation per Employee

Average Rate	Range of Rates	Standard Deviation
1.10	0.67 - 1.75	1.13

Data Plot and Equation

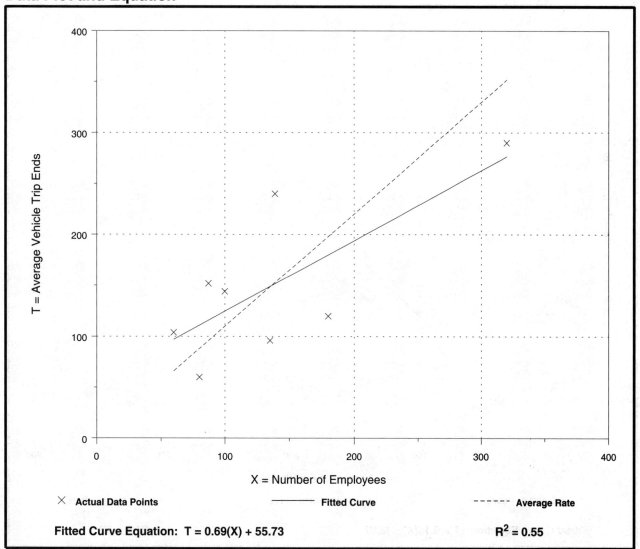

X = Number of Employees

$\times$ **Actual Data Points**   —— **Fitted Curve**   - - - - - **Average Rate**

Fitted Curve Equation: T = 0.69(X) + 55.73 $R^2 = 0.55$

Hotel
(310)

Average Vehicle Trip Ends vs: **Employees**
On a: **Sunday**

Number of Studies: 8
Avg. Number of Employees: 138
Directional Distribution: 50% entering, 50% exiting

Trip Generation per Employee

Average Rate	Range of Rates	Standard Deviation
8.92	5.21 - 17.06	4.71

Data Plot and Equation

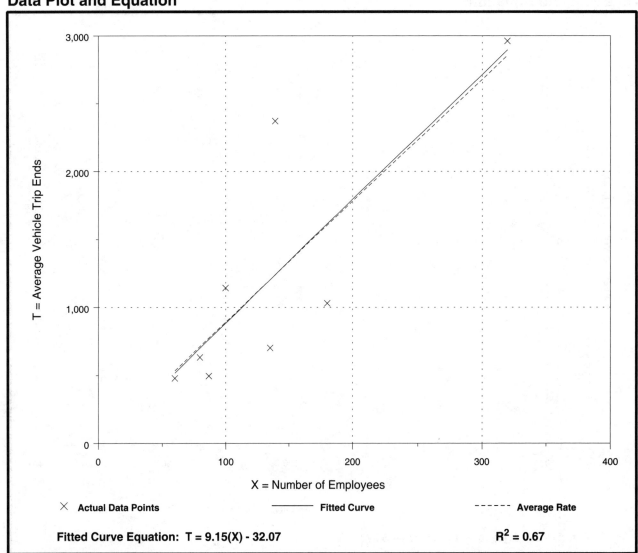

Fitted Curve Equation: T = 9.15(X) - 32.07   **R² = 0.67**

Hotel
(310)

Average Vehicle Trip Ends vs: Employees
On a: Sunday,
Peak Hour of Generator

Number of Studies: 8
Avg. Number of Employees: 138
Directional Distribution: 46% entering, 54% exiting

Trip Generation per Employee

Average Rate	Range of Rates	Standard Deviation
0.83	0.45 - 1.60	0.98

Data Plot and Equation

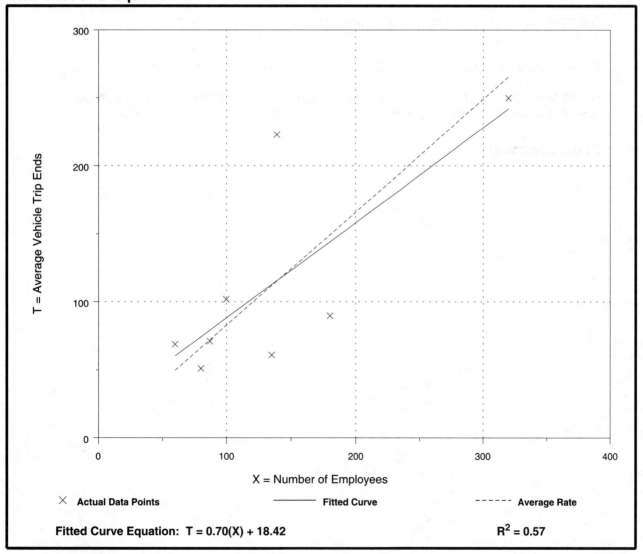

Fitted Curve Equation: T = 0.70(X) + 18.42 $R^2 = 0.57$

Land Use: 311
All Suites Hotel

Description

All suites hotels are places of lodging that provide sleeping accommodations, a small restaurant and lounge and small amounts of meeting space. Each suite includes a sitting room and separate bedroom; limited kitchen facilities are provided within the suite. These hotels are located primarily in suburban areas. Hotel (Land Use 310), business hotel (Land Use 312), motel (Land Use 320) and resort hotel (Land Use 330) are related uses.

Additional Data

Only one hotel provided employment data; this site had 0.10 employees per room.

Four studies provided information on occupancy rates at the time the studies were conducted. The average occupancy rate for these studies was approximately 74 percent.

The peak hour of the generator typically coincided with the peak hour of the adjacent street traffic.

The sites were surveyed in the mid-1980s and the 1990s in Georgia and Florida.

For all lodging uses, it is important to collect data on occupied rooms as well as total rooms in order to accurately predict trip generation characteristics for the site.

Source Numbers

216, 436

Land Use: 311
All Suites Hotel
Independent Variables with One Observation

The following trip generation data are for independent variables with only one observation. This information is shown in this table only; there are no related plots for these data.

Users are cautioned to use data with care because of the small sample size.

Independent Variable	Trip Generation Rate	Size of Independent Variable	Number of Studies	Directional Distribution
Employees				
Weekday a.m. Peak Hour of Adjacent Street Traffic	4.76	25	1	67% entering, 33% exiting
Weekday p.m. Peak Hour of Adjacent Street Traffic	4.44	25	1	37% entering, 63% exiting
Weekday a.m. Peak Hour of Generator	4.76	25	1	67% entering, 33% exiting
Weekday p.m. Peak Hour of Generator	4.44	25	1	37% entering, 63% exiting

All Suites Hotel
(311)

Average Vehicle Trip Ends vs: Occupied Rooms
On a: Weekday

Number of Studies: 3
Average Number of Occupied Rooms: 167
Directional Distribution: 50% entering, 50% exiting

Trip Generation per Occupied Room

Average Rate	Range of Rates	Standard Deviation
6.24	5.61 - 6.85	2.55

Data Plot and Equation

Caution - Use Carefully - Small Sample Size

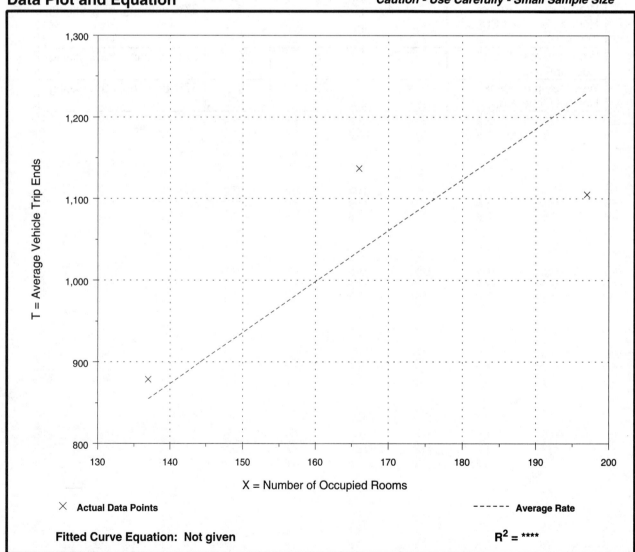

X   **Actual Data Points**

------ **Average Rate**

Fitted Curve Equation: Not given

$R^2 = ****$

All Suites Hotel
(311)

Average Vehicle Trip Ends vs: **Occupied Rooms**
On a: **Weekday,**
Peak Hour of Adjacent Street Traffic,
One Hour Between 7 and 9 a.m.

Number of Studies: 4
Average Number of Occupied Rooms: 157
Directional Distribution: 67% entering, 33% exiting

Trip Generation per Occupied Room

Average Rate	Range of Rates	Standard Deviation
0.48	0.31 - 0.94	0.73

Data Plot and Equation

Caution - Use Carefully - Small Sample Size

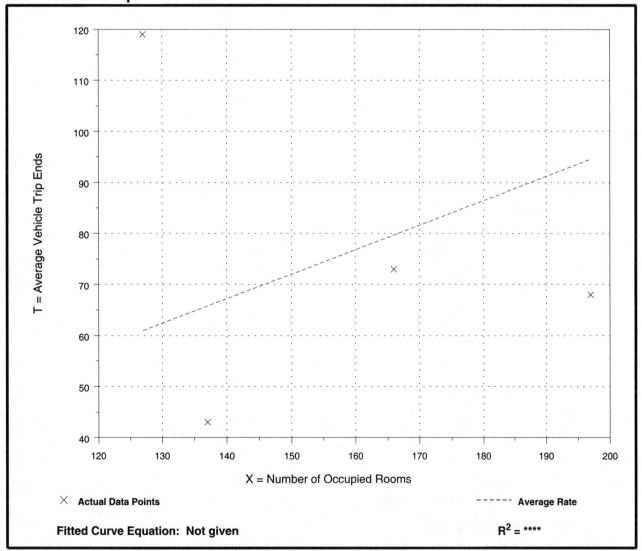

X **Actual Data Points**

- - - - - Average Rate

Fitted Curve Equation: Not given

$R^2 = ****$

All Suites Hotel
(311)

Average Vehicle Trip Ends vs: Occupied Rooms
On a: Weekday,
Peak Hour of Adjacent Street Traffic,
One Hour Between 4 and 6 p.m.

Number of Studies: 4
Average Number of Occupied Rooms: 157
Directional Distribution: 42% entering, 58% exiting

Trip Generation per Occupied Room

Average Rate	Range of Rates	Standard Deviation
0.55	0.40 - 0.87	0.76

Data Plot and Equation

Caution - Use Carefully - Small Sample Size

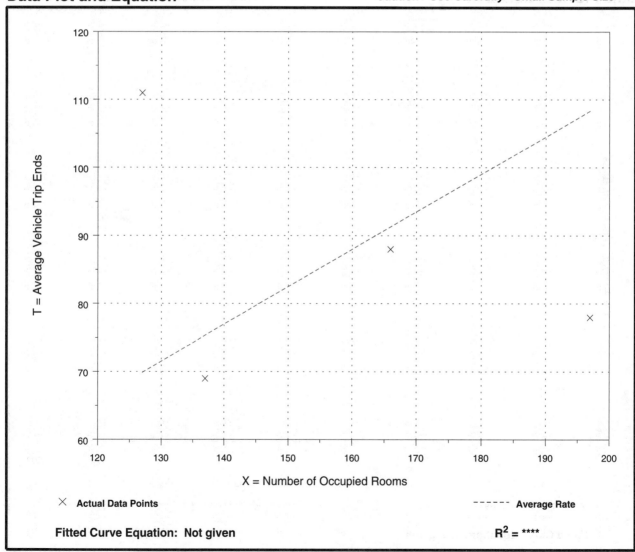

X   **Actual Data Points**

----- **Average Rate**

Fitted Curve Equation: Not given $R^2 = ****$

All Suites Hotel
(311)

Average Vehicle Trip Ends vs: Occupied Rooms
On a: Weekday,
A.M. Peak Hour of Generator

Number of Studies: 4
Average Number of Occupied Rooms: 157
Directional Distribution: 67% entering, 33% exiting

Trip Generation per Occupied Room

Average Rate	Range of Rates	Standard Deviation
0.52	0.39 - 0.94	0.75

Data Plot and Equation

Caution - Use Carefully - Small Sample Size

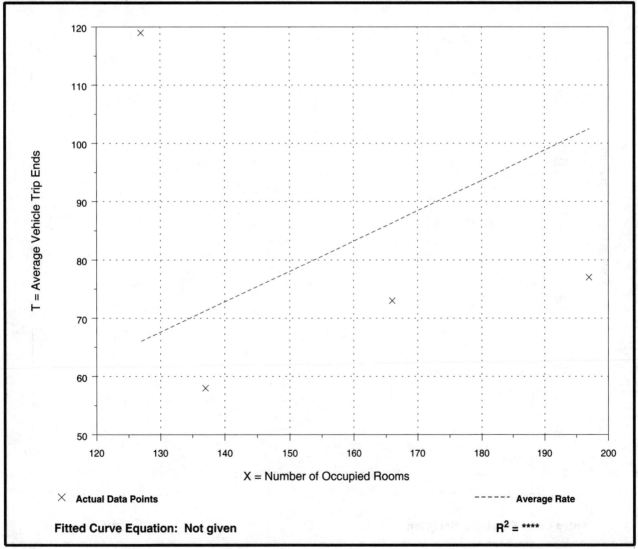

X **Actual Data Points**

----- **Average Rate**

Fitted Curve Equation: Not given

$R^2 = ****$

All Suites Hotel
(311)

Average Vehicle Trip Ends vs: Occupied Rooms
On a: Weekday,
P.M. Peak Hour of Generator

Number of Studies: 4
Average Number of Occupied Rooms: 157
Directional Distribution: 42% entering, 58% exiting

Trip Generation per Occupied Room

Average Rate	Range of Rates	Standard Deviation
0.55	0.40 - 0.87	0.76

Data Plot and Equation

Caution - Use Carefully - Small Sample Size

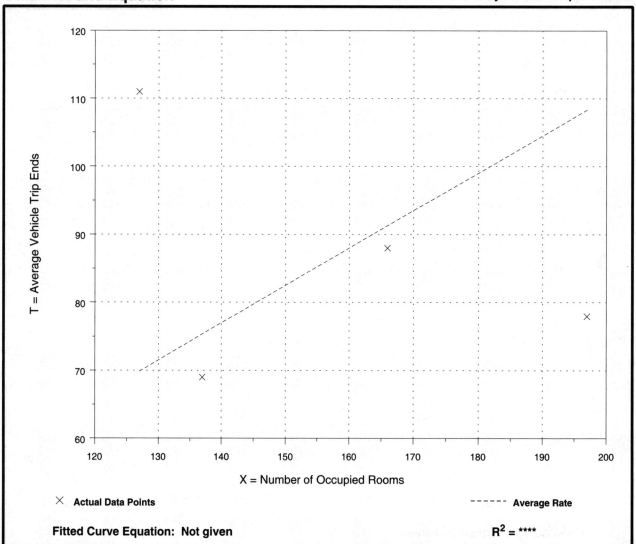

X **Actual Data Points**   - - - - - **Average Rate**

Fitted Curve Equation: Not given $R^2 = ****$

All Suites Hotel
(311)

Average Vehicle Trip Ends vs: Rooms
On a: Weekday

Number of Studies: 3
Average Number of Rooms: 212
Directional Distribution: 50% entering, 50% exiting

Trip Generation per Room

Average Rate	Range of Rates	Standard Deviation
4.90	4.49 - 6.02	2.29

Data Plot and Equation

Caution - Use Carefully - Small Sample Size

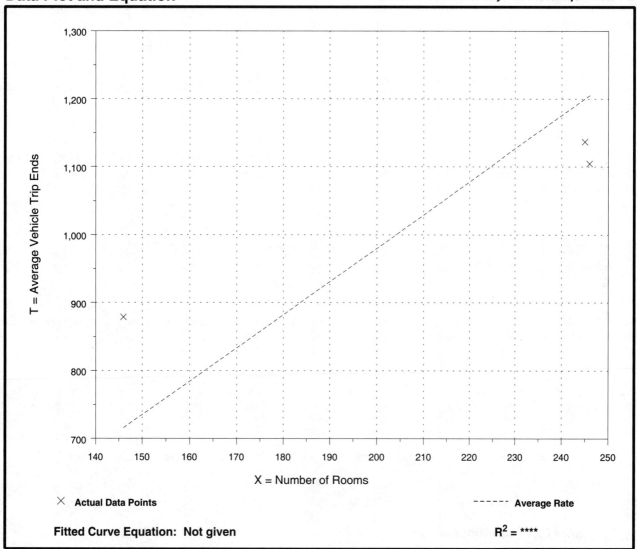

X **Actual Data Points**   - - - - - **Average Rate**

Fitted Curve Equation: Not given $R^2 = ****$

All Suites Hotel
(311)

Average Vehicle Trip Ends vs: **Rooms**
On a: **Weekday,**
  Peak Hour of Adjacent Street Traffic,
  One Hour Between 7 and 9 a.m.

Number of Studies: 5
Average Number of Rooms: 216
Directional Distribution: 55% entering, 45% exiting

Trip Generation per Room

Average Rate	Range of Rates	Standard Deviation
0.38	0.28 - 0.51	0.62

Data Plot and Equation

Caution - Use Carefully - Small Sample Size

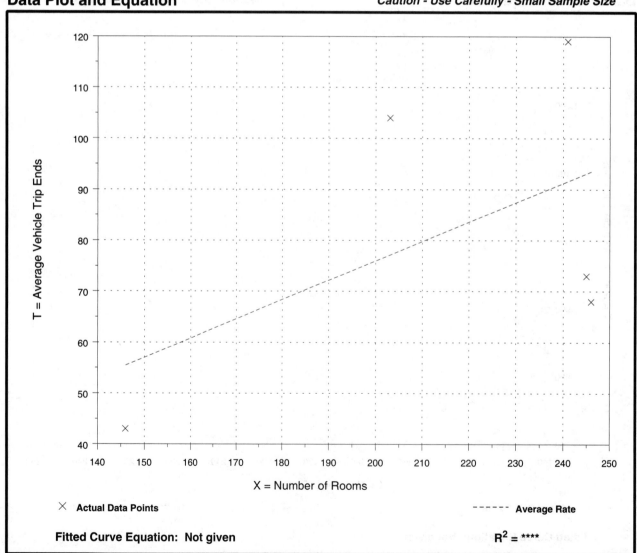

X   **Actual Data Points**

- - - - - **Average Rate**

Fitted Curve Equation: Not given $R^2 = ****$

All Suites Hotel
(311)

Average Vehicle Trip Ends vs: Rooms
On a: Weekday,
Peak Hour of Adjacent Street Traffic,
One Hour Between 4 and 6 p.m.

Number of Studies: 5
Average Number of Rooms: 216
Directional Distribution: 45% entering, 55% exiting

Trip Generation per Room

Average Rate	Range of Rates	Standard Deviation
0.40	0.32 - 0.47	0.63

Data Plot and Equation

Caution - Use Carefully - Small Sample Size

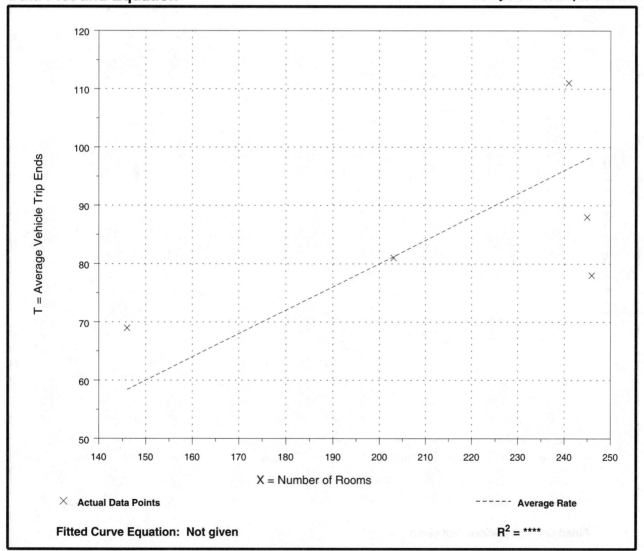

X Actual Data Points

----- Average Rate

Fitted Curve Equation: Not given

$R^2 = ****$

All Suites Hotel
(311)

Average Vehicle Trip Ends vs: **Rooms**
On a: **Weekday,**
A.M. Peak Hour of Generator

Number of Studies: 5
Average Number of Rooms: 216
Directional Distribution: 55% entering, 45% exiting

Trip Generation per Room

Average Rate	Range of Rates	Standard Deviation
0.40	0.30 - 0.51	0.64

Data Plot and Equation

Caution - Use Carefully - Small Sample Size

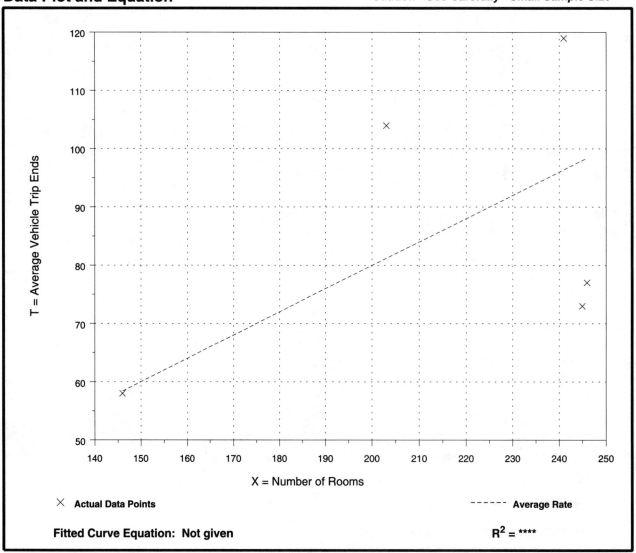

X **Actual Data Points**

-------- **Average Rate**

Fitted Curve Equation: Not given

$R^2 = ****$

All Suites Hotel
(311)

Average Vehicle Trip Ends vs: **Rooms**
On a: **Weekday,**
P.M. Peak Hour of Generator

Number of Studies: 5
Average Number of Rooms: 216
Directional Distribution: 45% entering, 55% exiting

Trip Generation per Room

Average Rate	Range of Rates	Standard Deviation
0.40	0.32 - 0.47	0.63

Data Plot and Equation

Caution - Use Carefully - Small Sample Size

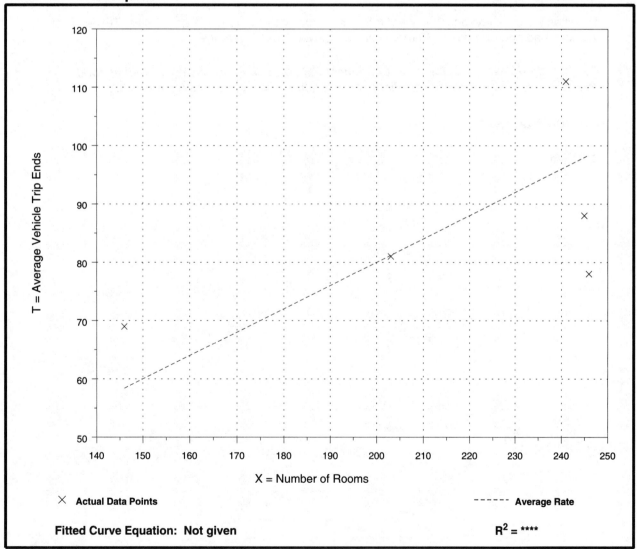

X **Actual Data Points**   - - - - - **Average Rate**

Fitted Curve Equation: Not given $R^2 = ****$

Land Use: 312
Business Hotel

Description

Business hotels are places of lodging aimed toward the business traveler. These hotels provide sleeping accommodations and other limited facilities, such as a breakfast buffet bar and afternoon beverage bar (no lunch or dinner is served and no meeting facilities are provided). Each unit is a large single room. Business hotels provide very few or none of the supporting facilities provided at hotels or suite hotels and are usually smaller in size. All locations nationwide are in suburban areas. Hotel (Land Use 310), all suites hotel (Land Use 311), motel (Land Use 320) and resort hotel (Land Use 330) are related uses.

Additional Data

The peak hour of the generator typically coincided with the peak hour of the adjacent street traffic.

The sites were surveyed in the late 1980s in suburban Atlanta, Georgia and Dallas, Texas; all of the sites had approximately 130 rooms and employed 8 to 12 persons.

For all lodging uses, it is important to collect data on occupied rooms as well as total rooms in order to accurately predict trip generation characteristics for the site.

Source Numbers

216, 306

Land Use: 312
Business Hotel
Independent Variables with One Observation

The following trip generation data are for independent variables with only one observation. This information is shown in this table only; there are no related plots for these data.

Users are cautioned to use data with care because of the small sample size.

Independent Variable	Trip Generation Rate	Size of Independent Variable	Number of Studies	Directional Distribution
Occupied Rooms				
Weekday	7.27	120	1	50% entering, 50% exiting
Employees				
Weekday	72.67	12	1	50% entering, 50% exiting

Business Hotel
(312)

Average Vehicle Trip Ends vs: **Occupied Rooms**
On a: **Weekday,**
Peak Hour of Adjacent Street Traffic,
One Hour Between 7 and 9 a.m.

Number of Studies: 3
Average Number of Occupied Rooms: 123
Directional Distribution: 59% entering, 41% exiting

Trip Generation per Occupied Room

Average Rate	Range of Rates	Standard Deviation
0.58	0.53 - 0.63	0.76

Data Plot and Equation

Caution - Use Carefully - Small Sample Size

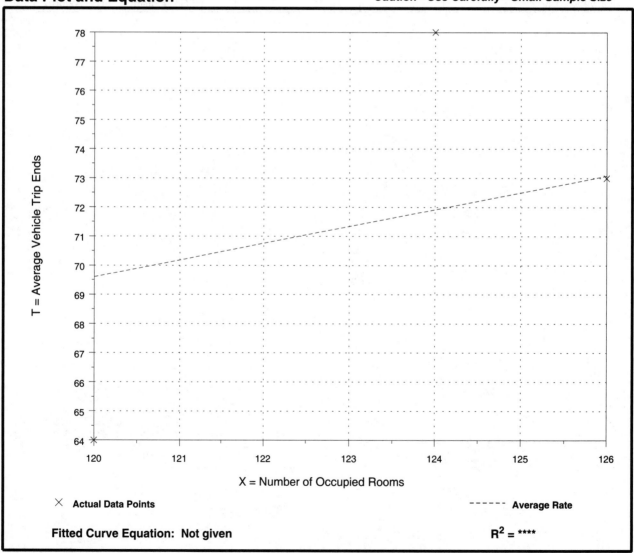

X **Actual Data Points**

------ **Average Rate**

Fitted Curve Equation: Not given $R^2 = ****$

Business Hotel
(312)

Average Vehicle Trip Ends vs: **Occupied Rooms**
On a: **Weekday,**
Peak Hour of Adjacent Street Traffic,
One Hour Between 4 and 6 p.m.

Number of Studies: 3
Average Number of Occupied Rooms: 123
Directional Distribution: 60% entering, 40% exiting

Trip Generation per Occupied Room

Average Rate	Range of Rates	Standard Deviation
0.62	0.44 - 0.75	0.79

Data Plot and Equation

Caution - Use Carefully - Small Sample Size

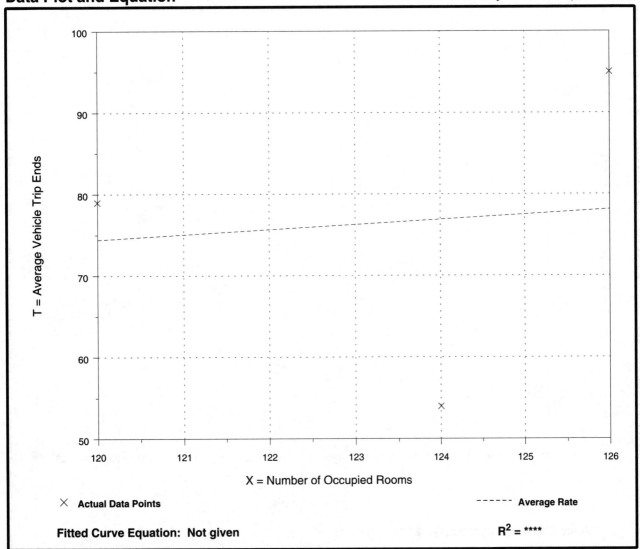

X **Actual Data Points**   - - - - - - **Average Rate**

Fitted Curve Equation: Not given $R^2 = ****$

Business Hotel
(312)

Average Vehicle Trip Ends vs: Occupied Rooms
On a: Weekday,
A.M. Peak Hour of Generator

Number of Studies: 4
Average Number of Occupied Rooms: 119
Directional Distribution: 54% entering, 46% exiting

Trip Generation per Occupied Room

Average Rate	Range of Rates	Standard Deviation
0.56	0.50 - 0.63	0.75

Data Plot and Equation

Caution - Use Carefully - Small Sample Size

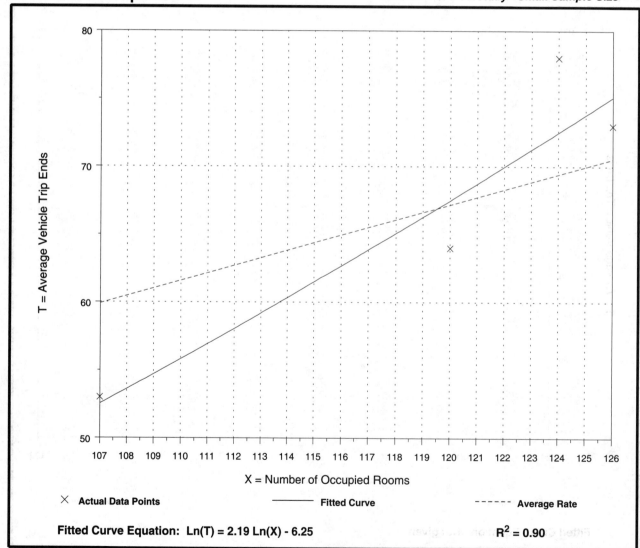

X **Actual Data Points**   ———— **Fitted Curve**   ----- **Average Rate**

Fitted Curve Equation: Ln(T) = 2.19 Ln(X) - 6.25 $R^2 = 0.90$

Business Hotel
(312)

Average Vehicle Trip Ends vs: Occupied Rooms
On a: Weekday,
P.M. Peak Hour of Generator

Number of Studies: 4
Average Number of Occupied Rooms: 119
Directional Distribution: 61% entering, 39% exiting

Trip Generation per Occupied Room

Average Rate	Range of Rates	Standard Deviation
0.57	0.41 - 0.75	0.77

Data Plot and Equation

Caution - Use Carefully - Small Sample Size

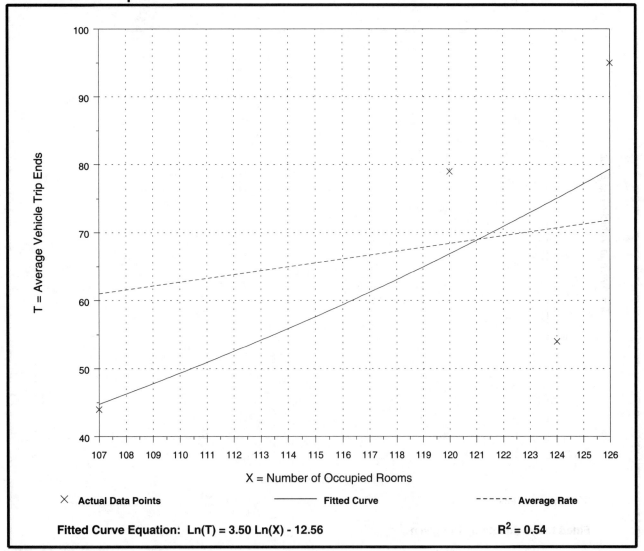

X = Number of Occupied Rooms

✕ **Actual Data Points** ——— **Fitted Curve** - - - - - **Average Rate**

Fitted Curve Equation: Ln(T) = 3.50 Ln(X) - 12.56 $R^2 = 0.54$

Business Hotel
(312)

Average Vehicle Trip Ends vs: **Employees**
On a: **Weekday,**
Peak Hour of Adjacent Street Traffic,
One Hour Between 7 and 9 a.m.

Number of Studies: 3
Avg. Number of Employees: 10
Directional Distribution: 59% entering, 41% exiting

Trip Generation per Employee

Average Rate	Range of Rates	Standard Deviation
7.17	5.33 - 9.75	3.14

Data Plot and Equation

Caution - Use Carefully - Small Sample Size

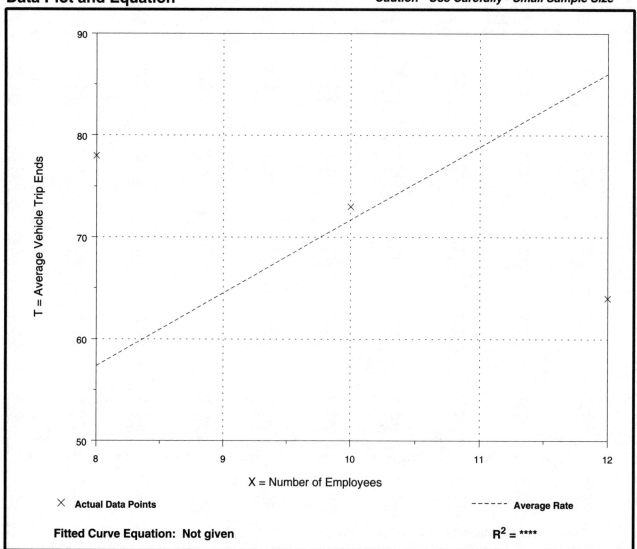

X = Number of Employees

✕ **Actual Data Points**   - - - - - **Average Rate**

Fitted Curve Equation: Not given $R^2 = ****$

Business Hotel
(312)

Average Vehicle Trip Ends vs: **Employees**
On a: **Weekday,**
Peak Hour of Adjacent Street Traffic,
One Hour Between 4 and 6 p.m.

Number of Studies: 3
Avg. Number of Employees: 10
Directional Distribution: 60% entering, 40% exiting

Trip Generation per Employee

Average Rate	Range of Rates	Standard Deviation
7.60	6.58 - 9.50	2.99

Data Plot and Equation

Caution - Use Carefully - Small Sample Size

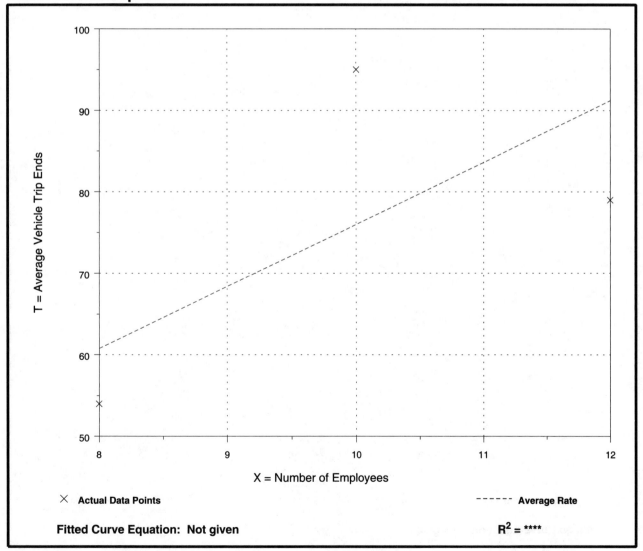

X Actual Data Points

- - - - - **Average Rate**

Fitted Curve Equation: Not given $R^2 = ****$

Business Hotel
(312)

Average Vehicle Trip Ends vs: Employees
On a: Weekday,
A.M. Peak Hour of Generator

Number of Studies: 3
Avg. Number of Employees: 10
Directional Distribution: 59% entering, 41% exiting

Trip Generation per Employee

Average Rate	Range of Rates	Standard Deviation
7.17	5.33 - 9.75	3.14

Data Plot and Equation

Caution - Use Carefully - Small Sample Size

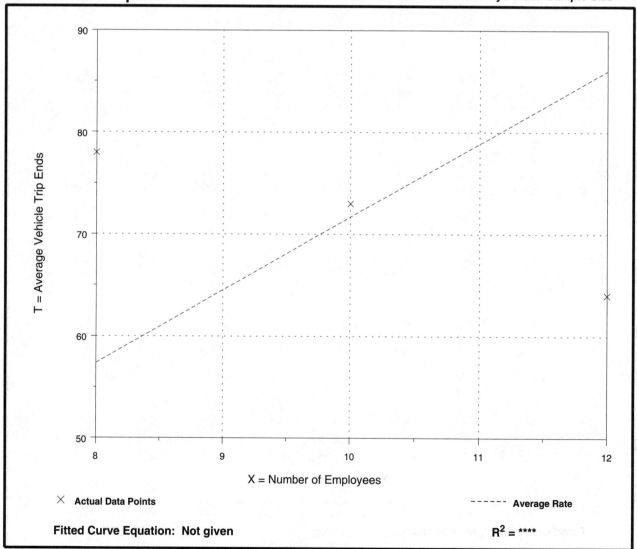

X **Actual Data Points**

- - - - - **Average Rate**

Fitted Curve Equation: Not given $R^2 = $ ****

Business Hotel
(312)

Average Vehicle Trip Ends vs: **Employees**
On a: **Weekday,**
  P.M. Peak Hour of Generator

Number of Studies: 3
Avg. Number of Employees: 10
Directional Distribution: 60% entering, 40% exiting

Trip Generation per Employee

Average Rate	Range of Rates	Standard Deviation
7.60	6.58 - 9.50	2.99

Data Plot and Equation

Caution - Use Carefully - Small Sample Size

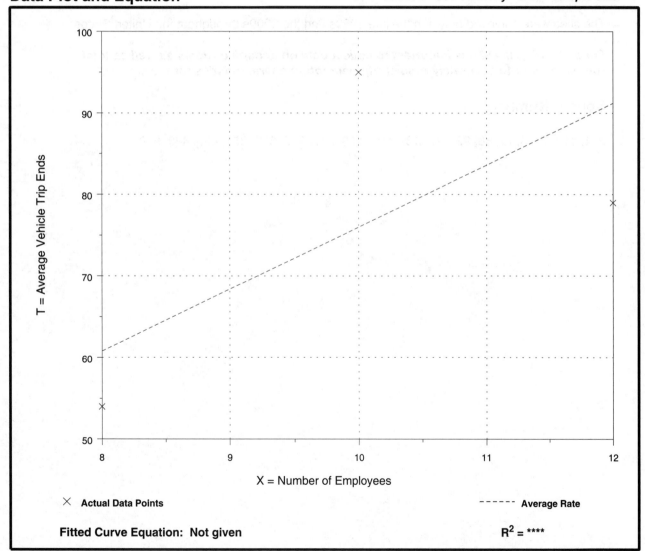

X   **Actual Data Points**

- - - - -   **Average Rate**

Fitted Curve Equation: Not given $R^2 = ****$

Land Use: 320
Motel

Description

Motels are places of lodging that provide sleeping accommodations and often a restaurant. Motels generally offer free on-site parking and provide little or no meeting space and few (if any) supporting facilities. Exterior corridors accessing rooms—immediately adjacent to a parking lot— commonly characterize motels. Hotel (Land Use 310), all suites hotel (Land Use 311), business hotel (Land Use 312) and resort hotel (Land Use 330) are related uses.

Additional Data

Typically, the average employment at motels is much lower than at hotels.

Twenty-six studies provided information on occupancy rates at the time the studies were conducted. The average occupancy rate for these studies was approximately 78 percent.

The sites were surveyed between the late 1960s and the 2000s throughout the United States.

For all lodging uses, it is important to collect data on occupied rooms as well as total rooms in order to accurately predict trip generation characteristics for the site.

Source Numbers

2, 4, 11, 12, 13, 72, 88, 92, 172, 187, 191, 193, 277, 295, 300, 357, 439, 443, 598

Motel
(320)

Average Vehicle Trip Ends vs: Occupied Rooms
On a: Weekday

Number of Studies: 15
Average Number of Occupied Rooms: 131
Directional Distribution: 50% entering, 50% exiting

Trip Generation per Occupied Room

Average Rate	Range of Rates	Standard Deviation
9.11	4.13 - 14.64	4.39

Data Plot and Equation

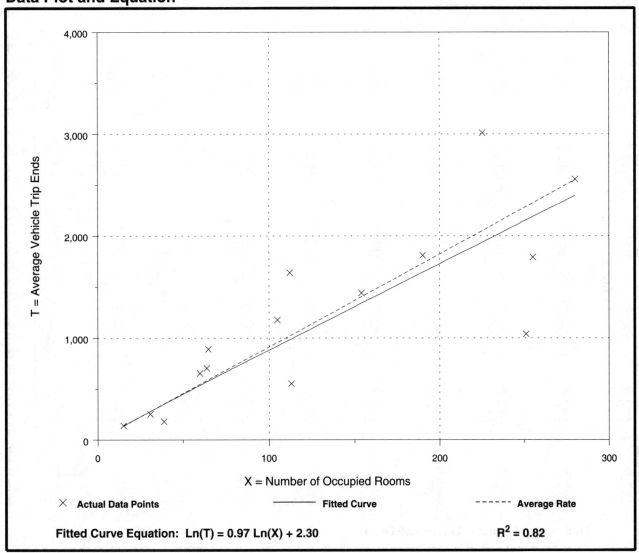

X = Number of Occupied Rooms

✕ Actual Data Points ——— Fitted Curve - - - - Average Rate

Fitted Curve Equation: Ln(T) = 0.97 Ln(X) + 2.30 $R^2 = 0.82$

Motel
(320)

Average Vehicle Trip Ends vs: **Occupied Rooms**
On a: **Weekday,**
Peak Hour of Adjacent Street Traffic,
One Hour Between 7 and 9 a.m.

Number of Studies: 21
Average Number of Occupied Rooms: 134
Directional Distribution: 36% entering, 64% exiting

Trip Generation per Occupied Room

Average Rate	Range of Rates	Standard Deviation
0.64	0.35 - 1.56	0.84

Data Plot and Equation

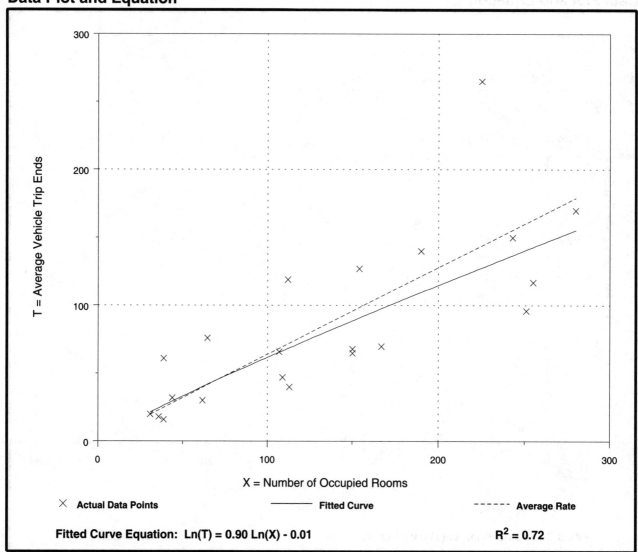

Fitted Curve Equation: $Ln(T) = 0.90\ Ln(X) - 0.01$ $R^2 = 0.72$

Motel
(320)

Average Vehicle Trip Ends vs:	**Occupied Rooms**
On a:	**Weekday,**
	Peak Hour of Adjacent Street Traffic,
	One Hour Between 4 and 6 p.m.

Number of Studies: 22
Average Number of Occupied Rooms: 133
Directional Distribution: 53% entering, 47% exiting

Trip Generation per Occupied Room

Average Rate	Range of Rates	Standard Deviation
0.58	0.26 - 1.33	0.78

Data Plot and Equation

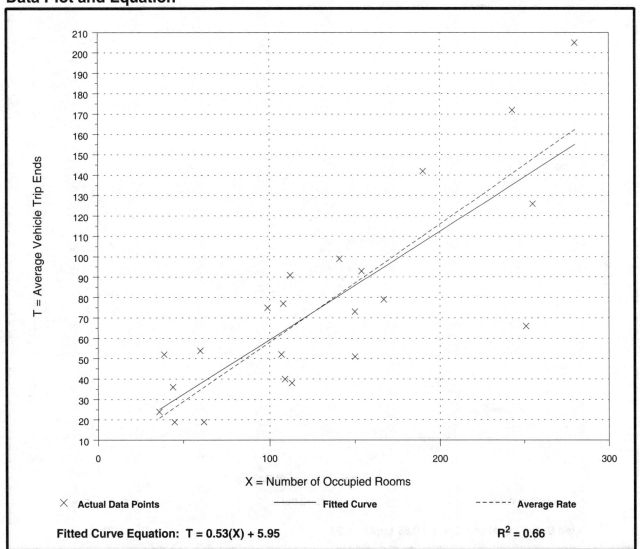

Fitted Curve Equation: T = 0.53(X) + 5.95 $R^2 = 0.66$

Motel
(320)

Average Vehicle Trip Ends vs: Occupied Rooms
On a: Weekday,
A.M. Peak Hour of Generator

Number of Studies: 23
Average Number of Occupied Rooms: 116
Directional Distribution: 39% entering, 61% exiting

Trip Generation per Occupied Room

Average Rate	Range of Rates	Standard Deviation
0.67	0.35 - 1.33	0.86

Data Plot and Equation

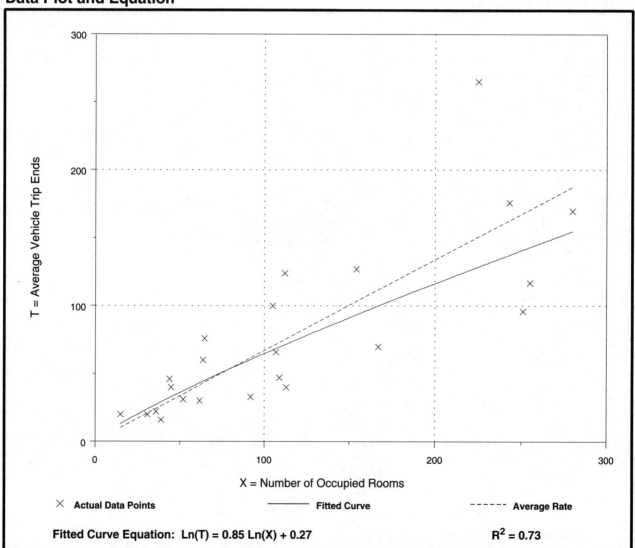

Fitted Curve Equation: Ln(T) = 0.85 Ln(X) + 0.27 $R^2 = 0.73$

Motel
(320)

Average Vehicle Trip Ends vs: Occupied Rooms
On a: Weekday,
P.M. Peak Hour of Generator

Number of Studies: 25
Average Number of Occupied Rooms: 120
Directional Distribution: 54% entering, 46% exiting

Trip Generation per Occupied Room

Average Rate	Range of Rates	Standard Deviation
0.69	0.29 - 1.33	0.87

Data Plot and Equation

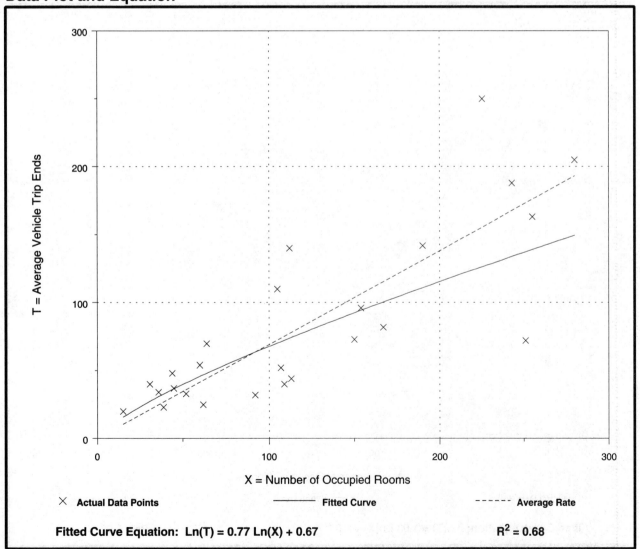

Fitted Curve Equation: Ln(T) = 0.77 Ln(X) + 0.67 $R^2 = 0.68$

Motel
(320)

Average Vehicle Trip Ends vs: Occupied Rooms
On a: Saturday

Number of Studies: 11
Average Number of Occupied Rooms: 141
Directional Distribution: 50% entering, 50% exiting

Trip Generation per Occupied Room

Average Rate	Range of Rates	Standard Deviation
8.84	4.72 - 12.57	3.62

Data Plot and Equation

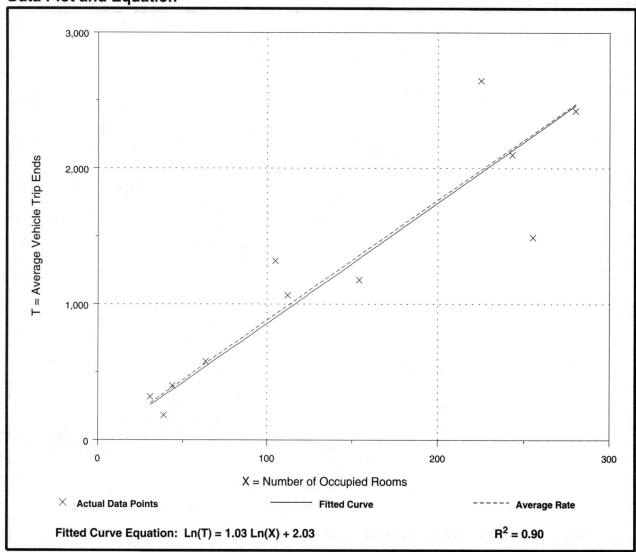

Fitted Curve Equation: Ln(T) = 1.03 Ln(X) + 2.03 $R^2 = 0.90$

Motel
(320)

Average Vehicle Trip Ends vs: Occupied Rooms
On a: Saturday,
Peak Hour of Generator

Number of Studies: 14
Average Number of Occupied Rooms: 124
Directional Distribution: 45% entering, 55% exiting

Trip Generation per Occupied Room

Average Rate	Range of Rates	Standard Deviation
0.76	0.45 - 1.94	0.93

Data Plot and Equation

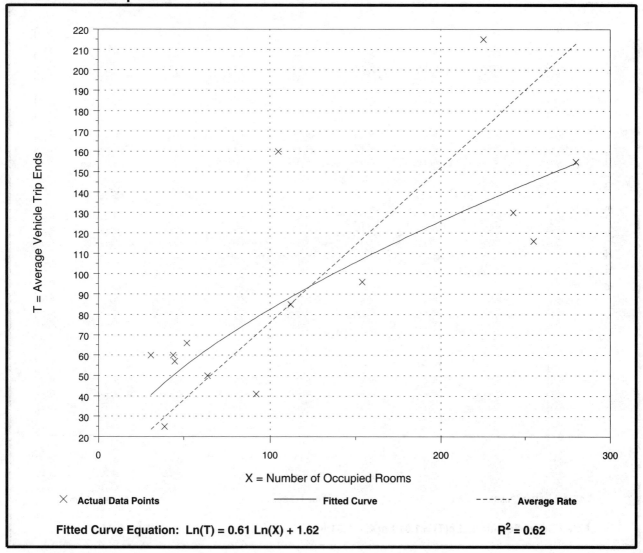

Fitted Curve Equation: Ln(T) = 0.61 Ln(X) + 1.62 $R^2 = 0.62$

Motel
(320)

Average Vehicle Trip Ends vs: Occupied Rooms
On a: Sunday

Number of Studies: 11
Average Number of Occupied Rooms: 141
Directional Distribution: 50% entering, 50% exiting

Trip Generation per Occupied Room

Average Rate	Range of Rates	Standard Deviation
7.39	3.81 - 11.81	3.76

Data Plot and Equation

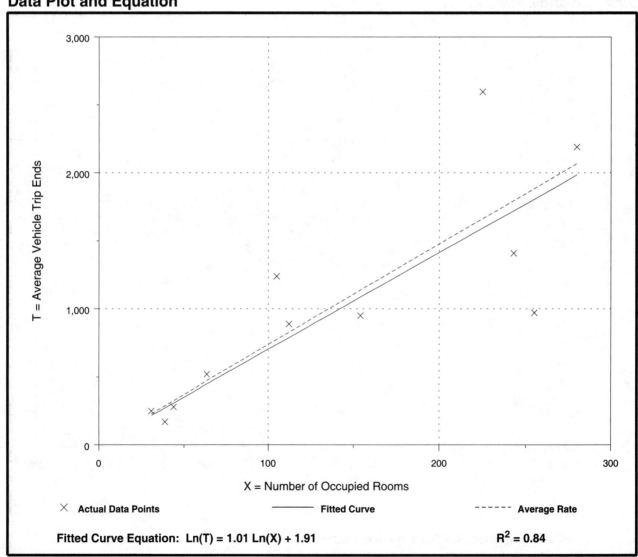

Fitted Curve Equation: Ln(T) = 1.01 Ln(X) + 1.91 $R^2 = 0.84$

Motel
(320)

Average Vehicle Trip Ends vs: Occupied Rooms
On a: Sunday,
Peak Hour of Generator

Number of Studies: 14
Average Number of Occupied Rooms: 124
Directional Distribution: 53% entering, 47% exiting

Trip Generation per Occupied Room

Average Rate	Range of Rates	Standard Deviation
0.60	0.36 - 1.13	0.80

Data Plot and Equation

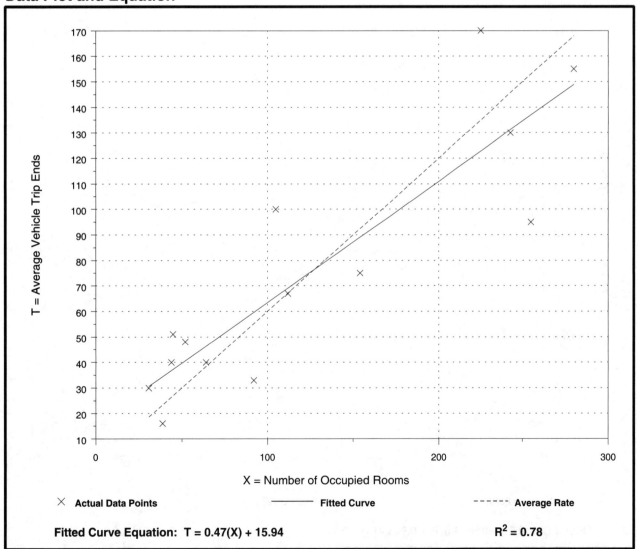

X   **Actual Data Points** ──────── **Fitted Curve** - - - - - **Average Rate**

Fitted Curve Equation: T = 0.47(X) + 15.94 $R^2 = 0.78$

Motel
(320)

Average Vehicle Trip Ends vs: Rooms
On a: Weekday

Number of Studies: 10
Average Number of Rooms: 216
Directional Distribution: 50% entering, 50% exiting

Trip Generation per Room

Average Rate	Range of Rates	Standard Deviation
5.63	3.47 - 10.04	3.31

Data Plot and Equation

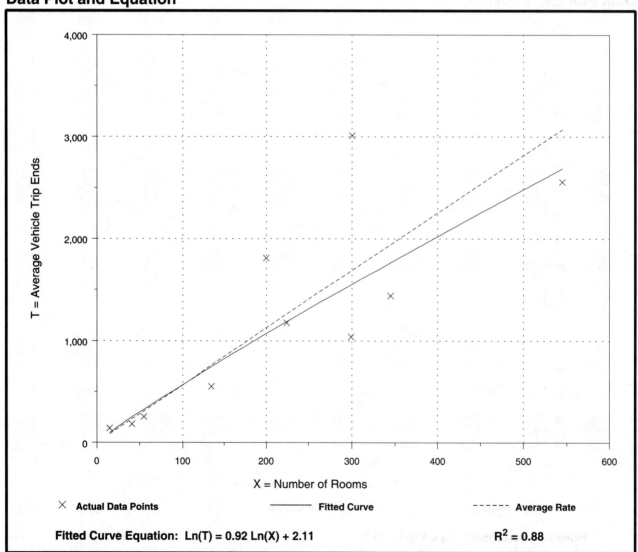

Fitted Curve Equation: $\text{Ln}(T) = 0.92\,\text{Ln}(X) + 2.11$ $\qquad$ $R^2 = 0.88$

Motel
(320)

Average Vehicle Trip Ends vs: **Rooms**
On a: **Weekday,**
Peak Hour of Adjacent Street Traffic,
One Hour Between 7 and 9 a.m.

Number of Studies: 24
Average Number of Rooms: 167
Directional Distribution: 36% entering, 64% exiting

Trip Generation per Room

Average Rate	Range of Rates	Standard Deviation
0.45	0.15 - 0.97	0.70

Data Plot and Equation

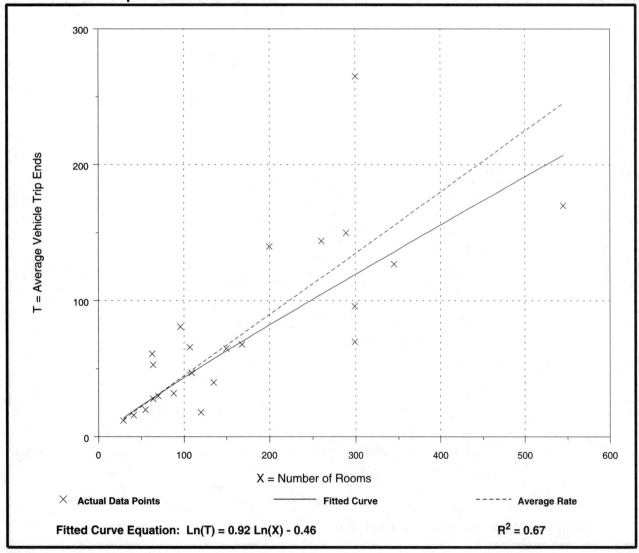

Fitted Curve Equation: Ln(T) = 0.92 Ln(X) - 0.46 $R^2 = 0.67$

Motel
(320)

Average Vehicle Trip Ends vs: **Rooms**
On a: **Weekday,**
Peak Hour of Adjacent Street Traffic,
One Hour Between 4 and 6 p.m.

Number of Studies: 26
Average Number of Rooms: 161
Directional Distribution: 54% entering, 46% exiting

Trip Generation per Room

Average Rate	Range of Rates	Standard Deviation
0.47	0.10 - 1.69	0.72

Data Plot and Equation

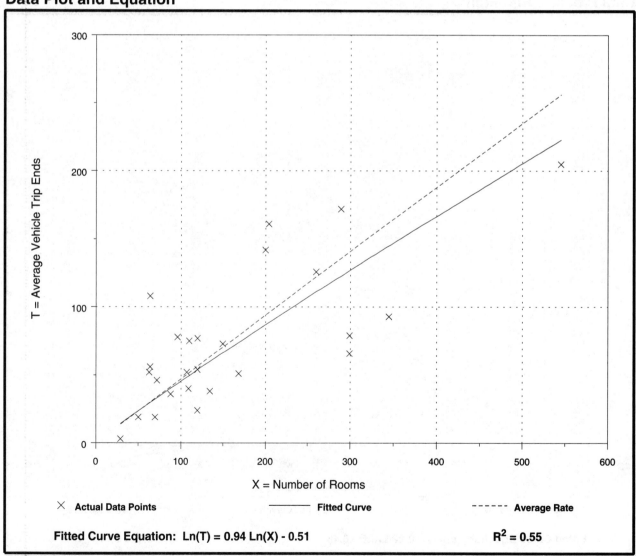

Fitted Curve Equation: $Ln(T) = 0.94\ Ln(X) - 0.51$ $\qquad$ $R^2 = 0.55$

Motel
(320)

Average Vehicle Trip Ends vs: Rooms
On a: Weekday,
A.M. Peak Hour of Generator

Number of Studies: 20
Average Number of Rooms: 171
Directional Distribution: 39% entering, 61% exiting

Trip Generation per Room

Average Rate	Range of Rates	Standard Deviation
0.44	0.18 - 1.33	0.69

Data Plot and Equation

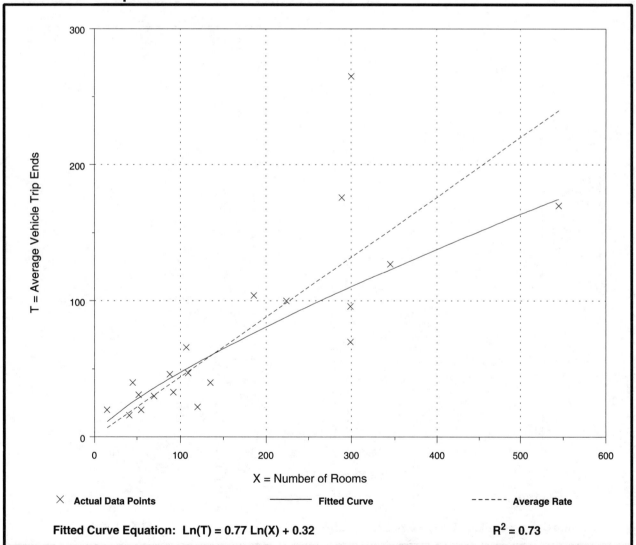

X = Number of Rooms

× **Actual Data Points**   —— **Fitted Curve**   - - - - - **Average Rate**

Fitted Curve Equation: Ln(T) = 0.77 Ln(X) + 0.32 $R^2 = 0.73$

Motel
(320)

Average Vehicle Trip Ends vs: Rooms
On a: Weekday,
P.M. Peak Hour of Generator

Number of Studies: 27
Average Number of Rooms: 165
Directional Distribution: 54% entering, 46% exiting

Trip Generation per Room

Average Rate	Range of Rates	Standard Deviation
0.56	0.24 - 1.83	0.81

Data Plot and Equation

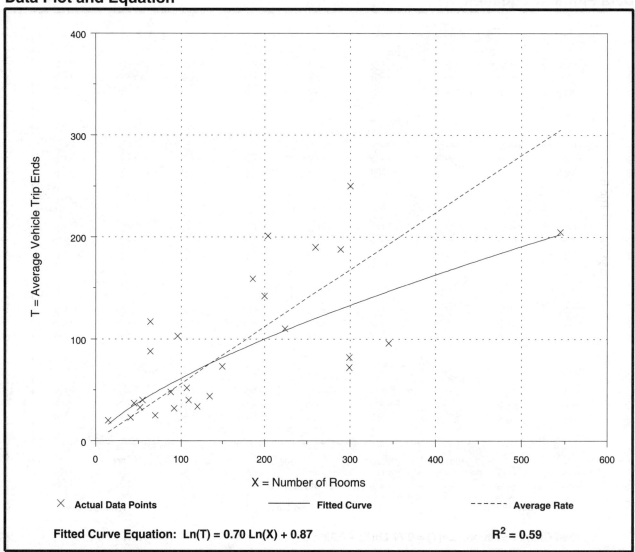

Fitted Curve Equation: Ln(T) = 0.70 Ln(X) + 0.87 $R^2 = 0.59$

Motel
(320)

Average Vehicle Trip Ends vs: Employees
On a: Weekday

Number of Studies: 10
Avg. Number of Employees: 101
Directional Distribution: 50% entering, 50% exiting

Trip Generation per Employee

Average Rate	Range of Rates	Standard Deviation
12.81	7.20 - 41.00	8.11

Data Plot and Equation

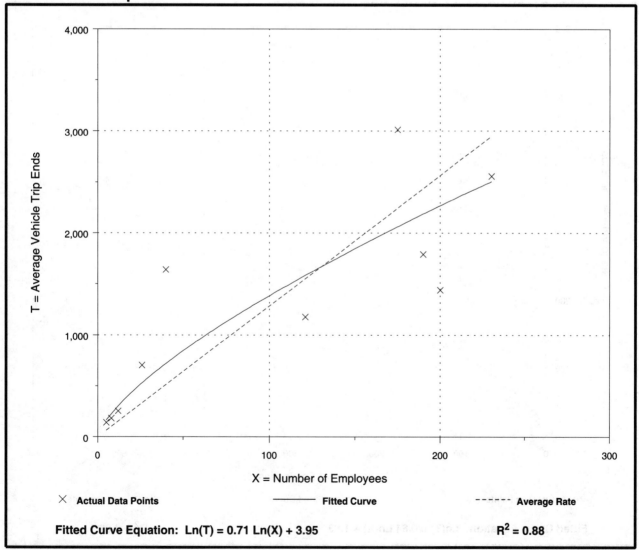

Fitted Curve Equation: Ln(T) = 0.71 Ln(X) + 3.95 $R^2 = 0.88$

Motel
(320)

Average Vehicle Trip Ends vs: Employees
On a: Weekday,
Peak Hour of Adjacent Street Traffic,
One Hour Between 7 and 9 a.m.

Number of Studies: 11
Avg. Number of Employees: 144
Directional Distribution: 54% entering, 46% exiting

Trip Generation per Employee

Average Rate	Range of Rates	Standard Deviation
0.91	0.60 - 3.30	1.12

Data Plot and Equation

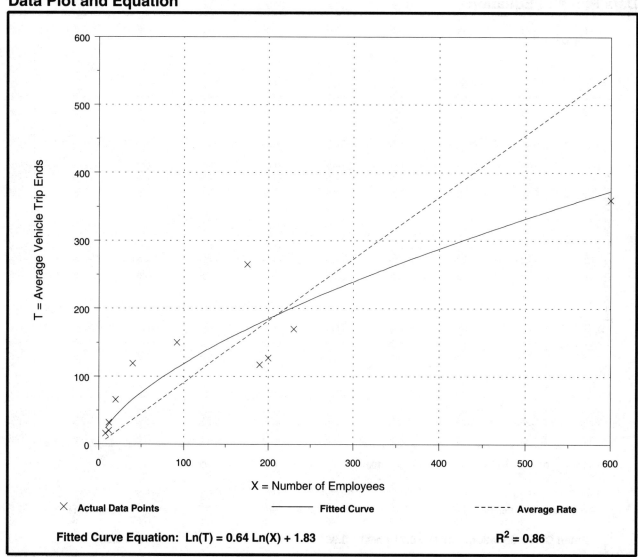

Fitted Curve Equation: Ln(T) = 0.64 Ln(X) + 1.83 $R^2 = 0.86$

Motel
(320)

Average Vehicle Trip Ends vs: Employees
On a: Weekday,
Peak Hour of Adjacent Street Traffic,
One Hour Between 4 and 6 p.m.

Number of Studies: 8
Avg. Number of Employees: 173
Directional Distribution: 54% entering, 46% exiting

Trip Generation per Employee

Average Rate	Range of Rates	Standard Deviation
0.73	0.40 - 3.00	1.02

Data Plot and Equation

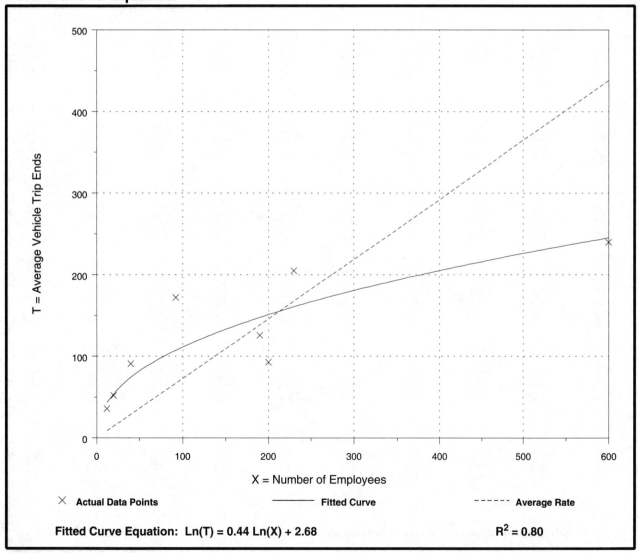

X Actual Data Points   —— Fitted Curve   ----- Average Rate

Fitted Curve Equation: Ln(T) = 0.44 Ln(X) + 2.68 $R^2 = 0.80$

Motel
(320)

Average Vehicle Trip Ends vs: Employees
On a: Weekday,
A.M. Peak Hour of Generator

Number of Studies: 13
Avg. Number of Employees: 87
Directional Distribution: 39% entering, 61% exiting

Trip Generation per Employee

Average Rate	Range of Rates	Standard Deviation
1.16	0.62 - 4.00	1.31

Data Plot and Equation

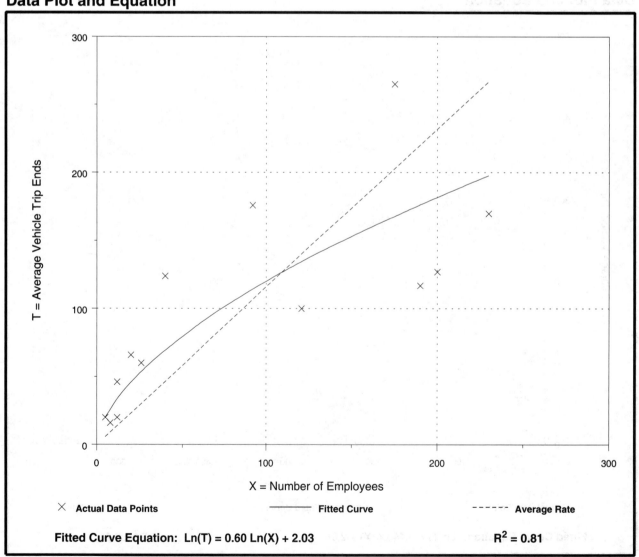

Fitted Curve Equation: $\text{Ln}(T) = 0.60\ \text{Ln}(X) + 2.03$ $R^2 = 0.81$

Motel
(320)

Average Vehicle Trip Ends vs: **Employees**
On a: **Weekday,**
P.M. Peak Hour of Generator

Number of Studies: 13
Avg. Number of Employees: 87
Directional Distribution: 59% entering, 41% exiting

Trip Generation per Employee

Average Rate	Range of Rates	Standard Deviation
1.24	0.48 - 4.00	1.37

Data Plot and Equation

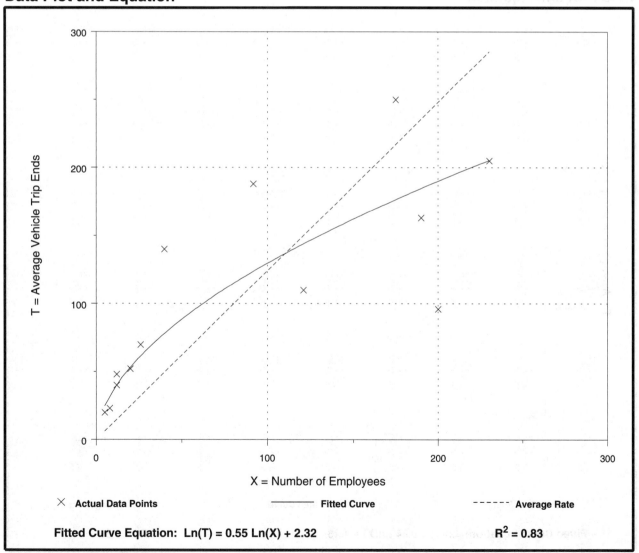

X   **Actual Data Points**   —— **Fitted Curve**   - - - - - **Average Rate**

Fitted Curve Equation: Ln(T) = 0.55 Ln(X) + 2.32 $R^2 = 0.83$

Motel
(320)

Average Vehicle Trip Ends vs: Employees
On a: Saturday

Number of Studies: 11
Avg. Number of Employees: 101
Directional Distribution: 50% entering, 50% exiting

Trip Generation per Employee

Average Rate	Range of Rates	Standard Deviation
12.40	5.90 - 33.33	7.22

Data Plot and Equation

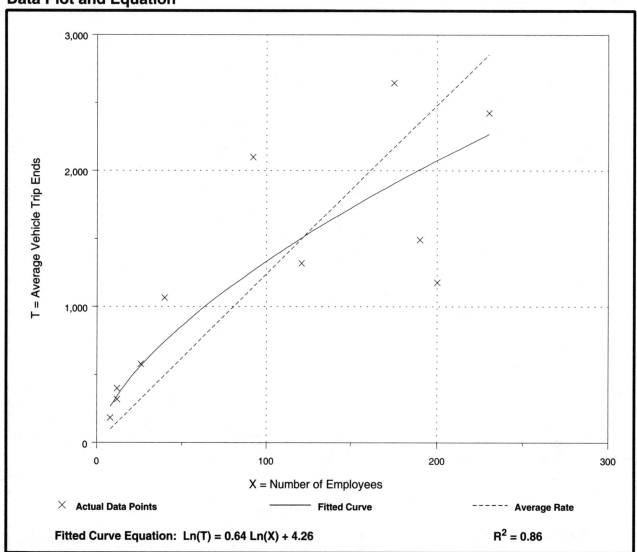

Fitted Curve Equation: Ln(T) = 0.64 Ln(X) + 4.26 $R^2 = 0.86$

Motel
(320)

Average Vehicle Trip Ends vs: Employees
On a: Saturday,
Peak Hour of Generator

Number of Studies: 11
Avg. Number of Employees: 101
Directional Distribution: 38% entering, 62% exiting

Trip Generation per Employee

Average Rate	Range of Rates	Standard Deviation
1.04	0.48 - 5.00	1.26

Data Plot and Equation

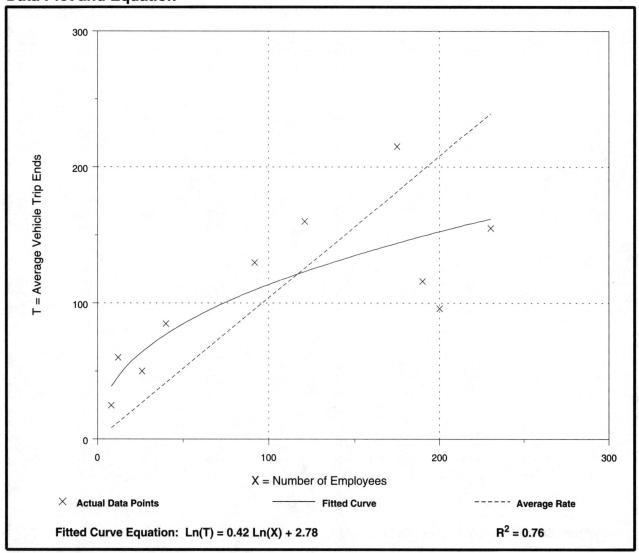

X = Number of Employees

$\times$ **Actual Data Points** — **Fitted Curve** ----- **Average Rate**

Fitted Curve Equation: Ln(T) = 0.42 Ln(X) + 2.78 $R^2 = 0.76$

Motel
(320)

Average Vehicle Trip Ends vs: Employees
On a: Sunday

Number of Studies: 11
Avg. Number of Employees: 101
Directional Distribution: 50% entering, 50% exiting

Trip Generation per Employee

Average Rate	Range of Rates	Standard Deviation
10.37	4.75 - 23.33	6.10

Data Plot and Equation

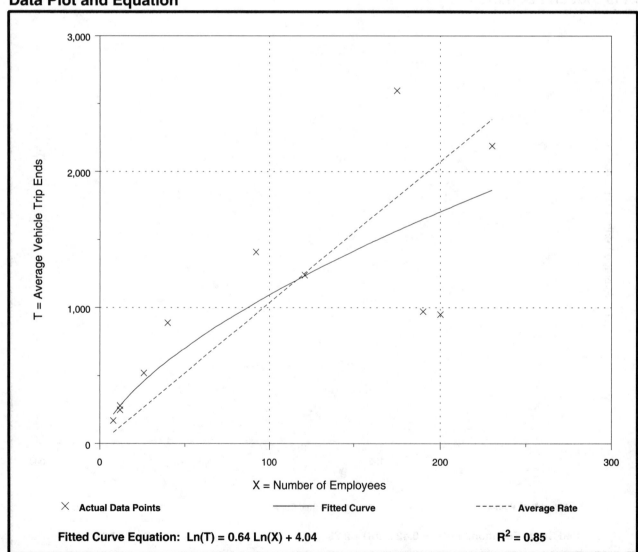

Fitted Curve Equation: Ln(T) = 0.64 Ln(X) + 4.04 $R^2 = 0.85$

Motel
(320)

Average Vehicle Trip Ends vs: Employees
On a: Sunday,
Peak Hour of Generator

Number of Studies: 11
Avg. Number of Employees: 101
Directional Distribution: 54% entering, 46% exiting

Trip Generation per Employee

Average Rate	Range of Rates	Standard Deviation
0.83	0.38 - 3.33	1.03

Data Plot and Equation

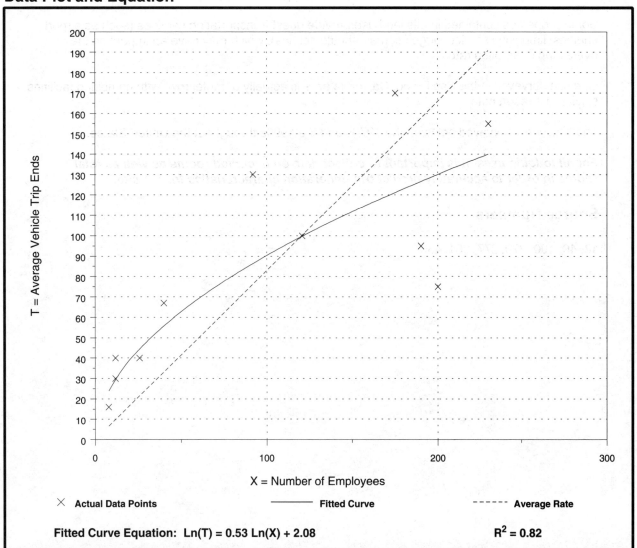

X   Actual Data Points   ——— Fitted Curve   - - - - Average Rate

Fitted Curve Equation: Ln(T) = 0.53 Ln(X) + 2.08 $R^2 = 0.82$

Land Use: 330
Resort Hotel

Description

Resort hotels are similar to hotels (Land Use 310) in that they provide sleeping accommodations, restaurants, cocktail lounges, retail shops and guest services. The primary difference is that resort hotels cater to the tourist and vacation industry, often providing a wide variety of recreational facilities/programs (golf courses, tennis courts, beach access, or other amenities) rather than convention and meeting business. Resort hotels are normally located in suburban or outlying locations on larger sites than conventional hotels. Hotel (Land Use 310), all suites hotel (Land Use 311), business hotel (Land Use 312) and motel (Land Use 320) are related uses.

Additional Data

Eleven studies provided information on occupancy rates at the time the studies were conducted. The average occupancy rate for these studies was approximately 82 percent.

Some properties contained in this land use provide guest transportation services (such as airport shuttles, limousine service, or golf course shuttle service), which may have an impact on the overall trip generation rates.

One site surveyed in the San Diego, California area is actually a "motel row" with combined facilities similar to a resort hotel.

The sites were surveyed between the 1970s and the 1990s throughout the United States.

For all lodging uses, it is important to collect data on occupied rooms as well as total rooms in order to accurately predict trip generation characteristics for the site.

Source Numbers

18, 40, 100, 270, 277, 381, 436

Land Use: 330
Resort Hotel
Independent Variables with One Observation

The following trip generation data are for independent variables with only one observation. This information is shown in this table only; there are no related plots for these data.

Users are cautioned to use data with care because of the small sample size.

Independent Variable	Trip Generation Rate	Size of Independent Variable	Number of Studies	Directional Distribution
Occupied Rooms				
Saturday	13.43	273	1	50% entering, 50% exiting
Saturday Peak Hour of Generator	1.23	273	1	Not available
Sunday	10.09	273	1	50% entering, 50% exiting
Employees				
Saturday	13.58	270	1	50% entering, 50% exiting
Saturday Peak Hour of Generator	1.25	270	1	Not available
Sunday	10.20	270	1	50% entering, 50% exiting

Resort Hotel
(330)

Average Vehicle Trip Ends vs: **Occupied Rooms**
On a: **Weekday,**
Peak Hour of Adjacent Street Traffic,
One Hour Between 7 and 9 a.m.

Number of Studies: 7
Average Number of Occupied Rooms: 434
Directional Distribution: 72% entering, 28% exiting

Trip Generation per Occupied Room

Average Rate	Range of Rates	Standard Deviation
0.37	0.28 - 0.59	0.61

Data Plot and Equation

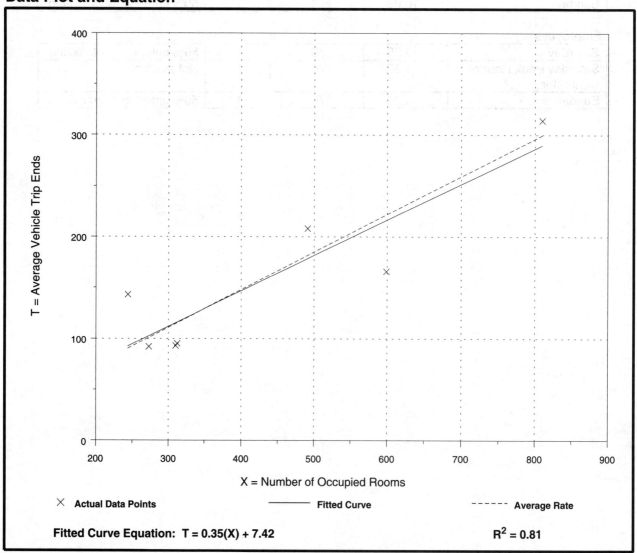

X Actual Data Points   **——— Fitted Curve**   **- - - - - Average Rate**

Fitted Curve Equation: T = 0.35(X) + 7.42   **$R^2 = 0.81$**

Resort Hotel
(330)

Average Vehicle Trip Ends vs: Occupied Rooms
On a: Weekday,
Peak Hour of Adjacent Street Traffic,
One Hour Between 4 and 6 p.m.

Number of Studies: 10
Average Number of Occupied Rooms: 429
Directional Distribution: 43% entering, 57% exiting

Trip Generation per Occupied Room

Average Rate	Range of Rates	Standard Deviation
0.49	0.27 - 0.72	0.70

Data Plot and Equation

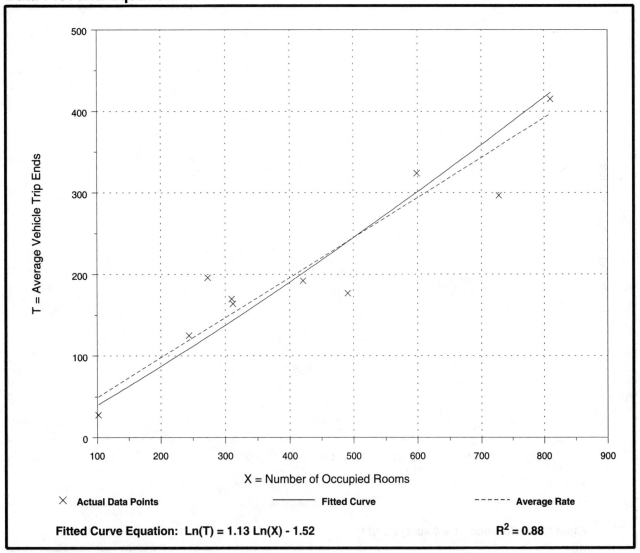

Fitted Curve Equation: $Ln(T) = 1.13 \, Ln(X) - 1.52$ $R^2 = 0.88$

Resort Hotel
(330)

Average Vehicle Trip Ends vs: Occupied Rooms
On a: Weekday,
A.M. Peak Hour of Generator

Number of Studies: 7
Average Number of Occupied Rooms: 434
Directional Distribution: 63% entering, 37% exiting

Trip Generation per Occupied Room

Average Rate	Range of Rates	Standard Deviation
0.47	0.34 - 0.67	0.70

Data Plot and Equation

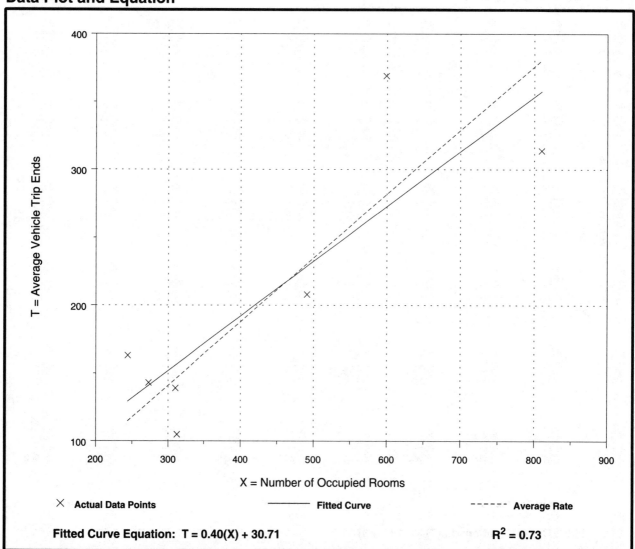

X = Number of Occupied Rooms

| × Actual Data Points | —— Fitted Curve | - - - - - Average Rate |

Fitted Curve Equation: T = 0.40(X) + 30.71　　　　　　　$R^2 = 0.73$

Resort Hotel
(330)

Average Vehicle Trip Ends vs: Occupied Rooms
On a: Weekday,
P.M. Peak Hour of Generator

Number of Studies: 7
Average Number of Occupied Rooms: 434
Directional Distribution: 50% entering, 50% exiting

Trip Generation per Occupied Room

Average Rate	Range of Rates	Standard Deviation
0.59	0.36 - 1.06	0.79

Data Plot and Equation

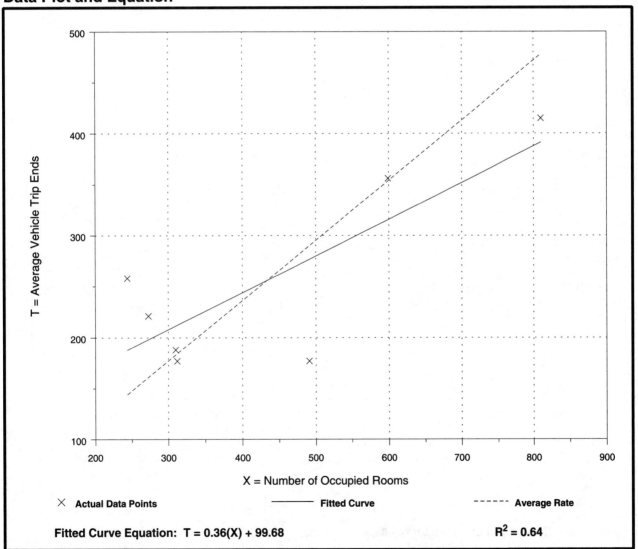

X   Actual Data Points   ———— Fitted Curve   - - - - - Average Rate

Fitted Curve Equation: T = 0.36(X) + 99.68 $R^2 = 0.64$

Resort Hotel
(330)

Average Vehicle Trip Ends vs: **Employees**
On a: **Weekday,**
Peak Hour of Adjacent Street Traffic,
One Hour Between 7 and 9 a.m.

Number of Studies: 4
Avg. Number of Employees: 818
Directional Distribution: 69% entering, 31% exiting

Trip Generation per Employee

Average Rate	Range of Rates	Standard Deviation
0.15	0.11 - 0.34	0.39

Data Plot and Equation

Caution - Use Carefully - Small Sample Size

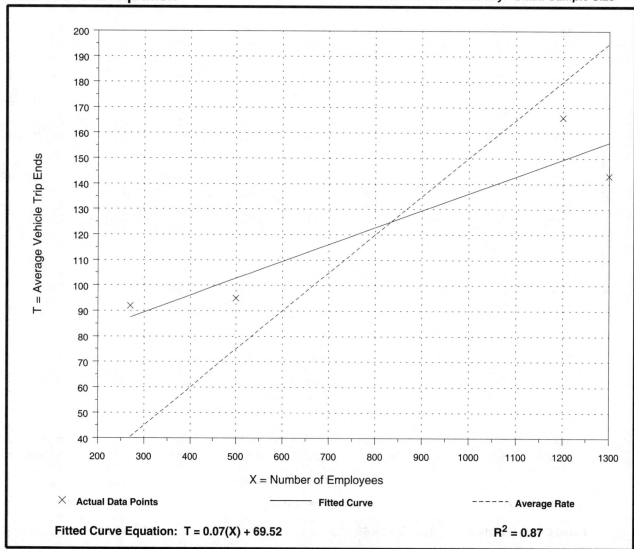

X = Number of Employees

X **Actual Data Points**   ——— **Fitted Curve**   - - - - - **Average Rate**

Fitted Curve Equation: T = 0.07(X) + 69.52 $R^2 = 0.87$

Resort Hotel
(330)

Average Vehicle Trip Ends vs: **Employees**
On a: **Weekday,**
Peak Hour of Adjacent Street Traffic,
One Hour Between 4 and 6 p.m.

Number of Studies: 4
Avg. Number of Employees: 818
Directional Distribution: 40% entering, 60% exiting

Trip Generation per Employee

Average Rate	Range of Rates	Standard Deviation
0.25	0.10 - 0.73	0.53

Data Plot and Equation

Caution - Use Carefully - Small Sample Size

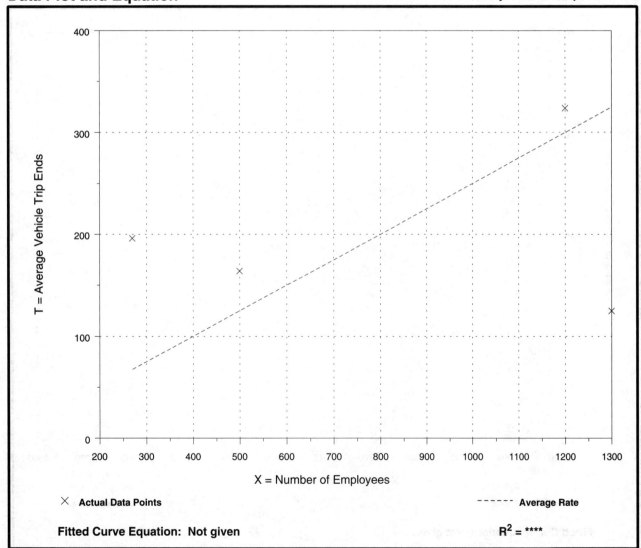

X **Actual Data Points**

- - - - - **Average Rate**

Fitted Curve Equation: Not given $R^2 = ****$

Resort Hotel
(330)

Average Vehicle Trip Ends vs: Employees
On a: Weekday,
A.M. Peak Hour of Generator

Number of Studies: 4
Avg. Number of Employees: 818
Directional Distribution: 58% entering, 42% exiting

Trip Generation per Employee

Average Rate	Range of Rates	Standard Deviation
0.24	0.13 - 0.53	0.50

Data Plot and Equation

Caution - Use Carefully - Small Sample Size

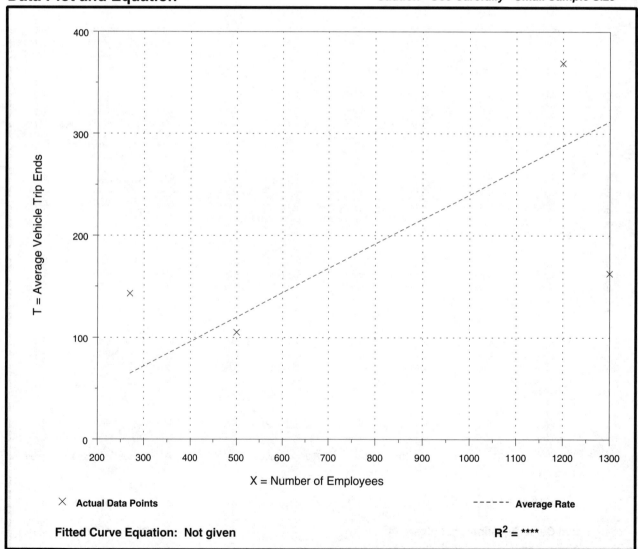

X **Actual Data Points**

------ **Average Rate**

Fitted Curve Equation: Not given

$R^2 = ****$

Resort Hotel
(330)

Average Vehicle Trip Ends vs: Employees
On a: Weekday,
P.M. Peak Hour of Generator

Number of Studies: 4
Avg. Number of Employees: 818
Directional Distribution: 51% entering, 49% exiting

Trip Generation per Employee

Average Rate	Range of Rates	Standard Deviation
0.31	0.20 - 0.82	0.58

Data Plot and Equation

Caution - Use Carefully - Small Sample Size

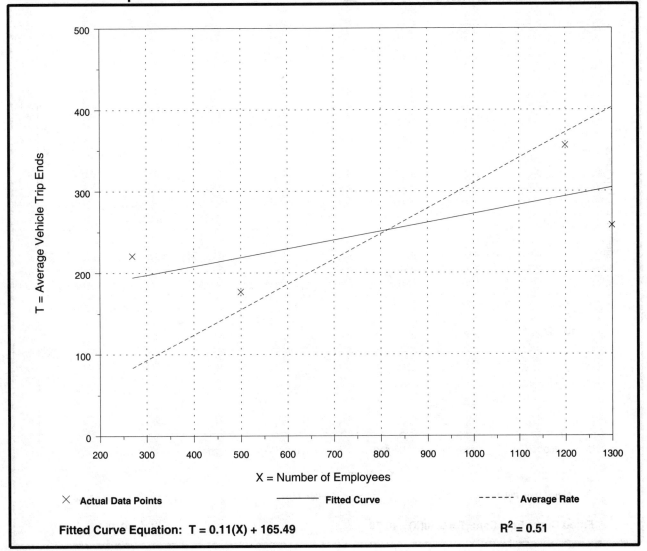

X = Number of Employees

✕ **Actual Data Points** ——— **Fitted Curve** ----- **Average Rate**

Fitted Curve Equation: T = 0.11(X) + 165.49 $R^2 = 0.51$

Resort Hotel
(330)

Average Vehicle Trip Ends vs: **Rooms**
On a: **Weekday,**
Peak Hour of Adjacent Street Traffic,
One Hour Between 7 and 9 a.m.

Number of Studies: 7
Average Number of Rooms: 504
Directional Distribution: 72% entering, 28% exiting

Trip Generation per Room

Average Rate	Range of Rates	Standard Deviation
0.31	0.24 - 0.41	0.57

Data Plot and Equation

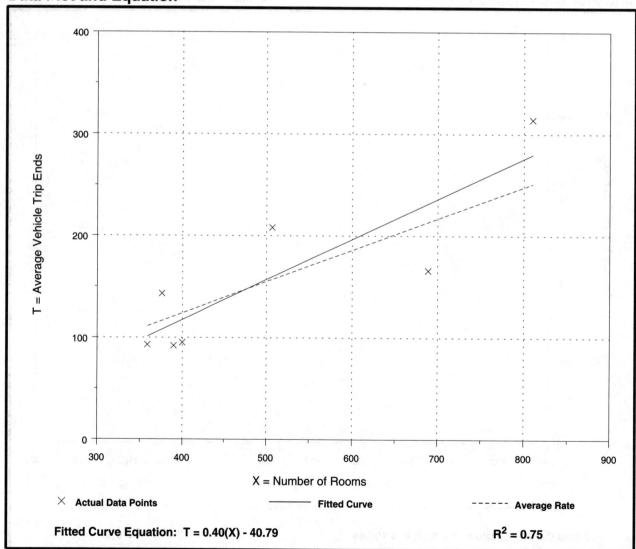

Fitted Curve Equation: T = 0.40(X) - 40.79 $R^2 = 0.75$

Resort Hotel
(330)

Average Vehicle Trip Ends vs: **Rooms**
On a: **Weekday,**
Peak Hour of Adjacent Street Traffic,
One Hour Between 4 and 6 p.m.

Number of Studies: 10
Average Number of Rooms: 495
Directional Distribution: 43% entering, 57% exiting

Trip Generation per Room

Average Rate	Range of Rates	Standard Deviation
0.42	0.19 - 0.51	0.65

Data Plot and Equation

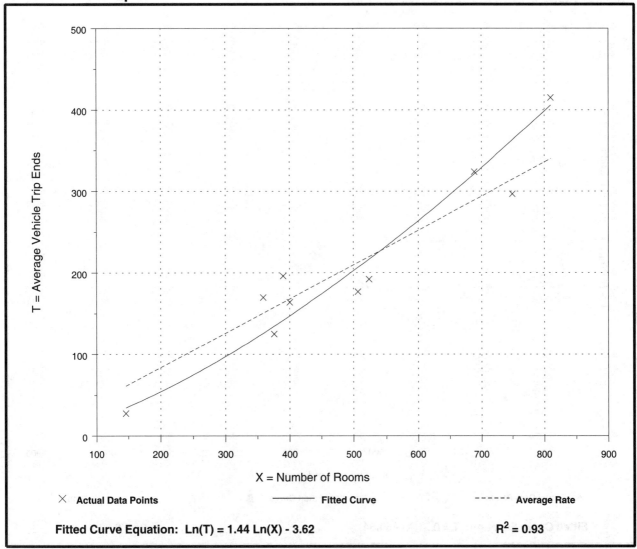

X Actual Data Points   —— Fitted Curve   ----- Average Rate

Fitted Curve Equation: Ln(T) = 1.44 Ln(X) - 3.62 $R^2 = 0.93$

Resort Hotel
(330)

Average Vehicle Trip Ends vs: **Rooms**
On a: **Weekday,**
A.M. Peak Hour of Generator

Number of Studies: 7
Average Number of Rooms: 504
Directional Distribution: 63% entering, 37% exiting

Trip Generation per Room

Average Rate	Range of Rates	Standard Deviation
0.41	0.26 - 0.54	0.64

Data Plot and Equation

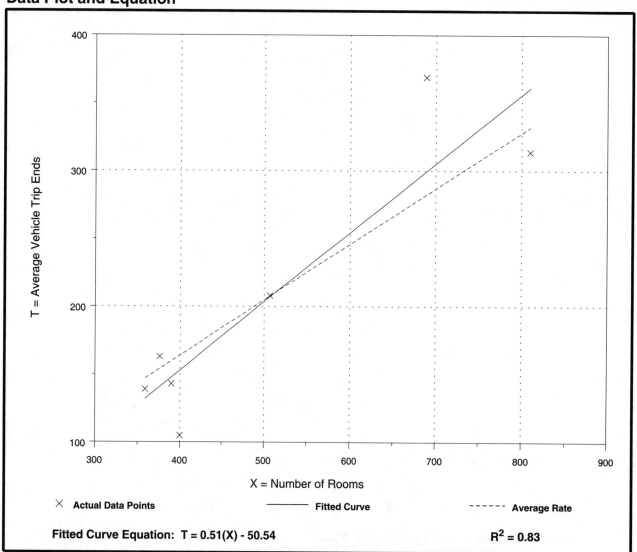

Fitted Curve Equation: T = 0.51(X) - 50.54 $R^2 = 0.83$

Resort Hotel
(330)

Average Vehicle Trip Ends vs: Rooms
On a: Weekday,
P.M. Peak Hour of Generator

Number of Studies: 7
Average Number of Rooms: 504
Directional Distribution: 50% entering, 50% exiting

Trip Generation per Room

Average Rate	Range of Rates	Standard Deviation
0.51	0.35 - 0.69	0.72

Data Plot and Equation

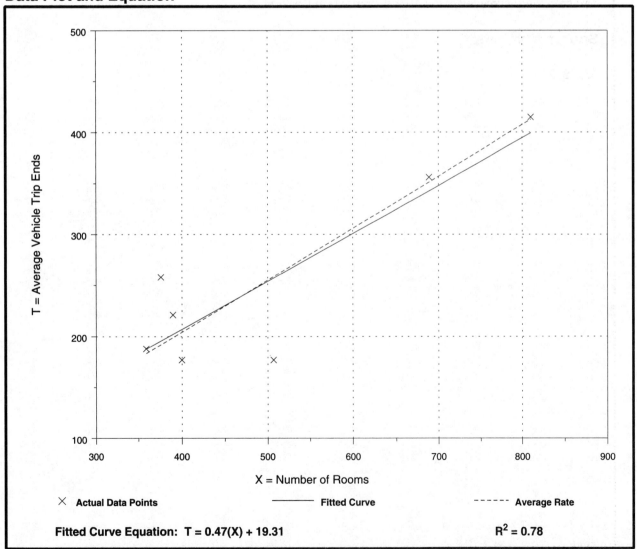

Fitted Curve Equation: T = 0.47(X) + 19.31 $R^2 = 0.78$

Land Use: 411
City Park

Description

City parks are owned and operated by a city. The city parks surveyed vary widely as to location, type and number of facilities, including boating or swimming facilities, ball fields, camp sites and picnic facilities. Seasonal use of the individual sites differs widely as a result of the varying facilities and local conditions, such as weather. For example, some of the sites are used primarily for boating or swimming; others are used for softball games.

Additional Data

The percentage of the park area that is used most intensively varies considerably within the studies contained in this land use; therefore, caution should be used when using acres as an independent variable.

The sites were surveyed in the 1970s, primarily in California.

Source Numbers

13, 18, 214

Land Use: 411
City Park
Independent Variables with One Observation

The following trip generation data are for independent variables with only one observation. This information is shown in this table only; there are no related plots for these data.

Users are cautioned to use data with care because of the small sample size.

Independent Variable	Trip Generation Rate	Size of Independent Variable	Number of Studies	Directional Distribution
Acres				
Sunday	16.00	15	1	50% entering, 50% exiting

City Park
(411)

Average Vehicle Trip Ends vs: Acres
On a: Weekday

Number of Studies: 3
Average Number of Acres: 142
Directional Distribution: 50% entering, 50% exiting

Trip Generation per Acre

Average Rate	Range of Rates	Standard Deviation
1.59	1.04 - 8.00	1.79

Data Plot and Equation

Caution - Use Carefully - Small Sample Size

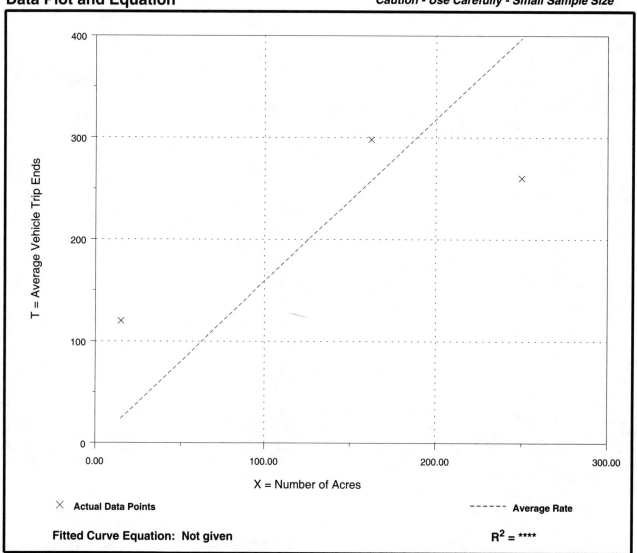

Fitted Curve Equation: Not given

$R^2 = ****$

City Park
(411)

Average Vehicle Trip Ends vs: Picnic Sites
On a: Weekday

Number of Studies: 2
Average Number of Picnic Sites: 48
Directional Distribution: 50% entering, 50% exiting

Trip Generation per Picnic Site

Average Rate	Range of Rates	Standard Deviation
5.87	4.58 - 8.67	*

Data Plot and Equation

Caution - Use Carefully - Small Sample Size

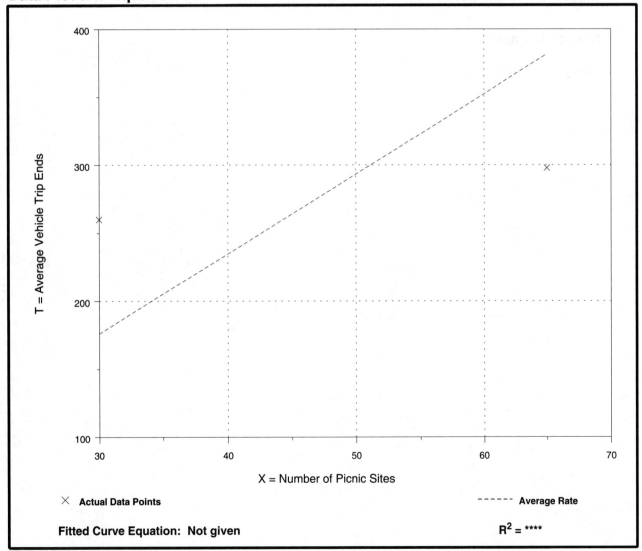

X **Actual Data Points**

- - - - - **Average Rate**

Fitted Curve Equation: Not given

$R^2 = ****$

Land Use: 412
County Park

Description

County parks are owned and operated by a county. The county parks surveyed vary widely as to location, type and number of facilities, including boating or swimming facilities, ball fields, camp sites, picnic facilities and general open space. Seasonal use of the individual sites differs widely as a result of the varying facilities and local conditions, such as weather. For example, some of the sites are used primarily for boating or swimming; others are used for softball games.

Additional Data

The percentage of the park area that is used most intensively varies considerably among the studies contained in this land use; therefore, caution should be used when using acres as an independent variable.

The sites were surveyed between the 1970s and the 1990s in New Jersey and California.

Source Numbers

13, 18, 186, 213, 407

County Park
(412)

Average Vehicle Trip Ends vs: **Acres**
On a: **Weekday**

Number of Studies: 22
Average Number of Acres: 349
Directional Distribution: 50% entering, 50% exiting

Trip Generation per Acre

Average Rate	Range of Rates	Standard Deviation
2.28	0.17 - 53.41	7.04

Data Plot and Equation

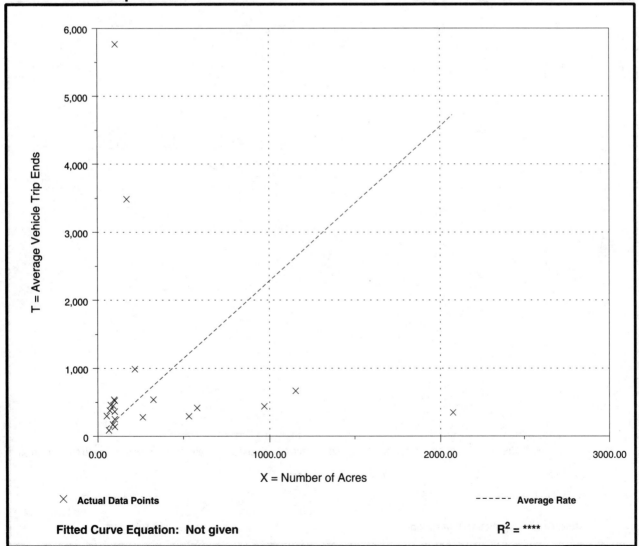

X Actual Data Points

------ Average Rate

Fitted Curve Equation: Not given

$R^2 = ****$

County Park
(412)

Average Vehicle Trip Ends vs: Acres
On a: Weekday,
Peak Hour of Adjacent Street Traffic,
One Hour Between 7 and 9 a.m.

Number of Studies: 3
Average Number of Acres: 650
Directional Distribution: 80% entering, 20% exiting

Trip Generation per Acre

Average Rate	Range of Rates	Standard Deviation
0.01	0.00 - 0.02	0.10

Data Plot and Equation

Caution - Use Carefully - Small Sample Size

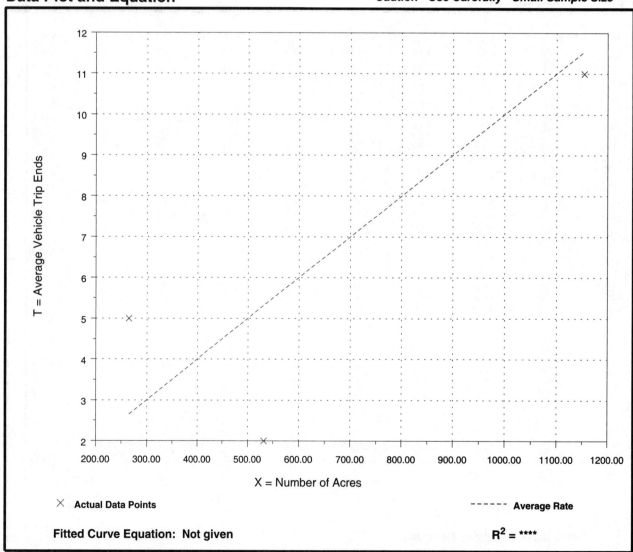

X   **Actual Data Points**   - - - - - **Average Rate**

Fitted Curve Equation: Not given $R^2 = ****$

County Park
(412)

Average Vehicle Trip Ends vs: **Acres**
On a: **Weekday,**
Peak Hour of Adjacent Street Traffic,
One Hour Between 4 and 6 p.m.

Number of Studies: 3
Average Number of Acres: 650
Directional Distribution: 41% entering, 59% exiting

Trip Generation per Acre

Average Rate	Range of Rates	Standard Deviation
0.06	0.05 - 0.08	0.25

Data Plot and Equation

Caution - Use Carefully - Small Sample Size

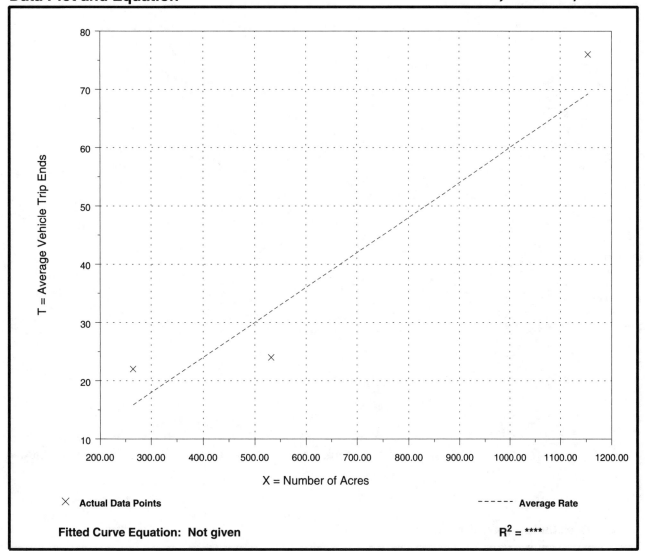

X **Actual Data Points** ----- **Average Rate**

Fitted Curve Equation: Not given $R^2 = ****$

County Park
(412)

Average Vehicle Trip Ends vs: **Acres**
On a: **Weekday,**
A.M. Peak Hour of Generator

Number of Studies: 7
Average Number of Acres: 335
Directional Distribution: 71% entering, 29% exiting

Trip Generation per Acre

Average Rate	Range of Rates	Standard Deviation
0.52	0.05 - 22.29	1.89

Data Plot and Equation

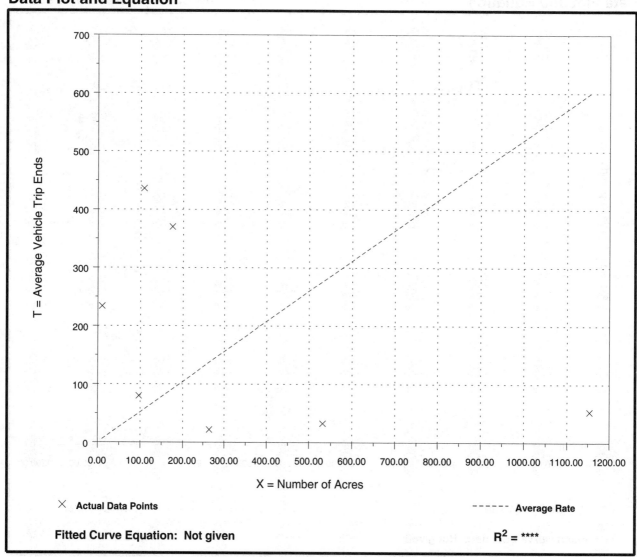

Fitted Curve Equation: **Not given** $R^2 = ****$

County Park
(412)

Average Vehicle Trip Ends vs: **Acres**
On a: **Weekday,**
P.M. Peak Hour of Generator

Number of Studies: 6
Average Number of Acres: 389
Directional Distribution: 35% entering, 65% exiting

Trip Generation per Acre

Average Rate	Range of Rates	Standard Deviation
0.59	0.08 - 5.30	1.50

Data Plot and Equation

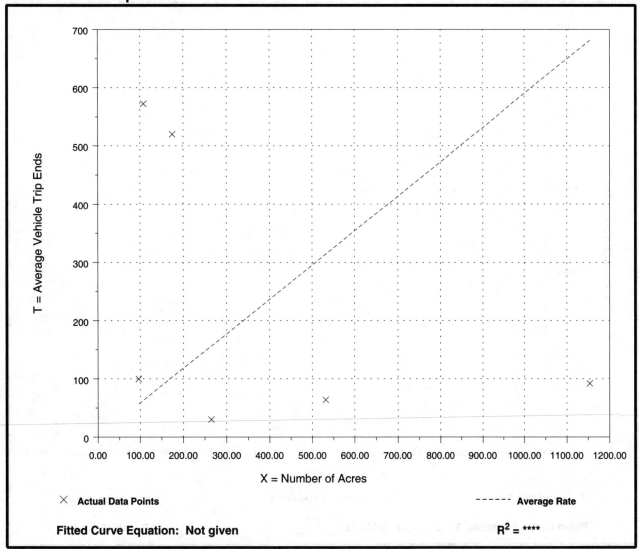

X = Number of Acres

✕ **Actual Data Points** - - - - - **Average Rate**

Fitted Curve Equation: Not given $R^2 = ****$

County Park
(412)

Average Vehicle Trip Ends vs: Acres
On a: Saturday

Number of Studies: 6
Average Number of Acres: 101
Directional Distribution: 50% entering, 50% exiting

Trip Generation per Acre

Average Rate	Range of Rates	Standard Deviation
12.14	4.04 - 24.74	9.63

Data Plot and Equation

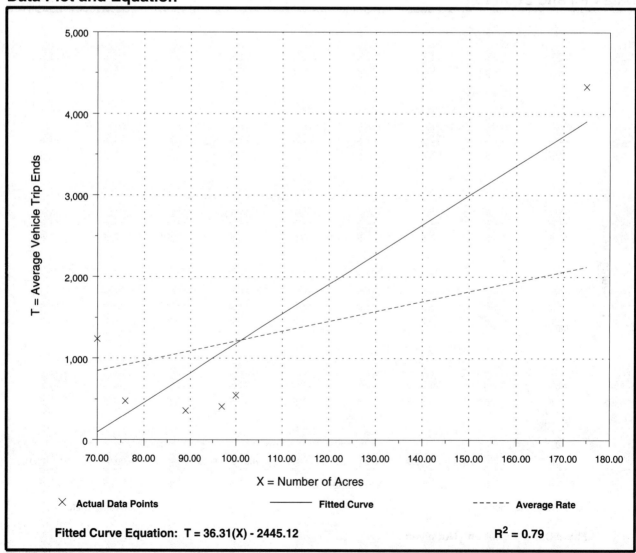

Fitted Curve Equation: T = 36.31(X) - 2445.12 $R^2 = 0.79$

County Park
(412)

Average Vehicle Trip Ends vs: Acres
On a: Saturday,
Peak Hour of Generator

Number of Studies: 2
Average Number of Acres: 136
Directional Distribution: 59% entering, 41% exiting

Trip Generation per Acre

Average Rate	Range of Rates	Standard Deviation
2.24	0.52 - 3.20	*

Data Plot and Equation

Caution - Use Carefully - Small Sample Size

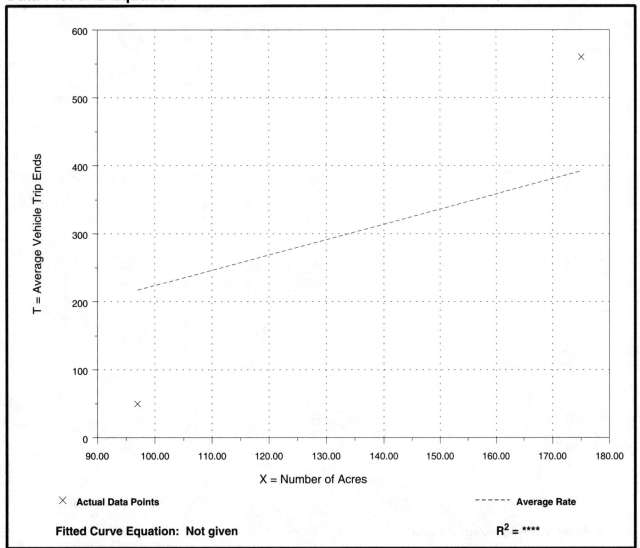

X **Actual Data Points**   - - - - - **Average Rate**

Fitted Curve Equation: Not given $R^2 = ****$

County Park
(412)

Average Vehicle Trip Ends vs: Acres
On a: Sunday

Number of Studies: 14
Average Number of Acres: 339
Directional Distribution: 50% entering, 50% exiting

Trip Generation per Acre

Average Rate	Range of Rates	Standard Deviation
4.13	0.32 - 38.46	8.07

Data Plot and Equation

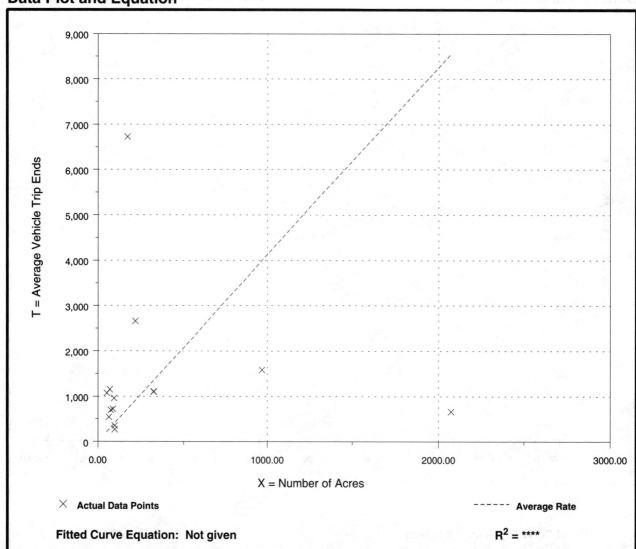

X **Actual Data Points**   - - - - - **Average Rate**

Fitted Curve Equation: Not given $R^2 =$ ****

County Park
(412)

Average Vehicle Trip Ends vs: **Acres**
On a: **Sunday,**
Peak Hour of Generator

Number of Studies: 2
Average Number of Acres: 136
Directional Distribution: 47% entering, 53% exiting

Trip Generation per Acre

Average Rate	Range of Rates	Standard Deviation
3.60	1.55 - 4.74	*

Data Plot and Equation

Caution - Use Carefully - Small Sample Size

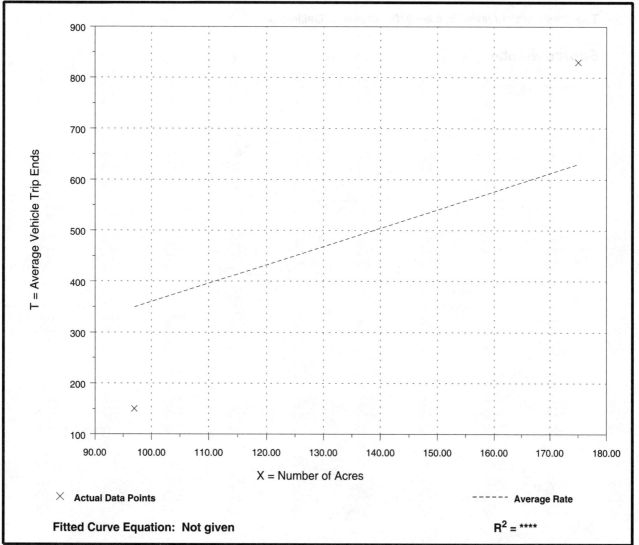

Fitted Curve Equation: Not given $R^2 = ****$

Land Use: 413
State Park

Description

State parks are owned and operated by a state. The state parks surveyed vary widely as to location, type and number of facilities, including beaches, hiking trails, boating or swimming facilities, ball fields, camp sites, picnic facilities and general open space. Seasonal use of the individual sites differs widely as a result of the varying facilities and local conditions, such as weather. For example, some of the sites are used primarily for boating or swimming; others are used for hiking or camping.

Additional Data

The percentage of the park area that is used most intensively varies considerably within the studies contained in this land use; therefore, caution should be used when using acres as an independent variable.

The sites were surveyed in the 1970s, mostly in California.

Source Numbers

11, 12, 13, 18, 213

Land Use: 413
State Park
Independent Variables with One Observation

The following trip generation data are for independent variables with only one observation. This information is shown in this table only; there are no related plots for these data.

Users are cautioned to use data with care because of the small sample size.

Independent Variable	Trip Generation Rate	Size of Independent Variable	Number of Studies	Directional Distribution
Picnic Sites				
Weekday p.m. Peak Hour of Adjacent Street Traffic	0.55	128	1	43% entering, 57% exiting
Employees				
Weekday p.m. Peak Hour of Adjacent Street Traffic	4.67	15	1	43% entering, 57% exiting

State Park
(413)

Average Vehicle Trip Ends vs: Acres
On a: Weekday

Number of Studies: 12
Average Number of Acres: 1,004
Directional Distribution: 50% entering, 50% exiting

Trip Generation per Acre

Average Rate	Range of Rates	Standard Deviation
0.65	0.05 - 183.33	3.36

Data Plot and Equation

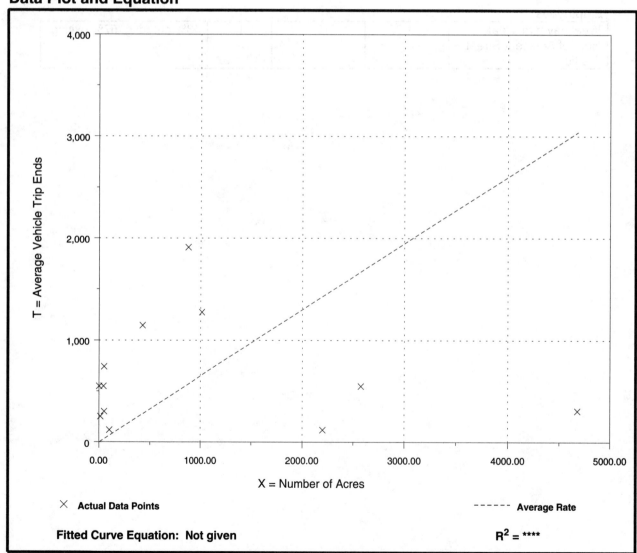

Fitted Curve Equation: Not given $R^2 = ****$

State Park
(413)

Average Vehicle Trip Ends vs: Acres
On a: Saturday

Number of Studies: 4
Average Number of Acres: 2,175
Directional Distribution: 50% entering, 50% exiting

Trip Generation per Acre

Average Rate	Range of Rates	Standard Deviation
0.61	0.10 - 2.94	1.26

Data Plot and Equation

Caution - Use Carefully - Small Sample Size

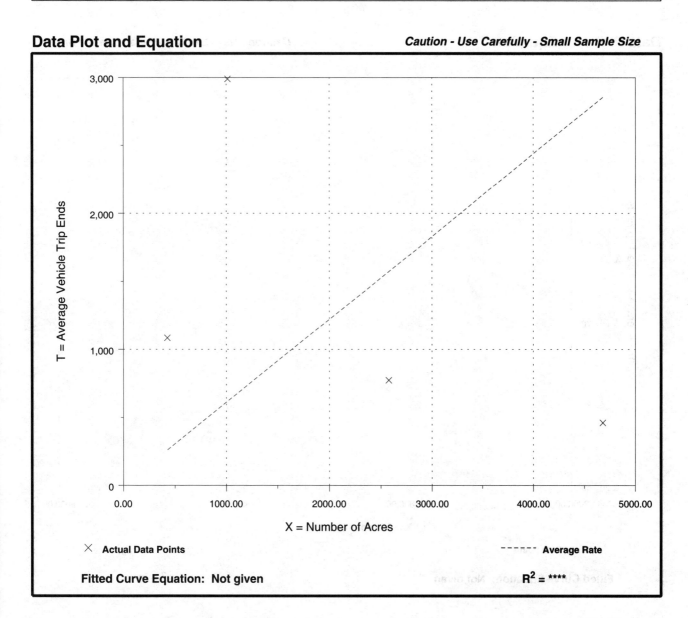

X   **Actual Data Points**

‑ ‑ ‑ ‑ ‑ **Average Rate**

Fitted Curve Equation: Not given

$R^2 = $ ****

State Park
(413)

Average Vehicle Trip Ends vs: Acres
On a: Saturday,
Peak Hour of Generator

Number of Studies: 2
Average Number of Acres: 3,628
Directional Distribution: 50% entering, 50% exiting

Trip Generation per Acre

Average Rate	Range of Rates	Standard Deviation
0.02	0.01 - 0.03	*

Data Plot and Equation

Caution - Use Carefully - Small Sample Size

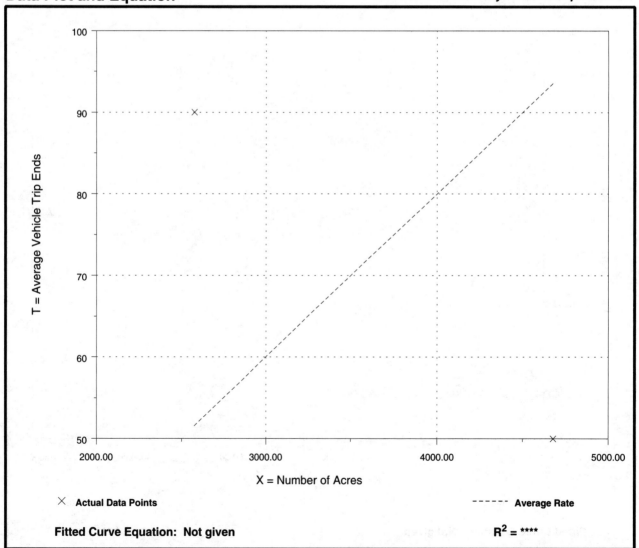

Fitted Curve Equation: Not given

$R^2 = ****$

State Park
(413)

Average Vehicle Trip Ends vs: Acres
On a: Sunday

Number of Studies: 11
Average Number of Acres: 1,015
Directional Distribution: 50% entering, 50% exiting

Trip Generation per Acre

Average Rate	Range of Rates	Standard Deviation
1.10	0.12 - 366.67	6.73

Data Plot and Equation

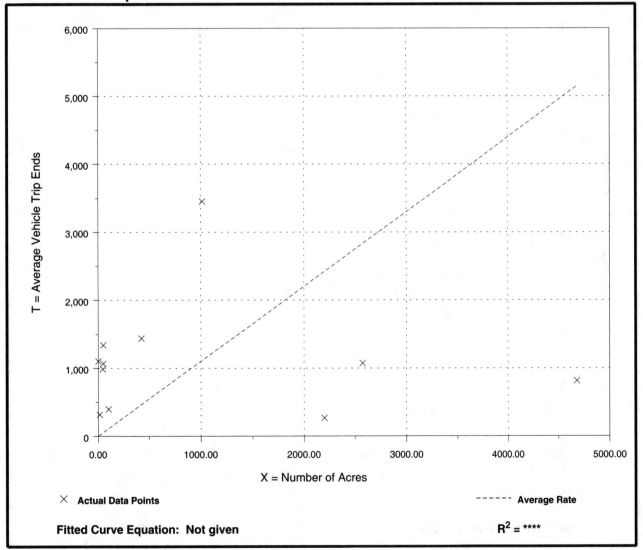

X = Number of Acres

× Actual Data Points   ----- Average Rate

Fitted Curve Equation: Not given R^2 = ****

State Park
(413)

Average Vehicle Trip Ends vs: **Acres**
On a: **Sunday,**
Peak Hour of Generator

Number of Studies: 2
Average Number of Acres: 3,628
Directional Distribution: 48% entering, 52% exiting

Trip Generation per Acre

Average Rate	Range of Rates	Standard Deviation
0.03	0.02 - 0.05	*

Data Plot and Equation

Caution - Use Carefully - Small Sample Size

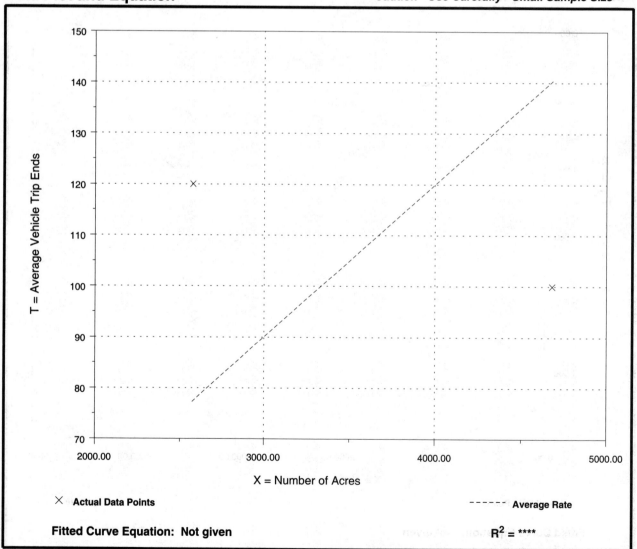

X **Actual Data Points**   - - - - - **Average Rate**

Fitted Curve Equation: Not given $R^2 = ****$

State Park
(413)

Average Vehicle Trip Ends vs: Picnic Sites
On a: Weekday

Number of Studies: 10
Average Number of Picnic Sites: 65
Directional Distribution: 50% entering, 50% exiting

Trip Generation per Picnic Site

Average Rate	Range of Rates	Standard Deviation
9.95	2.95 - 55.00	11.07

Data Plot and Equation

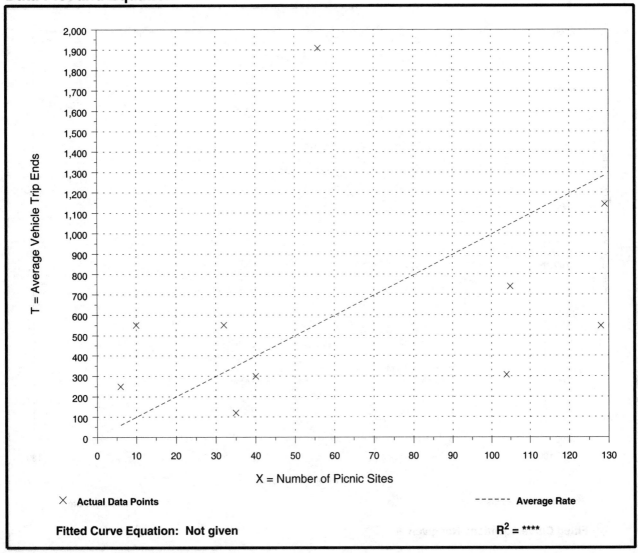

X **Actual Data Points**

- - - - - **Average Rate**

Fitted Curve Equation: Not given

$R^2 = ****$

State Park
(413)

Average Vehicle Trip Ends vs: Picnic Sites
On a: Saturday

Number of Studies: 3
Average Number of Picnic Sites: 120
Directional Distribution: 50% entering, 50% exiting

Trip Generation per Picnic Site

Average Rate	Range of Rates	Standard Deviation
6.42	4.42 - 8.41	3.00

Data Plot and Equation

Caution - Use Carefully - Small Sample Size

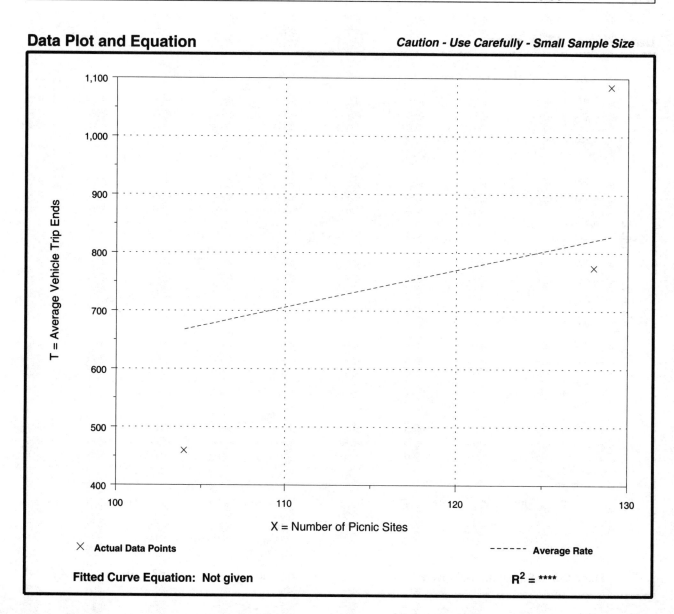

X **Actual Data Points**   - - - - - **Average Rate**

Fitted Curve Equation: Not given $R^2 = ****$

State Park
(413)

Average Vehicle Trip Ends vs: **Picnic Sites**
On a: **Saturday,**
Peak Hour of Generator

Number of Studies: 2
Average Number of Picnic Sites: 116
Directional Distribution: 50% entering, 50% exiting

Trip Generation per Picnic Site

Average Rate	Range of Rates	Standard Deviation
0.60	0.48 - 0.70	*

Data Plot and Equation

Caution - Use Carefully - Small Sample Size

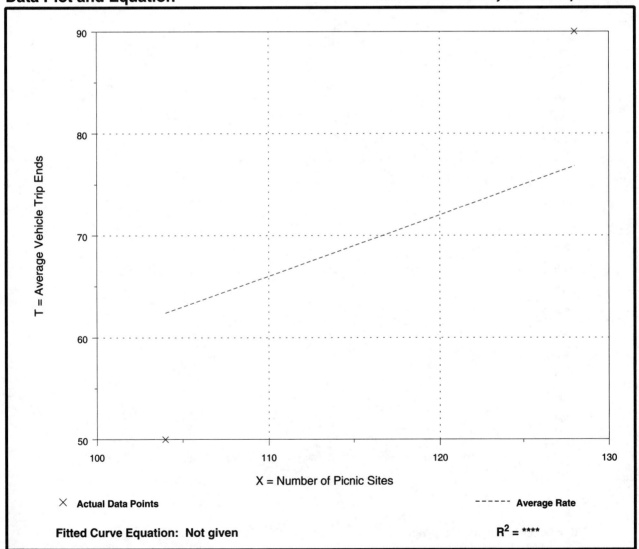

X **Actual Data Points**   - - - - - **Average Rate**

Fitted Curve Equation: Not given $R^2 = ****$

State Park
(413)

Average Vehicle Trip Ends vs: Picnic Sites
On a: Sunday

Number of Studies: 9
Average Number of Picnic Sites: 65
Directional Distribution: 50% entering, 50% exiting

Trip Generation per Picnic Site

Average Rate	Range of Rates	Standard Deviation
14.51	7.83 - 110.00	15.13

Data Plot and Equation

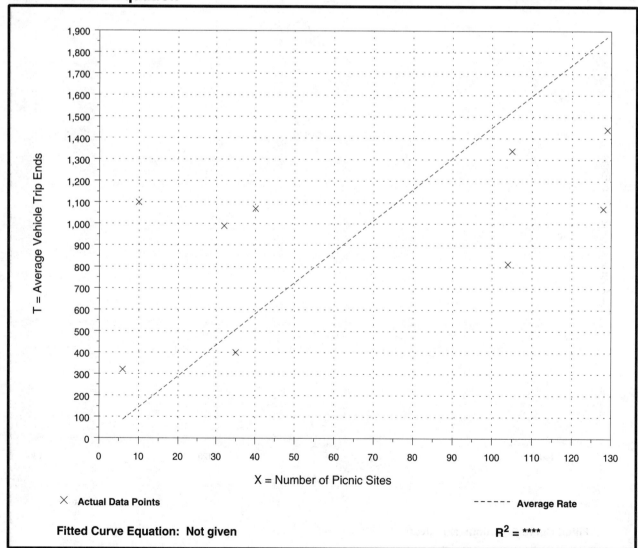

Fitted Curve Equation: Not given $R^2 = ****$

State Park
(413)

Average Vehicle Trip Ends vs: Picnic Sites
On a: Sunday,
Peak Hour of Generator

Number of Studies: 2
Average Number of Picnic Sites: 116
Directional Distribution: 48% entering, 52% exiting

Trip Generation per Picnic Site

Average Rate	Range of Rates	Standard Deviation
0.95	0.94 - 0.96	*

Data Plot and Equation

Caution - Use Carefully - Small Sample Size

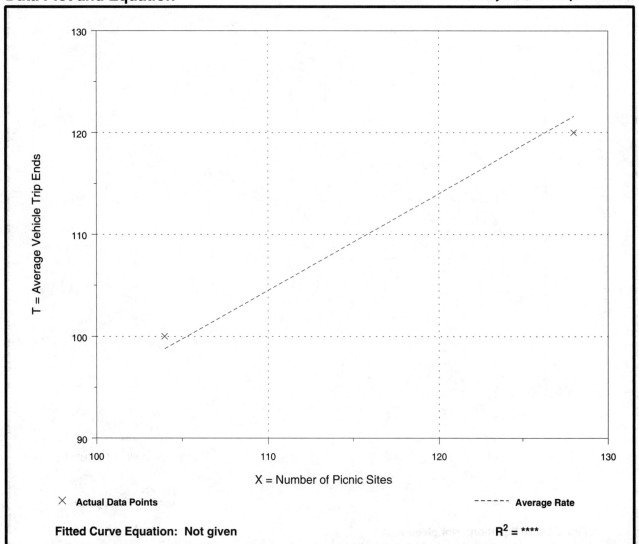

X **Actual Data Points**   - - - - - **Average Rate**

Fitted Curve Equation: Not given $R^2 =$ ****

State Park
(413)

Average Vehicle Trip Ends vs: Employees
On a: Saturday

Number of Studies: 2
Avg. Number of Employees: 15
Directional Distribution: 50% entering, 50% exiting

Trip Generation per Employee

Average Rate	Range of Rates	Standard Deviation
42.55	32.86 - 51.60	*

Data Plot and Equation

Caution - Use Carefully - Small Sample Size

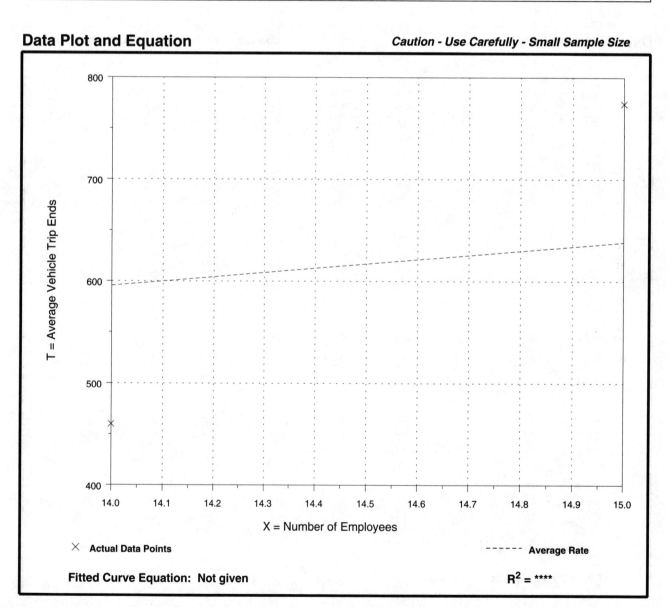

X = Number of Employees

✕ **Actual Data Points**   - - - - - **Average Rate**

Fitted Curve Equation: Not given $R^2 = ****$

State Park
(413)

Average Vehicle Trip Ends vs: Employees
On a: Saturday,
Peak Hour of Generator

Number of Studies: 2
Avg. Number of Employees: 15
Directional Distribution: 50% entering, 50% exiting

Trip Generation per Employee

Average Rate	Range of Rates	Standard Deviation
4.83	3.57 - 6.00	*

Data Plot and Equation

Caution - Use Carefully - Small Sample Size

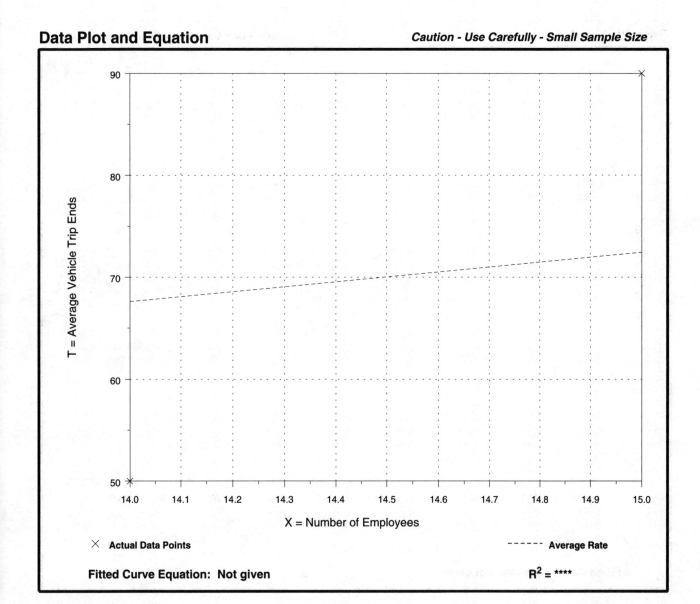

X **Actual Data Points**   ----- **Average Rate**

Fitted Curve Equation: Not given $R^2 = ****$

State Park
(413)

Average Vehicle Trip Ends vs: **Employees**
On a: **Sunday,**
Peak Hour of Generator

Number of Studies: 2
Avg. Number of Employees: 15
Directional Distribution: 48% entering, 52% exiting

Trip Generation per Employee

Average Rate	Range of Rates	Standard Deviation
7.59	7.14 - 8.00	*

Data Plot and Equation

Caution - Use Carefully - Small Sample Size

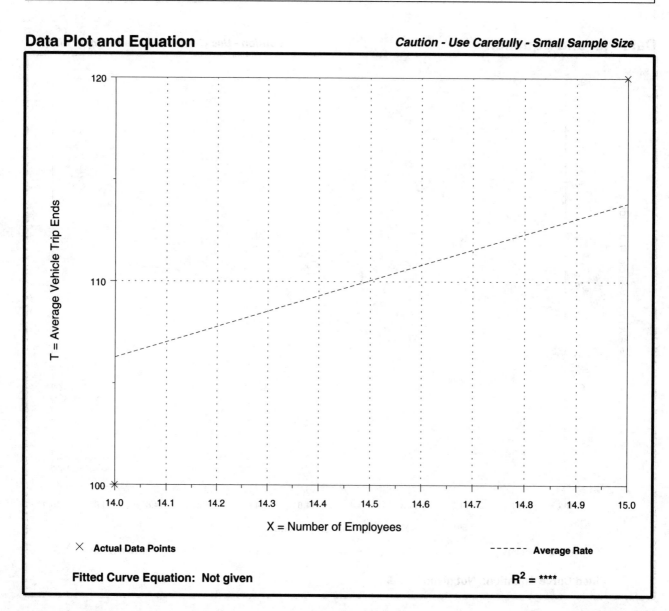

X **Actual Data Points**   ----- **Average Rate**

Fitted Curve Equation: Not given $R^2 = ****$

Land Use: 414
Water Slide Park

Description

Water slide parks contain water slides, wading pools, refreshment stands and picnic areas.

Additional Data

One site was surveyed in 1982 in Idaho with hours of operation between 10:00 a.m. and 9:00 p.m. Parking for this site was available for 299 vehicles. The other site was surveyed in 1999 in New Hampshire and had parking available for 1,500 vehicles.

Source Numbers

206, 617

Land Use: 414
Water Slide Park
Independent Variables with One Observation

The following trip generation data are for independent variables with only one observation. This information is shown in this table only; there are no related plots for these data.

Users are cautioned to use data with care because of the small sample size.

Independent Variable	Trip Generation Rate	Size of Independent Variable	Number of Studies	Directional Distribution
Parking Spaces				
Weekday a.m. Peak Hour of Adjacent Street Traffic	0.08	1500	1	70% entering, 30% exiting
Weekday p.m. Peak Hour of Adjacent Street Traffic	0.28	1500	1	21% entering, 79% exiting
Weekday a.m. Peak Hour of Generator	0.25	1500	1	89% entering, 11% exiting
Weekday p.m. Peak Hour of Generator	0.28	1500	1	21% entering, 79% exiting
Saturday	2.91	1500	1	50% entering, 50% exiting
Saturday Peak Hour of Generator	0.39	1500	1	13% entering, 87% exiting
Sunday	2.28	1500	1	50% entering, 50% exiting
Sunday Peak Hour of Generator	0.33	1500	1	21% entering, 79% exiting

Water Slide Park
(414)

Average Vehicle Trip Ends vs: Parking Spaces
On a: Weekday

Number of Studies: 2
Average Number of Parking Spaces: 900
Directional Distribution: 50% entering, 50% exiting

Trip Generation per Parking Space

Average Rate	Range of Rates	Standard Deviation
2.27	1.67 - 2.39	*

Data Plot and Equation

Caution - Use Carefully - Small Sample Size

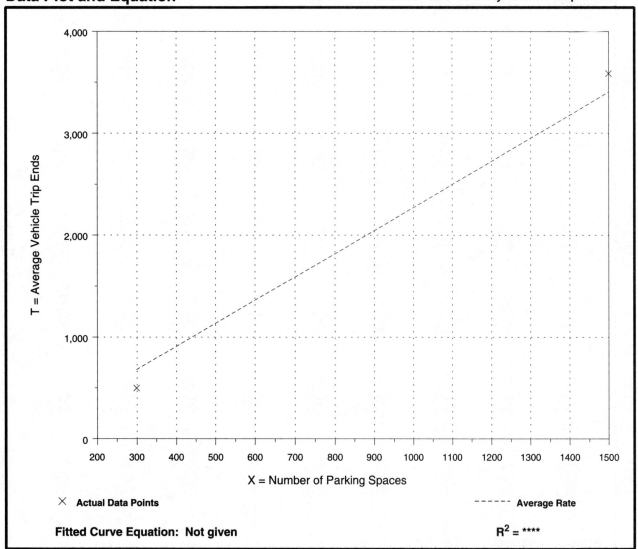

X Actual Data Points

- - - - - Average Rate

Fitted Curve Equation: Not given

$R^2 = ****$

Land Use: 415
Beach Park

Description

Beach parks consist of a beach and possibly other facilities such as changing rooms, restrooms, picnic facilities and hiking, fishing and camping facilities. In season, lifeguards are often provided. Seasonal use of the individual sites differs widely as a result of the varying facilities and local conditions, such as weather.

Additional Data

The sites were surveyed in the 1970s in California.

Source Numbers

11, 13, 214

Beach Park
(415)

Average Vehicle Trip Ends vs: Acres
On a: Weekday

Number of Studies: 10
Average Number of Acres: 81
Directional Distribution: 50% entering, 50% exiting

Trip Generation per Acre

Average Rate	Range of Rates	Standard Deviation
29.81	1.38 - 146.29	47.96

Data Plot and Equation

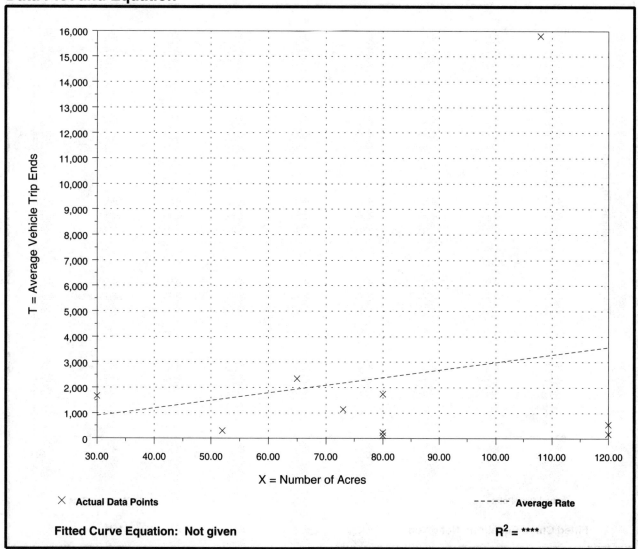

X   **Actual Data Points**   - - - - -   **Average Rate**

Fitted Curve Equation: Not given $R^2 = ****$

Beach Park
(415)

Average Vehicle Trip Ends vs: **Acres**
On a: **Weekday,**
Peak Hour of Adjacent Street Traffic,
One Hour Between 4 and 6 p.m.

Number of Studies: 2
Average Number of Acres: 63
Directional Distribution: 29% entering, 71% exiting

Trip Generation per Acre

Average Rate	Range of Rates	Standard Deviation
1.30	1.26 - 1.35	*

Data Plot and Equation

Caution - Use Carefully - Small Sample Size

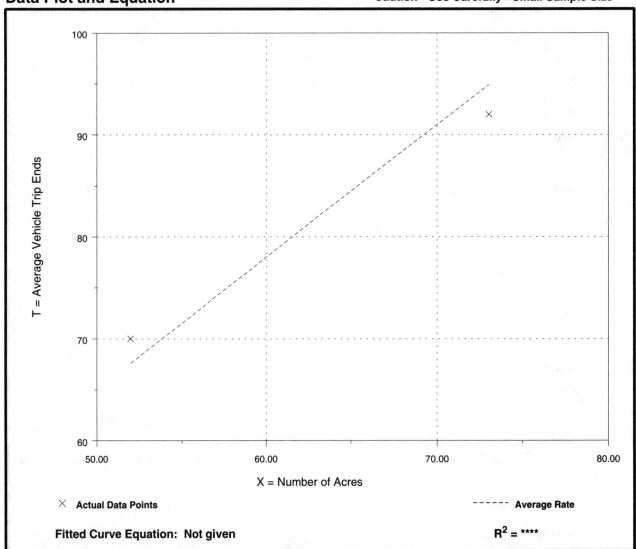

X Actual Data Points

----- **Average Rate**

Fitted Curve Equation: Not given

$R^2 = ****$

Beach Park
(415)

Average Vehicle Trip Ends vs: **Acres**
On a: **Weekday,**
A.M. Peak Hour of Generator

Number of Studies: 6
Average Number of Acres: 88
Directional Distribution: 59% entering, 41% exiting

Trip Generation per Acre

Average Rate	Range of Rates	Standard Deviation
0.48	0.08 - 1.49	0.84

Data Plot and Equation

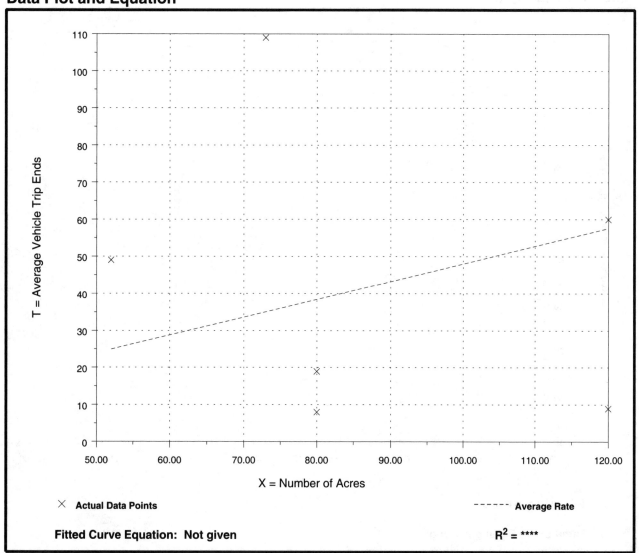

X **Actual Data Points** – – – – – **Average Rate**

Fitted Curve Equation: Not given $R^2 = ****$

Beach Park
(415)

Average Vehicle Trip Ends vs: **Acres**
On a: **Weekday,**
P.M. Peak Hour of Generator

Number of Studies: 6
Average Number of Acres: 88
Directional Distribution: 34% entering, 66% exiting

Trip Generation per Acre

Average Rate	Range of Rates	Standard Deviation
0.60	0.23 - 1.35	0.87

Data Plot and Equation

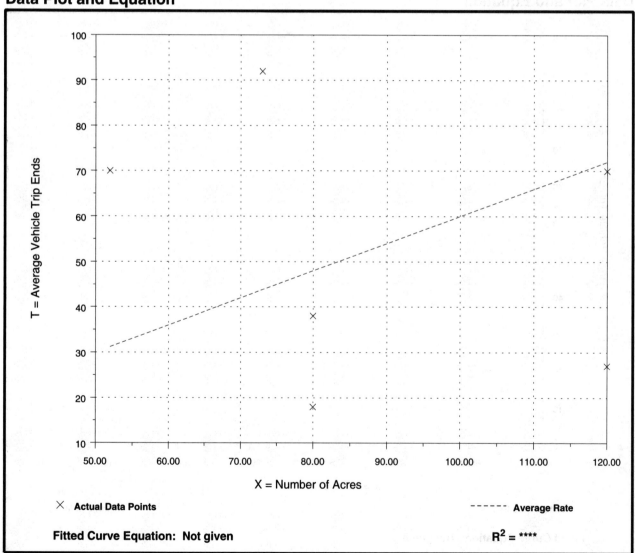

Fitted Curve Equation: Not given $R^2 = ****$

Beach Park
(415)

Average Vehicle Trip Ends vs: Acres
On a: Saturday

Number of Studies: 10
Average Number of Acres: 81
Directional Distribution: 50% entering, 50% exiting

Trip Generation per Acre

Average Rate	Range of Rates	Standard Deviation
66.47	4.13 - 355.74	116.34

Data Plot and Equation

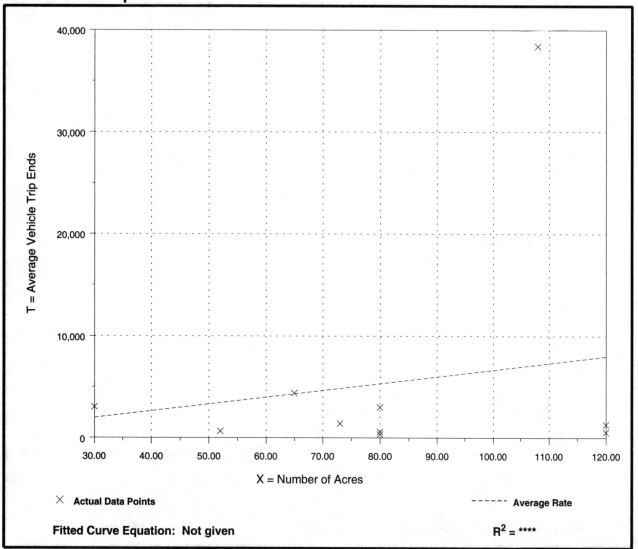

Fitted Curve Equation: Not given $R^2 = ****$

Beach Park
(415)

Average Vehicle Trip Ends vs: Acres
On a: Saturday,
Peak Hour of Generator

Number of Studies: 6
Average Number of Acres: 88
Directional Distribution: 46% entering, 54% exiting

Trip Generation per Acre

Average Rate	Range of Rates	Standard Deviation
1.18	0.69 - 2.60	1.25

Data Plot and Equation

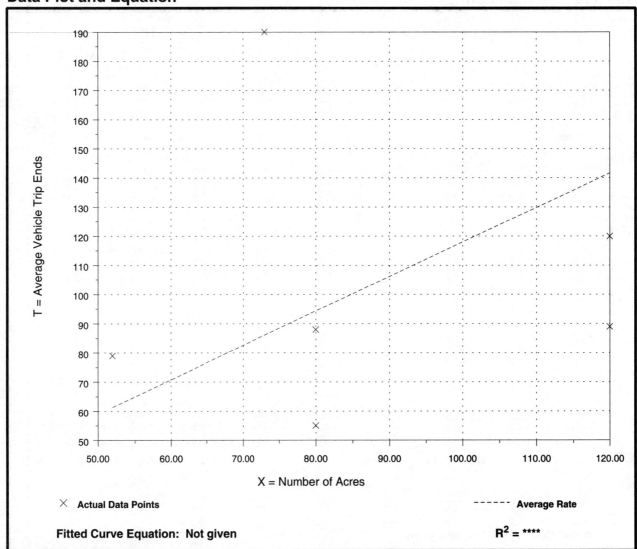

X = Number of Acres

✕ **Actual Data Points**   – – – – – **Average Rate**

Fitted Curve Equation: Not given $R^2 = ****$

Beach Park
(415)

Average Vehicle Trip Ends vs: **Acres**
On a: **Sunday**

Number of Studies: 10
Average Number of Acres: 81
Directional Distribution: 50% entering, 50% exiting

Trip Generation per Acre

Average Rate	Range of Rates	Standard Deviation
68.52	5.50 - 343.57	111.72

Data Plot and Equation

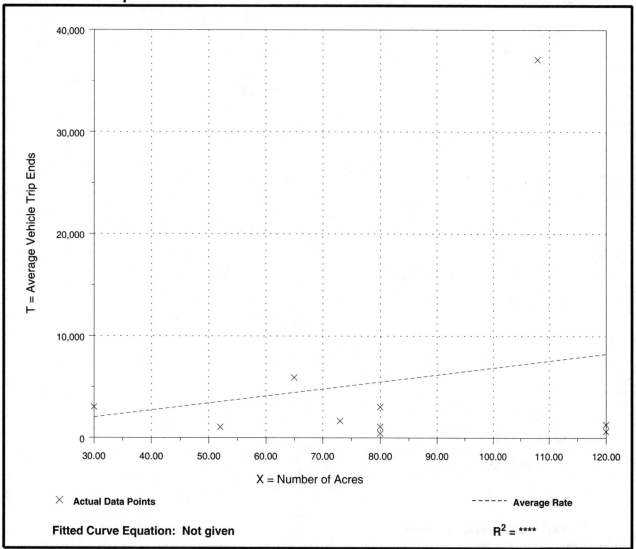

Fitted Curve Equation: Not given $R^2 = ****$

Beach Park
(415)

Average Vehicle Trip Ends vs: **Acres**
On a: **Sunday,**
Peak Hour of Generator

Number of Studies: 6
Average Number of Acres: 88
Directional Distribution: 51% entering, 49% exiting

Trip Generation per Acre

Average Rate	Range of Rates	Standard Deviation
1.54	0.83 - 2.56	1.42

Data Plot and Equation

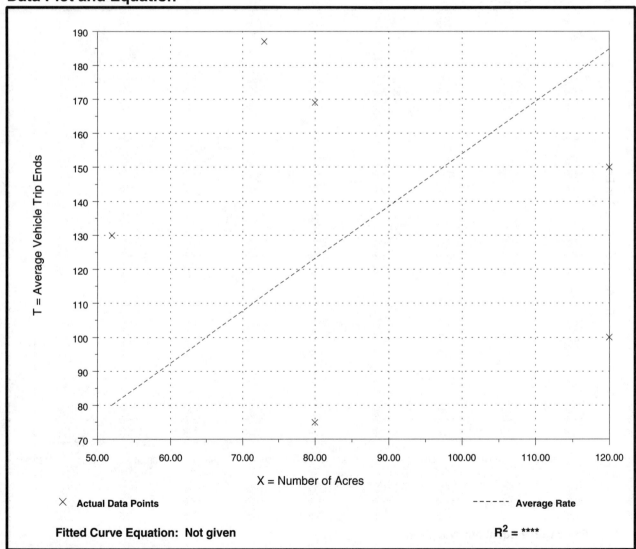

X **Actual Data Points**   - - - - - **Average Rate**

Fitted Curve Equation: Not given $R^2 = $ ****

Land Use: 416
Campground/Recreational Vehicle Park

Description

Campgrounds and recreational vehicle parks are recreational sites that accommodate campers, trailers, tents and recreational vehicles on a transient basis. They are found in a variety of locations and provide a variety of facilities, often including restrooms with showers, recreational facilities such as a swimming pool, convenience store and laundromat.

Additional Data

The sites were surveyed in the late 1980s, 1990s and 2000s in California, Rhode Island and Washington.

Source Numbers

264, 401, 559

Land Use: 416
Campground/Recreational Vehicle Park
Independent Variables with One Observation

The following trip generation data are for independent variables with only one observation. This information is shown in this table only; there are no related plots for these data.

Users are cautioned to use data with care because of the small sample size.

Independent Variable	Trip Generation Rate	Size of Independent Variable	Number of Studies	Directional Distribution
Acres				
Weekday a.m. Peak Hour of Adjacent Street Traffic	0.48	50	1	42% entering, 58% exiting
Weekday p.m. Peak Hour of Adjacent Street Traffic	0.98	50	1	69% entering, 31% exiting
Weekday a.m. Peak Hour of Generator	0.52	50	1	42% entering, 58% exiting
Weekday p.m. Peak Hour of Generator	1.06	50	1	62% entering, 38% exiting

Campground/Recreational Vehicle Park
(416)

Average Vehicle Trip Ends vs: Occupied Camp Sites
On a: Weekday,
Peak Hour of Adjacent Street Traffic,
One Hour Between 7 and 9 a.m.

Number of Studies: 3
Average Number of Occupied Camp Sites: 60
Directional Distribution: 42% entering, 58% exiting

Trip Generation per Occupied Camp Site

Average Rate	Range of Rates	Standard Deviation
0.20	0.18 - 0.35	0.45

Data Plot and Equation

Caution - Use Carefully - Small Sample Size

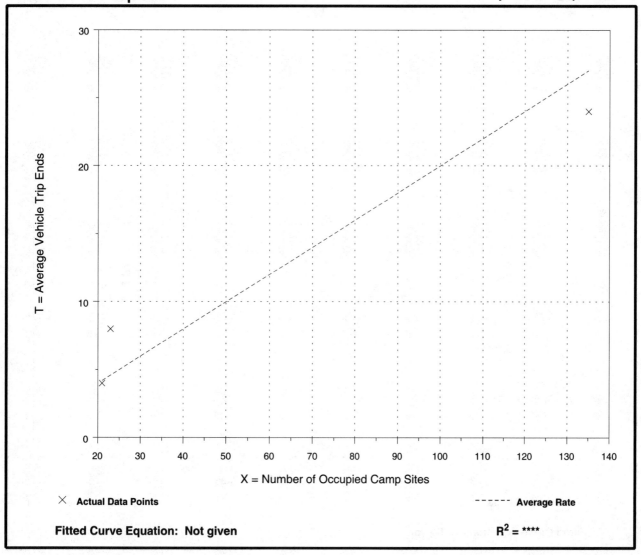

X **Actual Data Points**   ----- **Average Rate**

Fitted Curve Equation: Not given $R^2 = $ ****

Campground/Recreational Vehicle Park
(416)

Average Vehicle Trip Ends vs: **Occupied Camp Sites**
On a: **Weekday,**
Peak Hour of Adjacent Street Traffic,
One Hour Between 4 and 6 p.m.

Number of Studies: 3
Average Number of Occupied Camp Sites: 60
Directional Distribution: 69% entering, 31% exiting

Trip Generation per Occupied Camp Site

Average Rate	Range of Rates	Standard Deviation
0.37	0.33 - 0.43	0.60

Data Plot and Equation

Caution - Use Carefully - Small Sample Size

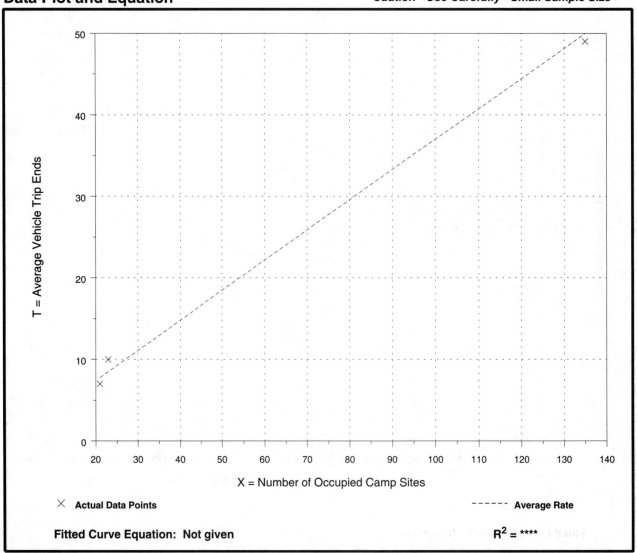

X = Number of Occupied Camp Sites

✕ **Actual Data Points** - - - - - **Average Rate**

Fitted Curve Equation: Not given $R^2 =$ ****

Campground/Recreational Vehicle Park
(416)

Average Vehicle Trip Ends vs: Occupied Camp Sites
On a: Weekday,
A.M. Peak Hour of Generator

Number of Studies: 3
Average Number of Occupied Camp Sites: 60
Directional Distribution: 42% entering, 58% exiting

Trip Generation per Occupied Camp Site

Average Rate	Range of Rates	Standard Deviation
0.22	0.19 - 0.35	0.47

Data Plot and Equation

Caution - Use Carefully - Small Sample Size

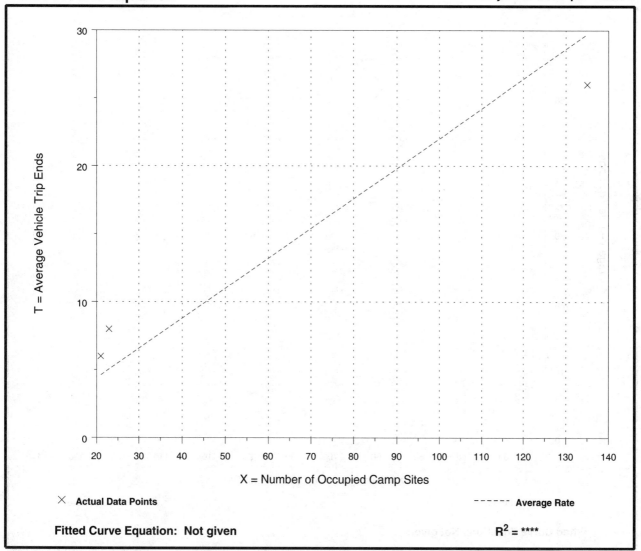

X = Number of Occupied Camp Sites

✕ **Actual Data Points**   ----- **Average Rate**

Fitted Curve Equation: Not given $R^2 = ****$

Campground/Recreational Vehicle Park
(416)

Average Vehicle Trip Ends vs: **Occupied Camp Sites**
On a: **Weekday,**
P.M. Peak Hour of Generator

Number of Studies: 3
Average Number of Occupied Camp Sites: 60
Directional Distribution: 62% entering, 38% exiting

Trip Generation per Occupied Camp Site

Average Rate	Range of Rates	Standard Deviation
0.41	0.38 - 0.57	0.64

Data Plot and Equation

Caution - Use Carefully - Small Sample Size

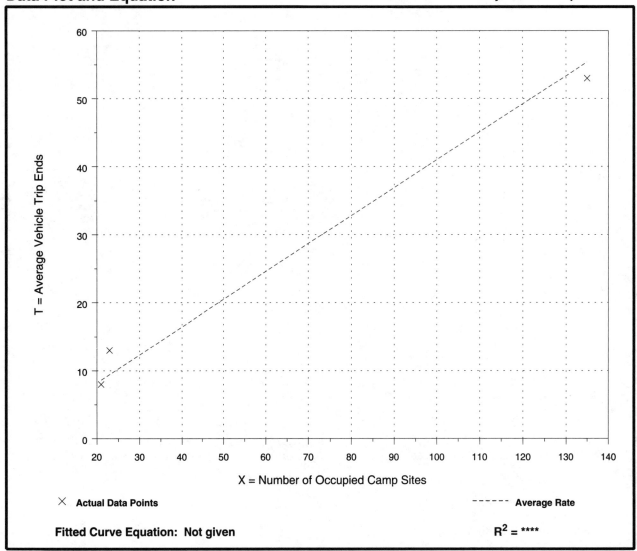

X **Actual Data Points**

‑ ‑ ‑ ‑ ‑ **Average Rate**

Fitted Curve Equation: Not given

$R^2 = ****$

Land Use: 417
Regional Park

Description

Regional parks are owned and operated by a regional park authority. The regional parks surveyed vary widely as to location, type and number of facilities, including hiking trails, lakes, pools, ball fields, camp sites, picnic facilities and general office space. Seasonal use of the individual sites differs widely as a result of the varying facilities and local conditions, such as weather. For example, some of the sites are used primarily for boating or swimming; others are used for hiking or camping, etc.

Additional Data

The percentage of the park area that is used most intensively varies considerably within the studies contained in this land use; therefore, caution should be used when using acres as an independent variable.

The sites were surveyed in the 1970s and 1990s in California.

Source Numbers

12, 13, 214, 392

Land Use: 417
Regional Park
Independent Variables with One Observation

The following trip generation data are for independent variables with only one observation. This information is shown in this table only; there are no related plots for these data.

Users are cautioned to use data with care because of the small sample size.

Independent Variable	Trip Generation Rate	Size of Independent Variable	Number of Studies	Directional Distribution
Picnic Sites				
Weekday a.m. Peak Hour of Generator	4.00	10	1	75% entering, 25% exiting
Weekday p.m. Peak Hour of Generator	9.60	10	1	41% entering, 59% exiting
Saturday Peak Hour of Generator	12.10	10	1	35% entering, 65% exiting
Sunday Peak Hour of Generator	16.70	10	1	47% entering, 53% exiting
Employees				
Weekday a.m. Peak Hour of Adjacent Street Traffic	4.59	17	1	65% entering, 35% exiting

Regional Park
(417)

Average Vehicle Trip Ends vs: **Employees**
On a: **Weekday**

Number of Studies: 3
Avg. Number of Employees: 9
Directional Distribution: 50% entering, 50% exiting

Trip Generation per Employee

Average Rate	Range of Rates	Standard Deviation
79.77	59.53 - 183.33	40.53

Data Plot and Equation

Caution - Use Carefully - Small Sample Size

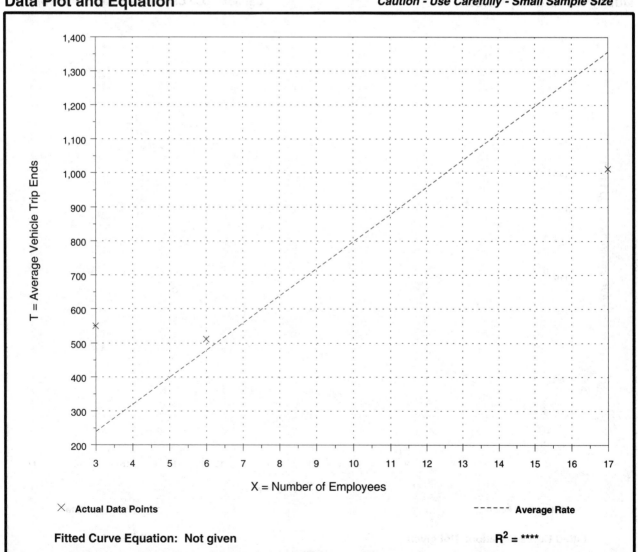

X **Actual Data Points**   ----- **Average Rate**

Fitted Curve Equation: Not given $R^2 = ****$

Regional Park
(417)

Average Vehicle Trip Ends vs: **Employees**
On a: **Weekday,**
Peak Hour of Adjacent Street Traffic,
One Hour Between 4 and 6 p.m.

Number of Studies: 2
Avg. Number of Employees: 12
Directional Distribution: 45% entering, 55% exiting

Trip Generation per Employee

Average Rate	Range of Rates	Standard Deviation
10.26	7.41 - 18.33	*

Data Plot and Equation

Caution - Use Carefully - Small Sample Size

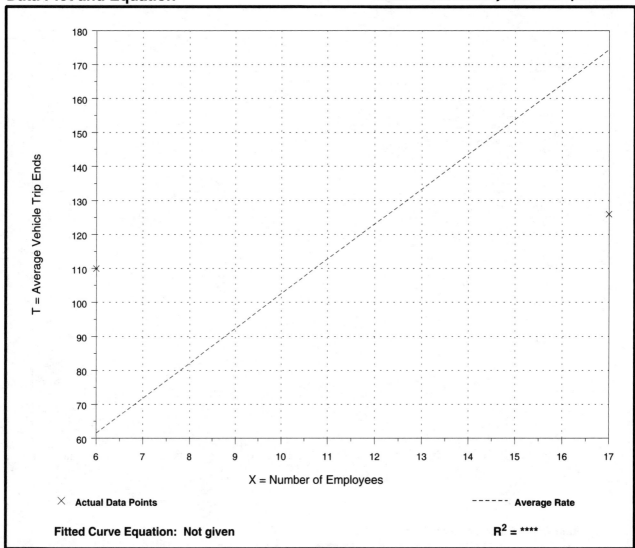

Fitted Curve Equation: Not given $R^2 = ****$

Regional Park
(417)

Average Vehicle Trip Ends vs: **Employees**
On a: **Weekday,**
A.M. Peak Hour of Generator

Number of Studies: 3
Avg. Number of Employees: 9
Directional Distribution: 57% entering, 43% exiting

Trip Generation per Employee

Average Rate	Range of Rates	Standard Deviation
7.23	5.18 - 13.33	3.94

Data Plot and Equation

Caution - Use Carefully - Small Sample Size

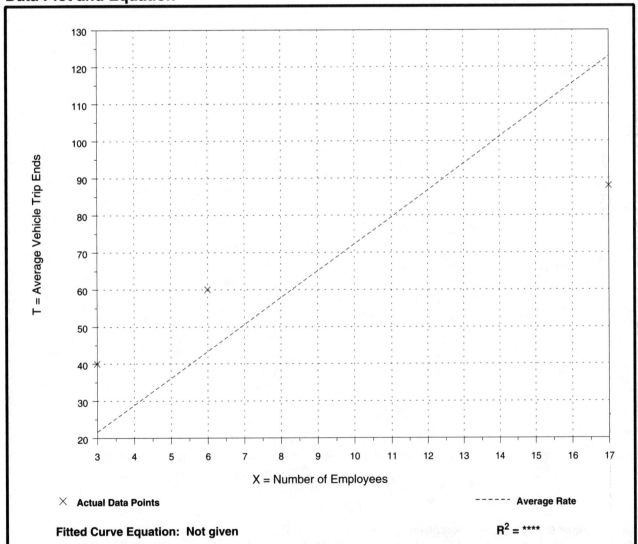

X **Actual Data Points**   - - - - - **Average Rate**

Fitted Curve Equation: Not given $R^2 = ****$

Regional Park
(417)

Average Vehicle Trip Ends vs: **Employees**
On a: **Weekday,**
P.M. Peak Hour of Generator

Number of Studies: 3
Avg. Number of Employees: 9
Directional Distribution: 44% entering, 56% exiting

Trip Generation per Employee

Average Rate	Range of Rates	Standard Deviation
12.77	7.41 - 32.00	9.07

Data Plot and Equation

Caution - Use Carefully - Small Sample Size

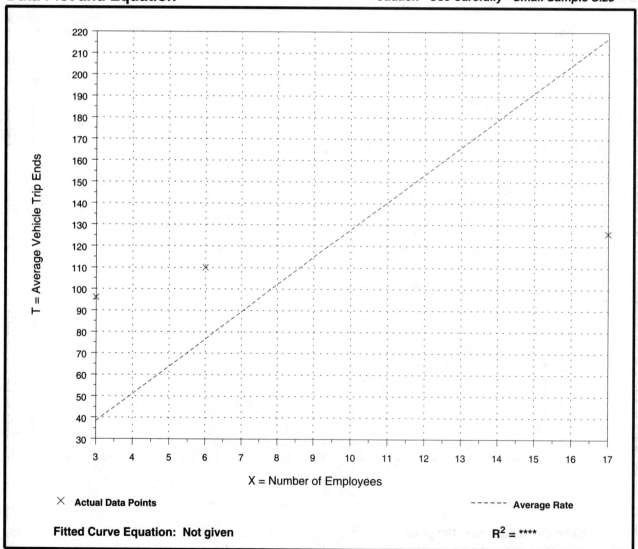

X **Actual Data Points**

----- **Average Rate**

Fitted Curve Equation: Not given $R^2 = ****$

Regional Park
(417)

Average Vehicle Trip Ends vs: Employees
On a: Saturday

Number of Studies: 3
Avg. Number of Employees: 9
Directional Distribution: 50% entering, 50% exiting

Trip Generation per Employee

Average Rate	Range of Rates	Standard Deviation
128.04	56.67 - 303.33	71.04

Data Plot and Equation

Caution - Use Carefully - Small Sample Size

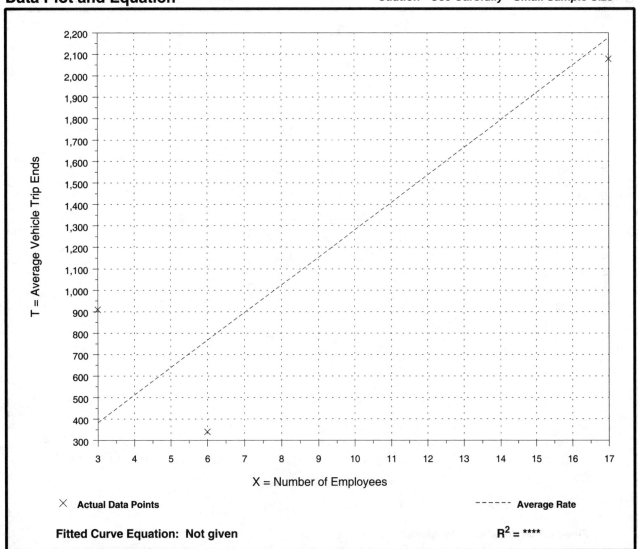

X   **Actual Data Points**   - - - - - - **Average Rate**

Fitted Curve Equation: Not given $R^2 =$ ****

Regional Park
(417)

Average Vehicle Trip Ends vs: **Employees**
On a: **Saturday,**
Peak Hour of Generator

Number of Studies: 3
Avg. Number of Employees: 9
Directional Distribution: 48% entering, 52% exiting

Trip Generation per Employee

Average Rate	Range of Rates	Standard Deviation
16.54	8.33 - 40.33	10.00

Data Plot and Equation

Caution - Use Carefully - Small Sample Size

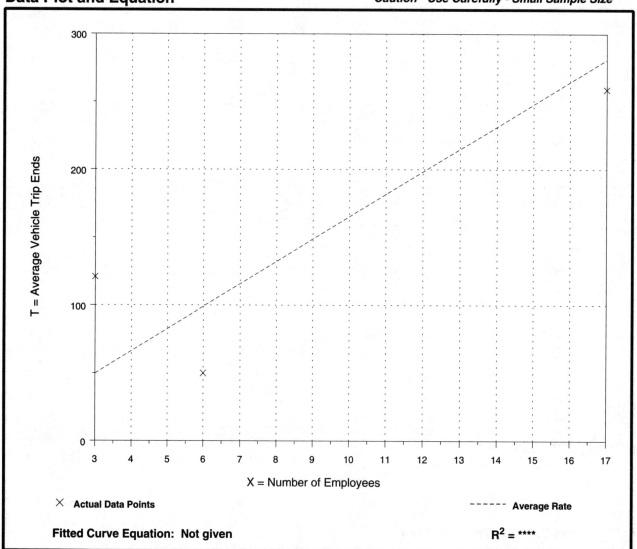

X **Actual Data Points**   — — — — — **Average Rate**

Fitted Curve Equation: Not given $R^2 = ****$

Regional Park
(417)

Average Vehicle Trip Ends vs: **Employees**
On a: **Sunday**

Number of Studies: 3
Avg. Number of Employees: 9
Directional Distribution: 50% entering, 50% exiting

Trip Generation per Employee

Average Rate	Range of Rates	Standard Deviation
162.81	131.67 - 366.67	76.08

Data Plot and Equation

Caution - Use Carefully - Small Sample Size

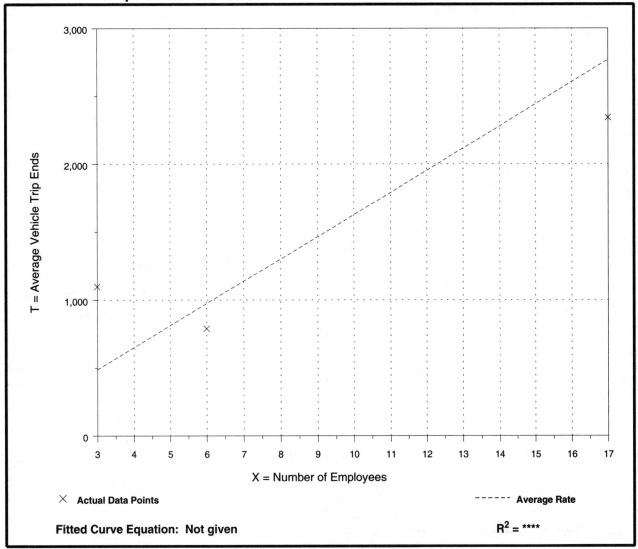

X   **Actual Data Points**

------ **Average Rate**

Fitted Curve Equation: Not given

$R^2 = ****$

Regional Park
(417)

Average Vehicle Trip Ends vs: Employees
On a: Sunday,
Peak Hour of Generator

Number of Studies: 3
Avg. Number of Employees: 9
Directional Distribution: 34% entering, 66% exiting

Trip Generation per Employee

Average Rate	Range of Rates	Standard Deviation
20.46	13.82 - 55.67	14.02

Data Plot and Equation

Caution - Use Carefully - Small Sample Size

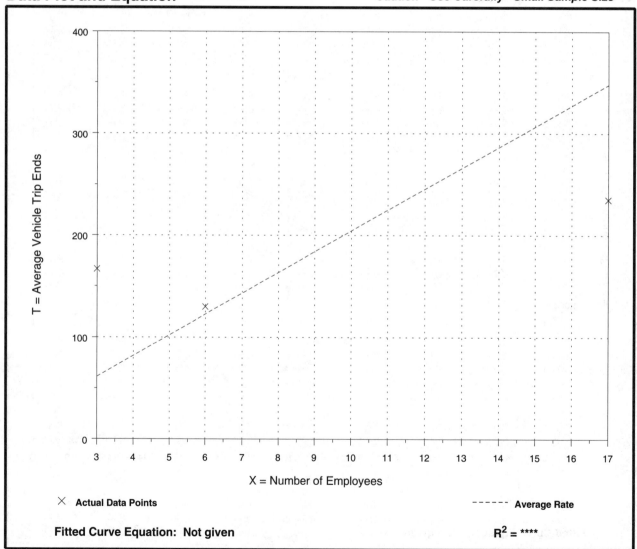

X **Actual Data Points**

- - - - - **Average Rate**

Fitted Curve Equation: Not given

$R^2 = ****$

Regional Park
(417)

Average Vehicle Trip Ends vs: Acres
On a: Weekday

Number of Studies: 5
Average Number of Acres: 310
Directional Distribution: 50% entering, 50% exiting

Trip Generation per Acre

Average Rate	Range of Rates	Standard Deviation
4.57	0.92 - 39.07	10.03

Data Plot and Equation

Caution - Use Carefully - Small Sample Size

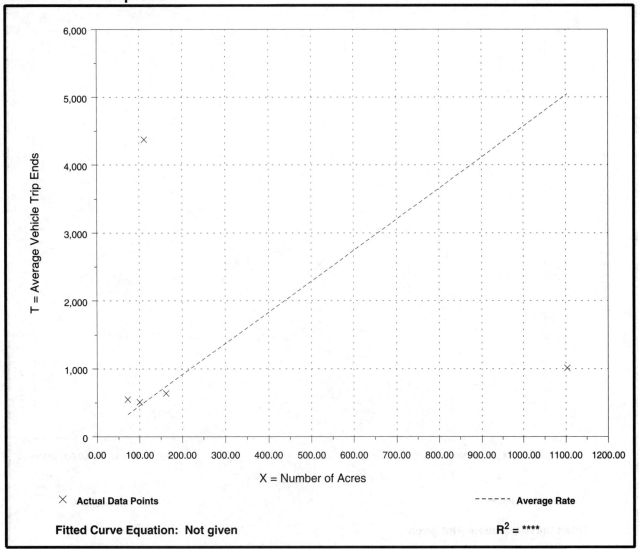

X = Number of Acres

× **Actual Data Points**   - - - - - **Average Rate**

Fitted Curve Equation: Not given $R^2 =$ ****

Regional Park
(417)

Average Vehicle Trip Ends vs:	**Acres**
On a:	**Weekday,**
	Peak Hour of Adjacent Street Traffic,
	One Hour Between 4 and 6 p.m.

Number of Studies: 2
Average Number of Acres: 602
Directional Distribution: 45% entering, 55% exiting

Trip Generation per Acre

Average Rate	Range of Rates	Standard Deviation
0.20	0.11 - 1.10	*

Data Plot and Equation

Caution - Use Carefully - Small Sample Size

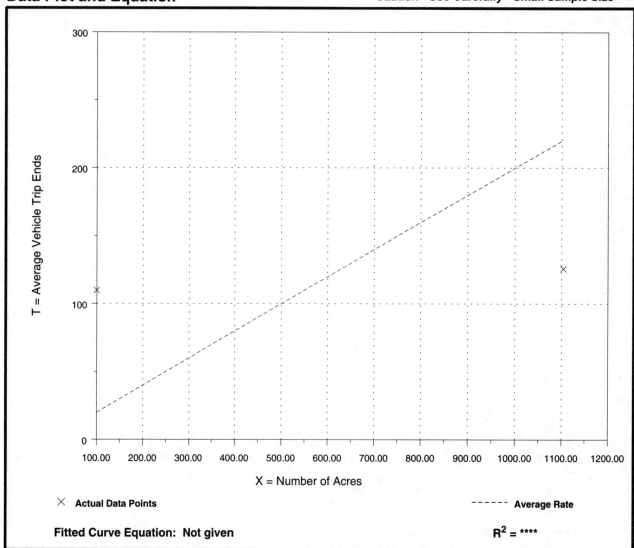

X   **Actual Data Points**   - - - - - **Average Rate**

Fitted Curve Equation: Not given $R^2 = $ ****

Regional Park
(417)

Average Vehicle Trip Ends vs: Acres
On a: Weekday,
A.M. Peak Hour of Generator

Number of Studies: 3
Average Number of Acres: 425
Directional Distribution: 57% entering, 43% exiting

Trip Generation per Acre

Average Rate	Range of Rates	Standard Deviation
0.15	0.08 - 0.60	0.42

Data Plot and Equation

Caution - Use Carefully - Small Sample Size

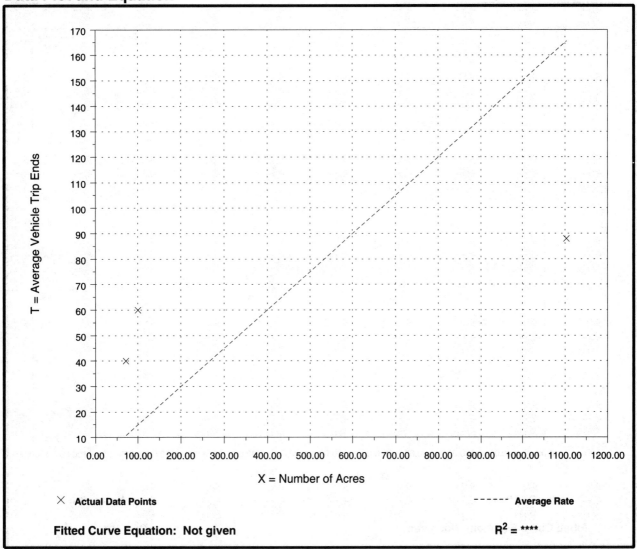

X = Number of Acres

× **Actual Data Points** - - - - - **Average Rate**

Fitted Curve Equation: Not given $R^2 = ****$

Regional Park
(417)

Number of Studies: 3
Average Number of Acres: 425
Directional Distribution: 44% entering, 56% exiting

Trip Generation per Acre

Average Rate	Range of Rates	Standard Deviation
0.26	0.11 - 1.33	0.63

Data Plot and Equation

Caution - Use Carefully - Small Sample Size

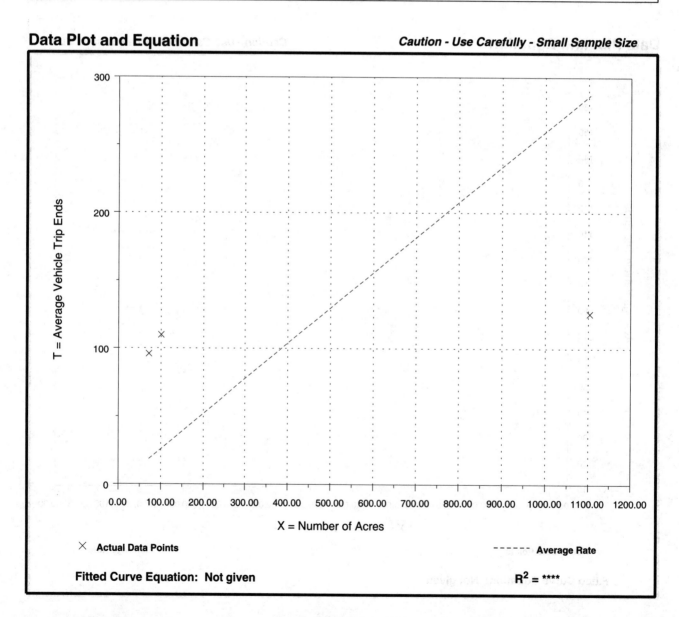

× **Actual Data Points**

------ **Average Rate**

Fitted Curve Equation: Not given

$R^2 = ****$

Regional Park
(417)

Average Vehicle Trip Ends vs: Acres
On a: Saturday

Number of Studies: 5
Average Number of Acres: 310
Directional Distribution: 50% entering, 50% exiting

Trip Generation per Acre

Average Rate	Range of Rates	Standard Deviation
5.65	1.88 - 43.04	10.94

Data Plot and Equation

Caution - Use Carefully - Small Sample Size

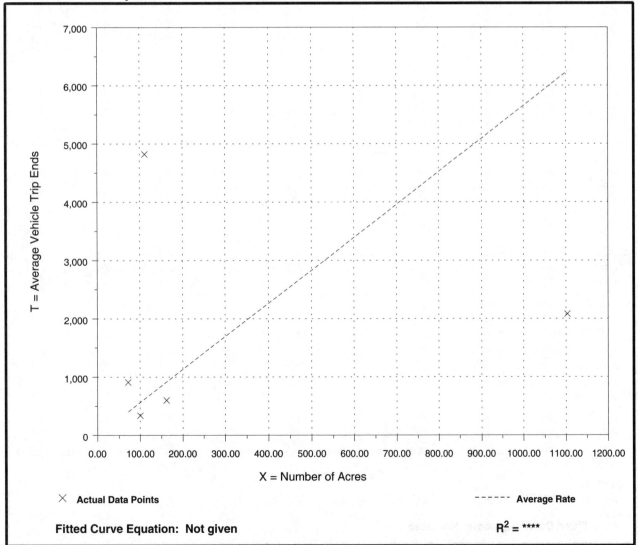

Fitted Curve Equation: Not given $R^2 = ****$

Regional Park
(417)

Average Vehicle Trip Ends vs: **Acres**
On a: **Saturday,**
Peak Hour of Generator

Number of Studies: 3
Average Number of Acres: 425
Directional Distribution: 48% entering, 52% exiting

Trip Generation per Acre

Average Rate	Range of Rates	Standard Deviation
0.34	0.23 - 1.68	0.67

Data Plot and Equation

Caution - Use Carefully - Small Sample Size

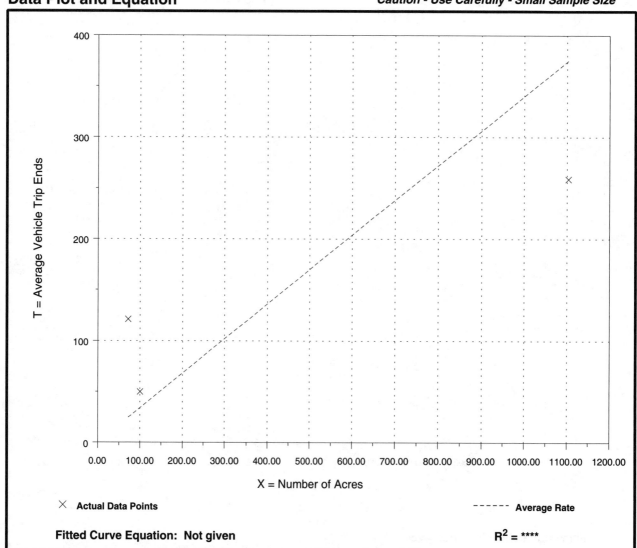

X **Actual Data Points**

- - - - - **Average Rate**

Fitted Curve Equation: Not given

$R^2 = $ ****

Regional Park
(417)

Average Vehicle Trip Ends vs: Acres
On a: Sunday

Number of Studies: 5
Average Number of Acres: 310
Directional Distribution: 50% entering, 50% exiting

Trip Generation per Acre

Average Rate	Range of Rates	Standard Deviation
6.44	2.12 - 44.11	11.24

Data Plot and Equation

Caution - Use Carefully - Small Sample Size

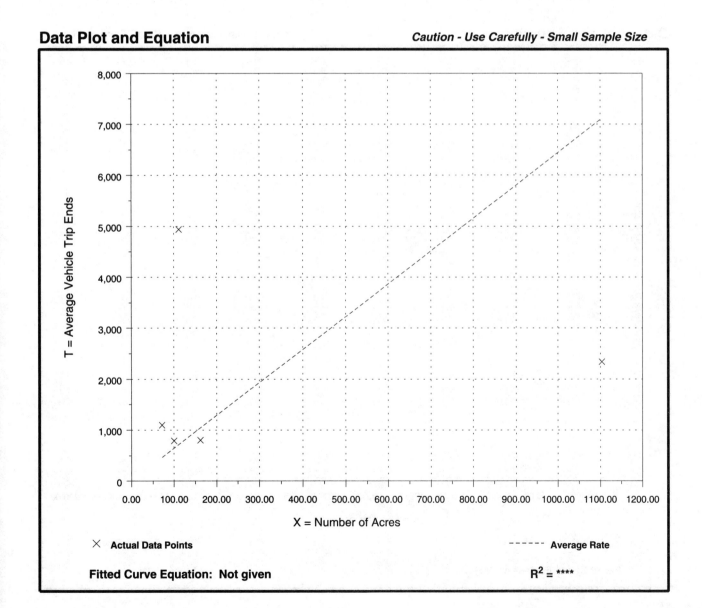

X Actual Data Points   **- - - - - Average Rate**

Fitted Curve Equation: Not given $R^2 =$ ****

Regional Park
(417)

Average Vehicle Trip Ends vs: **Acres**
On a: **Sunday,**
Peak Hour of Generator

Number of Studies: 3
Average Number of Acres: 425
Directional Distribution: 34% entering, 66% exiting

Trip Generation per Acre

Average Rate	Range of Rates	Standard Deviation
0.42	0.21 - 2.32	0.85

Data Plot and Equation

Caution - Use Carefully - Small Sample Size

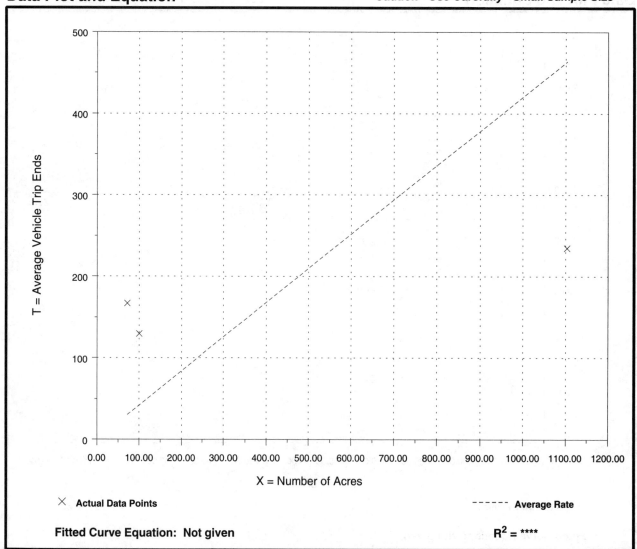

X **Actual Data Points**   - - - - - **Average Rate**

Fitted Curve Equation: Not given $R^2 = ****$

Regional Park
(417)

Average Vehicle Trip Ends vs: Picnic Sites
On a: Weekday

Number of Studies: 3
Average Number of Picnic Sites: 30
Directional Distribution: 50% entering, 50% exiting

Trip Generation per Picnic Site

Average Rate	Range of Rates	Standard Deviation
61.82	9.82 - 291.73	104.63

Data Plot and Equation

Caution - Use Carefully - Small Sample Size

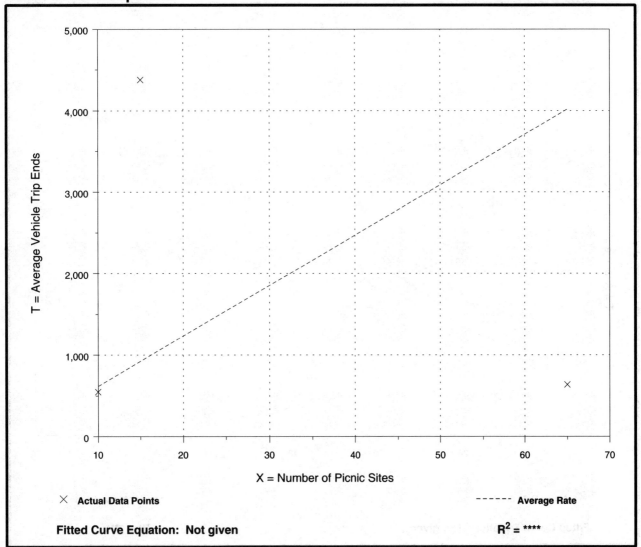

X **Actual Data Points**   - - - - - **Average Rate**

Fitted Curve Equation: Not given $R^2 = ****$

Regional Park
(417)

Average Vehicle Trip Ends vs: Picnic Sites
On a: Saturday

Number of Studies: 3
Average Number of Picnic Sites: 30
Directional Distribution: 50% entering, 50% exiting

Trip Generation per Picnic Site

Average Rate	Range of Rates	Standard Deviation
70.39	9.31 - 321.33	115.98

Data Plot and Equation

Caution - Use Carefully - Small Sample Size

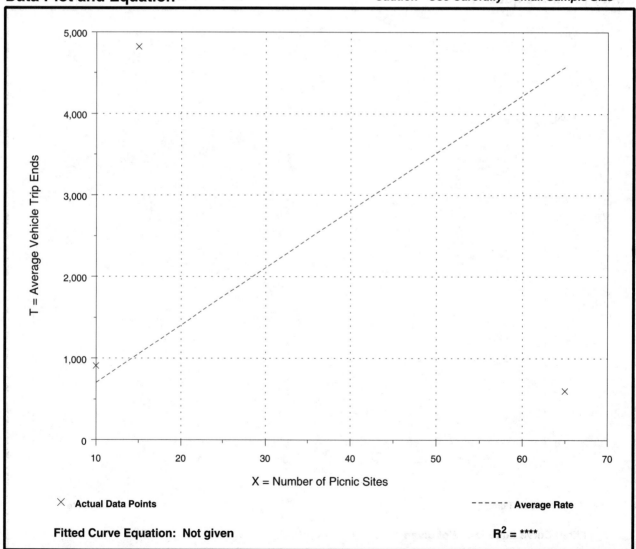

X **Actual Data Points**   - - - - - **Average Rate**

Fitted Curve Equation: Not given $R^2 = ****$

Regional Park
(417)

Average Vehicle Trip Ends vs: Picnic Sites
On a: Sunday

Number of Studies: 3
Average Number of Picnic Sites: 30
Directional Distribution: 50% entering, 50% exiting

Trip Generation per Picnic Site

Average Rate	Range of Rates	Standard Deviation
76.06	12.38 - 329.33	118.21

Data Plot and Equation

Caution - Use Carefully - Small Sample Size

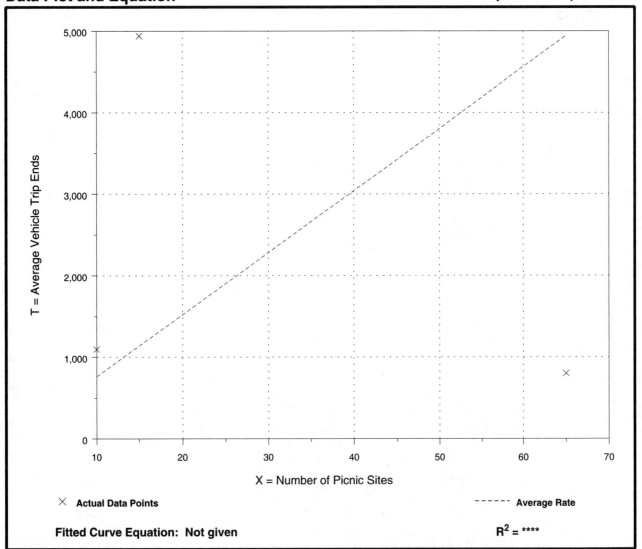

X = Number of Picnic Sites

× **Actual Data Points** ----- **Average Rate**

Fitted Curve Equation: Not given $R^2 = ****$

Land Use: 418
National Monument

Description

National monuments vary widely as to type of facilities and location. Many of them are scenic observation points, towers, or historical monuments.

Additional Data

The peak hour of the adjacent street traffic does not typically coincide with the peak hour of the generator.

The sites were surveyed in the 1970s in California.

Source Numbers

13, 213

Land Use: 418
National Monument
Independent Variables with One Observation

The following trip generation data are for independent variables with only one observation. This information is shown in this table only; there are no related plots for these data.

Users are cautioned to use data with care because of the small sample size.

Independent Variable	Trip Generation Rate	Size of Independent Variable	Number of Studies	Directional Distribution
Employees				
Weekday	31.05	38	1	50% entering, 50% exiting
Weekday a.m. Peak Hour of Generator	3.05	38	1	Not available
Weekday p.m. Peak Hour of Generator	5.58	38	1	Not available
Saturday	43.16	38	1	50% entering, 50% exiting
Saturday Peak Hour of Generator	6.18	38	1	Not available
Sunday	47.63	38	1	50% entering, 50% exiting
Sunday Peak Hour of Generator	6.68	38	1	Not available
Acres				
Weekday a.m. Peak Hour of Generator	0.23	502	1	Not available
Weekday p.m. Peak Hour of Generator	0.42	502	1	Not available
Saturday Peak Hour of Generator	0.47	502	1	Not available
Sunday Peak Hour of Generator	0.51	502	1	Not available

National Monument
(418)

Average Vehicle Trip Ends vs: **Acres**
On a: **Weekday**

Number of Studies: 2
Average Number of Acres: 323
Directional Distribution: 50% entering, 50% exiting

Trip Generation per Acre

Average Rate	Range of Rates	Standard Deviation
5.37	2.35 - 15.92	*

Data Plot and Equation

Caution - Use Carefully - Small Sample Size

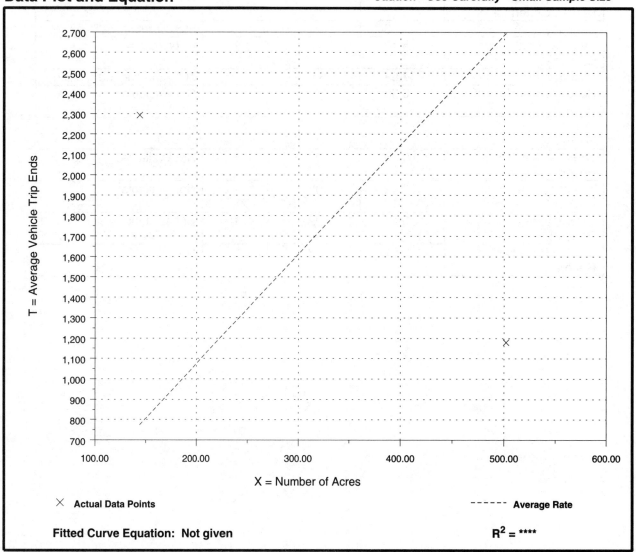

X   **Actual Data Points**

- - - - - **Average Rate**

Fitted Curve Equation: Not given $R^2 =$ ****

National Monument
(418)

Average Vehicle Trip Ends vs: Acres
On a: Saturday

Number of Studies: 2
Average Number of Acres: 323
Directional Distribution: 50% entering, 50% exiting

Trip Generation per Acre

Average Rate	Range of Rates	Standard Deviation
8.28	3.27 - 25.76	*

Data Plot and Equation

Caution - Use Carefully - Small Sample Size

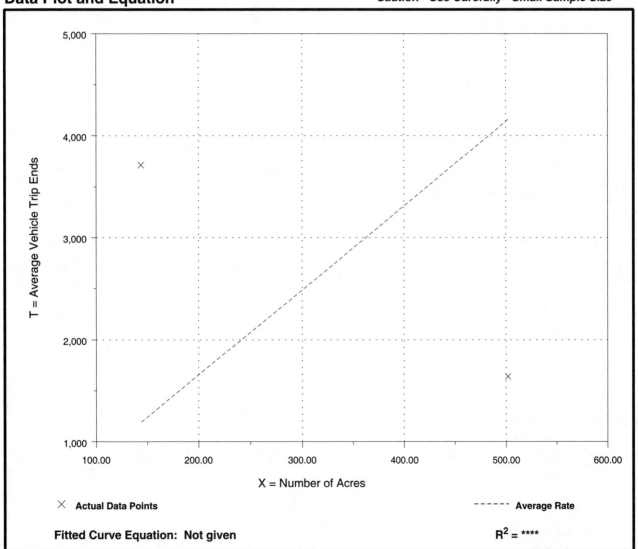

X   **Actual Data Points**

- - - - - **Average Rate**

Fitted Curve Equation: Not given $R^2 =$ ****

National Monument
(418)

Average Vehicle Trip Ends vs: Acres
On a: Sunday

Number of Studies: 2
Average Number of Acres: 323
Directional Distribution: 50% entering, 50% exiting

Trip Generation per Acre

Average Rate	Range of Rates	Standard Deviation
9.39	3.61 - 29.54	*

Data Plot and Equation

Caution - Use Carefully - Small Sample Size

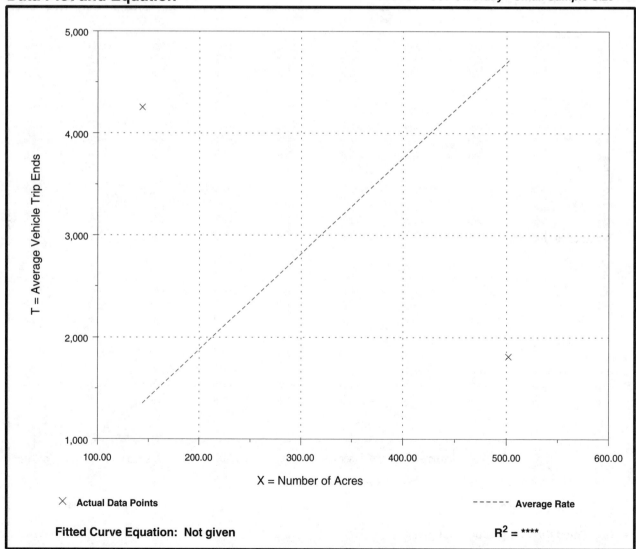

X **Actual Data Points**   - - - - - **Average Rate**

Fitted Curve Equation: Not given   **R^2 = ******

Land Use: 420
Marina

Description

Marinas are public or private facilities that provide docks and berths for boats and may include limited retail and restaurant space.

Additional Data

The number of boat berths ranged from 108 to 1,750; the number of acres ranged from 11 to 105; and the number of parking spaces ranged from 65 to 493.

The sites were surveyed between the late 1960s and the late 1980s in California and Washington.

Source Numbers

6, 12, 19, 101, 123, 265

Land Use: 420
Marina
Independent Variables with One Observation

The following trip generation data are for independent variables with only one observation. This information is shown in this table only; there are no related plots for these data.

Users are cautioned to use data with care because of the small sample size.

Independent Variable	Trip Generation Rate	Size of Independent Variable	Number of Studies	Directional Distribution
Berths				
Sunday Peak Hour of Generator	0.31	300	1	68% entering, 32% exiting

Marina
(420)

Average Vehicle Trip Ends vs: Berths
On a: Weekday

Number of Studies: 11
Average Number of Berths: 386
Directional Distribution: 50% entering, 50% exiting

Trip Generation per Berth

Average Rate	Range of Rates	Standard Deviation
2.96	1.91 - 10.04	2.26

Data Plot and Equation

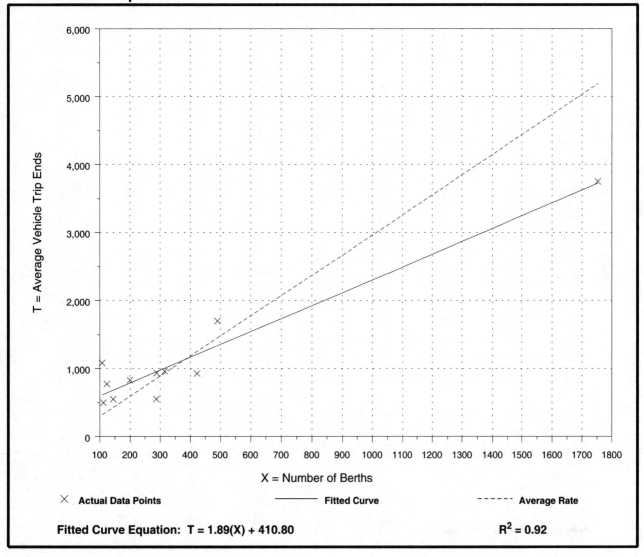

X = Number of Berths

| × | **Actual Data Points** | —— | **Fitted Curve** | - - - - | **Average Rate** |

Fitted Curve Equation: T = 1.89(X) + 410.80 $R^2 = 0.92$

Marina
(420)

Average Vehicle Trip Ends vs: **Berths**
On a: **Weekday,**
      Peak Hour of Adjacent Street Traffic,
      One Hour Between 7 and 9 a.m.

Number of Studies: 2
Average Number of Berths: 362
Directional Distribution: 33% entering, 67% exiting

Trip Generation per Berth

Average Rate	Range of Rates	Standard Deviation
0.08	0.07 - 0.09	*

Data Plot and Equation

Caution - Use Carefully - Small Sample Size

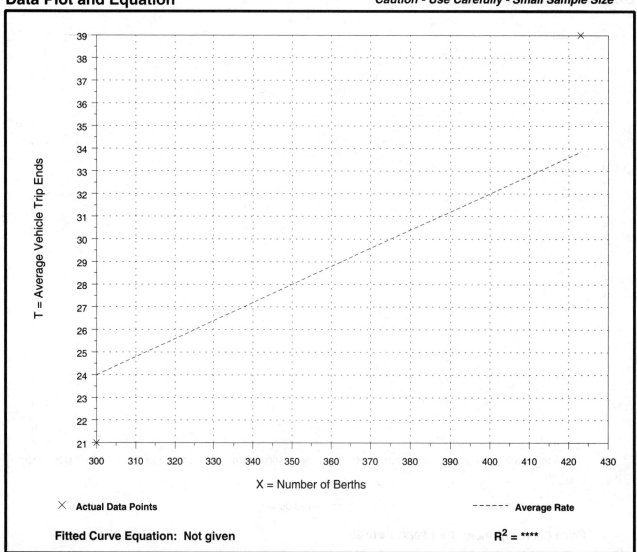

X **Actual Data Points**

------ **Average Rate**

Fitted Curve Equation: Not given $R^2 = $ ****

Marina
(420)

Average Vehicle Trip Ends vs: Berths
On a: Weekday,
Peak Hour of Adjacent Street Traffic,
One Hour Between 4 and 6 p.m.

Number of Studies: 2
Average Number of Berths: 362
Directional Distribution: 60% entering, 40% exiting

Trip Generation per Berth

Average Rate	Range of Rates	Standard Deviation
0.19	0.17 - 0.21	*

Data Plot and Equation

Caution - Use Carefully - Small Sample Size

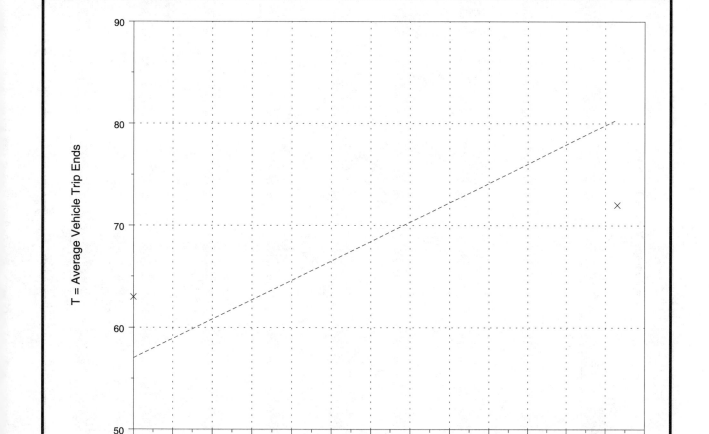

X = Number of Berths

× **Actual Data Points**   - - - - - **Average Rate**

Fitted Curve Equation: Not given $R^2 = ****$

Marina
(420)

Average Vehicle Trip Ends vs: **Berths**
On a: **Weekday,**
A.M. Peak Hour of Generator

Number of Studies: 2
Average Number of Berths: 362
Directional Distribution: 64% entering, 36% exiting

Trip Generation per Berth

Average Rate	Range of Rates	Standard Deviation
0.17	0.12 - 0.20	*

Data Plot and Equation

Caution - Use Carefully - Small Sample Size

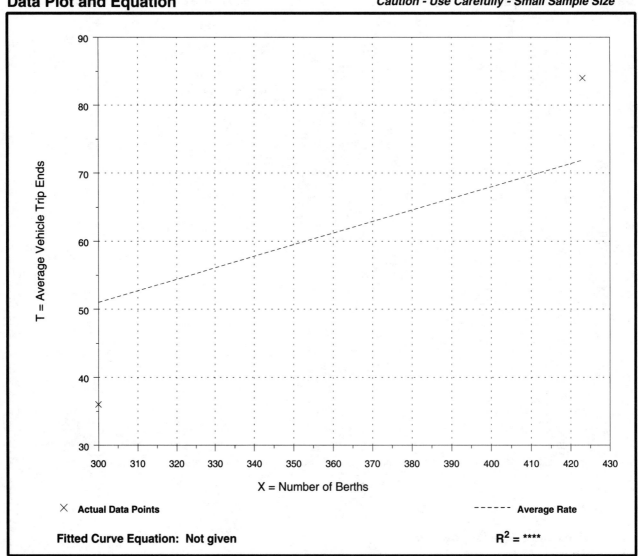

X **Actual Data Points**   ------ **Average Rate**

Fitted Curve Equation: Not given $R^2 = ****$

Marina
(420)

Average Vehicle Trip Ends vs: **Berths**
On a: **Weekday,**
P.M. Peak Hour of Generator

Number of Studies: 3
Average Number of Berths: 825
Directional Distribution: 51% entering, 49% exiting

Trip Generation per Berth

Average Rate	Range of Rates	Standard Deviation
0.21	0.18 - 0.30	0.46

Data Plot and Equation

Caution - Use Carefully - Small Sample Size

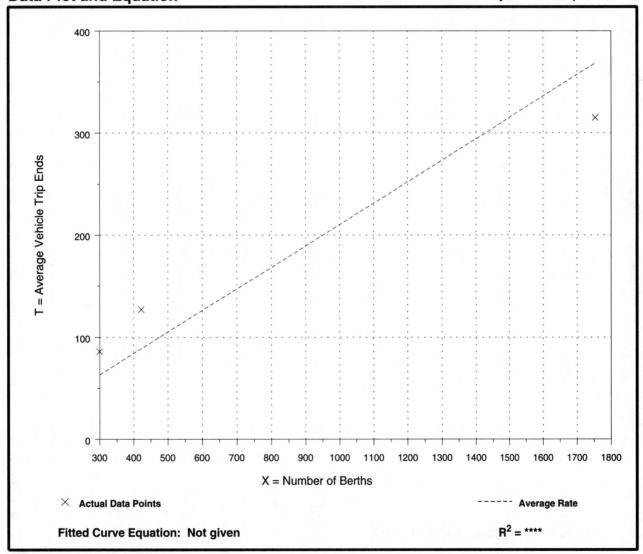

X **Actual Data Points**

---- **Average Rate**

Fitted Curve Equation: Not given

$R^2 = ****$

Marina
(420)

Average Vehicle Trip Ends vs: Berths
On a: Saturday

Number of Studies: 6
Average Number of Berths: 512
Directional Distribution: 50% entering, 50% exiting

Trip Generation per Berth

Average Rate	Range of Rates	Standard Deviation
3.22	2.47 - 12.78	2.64

Data Plot and Equation

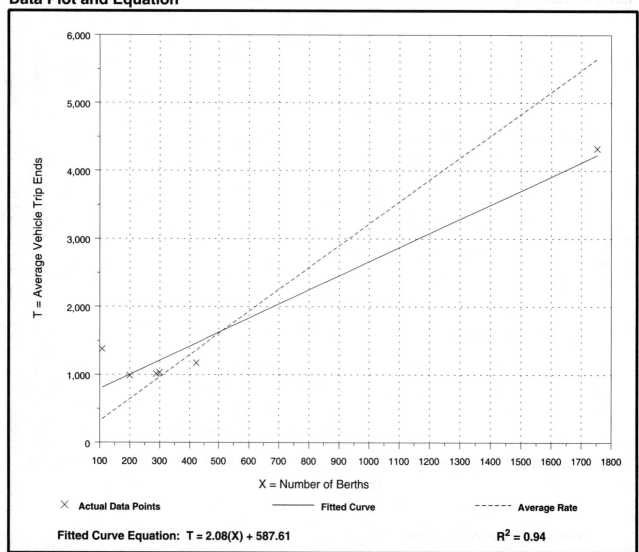

X **Actual Data Points**   —— **Fitted Curve**   - - - - **Average Rate**

Fitted Curve Equation: T = 2.08(X) + 587.61 $R^2 = 0.94$

Marina
(420)

Average Vehicle Trip Ends vs: Berths
On a: Saturday,
Peak Hour of Generator

Number of Studies: 3
Average Number of Berths: 825
Directional Distribution: 44% entering, 56% exiting

Trip Generation per Berth

Average Rate	Range of Rates	Standard Deviation
0.27	0.21 - 0.48	0.53

Data Plot and Equation

Caution - Use Carefully - Small Sample Size

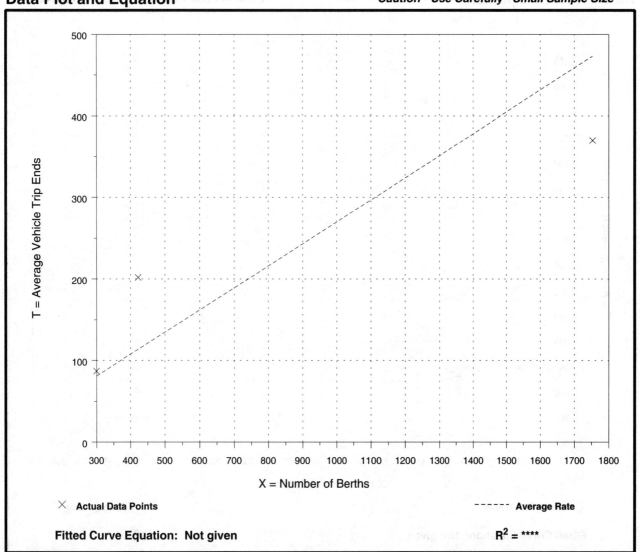

X **Actual Data Points**

------ **Average Rate**

Fitted Curve Equation: Not given

$R^2 = ****$

Marina
(420)

Average Vehicle Trip Ends vs: Berths
On a: Sunday

Number of Studies: 4
Average Number of Berths: 224
Directional Distribution: 50% entering, 50% exiting

Trip Generation per Berth

Average Rate	Range of Rates	Standard Deviation
6.40	3.49 - 20.00	5.75

Data Plot and Equation

Caution - Use Carefully - Small Sample Size

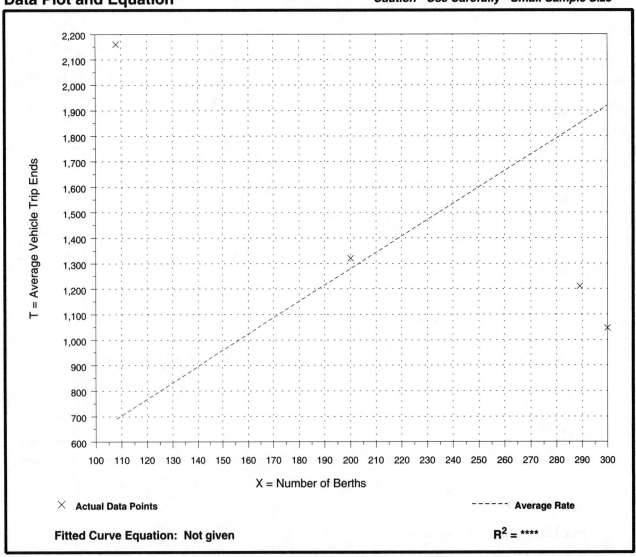

X **Actual Data Points**

----- **Average Rate**

Fitted Curve Equation: Not given

$R^2 = ****$

Trip Generation, 8th Edition   740   Institute of Transportation Engineers

Marina
(420)

Average Vehicle Trip Ends vs: Acres
On a: Weekday

Number of Studies: 3
Average Number of Acres: 45
Directional Distribution: 50% entering, 50% exiting

Trip Generation per Acre

Average Rate	Range of Rates	Standard Deviation
20.93	10.32 - 75.45	21.15

Data Plot and Equation

Caution - Use Carefully - Small Sample Size

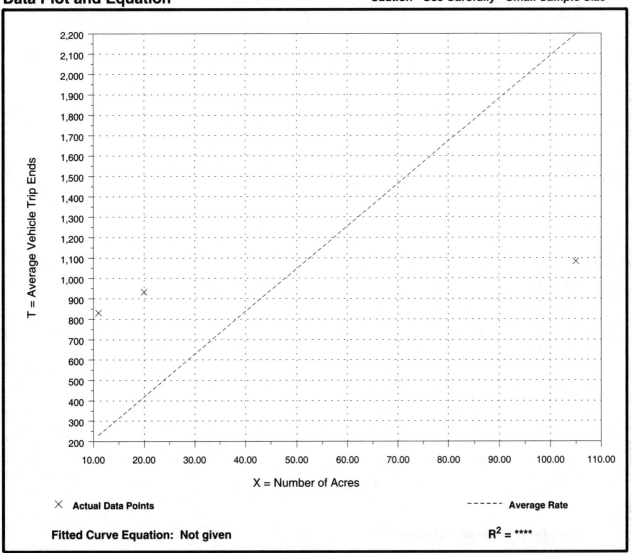

X = Number of Acres

$\times$ **Actual Data Points**   - - - - - **Average Rate**

Fitted Curve Equation: Not given $R^2 = ****$

Marina
(420)

Number of Studies: 3
Average Number of Acres: 45
Directional Distribution: 50% entering, 50% exiting

Trip Generation per Acre

Average Rate	Range of Rates	Standard Deviation
24.85	13.14 - 90.00	23.95

Data Plot and Equation

Caution - Use Carefully - Small Sample Size

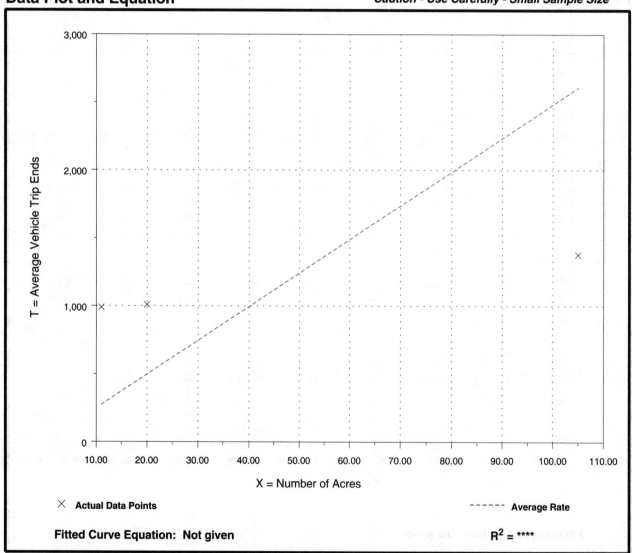

X **Actual Data Points**   - - - - - **Average Rate**

Fitted Curve Equation: Not given $R^2 = ****$

Marina
(420)

Average Vehicle Trip Ends vs: Acres
On a: Sunday

Number of Studies: 3
Average Number of Acres: 45
Directional Distribution: 50% entering, 50% exiting

Trip Generation per Acre

Average Rate	Range of Rates	Standard Deviation
34.49	20.57 - 120.00	29.66

Data Plot and Equation

Caution - Use Carefully - Small Sample Size

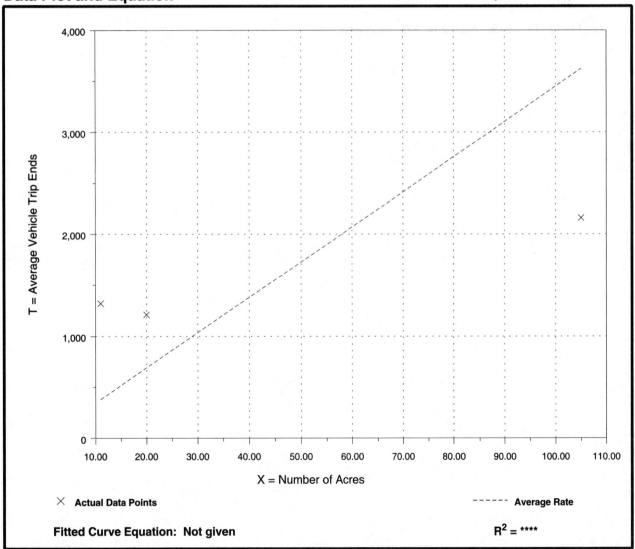

X   **Actual Data Points**

- - - - - **Average Rate**

Fitted Curve Equation: Not given

$R^2 = ****$

Land Use: 430
Golf Course

Description

Golf courses include 9-, 18-, 27- and 36-hole municipal courses. Some sites may also have driving ranges and clubhouses with a pro shop, restaurant, lounge and banquet facilities. Miniature golf course (Land Use 431), golf driving range (Land Use 432) and multipurpose recreational facility (Land Use 435) are related uses.

Additional Data

Most of the facilities were located in suburban areas; a few were in scenic, rural areas.

The sites were surveyed between the late 1960s and the 2000s throughout the United States.

Source Numbers

7, 11, 12, 13, 18, 98, 102, 214, 378, 407, 440, 629

Golf Course
(430)

Average Vehicle Trip Ends vs: **Employees**
On a: **Weekday**

Number of Studies: 16
Avg. Number of Employees: 38
Directional Distribution: 50% entering, 50% exiting

Trip Generation per Employee

Average Rate	Range of Rates	Standard Deviation
20.52	10.90 - 75.00	13.02

Data Plot and Equation

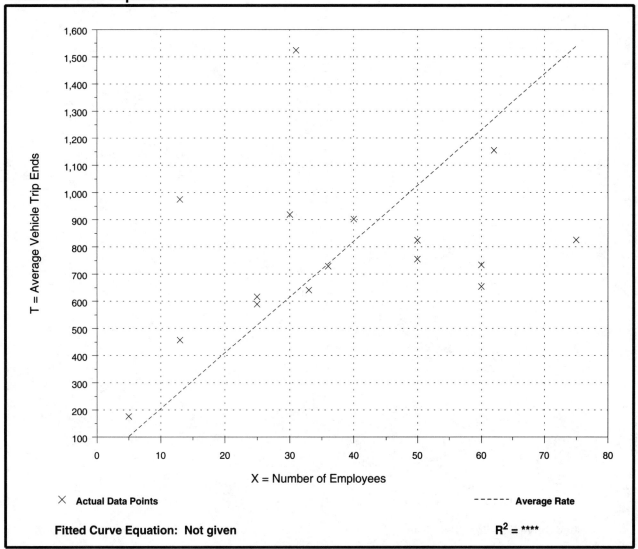

X **Actual Data Points** ----- **Average Rate**

Fitted Curve Equation: Not given $R^2 = ****$

Golf Course
(430)

Average Vehicle Trip Ends vs: **Employees**
On a: **Weekday,**
Peak Hour of Adjacent Street Traffic,
One Hour Between 7 and 9 a.m.

Number of Studies: 3
Avg. Number of Employees: 41
Directional Distribution: 68% entering, 32% exiting

Trip Generation per Employee

Average Rate	Range of Rates	Standard Deviation
1.01	0.84 - 1.28	1.01

Data Plot and Equation

Caution - Use Carefully - Small Sample Size

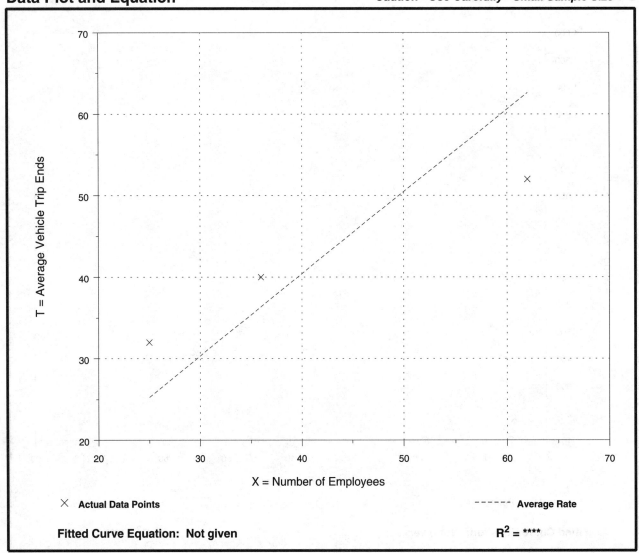

X **Actual Data Points**   - - - - - **Average Rate**

Fitted Curve Equation: Not given $R^2 = ****$

Golf Course
(430)

Average Vehicle Trip Ends vs: Employees
On a: Weekday,
Peak Hour of Adjacent Street Traffic,
One Hour Between 4 and 6 p.m.

Number of Studies: 3
Avg. Number of Employees: 41
Directional Distribution: 48% entering, 52% exiting

Trip Generation per Employee

Average Rate	Range of Rates	Standard Deviation
1.48	1.39 - 1.84	1.22

Data Plot and Equation

Caution - Use Carefully - Small Sample Size

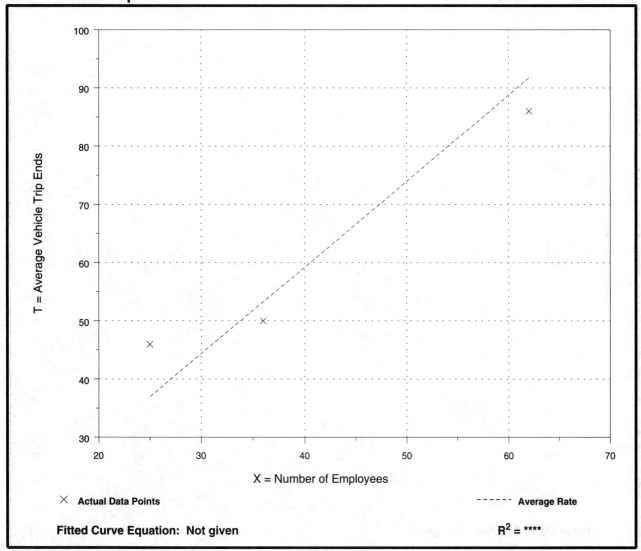

X   **Actual Data Points**   - - - - -   **Average Rate**

Fitted Curve Equation: Not given $R^2 = $ ****

Golf Course
(430)

Average Vehicle Trip Ends vs: **Employees**
On a: **Weekday,**
A.M. Peak Hour of Generator

Number of Studies: 3
Avg. Number of Employees: 41
Directional Distribution: 47% entering, 53% exiting

Trip Generation per Employee

Average Rate	Range of Rates	Standard Deviation
1.76	1.31 - 2.36	1.40

Data Plot and Equation

Caution - Use Carefully - Small Sample Size

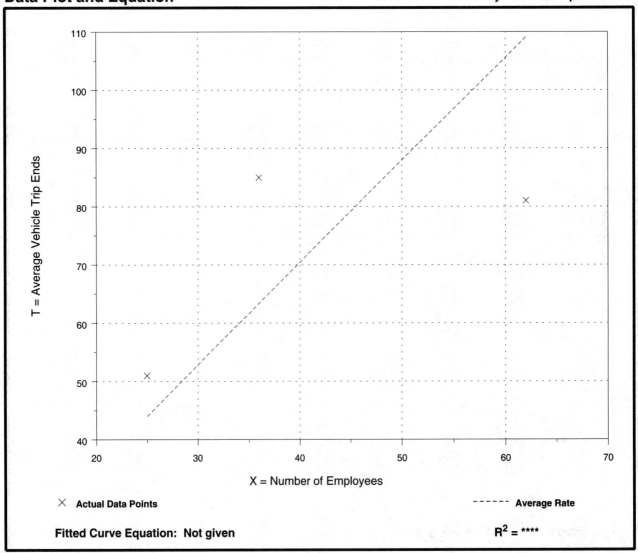

X **Actual Data Points**

----- **Average Rate**

Fitted Curve Equation: Not given

$R^2 = ****$

Golf Course
(430)

Average Vehicle Trip Ends vs: Employees
On a: Weekday,
P.M. Peak Hour of Generator

Number of Studies: 3
Avg. Number of Employees: 41
Directional Distribution: 43% entering, 57% exiting

Trip Generation per Employee

Average Rate	Range of Rates	Standard Deviation
2.08	1.92 - 2.56	1.45

Data Plot and Equation

Caution - Use Carefully - Small Sample Size

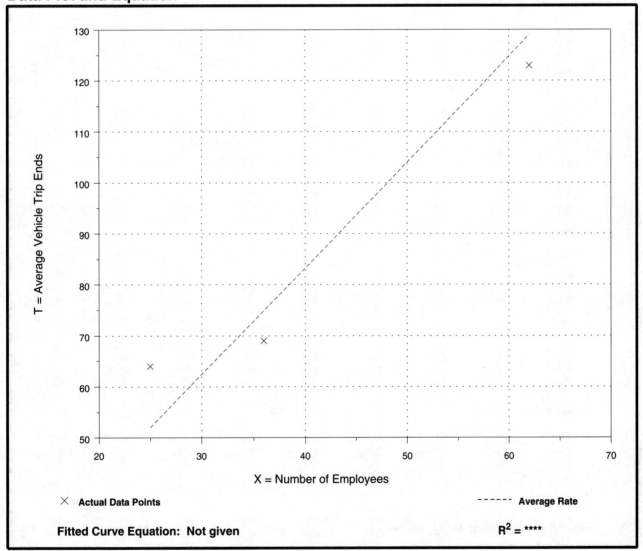

X **Actual Data Points**
----- **Average Rate**

Fitted Curve Equation: Not given $R^2 = ****$

Golf Course
(430)

Average Vehicle Trip Ends vs: Employees
On a: Saturday

Number of Studies: 12
Avg. Number of Employees: 35
Directional Distribution: 50% entering, 50% exiting

Trip Generation per Employee

Average Rate	Range of Rates	Standard Deviation
25.28	10.86 - 98.08	18.02

Data Plot and Equation

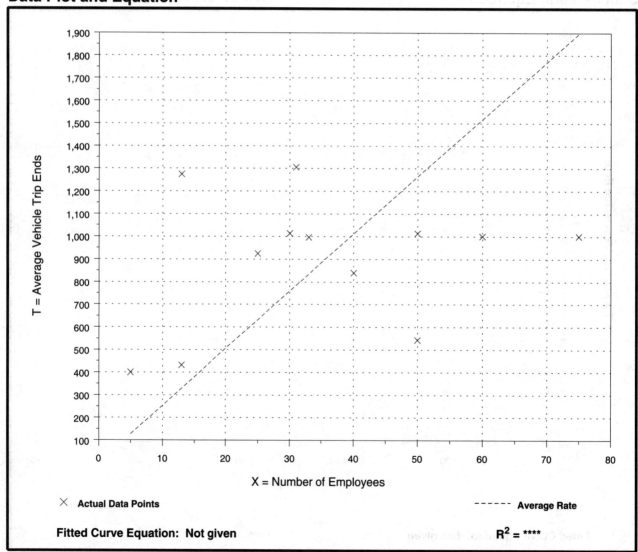

X   **Actual Data Points**

- - - - - **Average Rate**

Fitted Curve Equation: Not given $R^2 = ****$

Golf Course
(430)

Average Vehicle Trip Ends vs: **Employees**
On a: **Saturday,**
Peak Hour of Generator

Number of Studies: 9
Avg. Number of Employees: 39
Directional Distribution: Not available

Trip Generation per Employee

Average Rate	Range of Rates	Standard Deviation
2.58	1.06 - 9.15	2.32

Data Plot and Equation

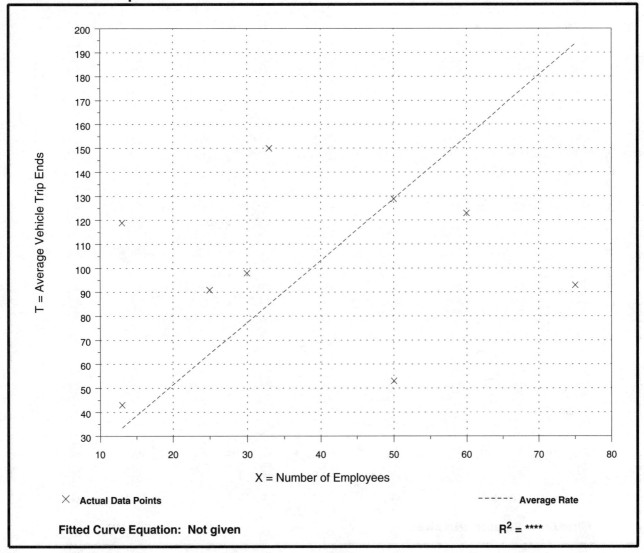

X **Actual Data Points**   - - - - - - **Average Rate**

Fitted Curve Equation: Not given $R^2 = ****$

Golf Course
(430)

Average Vehicle Trip Ends vs: Employees
On a: Sunday

Number of Studies: 11
Avg. Number of Employees: 37
Directional Distribution: 50% entering, 50% exiting

Trip Generation per Employee

Average Rate	Range of Rates	Standard Deviation
23.25	11.78 - 78.38	16.44

Data Plot and Equation

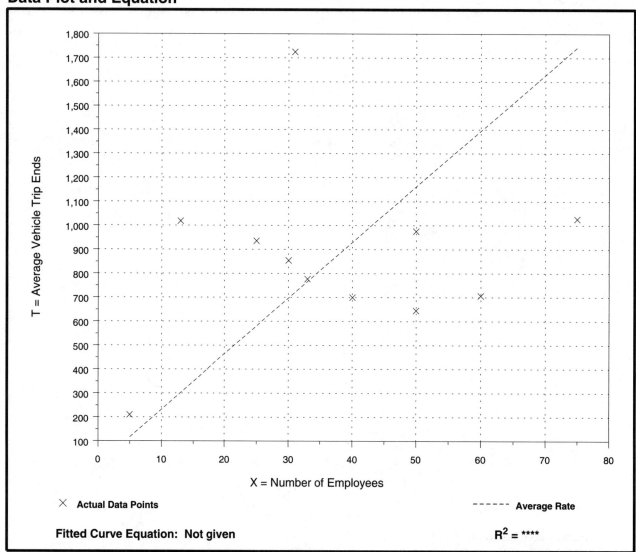

X Actual Data Points

- - - - - Average Rate

Fitted Curve Equation: Not given $R^2 = ****$

Golf Course
(430)

Average Vehicle Trip Ends vs: **Employees**
On a: **Sunday,**
Peak Hour of Generator

Number of Studies: 8
Avg. Number of Employees: 42
Directional Distribution: Not available

Trip Generation per Employee

Average Rate	Range of Rates	Standard Deviation
2.18	0.90 - 8.38	2.10

Data Plot and Equation

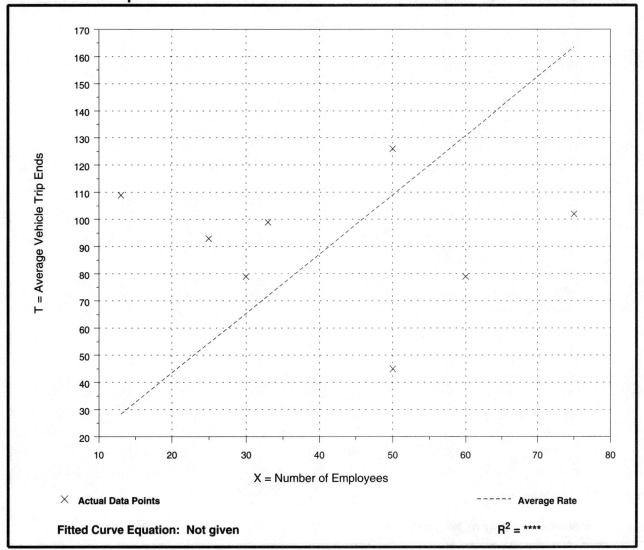

Fitted Curve Equation: Not given

$R^2 = ****$

Golf Course
(430)

Average Vehicle Trip Ends vs: Acres
On a: Weekday

Number of Studies: 24
Average Number of Acres: 143
Directional Distribution: 50% entering, 50% exiting

Trip Generation per Acre

Average Rate	Range of Rates	Standard Deviation
5.04	2.33 - 10.89	3.37

Data Plot and Equation

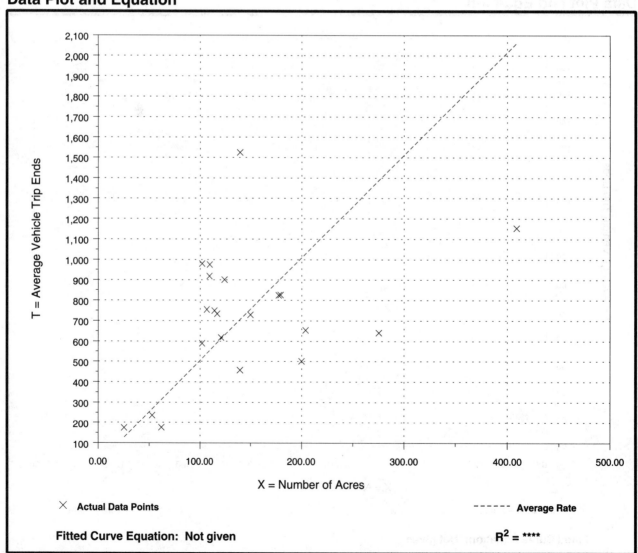

X **Actual Data Points**

- - - - - **Average Rate**

Fitted Curve Equation: Not given $R^2 = ****$

Golf Course
(430)

Average Vehicle Trip Ends vs: **Acres**
On a: **Weekday,**
Peak Hour of Adjacent Street Traffic,
One Hour Between 7 and 9 a.m.

Number of Studies: 5
Average Number of Acres: 177
Directional Distribution: 74% entering, 26% exiting

Trip Generation per Acre

Average Rate	Range of Rates	Standard Deviation
0.21	0.13 - 0.39	0.46

Data Plot and Equation

Caution - Use Carefully - Small Sample Size

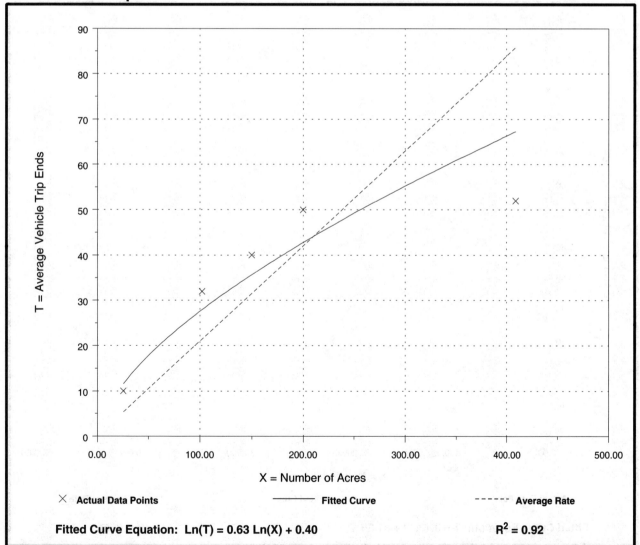

X Actual Data Points ——— Fitted Curve - - - - - Average Rate

Fitted Curve Equation: Ln(T) = 0.63 Ln(X) + 0.40 $R^2 = 0.92$

Golf Course
(430)

Average Vehicle Trip Ends vs: **Acres**
On a: **Weekday,**
Peak Hour of Adjacent Street Traffic,
One Hour Between 4 and 6 p.m.

Number of Studies: 5
Average Number of Acres: 177
Directional Distribution: 34% entering, 66% exiting

Trip Generation per Acre

Average Rate	Range of Rates	Standard Deviation
0.30	0.21 - 1.45	0.59

Data Plot and Equation

Caution - Use Carefully - Small Sample Size

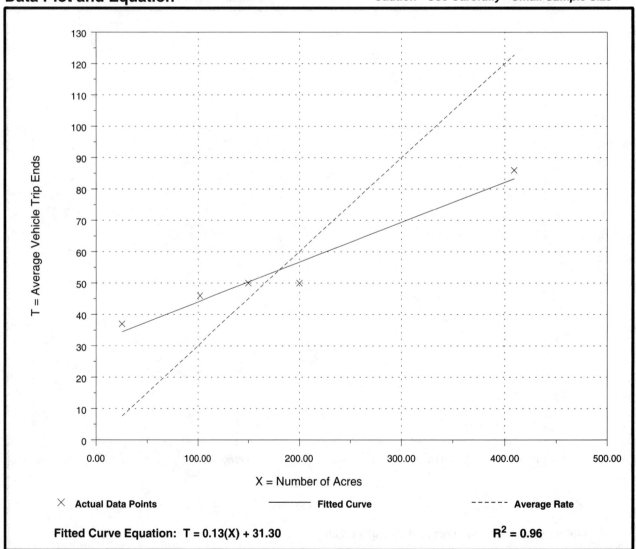

X **Actual Data Points** ——— **Fitted Curve** - - - - - **Average Rate**

Fitted Curve Equation: T = 0.13(X) + 31.30 $R^2 = 0.96$

Golf Course
(430)

Average Vehicle Trip Ends vs: Acres
On a: Weekday,
A.M. Peak Hour of Generator

Number of Studies: 3
Average Number of Acres: 220
Directional Distribution: 47% entering, 53% exiting

Trip Generation per Acre

Average Rate	Range of Rates	Standard Deviation
0.33	0.20 - 0.57	0.60

Data Plot and Equation

Caution - Use Carefully - Small Sample Size

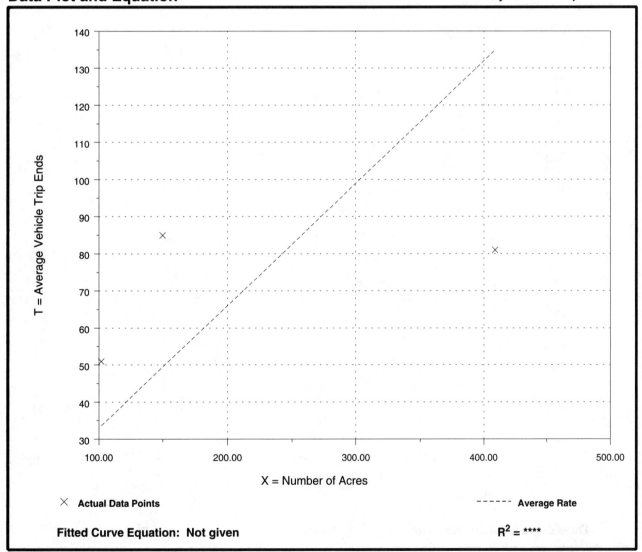

$\times$ **Actual Data Points**　　　　　　　　　- - - - - **Average Rate**

Fitted Curve Equation: Not given　　　　　$R^2 = ****$

Golf Course
(430)

Average Vehicle Trip Ends vs: **Acres**
On a: **Weekday,**
P.M. Peak Hour of Generator

Number of Studies: 3
Average Number of Acres: 220
Directional Distribution: 43% entering, 57% exiting

Trip Generation per Acre

Average Rate	Range of Rates	Standard Deviation
0.39	0.30 - 0.63	0.63

Data Plot and Equation

Caution - Use Carefully - Small Sample Size

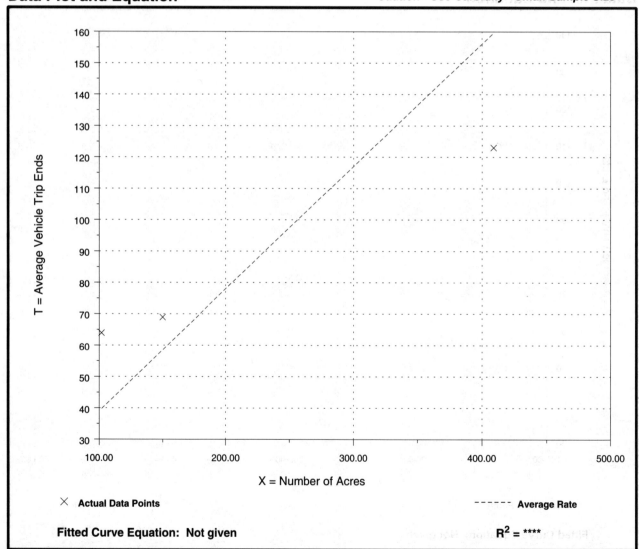

X **Actual Data Points**   ----- **Average Rate**

Fitted Curve Equation: Not given $R^2 = ****$

Golf Course
(430)

Average Vehicle Trip Ends vs: Acres
On a: Saturday

Number of Studies: 18
Average Number of Acres: 136
Directional Distribution: 50% entering, 50% exiting

Trip Generation per Acre

Average Rate	Range of Rates	Standard Deviation
5.82	2.20 - 11.59	3.64

Data Plot and Equation

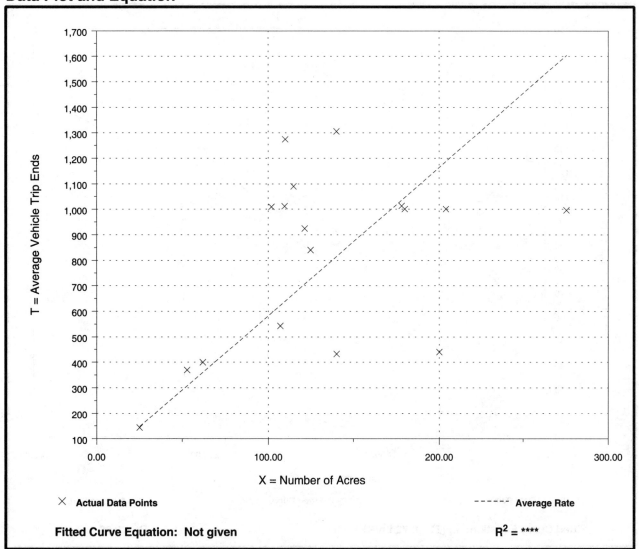

Fitted Curve Equation: Not given $R^2 = ****$

Golf Course
(430)

Average Vehicle Trip Ends vs: **Acres**
On a: **Saturday,**
Peak Hour of Generator

Number of Studies: 10
Average Number of Acres: 145
Directional Distribution: 52% entering, 48% exiting

Trip Generation per Acre

Average Rate	Range of Rates	Standard Deviation
0.64	0.31 - 1.08	0.82

Data Plot and Equation

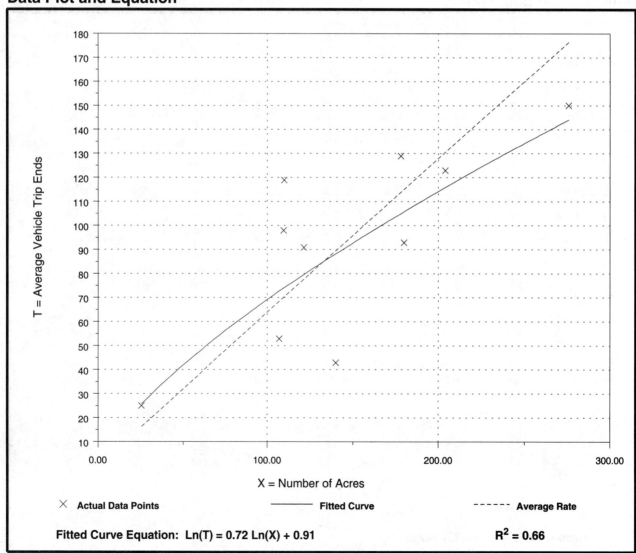

X **Actual Data Points**   ——— **Fitted Curve**   - - - - - **Average Rate**

Fitted Curve Equation: Ln(T) = 0.72 Ln(X) + 0.91 $R^2 = 0.66$

Golf Course
(430)

Average Vehicle Trip Ends vs: Acres
On a: Sunday

Number of Studies: 16
Average Number of Acres: 132
Directional Distribution: 50% entering, 50% exiting

Trip Generation per Acre

Average Rate	Range of Rates	Standard Deviation
5.88	2.00 - 12.32	3.73

Data Plot and Equation

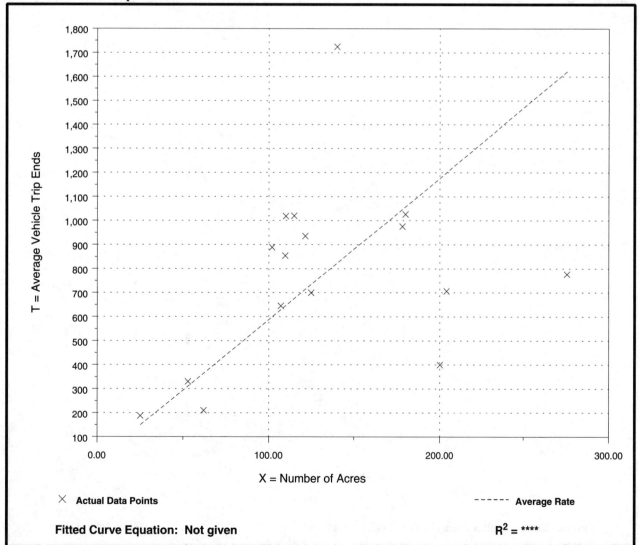

X = Number of Acres

✕ **Actual Data Points**   - - - - - **Average Rate**

Fitted Curve Equation: Not given $R^2 = ****$

Golf Course
(430)

Average Vehicle Trip Ends vs: **Acres**
On a: **Sunday,**
Peak Hour of Generator

Number of Studies: 9
Average Number of Acres: 146
Directional Distribution: Not available

Trip Generation per Acre

Average Rate	Range of Rates	Standard Deviation
0.58	0.36 - 0.99	0.78

Data Plot and Equation

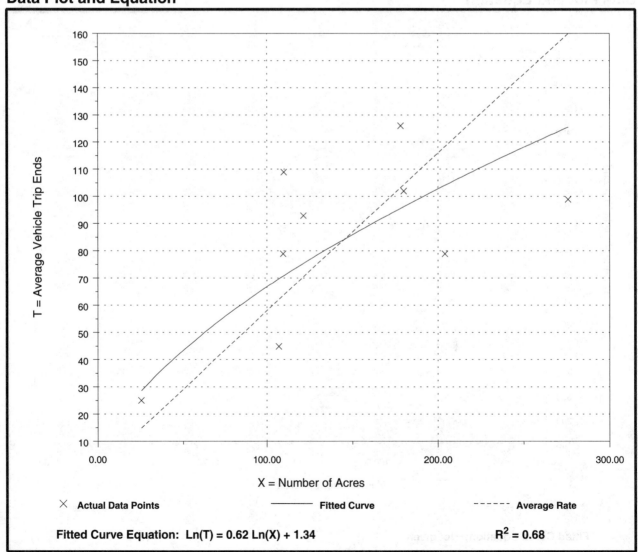

Fitted Curve Equation: Ln(T) = 0.62 Ln(X) + 1.34 R^2 = 0.68

Golf Course
(430)

Average Vehicle Trip Ends vs: **Holes**
On a: **Weekday**

Number of Studies: 18
Average Number of Holes: 20
Directional Distribution: 50% entering, 50% exiting

Trip Generation per Hole

Average Rate	Range of Rates	Standard Deviation
35.74	14.50 - 54.44	12.12

Data Plot and Equation

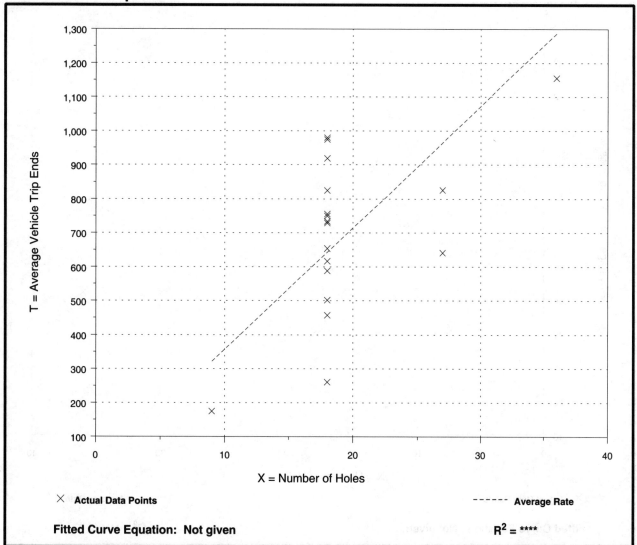

Fitted Curve Equation: Not given $R^2 = ****$

Golf Course
(430)

Average Vehicle Trip Ends vs: **Holes**
On a: **Weekday,**
Peak Hour of Adjacent Street Traffic,
One Hour Between 7 and 9 a.m.

Number of Studies: 11
Average Number of Holes: 21
Directional Distribution: 79% entering, 21% exiting

Trip Generation per Hole

Average Rate	Range of Rates	Standard Deviation
2.23	1.06 - 4.52	1.79

Data Plot and Equation

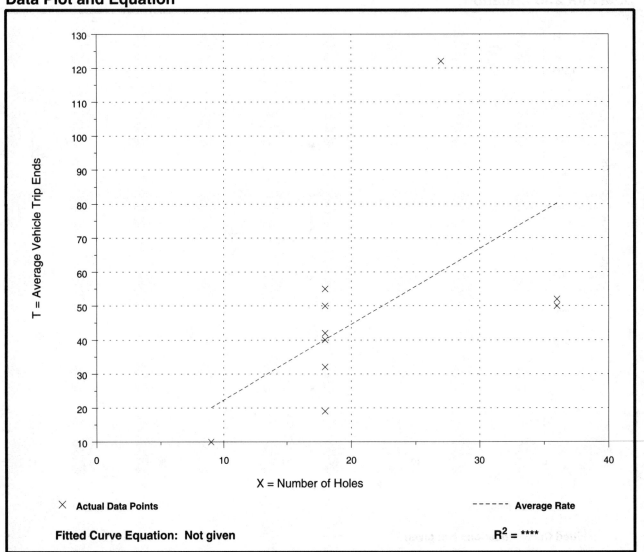

Fitted Curve Equation: Not given $R^2 = ****$

Golf Course
(430)

Average Vehicle Trip Ends vs: **Holes**
On a: **Weekday,**
Peak Hour of Adjacent Street Traffic,
One Hour Between 4 and 6 p.m.

Number of Studies: 12
Average Number of Holes: 21
Directional Distribution: 45% entering, 55% exiting

Trip Generation per Hole

Average Rate	Range of Rates	Standard Deviation
2.78	1.67 - 4.11	1.79

Data Plot and Equation

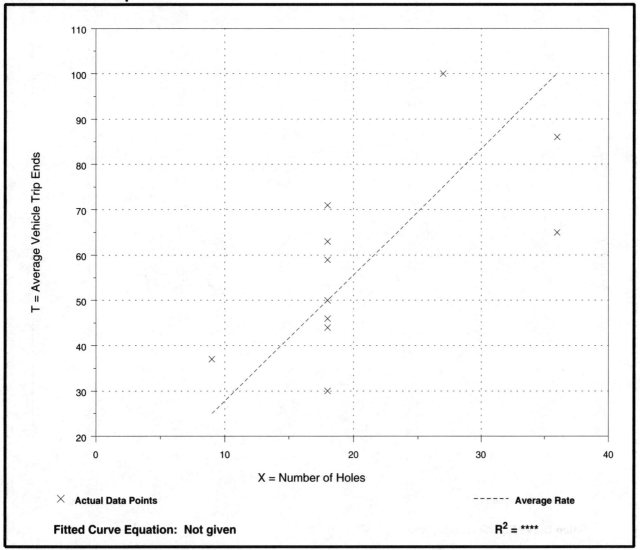

Fitted Curve Equation: Not given $R^2 = ****$

Golf Course
(430)

Average Vehicle Trip Ends vs: **Holes**
On a: **Weekday,**
A.M. Peak Hour of Generator

Number of Studies: 3
Average Number of Holes: 24
Directional Distribution: 47% entering, 53% exiting

Trip Generation per Hole

Average Rate	Range of Rates	Standard Deviation
3.01	2.25 - 4.72	1.99

Data Plot and Equation

Caution - Use Carefully - Small Sample Size

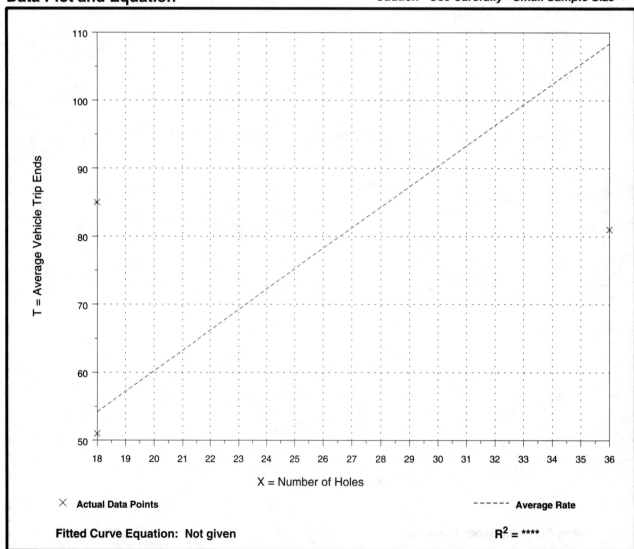

X Actual Data Points

- - - - - **Average Rate**

Fitted Curve Equation: Not given $R^2 = ****$

Golf Course
(430)

Average Vehicle Trip Ends vs: **Holes**
On a: **Weekday,**
P.M. Peak Hour of Generator

Number of Studies: 3
Average Number of Holes: 24
Directional Distribution: 43% entering, 57% exiting

Trip Generation per Hole

Average Rate	Range of Rates	Standard Deviation
3.56	3.42 - 3.83	1.87

Data Plot and Equation

Caution - Use Carefully - Small Sample Size

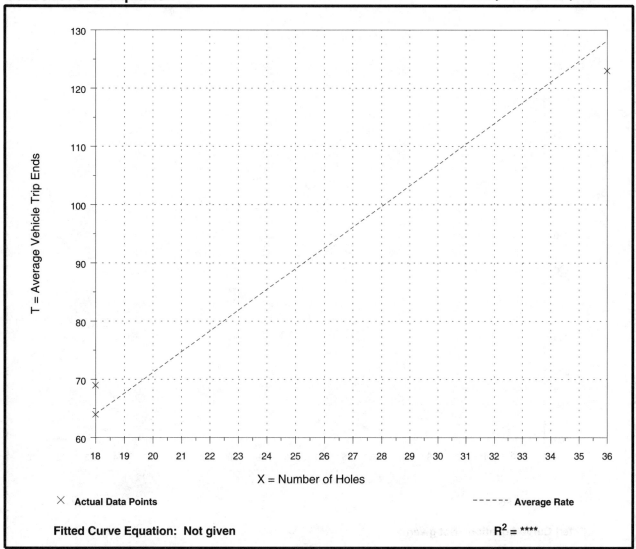

X = Number of Holes

✕ **Actual Data Points**   - - - - - **Average Rate**

Fitted Curve Equation: Not given $R^2 = ****$

Golf Course
(430)

Average Vehicle Trip Ends vs: Holes
On a: Saturday

Number of Studies: 12
Average Number of Holes: 19
Directional Distribution: 50% entering, 50% exiting

Trip Generation per Hole

Average Rate	Range of Rates	Standard Deviation
40.63	16.00 - 70.83	17.12

Data Plot and Equation

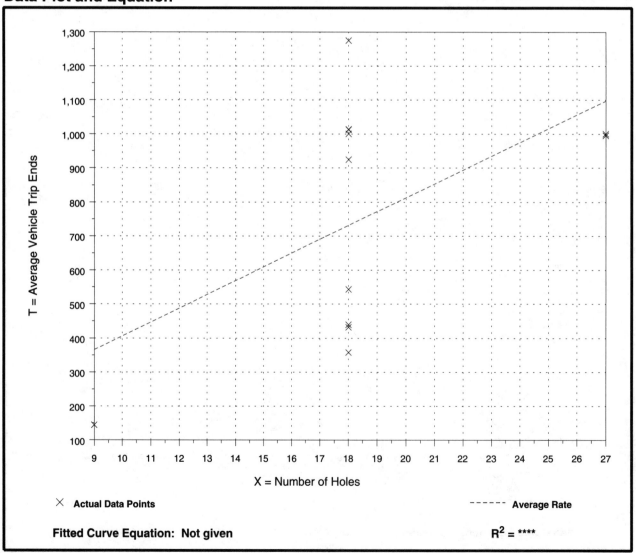

X **Actual Data Points**   — — — — — **Average Rate**

Fitted Curve Equation: Not given $R^2 = ****$

Golf Course
(430)

Average Vehicle Trip Ends vs: Holes
On a: Saturday,
Peak Hour of Generator

Number of Studies: 12
Average Number of Holes: 19
Directional Distribution: 49% entering, 51% exiting

Trip Generation per Hole

Average Rate	Range of Rates	Standard Deviation
4.59	1.61 - 7.17	2.73

Data Plot and Equation

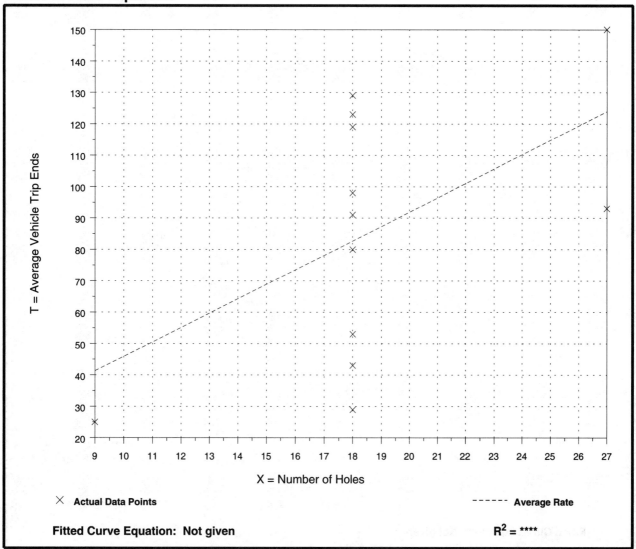

Fitted Curve Equation: Not given $R^2 = ****$

Golf Course
(430)

Average Vehicle Trip Ends vs: Holes
On a: Sunday

Number of Studies: 10
Average Number of Holes: 19
Directional Distribution: 50% entering, 50% exiting

Trip Generation per Hole

Average Rate	Range of Rates	Standard Deviation
39.53	18.89 - 56.61	13.52

Data Plot and Equation

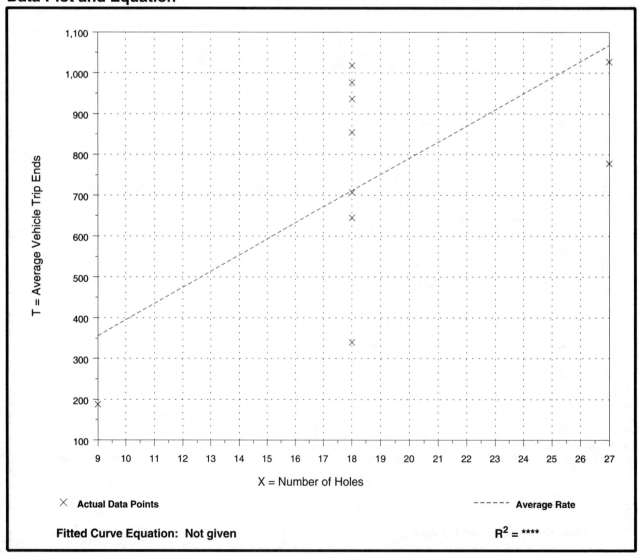

X **Actual Data Points**   - - - - - **Average Rate**

Fitted Curve Equation: Not given $R^2 = $ ****

Golf Course
(430)

Average Vehicle Trip Ends vs: **Holes**
On a: **Sunday,**
Peak Hour of Generator

Number of Studies: 9
Average Number of Holes: 19
Directional Distribution: Not available

Trip Generation per Hole

Average Rate	Range of Rates	Standard Deviation
4.43	2.50 - 7.00	2.44

Data Plot and Equation

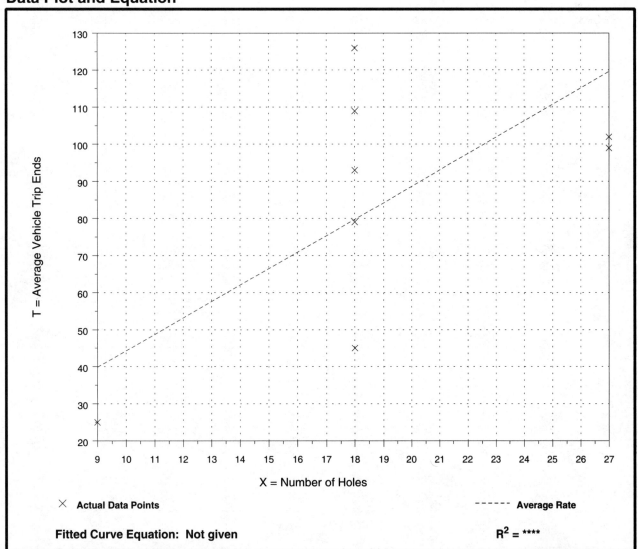

X **Actual Data Points**   ----- **Average Rate**

Fitted Curve Equation: Not given $R^2 = ****$

Land Use: 431
Miniature Golf Course

Description

Miniature golf courses consist of one or more individual putting courses. They may or may not include limited game rooms or refreshment services. This land use is a stand-alone facility and is not part of a larger multipurpose entertainment or recreational facility. Golf course (Land Use 430), golf driving range (Land Use 432) and multipurpose recreational facility (Land Use 435) are related uses.

Additional Data

The site was surveyed in 1991 in New Hampshire.

Source Number

393

Land Use: 431
Miniature Golf Course
Independent Variables with One Observation

The following trip generation data are for independent variables with only one observation. This information is shown in this table only; there are no related plots for these data.

Users are cautioned to use data with care because of the small sample size.

Independent Variable	Trip Generation Rate	Size of Independent Variable	Number of Studies	Directional Distribution
Holes				
Weekday p.m. Peak Hour of Adjacent Street Traffic	0.33	18	1	33% entering, 67% exiting

Land Use: 432
Golf Driving Range

Description

Golf driving ranges are outdoor facilities containing driving tees for golfers to practice. These facilities may also provide individual or small group lessons. Some sites have pro shops and/or small refreshment facilities. Driving ranges affiliated with full-sized golf courses are included in golf course (Land Use 430). Golf course (Land Use 430), miniature golf course (Land Use 431) and multipurpose recreational facility (Land Use 435) are related uses.

Additional Data

The sites were surveyed in the 1990s throughout the United States.

Source Numbers

361, 363, 365, 393, 426, 517

Land Use: 432
Golf Driving Range
Independent Variables with One Observation

The following trip generation data are for independent variables with only one observation. This information is shown in this table only; there are no related plots for these data.

Users are cautioned to use data with care because of the small sample size.

Independent Variable	Trip Generation Rate	Size of Independent Variable	Number of Studies	Directional Distribution
Tees				
Weekday	13.65	57	1	50% entering, 50% exiting
Weekday a.m. Peak Hour of Adjacent Street Traffic	0.40	57	1	61% entering, 39% exiting
Weekday a.m. Peak Hour of Generator	1.02	57	1	53% entering, 47% exiting
Weekday p.m. Peak Hour of Generator	1.65	57	1	50% entering, 50% exiting
Saturday	17.68	57	1	50% entering, 50% exiting
Sunday	14.32	57	1	50% entering, 50% exiting
Sunday Peak Hour of Generator	1.32	57	1	60% entering, 40% exiting
Employees				
Weekday	55.57	14	1	50% entering, 50% exiting
Weekday a.m. Peak Hour of Adjacent Street Traffic	1.64	14	1	61% entering, 39% exiting
Weekday a.m. Peak Hour of Generator	4.14	14	1	53% entering, 47% exiting
Weekday p.m. Peak Hour of Generator	6.71	14	1	50% entering, 50% exiting
Saturday	72.00	14	1	50% entering, 50% exiting
Sunday	58.29	14	1	50% entering, 50% exiting
Sunday Peak Hour of Generator	5.36	14	1	60% entering, 40% exiting

Golf Driving Range
(432)

Average Vehicle Trip Ends vs: Tees/Driving Positions
On a: Weekday,
Peak Hour of Adjacent Street Traffic,
One Hour Between 4 and 6 p.m.

Number of Studies: 7
Avg. Num. of Tees/Driving Positions: 41
Directional Distribution: 45% entering, 55% exiting

Trip Generation per Tee/Driving Position

Average Rate	Range of Rates	Standard Deviation
1.25	0.54 - 2.80	1.33

Data Plot and Equation

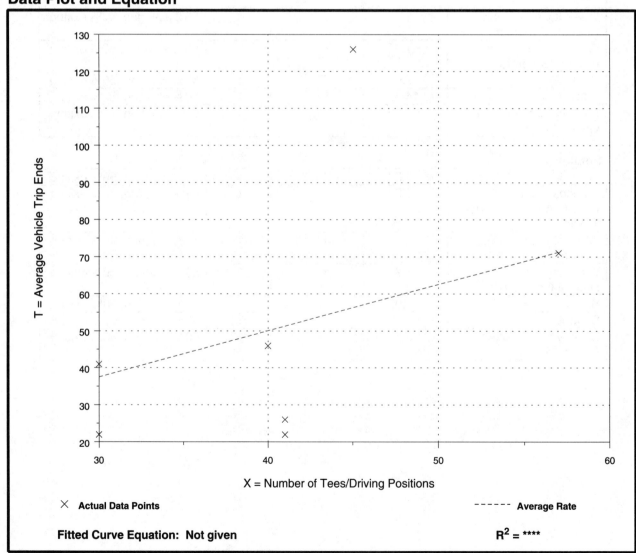

X Actual Data Points   - - - - - **Average Rate**

Fitted Curve Equation: Not given $R^2 = ****$

Golf Driving Range
(432)

Average Vehicle Trip Ends vs: **Tees/Driving Positions**
On a: **Saturday,**
Peak Hour of Generator

Number of Studies: 3
Avg. Num. of Tees/Driving Positions: 46
Directional Distribution: 50% entering, 50% exiting

Trip Generation per Tee/Driving Position

Average Rate	Range of Rates	Standard Deviation
1.30	0.66 - 2.00	1.28

Data Plot and Equation

Caution - Use Carefully - Small Sample Size

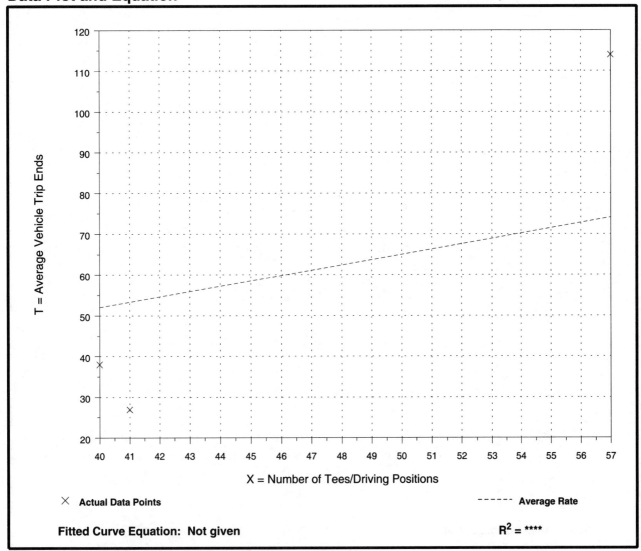

X = Number of Tees/Driving Positions

✕ **Actual Data Points**   - - - - - **Average Rate**

Fitted Curve Equation: Not given $R^2 = ****$

Golf Driving Range
(432)

Average Vehicle Trip Ends vs: Employees
On a: Weekday,
Peak Hour of Adjacent Street Traffic,
One Hour Between 4 and 6 p.m.

Number of Studies: 2
Avg. Number of Employees: 15
Directional Distribution: 50% entering, 50% exiting

Trip Generation per Employee

Average Rate	Range of Rates	Standard Deviation
5.48	5.07 - 5.87	*

Data Plot and Equation

Caution - Use Carefully - Small Sample Size

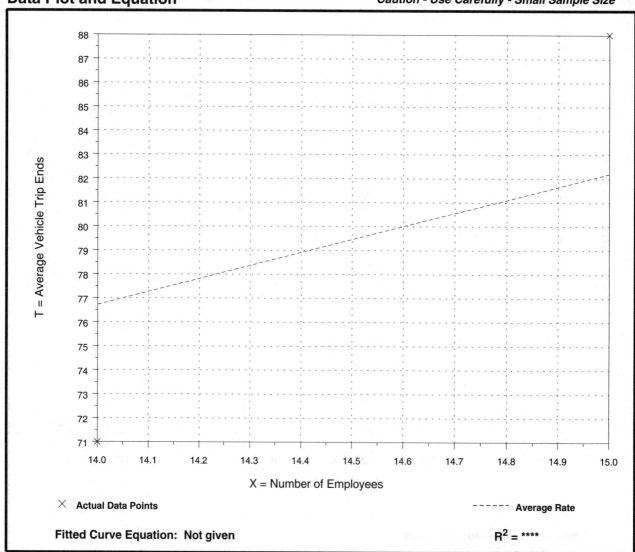

X **Actual Data Points**

‑ ‑ ‑ ‑ ‑ **Average Rate**

Fitted Curve Equation: Not given $R^2 = ****$

Golf Driving Range
(432)

Average Vehicle Trip Ends vs: **Employees**
On a: **Saturday,**
Peak Hour of Generator

Number of Studies: 2
Avg. Number of Employees: 15
Directional Distribution: 50% entering, 50% exiting

Trip Generation per Employee

Average Rate	Range of Rates	Standard Deviation
7.76	7.40 - 8.14	*

Data Plot and Equation

Caution - Use Carefully - Small Sample Size

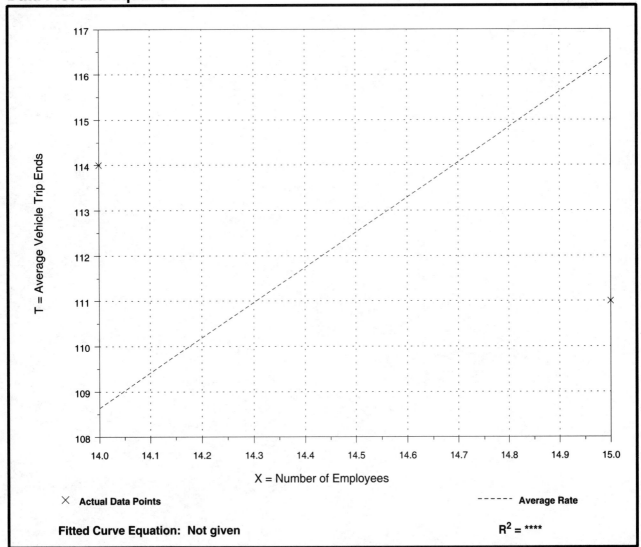

Fitted Curve Equation: Not given

$R^2 = ****$

Land Use: 433
Batting Cages

Description

These facilities consist of one or more individual batting cages. They may or may not include limited game rooms or refreshment services. This land use is a stand-alone facility and is not part of a larger multipurpose entertainment or recreational facility. Multipurpose recreational facility (Land Use 435) is a related use.

Additional Data

The sites were surveyed in the 1990s in California and New Hampshire.

Source Numbers

393, 441

Batting Cages
(433)

Average Vehicle Trip Ends vs: **Cages**
On a: **Weekday,**
Peak Hour of Adjacent Street Traffic,
One Hour Between 4 and 6 p.m.

Number of Studies: 3
Average Number of Cages: 6
Directional Distribution: 55% entering, 45% exiting

Trip Generation per Cage

Average Rate	Range of Rates	Standard Deviation
2.22	1.75 - 2.50	1.43

Data Plot and Equation

Caution - Use Carefully - Small Sample Size

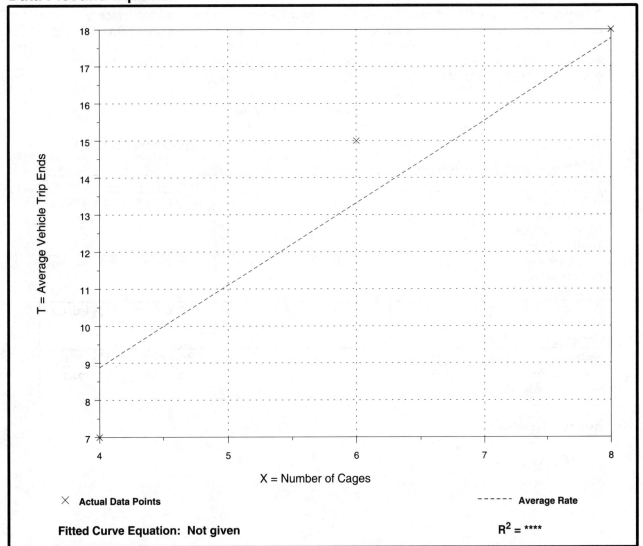

X = Number of Cages

✕ **Actual Data Points**   ----- **Average Rate**

Fitted Curve Equation: Not given $R^2 = ****$

Land Use: 435
Multipurpose Recreational Facility

Description

Multipurpose recreational facilities contain two or more of the following land uses combined at one site: miniature golf, batting cages, video arcade, bumper boats, go-carts and golf driving ranges. Refreshment areas may also be provided. Golf course (Land Use 430), miniature golf course (Land Use 431), golf driving range (Land Use 432) and batting cages (Land Use 433) are related uses.

Additional Data

These sites were surveyed in the 1990s and 2000s in California and Oregon.

Specialized Land Use Data

A survey conducted in Pennsylvania in 1998 was submitted for an indoor race track facility containing a go-cart racing track, arcade, laser tag, restaurant and party function rooms. The trip generation rates for this facility differ considerably from those contained in this land use. Therefore, the information collected on this facility is presented in the following table and was excluded from the data plots.

Day/Time Period	Trip Generation Rate	Size of Independent Variable	Number of Studies	Directional Distribution
1,000 Square Feet Gross Floor Area				
Weekday	1.99	118	1	52% entering, 48% exiting
Weekday p.m. Peak Hour of Adjacent Street Traffic	0.17	118	1	35% entering, 65% exiting
Weekday a.m. Peak Hour of Generator	0.24	118	1	71% entering, 29% exiting
Weekday p.m. Peak Hour of Generator	0.25	118	1	52% entering, 48% exiting
Saturday	2.35	118	1	52% entering, 48% exiting
Saturday Peak Hour of Generator	0.29	118	1	59% entering, 41% exiting

Source Numbers

441, 583, 611, 618

Land Use: 435
Multipurpose Recreational Facility
Independent Variables with One Observation

The following trip generation data are for independent variables with only one observation. This information is shown in this table only; there are no related plots for these data.

Users are cautioned to use data with care because of the small sample size.

Independent Variable	Trip Generation Rate	Size of Independent Variable	Number of Studies	Directional Distribution
Acres				
Weekday	90.38	4.1	1	50% entering, 50% exiting
Weekday a.m. Peak Hour of Adjacent Street Traffic	1.92	4.1	1	Not available
Weekday p.m. Peak Hour of Adjacent Street Traffic	5.77	4.1	1	Not available
Weekday a.m. Peak Hour of Generator	2.88	4.1	1	Not available
Weekday p.m. Peak Hour of Generator	11.54	4.1	1	Not available
Saturday	97.60	4.1	1	50% entering, 50% exiting
Saturday Peak Hour of Generator	12.26	4.1	1	Not available
Sunday	81.49	4.1	1	50% entering, 50% exiting
Sunday Peak Hour of Generator	9.38	4.1	1	Not available

Multipurpose Recreational Facility
(435)

Average Vehicle Trip Ends vs: **1000 Sq. Feet Gross Floor Area**
On a: **Weekday,**
Peak Hour of Adjacent Street Traffic,
One Hour Between 4 and 6 p.m.

Number of Studies: 3
Average 1000 Sq. Feet GFA: 21
Directional Distribution: 55% entering, 45% exiting

Trip Generation per 1000 Sq. Feet Gross Floor Area

Average Rate	Range of Rates	Standard Deviation
3.58	2.95 - 4.06	1.92

Data Plot and Equation

Caution - Use Carefully - Small Sample Size

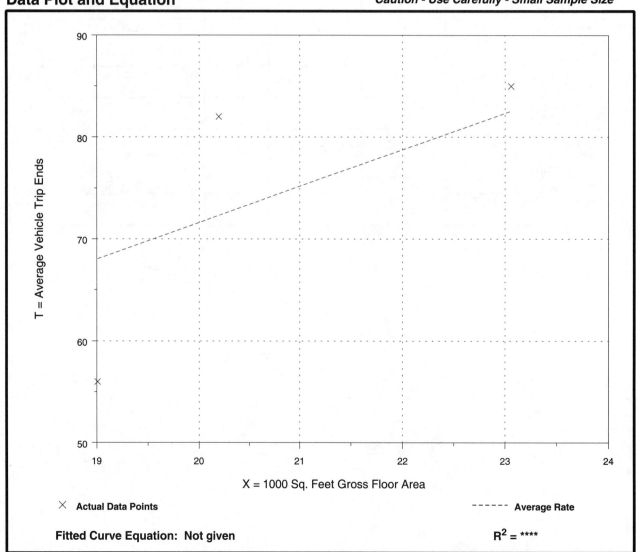

X = 1000 Sq. Feet Gross Floor Area

✕ **Actual Data Points**   - - - - - **Average Rate**

Fitted Curve Equation: Not given $R^2 = ****$

Land Use: 437
Bowling Alley

Description

Bowling alleys are recreational facilities that include bowling lanes. A small lounge, restaurant and/or snack bar, video games and pool tables may also be available.

Additional Data

The sites were surveyed in the 1960s and 1990s in California and Connecticut.

Source Numbers

8, 400

Land Use: 437
Bowling Alley
Independent Variables with One Observation

The following trip generation data are for independent variables with only one observation. This information is shown in this table only; there are no related plots for these data.

Users are cautioned to use data with care because of the small sample size.

Independent Variable	Trip Generation Rate	Size of Independent Variable	Number of Studies	Directional Distribution
Bowling Lanes				
Weekday	33.33	24	1	50% entering, 50% exiting
Weekday a.m. Peak Hour of Adjacent Street Traffic	3.13	24	1	60% entering, 40% exiting
Weekday p.m. Peak Hour of Adjacent Street Traffic	3.54	24	1	35% entering, 65% exiting
Weekday p.m. Peak Hour of Generator	4.50	32	1	83% entering, 17% exiting
Saturday Peak Hour of Generator	2.41	32	1	39% entering, 61% exiting
1,000 Square Feet Gross Floor Area				
Weekday	33.33	24	1	50% entering, 50% exiting
Weekday a.m. Peak Hour of Adjacent Street Traffic	3.13	24	1	60% entering, 40% exiting
Weekday p.m. Peak Hour of Adjacent Street Traffic	3.54	24	1	35% entering, 65% exiting

Land Use: 440
Adult Cabaret

Description

An adult cabaret is a nightclub with partially clothed or non-clothed live dancers (also known as an exotic dance club).

Additional Data

The site was surveyed in 1992 in California.

Source Number

374

Land Use: 440
Adult Cabaret
Independent Variables with One Observation

The following trip generation data are for independent variables with only one observation. This information is shown in this table only; there are no related plots for these data.

Users are cautioned to use data with care because of the small sample size.

Independent Variable	Trip Generation Rate	Size of Independent Variable	Number of Studies	Directional Distribution
1,000 Square Feet Gross Floor Area				
Weekday p.m. Peak Hour of Generator	38.67	1.5	1	64% entering, 36% exiting
Saturday Peak Hour of Generator	38.67	1.5	1	57% entering, 43% exiting

Land Use: 441
Live Theater

Description

Live theaters are situated in buildings or open-air settings and include a stage, backstage area, dressing rooms, seats for the audience and a lobby area.

Additional Data

The site was surveyed in 1979 in suburban New York City, New York.

Source Number

193

Land Use: 441
Live Theater
Independent Variables with One Observation

The following trip generation data are for independent variables with only one observation. This information is shown in this table only; there are no related plots for these data.

Users are cautioned to use data with care because of the small sample size.

Independent Variable	Trip Generation Rate	Size of Independent Variable	Number of Studies	Directional Distribution
Seats				
Weekday p.m. Peak Hour of Adjacent Street Traffic	0.02	4,400	1	50% entering, 50% exiting

Land Use: 443
Movie Theater without Matinee

Description

Movie theaters consist of audience seating, single or multiple screens and auditoriums, a lobby and a refreshment stand. Movie theaters without matinees show movies on weekday evenings and weekends only; there are no weekday daytime showings. Movie theater with matinee (Land Use 444) and multiplex movie theater (Land Use 445) are related uses.

Additional Data

Caution should be used when applying these data, as the peaking characteristics for this land use could have a significant impact on trip generation rates. Peaking at movie theaters typically occurred in time periods shorter than an hour.

Independent analyses of Friday trip generation data were not conducted, as was done for movie theater with matinee (Land Use 444) and multiplex movie theater (Land Use 445), because the studies did not distinguish data by day of the week.

The sites were surveyed in the late 1970s and the early 1980s throughout the United States at theaters with 1,200 to 2,500 seats; only one study identified the number of movie screens as six.

Source Numbers

193, 213, 215

Land Use: 443
Movie Theater without Matinee
Independent Variables with One Observation

The following trip generation data are for independent variables with only one observation. This information is shown in this table only; there are no related plots for these data.

Users are cautioned to use data with care because of the small sample size.

Independent Variable	Trip Generation Rate	Size of Independent Variable	Number of Studies	Directional Distribution
Employees				
Weekday	53.12	41	1	50% entering, 50% exiting
Weekday a.m. Peak Hour of Adjacent Street Traffic	0.15	41	1	Not available
Weekday p.m. Peak Hour of Adjacent Street Traffic	4.20	41	1	Not available
Weekday a.m. Peak Hour of Generator	1.95	41	1	Not available
Weekday p.m. Peak Hour of Generator	9.56	41	1	Not available
Saturday	67.56	41	1	50% entering, 50% exiting
Saturday Peak Hour of Generator	10.73	41	1	Not available
Sunday	55.73	41	1	50% entering, 50% exiting
Sunday Peak Hour of Generator	7.32	41	1	Not available
Seats				
Weekday	1.76	1,236	1	50% entering, 50% exiting
Weekday a.m. Peak Hour of Adjacent Street Traffic	0.01	1,236	1	Not available
Weekday a.m. Peak Hour of Generator	0.06	1,236	1	Not available
Weekday p.m. Peak Hour of Generator	0.32	1,236	1	Not available
Saturday	2.24	1,236	1	50% entering, 50% exiting
Saturday Peak Hour of Generator	0.36	1,236	1	Not available
Sunday	1.85	1,236	1	50% entering, 50% exiting
Sunday Peak Hour of Generator	0.24	1,236	1	Not available

Land Use: 443
Movie Theater without Matinee
Independent Variables with One Observation

Movie Screens

Weekday	220.00	6	1	50% entering, 50% exiting
Weekday p.m. Peak Hour of Adjacent Street Traffic	24.00	6	1	41% entering, 59% exiting
Weekday p.m. Peak Hour of Generator	37.83	6	1	52% entering, 48% exiting
Saturday	376.00	6	1	50% entering, 50% exiting
Saturday Peak Hour of Generator	64.50	6	1	61% entering, 39% exiting
Sunday	314.00	6	1	50% entering, 50% exiting
Sunday Peak Hour of Generator	45.17	6	1	52% entering, 48% exiting

1,000 Square Feet Gross Floor Area

Weekday	78.06	28	1	50% entering, 50% exiting
Weekday a.m. Peak Hour of Adjacent Street Traffic	0.22	28	1	Not available
Weekday p.m. Peak Hour of Adjacent Street Traffic	6.16	28	1	94% entering, 6% exiting
Weekday a.m. Peak Hour of Generator	2.87	28	1	Not available
Weekday p.m. Peak Hour of Generator	14.05	28	1	Not available
Saturday	99.28	28	1	50% entering, 50% exiting
Saturday Peak Hour of Generator	15.77	28	1	61% entering, 39% exiting
Sunday	81.90	28	1	50% entering, 50% exiting
Sunday Peak Hour of Generator	10.75	28	1	52% entering,48% exiting

Movie Theater without Matinee
(443)

Average Vehicle Trip Ends vs: **Seats**
               On a: **Weekday,**
                        Peak Hour of Adjacent Street Traffic,
                        One Hour Between 4 and 6 p.m.

Number of Studies: 2
Average Number of Seats: 1,868
Directional Distribution: 75% entering, 25% exiting

Trip Generation per Seat

Average Rate	Range of Rates	Standard Deviation
0.07	0.04 - 0.14	*

Data Plot and Equation

Caution - Use Carefully - Small Sample Size

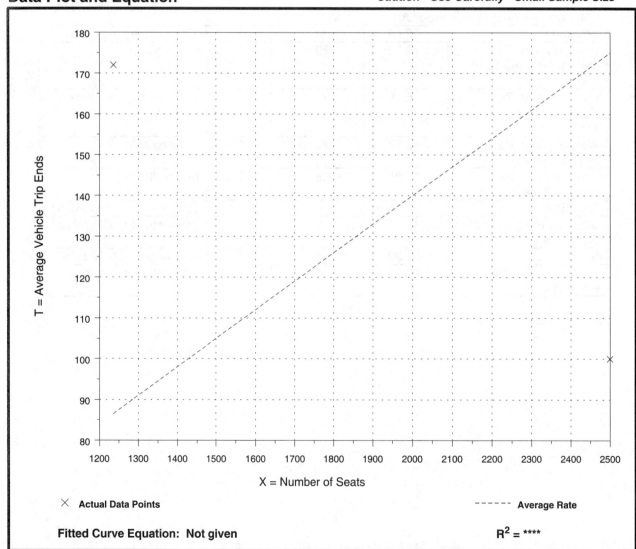

X   **Actual Data Points**
                  - - - - - **Average Rate**

Fitted Curve Equation: Not given $R^2 = $ ****

Land Use: 444
Movie Theater with Matinee

Description

Traditional movie theaters consist of audience seating, less than 10 screens, a lobby and a refreshment stand. These sites show movies on weekday afternoons and evenings as well as on weekends. Movie theater without matinee (Land Use 443) and multiplex movie theater (Land Use 445) are related uses.

Additional Data

Caution should be used when applying these data, as the peaking characteristics for this land use could have a significant impact on trip generation rates. Peaking at movie theaters typically occurred in time periods shorter than an hour. Some movie theaters' start and end times may be staggered to reduce peak surging impacts.

Friday trip generation was typically higher than other weekdays. Therefore, Friday's data have been excluded from the weekday analyses and have been independently studied. Additional data on daily variation for traditional movie theaters based on a 1985 study are reported in Table 1.

Table 1: Movie Theater Daily Traffic Variation	
Day of Week	Percent of Weekly Traffic (%)
Monday	11.1
Tuesday	12.0
Wednesday	9.9
Thursday	8.9
Friday	19.5
Saturday	21.0
Sunday	17.6

Trip generation data for movie theaters have also been found to vary by month. Information contained on the Box Office Guru Web site[1] and summarized in Table 2 provides a general overview of monthly variation. Table 2 is a summary of the box office data based on the gross revenue of the weekly top 15 films for 1997 through 1999.

The monthly factor, as it is defined for use in Table 2, represents the portion of revenue that was generated during an individual month as it relates to an average month during that year. For example, a factor of 0.93 for the month of January 1999 means that sales in January were approximately 93 percent of the sales for an average month in 1999. These monthly factors were calculated individually for 1997, 1998 and 1999. The final column in the table averages the factors by month over the 3-year period.

---

[1] Box Office Guru Web site: www.boxofficeguru.com/monthavg.htm.

Table 2: Average Gross Revenue of Weekly Top 15 Films with Calculated Monthly Factors for Traditional and Multiplex Movie Theaters							
Month	Year 1999		Year 1998		Year 1997		Average Factor
	U.S. Dollar Values	Monthly Factor	U.S. Dollar Values	Monthly Factor	U.S. Dollar Values	Monthly Factor	
January	82,498,100	0.93	94,393,900	1.12	73,549,300	0.95	1.00
February	75,466,600	0.85	79,949,200	0.95	86,008,600	1.12	0.97
March	67,702,700	0.76	77,418,200	0.92	74,936,400	0.97	0.88
April	66,678,600	0.75	68,172,800	0.81	65,277,200	0.85	0.80
May	95,492,000	1.08	76,713,600	0.91	77,545,000	1.01	1.00
June	112,014,200	1.26	95,786,900	1.13	79,501,000	1.03	1.14
July	122,131,500	1.38	113,032,500	1.34	105,286,300	1.37	1.36
August	108,967,400	1.23	90,890,100	1.08	84,620,400	1.10	1.13
September	76,152,200	0.86	61,879,600	0.73	52,495,000	0.68	0.76
October	72,788,900	0.82	68,203,000	0.81	61,671,500	0.80	0.81
November	105,310,500	1.19	101,168,800	1.20	76,778,200	1.00	1.13
December	79,125,400	0.89	86,232,200	1.02	87,596,400	1.14	1.02

Use of the information from Table 2 for trip generation estimates assumes that the amount of revenue generated by a film is directly related to the number of trips that are generated by movie theaters. A detailed analysis to confirm this assumption was not conducted; therefore, caution should be used in applying these data. Also, caution should be exercised when applying these factors during months with major holidays, such as December. Christmas week would likely increase the average value for the entire month. Future analysis should be conducted on a weekly basis to address this concern.

Traditional theaters characteristically house a larger number of seats per screen than multiplex theaters.

One study in this land use was conducted at a theater that runs movies previously introduced or made available to the public through theaters, television, or videotape.

For additional information on traditional movie theaters, refer to the ITE Informational Report, *Trip Generation Characteristics of Traditional and Multiplex Movie Theaters.*[2]

The sites were surveyed between the mid-1980s and the mid-1990s throughout the United States.

Source Numbers

215, 241, 283, 387, 397, 418, 433, 440, 544

---

[2] *Trip Generation Characteristics of Traditional and Multiplex Movie Theaters.* Washington, DC, USA: Institute of Transportation Engineers, March 2001.

Land Use: 444
Movie Theater with Matinee
Independent Variables with One Observation

The following trip generation data are for independent variables with only one observation. This information is shown in this table only; there are no related plots for these data.

Users are cautioned to use data with care because of the small sample size.

Independent Variable	Trip Generation Rate	Size of Independent Variable	Number of Studies	Directional Distribution
1,000 Square Feet Gross Floor Area				
Friday p.m. Peak Hour of Generator	26.70	31	1	56% entering, 44% exiting
Saturday	99.28	28	1	50% entering, 50% exiting
Sunday	81.90	28	1	50% entering, 50% exiting
Sunday Peak Hour of Generator	10.75	28	1	Not available
Movie Screens				
Weekday p.m. Peak Hour of Generator	37.83	6	1	52% entering, 48% exiting
Friday	348.33	6	1	50% entering, 50% exiting
Seats				
Friday p.m. Peak Hour of Generator	0.36	2,250	1	56% entering, 44% exiting
Saturday	2.24	1,236	1	50% entering, 50% exiting
Sunday	1.85	1,236	1	50% entering, 50% exiting
Sunday Peak Hour of Generator	0.24	1,236	1	Not available

Movie Theater with Matinee
(444)

Average Vehicle Trip Ends vs: 1000 Sq. Feet Gross Floor Area
On a: Friday,
Peak Hour of Adjacent Street Traffic,
One Hour Between 4 and 6 p.m.

Number of Studies: 2
Average 1000 Sq. Feet GFA: 31
Directional Distribution: 64% entering, 36% exiting

Trip Generation per 1000 Sq. Feet Gross Floor Area

Average Rate	Range of Rates	Standard Deviation
3.80	2.09 - 6.10	*

Data Plot and Equation

Caution - Use Carefully - Small Sample Size

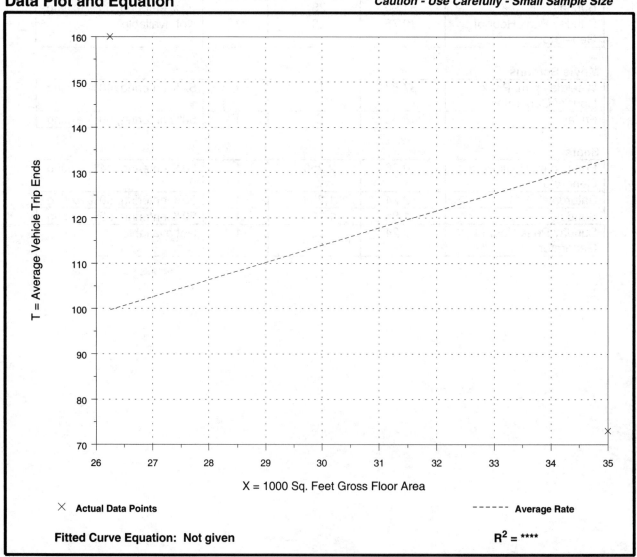

X **Actual Data Points**

- - - - - **Average Rate**

Fitted Curve Equation: Not given

$R^2 = ****$

Movie Theater with Matinee
(444)

Average Vehicle Trip Ends vs: **1000 Sq. Feet Gross Floor Area**
On a: **Saturday,**
          Peak Hour of Generator

Number of Studies: 2
Average 1000 Sq. Feet GFA: 29
Directional Distribution: 56% entering, 44% exiting

Trip Generation per 1000 Sq. Feet Gross Floor Area

Average Rate	Range of Rates	Standard Deviation
27.39	15.77 - 37.95	*

Data Plot and Equation

Caution - Use Carefully - Small Sample Size

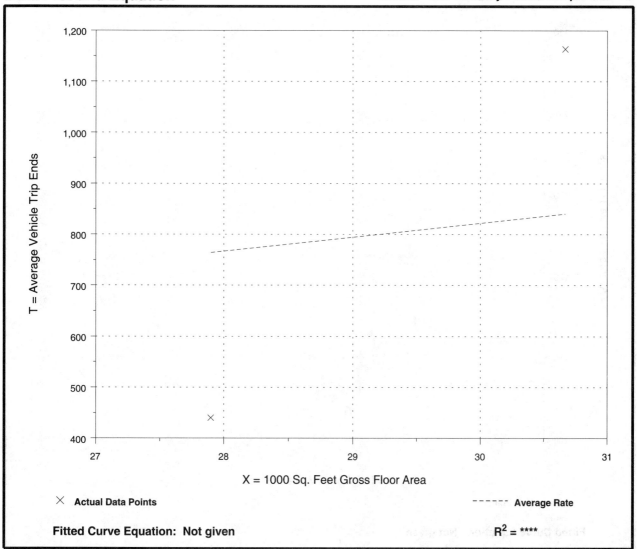

Fitted Curve Equation: Not given $R^2 = ****$

Movie Theater with Matinee
(444)

Average Vehicle Trip Ends vs: **Movie Screens**
On a: **Weekday,**
Peak Hour of Adjacent Street Traffic,
One Hour Between 4 and 6 p.m.

Number of Studies: 3
Average Number of Movie Screens: 6
Directional Distribution: 40% entering, 60% exiting

Trip Generation per Movie Screen

Average Rate	Range of Rates	Standard Deviation
20.22	18.17 - 24.17	5.11

Data Plot and Equation

Caution - Use Carefully - Small Sample Size

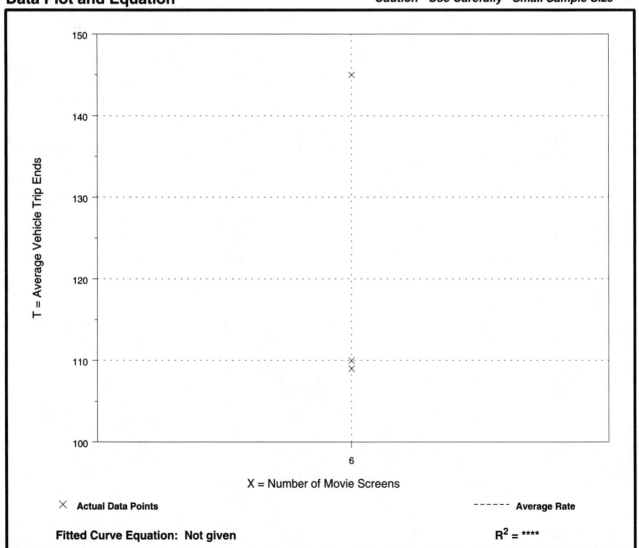

X Actual Data Points

----- Average Rate

Fitted Curve Equation: Not given

$R^2 = $ ****

Movie Theater with Matinee
(444)

Average Vehicle Trip Ends vs: **Movie Screens**
On a: **Friday,**
Peak Hour of Adjacent Street Traffic,
One Hour Between 4 and 6 p.m.

Number of Studies: 6
Average Number of Movie Screens: 6
Directional Distribution: 55% entering, 45% exiting

Trip Generation per Movie Screen

Average Rate	Range of Rates	Standard Deviation
45.91	12.17 - 106.50	37.26

Data Plot and Equation

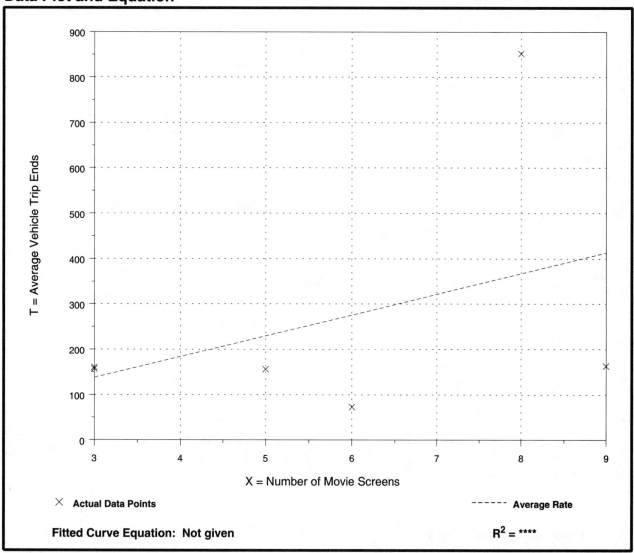

X Actual Data Points

- - - - - Average Rate

Fitted Curve Equation: Not given

$R^2 = {****}$

Movie Theater with Matinee
(444)

Average Vehicle Trip Ends vs: **Movie Screens**
On a: **Friday,**
P.M. Peak Hour of Generator

Number of Studies: 3
Average Number of Movie Screens: 8
Directional Distribution: 58% entering, 42% exiting

Trip Generation per Movie Screen

Average Rate	Range of Rates	Standard Deviation
102.87	67.33 - 127.00	26.01

Data Plot and Equation

Caution - Use Carefully - Small Sample Size

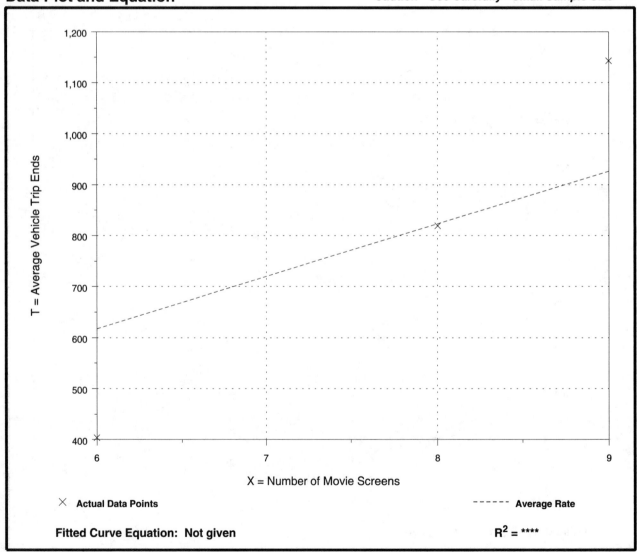

X = Number of Movie Screens

✕ **Actual Data Points**   - - - - - **Average Rate**

Fitted Curve Equation: Not given $R^2 = ****$

Movie Theater with Matinee
(444)

Average Vehicle Trip Ends vs: Movie Screens
On a: Saturday

Number of Studies: 3
Average Number of Movie Screens: 7
Directional Distribution: 50% entering, 50% exiting

Trip Generation per Movie Screen

Average Rate	Range of Rates	Standard Deviation
546.86	376.00 - 717.56	156.66

Data Plot and Equation

Caution - Use Carefully - Small Sample Size

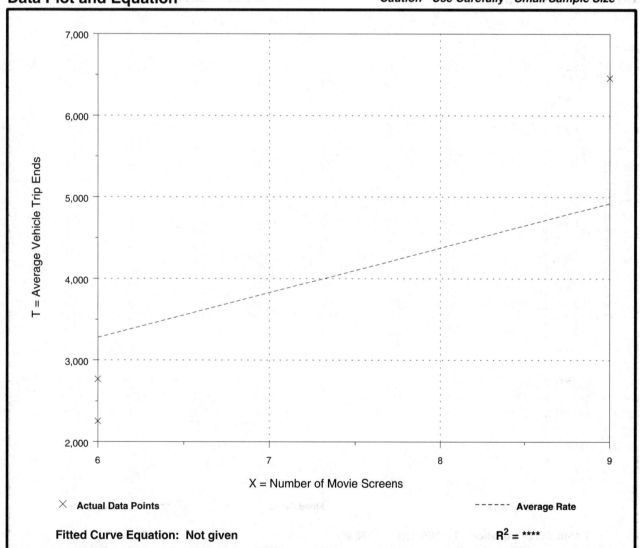

X **Actual Data Points**

- - - - - **Average Rate**

Fitted Curve Equation: Not given $R^2 = ****$

Movie Theater with Matinee
(444)

Average Vehicle Trip Ends vs: **Movie Screens**
On a: **Saturday,**
Peak Hour of Generator

Number of Studies: 4
Average Number of Movie Screens: 7
Directional Distribution: 60% entering, 40% exiting

Trip Generation per Movie Screen

Average Rate	Range of Rates	Standard Deviation
120.48	64.50 - 167.00	46.16

Data Plot and Equation

Caution - Use Carefully - Small Sample Size

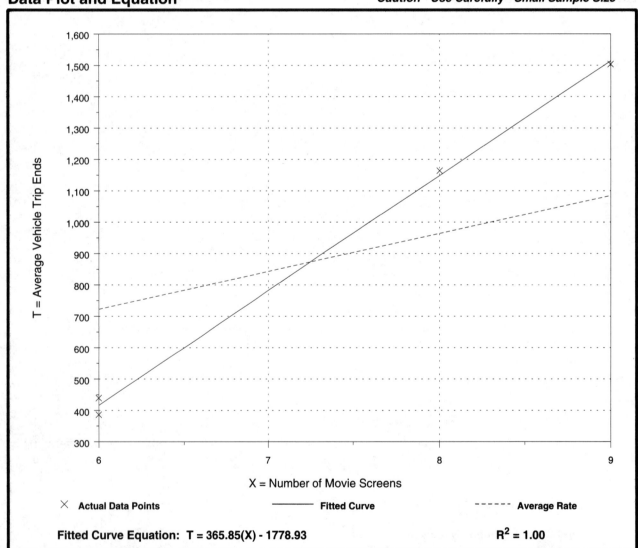

X = Number of Movie Screens

✕ **Actual Data Points**	——— **Fitted Curve**	- - - - - **Average Rate**

Fitted Curve Equation: T = 365.85(X) - 1778.93 $R^2 = 1.00$

Movie Theater with Matinee
(444)

Average Vehicle Trip Ends vs: Movie Screens
On a: Sunday

Number of Studies: 3
Average Number of Movie Screens: 7
Directional Distribution: 50% entering, 50% exiting

Trip Generation per Movie Screen

Average Rate	Range of Rates	Standard Deviation
420.71	314.00 - 518.44	92.59

Data Plot and Equation

Caution - Use Carefully - Small Sample Size

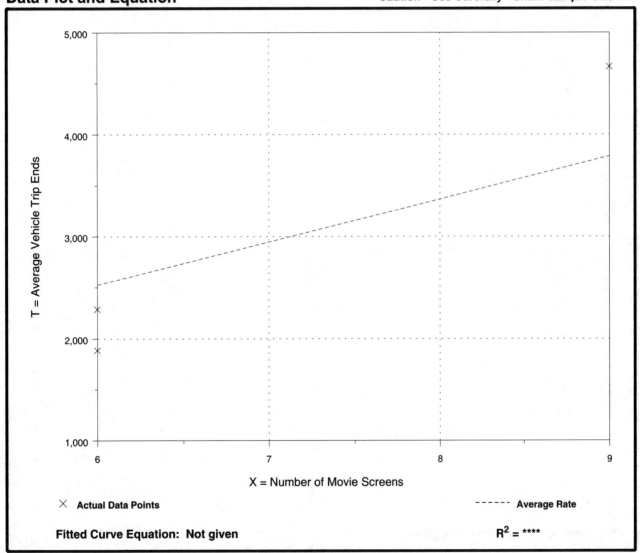

X **Actual Data Points**

- - - - - - **Average Rate**

Fitted Curve Equation: Not given $R^2 = $ ****

Movie Theater with Matinee
(444)

Average Vehicle Trip Ends vs: **Movie Screens**
On a: **Sunday,**
Peak Hour of Generator

Number of Studies: 3
Average Number of Movie Screens: 7
Directional Distribution: 60% entering, 40% exiting

Trip Generation per Movie Screen

Average Rate	Range of Rates	Standard Deviation
44.52	40.44 - 50.00	7.52

Data Plot and Equation

Caution - Use Carefully - Small Sample Size

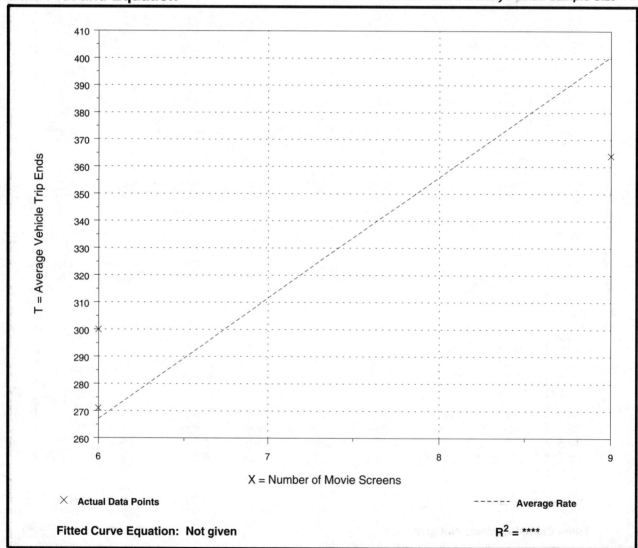

X   **Actual Data Points**   - - - - - **Average Rate**

Fitted Curve Equation: Not given $R^2 = ****$

Movie Theater with Matinee
(444)

Average Vehicle Trip Ends vs: Seats
On a: Weekday,
Peak Hour of Adjacent Street Traffic,
One Hour Between 4 and 6 p.m.

Number of Studies: 2
Average Number of Seats: 1,576
Directional Distribution: 39% entering, 61% exiting

Trip Generation per Seat

Average Rate	Range of Rates	Standard Deviation
0.07	0.07 - 0.07	*

Data Plot and Equation

Caution - Use Carefully - Small Sample Size

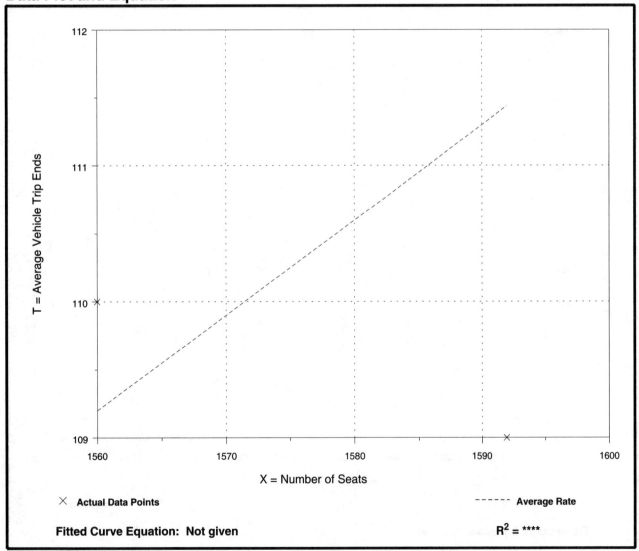

X **Actual Data Points**

– – – – – **Average Rate**

Fitted Curve Equation: Not given

$R^2 = ****$

Movie Theater with Matinee
(444)

Average Vehicle Trip Ends vs: **Seats**
On a: **Friday,**
Peak Hour of Adjacent Street Traffic,
One Hour Between 4 and 6 p.m.

Number of Studies: 4
Average Number of Seats: 2,031
Directional Distribution: 55% entering, 45% exiting

Trip Generation per Seat

Average Rate	Range of Rates	Standard Deviation
0.07	0.04 - 0.09	0.26

Data Plot and Equation

Caution - Use Carefully - Small Sample Size

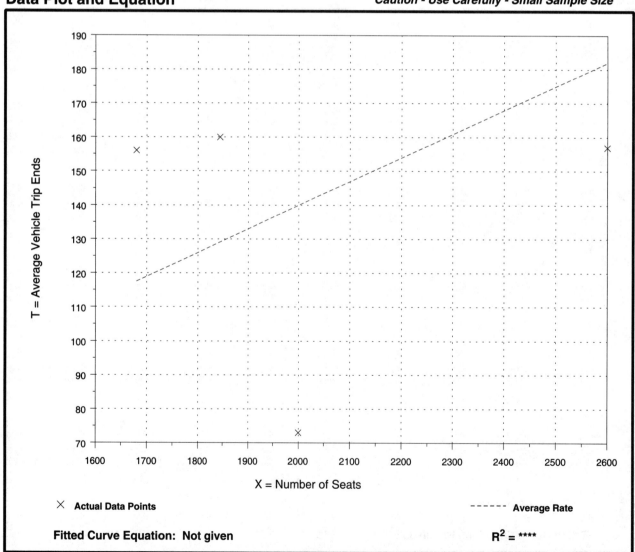

X **Actual Data Points**

----- **Average Rate**

Fitted Curve Equation: Not given $R^2 = ****$

Movie Theater with Matinee
(444)

Average Vehicle Trip Ends vs: **Seats**
On a: **Saturday,**
Peak Hour of Generator

Number of Studies: 2
Average Number of Seats: 1,743
Directional Distribution: 56% entering, 44% exiting

Trip Generation per Seat

Average Rate	Range of Rates	Standard Deviation
0.46	0.36 - 0.52	*

Data Plot and Equation

Caution - Use Carefully - Small Sample Size

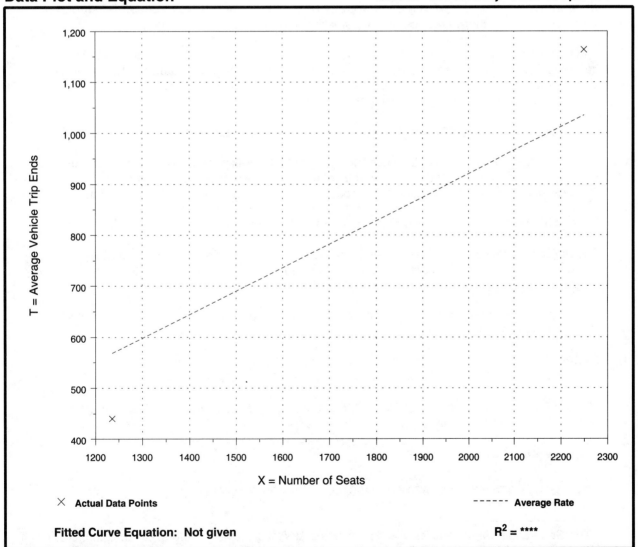

X **Actual Data Points**

- - - - - **Average Rate**

Fitted Curve Equation: Not given $R^2 = ****$

Land Use: 445
Multiplex Movie Theater

Description

A multiplex movie theater consists of audience seating, a minimum of 10 screens, a lobby and a refreshment area. The development generally has one or more of the following amenities: digital sound, tiered stadium seating and moveable or expandable walls. Theaters included in this category are primarily stand-alone facilities with separate parking and dedicated driveways. All theaters in the category show only first-run movies or movies not previously seen through any other media. They may also have matinee showings. Movie theater without matinee (Land Use 443) and movie theater with matinee (Land Use 444) are related uses.

Additional Data

Caution should be used when applying these data, as the peaking characteristics for this land use could have a significant impact on trip generation rates. Peaking at movie theaters typically occurred in time periods shorter than an hour. Movie theaters' start and end times may be staggered to reduce peak surging impacts.

Friday trip generation was typically higher than other weekdays. Therefore, Friday's data have been excluded from the weekday analyses and have been independently studied. Trip generation data for movie theaters have also been found to vary by month. Refer to Table 2 in movie theater with matinee (Land Use 444) for additional information.

Multiplex theaters typically house a smaller number of seats per screen than traditional theaters.

Data were collected throughout the year, excluding holiday peak periods. The majority of the theaters studied were open between 1 and 5 years at the time of the study. In addition, 10 theaters indicated that the distance to the closest competitor ranged from 1.5 miles to 5 miles.

Several of the study locations also had a game-room facility on site.

The majority of the surveyed sites consisted of stand-alone parking areas with minimal pedestrian and transit accessibility. One study reported that the theater was located on a bus route.

The peak hour of the generator for multiplex movie theaters occurred during Friday and Saturday evenings between 6:00 p.m. and 10:00 p.m.

For additional information on multiplex movie theaters, refer to the ITE Informational Report, *Trip Generation Characteristics of Traditional and Multiplex Movie Theaters.*[1]

The sites were surveyed in the 1990s and the 2000s throughout the United States. At least four of the studies were conducted near or in college towns.

Source Numbers

418, 433, 443, 450, 451, 452, 453, 455, 456, 457, 458, 459, 513, 618

---

[1] *Trip Generation Characteristics of Traditional and Multiplex Movie Theaters.* Washington, DC, USA: Institute of Transportation Engineers, March 2001.

Land Use: 445
Multiplex Movie Theater
Independent Variables with One Observation

The following trip generation data are for independent variables with only one observation. This information is shown in this table only; there are no related plots for these data.

Users are cautioned to use data with care because of the small sample size.

Independent Variable	Trip Generation Rate	Size of Independent Variable	Number of Studies	Directional Distribution
Seats				
Weekday p.m. Peak Hour of Generator	0.28	2,739	1	51% entering, 49% exiting

Multiplex Movie Theater
(445)

Average Vehicle Trip Ends vs: 1000 Sq. Feet Gross Floor Area
On a: Friday,
Peak Hour of Adjacent Street Traffic,
One Hour Between 4 and 6 p.m.

Number of Studies: 8
Average 1000 Sq. Feet GFA: 68
Directional Distribution: 62% entering, 38% exiting

Trip Generation per 1000 Sq. Feet Gross Floor Area

Average Rate	Range of Rates	Standard Deviation
4.91	3.07 - 9.40	3.04

Data Plot and Equation

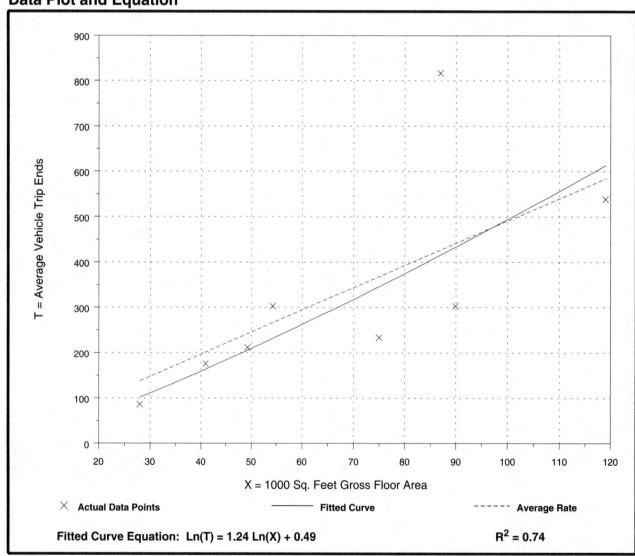

X **Actual Data Points**   —— **Fitted Curve**   - - - - - **Average Rate**

Fitted Curve Equation: Ln(T) = 1.24 Ln(X) + 0.49 $R^2 = 0.74$

Multiplex Movie Theater
(445)

Average Vehicle Trip Ends vs: 1000 Sq. Feet Gross Floor Area
On a: Friday,
P.M. Peak Hour of Generator

Number of Studies: 5
Average 1000 Sq. Feet GFA: 66
Directional Distribution: 58% entering, 42% exiting

Trip Generation per 1000 Sq. Feet Gross Floor Area

Average Rate	Range of Rates	Standard Deviation
17.87	9.83 - 20.59	5.15

Data Plot and Equation

Caution - Use Carefully - Small Sample Size

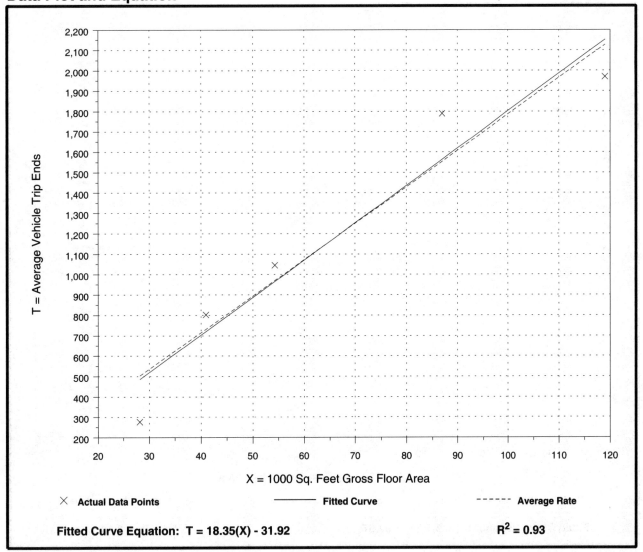

X Actual Data Points   ——— Fitted Curve   - - - - - Average Rate

Fitted Curve Equation: T = 18.35(X) - 31.92   **$R^2 = 0.93$**

Trip Generation, 8th Edition   813   Institute of Transportation Engineers

Multiplex Movie Theater
(445)

Average Vehicle Trip Ends vs: **1000 Sq. Feet Gross Floor Area**
           On a: **Saturday,**
                  Peak Hour of Adjacent Street Traffic,
                  One Hour between 11 a.m. and 1 p.m.

Number of Studies: 4
Average 1000 Sq. Feet GFA: 75
Directional Distribution: 75% entering, 25% exiting

Trip Generation per 1000 Sq. Feet Gross Floor Area

Average Rate	Range of Rates	Standard Deviation
4.70	4.22 - 6.93	2.33

Data Plot and Equation

Caution - Use Carefully - Small Sample Size

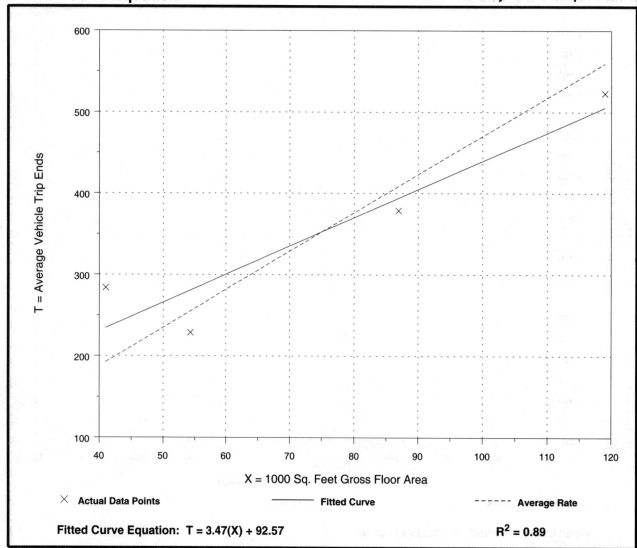

X   **Actual Data Points**   ——— **Fitted Curve**   - - - - - **Average Rate**

Fitted Curve Equation: T = 3.47(X) + 92.57   **$R^2 = 0.89$**

Multiplex Movie Theater
(445)

Average Vehicle Trip Ends vs: **1000 Sq. Feet Gross Floor Area**
On a: **Saturday,**
        Peak Hour of Generator

Number of Studies: 8
Average 1000 Sq. Feet GFA: 60
Directional Distribution: 52% entering, 48% exiting

Trip Generation per 1000 Sq. Feet Gross Floor Area

Average Rate	Range of Rates	Standard Deviation
16.76	10.22 - 26.34	6.58

Data Plot and Equation

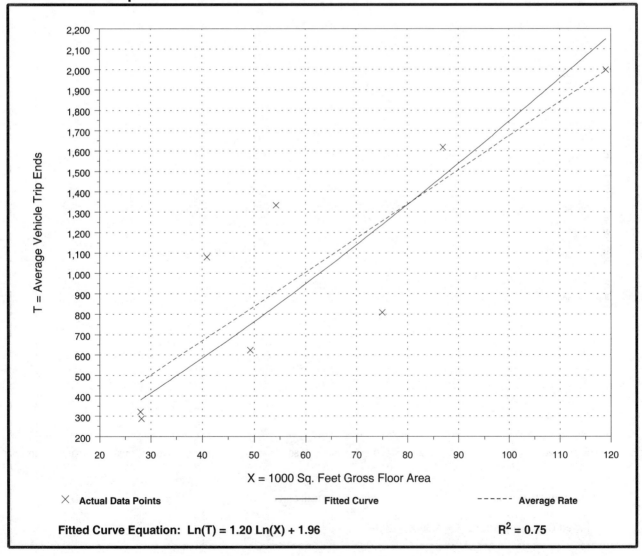

Fitted Curve Equation: Ln(T) = 1.20 Ln(X) + 1.96 $R^2 = 0.75$

Multiplex Movie Theater
(445)

Average Vehicle Trip Ends vs: Employees
On a: Friday,
Peak Hour of Adjacent Street Traffic,
One Hour Between 4 and 6 p.m.

Number of Studies: 6
Avg. Number of Employees: 82
Directional Distribution: 65% entering, 35% exiting

Trip Generation per Employee

Average Rate	Range of Rates	Standard Deviation
4.45	2.87 - 8.83	2.59

Data Plot and Equation

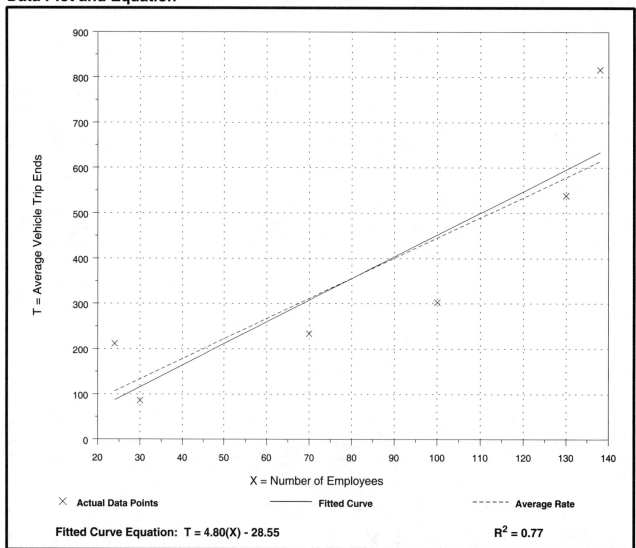

Fitted Curve Equation: T = 4.80(X) - 28.55 $R^2 = 0.77$

Multiplex Movie Theater
(445)

Average Vehicle Trip Ends vs: **Employees**
On a: **Friday,**
P.M. Peak Hour of Generator

Number of Studies: 4
Avg. Number of Employees: 96
Directional Distribution: 60% entering, 40% exiting

Trip Generation per Employee

Average Rate	Range of Rates	Standard Deviation
13.20	10.46 - 16.29	4.10

Data Plot and Equation

Caution - Use Carefully - Small Sample Size

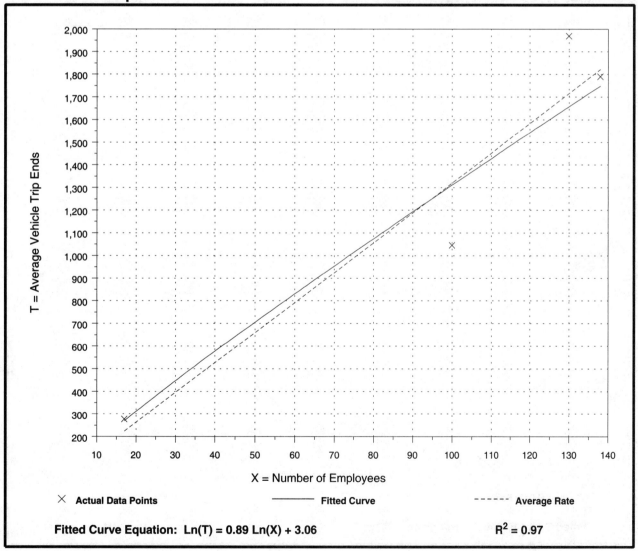

X = Number of Employees

✕ Actual Data Points	——— Fitted Curve	- - - - Average Rate

Fitted Curve Equation: Ln(T) = 0.89 Ln(X) + 3.06 $R^2 = 0.97$

Multiplex Movie Theater
(445)

Average Vehicle Trip Ends vs: **Employees**
On a: **Saturday,**
Peak Hour of Adjacent Street Traffic,
One Hour between 11 a.m. and 1 p.m.

Number of Studies: 3
Avg. Number of Employees: 123
Directional Distribution: 73% entering, 27% exiting

Trip Generation per Employee

Average Rate	Range of Rates	Standard Deviation
3.07	2.29 - 4.02	1.89

Data Plot and Equation

Caution - Use Carefully - Small Sample Size

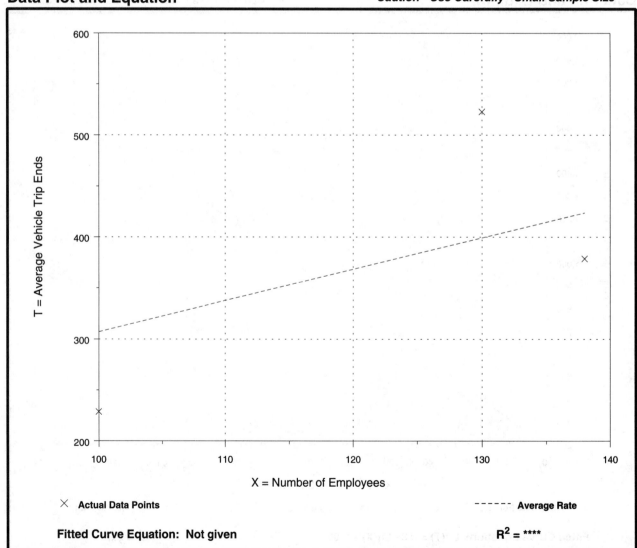

X   **Actual Data Points**

‑ ‑ ‑ ‑ ‑   **Average Rate**

Fitted Curve Equation: Not given $R^2 =$ ****

Multiplex Movie Theater
(445)

Average Vehicle Trip Ends vs: **Employees**
On a: **Saturday,**
Peak Hour of Generator

Number of Studies: 7
Avg. Number of Employees: 73
Directional Distribution: 53% entering, 47% exiting

Trip Generation per Employee

Average Rate	Range of Rates	Standard Deviation
13.74	10.77 - 25.96	4.89

Data Plot and Equation

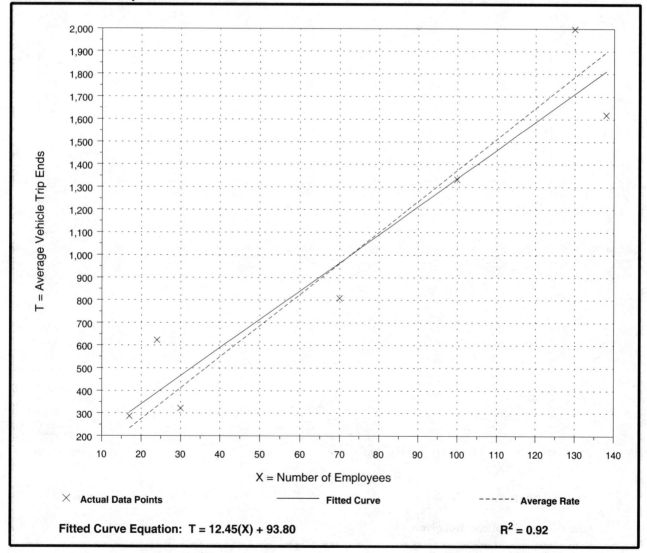

X = Number of Employees

✕ **Actual Data Points**   —— **Fitted Curve**   - - - - - **Average Rate**

Fitted Curve Equation: T = 12.45(X) + 93.80 $R^2 = 0.92$

Multiplex Movie Theater
(445)

Average Vehicle Trip Ends vs: **Movie Screens**
On a: **Weekday,**
Peak Hour of Adjacent Street Traffic,
One Hour Between 4 and 6 p.m.

Number of Studies: 4
Average Number of Movie Screens: 17
Directional Distribution: 45% entering, 55% exiting

Trip Generation per Movie Screen

Average Rate	Range of Rates	Standard Deviation
13.64	9.38 - 23.69	7.00

Data Plot and Equation

Caution - Use Carefully - Small Sample Size

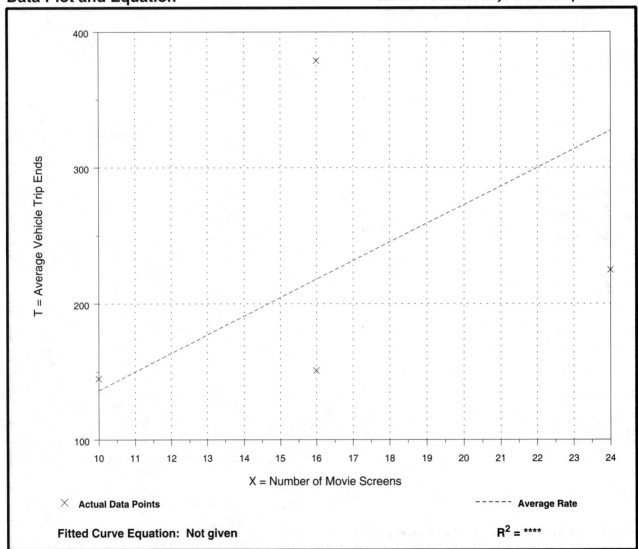

X = Number of Movie Screens

✕ **Actual Data Points**   - - - - - **Average Rate**

Fitted Curve Equation: Not given $R^2 = ****$

Multiplex Movie Theater
(445)

Average Vehicle Trip Ends vs: **Movie Screens**
On a: **Weekday,**
P.M. Peak Hour of Generator

Number of Studies: 3
Average Number of Movie Screens: 17
Directional Distribution: 49% entering, 51% exiting

Trip Generation per Movie Screen

Average Rate	Range of Rates	Standard Deviation
25.84	13.33 - 69.45	23.63

Data Plot and Equation

Caution - Use Carefully - Small Sample Size

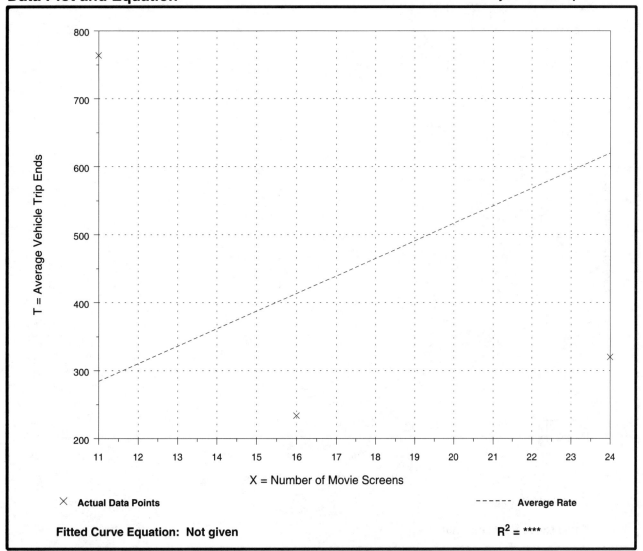

X = Number of Movie Screens

✕ **Actual Data Points**   - - - - - **Average Rate**

Fitted Curve Equation: Not given $R^2 = ****$

Multiplex Movie Theater
(445)

Average Vehicle Trip Ends vs: Movie Screens
On a: Friday

Number of Studies: 2
Average Number of Movie Screens: 20
Directional Distribution: 50% entering, 50% exiting

Trip Generation per Movie Screen

Average Rate	Range of Rates	Standard Deviation
292.50	289.94 - 294.21	*

Data Plot and Equation

Caution - Use Carefully - Small Sample Size

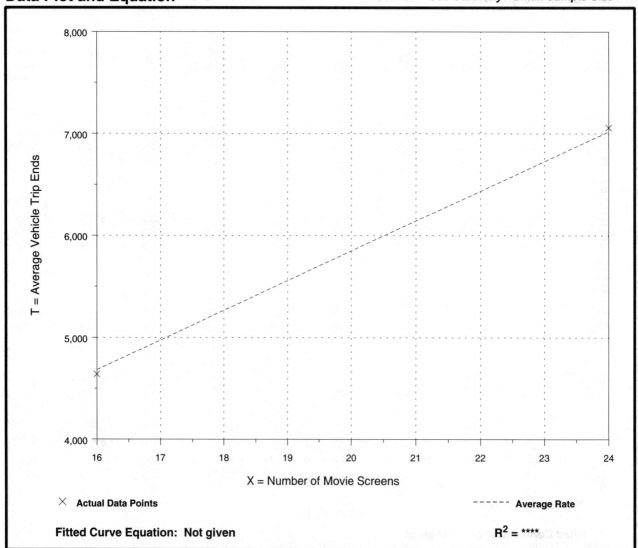

X **Actual Data Points**

- - - - - **Average Rate**

Fitted Curve Equation: Not given $R^2 = ****$

Multiplex Movie Theater
(445)

Average Vehicle Trip Ends vs: **Movie Screens**
On a: **Friday,**
Peak Hour of Adjacent Street Traffic,
One Hour Between 4 and 6 p.m.

Number of Studies: 16
Average Number of Movie Screens: 16
Directional Distribution: 59% entering, 41% exiting

Trip Generation per Movie Screen

Average Rate	Range of Rates	Standard Deviation
22.76	8.41 - 47.60	11.42

Data Plot and Equation

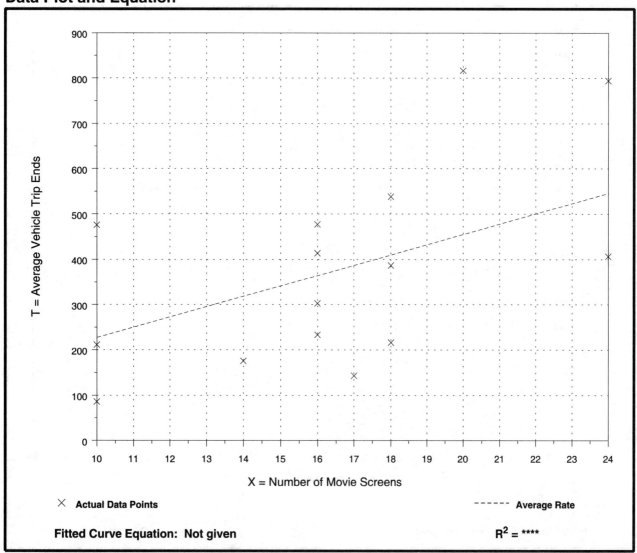

X Actual Data Points

---- **Average Rate**

Fitted Curve Equation: Not given $R^2 = ****$

Multiplex Movie Theater
(445)

Average Vehicle Trip Ends vs: Movie Screens
On a: Friday,
P.M. Peak Hour of Generator

Number of Studies: 13
Average Number of Movie Screens: 17
Directional Distribution: 57% entering, 43% exiting

Trip Generation per Movie Screen

Average Rate	Range of Rates	Standard Deviation
62.89	27.70 - 109.44	24.54

Data Plot and Equation

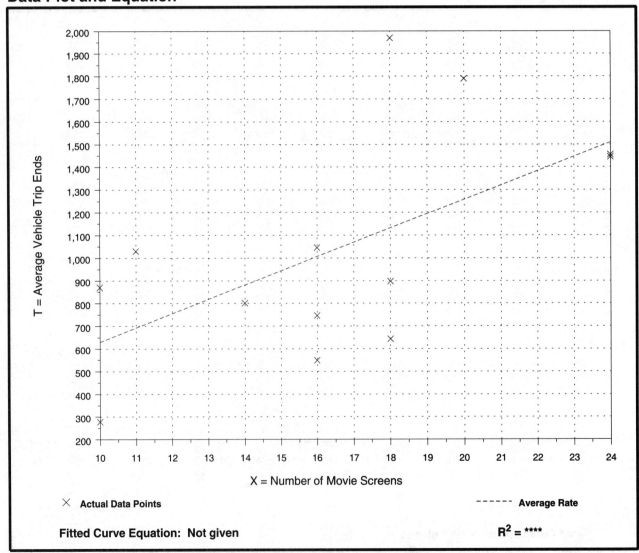

X **Actual Data Points**

- - - - - **Average Rate**

Fitted Curve Equation: Not given $R^2 = ****$

Multiplex Movie Theater
(445)

Average Vehicle Trip Ends vs: Movie Screens
On a: Saturday,
Peak Hour of Adjacent Street Traffic,
One Hour between 11 a.m. and 1 p.m.

Number of Studies: 7
Average Number of Movie Screens: 18
Directional Distribution: 72% entering, 28% exiting

Trip Generation per Movie Screen

Average Rate	Range of Rates	Standard Deviation
19.97	14.31 - 29.06	6.47

Data Plot and Equation

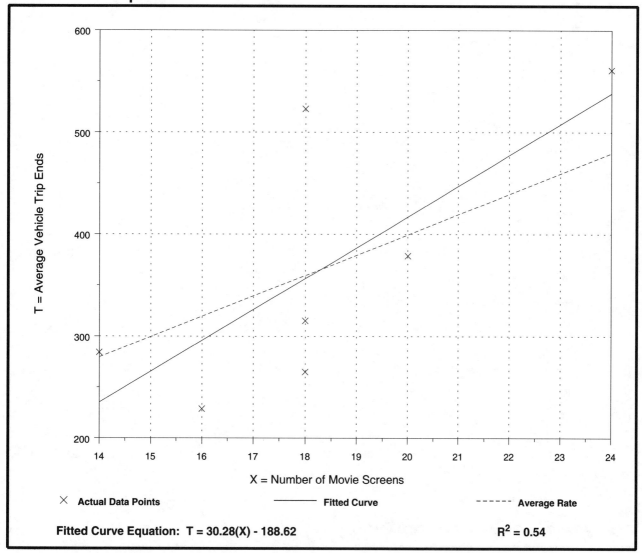

Fitted Curve Equation: T = 30.28(X) - 188.62 $R^2 = 0.54$

Multiplex Movie Theater
(445)

Average Vehicle Trip Ends vs: **Movie Screens**
On a: **Saturday,**
Peak Hour of Generator

Number of Studies: 16
Average Number of Movie Screens: 16
Directional Distribution: 52% entering, 48% exiting

Trip Generation per Movie Screen

Average Rate	Range of Rates	Standard Deviation
69.14	28.80 - 111.00	21.10

Data Plot and Equation

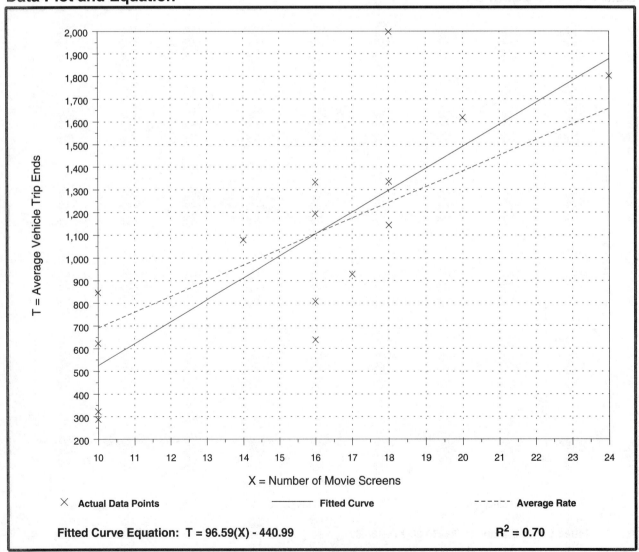

X **Actual Data Points** ——— **Fitted Curve** - - - - - **Average Rate**

Fitted Curve Equation: T = 96.59(X) - 440.99 $R^2 = 0.70$

Multiplex Movie Theater
(445)

Average Vehicle Trip Ends vs: **Seats**
On a: **Weekday,**
Peak Hour of Adjacent Street Traffic,
One Hour Between 4 and 6 p.m.

Number of Studies: 2
Average Number of Seats: 3,325
Directional Distribution: 36% entering, 64% exiting

Trip Generation per Seat

Average Rate	Range of Rates	Standard Deviation
0.08	0.06 - 0.09	*

Data Plot and Equation

Caution - Use Carefully - Small Sample Size

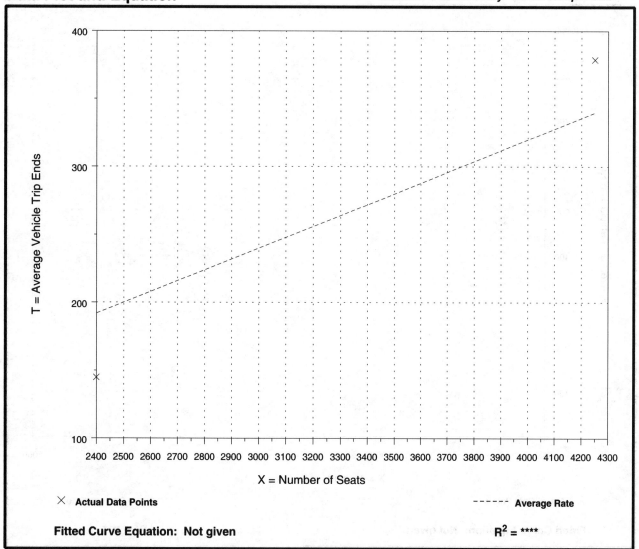

X   **Actual Data Points**   ----- **Average Rate**

Fitted Curve Equation: Not given $R^2 = ****$

Multiplex Movie Theater
(445)

Average Vehicle Trip Ends vs: **Seats**
On a: **Friday,**
Peak Hour of Adjacent Street Traffic,
One Hour Between 4 and 6 p.m.

Number of Studies: 14
Average Number of Seats: 3,609
Directional Distribution: 60% entering, 40% exiting

Trip Generation per Seat

Average Rate	Range of Rates	Standard Deviation
0.10	0.04 - 0.21	0.32

Data Plot and Equation

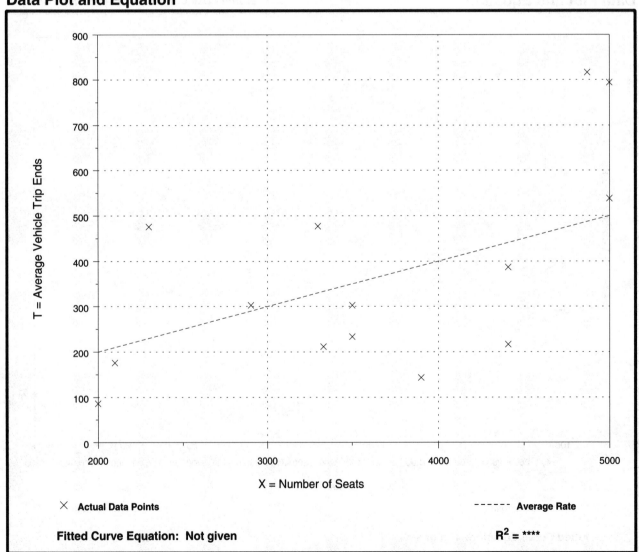

X Actual Data Points

- - - - - Average Rate

Fitted Curve Equation: Not given

$R^2 = ****$

Multiplex Movie Theater
(445)

Average Vehicle Trip Ends vs: **Seats**
On a: **Friday,**
P.M. Peak Hour of Generator

Number of Studies: 11
Average Number of Seats: 3,551
Directional Distribution: 59% entering, 41% exiting

Trip Generation per Seat

Average Rate	Range of Rates	Standard Deviation
0.29	0.14 - 0.39	0.55

Data Plot and Equation

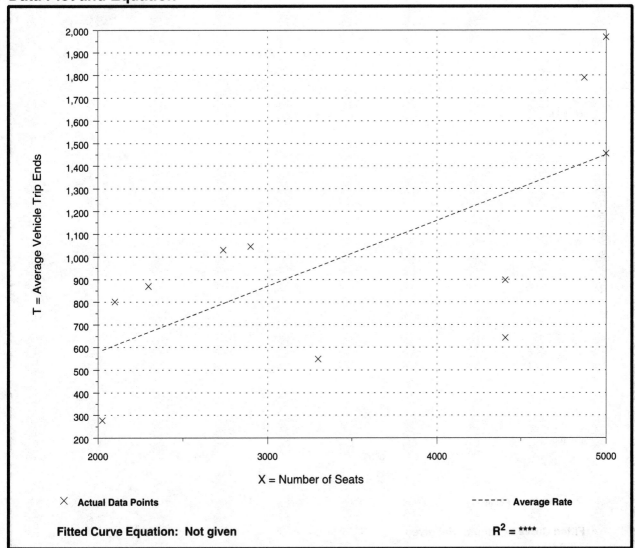

X **Actual Data Points**

- - - - - **Average Rate**

Fitted Curve Equation: Not given

$R^2 = ****$

Multiplex Movie Theater
(445)

Average Vehicle Trip Ends vs: **Seats**
On a: **Saturday,**
Peak Hour of Adjacent Street Traffic,
One Hour between 11 a.m. and 1 p.m.

Number of Studies: 7
Average Number of Seats: 4,099
Directional Distribution: 72% entering, 28% exiting

Trip Generation per Seat

Average Rate	Range of Rates	Standard Deviation
0.09	0.06 - 0.14	0.30

Data Plot and Equation

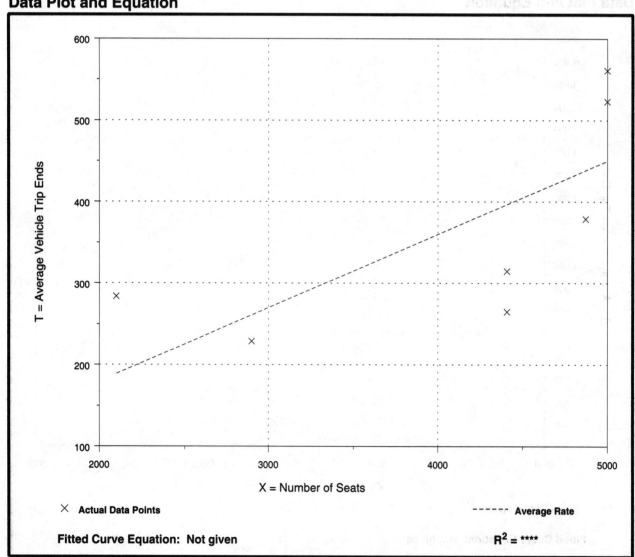

Fitted Curve Equation: Not given $R^2 = ****$

Multiplex Movie Theater
(445)

Average Vehicle Trip Ends vs: **Seats**
On a: **Saturday,**
      Peak Hour of Generator

Number of Studies: 14
Average Number of Seats: 3,504
Directional Distribution: 52% entering, 48% exiting

Trip Generation per Seat

Average Rate	Range of Rates	Standard Deviation
0.30	0.14 - 0.51	0.56

Data Plot and Equation

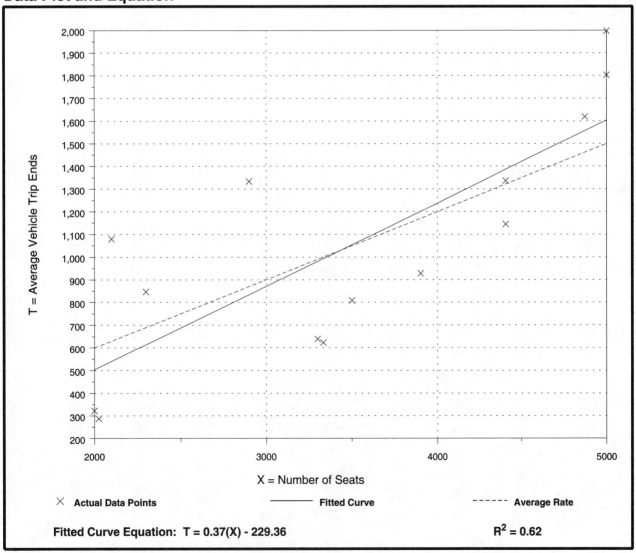

X = Number of Seats

X   **Actual Data Points**   —— **Fitted Curve**   - - - - **Average Rate**

Fitted Curve Equation: T = 0.37(X) - 229.36   **$R^2 = 0.62$**

Land Use: 452
Horse Racetrack

Description

A horse racetrack includes a spectator stadium, parking, track, stables and housing for workers.

Additional Data

The sites were surveyed in the late 1960s and late 1990s in southern California and Delaware.

Source Numbers

18, 529

Land Use: 452
Horse Racetrack
Independent Variables with One Observation

The following trip generation data are for independent variables with only one observation. This information is shown in this table only; there are no related plots for these data.

Users are cautioned to use data with care because of the small sample size.

Independent Variable	Trip Generation Rate	Size of Independent Variable	Number of Studies	Directional Distribution
Acres				
Weekday	43.00	200	1	50% entering, 50% exiting
Attendees				
Weekday a.m. Peak Hour of Adjacent Street Traffic	0.01	1,515	1	Not available
Weekday p.m. Peak Hour of Adjacent Street Traffic	0.13	1,515	1	66% entering, 34% exiting
Weekday a.m. Peak Hour of Generator	0.01	1,515	1	91% entering, 9% exiting
Weekday p.m. Peak Hour of Generator	0.22	1,515	1	91% entering, 9% exiting
Seats				
Weekday p.m. Peak Hour of Adjacent Street Traffic	0.06	3,000	1	66% entering, 34% exiting
Weekday a.m. Peak Hour of Generator	0.01	3,000	1	91% entering, 9% exiting
Weekday p.m. Peak Hour of Generator	0.11	3,000	1	91% entering, 9% exiting

Horse Racetrack
(452)

Average Vehicle Trip Ends vs: Seats
On a: Weekday

Number of Studies: 2
Average Number of Seats: 8,500
Directional Distribution: 50% entering, 50% exiting

Trip Generation per Seat

Average Rate	Range of Rates	Standard Deviation
0.61	0.60 - 0.61	*

Data Plot and Equation

Caution - Use Carefully - Small Sample Size

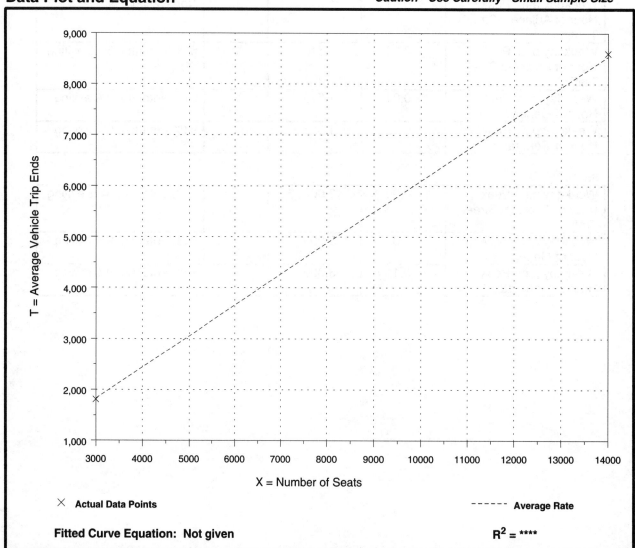

X = Number of Seats

✕ **Actual Data Points**   - - - - - **Average Rate**

Fitted Curve Equation: Not given $R^2 =$ ****

Horse Racetrack
(452)

Average Vehicle Trip Ends vs: **Attendees**
On a: **Weekday**

Number of Studies: 2
Average Number of Attendees: 4,758
Directional Distribution: 50% entering, 50% exiting

Trip Generation per Attendee

Average Rate	Range of Rates	Standard Deviation
1.09	1.08 - 1.19	*

Data Plot and Equation

Caution - Use Carefully - Small Sample Size

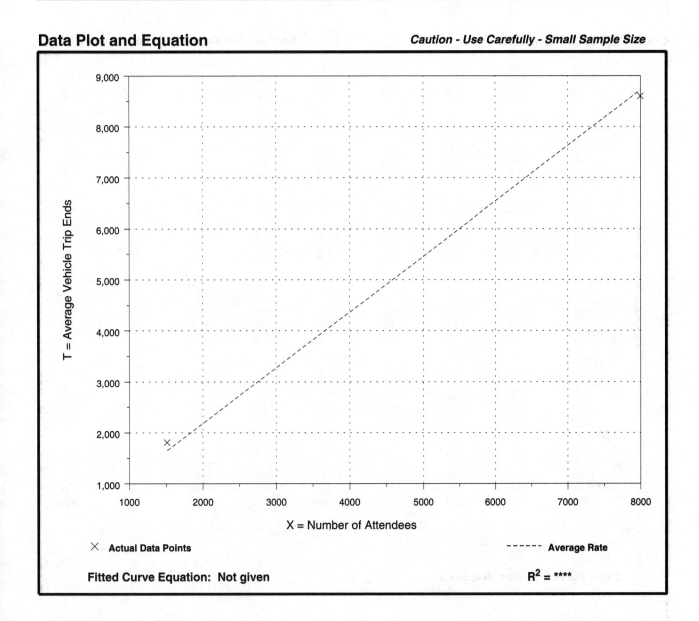

Fitted Curve Equation: Not given

$R^2 = ****$

Horse Racetrack
(452)

Average Vehicle Trip Ends vs: **Employees**
On a: **Weekday**

Number of Studies: 2
Avg. Number of Employees: 2,000
Directional Distribution: 50% entering, 50% exiting

Trip Generation per Employee

Average Rate	Range of Rates	Standard Deviation
2.60	1.81 - 2.87	*

Data Plot and Equation

Caution - Use Carefully - Small Sample Size

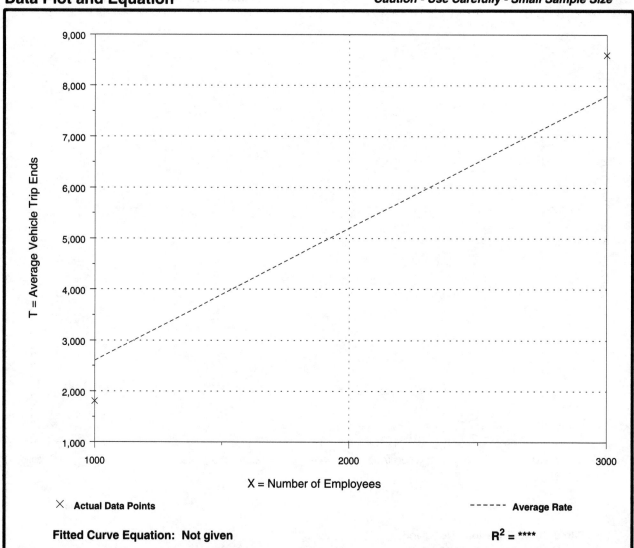

X = Number of Employees

✕ **Actual Data Points**   --------- **Average Rate**

Fitted Curve Equation: Not given $R^2 = ****$

Land Use: 453
Automobile Racetrack

Description

Automobile racetracks are facilities that contain a racetrack, spectator seating, parking and restaurant/refreshment areas.

Additional Data

The sites were surveyed in 1991 at stock car racetracks in suburban Florida.

Source Number

379

Automobile Racetrack
(453)

Average Vehicle Trip Ends vs: **Attendees**
On a: **Saturday,**
Peak Hour of Generator

Number of Studies: 2
Average Number of Attendees: 1,862
Directional Distribution: 1% entering, 99% exiting

Trip Generation per Attendee

Average Rate	Range of Rates	Standard Deviation
0.28	0.28 - 0.28	*

Data Plot and Equation

Caution - Use Carefully - Small Sample Size

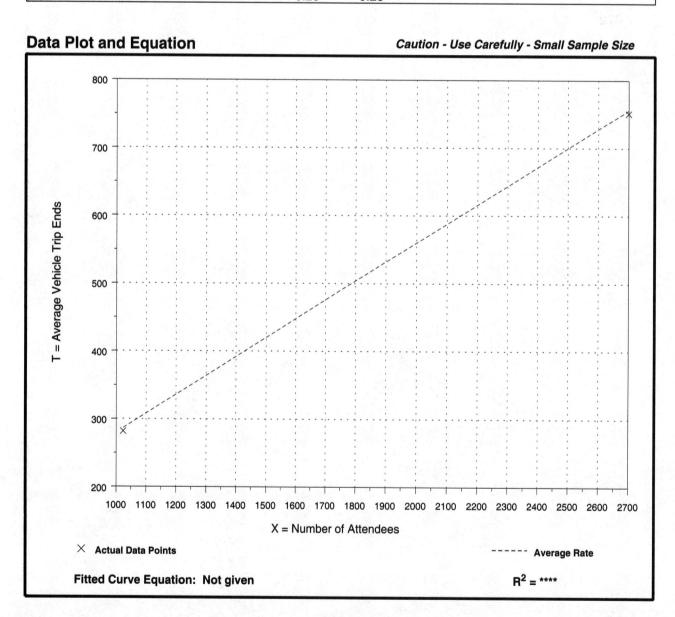

Fitted Curve Equation: Not given $R^2 =$ ****

Land Use: 454
Dog Racetrack

Description

Dog racetracks are facilities that contain a spectator stadium, parking, track and possibly stables and housing for workers.

Additional Data

Peak hour of the generator —
  The weekday p.m. peak hour was between 12:00 noon and 1:00 p.m.

The site was surveyed in 1990 at a greyhound racing facility in Massachusetts, with 2,875 attendees on the day that data were collected.

Source Number

329

Land Use: 454
Dog Racetrack
Independent Variables with One Observation

The following trip generation data are for independent variables with only one observation. This information is shown in this table only; there are no related plots for these data.

Users are cautioned to use data with care because of the small sample size.

Independent Variable	Trip Generation Rate	Size of Independent Variable	Number of Studies	Directional Distribution
Attendees				
Weekday p.m. Peak Hour of Adjacent Street Traffic	0.15	2,875	1	8% entering, 92% exiting
Weekday p.m. Peak Hour of Generator	0.41	2,875	1	92% entering, 8% exiting

Land Use: 460
Arena

Description

Arenas are large indoor structures in which spectator events are held. These events vary from professional ice hockey and basketball to non-sporting events such as concerts, shows, or religious services. Arenas generally have large parking facilities, except when located in or around the downtown of a large city.

Additional Data

The site was surveyed in 1970 in California at an arena used for ice hockey and basketball, with a seating capacity of 14,600 and 4,000 parking spaces.

Source Number

18

Land Use: 460
Arena
Independent Variables with One Observation

The following trip generation data are for independent variables with only one observation. This information is shown in this table only; there are no related plots for these data.

Users are cautioned to use data with care because of the small sample size.

Independent Variable	Trip Generation Rate	Size of Independent Variable	Number of Studies	Directional Distribution
Employees				
Weekday	10.00	110	1	50% entering, 50% exiting
Acres				
Weekday	33.33	33	1	50% entering, 50% exiting

Land Use: 465
Ice Skating Rink

Description

Ice skating rinks are stand-alone facilities used for ice-skating-oriented sports and entertainment activities. They may contain limited spectator seating, refreshment areas, locker rooms and arcades.

Additional Data

The sites were surveyed in California.

Source Number

441

Land Use: 465
Ice Skating Rink
Independent Variables with One Observation

The following trip generation data are for independent variables with only one observation. This information is shown in this table only; there are no related plots for these data.

Users are cautioned to use data with care because of the small sample size.

Independent Variable	Trip Generation Rate	Size of Independent Variable	Number of Studies	Directional Distribution
1,000 Square Feet Gross Floor Area				
Weekday p.m. Peak Hour of Adjacent Street Traffic	2.36	70	1	45% entering, 55% exiting
Seats				
Weekday	1.26	300	1	50% entering, 50% exiting
Weekday p.m. Peak Hour of Adjacent Street Traffic	0.12	300	1	Not available

Land Use: 473
Casino/Video Lottery Establishment

Description

Casino/video lottery establishments are businesses that provide electronic or manually-controlled slot machines. These facilities exist for the primary purpose of deriving revenue from gaming operations. Full food service is generally not provided at these facilities; however, refreshments and alcoholic beverages may be served. These facilities do not include full-service casinos or casino/hotel facilities such as those located in Las Vegas, Nevada or Atlantic City, New Jersey. Riverboat casinos are not included in this land use category.

Additional Data

Trip generation rates for full-service casinos and casino/hotel facilities are not included in this land use.

The sites were surveyed in the 1990s in South Dakota.

Source Number

359

Casino/Video Lottery Establishment
(473)

Average Vehicle Trip Ends vs: 1000 Sq. Feet Gross Floor Area
On a: Weekday,
Peak Hour of Adjacent Street Traffic,
One Hour Between 4 and 6 p.m.

Number of Studies: 6
Average 1000 Sq. Feet GFA: 2
Directional Distribution: 56% entering, 44% exiting

Trip Generation per 1000 Sq. Feet Gross Floor Area

Average Rate	Range of Rates	Standard Deviation
13.43	7.08 - 27.00	8.65

Data Plot and Equation

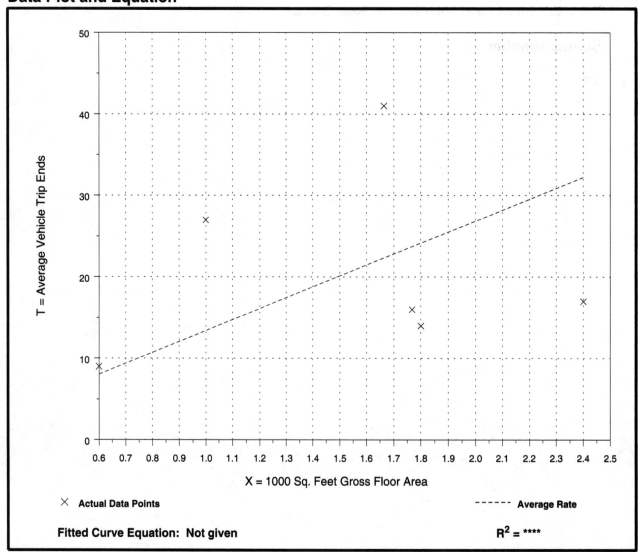

X = 1000 Sq. Feet Gross Floor Area

✕ **Actual Data Points**   - - - - - **Average Rate**

Fitted Curve Equation: Not given $R^2 =$ ****

Land Use: 480
Amusement Park

Description

An amusement park contains rides, entertainment, refreshment stands and picnic areas.

Additional Data

The sites were surveyed in 1970 and 1987 in California and Oklahoma. The California site, at the time of data collection (1970), had 600 employees and 3,000 parking spaces. The two sites located in Oklahoma had 108 employees and 697 parking spaces, and 300 employees and 2,200 parking spaces.

Source Numbers

18, 269

Land Use: 480
Amusement Park
Independent Variables with One Observation

The following trip generation data are for independent variables with only one observation. This information is shown in this table only; there are no related plots for these data.

Users are cautioned to use data with care because of the small sample size.

Independent Variable	Trip Generation Rate	Size of Independent Variable	Number of Studies	Directional Distribution
Employees				
Weekday	8.33	600	1	50% entering, 50% exiting
Weekday a.m. Peak Hour of Adjacent Street Traffic	0.03	300	1	88% entering, 12% exiting
Weekday p.m. Peak Hour of Adjacent Street Traffic	0.50	300	1	61% entering, 39% exiting
Weekday a.m. Peak Hour of Generator	0.09	300	1	46% entering, 54% exiting
Weekday p.m. Peak Hour of Generator	0.52	300	1	60% entering, 40% exiting
Acres				
Weekday	75.76	66	1	50% entering, 50% exiting
Weekday a.m. Peak Hour of Adjacent Street Traffic	0.21	38	1	88% entering, 12% exiting
Weekday p.m. Peak Hour of Adjacent Street Traffic	3.95	38	1	61% entering, 39% exiting
Weekday a.m. Peak Hour of Generator	0.68	38	1	46% entering, 54% exiting
Weekday p.m. Peak Hour of Generator	4.11	38	1	60% entering, 40% exiting

Amusement Park
(480)

Average Vehicle Trip Ends vs: Employees

On a: Saturday

Number of Studies: 2
Avg. Number of Employees: 204
Directional Distribution: 50% entering, 50% exiting

Trip Generation per Employee

Average Rate	Range of Rates	Standard Deviation
22.08	16.70 - 24.02	*

Data Plot and Equation

Caution - Use Carefully - Small Sample Size

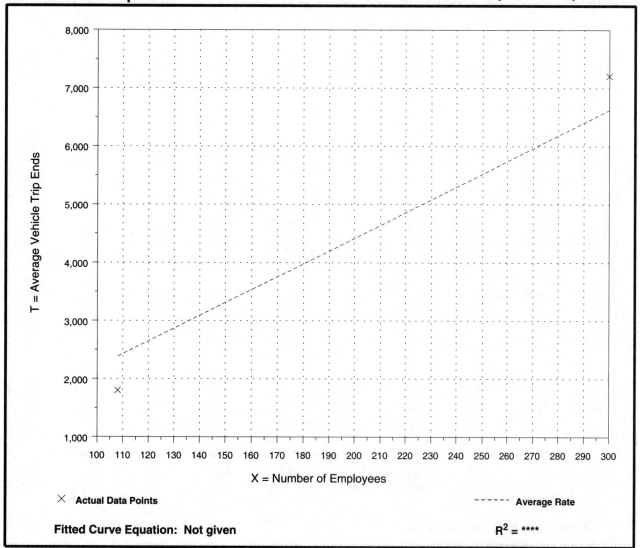

X **Actual Data Points**

- - - - - **Average Rate**

Fitted Curve Equation: Not given $R^2 =$ ****

Amusement Park
(480)

Average Vehicle Trip Ends vs: Employees
On a: Saturday,
Peak Hour of Generator

Number of Studies: 2
Avg. Number of Employees: 204
Directional Distribution: 58% entering, 42% exiting

Trip Generation per Employee

Average Rate	Range of Rates	Standard Deviation
2.31	2.23 - 2.55	*

Data Plot and Equation

Caution - Use Carefully - Small Sample Size

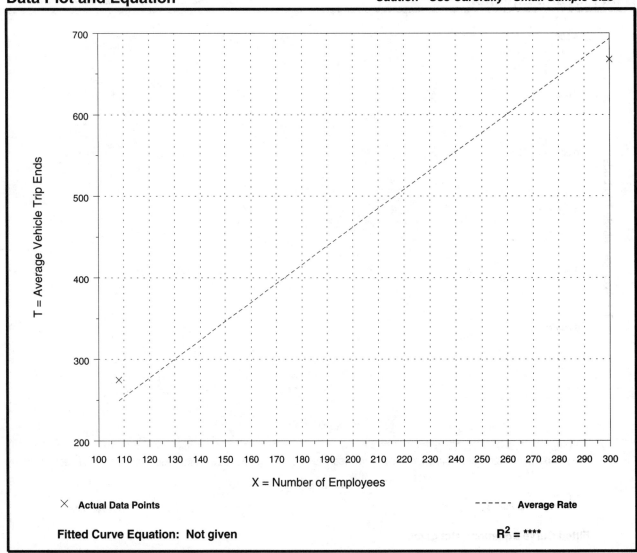

X   **Actual Data Points**

- - - - - **Average Rate**

Fitted Curve Equation: Not given

$R^2 = ****$

Amusement Park
(480)

Average Vehicle Trip Ends vs: Employees
On a: Sunday

Number of Studies: 2
Avg. Number of Employees: 204
Directional Distribution: 50% entering, 50% exiting

Trip Generation per Employee

Average Rate	Range of Rates	Standard Deviation
20.96	9.17 - 25.20	*

Data Plot and Equation

Caution - Use Carefully - Small Sample Size

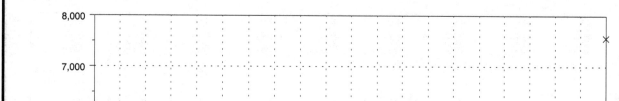

X = Number of Employees

✕ **Actual Data Points**   - - - - - **Average Rate**

Fitted Curve Equation: Not given $R^2 = ****$

Amusement Park
(480)

Average Vehicle Trip Ends vs: **Employees**
On a: **Sunday,**
  Peak Hour of Generator

Number of Studies: 2
Avg. Number of Employees: 204
Directional Distribution: 44% entering, 56% exiting

Trip Generation per Employee

Average Rate	Range of Rates	Standard Deviation
2.18	1.34 - 2.48	*

Data Plot and Equation

Caution - Use Carefully - Small Sample Size

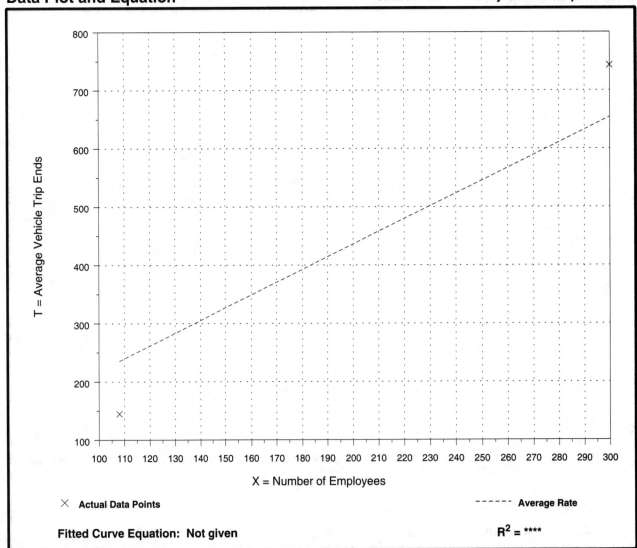

X **Actual Data Points**

- - - - -   **Average Rate**

Fitted Curve Equation: Not given

$R^2 = ****$

Amusement Park
(480)

Average Vehicle Trip Ends vs: Acres
On a: Saturday

Number of Studies: 2
Average Number of Acres: 25
Directional Distribution: 50% entering, 50% exiting

Trip Generation per Acre

Average Rate	Range of Rates	Standard Deviation
180.20	150.33 - 189.63	*

Data Plot and Equation

Caution - Use Carefully - Small Sample Size

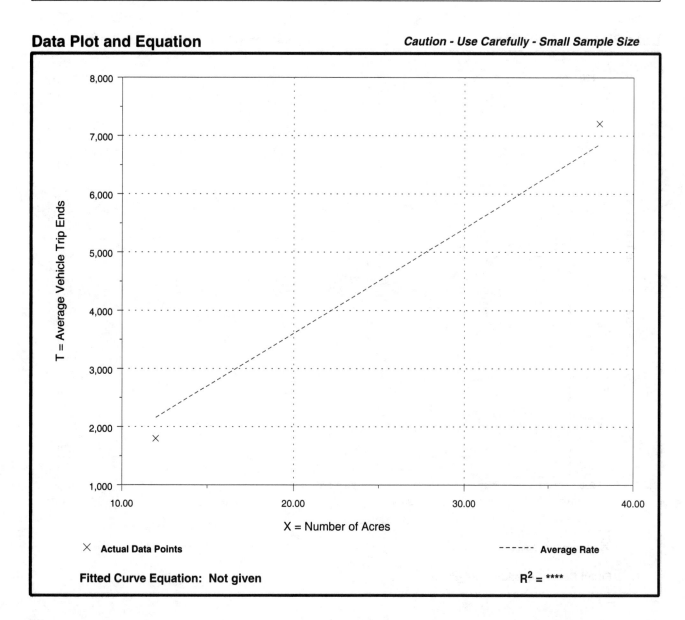

X = Number of Acres

× **Actual Data Points**   - - - - - **Average Rate**

Fitted Curve Equation: Not given $R^2 = ****$

Amusement Park
(480)

Average Vehicle Trip Ends vs: **Acres**
On a: **Saturday,**
Peak Hour of Generator

Number of Studies: 2
Average Number of Acres: 25
Directional Distribution: 58% entering, 42% exiting

Trip Generation per Acre

Average Rate	Range of Rates	Standard Deviation
18.86	17.58 - 22.92	*

Data Plot and Equation

Caution - Use Carefully - Small Sample Size

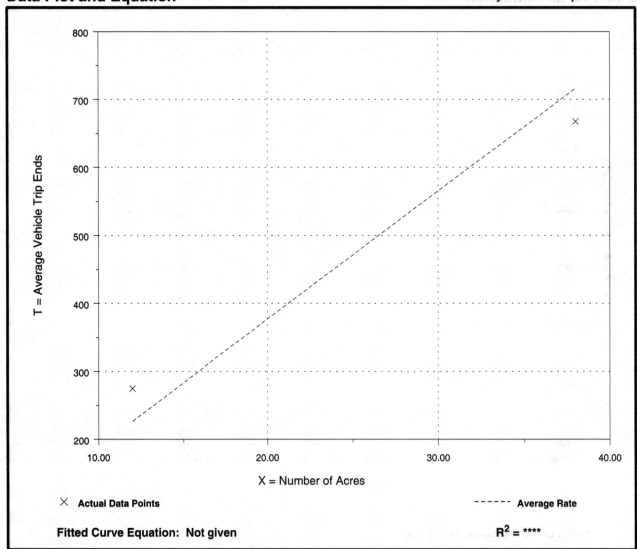

X   **Actual Data Points**   - - - - - **Average Rate**

Fitted Curve Equation: Not given $R^2 =$ ****

Amusement Park
(480)

Average Vehicle Trip Ends vs: **Acres**
On a: **Sunday**

Number of Studies: 2
Average Number of Acres: 25
Directional Distribution: 50% entering, 50% exiting

Trip Generation per Acre

Average Rate	Range of Rates	Standard Deviation
171.02	82.50 - 198.97	*

Data Plot and Equation

Caution - Use Carefully - Small Sample Size

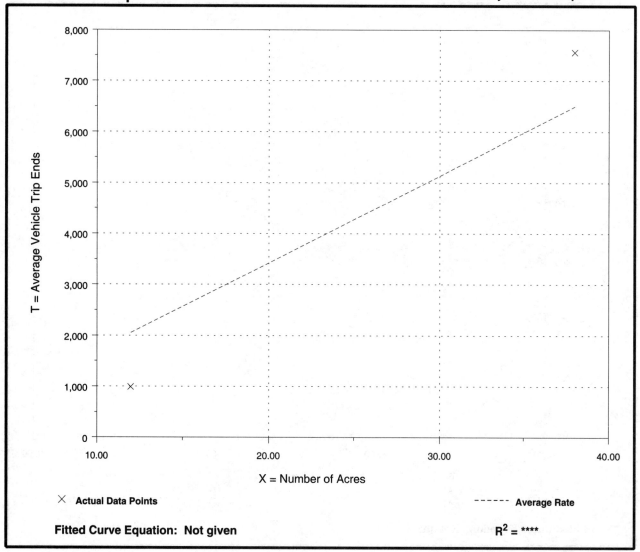

× **Actual Data Points** − − − − − **Average Rate**

Fitted Curve Equation: Not given $R^2 = ****$

Amusement Park
(480)

Average Vehicle Trip Ends vs: **Acres**
On a: **Sunday,**
  Peak Hour of Generator

Number of Studies: 2
Average Number of Acres: 25
Directional Distribution: 44% entering, 56% exiting

Trip Generation per Acre

Average Rate	Range of Rates	Standard Deviation
17.76	12.08 - 19.55	*

Data Plot and Equation

Caution - Use Carefully - Small Sample Size

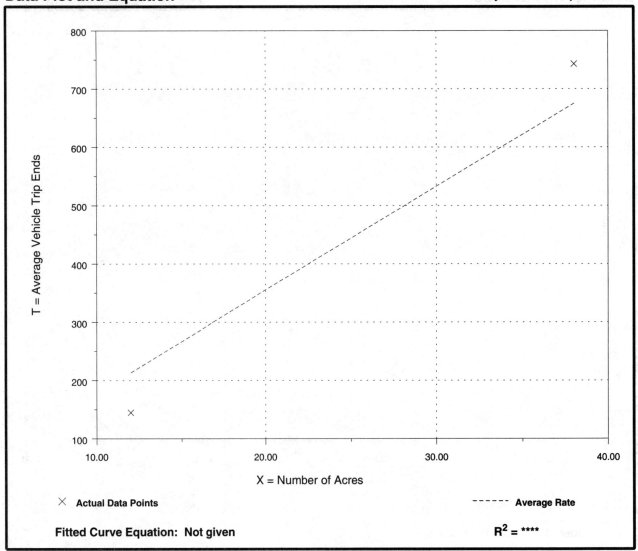

X   **Actual Data Points**

- - - - - **Average Rate**

Fitted Curve Equation: Not given

$R^2 = ****$

Land Use: 481
Zoo

Description

Zoos contain wild animals in cages or enclosed areas, refreshment stands, souvenir stands and picnic areas.

Additional Data

This site was surveyed in 1970 in San Diego, California. At the time of the survey, the San Diego Zoo had 3,251 parking spaces and 600 employees on 125 acres.

Source Number

18

Land Use: 481
Zoo
Independent Variables with One Observation

The following trip generation data are for independent variables with only one observation. This information is shown in this table only; there are no related plots for these data.

Users are cautioned to use data with care because of the small sample size.

Independent Variable	Trip Generation Rate	Size of Independent Variable	Number of Studies	Directional Distribution
Employees				
Weekday	23.93	600	1	50% entering, 50% exiting
Acres				
Weekday	114.88	125	1	50% entering, 50% exiting

Land Use: 488
Soccer Complex

Description

Soccer complexes are outdoor parks that are used for non-professional soccer games. They may consist of one or more fields, and the size of each field within the land use may vary to accommodate games for different age groups. Ancillary amenities may include a fitness trail, activities shelter, aquatic center, picnic grounds, basketball and tennis courts and a playground.

Additional Data

Caution should be used when applying these data. Peaking at soccer complexes typically occurred in time periods shorter than one hour. These peaking periods may have durations of 10 to 15 minutes.

One study noted that ridesharing was common for teams traveling to out-of-town matches.

The sites were surveyed in the 1990s in Indiana and Washington.

To assist in the future analysis of this land use, it is important to collect driveway counts in 10-minute intervals.

Source Numbers

377, 519, 565

Land Use: 488
Soccer Complex
Independent Variables with One Observation

The following trip generation data are for independent variables with only one observation. This information is shown in this table only; there are no related plots for these data.

Users are cautioned to use data with care because of the small sample size.

Independent Variable	Trip Generation Rate	Size of Independent Variable	Number of Studies	Directional Distribution
Fields				
Saturday	117.43	7	1	50% entering, 50% exiting

Soccer Complex
(488)

Average Vehicle Trip Ends vs: **Fields**
On a: **Weekday**

Number of Studies: 3
Average Number of Fields: 10
Directional Distribution: 50% entering, 50% exiting

Trip Generation per Field

Average Rate	Range of Rates	Standard Deviation
71.33	42.86 - 90.81	23.12

Data Plot and Equation

Caution - Use Carefully - Small Sample Size

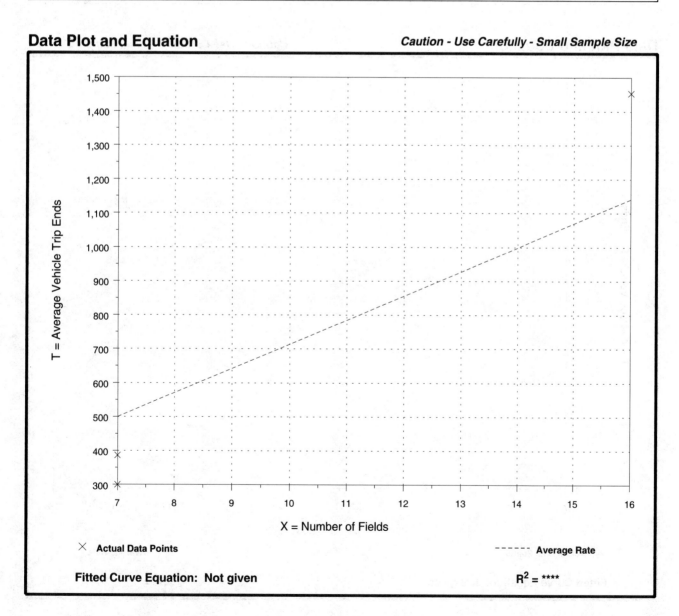

X = Number of Fields

✕ **Actual Data Points** - - - - - **Average Rate**

Fitted Curve Equation: Not given $R^2 = ****$

Soccer Complex
(488)

Average Vehicle Trip Ends vs:	**Fields**
On a:	**Weekday,**
	Peak Hour of Adjacent Street Traffic,
	One Hour Between 7 and 9 a.m.

Number of Studies: 3
Average Number of Fields: 10
Directional Distribution: 50% entering, 50% exiting

Trip Generation per Field

Average Rate	Range of Rates	Standard Deviation
1.40	0.29 - 1.88	1.32

Data Plot and Equation

Caution - Use Carefully - Small Sample Size

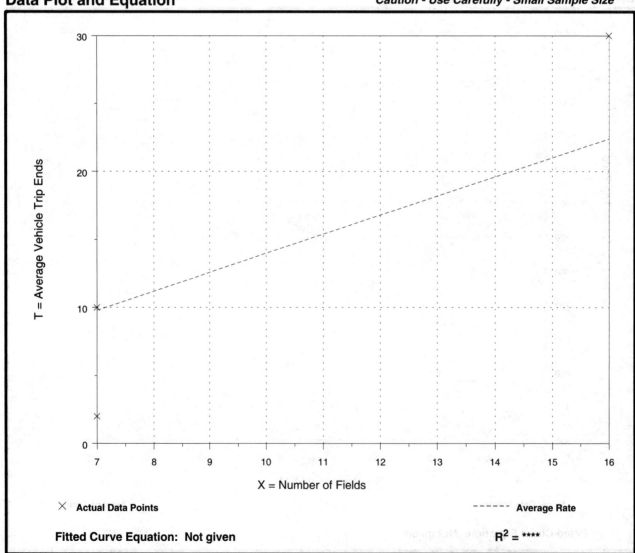

X **Actual Data Points**   - - - - - **Average Rate**

Fitted Curve Equation: Not given $R^2 = $ ****

Soccer Complex
(488)

Average Vehicle Trip Ends vs: **Fields**
On a: **Weekday,**
Peak Hour of Adjacent Street Traffic,
One Hour Between 4 and 6 p.m.

Number of Studies: 3
Average Number of Fields: 10
Directional Distribution: 69% entering, 31% exiting

Trip Generation per Field

Average Rate	Range of Rates	Standard Deviation
20.67	8.71 - 24.88	8.06

Data Plot and Equation

Caution - Use Carefully - Small Sample Size

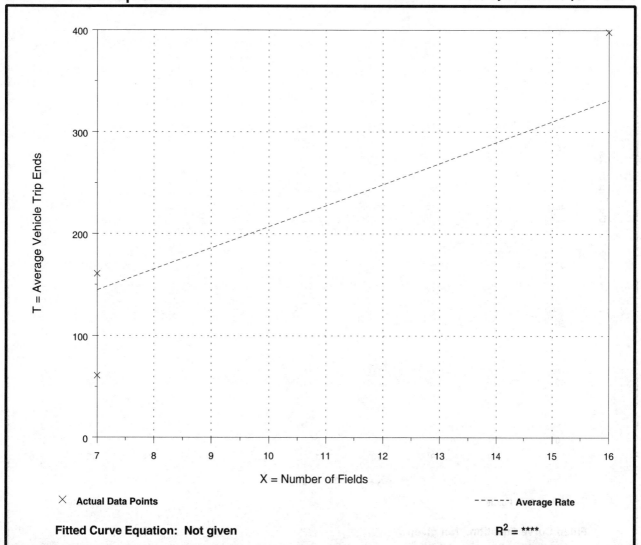

X **Actual Data Points** - - - - - **Average Rate**

Fitted Curve Equation: Not given $R^2 = ****$

Soccer Complex
(488)

Average Vehicle Trip Ends vs: **Fields**
On a: **Weekday,**
A.M. Peak Hour of Generator

Number of Studies: 3
Average Number of Fields: 10
Directional Distribution: 54% entering, 46% exiting

Trip Generation per Field

Average Rate	Range of Rates	Standard Deviation
2.90	0.29 - 3.81	2.22

Data Plot and Equation

Caution - Use Carefully - Small Sample Size

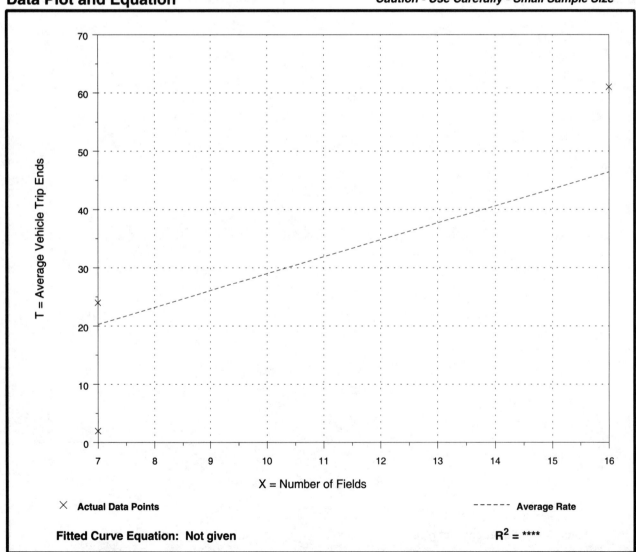

X **Actual Data Points**   - - - - - **Average Rate**

Fitted Curve Equation: Not given $R^2 = ****$

Soccer Complex
(488)

Average Vehicle Trip Ends vs: **Fields**
                   On a: **Weekday,**
                          P.M. Peak Hour of Generator

Number of Studies: 3
Average Number of Fields: 10
Directional Distribution: 33% entering, 67% exiting

Trip Generation per Field

Average Rate	Range of Rates	Standard Deviation
21.77	9.71 - 26.50	8.26

Data Plot and Equation

Caution - Use Carefully - Small Sample Size

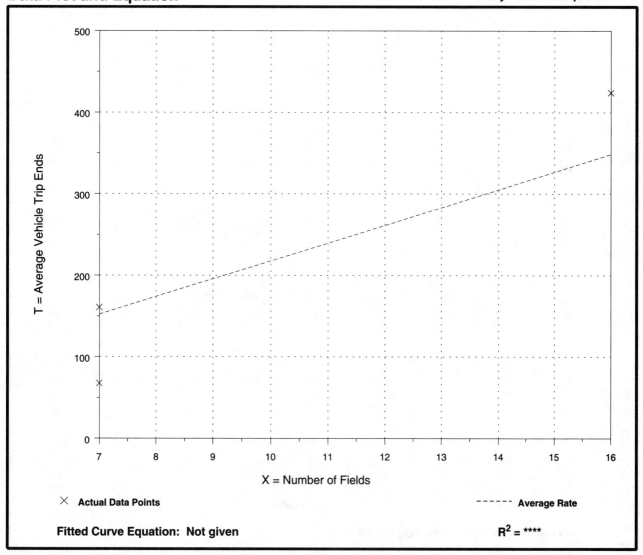

$\times$ **Actual Data Points**   - - - - - **Average Rate**

Fitted Curve Equation: Not given $R^2 = ****$

Soccer Complex
(488)

Average Vehicle Trip Ends vs: **Fields**
On a: **Saturday,**
Peak Hour of Generator

Number of Studies: 5
Average Number of Fields: 10
Directional Distribution: 48% entering, 52% exiting

Trip Generation per Field

Average Rate	Range of Rates	Standard Deviation
28.73	17.14 - 33.56	7.47

Data Plot and Equation

Caution - Use Carefully - Small Sample Size

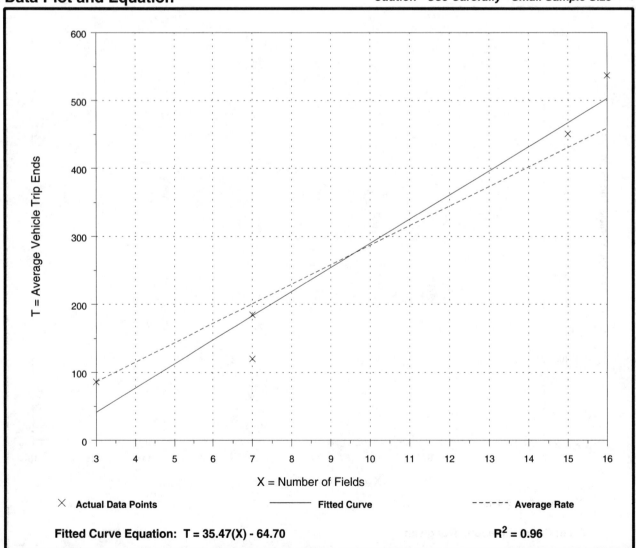

Fitted Curve Equation: T = 35.47(X) - 64.70 $R^2 = 0.96$

Land Use: 490
Tennis Courts

Description

Tennis courts are indoor or outdoor facilities specifically designed for playing tennis. Tennis courts can either be public or private facilities and do not typically include any ancillary facilities other than limited spectator seating. Racquet/tennis club (Land Use 491) is a related use.

Additional Data

One of the sites was surveyed in 1979 in California.

Source Numbers

113, 440, 441

Land Use: 490
Tennis Courts
Independent Variables with One Observation

The following trip generation data are for independent variables with only one observation. This information is shown in this table only; there are no related plots for these data.

Users are cautioned to use data with care because of the small sample size.

Independent Variable	Trip Generation Rate	Size of Independent Variable	Number of Studies	Directional Distribution
Tennis Courts				
Weekday a.m. Peak Hour of Adjacent Street Traffic	1.67	6	1	Not available
Weekday a.m. Peak Hour of Generator	1.83	6	1	Not available
Weekday p.m. Peak Hour of Generator	3.67	6	1	Not available
Saturday	27.83	6	1	50% entering, 50% exiting
Saturday Peak Hour of Generator	3.00	6	1	Not available
Sunday	37.83	6	1	50% entering, 50% exiting
Sunday Peak Hour of Generator	5.00	6	1	Not available
Acres				
Weekday	16.26	12	1	50% entering, 50% exiting
Weekday a.m. Peak Hour of Adjacent Street Traffic	0.81	12	1	Not available
Weekday p.m. Peak Hour of Adjacent Street Traffic	1.38	12	1	Not available
Weekday a.m. Peak Hour of Generator	0.89	12	1	Not available
Weekday p.m. Peak Hour of Generator	1.79	12	1	Not available
Saturday	13.58	12	1	50% entering, 50% exiting
Saturday Peak Hour of Generator	1.46	12	1	Not available
Sunday	18.46	12	1	50% entering, 50% exiting
Sunday Peak Hour of Generator	2.44	12	1	Not available

Land Use: 490
Tennis Courts
Independent Variables with One Observation

Employees

Weekday	66.67	3	1	50% entering, 50% exiting
Weekday a.m. Peak Hour of Adjacent Street Traffic	3.33	3	1	Not available
Weekday p.m. Peak Hour of Adjacent Street Traffic	5.67	3	1	Not available
Weekday a.m. Peak Hour of Generator	3.67	3	1	Not available
Weekday p.m. Peak Hour of Generator	7.33	3	1	Not available
Saturday	55.67	3	1	50% entering, 50% exiting
Saturday Peak Hour of Generator	6.00	3	1	Not available
Sunday	75.67	3	1	50% entering, 50% exiting
Sunday Peak Hour of Generator	10.00	3	1	Not available

Tennis Courts
(490)

Average Vehicle Trip Ends vs: **Tennis Courts**
On a: **Weekday**

Number of Studies: 3
Avg. Number of Tennis Courts: 8
Directional Distribution: 50% entering, 50% exiting

Trip Generation per Tennis Court

Average Rate	Range of Rates	Standard Deviation
31.04	20.17 - 47.71	13.02

Data Plot and Equation

Caution - Use Carefully - Small Sample Size

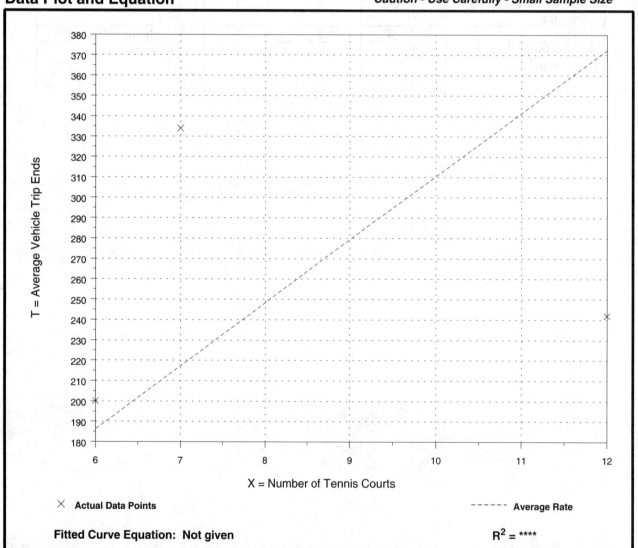

X = Number of Tennis Courts

× **Actual Data Points** ----- **Average Rate**

Fitted Curve Equation: Not given $R^2 = ****$

Tennis Courts
(490)

Average Vehicle Trip Ends vs: Tennis Courts
On a: Weekday,
Peak Hour of Adjacent Street Traffic,
One Hour Between 4 and 6 p.m.

Number of Studies: 3
Avg. Number of Tennis Courts: 8
Directional Distribution: Not available

Trip Generation per Tennis Court

Average Rate	Range of Rates	Standard Deviation
3.88	2.83 - 5.71	2.23

Data Plot and Equation

Caution - Use Carefully - Small Sample Size

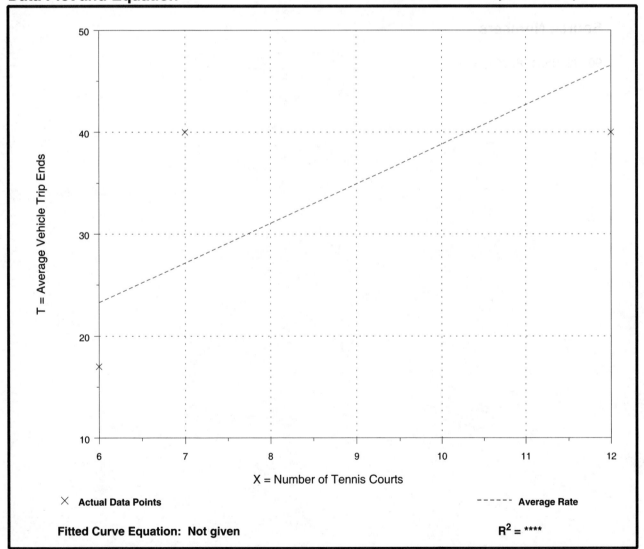

Actual Data Points   ----- **Average Rate**

Fitted Curve Equation: Not given $R^2 = $ ****

Land Use: 491
Racquet/Tennis Club

Description

Racquet/tennis clubs are privately-owned facilities that primarily cater to racquet sports (tennis, racquetball, or squash—indoor or outdoor). This land use may also provide ancillary facilities, such as swimming pools, whirlpools, saunas, weight rooms, snack bars and retail stores. These facilities are membership clubs that may allow access to the general public for a fee. Tennis courts (Land Use 490), health/fitness club (Land Use 492), athletic club (Land Use 493) and recreational community center (Land Use 495) are related uses.

Additional Data

Some of the sites in this land use offered racquet/tennis competitions.

The majority of the sites were surveyed in the 1970s throughout the West Coast and Connecticut.

Source Numbers

90, 92, 95, 158, 214, 440

Land Use: 491
Racquet/Tennis Club
Independent Variables with One Observation

The following trip generation data are for independent variables with only one observation. This information is shown in this table only; there are no related plots for these data.

Users are cautioned to use data with care because of the small sample size.

Independent Variable	Trip Generation Rate	Size of Independent Variable	Number of Studies	Directional Distribution
1,000 Square Feet Gross Floor Area				
Weekday p.m. Peak Hour of Adjacent Street Traffic	1.06	54	1	Not available

Racquet/Tennis Club
(491)

Average Vehicle Trip Ends vs: Employees
On a: Weekday

Number of Studies: 8
Avg. Number of Employees: 9
Directional Distribution: 50% entering, 50% exiting

Trip Generation per Employee

Average Rate	Range of Rates	Standard Deviation
45.71	19.65 - 87.67	26.08

Data Plot and Equation

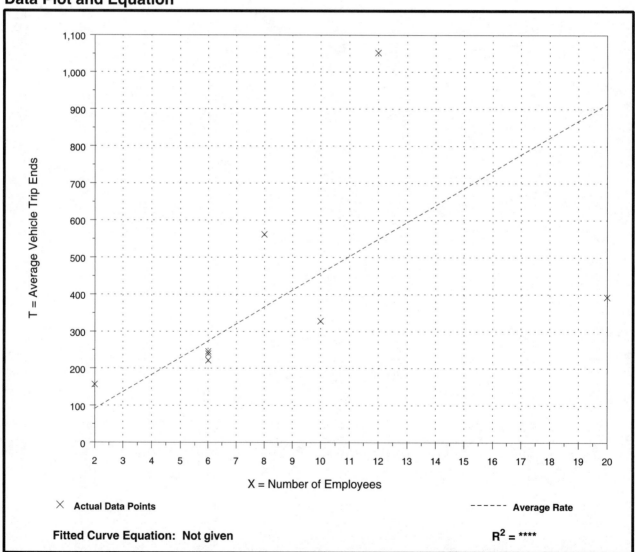

X **Actual Data Points**   - - - - - **Average Rate**

Fitted Curve Equation: Not given $R^2 = ****$

Racquet/Tennis Club
(491)

Average Vehicle Trip Ends vs: **Employees**
On a: **Weekday,**
Peak Hour of Adjacent Street Traffic,
One Hour Between 7 and 9 a.m.

Number of Studies: 3
Avg. Number of Employees: 5
Directional Distribution: Not available

Trip Generation per Employee

Average Rate	Range of Rates	Standard Deviation
1.86	1.17 - 3.00	1.41

Data Plot and Equation

Caution - Use Carefully - Small Sample Size

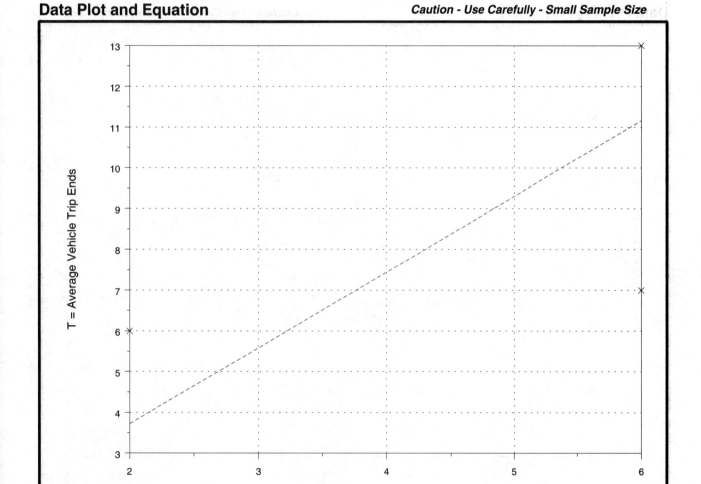

X **Actual Data Points**

- - - - - **Average Rate**

Fitted Curve Equation: Not given $R^2 =$ ****

Racquet/Tennis Club
(491)

Average Vehicle Trip Ends vs: **Employees**
On a: **Weekday,**
Peak Hour of Adjacent Street Traffic,
One Hour Between 4 and 6 p.m.

Number of Studies: 4
Avg. Number of Employees: 6
Directional Distribution: Not available

Trip Generation per Employee

Average Rate	Range of Rates	Standard Deviation
4.95	3.17 - 7.13	2.81

Data Plot and Equation

Caution - Use Carefully - Small Sample Size

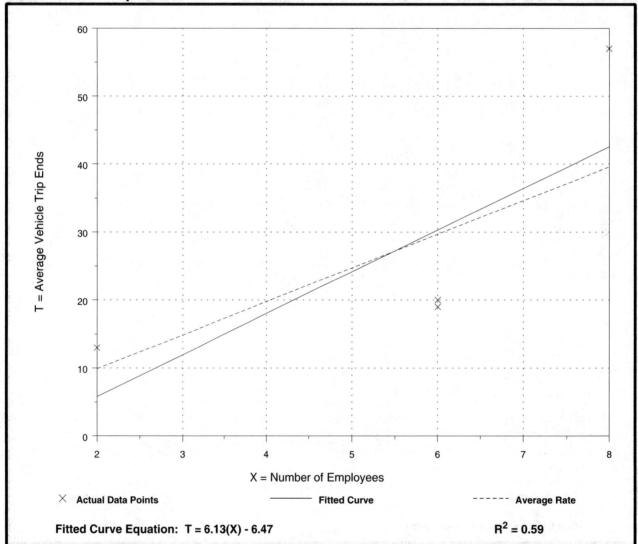

X **Actual Data Points** —————— **Fitted Curve** - - - - - **Average Rate**

Fitted Curve Equation: T = 6.13(X) - 6.47 $R^2 = 0.59$

Racquet/Tennis Club
(491)

Average Vehicle Trip Ends vs: **Employees**
On a: **Weekday,**
     A.M. Peak Hour of Generator

Number of Studies: 3
Avg. Number of Employees: 5
Directional Distribution: Not available

Trip Generation per Employee

Average Rate	Range of Rates	Standard Deviation
3.64	3.00 - 6.00	2.00

Data Plot and Equation

Caution - Use Carefully - Small Sample Size

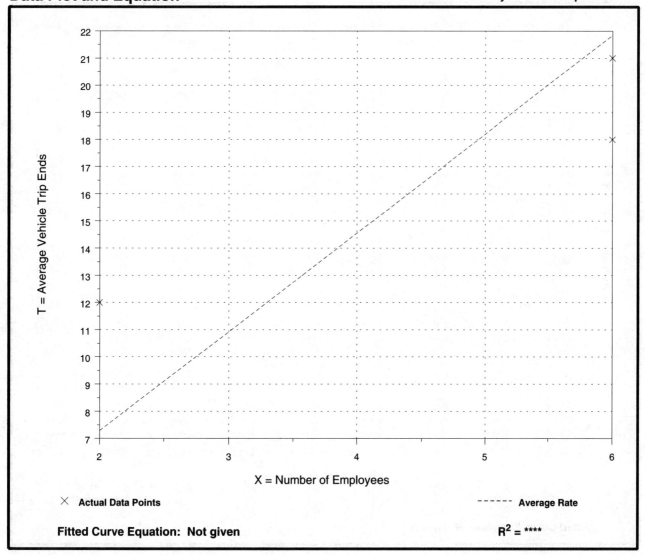

X   **Actual Data Points**   - - - - - **Average Rate**

Fitted Curve Equation: Not given $R^2 = ****$

Racquet/Tennis Club
(491)

Average Vehicle Trip Ends vs: **Employees**
On a: **Weekday,**
P.M. Peak Hour of Generator

Number of Studies: 6
Avg. Number of Employees: 9
Directional Distribution: Not available

Trip Generation per Employee

Average Rate	Range of Rates	Standard Deviation
3.40	1.65 - 8.00	2.68

Data Plot and Equation

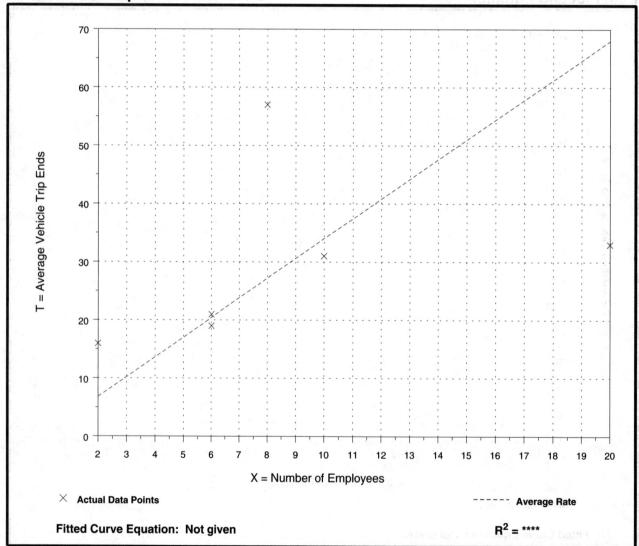

Fitted Curve Equation: Not given $R^2 = ****$

Racquet/Tennis Club
(491)

Average Vehicle Trip Ends vs: Employees
On a: Saturday

Number of Studies: 5
Avg. Number of Employees: 6
Directional Distribution: 50% entering, 50% exiting

Trip Generation per Employee

Average Rate	Range of Rates	Standard Deviation
49.69	19.67 - 109.00	22.77

Data Plot and Equation

Caution - Use Carefully - Small Sample Size

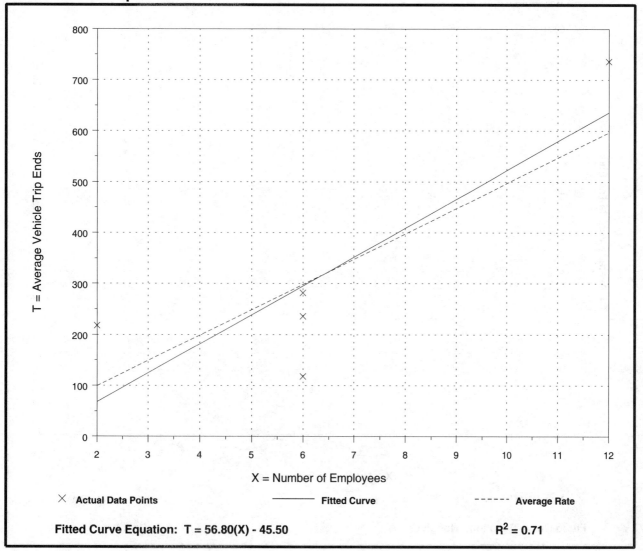

X **Actual Data Points**   ———— **Fitted Curve**   - - - - - **Average Rate**

Fitted Curve Equation: T = 56.80(X) - 45.50 $R^2 = 0.71$

Racquet/Tennis Club
(491)

Average Vehicle Trip Ends vs: **Employees**
On a: **Saturday,**
Peak Hour of Generator

Number of Studies: 3
Avg. Number of Employees: 5
Directional Distribution: Not available

Trip Generation per Employee

Average Rate	Range of Rates	Standard Deviation
7.71	4.50 - 14.00	4.20

Data Plot and Equation

Caution - Use Carefully - Small Sample Size

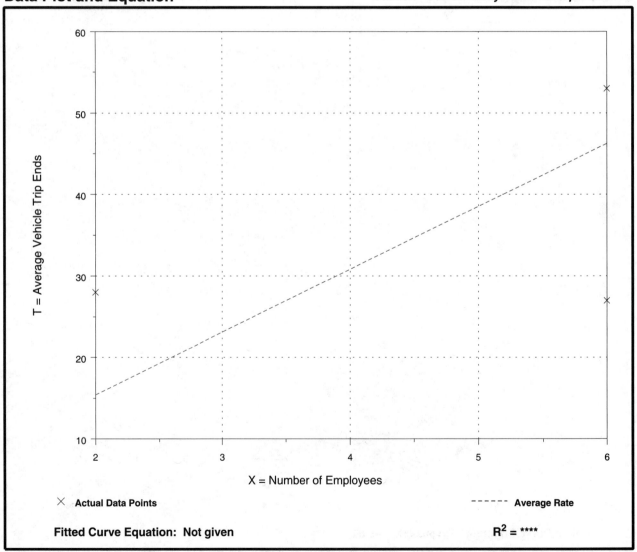

X = Number of Employees

× **Actual Data Points**   ----- **Average Rate**

Fitted Curve Equation: Not given $R^2 = ****$

Racquet/Tennis Club
(491)

Average Vehicle Trip Ends vs: Employees
On a: Sunday

Number of Studies: 5
Avg. Number of Employees: 6
Directional Distribution: 50% entering, 50% exiting

Trip Generation per Employee

Average Rate	Range of Rates	Standard Deviation
40.91	15.33 - 77.50	16.91

Data Plot and Equation

Caution - Use Carefully - Small Sample Size

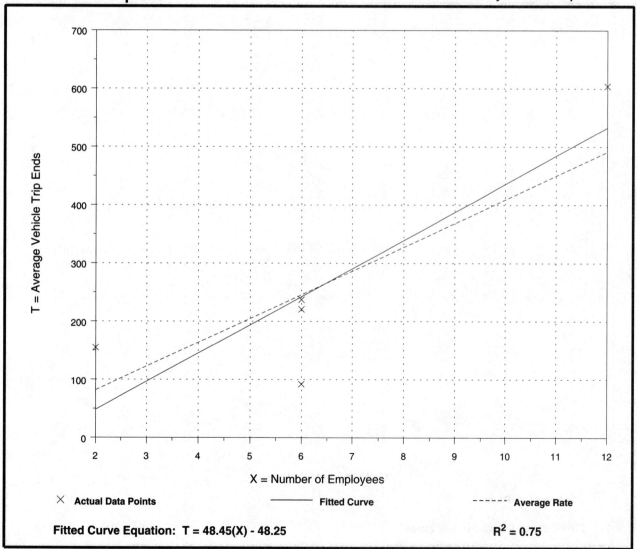

Actual Data Points ✕   Fitted Curve ——   Average Rate -----

Fitted Curve Equation: T = 48.45(X) - 48.25 $R^2 = 0.75$

Racquet/Tennis Club
(491)

Average Vehicle Trip Ends vs: **Employees**
On a: **Sunday,**
Peak Hour of Generator

Number of Studies: 3
Avg. Number of Employees: 5
Directional Distribution: Not available

Trip Generation per Employee

Average Rate	Range of Rates	Standard Deviation
6.00	5.17 - 10.50	2.91

Data Plot and Equation

Caution - Use Carefully - Small Sample Size

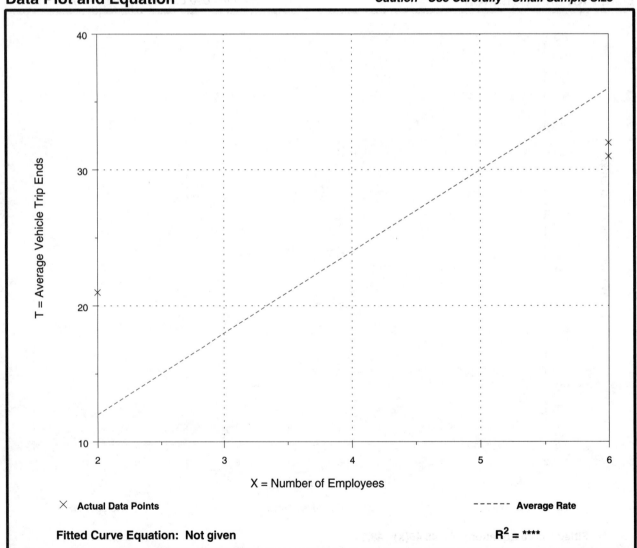

X = Number of Employees

✕ **Actual Data Points**   - - - - - **Average Rate**

Fitted Curve Equation: Not given $R^2 = $ ****

Racquet/Tennis Club
(491)

Average Vehicle Trip Ends vs: Courts
On a: Weekday

Number of Studies: 9
Avg. Number of Courts: 9
Directional Distribution: 50% entering, 50% exiting

Trip Generation per Court

Average Rate	Range of Rates	Standard Deviation
38.70	20.18 - 70.25	17.15

Data Plot and Equation

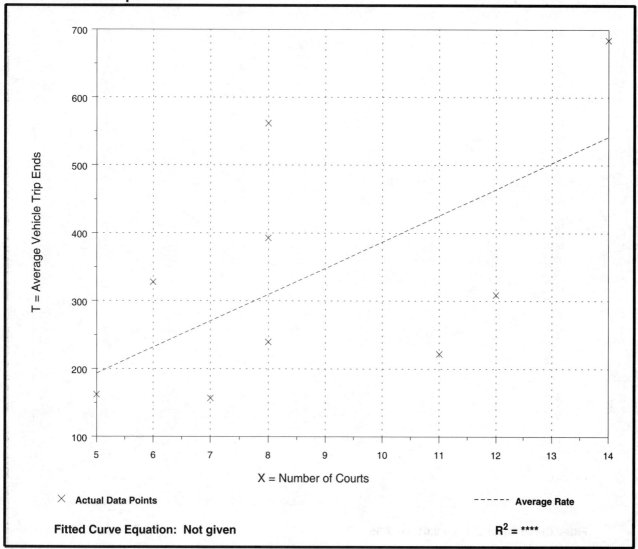

X = Number of Courts

$\times$ **Actual Data Points**   - - - - - **Average Rate**

Fitted Curve Equation: Not given $R^2 = ****$

Racquet/Tennis Club
(491)

Average Vehicle Trip Ends vs: **Courts**
On a: **Weekday,**
Peak Hour of Adjacent Street Traffic,
One Hour Between 7 and 9 a.m.

Number of Studies: 5
Avg. Number of Courts: 11
Directional Distribution: Not available

Trip Generation per Court

Average Rate	Range of Rates	Standard Deviation
1.31	0.64 - 1.79	1.19

Data Plot and Equation

Caution - Use Carefully - Small Sample Size

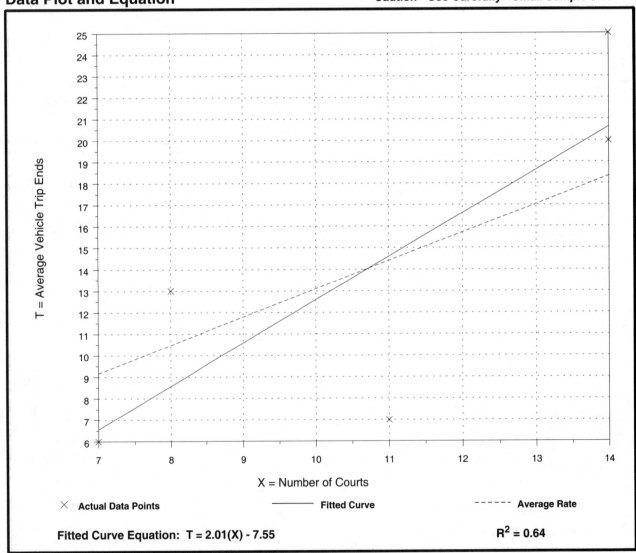

X = Number of Courts

✕ **Actual Data Points**   ——— **Fitted Curve**   - - - - - **Average Rate**

Fitted Curve Equation: T = 2.01(X) - 7.55 $R^2 = 0.64$

Racquet/Tennis Club
(491)

Average Vehicle Trip Ends vs: **Courts**
On a: **Weekday,**
Peak Hour of Adjacent Street Traffic,
One Hour Between 4 and 6 p.m.

Number of Studies: 8
Avg. Number of Courts: 10
Directional Distribution: Not available

Trip Generation per Court

Average Rate	Range of Rates	Standard Deviation
3.35	1.73 - 7.13	2.31

Data Plot and Equation

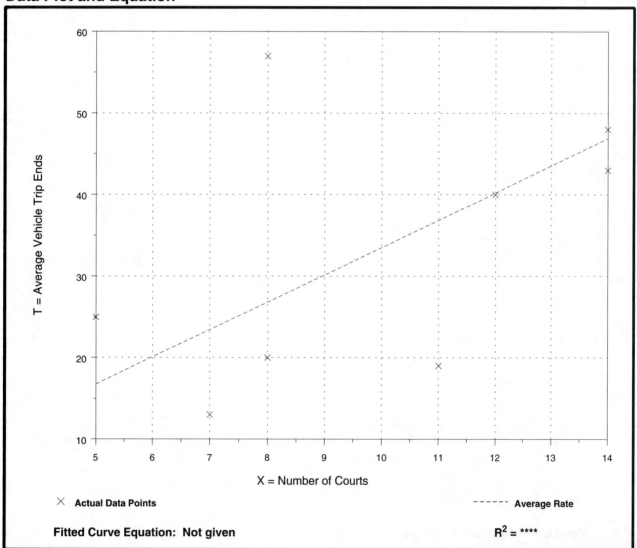

X Actual Data Points

- - - - - Average Rate

Fitted Curve Equation: Not given

$R^2 = ****$

885

Institute of Transportation Engineers

Racquet/Tennis Club
(491)

Average Vehicle Trip Ends vs: **Courts**
On a: **Weekday,**
A.M. Peak Hour of Generator

Number of Studies: 4
Avg. Number of Courts: 10
Directional Distribution: Not available

Trip Generation per Court

Average Rate	Range of Rates	Standard Deviation
2.30	1.71 - 2.93	1.54

Data Plot and Equation

Caution - Use Carefully - Small Sample Size

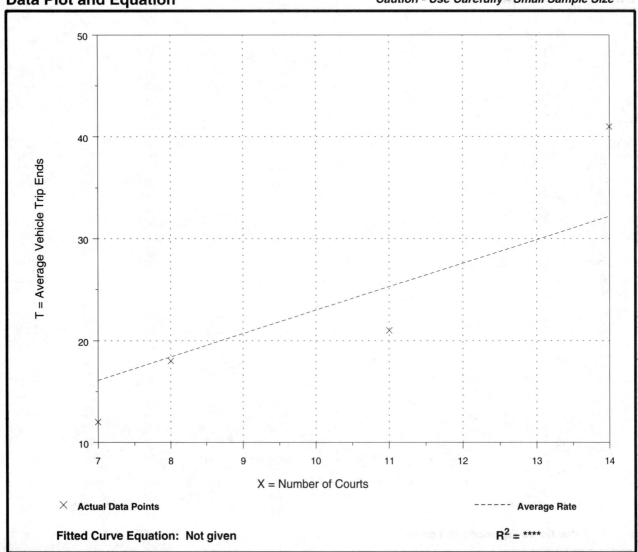

X **Actual Data Points**   - - - - - **Average Rate**

Fitted Curve Equation: Not given $R^2 = ****$

Racquet/Tennis Club
(491)

Average Vehicle Trip Ends vs: **Courts**
On a: **Weekday,**
P.M. Peak Hour of Generator

Number of Studies: 8
Avg. Number of Courts: 10
Directional Distribution: Not available

Trip Generation per Court

Average Rate	Range of Rates	Standard Deviation
4.38	1.73 - 7.21	2.86

Data Plot and Equation

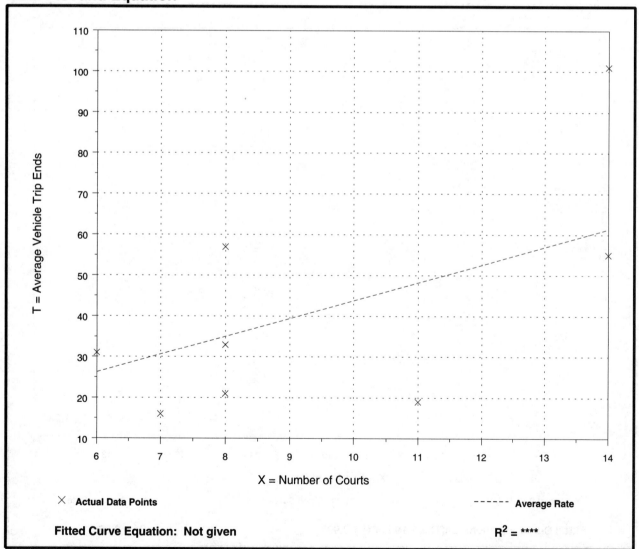

X **Actual Data Points** - - - - - **Average Rate**

Fitted Curve Equation: Not given $R^2 = $ ****

Racquet/Tennis Club
(491)

Average Vehicle Trip Ends vs: **Courts**
On a: **Saturday**

Number of Studies: 4
Avg. Number of Courts: 10
Directional Distribution: 50% entering, 50% exiting

Trip Generation per Court

Average Rate	Range of Rates	Standard Deviation
31.60	25.64 - 37.71	7.32

Data Plot and Equation

Caution - Use Carefully - Small Sample Size

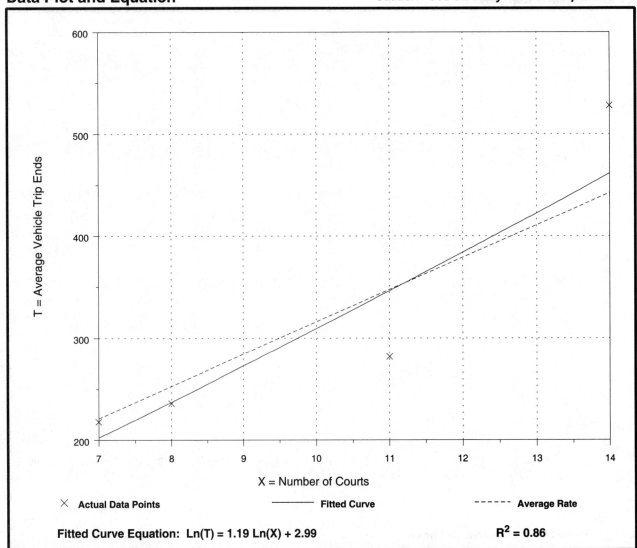

X Actual Data Points — Fitted Curve ----- Average Rate

Fitted Curve Equation: $Ln(T) = 1.19\ Ln(X) + 2.99$ $R^2 = 0.86$

Racquet/Tennis Club
(491)

Average Vehicle Trip Ends vs: **Courts**
On a: **Saturday,**
Peak Hour of Generator

Number of Studies: 5
Avg. Number of Courts: 11
Directional Distribution: Not available

Trip Generation per Court

Average Rate	Range of Rates	Standard Deviation
3.93	3.38 - 4.82	1.97

Data Plot and Equation

Caution - Use Carefully - Small Sample Size

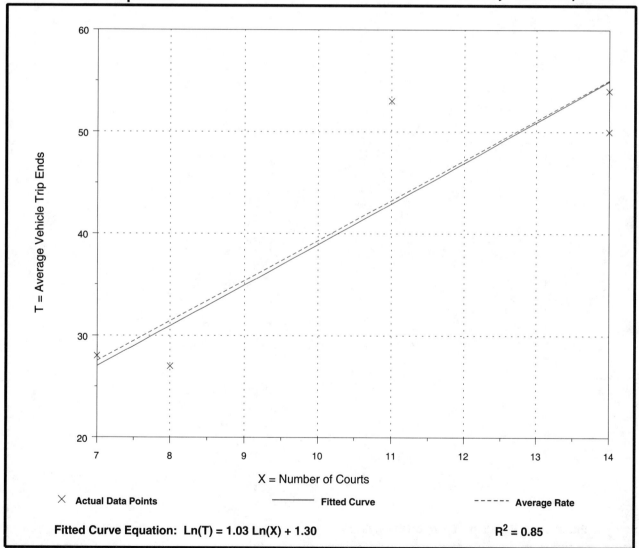

X **Actual Data Points** ——— **Fitted Curve** - - - - - **Average Rate**

Fitted Curve Equation: Ln(T) = 1.03 Ln(X) + 1.30 $R^2 = 0.85$

Racquet/Tennis Club
(491)

Average Vehicle Trip Ends vs: Courts
On a: Sunday

Number of Studies: 4
Avg. Number of Courts: 10
Directional Distribution: 50% entering, 50% exiting

Trip Generation per Court

Average Rate	Range of Rates	Standard Deviation
24.48	20.09 - 29.63	5.95

Data Plot and Equation

Caution - Use Carefully - Small Sample Size

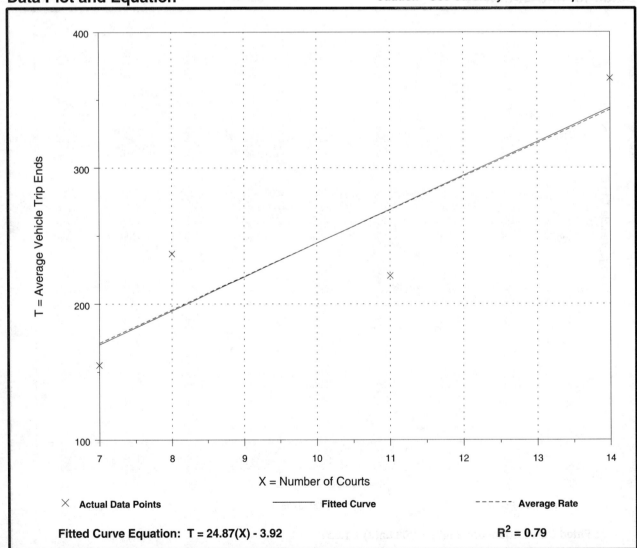

X **Actual Data Points**   —— **Fitted Curve**   - - - - - **Average Rate**

Fitted Curve Equation: T = 24.87(X) - 3.92 $R^2 = 0.79$

Racquet/Tennis Club
(491)

Average Vehicle Trip Ends vs: **Courts**
On a: **Sunday,**
Peak Hour of Generator

Number of Studies: 5
Avg. Number of Courts: 11
Directional Distribution: Not available

Trip Generation per Court

Average Rate	Range of Rates	Standard Deviation
3.15	2.57 - 4.00	1.78

Data Plot and Equation

Caution - Use Carefully - Small Sample Size

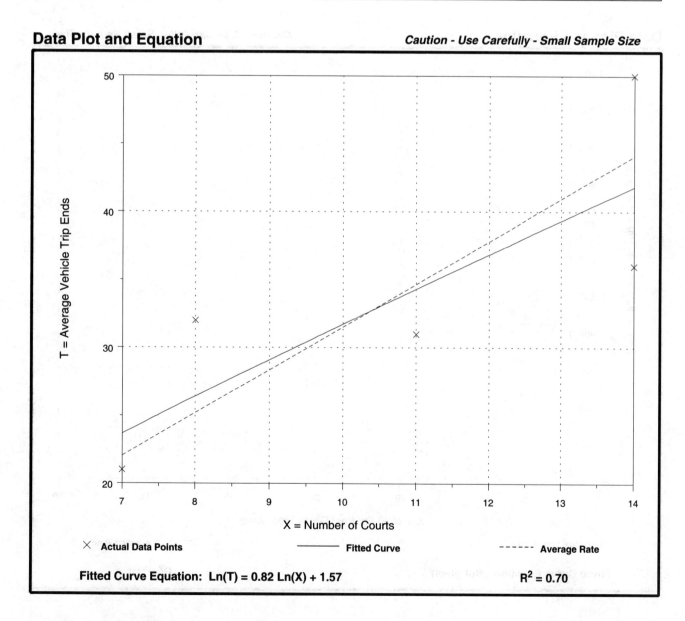

Fitted Curve Equation: Ln(T) = 0.82 Ln(X) + 1.57 $R^2 = 0.70$

Racquet/Tennis Club
(491)

Average Vehicle Trip Ends vs: 1000 Sq. Feet Gross Floor Area
On a: Weekday

Number of Studies: 5
Average 1000 Sq. Feet GFA: 37
Directional Distribution: 50% entering, 50% exiting

Trip Generation per 1000 Sq. Feet Gross Floor Area

Average Rate	Range of Rates	Standard Deviation
14.03	7.63 - 61.50	11.40

Data Plot and Equation

Caution - Use Carefully - Small Sample Size

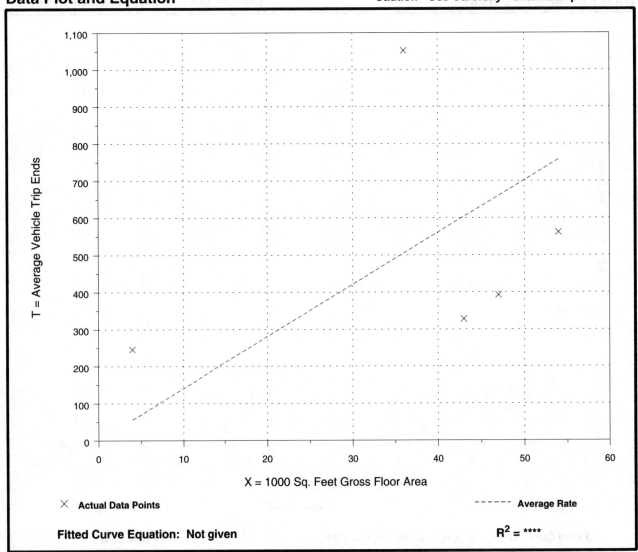

X **Actual Data Points**

- - - - - **Average Rate**

Fitted Curve Equation: Not given

$R^2 = ****$

Racquet/Tennis Club
(491)

Average Vehicle Trip Ends vs: 1000 Sq. Feet Gross Floor Area
On a: Weekday,
P.M. Peak Hour of Generator

Number of Studies: 3
Average 1000 Sq. Feet GFA: 48
Directional Distribution: Not available

Trip Generation per 1000 Sq. Feet Gross Floor Area

Average Rate	Range of Rates	Standard Deviation
0.84	0.70 - 1.06	0.93

Data Plot and Equation

Caution - Use Carefully - Small Sample Size

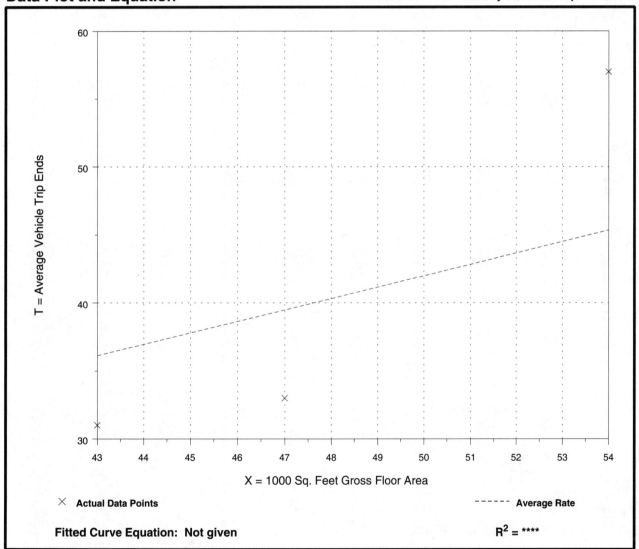

X **Actual Data Points**

- - - - - **Average Rate**

Fitted Curve Equation: Not given $R^2 = ****$

Racquet/Tennis Club
(491)

Average Vehicle Trip Ends vs: **1000 Sq. Feet Gross Floor Area**
On a: **Saturday**

Number of Studies: 2
Average 1000 Sq. Feet GFA: 20
Directional Distribution: 50% entering, 50% exiting

Trip Generation per 1000 Sq. Feet Gross Floor Area

Average Rate	Range of Rates	Standard Deviation
21.35	20.44 - 29.50	*

Data Plot and Equation

Caution - Use Carefully - Small Sample Size

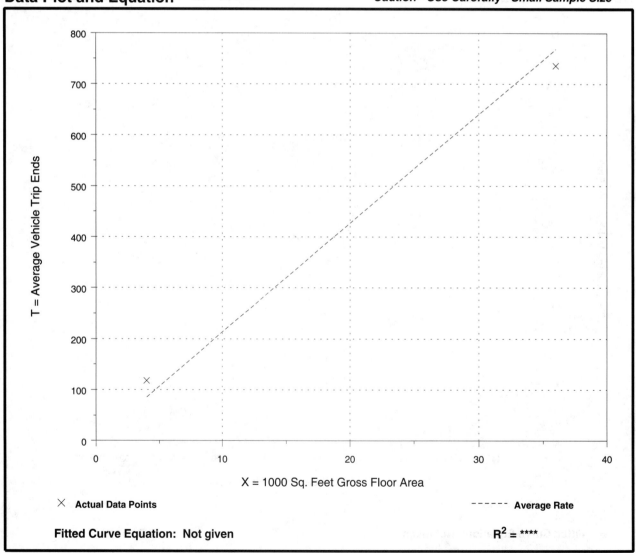

X **Actual Data Points** - - - - - **Average Rate**

Fitted Curve Equation: Not given $R^2 = ****$

Racquet/Tennis Club
(491)

Average Vehicle Trip Ends vs: 1000 Sq. Feet Gross Floor Area
On a: Sunday

Number of Studies: 2
Average 1000 Sq. Feet GFA: 20
Directional Distribution: 50% entering, 50% exiting

Trip Generation per 1000 Sq. Feet Gross Floor Area

Average Rate	Range of Rates	Standard Deviation
17.40	16.78 - 23.00	*

Data Plot and Equation

Caution - Use Carefully - Small Sample Size

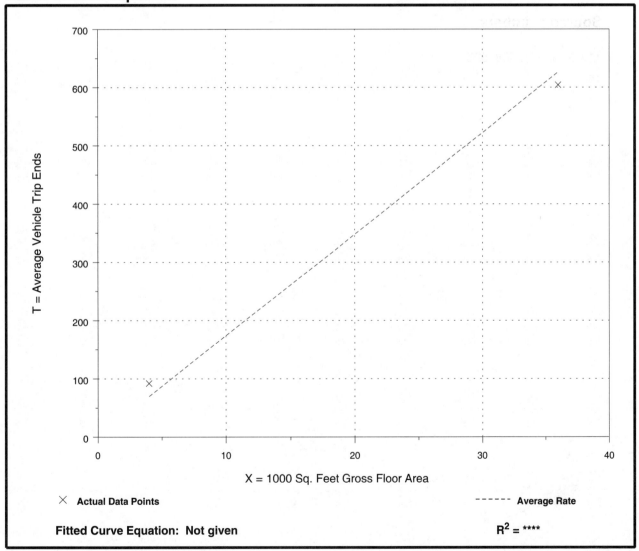

X **Actual Data Points**　　　　　　　　　　　　　- - - - - **Average Rate**

Fitted Curve Equation: Not given　　　　　　　　$R^2 = ****$

Land Use: 492
Health/Fitness Club

Description

Health/fitness clubs are privately-owned facilities that primarily focus on individual fitness or training. Typically they provide exercise classes; weightlifting, fitness and gymnastics equipment; spas; locker rooms; and small restaurants or snack bars. This land use may also include ancillary facilities, such as swimming pools, whirlpools, saunas, tennis, racquetball and handball courts and limited retail. These facilities are membership clubs that may allow access to the general public for a fee. Racquet/tennis club (Land Use 491), athletic club (Land Use 493) and recreational community center (Land Use 495) are related uses.

Additional Data

The sites were surveyed between the1970s and the 2000s in California, Pennsylvania, Connecticut and New Jersey.

Source Numbers

113, 253, 571, 588, 598

Land Use: 492
Health/Fitness Club
Independent Variables with One Observation

The following trip generation data are for independent variables with only one observation. This information is shown in this table only; there are no related plots for these data.

Users are cautioned to use data with care because of the small sample size.

Independent Variable	Trip Generation Rate	Size of Independent Variable	Number of Studies	Directional Distribution
1,000 Square Feet Gross Floor Area				
Weekday	32.93	15	1	50% entering, 50% exiting
Saturday	20.87	15	1	50% entering, 50% exiting
Sunday	26.73	15	1	50% entering, 50% exiting
Sunday Peak Hour of Generator	2.47	15	1	Not available

Health/Fitness Club
(492)

Average Vehicle Trip Ends vs: 1000 Sq. Feet Gross Floor Area
On a: Weekday,
Peak Hour of Adjacent Street Traffic,
One Hour Between 7 and 9 a.m.

Number of Studies: 5
Average 1000 Sq. Feet GFA: 37
Directional Distribution: 45% entering, 55% exiting

Trip Generation per 1000 Sq. Feet Gross Floor Area

Average Rate	Range of Rates	Standard Deviation
1.38	0.30 - 2.00	1.33

Data Plot and Equation

Caution - Use Carefully - Small Sample Size

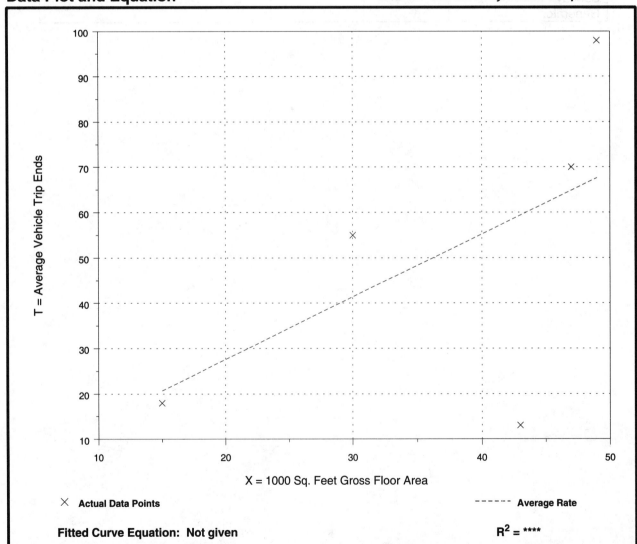

X Actual Data Points

- - - - - Average Rate

Fitted Curve Equation: Not given

$R^2 = ****$

Health/Fitness Club
(492)

Average Vehicle Trip Ends vs: **1000 Sq. Feet Gross Floor Area**
On a: **Weekday,**
Peak Hour of Adjacent Street Traffic,
One Hour Between 4 and 6 p.m.

Number of Studies: 6
Average 1000 Sq. Feet GFA: 42
Directional Distribution: 57% entering, 43% exiting

Trip Generation per 1000 Sq. Feet Gross Floor Area

Average Rate	Range of Rates	Standard Deviation
3.53	2.35 - 4.30	2.00

Data Plot and Equation

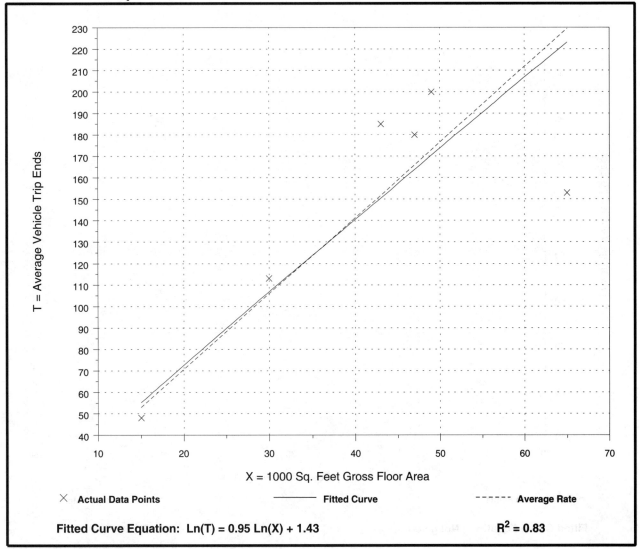

Fitted Curve Equation: Ln(T) = 0.95 Ln(X) + 1.43 $R^2 = 0.83$

Health/Fitness Club
(492)

Average Vehicle Trip Ends vs: **1000 Sq. Feet Gross Floor Area**
On a: **Weekday,**
A.M. Peak Hour of Generator

Number of Studies: 3
Average 1000 Sq. Feet GFA: 36
Directional Distribution: 42% entering, 58% exiting

Trip Generation per 1000 Sq. Feet Gross Floor Area

Average Rate	Range of Rates	Standard Deviation
1.41	0.30 - 2.67	1.50

Data Plot and Equation

Caution - Use Carefully - Small Sample Size

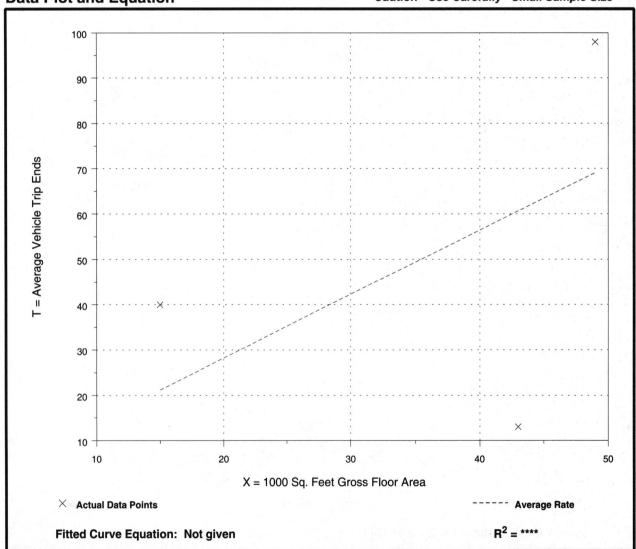

X = 1000 Sq. Feet Gross Floor Area

✕ **Actual Data Points**   - - - - - **Average Rate**

Fitted Curve Equation: Not given $R^2 = ****$

Health/Fitness Club
(492)

Average Vehicle Trip Ends vs: 1000 Sq. Feet Gross Floor Area
On a: Weekday,
P.M. Peak Hour of Generator

Number of Studies: 3
Average 1000 Sq. Feet GFA: 36
Directional Distribution: 51% entering, 49% exiting

Trip Generation per 1000 Sq. Feet Gross Floor Area

Average Rate	Range of Rates	Standard Deviation
4.06	3.27 - 4.30	2.02

Data Plot and Equation

Caution - Use Carefully - Small Sample Size

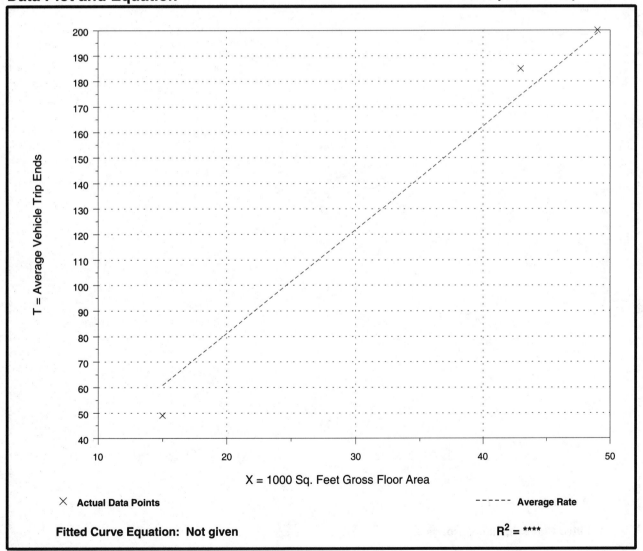

X   **Actual Data Points**   - - - - - **Average Rate**

Fitted Curve Equation: Not given $R^2 =$ ****

Health/Fitness Club
(492)

Average Vehicle Trip Ends vs: 1000 Sq. Feet Gross Floor Area
On a: Saturday,
Peak Hour of Generator

Number of Studies: 2
Average 1000 Sq. Feet GFA: 23
Directional Distribution: 45% entering, 55% exiting

Trip Generation per 1000 Sq. Feet Gross Floor Area

Average Rate	Range of Rates	Standard Deviation
2.78	2.60 - 2.87	*

Data Plot and Equation

Caution - Use Carefully - Small Sample Size

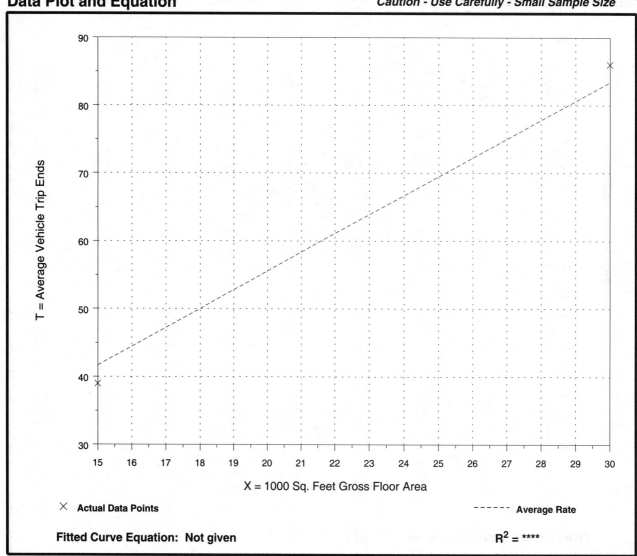

X **Actual Data Points**

----- **Average Rate**

Fitted Curve Equation: Not given

$R^2 = ****$

Land Use: 493
Athletic Club

Description

Athletic clubs are privately-owned facilities that offer comprehensive athletic facilities. These clubs typically have one or more of the following: tennis, racquetball, squash, handball, basketball and volleyball courts; swimming pools; whirlpools; saunas; spas; and exercise and weight rooms. They often offer diverse, competitive team sport activities and social facilities. These facilities are membership clubs that may allow access to the general public for a fee. Racquet/tennis club (Land Use 491), health/fitness club (Land Use 492) and recreational community center (Land Use 495) are related uses.

Additional Data

The sites were surveyed in 1978, 1985, 2002 and 2003 in California, Pennsylvania and Connecticut.

Source Numbers

113, 422, 571, 588

Land Use: 493
Athletic Club
Independent Variables with One Observation

The following trip generation data are for independent variables with only one observation. This information is shown in this table only; there are no related plots for these data.

Users are cautioned to use data with care because of the small sample size.

Independent Variable	Trip Generation Rate	Size of Independent Variable	Number of Studies	Directional Distribution
Employees				
Weekday	93.17	6	1	50% entering, 50% exiting
Weekday a.m. Peak Hour of Adjacent Street Traffic	3.83	6	1	Not available
Weekday p.m. Peak Hour of Adjacent Street Traffic	7.50	6	1	Not available
Weekday a.m. Peak Hour of Generator	5.17	6	1	Not available
Weekday p.m. Peak Hour of Generator	8.33	6	1	Not available
Saturday	83.33	6	1	50% entering, 50% exiting
Saturday Peak Hour of Generator	8.00	6	1	Not available
Sunday	79.67	6	1	50% entering, 50% exiting
Sunday Peak Hour of Generator	7.83	6	1	Not available

Independent Variable	Trip Generation Rate	Size of Independent Variable	Number of Studies	Directional Distribution
1,000 Square Feet Gross Floor Area				
Weekday	43.00	13	1	50% entering, 50% exiting
Saturday	38.46	13	1	50% entering, 50% exiting
Sunday	36.77	13	1	50% entering, 50% exiting
Sunday Peak Hour of Generator	3.62	13	1	Not available

Land Use: 493
Athletic Club
Independent Variables with One Observation

Members

Weekday	1.86	300	1	50% entering, 50% exiting
Weekday a.m. Peak Hour of Adjacent Street Traffic	0.08	300	1	Not available
Weekday a.m. Peak Hour of Generator	0.10	300	1	Not available
Weekday p.m. Peak Hour of Generator	0.17	300	1	Not available
Saturday	1.67	300	1	50% entering, 50% exiting
Saturday Peak Hour of Generator	0.16	300	1	Not available
Sunday	1.59	300	1	50% entering, 50% exiting
Sunday Peak Hour of Generator	0.16	300	1	Not available

Athletic Club
(493)

Average Vehicle Trip Ends vs: **1000 Sq. Feet Gross Floor Area**
On a: **Weekday,**
Peak Hour of Adjacent Street Traffic,
One Hour Between 7 and 9 a.m.

Number of Studies: 3
Average 1000 Sq. Feet GFA: 31
Directional Distribution: 61% entering, 39% exiting

Trip Generation per 1000 Sq. Feet Gross Floor Area

Average Rate	Range of Rates	Standard Deviation
2.97	1.77 - 3.40	1.80

Data Plot and Equation

Caution - Use Carefully - Small Sample Size

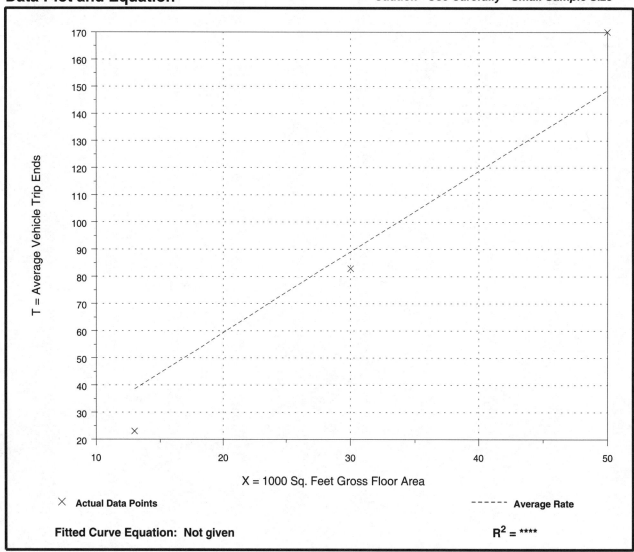

X   **Actual Data Points**   - - - - - **Average Rate**

Fitted Curve Equation: Not given $R^2 = $ ****

Athletic Club
(493)

Average Vehicle Trip Ends vs: **1000 Sq. Feet Gross Floor Area**
On a: **Weekday,**
Peak Hour of Adjacent Street Traffic,
One Hour Between 4 and 6 p.m.

Number of Studies: 4
Average 1000 Sq. Feet GFA: 28
Directional Distribution: 62% entering, 38% exiting

Trip Generation per 1000 Sq. Feet Gross Floor Area

Average Rate	Range of Rates	Standard Deviation
5.96	3.46 - 8.30	2.82

Data Plot and Equation

Caution - Use Carefully - Small Sample Size

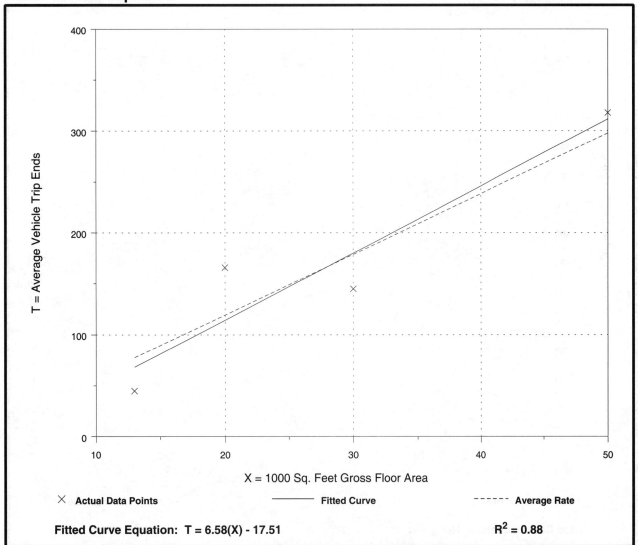

X **Actual Data Points**   —— **Fitted Curve**   - - - - **Average Rate**

Fitted Curve Equation: T = 6.58(X) - 17.51 $R^2 = 0.88$

Athletic Club
(493)

Average Vehicle Trip Ends vs: 1000 Sq. Feet Gross Floor Area
On a: Weekday,
A.M. Peak Hour of Generator

Number of Studies: 2
Average 1000 Sq. Feet GFA: 32
Directional Distribution: 58% entering, 42% exiting

Trip Generation per 1000 Sq. Feet Gross Floor Area

Average Rate	Range of Rates	Standard Deviation
3.19	2.38 - 3.40	*

Data Plot and Equation

Caution - Use Carefully - Small Sample Size

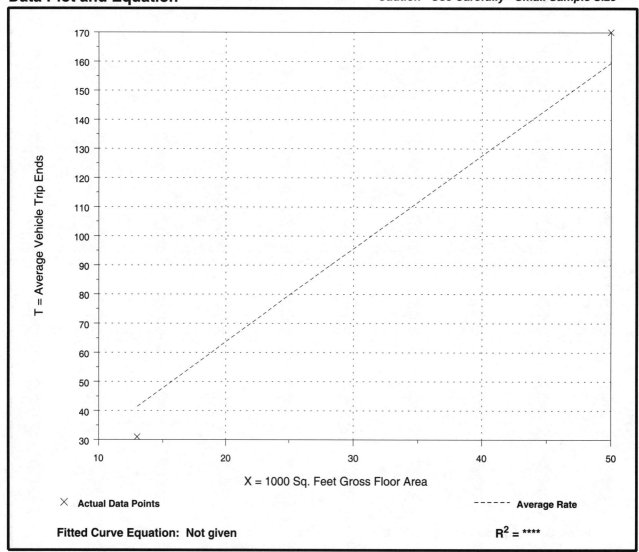

X = 1000 Sq. Feet Gross Floor Area

✕ **Actual Data Points**   - - - - - **Average Rate**

Fitted Curve Equation: Not given $R^2 = ****$

Athletic Club
(493)

Average Vehicle Trip Ends vs: **1000 Sq. Feet Gross Floor Area**
On a: **Weekday,**
P.M. Peak Hour of Generator

Number of Studies: 2
Average 1000 Sq. Feet GFA: 32
Directional Distribution: 63% entering, 37% exiting

Trip Generation per 1000 Sq. Feet Gross Floor Area

Average Rate	Range of Rates	Standard Deviation
5.84	3.85 - 6.36	*

Data Plot and Equation

Caution - Use Carefully - Small Sample Size

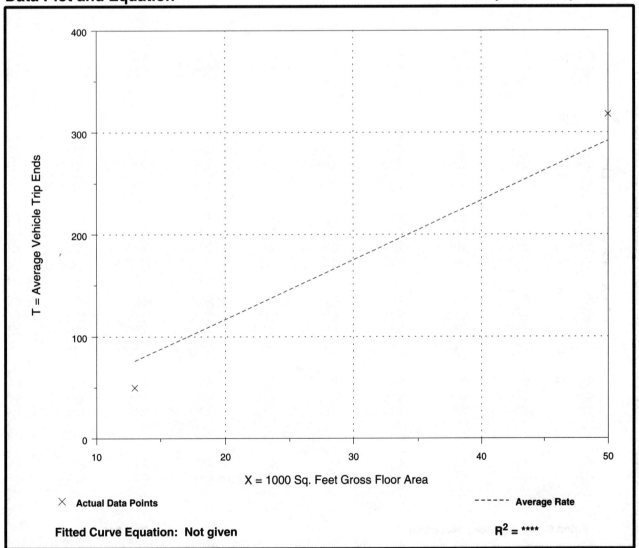

X **Actual Data Points**   - - - - - **Average Rate**

Fitted Curve Equation: Not given $R^2 = ****$

Athletic Club
(493)

Average Vehicle Trip Ends vs: 1000 Sq. Feet Gross Floor Area
On a: Saturday,
Peak Hour of Generator

Number of Studies: 2
Average 1000 Sq. Feet GFA: 17
Directional Distribution: 49% entering, 51% exiting

Trip Generation per 1000 Sq. Feet Gross Floor Area

Average Rate	Range of Rates	Standard Deviation
6.67	3.69 - 8.60	*

Data Plot and Equation

Caution - Use Carefully - Small Sample Size

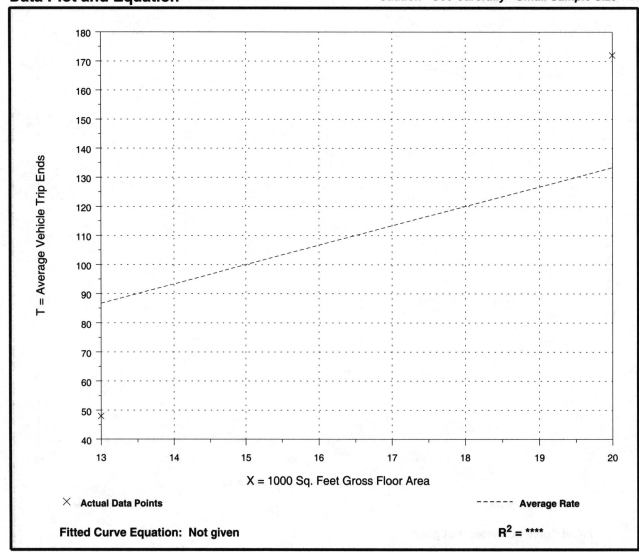

$\times$ **Actual Data Points**   ----- **Average Rate**

Fitted Curve Equation: Not given $R^2 = ****$

Athletic Club
(493)

Average Vehicle Trip Ends vs: **Members**
On a: **Weekday,**
Peak Hour of Adjacent Street Traffic,
One Hour Between 4 and 6 p.m.

Number of Studies: 2
Average Number of Members: 1,650
Directional Distribution: 61% entering, 39% exiting

Trip Generation per Member

Average Rate	Range of Rates	Standard Deviation
0.08	0.07 - 0.15	*

Data Plot and Equation

Caution - Use Carefully - Small Sample Size

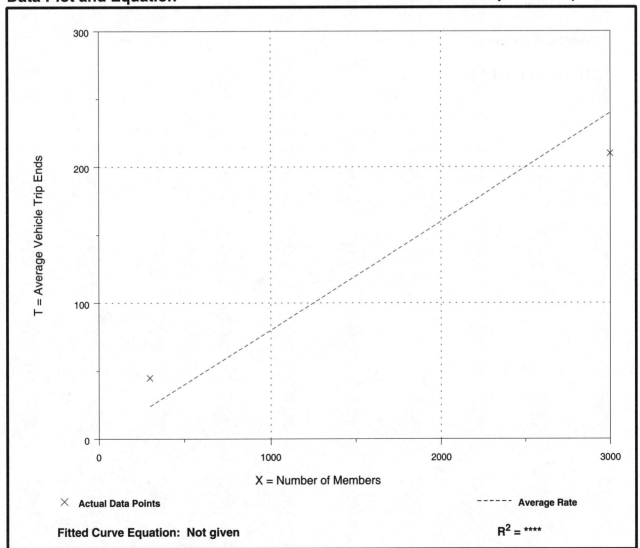

X **Actual Data Points**

- - - - - **Average Rate**

Fitted Curve Equation: Not given $R^2 = ****$

Land Use: 495
Recreational Community Center

Description

Recreational community centers are stand-alone public facilities similar to and including YMCAs. These facilities often include classes and clubs for adults and children; a day care or nursery school; meeting rooms; swimming pools and whirlpools; saunas; tennis, racquetball, handball, basketball and volleyball courts; outdoor athletic fields/courts; exercise classes; weightlifting and gymnastics equipment; locker rooms; and a restaurant or snack bar. Public access is typically allowed, but a fee may be charged. Racquet/tennis club (Land Use 491), health/fitness club (Land Use 492) and athletic club (Land Use 493) are related uses.

Additional Data

One surveyed site recorded significant pedestrian trips.

The sites were surveyed in the 1990s and 2000s throughout the United States.

Source Numbers

281, 410, 443, 571, 618

Land Use: 495
Recreational Community Center
Independent Variables with One Observation

The following trip generation data are for independent variables with only one observation. This information is shown in this table only; there are no related plots for these data.

Users are cautioned to use data with care because of the small sample size.

Independent Variable	Trip Generation Rate	Size of Independent Variable	Number of Studies	Directional Distribution
Members				
Weekday a.m. Peak Hour of Adjacent Street Traffic	0.01	14,000	1	62% entering, 38% exiting
Weekday p.m. Peak Hour of Adjacent Street Traffic	0.01	14,000	1	28% entering, 72% exiting
Weekday a.m. Peak Hour of Generator	0.03	14,000	1	58% entering, 42% exiting
Weekday p.m. Peak Hour of Generator	0.02	14,000	1	39% entering, 61% exiting
Saturday	0.07	14,000	1	50% entering, 50% exiting
Saturday Peak Hour of Generator	0.01	14,000	1	47% entering, 53% exiting
Sunday	0.15	14,000	1	50% entering, 50% exiting
Sunday Peak Hour of Generator	0.02	14,000	1	60% entering, 40% exiting
Employees				
Weekday	27.25	32	1	50% entering, 50% exiting
Weekday a.m. Peak Hour of Adjacent Street Traffic	2.66	32	1	72% entering, 28% exiting
Weekday p.m. Peak Hour of Adjacent Street Traffic	2.44	32	1	27% entering, 73% exiting
Weekday a.m. Peak Hour of Generator	3.50	32	1	38% entering, 62% exiting
Weekday p.m. Peak Hour of Generator	3.16	32	1	44% entering, 56% exiting
Saturday	18.34	32	1	50% entering, 50% exiting
Saturday Peak Hour of Generator	2.59	32	1	53% entering, 47% exiting
Sunday	12.03	32	1	50% entering, 50% exiting
Sunday Peak Hour of Generator	1.66	32	1	43% entering, 57% exiting
1,000 Square Feet Gross Floor Area				
Weekday	22.88	38	1	50% entering, 50% exiting

Recreational Community Center
(495)

Average Vehicle Trip Ends vs:	1000 Sq. Feet Gross Floor Area
On a:	Weekday,
	Peak Hour of Adjacent Street Traffic,
	One Hour Between 7 and 9 a.m.

Number of Studies: 3
Average 1000 Sq. Feet GFA: 76
Directional Distribution: 61% entering, 39% exiting

Trip Generation per 1000 Sq. Feet Gross Floor Area

Average Rate	Range of Rates	Standard Deviation
1.62	1.08 - 2.71	1.45

Data Plot and Equation

Caution - Use Carefully - Small Sample Size

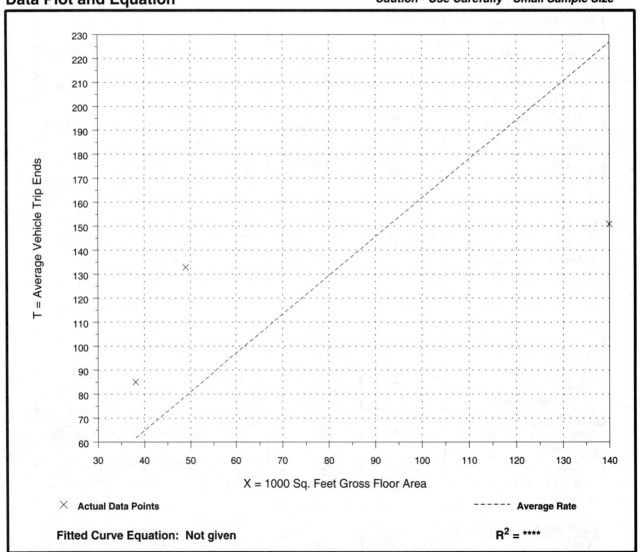

X   **Actual Data Points** - - - - - **Average Rate**

Fitted Curve Equation: Not given $R^2 = $ ****

Recreational Community Center
(495)

Average Vehicle Trip Ends vs:	1000 Sq. Feet Gross Floor Area
On a:	Weekday,
	Peak Hour of Adjacent Street Traffic,
	One Hour Between 4 and 6 p.m.

Number of Studies:	4
Average 1000 Sq. Feet GFA:	73
Directional Distribution:	37% entering, 63% exiting

Trip Generation per 1000 Sq. Feet Gross Floor Area

Average Rate	Range of Rates	Standard Deviation
1.45	1.05 - 2.78	1.28

Data Plot and Equation

Caution - Use Carefully - Small Sample Size

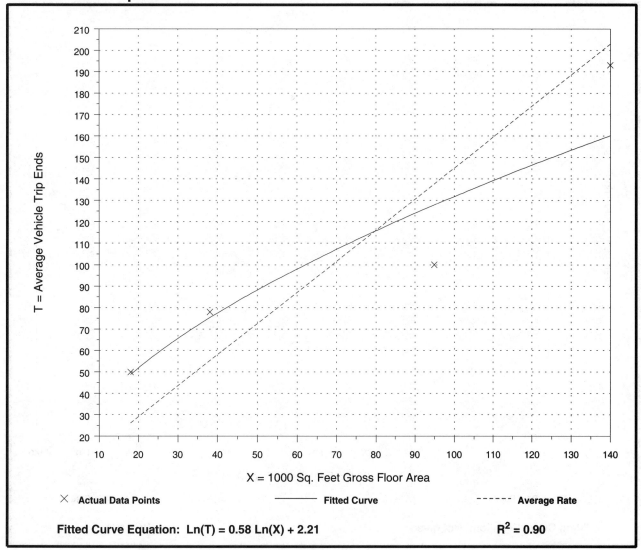

Fitted Curve Equation: Ln(T) = 0.58 Ln(X) + 2.21 $R^2 = 0.90$

Recreational Community Center
(495)

Average Vehicle Trip Ends vs: 1000 Sq. Feet Gross Floor Area
On a: Weekday,
A.M. Peak Hour of Generator

Number of Studies: 3
Average 1000 Sq. Feet GFA: 76
Directional Distribution: 53% entering, 47% exiting

Trip Generation per 1000 Sq. Feet Gross Floor Area

Average Rate	Range of Rates	Standard Deviation
2.69	2.61 - 2.94	1.64

Data Plot and Equation

Caution - Use Carefully - Small Sample Size

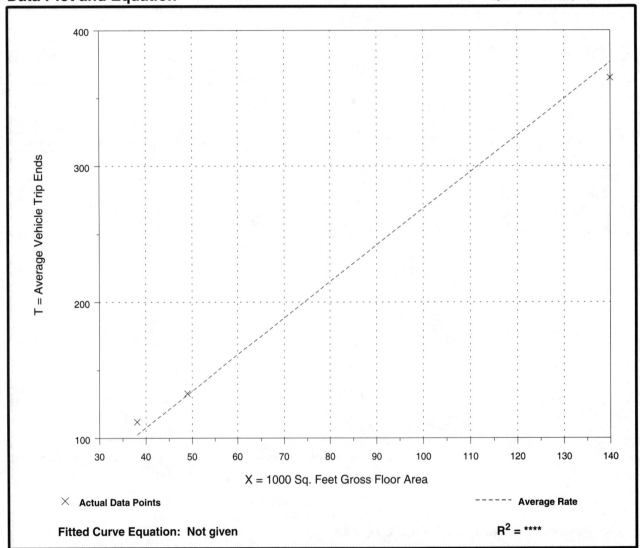

X **Actual Data Points** - - - - - **Average Rate**

Fitted Curve Equation: Not given $R^2 = ****$

Recreational Community Center
(495)

Average Vehicle Trip Ends vs: 1000 Sq. Feet Gross Floor Area
On a: Weekday,
P.M. Peak Hour of Generator

Number of Studies: 2
Average 1000 Sq. Feet GFA: 89
Directional Distribution: 40% entering, 60% exiting

Trip Generation per 1000 Sq. Feet Gross Floor Area

Average Rate	Range of Rates	Standard Deviation
2.39	2.31 - 2.65	*

Data Plot and Equation

Caution - Use Carefully - Small Sample Size

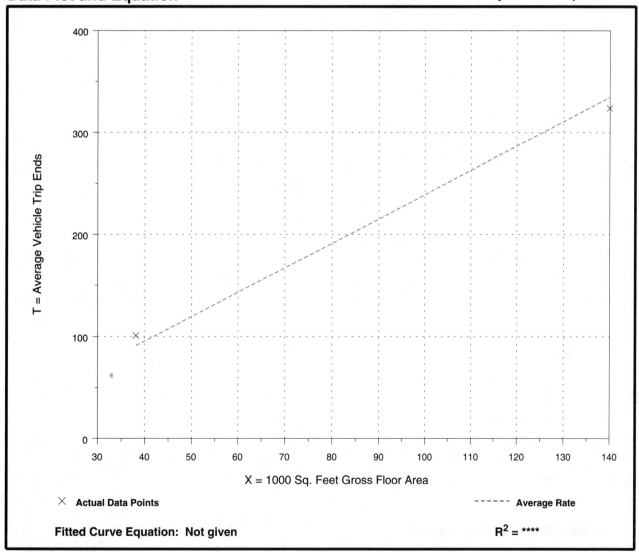

X **Actual Data Points**   - - - - - **Average Rate**

Fitted Curve Equation: Not given $R^2 = ****$

Recreational Community Center
(495)

Average Vehicle Trip Ends vs: 1000 Sq. Feet Gross Floor Area
On a: Saturday

Number of Studies: 2
Average 1000 Sq. Feet GFA: 89
Directional Distribution: 50% entering, 50% exiting

Trip Generation per 1000 Sq. Feet Gross Floor Area

Average Rate	Range of Rates	Standard Deviation
9.10	7.39 - 15.40	*

Data Plot and Equation

Caution - Use Carefully - Small Sample Size

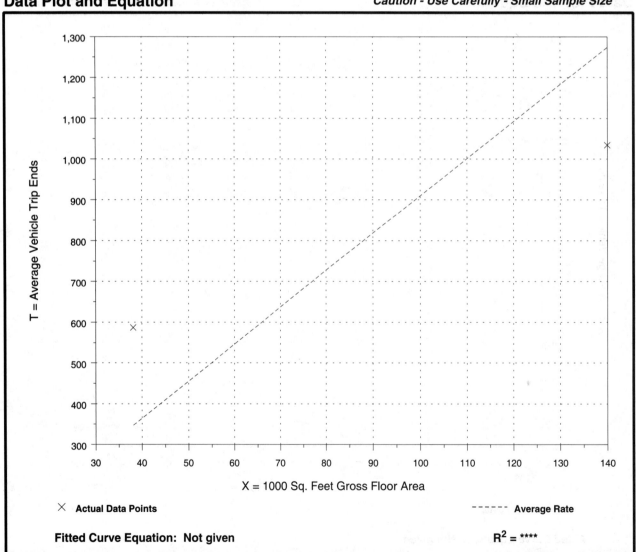

X **Actual Data Points**

‑ ‑ ‑ ‑ ‑ **Average Rate**

Fitted Curve Equation: Not given

$R^2 = ****$

Recreational Community Center
(495)

Average Vehicle Trip Ends vs: 1000 Sq. Feet Gross Floor Area
On a: Saturday,
Peak Hour of Generator

Number of Studies: 4
Average 1000 Sq. Feet GFA: 81
Directional Distribution: 54% entering, 46% exiting

Trip Generation per 1000 Sq. Feet Gross Floor Area

Average Rate	Range of Rates	Standard Deviation
1.07	0.58 - 2.18	1.14

Data Plot and Equation

Caution - Use Carefully - Small Sample Size

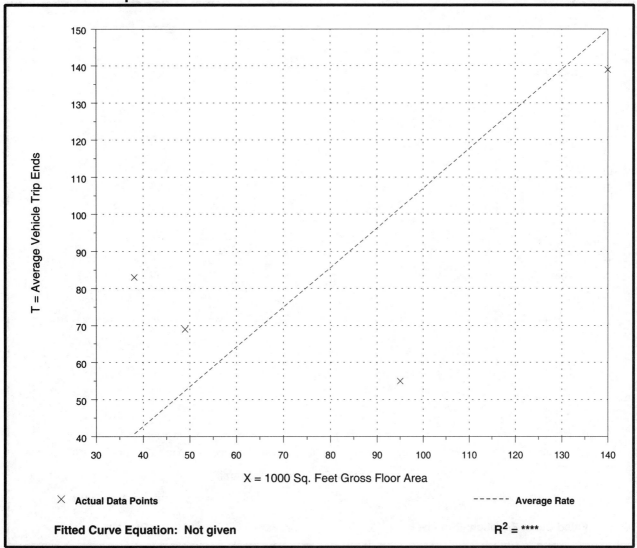

X **Actual Data Points**　　　　　　　　　　　　　　　----- **Average Rate**

Fitted Curve Equation: Not given　　　　　　　　　　$R^2 = $ ****

Recreational Community Center
(495)

Average Vehicle Trip Ends vs: 1000 Sq. Feet Gross Floor Area
On a: Sunday

Number of Studies: 2
Average 1000 Sq. Feet GFA: 89
Directional Distribution: 50% entering, 50% exiting

Trip Generation per 1000 Sq. Feet Gross Floor Area

Average Rate	Range of Rates	Standard Deviation
13.60	10.10 - 14.55	*

Data Plot and Equation

Caution - Use Carefully - Small Sample Size

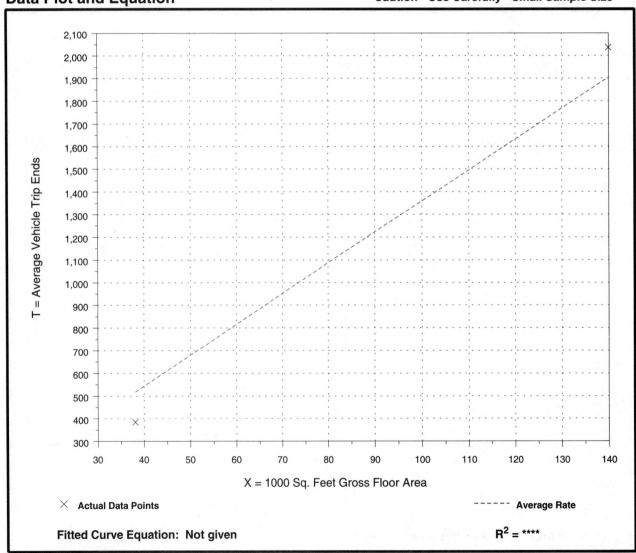

X **Actual Data Points**   - - - - - **Average Rate**

Fitted Curve Equation: Not given $R^2 = ****$

Recreational Community Center
(495)

Average Vehicle Trip Ends vs: 1000 Sq. Feet Gross Floor Area
On a: Sunday,
Peak Hour of Generator

Number of Studies: 2
Average 1000 Sq. Feet GFA: 89
Directional Distribution: 56% entering, 44% exiting

Trip Generation per 1000 Sq. Feet Gross Floor Area

Average Rate	Range of Rates	Standard Deviation
1.48	1.39 - 1.51	*

Data Plot and Equation

Caution - Use Carefully - Small Sample Size

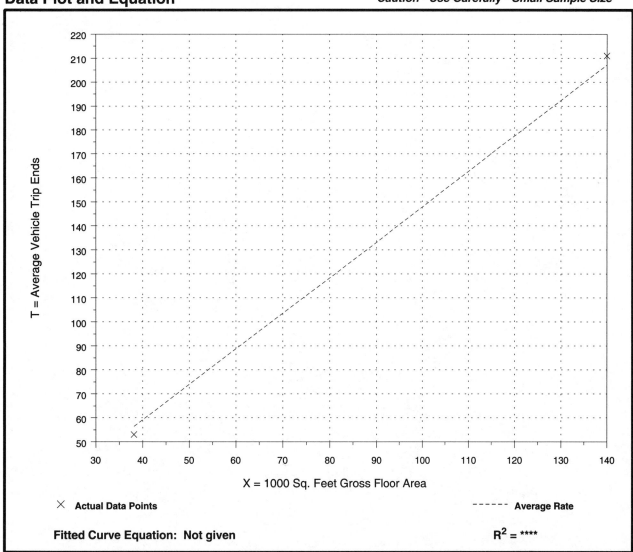

X Actual Data Points

- - - - - **Average Rate**

Fitted Curve Equation: Not given $R^2 = ****$